UNLEASHING BLACK POWER

THE CARTER G. WOODSON INSTITUTE SERIES
Black Studies at Work in the World

Deborah E. McDowell, Shawn Leigh Alexander, and Robert T. Vinson, Editors

UNLEASHING BLACK POWER

Grassroots Organizing in Harlem and the
Advent of the Long, Hot Summers

PETER D. BLACKMER

UNIVERSITY OF VIRGINIA PRESS
Charlottesville and London

Published in association with the
University of Virginia's Carter G. Woodson Institute

The University of Virginia Press is situated on the traditional lands of the Monacan Nation, and the Commonwealth of Virginia was and is home to many other Indigenous people. We pay our respect to all of them, past and present. We also honor the enslaved African and African American people who built the University of Virginia, and we recognize their descendants. We commit to fostering voices from these communities through our publications and to deepening our collective understanding of their histories and contributions.

University of Virginia Press
© 2025 by the Rector and Visitors of the University of Virginia
All rights reserved
Printed in the United States of America on acid-free paper

First published 2025

9 8 7 6 5 4 3 2 1

LIBRARY OF CONGRESS CATALOGING-IN-PUBLICATION DATA
Names: Blackmer, Peter D., author.
Title: Unleashing Black Power : grassroots organizing in Harlem and the advent of the long, hot summers / Peter D. Blackmer.
Description: Charlottesville : University of Virginia Press, 2025. | Series: Carter G. Woodson Institute series | Includes bibliographical references and index.
Identifiers: LCCN 2024060662 (print) | LCCN 2024060663 (ebook) | ISBN 9780813953755 hardback | ISBN 9780813953762 trade paperback | ISBN 9780813953779 ebook
Subjects: LCSH: Harlem (New York, N.Y.)—History—20th century | Black power—New York (State)—New York—History—20th century | African Americans—Civil rights—New York (State)—New York—History—20th century | African Americans—Social conditions—New York (State)—New York—History—20th century | Civil rights movements—New York (State)—New York—History—20th century | New York (N.Y.)—Race relations—History—20th century | BISAC: HISTORY / African American & Black | SOCIAL SCIENCE / Activism & Social Justice
Classification: LCC F128.68.H3 B54 2025 (print) | LCC F128.68.H3 (ebook) | DDC 323.1196/073074710904—dc23/eng/20250610
LC record available at https://lccn.loc.gov/2024060662
LC ebook record available at https://lccn.loc.gov/2024060663

Cover art: Students lead a march from JHS 167 (now Robert F. Wagner Middle School) on East 76th Street to the 19th Precinct on East 67th Street on July 17, 1964, to protest the killing of James Powell by NYPD Lieutenant Thomas Gilligan. (Photo by Dick DeMarsico; Library of Congress, Prints and Photographs Division, New York World-Telegram and the Sun Newspaper Photograph Collection, [LC-DIG-ds-17338])
Cover design: Cecilia Sorochin

To Bill Strickland, a long-distance runner
in the struggle for Black liberation

CONTENTS

List of Abbreviations | ix

Introduction	1
1 A "Rising Tide" Coming In, 1954–1957	15
2 "The Negro Revolt," 1958–1959	51
3 The Limits of Liberalism in Harlem, 1959–1960	83
4 The Spirit of Bandung, 1959–1961	111
5 The New Afro-American Nationalism, 1961–1963	145
6 Interracial Organizing and Black Self-Determination, 1960–1963	179
7 Rent Strikes and Repression, 1963–1964	215
8 The Time Has Come, 1964	254
Conclusion	301

Acknowledgments | 307
Notes | 313
Bibliography | 373
Index | 387

ABBREVIATIONS

AAAA	Afro-American Alliance for Action
ANPM	African Nationalist Pioneer Movement
BOSS	Bureau of Special Services
CAWAH	Cultural Association for Women of African Heritage
CCH	Community Council on Housing
CCRB	Civilian Complaint Review Board
CHA	Committee on Harlem Affairs
CORE	Congress of Racial Equality
EHTC	East Harlem Tenants Council
FNP	Freedom Now Party
FPCC	Fair Play for Cuba Committee
HARYOU	Harlem Youth Opportunities Unlimited
HDC	Harlem Defense Council
HEP	Harlem Education Project
HTC	Harlem Tenants Council
HWG	Harlem Writers Guild
LCA	Liberation Committee for Africa

LHTC	Lower Harlem Tenants Council
MDC	Monroe Defense Committee
MMI	Muslim Mosque, Inc.
NAACP	National Association for the Advancement of Colored People
NMU	National Maritime Union
NOI	Nation of Islam
NSM	Northern Student Movement
OAAU	Organization of Afro-American Unity
OGFF	On Guard Committee for Freedom
RAM	Revolutionary Action Movement
RRA	Rent and Rehabilitation Administration
SCLC	Southern Christian Leadership Conference
SNCC	Student Nonviolent Coordinating Committee
TPF	Tactical Patrol Force
UANM	United African Nationalist Movement
UCAAH	United Committee Against Alexander Hamilton Houses
UNIA	Universal Negro Improvement Association

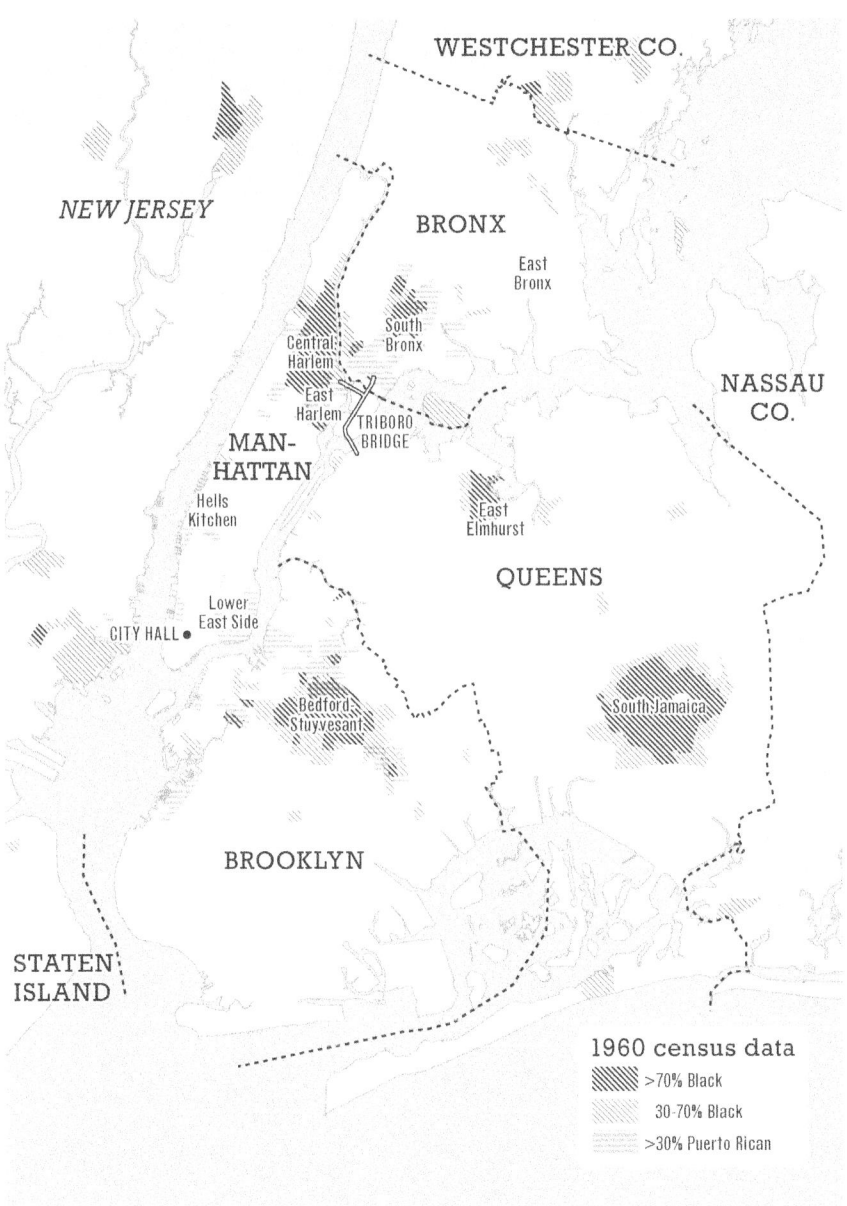

MAP 1 New York City with 1960 US census data for Black and Puerto Rican residents. (Data from IPUMS NHGIS, University of Minnesota, www.nhgis.org; map created by Nat Case, INCase, LLC)

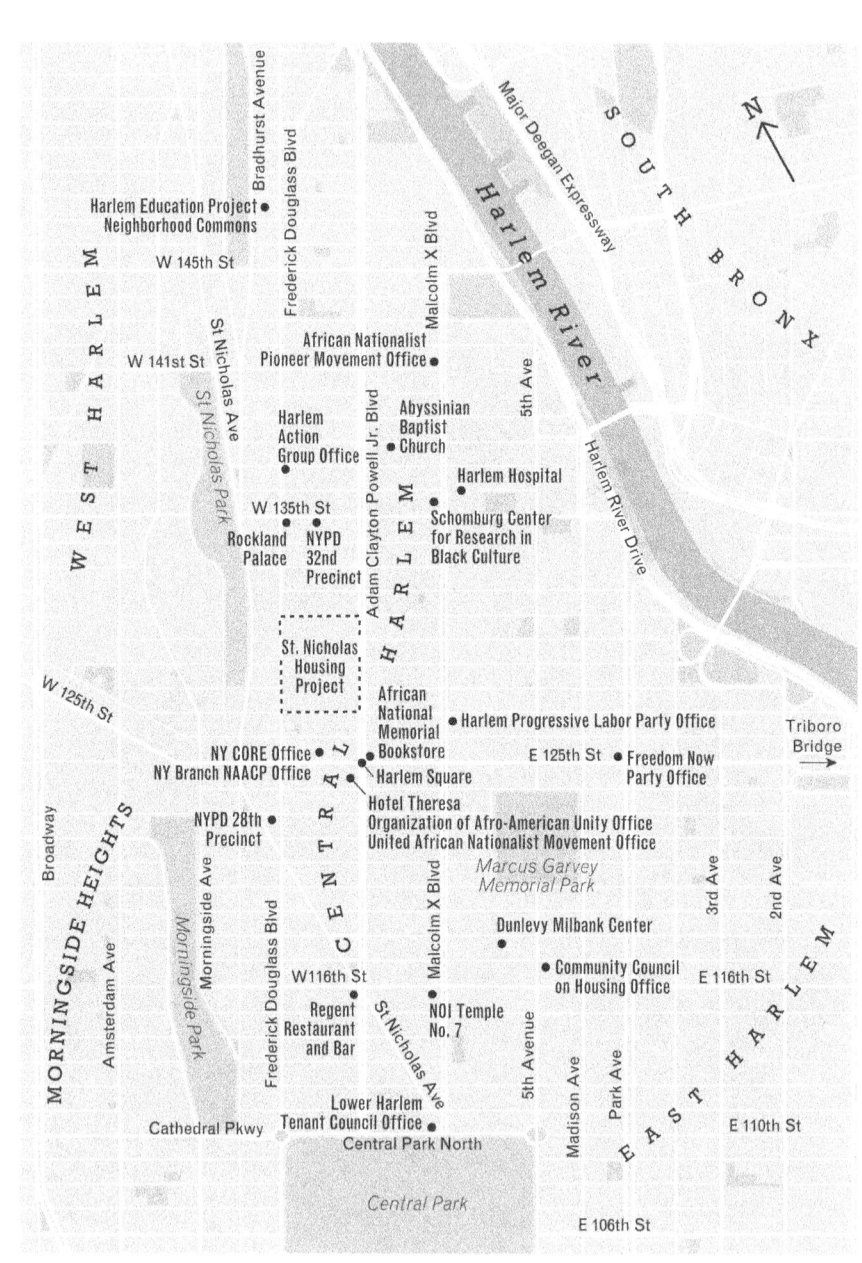

MAP 2 Harlem with key movement spaces. (Data from © OpenStreetMap contributors; map created by Nat Case, INCase, LLC)

UNLEASHING BLACK POWER

INTRODUCTION

> Harlem is the Black World.
> —ORGANIZATION OF AFRO-AMERICAN UNITY WORKING PAPER, 1964

ON A COLD JANUARY NIGHT in 1964, hundreds of Harlem residents crowded into the small gymnasium of the Dunlevy Milbank Community Center on West 118th Street. At one end of the room, writer James Baldwin sat at a long table alongside tenant organizer Jesse Gray, novelist John O. Killens, and Southern civil rights activist John Lewis. The makeshift speakers' platform was surrounded by local people, community organizers, labor leaders, and elected officials who came to show their support for a massive rent strike underway. Rising from his seat, Baldwin explained to the audience that, as a native son of Harlem, he came to testify against those responsible for the cruel and dangerous housing conditions that fueled a surging tenant movement in Harlem. The housing crisis in Harlem was not a local, isolated issue, Baldwin contended, but rather symptomatic of broader systems of racist oppression and exploitation in the urban North. "It is a more complex situation in the North," he explained. Compared to Southern states, where the perpetrators of racism were easy to identify, those responsible for crumbling apartments, segregated schools, and economic inequality in the urban North were often harder to pinpoint. "It's hard to find the landlord," Baldwin continued, "it's hard to know where the enemy is."[1] With the rent strike in its fifth month amid an escalating Black freedom movement, though, Harlem residents had begun naming and challenging the individuals and institutions responsible for systemic racism in Harlem and throughout the Jim Crow North.[2]

Much more than a lament of racial inequality in Harlem, Baldwin's comments offer critical insights into how many residents and activists understood the institutional nature of racism in the urban North. "There is a contradiction between the lives white people live and the lives we live," Baldwin argued, and "the landlords, the city and the state *are* responsible."[3] With this statement, Baldwin issued a fundamental challenge to one of the most popular and enduring perceptions of Jim Crow society. Popular and legal discourse hold that two distinct forms of racial subordination existed in the United States: one de jure, the other de facto. This enduring understanding of de jure segregation explains the system of racial oppression as one defined and codified by racist laws and regulations that governed the political, economic, and social aspects of life in the Jim Crow South. Conversely, a de facto system of racist oppression existed in the North, in which racism existed and was practiced on a personal and social level, but not officially sanctioned by governing structures.[4] By naming the city and the state as responsible for establishing, maintaining, and enforcing white supremacy in Harlem, Baldwin exposed these flawed perceptions of American racism and offered a clear directive. Black liberation would come not from changing hearts and minds but by transforming institutions and systems.

In doing so, Baldwin illuminated the nature and scope of the Black freedom movement in Harlem to upend these complex systems of oppression. Declaring that those who filled the gymnasium were part of a revolution, Baldwin warned that in the months ahead the struggle would get "harder and harder because the revolution has to revise the entire system" and that "people in power . . . are determined with everything they have in their hands to prevent such a transformation."[5] Such an appraisal was hardly romantic or hyperbolic. By the time Baldwin delivered this address, thousands of Harlem residents had already come to similar conclusions after nearly a decade of confrontations with various levels of the city's power structure. Through their experiences in grassroots organizing around housing, education, employment, and policing, local people faced violent repression as they pushed against the limits of liberalism in New York City. In the process, they developed systemic understandings of racial oppression which fueled increasingly radical struggles for rights and power in the heart of the Jim Crow North and global capitalism.

Despite the daunting odds and a determined opposition, Baldwin made clear that Harlem activists were far from alone in carrying out their revolutionary mandate. In the process of challenging racism in the largest city in the United States, Harlem residents and activists were influencing and being influenced by national and global movements for Black liberation. Baldwin proclaimed that oppressive conditions and radical organizing in Harlem were inherently linked to the Southern civil rights movement and anticolonial revolutions taking place throughout the Global South. As a destination for Black migrants within a global city, Harlem had long been a nexus between local, national, and global Black freedom struggles. Baldwin drew from this tradition as he stretched over the low table to deliver his closing remarks. "Things *can* be corrected but only if we force them to act," he exhorted, noting that the gains of the Southern civil rights movement were "precipitated by the Negro people in the streets" who "couldn't wait for Mr. Charlie to give them their freedom."[6]

While Baldwin urged the crowd to look South for inspiration, Student Nonviolent Coordinating Committee (SNCC) Chairman John Lewis explained that he and others were looking North. "Those of us who live and

FIG 1 James Baldwin addresses a rent strike rally in the gymnasium of the Dunlevy Milbank Community Center in January 1964. (*Saturday Evening Post*)

work in the Deep South have been following the struggle here in Harlem with great interest," Lewis explained. "Some of us have been saying all along that when the masses get moving in Harlem, the masses in the whole nation will move."[7] While much of the nation's gaze was fixed on dramatic struggles for civil rights in the Jim Crow South, Lewis recognized that decades of grassroots organizing were finally converging into a mass movement in Harlem that held great power and possibility for the national civil rights movement. Describing Harlem as "the only community in this nation . . . that is mobilized and prepared to move," Lewis declared the time had come for Harlem residents to "rise up and use new means to complete this revolution."[8] It was a prescient observation of Harlem's historical and contemporary importance in Black freedom struggles, which the nation was forced to reckon with in the months that followed.

With a nod to Lewis's assessment of Harlem's political significance, *Unleashing Black Power* explores the local dynamics, national connections, and global context of the Black freedom movement in Harlem. This book illuminates how activists, organizers, and local people drew from local organizing traditions and global Black liberation struggles as they theorized and organized their resistance to systemic racism in the Jim Crow North from 1954 to 1964. The richness of Black radical thought and action in this period made Harlem a key battleground in the national civil rights movement, transformed local Black grassroots politics, and facilitated the rise of Black Power in New York City. At the same time, the city's attempts to impede grassroots campaigns for human rights, power, and self-determination revealed the repressive nature of Northern liberalism and contributed to the expansion of the carceral state in the urban North. *Unleashing Black Power* argues that this decade of confrontations between Black communities and white state power caused Harlem residents and activists to seek "new means" for achieving freedom in a city, state, and nation determined to deny it. By tracing the evolution of Black radicalism and white resistance, this book offers a framework for analyzing the urban uprisings in the 1960s not as "race riots" but as rebellions *against* white supremacy and *for* Black liberation.

"HARLEM IS THE BLACK WORLD"

Despite its singular place in African American history and immense contributions to Black freedom struggles, Harlem has yet to be featured in a local study of the Black freedom movement. *Unleashing Black Power* builds on the important work scholars have done to analyze long histories of systemic racism and resistance in New York City, uplift the significance of local campaigns around housing, education, and policing during the modern civil rights era, and trace Harlem's dynamic traditions of resistance through thematic anthologies.[9] Yet, a comprehensive analysis of Harlem's place within and contributions to the Black freedom movement requires an extensive exploration of the local conditions, grassroots organizing, and global connections that shaped Black politics during that era. In centering Harlem within an expansive history of the Black freedom movement, *Unleashing Black Power* argues that the history of grassroots Black radicalism in Harlem is vital for understanding the evolution of Black liberation struggles, urban politics, and rebellions in the Jim Crow North and beyond.

Harlem has long occupied a prominent and unique place in the popular pantheon of Black political thought and cultural production. From the Pan-Africanism of Marcus Garvey to the consciousness-raising of the Harlem Renaissance, from the class struggle waged by the Communist Party during the Great Depression to the New Afro-American Nationalism in the era of anticolonial revolutions, Harlem was—and remains—at once a neighborhood, a political training ground, and a diasporic hub of Black radicalism and culture(s). While Brooklyn, the Bronx, Queens—and even Staten Island—had important pockets of Black radicalism and grassroots organizing during the Black freedom movement, Harlem's geographic location in Manhattan, storied artistic and political reputation, and cultural designation as a "Black Mecca" make it unique. When anticolonial leaders, dignitaries, and heads of state from the African diaspora visited New York, or when civil rights organizations wanted to connect with the city's Black community, they went to Harlem. As the Organization of Afro-American Unity put it in the spring of 1964, "Harlem is the Black World."[10]

To be clear, Harlem did not have a monopoly on Black radicalism during the Black freedom movement. It was, however, a well-connected and widely and historically respected political space with a deeply rooted Black radical tradition.[11] When we explore the work of grassroots organizers during the modern civil rights era in Harlem at a more granular level, we can see the formative influences that local people there had on the national trajectory of the broader Black freedom movement. As an international hub of Black political thought and cultural production, Harlem was home to organizers, artists, intellectuals, and local people whose contributions to Black liberation struggles throughout the African diaspora complicate popular narratives of the civil rights movement and challenge the geographies and periodization of the Black Power movement. By carefully tracing the development of local organizing campaigns within their national and international contexts, *Unleashing Black Power* argues that grassroots organizers moved beyond the framework of "civil rights" as they built a movement for Black Power and self-determination in the nation's largest city. As Northern Student Movement national director Bill Strickland put it in the fall of 1963, "It is becoming increasingly evident that 'civil rights' is no longer either an adequate term or an accurate description of the quest for full freedom which is now challenging our society."[12]

LOCAL STUDIES AND GRASSROOTS ORGANIZING

For those in attendance at the rent strike rally, the remarks of civil rights luminaries like Baldwin and Lewis were likely received not as a revelation but as an acknowledgment of a dynamic mass movement built by working-class Black and Puerto Rican residents, activists, and organizers over the past decade or more.[13] Their ideas and exhortations would have sounded familiar to anyone who heard Harlem's famed street orators at Speakers' Corner or Harlem Square, read the pages of the *Amsterdam News, Muhammad Speaks,* or *Liberator,* attended tenant organizing meetings in the basement of the Milbank Center, participated in boycotts or marches to desegregate public schools, shut down construction sites to demand jobs for Black workers, or challenged police brutality in Black and Puerto Rican communities. The presence of Baldwin and Lewis—now household names—demonstrated their respect and support for the work of local people and grassroots organizers, who have received far less popular recognition for their contributions to the Black freedom movement. It was this "spadework" of community organizing, as Ella Baker called it, that made the "revolution" Baldwin and Lewis spoke of seem like not just a necessity but a real possibility in 1964.[14]

As a local case study, *Unleashing Black Power* centers the experiences of local people and grassroots organizers in Harlem to explore broader histories of systemic racism, community organizing, and social movements in the urban North. Over the past thirty years, scholars have followed the lead of historians like John Dittmer and Charles Payne, producing important works that push against top-down accounts privileging the roles of national leaders and organizations in histories of the Black freedom movement.[15] Taking direction from this growing body of scholarship, this book proceeds from an understanding that transformative social movements are built by local people working to resolve immediate, material conditions in their communities within broader local, national, and global political contexts. In working to solve these problems, activists and organizers drew from relationships, resources, institutions, and traditions in local communities to diagnose their causes, develop potential solutions, and build the power to resolve them. Through such organizing work, residents and activists developed new ideas, strategies, and networks as they came into contact and confrontation with the individuals and institutions that maintained and defended white supremacy in Jim Crow New York. While mainstream leaders and national organizations have played important roles in social movements, the real work of organizing and movement building happens at the grass roots. Therefore, local studies offer vital insights into the emergence, mechanics, and evolution of the Black freedom movement that help us better understand its complexities, lessons, and legacies.

Local studies also allow us to better understand the nuances of the political, economic, and social landscapes people lived and organized in. Like most neighborhoods, Harlem was not a monolith, and the local Black freedom movement comprised a variety of political ideologies and interests. While the neighborhood was majority Black, experiences with systemic racism took different forms based on one's class, gender, religion, sexuality, and other identities. These experiences, in turn, often shaped individual and collective politics.[16] For example, a working-class Black woman living in a crumbling apartment on West 116th experienced racism differently from a middle-class Black man living in a stately townhouse on Striver's Row, and the two were likely to have different ideas about how racism functioned, what liberation required, and how it could be achieved.

As a study of grassroots Black radicalism, *Unleashing Black Power* focuses on the experiences, ideas, and actions of working-class Black residents who were the driving force of the Black freedom movement in Harlem. Through participation in local efforts to improve living conditions, dismantle systemic racism, advance national and global freedom struggles, and achieve Black self-determination, some of the most oppressed and exploited communities in New York City developed radical critiques of oppressive urban power structures and ushered in a new era of Black freedom struggles at the advent of the long, hot summers of the 1960s.

Throughout the book, the term "grassroots" is generally used to describe the membership and approach of certain organizations in the Black freedom movement. In this context, I consider grassroots organizations to be unaffiliated with national civil rights organizations, major institutions, or the political establishment, and composed primarily of, and led by, local working-class communities. At the same time, Black communities often saw local chapters of national organizations like the NAACP or CORE as vehicles for engaging in the civil rights movement and subsequently pushed for greater local agency that reflected their needs and aspirations. Such efforts illustrated a grassroots approach to organizing that was characterized by local leadership, a focus on working-class base building, the mobilization of community resources and institutions, a rejection of respectability politics and prescribed channels of dissent, a commitment to direct action, and a willingness to adapt to evolving conditions and needs.[17]

The proliferation of radical grassroots organizing in Harlem during the Black freedom movement was an outgrowth of local community organizing traditions, a reaction to the limits of liberalism, and a response to alienation from the mainstream civil rights movement. As historian Shannon King argues, grassroots political activism in Harlem emerged from a rich tradition of organizing for "community rights," which he defines as the "ideals, expectations, and objectives" Black residents held for their communities. Local organizing traditions, like the formation of social clubs, youth sporting teams, cultural institutions, church committees, mutual aid efforts, or political organizations, fostered a spirit of collectivity and helped shape what King calls "community politics" in Harlem. Through individual and collective struggles to realize "community rights" and build power in the early twentieth century, working-class communities created a deeply rooted and dynamic political culture of grassroots organizing.[18] In this book, I pick up decades after King, using a similar general focus while making critical interventions regarding the Northern Black freedom movement, postwar liberalism, and diasporic radical movements in Harlem.

As the Black freedom movement gradually emerged in the post–World War II era, activists and organizers drew from these traditions as they engaged with campaigns around education, housing, employment, and policing in Jim Crow New York. In the process, many working-class Harlem residents became disillusioned with mainstream civil rights organizations and city government. This alienation derived from a sense that civil rights and political establishments had abandoned the needs and aspirations of working-class

Black communities, especially as Africans throughout the Diaspora were rising up to seize their liberation by any means necessary. Through their experiences with local campaigns and engagement with national and global Black freedom struggles, many Harlem residents lost faith that the analyses, visions, strategies, and tactics of moderate, integrationist organizations would produce meaningful change and looked for alternative approaches to achieve more-expansive rights and transformative power.

THE GRASSROOTS EMERGENCE OF BLACK POWER

From the mid-1950s to early 1960s, residents and activists increasingly drew from local traditions of community organizing and Black radicalism as they forged a grassroots movement for Black Power in Harlem. While popular understandings of the civil rights movement hold that Black Power emerged in the aftermath of what Peniel Joseph describes as the "heroic period" of the Southern civil rights movement and the urban rebellions of the mid-1960s, *Unleashing Black Power* contributes to a growing body of scholarship that challenges the periodization and geography of the Black Power movement.[19] I argue that Black Power developed alongside the civil rights movement in the urban North as a grassroots response to local conditions, national and global movements, and state repression. Furthermore, tracing the evolution of grassroots Black radicalism in Harlem from 1954 to 1964 reveals a more complex picture of systemic racism in the Jim Crow North, the national Black freedom movement, and the outbreak of urban rebellions in the 1960s.

While Harlem's emergent Black Power movement was not monolithic, it had several defining characteristics expressed through the political analyses, strategies, and tactics of different organizing efforts. Analytically, the prevailing understanding of systemic racism in the Jim Crow North was fundamentally shaped by an analysis of capitalism and colonialism and an embrace of internationalism and Pan-Africanism. Inspired by Harlem's Black Left and Nationalist traditions, as well as anticolonial and socialist revolutions in Africa and the Caribbean, activists, artists, and intellectuals fostered popular consciousness about the root causes and global systems behind local conditions. Strategically, such analyses led to a general rejection of civil rights as an objective and integration as a strategy. Black radicals questioned both the efficacy of civil rights and the desirability of integrating "into a burning house," as Baldwin put it, calling instead for Black self-determination.[20]

Rather than gaining civil rights and breaking down the walls of segregated "ghettos," residents and activists called for more-expansive human rights and building power to gain Black community control of political, economic, and social institutions. Additionally, this power was to be built from the bottom up and wielded under the local leadership of working-class people, rather than through the bureaucratic hierarchies of national organizations.

Tactically, there was a rejection of nonviolence as an ideology and an embrace of self-defense and armed struggle to protect Black communities and achieve Black liberation. While extensive work has been done on the use of self-defense in the Southern civil rights movement, it has yet to be taken seriously and addressed systematically in the urban North, with a few exceptions.[21] Like Charles Cobb and Akinyele Umoja in their analyses of the Southern movement, I argue that nonviolence and self-defense were not contradictory but complementary, and necessary to the movement in Harlem. Harlem residents and activists practiced strategic nonviolence and self-defense based on their assessment of the material conditions they faced, actively supported armed self-defense in the South, and debated the use of armed struggle to advance Black liberation. As racist police violence escalated in the years leading up to the rebellion, Harlem residents used nonviolent direct action *and* demonstrated a growing embrace of organized self-defense—both unarmed and armed—to protect their communities when nonviolence proved ineffective.

RADICALISM, REPRESSION, AND REBELLION

As Baldwin predicted at the rent strike rally, the popular resurgence of Black radicalism was met with increasingly repressive measures from white New Yorkers. As Harlem residents demanded more-expansive rights and organized for power throughout the 1950s and early 1960s, they routinely pushed against the limits of liberalism and confronted the individuals and institutions upholding them. White New Yorkers used a variety of means to set and enforce these limits to maintain their power and privilege, even as many tried to distinguish themselves from their Southern counterparts through an imagined embrace of racial egalitarianism. In crafting a popular narrative of New York as an open city devoid of structural barriers to equality, white liberals narrowly considered racism to be an issue of personal prejudice, obscured the systemic forces of racism in the Jim Crow North, blamed inequality on both interpersonal racism *and* the supposed pathologies of Black communities, absolved the government of responsibility for ensuring equality, and criminalized those who challenged a status quo that was perceived as basically right and just.[22] When challenges emerged, the state routinely sought to pacify protests with lofty promises and meager reforms, while expanding policing to enforce and defend the interests of white supremacy. With liberalism as their shield, city officials, business leaders, the media, and white residents wielded state power as their sword to maintain inequality, suppress dissent, and prevent the kind of systemic transformation activists increasingly sought in the early 1960s.

Unleashing Black Power examines the practices, policies, and discourses of postwar racial liberalism in New York City to illustrate how state power was organized and mobilized to suppress Black liberation struggles and maintain a racist status quo in a supposedly open city. Through chronicling the intense and often violent resistance of city officials, industries, mainstream media, and residents to Black demands for rights and power in the decade before urban rebellions swept the nation, I argue that liberal repression of Black radicalism fomented rebellion in Northern cities. While recent scholarship on the 1964 Harlem rebellion has explored the forces of systemic racism acting on Black communities and the rebellion's impact on national policies on crime and policing, *Unleashing Black Power* contributes to a growing body of scholarship that centers the political agency and consciousness of Black communities and activists in reframing our understandings of the "long, hot summers" of the 1960s.[23] These histories of resistance are critical for understanding the escalation of state repression and police brutality that sparked nearly every rebellion of the 1960s and for challenging dominant narratives that depoliticize and criminalize uprisings while legitimizing the state's monopoly on violence. The absence of a comprehensive analysis of grassroots organizing in the ten-year period preceding the Harlem rebellion has enabled such narratives to persist, while marginalizing the significant roles played by local people and nationally recognized grassroots organizers—including Jesse Gray, Mae Mallory, and Malcolm X—in organizing Harlem residents to challenge systemic racism, thus incurring the wrath of the state to maintain the racist status quo.

By closely analyzing the escalation of confrontations with city officials and the New York Police Department (NYPD) from 1954 to 1964, *Unleashing Black Power* chronicles how police violence and repression of protest spurred Harlem residents to develop more radical analyses and strategies in their struggles for civil and human rights and power in New York City. Examining it within the context of national and global anticolonial struggles for self-determination, I argue that the outbreak of the 1964 Harlem rebellion—and the era of urban rebellions it ushered in—marked the collective rejection of postwar liberalism in an era of global revolution. By centering the experiences of grassroots organizers and local people who envisioned and fought for a radically different world in the face of systemic racism and violent repression, *Unleashing Black Power* offers a critical intervention in popular discourse around the urban rebellions of the 1960s and their legacies and recurrence today.

STRUCTURE OF THIS BOOK

The structure of the book is generally laid out chronologically, with each chapter covering a few years through a different thematic lens, all building toward the outbreak of the rebellion in July 1964. Chapter 1 surveys the political, economic, and social landscape in Harlem at the dawn of the national civil rights movement. This period was bookended by struggles against school segregation and the return of Malcolm X in 1954 and the 1957 police beating of Johnson X Hinton that heralded Malcolm's emergence as a leader in New York City. This chapter explores how grassroots organizers drew from Harlem's Black radical tradition to lay the groundwork for the Black freedom movement of the 1950s–60s.

Chapter 2 examines how Jesse Gray, Mae Mallory, and Malcolm X charted a more radical course for the movement in Harlem in the late 1950s by mounting campaigns and confrontations around housing, education, and policing. Intersecting with the efforts of an array of local, national, and international figures, their work demonstrated growing popular support for self-determination and self-defense in the months preceding a momentous protest against police brutality in the summer of 1959. The outcomes and impacts of this "near riot" are analyzed in chapter 3, which illuminates both a growing popular militancy against police violence and the methods city officials used in their attempts to ease racial tensions and prevent future unrest from 1959 to 1960. Coupled with promises of reform and minor concessions, the Wagner administration's expansion of police power revealed a commitment to using the police to maintain white supremacy and suppress dissent in New York City. This chapter also reveals how police, politicians, and press manufactured popular support for the expansion of policing, with predictably violent consequences.

While Harlem residents were confronting local conditions, many were also acting in solidarity with global freedom struggles. Set between the years of the Cuban Revolution (1959) and assassination of Patrice Lumumba (1961), chapter 4 explores how anticolonial revolutions throughout the African diaspora influenced the popular resurgence of Black radicalism in Harlem. By tracing connections between Harlem, Cuba, and Congo, this chapter explains how activists, organizers, and intellectuals helped forge a popular anticolonial consciousness in Harlem, culminating in dramatic confrontations at the United Nations in February 1961.

Set in the wake of Lumumba's assassination, chapter 5 explains how grassroots activists channeled the "spirit of Bandung" into local organizing campaigns in Harlem from 1961 to 1963, marking the emergence of what Dr. John Henrik Clarke called the "New Afro-American Nationalism." Through exploring the evolving political thought and actions of Mae Mallory and Malcolm X, the chapter details how local people theorized Harlem's place within national and global struggles for Black liberation and applied these politics to local struggles—while drawing the attention and ire of local and federal law enforcement in the process.

In chapter 6, I trace the development of both the Congress of Racial Equality (CORE) and the Northern Student Movement (NSM) in Harlem from 1960 to 1963 to analyze how local people shaped the evolution of national civil rights organizations. While this chapter covers the same years as chapter 5, the thematic split reflects the real divisions between different factions of the Black freedom movement in Harlem, namely, Black nationalists and integrationists. The involvement of local activists and organizers transformed the political thought and action of these organizations as they emerged at the forefront of Northern Black freedom struggles.

Chapter 7 examines the emergence, evolution, and impacts of the Harlem rent strikes of 1963–64, which launched tenant organizing into the vanguard of the Northern Black freedom movement. Met with meager concessions from the city and mounting repression from the NYPD, Harlem residents and grassroots organizers adopted more radical analyses and militant tactics as they fought to secure housing as a human right for Black communities.

The final chapter examines how the NYPD became the focal point of struggles for Black liberation in the days leading up to the 1964 rebellion. By the spring of 1964, heightened police surveillance, the violent repression of activists and organizations, and a war on Black and Puerto Rican youth prompted a widespread recognition of the NYPD as the enforcement arm of white supremacy. Harlem residents challenged police power through direct action, legal challenges, and self-defense in grassroots campaigns that coalesced into an emergent Black Power movement. With each successive challenge to state power, Harlem residents became increasingly radicalized, while the Wagner administration doubled down on repression and prepared for war against Black communities. This chapter ultimately argues that in its efforts to smash Black radicalism and prevent urban rebellions through a show of force, the Wagner administration provoked an open confrontation with Harlem residents who refused to submit to police terror and sought their freedom by any means necessary.

1

A "RISING TIDE" COMING IN

1954-1957

> In final analysis, Harlem is neither slum, ghetto, resort or colony, though it is in part all of them. It is—or promises at least to be—a race capital.
> —ALAIN LOCKE, "Harlem," 1925

JUST BELOW A DRAWING OF Roland Hayes on the front cover of the March 1925 issue of *Survey Graphic* magazine, the words "Harlem: Mecca of the New Negro" were printed in large, bold font. The *Survey Graphic,* which appealed mostly to a readership interested in social work and philanthropy, was inspired to publish the issue after the magazine's editor met Alain Locke at a debutante dinner, organized by Charles S. Johnson, honoring the young artists, writers, and intellectuals of the "New Negro Movement."[1] This movement represented the expressions of the social, artistic, and political consciousness of a new generation of African Americans, born after slavery, that converged in urban centers like Harlem and Chicago during the Great Migrations. In his preface to the issue, editor Alain Locke introduced readers to the social intricacies and dynamics of the neighborhood that provided fertile ground for the development of this new generation of race women and men. "The reformers, the fighting advocates, the inner spokesmen, the poets, artists and social prophets are here," Locke wrote, "and pouring in toward them are the fluid ambitious youth and pressing in upon them the migrant masses." Locke went on to contend that though surrounding communities may have been aware of the Great Migrations into Harlem and other urban centers around World War I and its ensuing social impacts, they remained "largely unaware of the psychology of it, of the galvanizing shocks and reactions, which mark the social awakening and internal reorganization which are making a race out of its own disunited elements."[2] To Locke, and many other conscious observers, this "social awakening" and unifying social reorganization taking place in Harlem signified the potential of the neighborhood as a "race capital," a Black Mecca.

This vision of Harlem as a Black Mecca put forth by Locke and others during the "New Negro Movement" was not merely an observation of contemporary social phenomena—it was a proclamation of Black survival, achievement, and empowerment. Through community organizing, political struggle, and cultural production, Harlem communities in the early twentieth century laid the groundwork for a new generation of race leaders to emerge and struggle to remake the city, nation, and world. Though there were certainly political, economic, and social forces unique to New York City that enabled the growth and development of Harlem's Black communities, this same growth was often achieved *in spite* of systemic racism in Jim Crow New York. It was, in fact, these conflicting forces of opportunity and oppression that made Harlem unique and contributed to its canonization as a "race capital."

Giving voice to this unique potential that Harlem represented for the Black world, writer James Weldon Johnson predicted in the same 1925 issue of *Survey Graphic* that "Harlem will become the intellectual, the cultural and the financial center for Negroes of the United States, and will exert a vital influence upon all Negro peoples."[3] Johnson's words proved prophetic, as Harlem's community swelled in size, reputation, and influence in the following decades. New generations of artists, activists, scholars, and politicians entered into the fray, each influenced by Harlem's cultural and political traditions. By the 1960s Harlem fostered the development of a wide array of homegrown and migrant race leaders, such as Marcus Garvey, Claude McKay, Audley Moore, Adam Clayton Powell Jr., Ella Baker, Malcolm X, Mae Mallory, and Jesse Gray, whose experiences in the neighborhood would shape political movements from the grassroots to international arenas for generations to follow.

This chapter explores the major traditions of Black political, social, and economic consciousness and organizing in Harlem that laid the groundwork for the emergence of the civil rights movement in New York City in the mid-1950s. The years from 1954 to 1957, particularly, represented a formative period in Harlem's political development, during which local activists and grassroots organizers drew from rich and diverse traditions of resistance to confront local and national issues and laid foundations for the transformative social movements of the early 1960s.

MALCOLM X AND BLACK NATIONALIST TRADITIONS IN HARLEM

Over a decade had passed since Harlem's last rebellion when Malcolm X returned in June of 1954 to lead the Nation of Islam's Temple No. 7. In the wake of World War II, white hostility toward Black claims to dignity, equality, and mobility led to a rebellion against police brutality and Northern racism following the shooting of a Black military veteran by a white police officer in 1943. Among the thousands who witnessed the mass demonstration was Malcolm Little, who had moved to Harlem the year before and immersed himself in its bustling night life and underground economy. Though raised by devoted followers of Black nationalist leader Marcus Garvey, Little was more concerned at the time with the rebellion's impacts on his livelihood than its political significance. After the death of his father and the commitment of his mother to a psychiatric facility, the teenage Little bounced between foster homes and stayed with family members from Lansing, Michigan, to Boston, Massachusetts, where he began building a reputation as a young hustler that he would carry with him to New York as a teenager. Shortly after the rebellion, financial hardship landed Malcolm back in Boston, where he was arrested and sentenced to eight to ten years on larceny and weapons charges. While incarcerated in Massachusetts state prisons, Malcolm experienced a spiritual and political awakening through his introduction to the Nation of Islam (NOI). Rejecting his past lifestyle as a symptom of white supremacy and reclaiming his dignity as a Black man, after a decade away he returned to Harlem as Malcolm X.[4]

The NOI's theology and programs were steeped in Black nationalist traditions cultivated by Marcus Garvey's Universal Negro Improvement Association (UNIA) and Noble Drew Ali's Moorish Science Temple of America. A

Jamaican migrant who settled in Harlem in 1916 and founded the UNIA the following year, Garvey built a mass movement of working-class Black people by promoting racial pride, economic nationalism, and Pan-Africanism during a period of immense racist violence.[5] Garvey's program on economic nationalism was particularly well received in Harlem, where Black residents were exploited by the white business owners and landlords who largely controlled the economy of their community. Although Garvey's movement ultimately crumbled under the weight of government repression, organizational shortcomings, and contentious relationships with other Black liberation groups, his meteoric rise had formative impacts on the political development of generations of Harlem activists, including Carlos Cooks, James Lawson, Audley and Eloise Moore, Hugh Mulzac, and Malcolm X, who carried the torch of Garveyism into subsequent eras of Black freedom struggles.[6]

While Malcolm had great successes in organizing temples in Boston and Philadelphia before arriving in Harlem, the opportunity to lead the storefront temple on the corner of West 116th Street and Lenox Avenue felt different. This homecoming of sorts reconnected Malcolm with his Garveyite roots and offered a unique opportunity to grow the NOI in an international city with a Black population that would swell to over one million by the end of the decade.[7] The temple's physical location also exposed Malcolm to Harlem's radical political culture. While receiving formal training in the NOI's brand of Black nationalism from Elijah Muhammad, Malcolm was also being influenced by street corner speakers, grassroots organizers, and radical intellectuals who shaped his evolution over the following decade.[8]

The political scene that Malcolm returned to in June 1954 was cultivated by a diverse bridge generation of Black radicals who carried Left and nationalist organizing traditions from the 1920s–40s into the postwar era through grassroots organizations, institutions, and literary collectives. As historian John Munro points out, Black anticolonialism was kept alive amid the repression of McCarthyism through "a movement culture of solidarity in spaces beyond the political spotlight."[9] These spaces included bookstores, like Lewis Michaux's National Memorial African Bookstore and Richard B. Moore's Frederick Douglass Book Centre, tenant organizations like the Harlem Tenants Council, labor organizations like the Civil Rights Congress and National Negro Labor Council, literary groups like the Harlem Writers Guild, and nationalist street rallies. Through mass rallies, parades, cultural festivals, and literature, these organizations nurtured racial pride, Pan-African identity, and grassroots anticolonial solidarity while inspiring new ideas and strategies for achieving Black liberation in the United States.

One of the most visible signs of Garvey's legacy in Harlem was (and remains) the annual Marcus Garvey Day parade, first organized by former UNIA member Carlos Cooks in the late 1940s.[10] Cooks, who formed the African Nationalist Pioneer Movement (ANPM) in 1941, was an important link between the Garvey generation and civil rights movement. Cooks conceived of the celebration as a way to forge racial identity, which he described as "the magnet that fuses and welds people . . . together for mutual advancement." The full-day affair consisted of a grand parade, eulogy and tributes to Garvey, beauty contest, raffle, music, and dance, with each part designed to cultivate Pan-African identity and pride, while raising consciousness about unity in the global struggle for African liberation throughout the diaspora.[11]

While consciousness-raising was a foundational part of these organizers' work, like Garvey they also developed pragmatic programs to translate Black nationalist and Pan-African consciousness into political action. The programs of the ANPM and United African Nationalist Movement (UANM), for example, offered pathways for Harlem residents to engage in struggles for Black self-determination at home and abroad, largely based on economic nationalism and Black capitalism. Formed by Garveyite and anticommunist James Lawson in 1948, the UANM became one of the most visible Black nationalist organizations in Harlem in the 1950s.[12] The UANM's aims and objectives for 1958–59 included international and domestic programs under the Garvey-inspired slogans of "Africa for the Africans" and "Harlem for the Harlemites." To build a "militant and consistent campaign" against colonialism, the UANM called for Afro-Americans to make capital investments and lend their technical skills "to help develop Africa," raise popular consciousness about African independence in the United States, and lobby Congress on behalf of the "needs and aspirations of Africa." In their blueprint for Harlem, the UANM called for Black-owned businesses, housing, banks, and media, as well as greater Black representation in schools and government.[13]

As a stepping-stone toward this larger goal of economic self-determination, the UANM urged Harlem residents to "Buy Black," a staple of Black nationalist programs in Harlem that was also promoted by the ANPM and NOI. For Cooks, "Buy Black" campaigns and economic boycotts were an integral part of the ANPM's program of achieving "complete economic control by the Blacks of all African Communities in America, creating thereby Self-Determination and Race Pride." To support Black communities in fulfilling this charge, the ANPM published a "Buy Black Shopper's Directory" of Black-owned businesses in their newspaper, *The Black Challenge*. In addition to supporting economic nationalism, ANPM members also pledged to promote racial consciousness and nationalist unity within Black communities and to dedicate themselves to the liberation of Africa, including vowing to volunteer as a soldier when "Africa strikes physically for freedom."[14]

The popular resurgence of Black internationalism and anticolonialism that Black nationalist organizations cultivated in the 1950s was also a response to the call of African nationalism and anticolonial revolutions sweeping the continent. The power and possibilities of Third World anticolonial struggle were heralded at the 1955 Asian-African Conference in Bandung, Indonesia. Rejecting alignment with the superpowers of Cold War imperialism (the US and USSR were not invited), representatives from twenty-nine Asian and African nations gathered to chart a cooperative course for postcolonial solidarity and self-determination.[15] The Bandung conference inspired the radical imaginations of Harlem activists and residents who were called into a global movement for self-determination by the "spirit of Bandung." Harlem residents kept up with the proceedings through coverage in *Freedom* and the *Amsterdam News,* which urged its readers to pay attention to what "looks like the beginning of a united struggle for first class citizenship on a global scale," and through Black nationalist rallies and forums to discuss its implications and outcomes.[16]

As anticolonial revolutions surged across the continent, Black nationalists in Harlem worked to cultivate a popular identification with Africa and raise critical consciousness about the significance of African independence struggles. While Cold War liberals embraced racist myths about Africa as a "dark continent" in need of American intervention to aid development and save it from communism, Black radicals sought to forge relationships between continental and diasporic Africans based on shared experiences of oppression and resistance.[17] Speaking at a rally in 1959, Malcolm X declared that "it has been since the Bandung Conference that all dark people of earth have been striding toward freedom" and urged Harlem residents not just to celebrate African independence but to "study the methods used by our darker brothers in Africa and Asia to get their freedom."[18] To veteran Black communist Alphaeus Hunton, the Bandung conference also expanded the arena of African freedom struggles and demonstrated that Black communists, non-communists, and anticommunists could find common ground in anticolonial struggle for Black liberation.[19] Hunton's analysis proved prescient in Harlem, where oft-competing organizations like the UANM, ANPM, NOI, and the International Committee in Defense of Africa rekindled the flame of Pan-Africanism lit by Marcus Garvey.

The most visible manifestation of Harlem's Black nationalist political culture was Speakers' Corner. Twenty blocks north of Temple No. 7, the corner of 135th Street and Lenox Avenue served as an informal, open-air classroom, theater, and church, depending on the orator and audience. From spring to fall, speakers on stepladders and makeshift platforms called out to passersby at the busy intersection, "raining abuse" on Jim Crow society, exhorting racial pride and dignity, and recruiting members for their organizations.[20] Speakers like Carlos Cooks—who was a major influence on Malcolm X—used a booming voice, sharp wit, and a preacher's flair to captivate transient audiences and bring Black radical thought to the street level.[21] In doing so, they created a popular forum for political debate and played a significant role in promoting popular political consciousness for generations of Harlem residents. "Speakers' Corner made it easy to raise critical questions, to be concerned about what's happening locally and internationally," writer Toni Cade Bambara later reflected. "It shaped the political perceptions of at least three generations."[22] Among those who cut their teeth as orators and organizers there in the first half of the 1900s were Garvey, Cooks, Lawson, Edward "Pork Chop" Davis, Hubert Harrison, Audley Moore, Richard B. Moore, Bessie Philips, Adam Clayton Powell Jr., and A. Philip Randolph, all of whom laid ideological and organizational foundations for the burgeoning civil rights movement in the mid-1950s.

Malcolm X's entrée to Harlem's street speaking scene came through another former Garveyite, Lewis Michaux, whose National Memorial African Bookstore on 125th and 7th Avenue was a Harlem landmark and a key site for the dissemination of Black radical thought.[23] In Michaux, Malcolm found another teacher and mentor in connecting with Black nationalists in Harlem. When local churches turned Black nationalists away from using their spaces for meetings, Michaux offered speakers a platform in front of his store—which he dubbed Harlem Square—to hold open-air rallies and meetings, where Malcolm became a regular fixture in the years that followed.[24] Through listening to and learning from veteran orators "making it plain and analytical all at the same time," Malcolm quickly established himself as an electrifying speaker and grassroots teacher.[25]

In addition to the political, economic, and spiritual education he was receiving through the NOI and Harlem's Black nationalist circles in the mid-1950s, Malcolm X was also studying with veteran radical organizers. With deep roots in Harlem's Black Left and nationalist movements during the Great Depression and post–World War II era, "Queen Mother" Audley Moore and Vicki Garvin were pillars of the political culture that Malcolm stepped into when he returned to Harlem in 1954. A Pan-Africanist and former Garveyite like Malcolm's parents, Moore established herself as a legendary street corner speaker during the Depression and was active in Left-led tenant organizing and anti-eviction campaigns. Garvin's family migrated north to Harlem during the Depression, where she cut her teeth as a young activist in Adam Clayton Powell's "Don't Buy Where You Can't Work" campaign, immersed herself in labor organizing with the National Negro Congress, and joined the Communist Party in 1947. By the 1950s she was a founding member of the Black Left newspaper *Freedom* and an active member of the Harlem Trade Union Council, a mass-based Black labor organization that laid the foundations for the National Negro Labor Council.[26] Garvin attempted to recruit Malcolm Little into the Communist Party in the 1940s during his days as a hustler in Harlem. And as Malcolm was beginning to make a name for himself with the Nation of Islam in the mid-1950s, Moore spread the word about his potential to her network of revolutionary nationalists, including Cyril Briggs and Harry Haywood. Through their continued contact with Malcolm, these radical Black women were "forging his approach to community organizing in Harlem during the 1950s and early 1960s."[27]

Before her death in 1963, Moore's younger sister Eloise Moore also played a formative role in shaping Malcolm's budding Pan-Africanist consciousness. Elijah Muhammad's insistence on the Asiatic origins of Black Americans and condescending views toward Africans had hamstrung Malcolm's outward embrace of Pan-African thought in the mid-1950s. But as the elder Moore later explained in multiple interviews, her younger sister had fueled Malcolm's international perspective by the end of the decade. "Eloise taught Malcolm about Africa," Moore recalled, "and I can tell you that when I wanted to talk to Malcolm about Africa, he couldn't mention the word." According to Queen Mother Moore, she made a trip to Chicago to confront Elijah Muhammad about his disavowal of the African heritage of Black Americans but was unsuccessful in changing his perspective after three days of debate. Undeterred, the Moore sisters took it upon themselves to teach Malcolm about Africa and guide his growth as a Pan-Africanist. "We had to teach Malcolm, you hear, and that's how he was able to get a new insight, put that to work."²⁸ It was a role that Queen Mother Moore would play for an emerging generation of Black radicals.

With a community of mentors guiding his steps at the dawn of the civil rights movement, Malcolm X rapidly expanded Temple No. 7 by awakening and organizing working-class communities. For years, the Nation's primary recruiting base was the American carceral system, where ministers offered visions of redemption and reclamation through racial pride, knowledge of self, and a strict code of personal conduct. Beyond merely instilling racial dignity and personal reform, ministers guided converts in developing analyses of systemic racism that made sense of their incarceration and social marginalization as symptoms of systemic racism imposed and enforced by a morally corrupt white society. Furthermore, the "morality" that the Nation promoted and instilled in its converts and sympathizers, though expressed in theological terms, was couched within a sense of social, political, and economic responsibility to racial advancement. While its moral code was inherently conservative, the NOI nonetheless promoted the notion of the personal as inherently political, which provided an accessible vehicle for racial consciousness and empowerment among populations that represented an "untapped reservoir of Black political power."²⁹

These were the messages that Malcolm X carried to the streets, pool halls, nationalist meetings, and Christian churches as he worked to expand the Nation's recruitment and organizing of this "untapped" power base in Harlem. Recognizing the competition that existed among nationalist organizations for the attention and loyalties of Harlem residents, Malcolm sought to distinguish the NOI through aggressive "fishing" campaigns throughout the neighborhood. By Malcolm's estimation, there was hardly a street that he and a few other ministers had missed. "We would step right in front of a walking black man or woman so that they had to accept our leaflet," he explained. "And if they hesitated one second, they had to hear us saying some catch thing such as 'Hear how the white man kidnapped and robbed and raped our black race.'"³⁰ It was through this provocative rhetoric that Malcolm was able to reach and engage broad audiences by breaking down complex analyses of racism in plain terms while also giving public voice to conversations that many were already thinking about or having behind closed doors. As Malcolm and his other ministers took this approach to the fringes of nationalist meetings and to the sidewalks of storefront churches, they "began to get visible results almost immediately."³¹

Eschewing notions of respectability politics that constrained participation in established civil rights organizations like the NAACP, Malcolm reached people where they were and captivated them with rhetoric that inspired a heightened political consciousness steeped in racial pride and empowerment. According to poet and activist Sonia Sanchez, a Harlem resident in the 1940s–50s who later joined the NOI in the 1970s, "He articulated that kind of oppression and what we needed to do to feel good about ourselves and to make for some kind of movement … he said it in a voice like we had never heard before … he said it for even the brothers on our block who didn't go to church, so couldn't involve themselves in the Civil Rights Movement … who were hanging out on corners."[32]

In addition to reaching out to the "brothers" on street corners or at nationalist meetings attended predominantly by men, Malcolm and his ministers also made concerted efforts to recruit Black women to the Nation. Recognizing that the majority of the "storefront Christians" they "fished" were women, Malcolm tailored his after-church messages along gender lines. Proclaiming the dignity and beauty of Black women in the face of an oppressive white society where racist caricatures dominated popular culture and ads for skin-lightening creams and hair-straightening products proliferated in Black media outlets, Malcolm promoted a gendered sense of racial pride in his speeches to these audiences. In these same speeches, he also invoked gendered notions of "respect" and "protection" to appeal to his audience, preaching, "The black man needs to start today to shelter and protect and *respect* his black women!"[33] While problematic for its inherently patriarchal nature, as scholar Farah Jasmine Griffin points out, Malcolm's gendered appeals to a popular desire for safety and protection from hostile and violent oppression at the hands of the police in Harlem, and at the hands of lynch mobs in the South, found receptive audiences in the late 1950s.[34]

However compelling many found the rhetoric of the NOI to be, few were lining up outside the doors of Temple No. 7 to convert in the mid-1950s.[35] As continuous acts of racist violence demonstrated a white backlash to the struggle for Black equality, though, the NOI's critique of the integrationist Southern civil rights movement became increasingly well-received in Northern cities. Indeed, a growing number saw the NOI as a useful alternative to integrationist organizing as Black Americans received a clear message that steps toward rights and power would be met with violent retribution and that local and federal governments would not be willing to intercede for their protection. As Harlem residents critiqued the futility of relying on local and federal authorities for protection and challenged the lack of initiative from civil rights organizations to protect Black communities, they found possible recourse in the theology and praxis of the NOI. In the years that followed, local, national, and global events and trends would coalesce to propel Malcolm X and his brand of Black political empowerment to the forefront of struggles for Black liberation in Harlem and beyond.

MAE MALLORY AND THE STRUGGLE FOR SCHOOL DESEGREGATION

In May 1954, just weeks before Malcolm's return to Harlem, the Supreme Court's decision in *Brown v. Board of Education* altered the course of struggles for Black liberation in the city, nation, and world. Ruling that the doctrine of "separate but equal" that sanctioned racial segregation was "inherently unequal," the Court's decision stretched beyond the lawsuit's initial intent of ensuring equal educational opportunity for African American children to challenging the legitimacy of the racial segregation that underwrote the segregation of schools. For this reason, an editorial in the *New York Amsterdam News* referred to the *Brown* decision as a "second emancipation for the Negro in America."[36]

While the case was being heard in Washington, parents, activists, and intellectuals were organizing to desegregate schools in Jim Crow New York. Two weeks before the *Brown* decision, the Intergroup Committee on New York's Public Schools held a conference in Harlem to call attention to the conditions and impacts of segregated schools in the city.[37] The committee's leaders included Ella Baker, leader of the New York branch of the NAACP (NY NAACP), Judge Hubert Delany, and Harlem psychologists Drs. Kenneth and Mamie Clark, whose testimony about the harms of segregation influenced the Supreme Court's decision in *Brown*.[38] Titled "Children Apart," the conference made clear that the problem of school segregation was not just a Southern one. Though segregated schools had been outlawed for decades in New York State, schools in the city remained separate and unequal well through the 1950s and beyond. The student body in Central Harlem's twenty-four schools was over 90 percent Black, and 71 percent of the city's elementary schools were considered segregated.[39] Compared to their white peers, the segregated schools that Black and Puerto Rican students attended were largely characterized by dilapidated buildings, overcrowded classrooms, split sessions (students attended for half days to reduce overcrowding), inexperienced, uncertified, and substitute teachers, ineffective and inappropriate curricula, and lower academic standards.[40]

Throughout the conference, the 175 delegates explained the conditions in Harlem's schools as symptomatic of systemic racism and sanctioned by city officials. Conference delegates challenged popular perceptions of "de facto" segregation in the urban North, which held that segregation was the result of social practices rather than official policies.[41] Delegates argued that the disparate adverse impacts public policies had on Black and Puerto Rican communities made city hall complicit in maintaining Jim Crow. As conference delegates pointed out, this culpability was seen most clearly through zoning policies that drew school district lines based on segregated neighborhoods and effectively maintained and enforced segregated schools.[42] Furthermore, teacher quality and assignment, student population and overcrowding, and the physical condition of school buildings all resulted from policy decisions that "created inferiority" for Black and Puerto Rican students.[43]

The "Children Apart" conference concluded with a series of resolutions to address the systemic factors behind segregated schools. Delegates resolved to establish a permanent committee that would cooperate with the Board of Education to conduct a "full and objective" study of the effects of segregation on students, meet with the Board of Estimate to discuss how housing, city planning, and zoning policies impacted education, and organize around a fair housing practices law.[44] The momentum generated by the conference coupled with the *Brown* decision spurred the Board of Education to heed the resolution for a study to investigate segregation in the city's schools. Ultimately however, like many government-sponsored studies or investigations, the study and subsequent formation of the city's Commission on Integration represented little more than a token concession to the pressure brought by the *Brown* decision and Black community leaders.[45] To many conference delegates, it quickly became clear that educational justice for Black children would not be won through city hall but through grassroots organizing for community power.

Beyond the resolutions and engagement with city officials, the real significance of the "Children Apart" conference came from activating Harlem residents and thrusting educational justice to the forefront of Black liberation struggles in New York City.[46] To *Freedom* editor Louis Burnham, the conference was "the first step in uniting parents, teachers and civic organizations" in a "movement for democracy in education in New York."[47] While many prominent activists were responsible for this development, few made greater contributions than Ella Baker. After playing a central role in organizing the conference and lobbying city officials with the Intergroup Committee on New York's Public Schools, Baker decided to change her focus "from debate to direct action."[48] Her shift reflected a growing trend in Black freedom struggles in the city and necessitated a reconsideration of her organizational approach.

Though the New York branch of the NAACP had been active in struggles for equality in education, housing, and employment for decades, by the 1950s the branch's influence in grassroots organizing had significantly waned. As the Red Scare intensified in the postwar era, the NAACP was mired in internal debates over communist involvement and ultimately banned and purged communists from the organization in 1950 to ward off repression and maintain political standing.[49] Even before the organization's capitulation to McCarthyism, which led to a steep decline in membership from 1946 to 1952, many of the NY NAACP's more progressive members had grown critical of the branch's slow-moving and compromising approach. Baker, for instance, resigned as branch secretary in 1946, citing an air of condescension toward local people and a general antagonism toward grassroots involvement.[50] Though she stayed involved for several more years, the nature of her disillusionment was an early indicator of a trending popular movement away from mainstream moderate organizations and toward independent grassroots organizing in Harlem in the mid-1950s.

Things began to change when Baker was elected as the first woman president of the branch. Under her leadership from 1952 to 1953, the branch took a more assertive approach to civil rights issues, particularly educational justice and police reform. Moving beyond the national organization's legal strategy, Baker steered the New York branch into the current of grassroots organizing by identifying pressing issues in Black communities and building direct-action campaigns with local people to solve them. "We tried to bring the NAACP back, as I called it, to the people," she later explained.[51] Baker's emphasis on grassroots organizing also informed her decision to move the branch's headquarters from its downtown location to Harlem. The move was both emblematic of Harlem's significance as a site of struggle and representative of Baker's dedication to involving local people in organizational direction, decision making, and action.[52]

In the aftermath of the "Children Apart" conference, Baker drew on her grassroots approach to advance its resolutions and demand enforcement of the *Brown* decision. "New York City didn't act right after the '54 decision," she later recalled. "It didn't have any reason to act so you had to help it to realize it."[53] Recognizing the limitations of working from within the NAACP, Baker helped found Parents in Action Against Educational Discrimination, a grassroots organization of primarily Black and Puerto Rican parents, to organize a direct-action campaign for quality education and greater parental agency in public schools.[54] Calling for a citywide campaign of political education and mass action, Parents in Action urged parents to tune into a weekly radio program on educational discrimination, write to the Board of Education with their complaints, and sign petitions. Additionally, Ella Baker and other organizers held weekly workshops to educate parents on their rights and to organize collective action.[55]

Through these efforts, Parents in Action essentially created a training institute for working-class parents to prepare for participation in mass political action, culminating in a rally at city hall in September 1957. Speaking at the rally just two weeks after Governor Orval Faubus used the Arkansas National Guard to physically prevent the integration of Little Rock High School, Baker criticized Mayor Robert F. Wagner's "hands-off policy" in allowing the city's schools to remain separate and unequal. In concluding her address, which included demands for experienced teachers in Black communities, an open transfer policy, greater parental power, and improved services in predominantly Black schools, Baker called Wagner's attention to the upcoming mayoral election. "It is with this fully in mind," Baker cautioned, "that we have instituted among parents of the subject schools a registration and voting drive."[56] If Mayor Wagner was not willing to take action on school segregation and inequality in New York City, Parents in Action intended to replace him with someone else who would.

The emphasis Baker placed on building grassroots power through Parents in Action had significant impacts on the growing militancy of many Black parents in New York, including Mae Mallory, who would mount an attack on educational inequality and systemic racism in the years that followed.[57] Born Willie Mae Range in Macon, Georgia, in 1927 and raised by a community of Southern Black women who demanded equality and advocated self-defense, Mae was taught at a young age to "hold your head up, stick your chest out, and march to the tune of 'The World Is Mine.'"[58] After a series of clashes with white children in Macon—one in which she "bloodied" the heads of a group of children who tried to stop her from roller-skating on the paved streets of a white neighborhood—Mae's mother sent her to live with her grandmother in Brooklyn when she was nine years old.[59] After a brief marriage to Keefer Mallory as a teenager, Mae Mallory moved to Harlem in the late 1940s.[60]

As a single Black mother of two children, oscillating between various jobs and welfare support, Mallory was acutely aware of how she experienced oppression and exploitation at the intersections of her race, gender, and class identities. Like Audley Moore, Mallory's search for meaningful ways to fight for rights and power in the face of this triple oppression led her to the Communist Party (CPUSA) in the early 1950s. "Every time I raised a question of better wages, better working conditions, and equality for black people," Mallory explained, "somebody would tell me that was communist . . . so I decided I better seek out the communists." The party had earned a favorable reputation in Harlem through their anti-eviction work during the Great Depression and defense of the Scottsboro Boys, yet when Mallory was fired from a job for organizing workers and the party-affiliated union hung her out to dry, she became disillusioned with white communists. "I could see that they didn't have answers . . . they didn't really want to challenge the system," Mallory recalled, "and it was impossible for me to exist without challenging the system because the system denied my very existence."[61]

After leaving the Communist Party, Mallory sought out Harlem's Black nationalist scene in the mid-1950s. Her involvement, however, went no further than attending some meetings of various organizations. "They talked a real militant thing but nobody did anything," Mallory explained. "They didn't have any answers and the men had contempt for the women." Finding these organizations to be militant in rhetoric but lacking in practical work and gender equity, Mallory decided to set her own course in the struggle for Black liberation, free from the doctrinaire confines of the Communist Party and Black nationalist organizations.[62]

Mallory hardly limited her critique of civil rights leadership to the CPUSA and Black Nationalist organizations. In a letter to the *Amsterdam News* in 1956, she criticized gradualist, middle-class organizations and emphasized the necessity of independent and local leadership for effectively mobilizing the masses for political action. Proudly declaring herself a "maladjusted Negro," Mallory criticized leaders in Black communities for "being followers themselves of certain groups that dictate to them" and therefore not being "maladjusted enough." In the letter, Mallory concerned herself with the daily labors of grassroots organizing, placing a premium on educating the "stragglers" in Harlem to become actively involved as "hopeful followers" in the struggle for Black liberation. Like Ella Baker and Malcolm X, Mallory believed that this vast pool of "stragglers" represented an essential wellspring of political power. "All the progress to be made," Mallory argued, "will be made by maladjusted Negroes."[63]

For the next two years, Mallory set her sights on making progress in public schools as she found her lane in the struggle. Beginning in 1956, she led a yearlong charge for the construction of a new school after the death of a Black child who was hit by a truck during recess prompted her to inspect the conditions of her children's school. What she found was a building in "deplorable condition" with no playground, only two decrepit bathrooms for 1,700 children, apathetic teachers, faculty shortages, and physical abuse of students. Mallory and twelve other Harlem mothers formed the Parents Committee for Better Education and joined the broader fight against Jim Crow education in New York City. The Parents Committee quickly grew to four hundred members and, after battling with city and state officials, was ultimately successful in getting a new school built. Reflecting on the struggle, Mallory later wrote that the state officials she sparred with in the state capital of Albany "were not quite prepared for this angry Black woman."[64]

Nor were local media outlets prepared to recognize her efforts. Like many Black women organizers in the civil rights movement, Mallory found that her contributions were marginalized by media outlets who credited men with leading the fight. Numerous newspaper articles credited Councilman Earl Brown or Reverend Eugene Callender with leading the group of mothers in the struggle for the new school.[65] Although Mallory and her comrades were heralded by the local Black press as courageous mothers and garnered favorable comparisons to Daisy Bates and Rosa Parks, journalists minimized their agency as leaders and thinkers in the struggle by associating these women with middle-class Black men such as Brown and Callender.[66] In this way, journalists contributed to a popular narrative that marginalized the leadership of working-class Black women and reified the assumed authority of middle-class Black men in civil rights organizations.

Nevertheless, the victory was a formative experience in Mallory's political development. "Getting that school was quite an achievement," she later wrote, "and gave me so much confidence in the fact that you *can* fight City Hall and win!" Furthermore, the fight for a new school offered an entry point and learning experience for dozens of Black women who joined the broader struggle against Jim Crow schools in Harlem. Parent-activists gained the type of political education that can only be earned through active struggle against systems of oppression. "The struggle for the new building had opened my eyes to a host of ills of the New York School System," she later reflected.[67]

On the heels of her victory in getting a new school, Mallory jumped right back in the ring with city officials when her daughter was denied registration at a nearby junior high school. While working with Parents in Action in July 1957, she filed a lawsuit in the state Supreme Court against the New York City Board of Education to challenge the legality of the BOE's zoning policy, which prevented her daughter Patricia from enrolling in a "substantially better" school. Represented by Paul Zuber, a young Black attorney and fellow member of the Parents Committee for Better Education (seen standing between Mae and Patricia Mallory in fig. 2), the suit built upon the legal precedent of the *Brown* decision by arguing that zoning policies effectively forced parents to send their children to segregated schools.[68] "The first thing that we are going to have to do is to be realistic and . . . stop calling this de facto segregation," Zuber argued. "Where we call it de jure or de facto it is still segregation under the law."[69] At a public hearing earlier that year, Mallory also blurred the lines between the racist South and the supposedly liberal North in explaining that the school her daughter now attended in Harlem was "just as Jim Crow" as the school she herself attended as a child in Macon. Like Zuber, Mallory laid the blame for separate and unequal schools at the feet of elected officials and the BOE.[70] While Mallory's lawsuit ultimately failed, it was an important contribution to mounting challenges to "segregation under the law" in Jim Crow New York.

Of course, the BOE claimed not to be responsible for residential segregation. A self-styled housing reformer, Mayor Wagner acknowledged that segregated schools were the result of "old established housing patterns" and argued that the solution to the education problem lay in the enforcement of fair housing practices.[71] The mayor's sentiment was echoed by Algernon Black of the New York Society for Ethical Culture in his support of the Sharkey-Brown-Isaacs Bill of 1957, which extended protections for fair housing practices in public housing to include privately owned dwellings. Black referred to the bill as the "Number One civil rights action which must be taken in the North if we are to implement desegregation in the schools."[72] Segregated housing was certainly a core factor in the proliferation of segregated schools in the Jim Crow North. At the same time, by tying the fate of schools to that of housing in their assessment of the problem, these white liberal leaders sought to absolve the BOE of responsibility for educational inequality, ignored the issue of racist zoning policies, and took a gradualist approach to resolving the crisis.

FIG 2 Mae Mallory (*left*) stands with her attorney, Paul Zuber (*center*), and her daughter, Patricia Mallory, in 1957. (Photo by Burley Versatile Photography; *Amsterdam News* Photograph Archive, Cornell University Library Rare and Manuscript Collections)

In doing so, they glossed over the reality that the board was neither innocent nor powerless to address separate and unequal schools in the city.

Just months before Mallory's lawsuit, the BOE's Commission on Integration—which counted Ella Baker among its members—presented two reports with plans to advance integration through revised zoning and teacher assignment policies. The BOE created the commission in 1955 to "show good faith" and evaluate potential means of desegregating schools. While acknowledging that systemic changes were needed to truly achieve educational justice for Black and Puerto Rican students, the commission showed how the BOE could take immediate action to create better, integrated schools. The reports called for the BOE to play a more assertive role in promoting equity in the city's schools through the creation of a new zoning unit with the power to integrate schools by drawing new borders, the "selective" use of busing to facilitate integration, the reduction of class sizes, and the assignment of more experienced and certified teachers to schools in Black and Puerto Rican communities.[73] Speaking before the BOE in January 1957, Hubert T. Delany, chairman of the Intergroup Committee on New York Public Schools, described the reports as an opportunity "to test the willingness of New York City to abide by its firm moral obligation" to adhere to the mandates of the *Brown* decision. The zoning report in particular, Delany argued, offered "a clear path" toward integration.[74]

While parents and activists pushed for immediate integration and equality, Superintendent William Jansen held tight to a narrow understanding of de jure segregation as a uniquely Southern phenomenon and maintained that segregated schools did not exist in New York City. Cloaking his objections to desegregation with support for "neighborhood schools," Jansen was joined by the BOE and many white New Yorkers in resisting the plans. Ella Baker spoke throughout the city on behalf of the reports and found that liberal white people "very eagerly said they wanted integration," yet when asked "whether they would permit or would welcome Blacks to live in the same houses with them, which was the only practical way at that stage to achieve integration, they squirmed." It was clear that while white liberals may have supported integration in the abstract, most were unwilling to actually "pay the price of integration," as Baker put it.[75]

Mallory, however, was less concerned with breaking down the barriers of residential segregation than she was with ensuring that Black children received quality education, regardless of where they lived. Notably absent in Mayor Wagner's assessment of desegregation was any mention of plans to resolve the rampant problems of unqualified teachers, substandard curricula, and hazardous buildings in Black and Puerto Rican communities. To Mallory, the desegregation of New York's public schools was a means by which Black students could gain access to quality education, and therefore better employment opportunities. "I don't want my child to just sit side by side with white children," Mallory later explained in a televised interview, "I just want the same classrooms with equal opportunity for my child."[76] Mallory essentially saw school desegregation as a tactic that had the potential to force the city to provide equal resources to all schools, because the fates of white and Black students would be bound together.

Through her involvement in these struggles against school segregation, Mallory also learned the risks that came with political agitation. After earlier attempts by her children's school principal to paint her as a "Communist" and troublemaker failed to deter her from demanding and winning the construction of the new school, Mallory was arrested on felony charges of fraud and grand larceny in June 1957 for briefly receiving welfare benefits while she was employed. Mallory understood the charges—which came four years after she allegedly committed the crime—as clear acts of political retribution.[77] "I had never been to jail in my life," Mallory recalled, "but this whole furor around the schools stirred up such a thing until the power structure decided that they would try to find something that they could discredit me with."[78] With the help of Ramona Garrett, a former CPUSA member and longtime Pan-Africanist organizer in Harlem, Mallory had a three-year sentence reduced to thirty days. Nonetheless, the charges made it hard for her to find work as a self-described "ex-convict" and led to her eviction from her home on Morningside Drive. Child protective services also took Mallory's son, Keefer Jr., based on claims that he was "a delinquent" (while alluding to her political activities as a source of his supposed delinquency) and put him in the care of her aunt. "They tried to make life miserable for me and I just fought back," Mallory recalled.[79] The experience left Mallory embittered by New York's racist power structure and determined to overthrow it, setting the stage for a dramatic confrontation the following year when she joined a group of mothers in organizing a landmark boycott of public schools in Harlem.

JESSE GRAY AND THE HOUSING QUESTION

As Mallory immersed herself in the struggle for educational justice, Jesse Gray was reinvigorating tenant organizing in the city. In many ways, Gray's history as an organizer is representative of a bridge generation of African Americans who carried the torch of Black radicalism from the postwar period through the emergence of the civil rights era. Gray was born in 1923 to a large family in Tunica, Louisiana, a small town on the banks of the Mississippi River and in the shadow of the notorious Angola Prison where one white sheriff reigned for nearly five decades. After moving to New Orleans as a teenager, Gray felt the brunt of Jim Crow racism and decided "to go to war against" it by challenging racist hiring practices and resisting segregated seating on street cars. As a college student at the historically Black Xavier University, he and classmate Jack O'Dell were drafted into World War II and joined the Merchant Marine, the only nonsegregated branch of the armed services.[80] The Merchant Marine also introduced them to the National Maritime Union (NMU), an 80,000-member seafarers' union and Left-led affiliate of the Congress of Industrial Organizations (CIO) that was renowned for its militant dedication to racial equality as a prerequisite for class struggle.[81]

"In the thirties and even the early forties there were only two places in the South where black and white could meet together," Gray's NMU comrade Josh Lawrence explained, "in the black churches and the halls of the NMU."[82]

The NMU offered Gray "a tremendous education" that shaped his political thought and organizing praxis.[83] Under the leadership of Black communists, like cofounder and first vice president Ferdinand Smith, the NMU emerged as a force in the labor movement and a training ground for a generation of Black radicals.[84] In addition to the leadership opportunities and organizing experience the NMU offered Black workers through its various committees, union policy required that each ship have a library and that union leaders should decide what books lined its shelves. This leadership position offered the significant opportunity to influence the nature of onboard political dialogue. As ship chairman of the SS *Washington,* Gray lined the shelves with Marxist and Black nationalist literature, introduced his comrades to the works of W. E. B. Du Bois, and facilitated discussions about the intersections of race and class in the creation and maintenance of oppressive power structures.[85] With their organizing and studies supplemented by mentorship from Black communists like Harry Haywood—who championed Black nationalism within the Communist Party through the "Black Belt" thesis—Gray and O'Dell acquired "tremendous experience; organizationally, politically, and everything else" and established themselves among Black radicals whom Gray described as the "most advanced workers in the country."[86] By 1950 both men had joined the Communist Party to apply the training they received at sea to organizing for rights and power on land.[87]

The Communist Party made strong inroads in Harlem during the Great Depression through its involvement in struggles for civil rights and Black equality, particularly with its defense of the Scottsboro Boys. Recognizing Harlem's significance within national Black consciousness, the party focused its efforts there as a means of organizing the Black working-class through direct-action campaigns, including mass marches, rent strikes, and economic boycotts.[88] The party's early advocacy of Black equality and support for Black Nationalism attracted the membership of many radical Black women in Harlem, including Vicki Garvin and Queen Mother Audley Moore, who credited the party as where she "really learned to struggle," in part through tenant organizing and anti-eviction protests during the Depression.[89]

Like Moore and other Harlem organizers who cut their teeth with the Communist Party, O'Dell and Gray carried the training and lessons they received in the NMU and the party into the burgeoning civil rights movement in the mid-1950s. After the war, Gray and O'Dell set up shop at NMU headquarters in New York City until the anticommunist purges of the postwar era resulted in their ouster from the NMU.[90] The purges were part of an onslaught of communist persecution after the war designed to dismantle Left labor-led struggles for racial equality and class solidarity. Following his ouster around 1952, the twenty-eight-year-old Gray slid into housing activism and Left political organizing in New York City.[91] While other party members went underground to escape political persecution, O'Dell and Gray remained heavily involved in mass organizing work.[92] "During this period the housing movement was really growing," Gray recalled, "we couldn't go underground."[93] Like Ella Baker, who took charge of the NY NAACP that year on the heels of their own communist purge, Gray built upon his political education and organizing experience in the NMU, as well as traditions of organizing in Harlem, to chart a new course for grassroots tenant organizing in the neighborhood and beyond.

Gray's analysis of the housing situation and approach to tenant organizing in Harlem was shaped by his experiences in the NMU. Aboard ship, Gray and O'Dell had been transformed by their reading of *The Housing Question,* Friedrich Engels's 1872 discourse on capitalism and housing conditions in urban centers.[94] "The housing shortage is no accident," Engels argued, "it is a necessary institution and it can be abolished together with all its effects on health, etc., only if the whole social order from which it springs is fundamentally refashioned."[95] In his analysis, inhumane housing conditions (shortage, overcrowding, and poor quality) were symptoms of capitalist exploitation, and therefore housing justice required the overthrow of capitalist society. While working to eradicate the root causes of housing injustice, Engels explained that "each social revolution will have to take things as it finds them and do its best to get rid of the most crying evils with the means at its disposal."[96]

The analysis was revelatory for the two young radicals as they developed a systemic analysis of housing conditions in urban Black communities and a strategy for resolving them. Through their discussions, Gray and O'Dell also came to recognize "the housing question" as an inherently racial one in American society, which could be seen most clearly in Black enclaves in the urban North. The "most crying evils" of housing revealed the intersections of capitalist exploitation and racial oppression and provided an immediate issue that working-class Black communities could be organized around to mount a political challenge to the political structures that created and maintained them. "The fact is that housing isn't just another issue," O'Dell later asserted, "housing is like bread and butter and a job."⁹⁷ As the duo read and discussed, the lesson became clear: organizing the urban Black working class around their dire housing conditions represented a pathway for engaging in revolutionary struggle for Black liberation.

During a crossing to Great Britain in the mid-1940s, the two found inspiration for putting this analysis into action. While in port, Gray and O'Dell learned that the tenant movement in Scotland had "made a breakthrough" in electing representatives to Parliament. Influenced by an era of militant labor organizing in nearby Glasgow, poor and working-class tenants in Clydebank had launched a widespread rent strike in 1920 as a means of challenging housing and labor exploitation. As a result of their seven-year rent strike, tenants achieved two immediate feats. First, they prevented the repeal of rent controls and protected their standard of living amid a period of intense economic hardships for the working class. Most significantly, though, the Clydebank rent strikers were able to form a political base among the working class that was capable of electing radical representatives to Parliament.⁹⁸

While certainly far short of a fundamental refashioning of society, the successes of the tenant movement in Scotland signaled to Gray and O'Dell the potential political power of working-class Black renters in the United States. According to O'Dell, the two men "felt that [the Glasgow residents' accomplishment] was our goal too, to develop a kind of tenants' movement, out of these slums and ghettoes, people who would fight for a national housing policy that guaranteed that working people had decent housing."⁹⁹ Gray had visions of even more expansive possibilities for tenant organizing. The housing question, to Gray, had the potential to mobilize the latent political power of the Black working class. "Rent is like that; housing can do it," Gray later argued. "We can base a party in the ghetto, we can bring in the mass of people of unrest, progressives with no place to go."¹⁰⁰

Gray found his political home in the Harlem Tenants Council (HTC), a tenants' rights initiative of the American Labor Party—an electoral front organization for the CPUSA.¹⁰¹ Left-led tenant organizing had deep roots in the city, and the American Labor Party made housing a central issue of its political platform as a means of base building among working-class Black, Puerto Rican, and Jewish communities.¹⁰² Restricted from living-wage jobs by employment discrimination, denied mortgages by racist lending practices, and kept out of majority-white communities by racist landlords and developers, many Black New Yorkers paid high rents to live in overcrowded older buildings where absentee landlords refused to make repairs. In the 1950s only

51 percent of Harlem's housing stock was classified as "sound," compared to 85 percent citywide, and over 20 percent of units were considered overcrowded, nearly doubling the citywide rate of 12 percent.[103] Although nearly 400,000 housing units were created from 1950 to 1959, by 1960 the city was still short another 430,000 units needed to replace substandard units, accommodate a growing population, and maintain a sufficient vacancy rate—a gap that city officials predicted would take another twenty-five years to fulfill.[104] Furthermore, Black and Puerto Rican residents had no representation in the agencies charged with addressing housing conditions in the city, including the Housing and Rent Commission and the Committee on Slum Clearance.

With the city's Black population growing amid a housing shortage, white landlords had free rein to exploit Black renters hemmed into segregated neighborhoods. Segregation played into the hands of slumlords who maximized their profits in captive markets by cutting costs of maintenance and repairs, while also reducing their federal income tax liability by claiming property depreciation.[105] As a result, tenants routinely complained of collapsed ceilings, busted pipes, no heat or hot water, trash-filled hallways and alleys, infestations of rats and roaches, inebriated superintendents, and absentee landlords who were nowhere to be found. The public health implications were disastrous: rates of infant mortality and deaths from home accidents in Harlem were nearly double the rest of the city.[106] In 1954 alone, Harlem residents filed more than ten thousand complaints for lack of heat in their buildings, including some that were without heat and hot water for an entire winter. Over a two-month span in the winter of 1953–54, ten Harlem residents were killed in building fires caused by landlord violations.[107] Weak code enforcement policies effectively made the city complicit in these conditions, and the lack of political representation limited the abilities of Black renters to challenge the racist exploitation of slumlords. "Landlords are literally getting away with murder," *Freedom* reported in early 1955. Explaining housing conditions in Harlem as symptoms of racist oppression and exploitation in the Jim Crow North, the radical monthly newspaper founded by Paul Robeson and Louis Burnham urged Harlem residents to see housing as a civil rights issue and join their local tenant organization as their "best insurance against landlord abuse, bad housing—and possible sudden death."[108]

With Gray at the helm, the Harlem Tenants Council organized tenants to demand safe and affordable housing as a civil rights issue through political advocacy, tenant support, and direct action. Shortly after assuming leadership in 1953, Gray borrowed a page from the Clydebank tenants' playbook and joined a major campaign to save rent control in the city when Governor Thomas Dewey moved to lift state rent control and allow a 15 percent rent hike to make up for the wartime freeze.[109] Warning that Dewey's plan would "hit the whole Harlem community hard" and further empower slumlords to exploit Harlem tenants, Gray and the HTC organized tenants to pressure Harlem congressmen and city officials in opposition.[110] While the struggle was unsuccessful, it illuminated the need for Black representation in housing policy. In the spring of 1954, Gray and the HTC called out the "lily-white leadership" of the Department of Housing and Building, demanded representation of Black tenants in policy-making positions, and campaigned for political candidates that supported the interests of working-class renters.[111] The following year, the HTC met with the city's Housing commissioner to demand that he hold landlords accountable and take responsibility for maintaining safe housing conditions in Harlem. One of the key demands they presented during the meeting was a "lien law," which would permit the city to make repairs on privately owned housing units and bill noncompliant landlords for the costs.[112]

Gray approached the HTC's policy campaigns as vehicles for activating and organizing tenants. In a leaflet from the rent control campaign, the HTC informed tenants of their rights, instructed them to seek rent reductions for poor conditions, and heralded the victories of organized tenants. Furthermore, they called tenants into the broader Black freedom struggle with a declaration that "THE END OF DISCRIMINATION IN ALL HOUSING IS THE KEY TO THE END OF DISCRIMINATION IN EVERYTHING."[113] Likewise, Gray saw the campaign for the lien law (also known as the receivership law) as an opportunity to raise consciousness about the housing question and advance a transitional demand toward what he described as "a fundamental objective which makes people first and property second."[114] In Gray's analysis, empowering the city to take control of private property would expedite improvements for Harlem tenants in the short term and move the city toward public control of housing in the long run.

Above and beyond the HTC's involvement in policy campaigns, it was Gray's day-to-day work of supporting and advocating for tenants that earned him respect and allowed the HTC to begin building a base in the community. Organizers routinely distributed fliers throughout Harlem urging tenants to visit the HTC office on 125th Street and Lenox Avenue, where they could learn about their rights, find help in filing complaints and navigating city departments, and get support for organizing their buildings. Among their most impactful work, though, was helping Harlem tenants resist unjust evictions. When two Black families were wrongfully evicted in the winter of 1953, Gray helped them file complaints with city agencies and successfully fought the local rent office to keep them in their homes, all while denouncing city housing agencies for protecting exploitative landlords and not tenants.[115] While the HTC's day-to-day work may have seemed more like the work of a social service agency than a radical political organization, it was a vital part of Gray's strategy of base building. By supporting and organizing tenants to address their immediate needs, he was activating working-class communities in struggles against racist oppression and exploitation at the dawn of the civil rights movement.

One of Gray's most common tactics to activate and empower tenants was going after their slippery landlords. Many Harlem tenants had little contact with—or knowledge of—their absentee landlords, and many feared that filing complaints could lead to retaliatory evictions. Gray understood that by bringing landlords out of the shadows and holding them accountable for providing safe and decent housing, tenants could improve their housing conditions and gain confidence in challenging their oppressors. Two days before the *Brown v. Board* decision in May 1954, Gray published the names and misdeeds of a hundred Harlem slumlords in the *Amsterdam News* and staged a direct-action protest against the landlord of a building who boasted to tenants "that they would never force him to repair the house." When the landlord was jailed two weeks later for evading a court summons to replace windows and repair the heating system, Gray and the HTC earned the respect of tenants for proving that racist slumlords were not untouchable and that organized action brought results.[116]

To Gray and the HTC, Harlem's housing conditions were interconnected with the emergence of urban renewal projects that washed over New York City in the 1950s and intensified the housing crisis. Spearheaded by planning czar Robert Moses and fueled by Title I of the 1949 Federal Housing Act—which subsidized the mass demolition of so-called slums to clear entire neighborhoods for private development—"urban renewal" hit Black communities particularly hard and resulted in widespread displacement of working-class residents. Entire blocks lined by brick rowhouses with low-rent units were replaced with new superblocks of high-rise apartments with higher rents, scattering residents and destroying the social fabric of communities. In true colonial fashion, Moses selected several sites comprising dozens of acres of primarily residential blocks in Harlem without community input, sparking over a decade of protests by residents who saw "urban renewal" as code for "Negro removal."[117] Like many Harlem residents, *Amsterdam News* columnist Richard Lincoln saw the urban renewal projects as calculated plans to "increase Jim Crow" by dislocating growing Black political power in Harlem. Between 1947 and 1953, nearly 150,000 Harlem residents were displaced, with another 21,000 Black and Puerto Rican families expected to be made homeless by 1956.[118]

One of the most contentious urban renewal projects of the 1950s was the Godfrey Nurse Houses, which were slated to be built on an area bounded by Lenox Avenue and 5th Avenue from 132nd Street to 135th Street. Led by white developers with public funding, the project was designed to house two thousand people in a neighborhood where eight thousand people lived with no provisions for their relocation. Furthermore, rents in the middle-class development were expected to be three times the amount the largely working-class Black community was paying. After acquiring the land in late 1952, the developers tried to force tenants out by letting buildings deteriorate to the point of being condemned. Rather than leave, Harlem tenants organized to fight back against racist displacement. "We don't want to leave this neighborhood," one longtime tenant said. "What we want is some repairs and some painting and some heat." Another tenant told reporters she had to "fight her landlord for a year" by withholding rent and taking him to court before he finally fixed a gaping hole in her ceiling.[119] In February 1955 an elderly woman living in an apartment with no heat was burned to death when a kerosene heater caught fire, leading Gray to call for a mass march on the state capital in Albany and Rep. Adam Clayton Powell Jr. to call for a federal investigation of Title I projects in Harlem.[120]

Within months of taking leadership of the HTC, Gray began organizing tenants in the project site to demand repairs, prevent evictions, and fight against demolitions. In early 1953 the HTC joined with the Urban League to organize a community meeting for residents to get answers from the developers and demand action from the city. The five hundred residents who turned out were enraged when the developers refused to attend the meeting because they heard from Robert Moses that it would be "invaded" by communist groups.[121] Gray, however, saw the developers' absence as a sign that they feared facing "the tremendous fighting spirit and sentiment in the area."[122] On the heels of the meeting, the HTC called for "a merger of all tenant groups fighting the common battle for decent housing, strengthening of rent controls, against all evictions, and for a program of forcing the city administration to assume its responsibility of forcing landlords to correct violations."[123]

At the same time, they also waged a successful campaign for legislation to protect rooming house tenants from displacement by urban renewal projects. While often characterized as sources of blight, vice, and crime—and therefore targeted for "slum clearance"—rooming houses were often the only housing options tens of thousands of working-class Black families could afford, or find, given the severe housing shortage in Harlem.[124] Passed in 1956, the rooming house law guaranteed legal rights to tenants and protected them from summary evictions.[125] Through these grassroots organizing and policy advocacy campaigns, the HTC helped to prevent countless evictions and helped make urban renewal a key political and civil rights issue in the city.

After nearly four years, the Godfrey Nurse Houses still were not built, yet countless residents had been displaced. In what became a national trend with urban renewal projects, the *Amsterdam News* reported in 1956 that "we now see hundreds of homeless Harlemites . . . walking the streets looking for homes."[126] In the spring of 1956, a thousand residents turned out for a public hearing on urban renewal projects in Harlem. It was the first time a city body came to Harlem for a public hearing on housing, and reporters said it was "one of the most stirring community meetings on housing in years." Speakers called for protests at city hall, the formation of a relocation bureau, building on vacant lands instead of occupied blocks, and city repossession of the land for the Godfrey Nurse project.[127] Despite immense pressure from Harlem tenants and sympathetic city officials, the city ultimately refused to repossess the land or pull funding, and the project was later rebranded and built as Lenox Terrace Apartments. The years-long campaign against the Godfrey Nurse project left many Harlem tenants bitter toward city officials and laid the groundwork for ongoing struggles against urban renewal in Harlem in the years to come.

Through their organizing campaigns in the mid-1950s, Gray and the HTC revived tenant organizing as an essential part of broader struggles against racist oppression and exploitation in Jim Crow New York. While Gray's tireless organizing work in these years earned him respect from Harlem tenants, it also heightened attention from the FBI, which escalated its anticommunist investigations of Gray in early 1956.[128] With the FBI hounding his tracks on the heels of the Godfrey Nurse campaign, Gray headed south to North Carolina sometime in 1956 before returning to Harlem the following year to form the Lower Harlem Tenants Council (LHTC). With Gray's return and the rise of the national civil rights movement, demands for tenants' rights and political power escalated, and Gray began to build a local political movement around housing.

POLICING JIM CROW AND STRUGGLES FOR REFORM

In organizing Black communities to challenge systemic racism, Gray, Mallory, and Malcolm X each came into confrontation with the institution charged with maintaining and enforcing the political, economic, and social status quo—the police. As racist violence escalated throughout the South in response to emergent challenges to Jim Crow, Northern activists increasingly came to identify police violence within a national context of racist violence as a tool of social control.[129] In the years following the 1943 uprising, which Rep. Adam Clayton Powell Jr. attributed to the actions of "bigots in high places [who] tried to hold back" a "rising tide" of Black activism, the daily brutality, corruption, negligence, and repression of white NYPD officers in Harlem made policing a core focus of struggles for Black rights and power.[130]

In 1947 Powell's successor as Harlem's representative on the city council, Benjamin Davis Jr., published a pamphlet titled *Lynching Northern Style: Police Brutality*. Davis, a lawyer and Communist Party member, had been elected to fill Powell's seat when the latter embarked on his first congressional campaign in 1943. The pamphlet was published in response to the inaction of police commissioner Arthur Wallander in twenty-six cases of alleged brutality brought to his attention in an eighteen-month span. Davis argued that, as with lynching in the South, the uptick in police violence since the end of World War II in the North was driven by an intention to "keep the Negroes 'in their place'"; to "create the impression that Negroes are unworthy of the full citizenship which they rightfully demand"; to "divide Negro and white" to undermine trade union organizing; and to make Black and nonwhite communities "the scapegoat of repeated 'crime wave' slanders against Harlem and other Negro communities."[131]

Although police officials characterized such analyses as subversive attacks on the department, Davis had hit on many of the core functions of racist policing in Jim Crow New York. Judge Hubert Delany, a member of the NAACP Legal Defense Fund and the Intergroup Committee on New York's Public Schools, was no stranger to the realities many Harlem residents lived with. Just months before the Civil Rights Congress delivered their petition "We Charge Genocide" to the United Nations in 1951, white NYPD officers brutally assaulted Delany's nephew outside his home on Bradhurst Avenue in Harlem. William Delany, a twenty-nine-year-old Black man whom the polio virus left disabled as a child, was beaten unconscious and kicked in the face after the white officers ordered him off his own front stoop.[132] The beating came during a five-year period from 1947 to 1952 in which forty-six unarmed African Americans were killed by police in the state of New York, according to investigations by the NAACP.[133] In response to the brutal beating of his nephew, Judge Delany penned a biting statement about police brutality that ran on the front page of the *New York Amsterdam News*. Delany charged that "police in Harlem consider that they have the God-given right in a poor community... to keep the peace with the nightstick and blackjack whenever a Negro attempts to question their right to restrict the individual's freedom of movement." To further emphasize the weight and urgency of his criticism of the heavy-handed practices of police officers, Delany pointed out that "such actions on their part lead to riots."[134]

Ten years after the 1943 rebellion, and two years after Delany's article, a 1953 scandal involving the NYPD and the FBI finally gave way to a modicum of police reform in New York City. Following an investigation into the brutal beatings of Jacob Jackson, a Black truck driver, and his neighbor Samuel Crawford in Hell's Kitchen in 1952, the *New York Telegram and Sun* newspaper reported on a secret agreement that existed between the NYPD and the FBI to block federal investigations of police brutality cases in the city.[135] In an open letter to the mayor, Ella Baker demanded "the immediate resignation" of the police commissioner, while the NY NAACP and Adam Clayton Powell Jr. organized mass meetings to protest police brutality.[136] As a result of the protests and organizing work of a coalition of nineteen community organizations, including the NAACP, ACLU, National Urban League, and the AFL, the NYPD implemented "antibias training" for officers and established the Civilian Complaint Review Board (CCRB).[137] This internal panel, staffed by three non-uniformed members of the NYPD who served in administrative roles in the Community Relations Division, conducted no hearings—its members simply reviewed reports from commanding officers and recommended any disciplinary actions to the police commissioner.[138] Furthermore, the police commissioner was not mandated to implement any recommendations of this advisory panel.

As tensions continued to rise with the growth of the modern civil rights movement in the mid-1950s at local and national levels, the internal-review structure of the CCRB came under increased fire from Black and Puerto Rican communities, who were disproportionately targeted and abused by an overwhelmingly white NYPD. Reflecting popular opinion, Councilman Earl Brown declared that the new review board was nothing more than "the same old system with a new coat of whitewash."[139] The only modification of the CCRB's procedures, before its short-lived reform under Mayor John Lindsay in 1966, came as a concession to community demands in May 1955. In essence, the only changes were the ability of complainants to file a claim of misconduct at any precinct and the shift of handling of complaints to the deputy commissioner of community relations.[140]

It took less than a week for complaints to flow into the new system. One of the first came from nine-year-old Elbert Dukes, a Harlem resident who filed a complaint with the assistance of the NY NAACP. Dukes, an honor student at PS 181, was beaten with a pair of handcuffs by officers inside the 28th Precinct, where his mother found him handcuffed to a steam pipe with blood on his head, face, neck, and chest.[141] While Dukes's case drew scant attention from media outlets and civil rights organizations in New York, the murder of fourteen-year-old Emmett Till in Money, Mississippi, just months later sent shockwaves through the city, nation, and world. Illustrating Davis's arguments in *Lynching Northern Style,* the two men who savagely murdered Till believed it their mission to uphold white supremacy. According to reporter William Bradford Huie, a white journalist who interviewed Till's killers, the two men felt they "had to make an example of a young man like Emmett Till." "They were told," Huie said when asked about their motives, "that with the beginning of the Supreme Court decision [in *Brown v. Board*], this was a war."[142] The lack of justice for Till's gruesome murder was a grim reminder that each step toward Black equality would be met with pushback. It was also a "clarion call" to an emergent generation of young African Americans far beyond the South who would shape the civil rights movement in the following years.[143]

In New York, Till's murder and trial were covered in newspapers for months and became a focal point of sermons, speeches, mass meetings, and rallies.[144] Advertisements promoting voter registration campaigns filled newspapers like the *Amsterdam News,* and crowds flocked to mass meetings and rallies in Harlem. A wave of mass demonstrations, meetings, and rallies washed over Harlem in early October (as seen in fig. 3), with crowds filling entire city blocks during protests. Commenting on a meeting held at Williams Institutional (CME) Church, Councilman Earl Brown wrote, "Never before in Harlem's history has a crowd been so big and shown so much determination to do something about the way their people are brutalized in their own country. They want action."[145] At another early October rally organized by the NY NAACP, three thousand people packed the Lawson Auditorium on 125th Street while another five thousand reportedly "pushed against police lines" outside.[146]

Although these demonstrations and campaigns were carried out with a greater sense of urgency in the latter months of 1955, they represented moderate approaches to civil rights agitation. Despite the large turnout, the resolutions passed at the NAACP rally were indicative of the organization's moderate approach that would be challenged in New York in the following months. The gathering voted to send resolutions to Mississippi Governor Hugh White and President Eisenhower protesting the handling of the Till trial and the "atmosphere of lawlessness" in the state; to appeal to New York voters to prevent white supremacists from being elected to Congress;

FIG 3 Thousands gather for a mass rally in New York City on October 11, 1955, to protest the murder of fourteen-year-old Emmett Till in Money, Mississippi. (Photo by Layne's Studio; Library of Congress, Prints and Photographs Division, Visual Materials from the NAACP Records [LC-USZ62-131058])

and to call for federal investigations into denial of voting rights in the recent Democratic primary in Mississippi and the recent murders in the state.[147] Though these resolutions were noteworthy for their approach in seeking federal intervention in matters of civil rights, which would become common practice throughout the burgeoning civil rights movement, it was becoming clear that a growing number of Black communities were anxious to explore new routes toward liberation.

In Harlem, this was particularly evident in the budding popularity of Malcolm X and the Nation of Islam, which sought to mobilize Black outrage in new organizational directions in the late 1950s. Like Ella Baker, who drew on her postwar organizing roots to influence the grassroots trajectory of Black freedom struggles in the mid-1950s, in the wake of Emmett Till's murder the Nation of Islam found fertile ground for cultivating local traditions of militant Black nationalism. The Nation of Islam fervently critiqued the integrationist approach to civil rights advocacy that undergirded the *Brown* decision and emergent Montgomery bus boycott. Elijah Muhammad, who claimed a causal relationship between acts of lynching and increased NOI recruitment, argued that the murder of Till was a "lesson" for those who sought integration with an inhumane white society built on Black oppression and exploitation.[148]

Malcolm's active presence on the streets of Harlem finally paid off in 1957, when an incident of police brutality provided a platform that would propel him and the Nation into the public eye in New York City. On a late April night, Johnson X Hinton, a member of Temple No. 7, and two other men intervened as NYPD officers were "working over" a Black man with their nightsticks at the corner of 125th Street and Lenox Avenue. Hinton approached the officers and asked them, "Why don't you carry the man on to jail?" before walking back into the small crowd, which was growing as more police cars arrived at the scene. Not satisfied with the rate at which the crowd was dispersing, the responding officers began swinging their nightsticks to speed up the process, cracking Hinton in the head in the process. As Hinton yelled a prayer in agony, more officers rushed at him, knocking him down as "blood gushed" from his head, and continued to attack him as he lay bleeding on the ground. Hinton was then taken to the notorious 28th Precinct on 123rd Street and 8th Avenue, where the relentless beating continued while he was handcuffed to a chair.[149]

As word spread of Hinton's beating, a crowd of five hundred, including members of the Nation of Islam led by Malcolm X, gathered outside the precinct, demanding that the injured man be provided medical attention. After initially being told that there was no such man in the precinct, police eventually permitted Malcolm inside to examine Hinton, as the crowd continued to swell outside. Upon seeing his condition, Malcolm demanded that the man be taken to the hospital. While Malcolm met with police officials, members of the Fruit of Islam, the NOI's regimented unarmed security detail, formed perimeters outside the precinct, "arms folded, like a battalion awaiting orders," as an increasingly volatile crowd continued to grow behind them. Hearing of Hinton's transfer to Harlem Hospital, the crowd marched to 135th Street and Lenox Avenue, where two thousand assembled, eager to learn of Hinton's condition. After being treated, he was quickly released back to police custody and returned to the 28th Precinct, where the crowd continued to swell to an estimated four thousand. While Hinton remained in a cell, Malcolm X once again negotiated with "nervous" police officials who feared that the situation outside the precinct was teetering on the edge of a "riot."[150] Malcolm was assured that Hinton would continue to receive medical treatment, and in return he agreed to calm the crowd outside. Upon exiting the precinct, *Amsterdam News* editor James Hicks reported, Malcolm "gave one brief command to his followers and they disappeared as if in thin air."[151] Astounded by the swift, disciplined dispersal of the NOI and massive crowd, a policeman on the scene infamously commented, "No one man should have that much power!"[152]

The "power" that Malcolm demonstrated outside the 28th Precinct garnered front-page attention in the *Amsterdam News,* under the subheading "'God's Angry Men' Tangle with Police." After the story ran, "for the first time," Malcolm later recalled, "the black man, woman, and child in the streets was discussing 'those Muslims.'"[153] The standoff on 123rd Street was a major victory for the NOI and Malcolm in Harlem. Not only did Johnson X Hinton later receive the highest police brutality settlement in city history at the time, the Nation also demonstrated to audiences in Harlem and beyond that they wielded the power to confront racist forces in the city—and win.[154] "What Harlem wanted from Malcolm and the Muslims," journalist Peter Goldman wrote, "was proof that they were as big and bad as they claimed to be."[155] At a moment when justice for victims of racist violence was in short supply locally and nationally, the Nation's offer of protection against a police department that functioned, as many believed, to "keep the Negroes 'in their place,'" drew many new converts into their ranks.

One such convert was Benjamin Goodman, an Air Force veteran who was struck by "how this man Malcolm X was out front protesting against that act and how the Muslim brothers and sisters reacted. The brotherhood is what attracted me. The unity. How a Muslim goes to the aid of a brother when he is mistreated. It seemed like unity and brotherhood and—*love*. So I went there to seek out the Muslims."[156] Goodman, who was underemployed and "born dissatisfied" with racism in America, was one of many in Harlem who found in Malcolm and the NOI a sense of empowerment and a way of confronting the oppressive white institutions that colored their lives. In the wake of Hinton's beating, the Nation grew from "a few hundred" to an estimated two thousand, "with a presence and impact far larger than the actual number."[157] Malcolm had effectively proven to the grassroots bases he sought to reach that he could back up his powerful rhetoric with concrete action, and from these populations at the margins of urban society, built "an army of people nobody wanted."[158]

In the waning days of the year, *Amsterdam News* editor James Hicks declared 1957 to be the "year Negroes fought back."[159] In the South, nine Black students in Little Rock, Arkansas, braved crowds of intransigent segregationists, supported by police and the governor, to compel federal enforcement of the *Brown* decision and successfully desegregate Little Rock Central High School. In New York, Malcolm X and the Nation of Islam faced down the New York Police Department in a startling display of power to signal a new challenge to age-old practices of racist policing in Harlem. Across the Atlantic, Ghanaians celebrated their independence from Britain, elevating Kwame Nkrumah to international acclaim and heralding an era of anticolonial revolutions in Africa.

Local, national, and global developments in the three years following the *Brown v. Board of Education* decision marked a new chapter in the long struggle for Black equality in Harlem, during which communities built upon traditions of political consciousness and action in the neighborhood to engage in new struggles for rights, power, and liberation. Drawing from postwar struggles for civil rights, along with Left and nationalist movements in the city, the surging grassroots organizing efforts of Ella Baker, Malcolm X, Mae Mallory, and Jesse Gray came to shape the civil rights movement in New York City and beyond in the next decade. Largely eschewing the moderate approaches and middle-class respectability politics of established civil rights organizations, these organizers sought to build their bases among working-class Black communities as a way of mobilizing an untapped well of potential political power.

It was also during this period that a new generation of future activists and organizers began to come of age in their racial and political consciousness. With the murder of Emmett Till in 1955 broadcast nationwide, the wanton brutality of white supremacy in the face of Black uplift sounded a call to action for young people across the nation who saw their reflection in the face of the fourteen-year-old. With the guidance of veteran organizers like Baker, it was this generation of Till's peers who would take to the streets in the early 1960s to alter the trajectory of the burgeoning civil rights movement in the South, as well as the North.

In Harlem, this period laid the groundwork for protracted struggles for rights and power in New York City and beyond in the following years. Though Malcolm X would rise to international acclaim in the 1960s for his piercing rhetoric that awakened and empowered people of African descent while stripping white supremacy to its core, his rise in Harlem in the mid-1950s was characterized by his dogged grassroots organizing efforts. Likewise, the successes of Gray, Baker, Mallory, and many other organizers in Harlem were grounded in their mobilization of resources that were "not only material but intellectual and emotional."[160] The grassroots organizing of these leaders during an era that represented real possibilities for fundamental societal change empowered local people in Harlem to become active in their communities and build movements that would have far-reaching impacts on the national civil rights movement in the coming years.

2

"THE NEGRO REVOLT"

1958-1959

> You see, Sir, I am also a maladjusted Negro and I wonder why the thousands of other maladjusted Negroes can't get all other Negroes to become maladjusted too. All the progress to be made will be made by maladjusted Negroes.
> —**MAE MALLORY**, *"Maladjusted Follower," New York Amsterdam News, 1956*

AS DAWN FILTERED INTO THE city on Independence Day in 1959, New Yorkers opened the Saturday edition of the *New York Times* to find a transcript of President Eisenhower's Fourth of July address. Eisenhower asked Americans to renew their dedication to "the principles of freedom, of government elected by the people, of equal opportunity for all" and called upon them to "state the facts of freedom and trust in God, as we have ever done. Thus, we know that truth will triumph."[1] In contrast, the morning edition of the *New York Amsterdam News* carried a starkly different message. Covering nearly half of the front fold in the largest, boldest, and blackest font the press had, the headline "Negro Revolt" exposed the hollowness of Eisenhower's rhetoric by highlighting recent struggles for "peace with justice" in the Jim Crow North. Beneath the headline, the front page was packed with reports of emergent rent strikes, NAACP pickets over employment discrimination, backlash from white parents over school desegregation in Queens, and political struggles for control of the Harlem Democratic Party. Warning that the city's largest Black community was "seething with grim unrest," the weekly paper reported that "more than one million Negroes were virtually in revolt this week, taking action into their own hands in bold moves."[2] While the nation celebrated its independence based on principles of freedom, justice, and democracy, the *Amsterdam News* evoked a vision of impending mass upheaval for civil and human rights in Harlem.

The political climate that marked the emergence of this "Negro revolt" in Harlem did not appear overnight—it was fostered by the efforts of local grassroots organizers like Jesse Gray, Mae Mallory, and Malcolm X in the latter years of the 1950s. The work of these three leaders drew from traditions of Black radicalism in Harlem, intersected with a wide array of influential local, national, and international figures, and laid a foundation for the evolution of Black radicalism in Harlem and beyond in the 1960s. The demands they raised for immediate systemic change and self-determination of working-class Black communities represented a fundamental challenge to racial liberalism and moderate civil rights organizations in the urban North. Through mounting confrontations around housing, education, policing, and political power, these grassroots organizers charted a more radical course for the Black freedom movement in Jim Crow New York.

As the national civil rights movement evolved throughout the South in the late 1950s, Black communities in New York City waged struggles of their own for equal educational opportunities, fair employment practices, access to safe and affordable housing, and protection from racist policing. Weaving together threads of Black nationalist, Left, anticolonial, and Pan-African thought, organizers saw these campaigns around the material needs of working-class Black communities as vital ways of engaging local people in a global struggle against white supremacy. Building upon national and local organizing in Harlem during the post–World War II era, Gray, Mallory, and Malcolm X steered a shift away from middle-class, integrationist approaches to civil rights toward building grassroots political power for human rights, self-determination, and a more fundamental transformation of society. In 1959 the growing power and influence of this swelling grassroots militancy became abundantly clear in New York City as a series of local and national events coalesced in Harlem to issue a challenge—and a warning—to Jim Crow in the nation's largest city.

THE HARLEM NINE AND MILITANT BLACK MOTHERS

In September of 1958 a group of nine Black mothers began a boycott of three junior high schools in Harlem to protest the inferior education their children were receiving in segregated schools. With the limitations of the *Brown* decision in New York City made clear over the past four years, Black women took the lead in escalating campaigns against separate and unequal schools. Influenced by Ella Baker's approach to grassroots organizing in the mid-1950s, they operated outside the confines of national civil rights organizations, "choosing the boycott rather than the boardroom as the tactic for demanding integrated schools in New York City."[3] The approach of these mothers was indicative of a more general impatience among working-class Black New Yorkers with the gradualist, middle-class approach to civil rights organizing through legal challenges that the NAACP championed in the late 1950s.

The growing rejection of gradualism and embrace of direct action had inspired members of Ella Baker's Parents in Action, including Mae Mallory, to form the Junior High School Coordinating Committee in 1957. Under the banner "Freedom of Choice of Junior High Schools," the committee set out to desegregate schools through permissive zoning policies that would allow Black and Puerto Rican students to attend schools of their choice.[4] Finding little recourse through the city's Board of Education (BOE) or the courts, the group of mothers decided to escalate their tactics by engaging in civil disobedience. When the new school year began in 1958, Mallory and the Junior High School Coordinating Committee announced their boycott of three junior high schools in Harlem. On the first day of the new school year, committee spokeswoman Carrie Haynes announced that nine parents of fifteen students in Harlem would be keeping their children out of school to protest the segregated schools they were assigned to. "We're not letting up until we get a decent program on the junior high school level," Haynes told reporters.[5]

Though by this point Baker had left New York for Atlanta to work with Dr. Martin Luther King Jr.'s Southern Christian Leadership Conference, the collective action of the boycott demonstrated the power of local leadership that she had championed during her years in Harlem. Indeed, Carrie Haynes, Mae Mallory, Viola Waddy, and the other working-class Black women—who were dubbed the "Little Rock Nine of Harlem" by the *Amsterdam News*—built upon the organizational foundation laid by the

Parents Committee for Better Education and Parents in Action to mount a direct-action challenge to systemic racism in New York City. "Conference upon conference has procured nothing," Carrie Haynes explained to a reporter in defense of the boycott, adding, "We're going to see this through to the bitter end."[6] In the wake of the *Brown* decision four years earlier, the boycott launched these Harlem parents and organizers to the forefront of national struggles for school desegregation and educational justice.

With support from community leaders, including Rev. Eugene Callender and attorney Paul Zuber, the boycotting parents arranged private tutoring sessions for their children to comply with the state's compulsory education law, foreshadowing the freedom schools that civil rights organizations would organize during subsequent boycotts. However, when the BOE expressed satisfaction with the education the children were receiving in these ad hoc schools, the mothers canceled the sessions to purposefully violate the law and force a confrontation with the BOE and city government. To up the ante, the parents also filed a $1 million lawsuit against the BOE, its superintendent, the Board of Estimates, and Mayor Robert F. Wagner, all of whom they accused of "sinister and discriminatory purpose" in maintaining racial segregation in Harlem.[7] These actions proved successful in finally provoking a response from the BOE when recently appointed Superintendent John Theobald requested a state investigation of the schools—and summoned the mothers before the Domestic Relations Court.

The ensuing trials of the Harlem Nine proved momentous for Black freedom struggles in New York. In the first wave of trials brought against six of the boycotting parents that December, Judge Nathaniel Kaplan ruled that the mothers were guilty of violating the state's compulsory education law. Two of the women folded and agreed to send their children back to school, but the other four, including Viola Waddy and Mae Mallory, were steadfast. "We will go to jail and rot there, if necessary," Waddy told a reporter, "but our children will not go to Jr. High Schools 136, 139, or 120."[8] Though they had their toothbrushes packed and affairs in order, the women avoided jail time when Justice Justine Polier issued a landmark decision in favor of two of the other boycotting mothers a week later.

In her decision, which Haynes later praised as "one of the great historical documents of our nation," Judge Polier argued that although the BOE was not responsible for the conditions of residential segregation that created segregated schools, the board had "done substantially nothing to rectify a situation it should never have allowed to develop."[9] Citing the stark contrast in the quality of education provided to students in predominantly Black schools compared to their white counterparts, Judge Polier held the BOE responsible for the unequal conditions created by segregated schools. Whereas the Supreme Court's *Brown* decision had ruled de jure segregation to be unconstitutional, Judge Polier's decision in New York City's Domestic Relations Court was celebrated as the first ruling against de facto segregation in schools.[10]

While the Polier decision was lauded by the Black press and community organizations, the ire it elicited from the BOE and white city residents demonstrated a collective effort to defend the city's racial status quo from forced integration. When the predominantly white BOE decided to appeal the decision, Black community leaders and organizations rallied in opposition. The 350,000-member Empire State Baptist Convention, for example, called for Mayor Wagner to dismiss all white members of the board and threatened a mass march on city hall if the appeal was not withdrawn. Dr. Gardner Taylor, a Baptist minister and the lone Black member of the board, asserted that by appealing the decision the city was essentially telling Black and Puerto Rican students, "You can't go to schools that are equal, you can't have equal opportunities here." With the appeal, he added, "the board erased the last line of differences between Little Rock and New York."[11]

The city's gendered attacks on the Black mothers of the Harlem Nine confirmed Taylor's point. As the boycott was underway in the fall of 1958, the New York City Housing Authority moved to evict Carrie Haynes and her five children from their home of ten years in the Lincoln Project in East Harlem. Without warning, housing authority police and the city marshal showed up with an eviction notice and movers to haul away Haynes's belongings while she frantically phoned for help with her three-month-old child in her arms. The eviction was only stopped when Bayard Rustin provided a loan from the In Friendship Fund to cover the back rent.[12] Coming on the heels of her own arrest, eviction, and loss of custody of her son the year before, Mallory saw these gendered acts of state violence as attempts to suppress political dissent by constraining the ability of Black women activists to find employment and housing and care for their children. "They try to pile as much on you as they can pile on you to see if you will snap, to see if you will break," Mallory said of her political persecution, "and I am just determined that I'm not going to."[13] While this repression put hurdles in the path of her political work and created real challenges for her and her family, it also sharpened Mallory's analysis of the systems that Black New Yorkers were up against.

For their part, everyday white New Yorkers also helped to blur the lines between Little Rock and New York. Objecting to the prospect of school desegregation, white residents took public and private actions to stifle the struggle. Mallory received several threatening letters from individuals who opposed her work to desegregate public schools. One anonymous letter she received from a former resident of Alabama read: "You should have lived down there and told them which school you wanted your daughter to go to. They would have hung you from a tree."[14] Though Judge Polier's ruling marked a victory for the Harlem Nine, it quickly became clear that their struggles for educational equality would continue to be met by staunch opposition in the city.

In spite of such resistance, the struggles for educational equality these Black women waged in Harlem represented a formative moment for the Black freedom struggle in New York City. In the long run, their boycott laid the groundwork for future school boycotts and forced the city to confront its complicity in establishing and maintaining segregated schools and systemic racism. In the short run, their actions won immediate, tangible benefits for Black children, demonstrated the collective power of Black women organizers, and spurred political education and radicalization. Local people emerged as powerful organizers and forged relationships and networks they would build upon as the emergent Black freedom movement progressed.

Additionally, the boycotts contributed to broader debates about strategies in local and national struggles for liberation. On the one hand, Harry Haywood, an influential Black communist leader and mentor of Jesse Gray, characterized such boycotts as "futile protests against de facto segregation" that merely supplemented the "legalistic and legislative approach of NAACP with demonstrations" and avoided "basic economic issues" in the North.[15] To Mae Mallory, on the other hand, educational activism was inseparable from "basic economic issues," particularly the ability of Black women to find decent employment opportunities. "I wanted both my children to get the best possible public education that they could," Mallory later explained, "because I wanted to break the cycle of women doing days work or factory work."[16] In this sense, Mallory essentially saw desegregation as a tactic in a broader struggle for economic, political, and social empowerment, leading to Black self-determination. Guided by the influence of Ella Baker's emphasis on building grassroots political power, the organizing efforts of Mae Mallory and the Harlem Nine in the waning years of the 1950s epitomized rising demands for immediate rights and self-determination through the local leadership of working-class Black women.

TENANT ORGANIZING AND THE 1959 RENT STRIKE

When Jack O'Dell returned to Harlem in 1958 to work with Jesse Gray and his newly formed Lower Harlem Tenants Council, he found a "community that had a rhythm of organization," with the tempo being set by Black women.[17] Having participated in some of the opening salvos of the Southern civil rights movement with the CIO's Operation Dixie and the Southern Negro Youth Conference, O'Dell "saw a movement was emerging" and knew that he had to be involved.[18] Having fled the South amid rabid anticommunist persecution, O'Dell found fertile ground in Harlem for continuing his work among the Black Left. While integrationist organizations sought to break down the institutional barriers that established Northern "ghettos," O'Dell and Gray sought to organize communities within these confines to seize control of the social, economic, and political levers of power. Tenant organizing, then, was a means of organizing working-class Black communities around their material needs to build political power and achieve Black liberation.

Though tenant organizing had deep roots in Harlem, the experiences that informed Gray and O'Dell's analysis of "the housing question" in Black freedom struggles distinguished their organizing from that of more moderate civil rights organizations and tenant councils. Unlike the more bureaucratic approach of the newly formed Metropolitan Council on Housing, which one activist described as being made up of "older white liberal types, social worker types as opposed to activist types," the Lower Harlem Tenants Council (LHTC) adopted strategies, tactics, and rhetoric that were more reflective of growing demands for immediate rights and self-determination.[19] The LHTC's approach, according to O'Dell, was that of "a tenant movement ... trying to empower itself," as opposed to "a social service thing."[20] Furthermore, while the Metropolitan Council on Housing operated on a citywide basis, which O'Dell saw as being spread too thin, the LHTC sought to grow grassroots community power in Harlem—building by building, block by block.[21]

Even in limiting their organizing to Harlem, the LHTC was still strained by the variety and complexity of housing issues renters faced, which forced the organization to fight on multiple fronts at once. Gray and O'Dell struggled in the mid-1950s to build a tenant movement capable of simultaneously taking on slumlords, city agencies and officials, state legislators, and the federal government. Initially operating out of a storefront office on 110th Street between Lenox and 7th Avenues before moving their headquarters in 1960 to West 116th Street—on the same block as the Nation of Islam's Temple No. 7—the LHTC found it challenging to establish a substantial base of local leaders who were committed to taking on the responsibilities of organizing.[22] "They were spotty," O'Dell recalled. "You'd do a rally on heat and hot water, and people would come by two months later and say, 'I got this leaflet on heat and hot water.'"[23] Despite its challenges and frustrations, this "spadework," as Ella Baker called it, was necessary for base building and endeared the LHTC to the community they were dedicated to organizing from 110th to 150th Street.

Alongside the rigors of organizing tenants, political education was a vital component of the LHTC's vision of building a tenant movement for collective power and liberation. Recognizing the transformative impacts of the political education they received through the National Maritime Union and the Communist Party, Gray and O'Dell placed a premium on study to advance the struggle. "One of the things the nation lacks today," Gray later explained, "is that tremendous education that the Left was able to offer this nation in the thirties and in the forties."[24] With his experience gained from the NMU Labor School and organizing in the South, O'Dell stepped into the role of educational director of the LHTC. In that capacity, he spent countless hours in the Schomburg Collection at the 135th Street Branch of the New York Public Library (now the Schomburg Center for Research in Black Culture), studying the histories of tenant movements in New York City to inform the LHTC's organizing work.[25]

Through consistent study and struggle, Gray, O'Dell, and the LHTC began to build a base of tenant organizers in Harlem that proved capable of winning battles at the city and state levels in the late 1950s.[26] On the heels of the long struggle against the Godfrey-Nurse housing project, the LHTC organized massive resistance to a plan to construct a new public housing project in Harlem in 1958. The Alexander Hamilton Houses were planned to house 1,200 families on four city blocks from 141st to 144th Street between 7th and 8th Avenues. The plan for the Hamilton Houses called for razing dozens of residential buildings and displacing anywhere from 8,000 to 15,000 residents without any guarantees or support from the city for their relocation.²⁷ The prospect of being displaced was particularly alarming to residents of that neighborhood, given the low vacancy rates and dire lack of safe and affordable housing in Harlem.

To combat the project, the LHTC forged a coalition of affected residents and organizations under the umbrella of the United Committee Against Alexander Hamilton Houses (UCAAH). "We built the broadest coalition against any development," Gray recalled of the coalition whose ranks included the LHTC, United African Nationalist Movement (UANM), Urban League, Committee for Racial Equality (later Congress of Racial Equality, CORE), NY NAACP, members of the Nation of Islam, and several local tenant and business associations. Like any coalition, the ideological and demographic diversity that member organizations brought to the UCAAH contributed to building a larger and more powerful base. While these organizations were united in opposition to the project, however, their analyses of the housing problem clearly diverged along class lines. Middle-class, integrationist organizations like the Urban League and CORE couched their objections to the project in terms of housing segregation and the concentration of low-income housing in Black and Puerto Rican communities. Meanwhile, the LHTC's objections to mass demolitions and the net loss of housing units were informed by the concerns and material needs of working-class Black and Puerto Rican residents who faced the threat of displacement.

The emphasis on demolition and displacement as issues of racial oppression and Black liberation echoed the great anti-eviction protests of the Great Depression in Harlem and garnered support from veterans of those struggles, including Rep. Adam Clayton Powell Jr. Speaking alongside Jesse Gray, UANM leader James Lawson, and other coalition members at a mass meeting at Abyssinian Baptist Church that April, Powell described the project as part of a "master plan to destroy Harlem" and called for mass civil disobedience to prevent evictions if it moved forward. The meeting opened with one thousand voices singing "We Shall Not Be Moved" before Powell took to the lectern and declared that "there aren't enough police in the city to move 15,000 women and children." Tenant organizer Eloise Richardson proudly announced that she had been "offered an apartment to keep my mouth shut, but I'm too much of a race woman. I will not walk out on my people."²⁸ The mass meeting showcased a growing militancy among Harlem residents who staked a claim to their neighborhood and understood their struggle as an important battlefront in the fight against Jim Crow. Powered by this grassroots militancy, the UCAAH was ultimately successful in forcing the city to scale back the project, thereby preventing mass demolition and the displacement of working-class Black residents.[29]

In addition to fighting against displacement, the LHTC also organized Harlem tenants to protect affordable housing in the city. Building on their 1953 effort to save rent control in the state, the LHTC once again helped organize a coalition when it came up for renewal in early 1959. That January the LHTC organized a petition drive and letter-writing campaign urging Governor Nelson Rockefeller to call a public hearing on rent control. When state legislators called a hearing the following month, seventy-five tenants and community leaders—including Jesse Gray and attorney Paul Zuber—boarded a bus to Albany to observe and testify in the proceedings. After seven hours of testimony, debate, and verbal clashes between tenants and landlords, including a rousing speech by Zuber, the state assembly voted to extend and strengthen rent control protections for another two years.[30]

Thanks to these successes, Gray and the LHTC showed signs of gaining traction as a burgeoning movement of working-class Black renters in Harlem. Building on the momentum generated by the struggle against the Hamilton Houses, Gray and the LHTC organized tenants in the Stephen Foster Houses to demand better maintenance services and increased police protection in the spring of 1959. Earlier that year, tenants of the 1,500-family project on Lenox Avenue and 115th Street had agreed to a steep six dollars per month increase in rent with the expectation that the higher rate would lead to better services. But after three months of waiting for elevator repairs, more frequent garbage collection, and more housing police, "the tenants were sick and tired of being forced to take whatever treatment is handed to them," Gray told reporters.[31] With the support of the LHTC, tenant organizers in the Foster homes launched a petition drive to pressure the city to act on their complaints. In late March a delegation of tenants hand-delivered the petition bearing a thousand signatures to the city's housing authority chairman, William Reid, who vowed to address the situation within a week. "By working together," Gray declared, "we'll be able to get more immediate action like that promised by Mr. Reid."[32] Reid's swift response showed tenants the power of organized action and demonstrated their ability to force concessions from city officials to address their material needs.

In the months following the petition drive at the Foster Houses, all eyes were on Gray and the LHTC as they brought the Depression-era direct-action tactics Powell had threatened back into the playbook of the growing tenant movement. Despite Mayor Wagner having announced a "massive new attack on slum conditions" the previous year, including building inspections, tenant-landlord education, and swifter punishment for violations, housing conditions in Harlem remained dire.[33] With 49 percent of its housing stock characterized as either "deteriorating" or "dilapidated," deaths from home accidents in Harlem were nearly double those of the rest of the city.[34] In January 1959 a two-year-old boy was killed in an apartment building fire on West 116th Street. In addition to the collective trauma and outrage caused by the child's death, tenants also complained that the structural damages caused by the fire had yet to be repaired months later.[35]

On the first day of July 1959, tenants from four dilapidated apartment buildings on West 116th Street—including the one where the child was killed—declared a rent strike to force their landlords to repair the buildings. Chanting "No repairs, no rent," a group of fifty tenants—primarily women—walked a picket line in front of the four adjacent six-story brick buildings carrying signs that read "My Baby Is Too Pretty to Die!," "Act Like Landlords: They Do Nothing, We Pay Nothing," and "Restore Law to Housing."[36] As the tenants walked the picket line, Gray patrolled the block, giving instructions to the picketers and passing out leaflets with details about the tenants' case. "The charges run the same through all the houses," he told a reporter at the scene. "No paint, falling ceilings, no hot water for months at a time and this terrible plague of rats. Babies can't sleep at night for them."[37] Though Gray was the leading organizer of the strike, the foot soldiers of the rent strike and broader tenant movement consisted mainly of working-class Black women. Gray's "militant, maternalistic rhetoric" emphasized the conditions faced by Black women and children in order to organize Black mothers in defense of their families and elicit dramatic and empathetic headlines publicizing protest actions.[38] It was an effective rhetorical and organizational tactic that Gray would refine in the years to come.

Coverage of the strike appeared in the pages of the *New York Times* and drew front-page attention in the *Amsterdam News*.[39] Citing Gray's claims that the LHTC had organized six thousand tenants in forty other buildings who were prepared to join the rent strike, one reporter declared that their actions represented "one of Harlem's first major rent rebellions."[40] The coverage provided important visibility and leverage for the LHTC and helped thrust tenant organizing into the fore of popular discourse about the civil rights movement in Harlem.

Within a week of launching the rent strike, the LHTC again proved its ability to score some immediate victories for tenants. By withholding rent

FIG 4 Tenants walk a picket line in front of their buildings on West 116th Street during a rent strike organized by the Lower Harlem Tenants Council in July 1959. (Photo by Richard A. Martin; Photographs and Prints Division, Schomburg Center for Research in Black Culture, The New York Public Library)

and staging direct-action protests at the buildings, the striking tenants compelled the city's Department of Housing and Buildings to order building inspections and rent reductions pending the completion of repairs. They also compelled some other landlords on West 116th Street to start fixing up their buildings voluntarily to avoid future rent strikes. The energy, publicity, and wins generated by the rent strike also motivated tenants in other buildings to get organized, become part of the LHTC, and join the strike.[41]

The surging momentum of the rent strike was on full display on July 11 as the city geared up for the fiftieth anniversary convention of the NAACP, which was scheduled to begin two days later. At a mass meeting in Dewey Square (110th Street and Lenox Avenue) that night, Gray and the LHTC reported on the progress and successes of the strike, which had by then spread to seventeen other buildings in the neighborhood, and encouraged striking tenants to hold the line until all violations were resolved. With new buildings getting organized and joining the LHTC at a rate of two per day in the first week, there were no signs of the strike slowing down.[42] The militant spirit of the striking tenants was enlivened the following night, when North Carolina

NAACP leader Robert F. Williams spoke at a rally just blocks away, advocating armed self-defense in domestic and international struggles for Black liberation.[43]

Though the *Amsterdam News* used the terms "protest," "revolt," and "revolution" loosely and interchangeably in their coverage of the rent strikes and other recent protest campaigns to present a provocative vision of an emergent mass movement in Harlem, the paper acknowledged that the "series of revolts" resulted from spontaneous actions by various organizations. These simultaneous, yet uncoordinated actions illuminated the diversity of political interests and priorities at play in Harlem. While the NY NAACP focused on civil rights agitation for the rights of the Black middle class to integrate into a white-dominated capitalist economy, the LHTC's approach to tenant organizing was grounded in Left and nationalist politics and a rejection of the supposed panacea of integration. Instead, they believed in the possibilities of revolutionary struggle and Black liberation through a mass mobilization of working-class people who were most oppressed and exploited in the Jim Crow North.

Despite these differences, in praxis a common sense of immediacy over gradualism and emphasis on direct-action campaigns over litigation emerged, revealing the vitality of Harlem's Black radical tradition in the late 1950s. It sustained a popular culture of militant struggle for rights and power in America's largest city, and as the rent strike continued to grow, the national spotlight fell on Harlem as local and national struggles for Black liberation intersected in an explosive manner that July.

THE 1959 NAACP CONVENTION AND THE QUESTION OF NONVIOLENCE

As the masses in Harlem began to mobilize through rent strikes and boycotts in the spring of 1959, several acts of racist violence rocked the South and sent shockwaves throughout the nation. In late April a lynch mob dragged twenty-three-year-old Mack Charles Parker from a Mississippi jail cell, where he was being held for the alleged rape of a white woman. As with the brutal murder of Emmett Till four years earlier, the white Southern justice system—with the assistance of federal agencies—allowed Parker's killers to walk free after his body was pulled from a nearby river. The responses of Southern civil rights leaders to the lynching of Mack Parker revealed a disillusionment with the limits of nonviolence and contributed to a growing national dialogue over the role of self-defense in Black freedom struggles.[44]

When the news of the lynching reached NAACP field secretary Medgar Evers, he told his wife, Myrlie, "I'd like to get a gun and start shooting."[45] In Monroe, North Carolina, where members of the local NAACP branch had formed a rifle club and engaged in shootouts with the Ku Klux Klan two years earlier, branch president Robert F. Williams argued that the tragedy could have been prevented with armed self-defense.[46] In New York City, readers of the *Amsterdam News* followed the case in weekly installments with headlines such as "Mississippi Is Hell," and editorials sprang up in support of armed self-defense. In a May 16 column titled "They Lynched Us All," city councilman Earl Brown charged that "the only way to break the chain of one-way death in Dixie would be for the Negroes to kill when attacked."[47] In a letter to the editor a week later, a Brooklyn resident made the case for the establishment of an armed organization that could move throughout the country and "take reprisals on whatever bigot is unfortunate to find himself within our reach."[48]

These sentiments demonstrated not only the national reach of the Parker lynching but also the reverberations of a thunderous declaration made by Williams the day after Mack Parker's body was found in the Pearl River. On May 5 two cases came to trial in Monroe, both involving white men accused of brutal assaults on Black women. Before the trials, when Black women and men in Monroe had sought to bring these white attackers to justice through violent retribution, Williams urged restraint and faith in the legal system. However, when charges were dropped in the first case and a verdict of not guilty swiftly reached in the second, this blatant yet predictable denial of justice brought the ire of Monroe's Black women down upon Williams.[49] "These people have declared open season on Black women," Mabel Williams recalled one woman telling her husband outside the courtroom. "What are you gonna say now?"[50] Their anger, Williams later said, "made me realize that this was the last straw, that we didn't have as much protection as a dog down there, and the Government didn't care about us." At that point, he turned to reporters on the scene and declared that the time had come for Black people to "meet violence with violence," and that "we must be willing to kill if necessary."[51] With these words, Williams aroused within white communities an age-old fear of Black rebellion and stirred the radical imaginations of Black communities that were growing increasingly indignant over the daily violence of American racism.

In the following months, Williams became a national cause célèbre, attracting loyal supporters and fervent detractors alike. Outside Monroe, Williams found some of his greatest advocates among Harlem's Black radical intellectuals, writers, and organizers, including John Henrik Clarke, Julian Mayfield, Audley and Eloise Moore, and Malcolm X. He also drew support from the International Committee in Defense of Africa (ICDA), a Harlem-based organization of Garveyites and Black nationalists that advocated for decolonization and Pan-African solidarity to "widen the scope of the struggle for freedom."[52] Led by veteran organizers Ennis Francis and Eloise Moore, the organization drew respected local Black nationalists into the fray, hosted public forums, and coordinated deliveries of donated supplies to the town of Monroe.

Williams had first met Malcolm X during a trip to New York in 1958 and found an ardent supporter in the minister and his congregation at Temple No. 7. "Every time I used to go to New York he would invite me to speak," Williams said in a 1968 interview.[53] As a working-class Southern Black man with personal ties to Harlem, support for Black nationalism, and experience in armed self-defense against the Ku Klux Klan, Williams was the type of secular leader that members of the Nation of Islam could rally behind. While Malcolm routinely exhorted but seldom practiced self-defense against white vigilantes and police, Williams had lived experience in organizing and using gun clubs for active self-defense against the KKK. During these visits to Temple No. 7, Malcolm X would take up a collection for Williams by explaining that "our brother is here from North Carolina, and he is the only fighting man that we got and we have to help him so he can stay down there."[54] With the support of Malcolm, Clarke, Mayfield, Moore, and others, Williams was able to build a veritable arsenal for his well-trained organization in Monroe, including military carbines, dynamite, and machine guns, the latter of which Mayfield was rumored to have brought down from New York.[55]

Family members also played important roles in forging personal relationships and political networks between New York and Monroe. Having lived with his aunt Estelle Williams on 117th Street for a time in the early 1950s, Williams had become acquainted with members of the CPUSA and American Labor Party and gotten a taste of the neighborhood's living traditions of radical politics.[56] His cousin Ora Mae Mobley (née Williams), who had fled Klan violence by moving from North Carolina to Harlem in 1951, was well connected in Harlem's diverse political circles and became an important comrade there. When he wasn't staying with his aunt Estelle during trips to New

York, Williams could often be found with Mobley, her husband Ezekiel, and two children in the St. Nicholas Housing Project at 127th Street and 7th Avenue. Mobley had gotten her start as an organizer through working with her tenants association before getting involved with campaigns for educational justice in Harlem alongside Mae Mallory and ICDA member Ennis Francis. The housing project—where Mallory also lived—proved a vital training ground and springboard for her involvement in city politics, African independence struggles, and various Black radical organizations in Harlem.[57] By the time the national spotlight fell on Williams, these Black women had built upon their organizing experience to create a powerful network to support Williams and advance more radical forms of political struggle in Harlem.

As the NAACP prepared for its fiftieth annual convention that summer, Williams made several trips to the association's headquarters in New York City to deal with the fallout from his advocacy of armed self-defense. In the wake of intense backlash, media fearmongering, and condemnation by moderate civil rights leaders, NAACP executive secretary Roy Wilkins announced in June that Williams had been suspended from his position as branch president. Though Williams made these trips for the purpose of appealing his suspension, the visits also allowed him to strengthen connections with his comrades and supporters in the North. He was a regular visitor to Lewis Michaux's National Memorial African Bookstore on 125th Street and 7th Avenue. In addition to speaking with crowds at street rallies and in barrooms, Williams was invited to use the store's famed platform to spread the word about what was happening in Monroe and share his analysis on armed resistance in domestic and international struggles for Black liberation.[58] "I was the only leader of the NAACP who could have associated with all kinds of people—the nationalists and all," Williams later explained. "I was the only one from the NAACP who could go down in Harlem and stand on a ladder on a corner and speak there."[59]

Though Williams had the fervent support of radical activists and intellectuals in Harlem and throughout the nation, he faced reactionary responses from inside and outside the NAACP. His frequent trips to New York that year drew the attention of FBI Director J. Edgar Hoover, who was particularly troubled by Williams's budding relationship with Malcolm X and the Nation of Islam. That June, Hoover instructed the Charlotte, North Carolina, office to "immediately open a case against" Williams and the Nation of Islam in light of his "recent activities in connection with the Nation of Islam at New York City."[60] Through heightened surveillance, Hoover sought to contain the influence of both Williams and the NOI within the broader civil rights movement. If left unchecked, such influence, the bureau argued, would "inflame racial disturbances and create racial violence."[61] Hoover was equally concerned by the prospect of Williams and the NOI joining forces under a shared banner of self-defense and self-determination. He instructed the Charlotte office to "remain alert for any attempt on the part of [Williams] to organize a Nation of Islam group in the area" and the New York office to "follow and promptly report all activities . . . while he remains in New York City."[62] Although the FBI had already been keeping tabs on Williams, Malcolm, and the NOI, the threat of their collaboration spurred an escalation of government surveillance in the weeks, months, and years that followed.

The late spring and early summer of 1959 also saw a dramatic struggle between Williams and the national NAACP, which sought to distance itself from his open advocacy of armed self-defense. Though NAACP Executive Secretary Roy Wilkins privately acknowledged that "the thought of using violence has been in the minds of Negroes," he feared the backlash that would follow any endorsement of Williams's position and actively maneuvered to discredit Williams and undermine his growing influence in the organization.[63] Even though armed self-defense was common practice as a means of protection, survival, and resistance for civil rights leaders throughout the South, the national leadership of the NAACP was not willing to publicly affirm a general policy in support of this constitutionally protected right for fear of political retribution and alienating its white and moderate supporters.[64] Furthermore, NAACP leaders justifiably feared that a public embrace of armed self-defense would be used as a pretext for government, law enforcement agencies, and white supremacists to crush the organization and the broader civil rights movement.

The bitter debate between Williams and Wilkins clearly reflected a widening rift in the NAACP over nonviolence and self-defense. More broadly, it also demonstrated a growing disillusionment over the constraining relationship between the national organization and its local branches. These debates came to a dramatic head during the "Golden Jubilee" convention, held the week of July 13, 1959, in New York City. In the weeks leading up to the historic convention, journalist Louis Lomax reported that there were "deep rumblings of unrest and discontent" over the organization's reticence to embrace the tactics of nonviolent direct action. As the convention neared, this was the primary issue that many delegates sought to raise for debate, in hopes of convincing the executive board to "relinquish its absolute power and institute a more democratic procedure," Lomax noted. The larger goal of these delegates, then, beyond the embrace of nonviolent direct action, was to compel the highly bureaucratic organization to develop a more expansive tactical approach that would empower local branches and local people to shape the course of the movement.[65]

As the convention opened, however, it quickly became clear that this was not the core debate of the gathering. With the firestorm surrounding the suspension of Robert F. Williams and his position on armed self-defense, those delegates who supported direct action and the democratization of the national organization hitched their wagons to Williams's case, and their arguments were subsumed within a defense of the embattled leader from Monroe. By conflating the two issues, these delegates played into the hand of Roy Wilkins, who had worked to set a tone of moderate, middle-class respectability in the convention's opening session, when Governor Nelson Rockefeller took to the stage to address the crowd of three thousand gathered in the New York Coliseum the evening of July 13.[66]

After assuring the crowd that segregation was "on its way out" in New York state and in the nation, the Republican governor proclaimed that America had been "fortunate in the kind of leadership the NAACP has given in this great struggle for civil rights." Furthermore, the *New York Times* reported, Rockefeller lauded the gathered delegates for having "made no appeal to violence," for having "rejected retaliation in kind to threat and terrorism," and—adding the tried and true tactic of red-baiting to the mix for good measure—for having "repulsed the threat of communism to invade your ranks."[67] The governor's address was a thinly veiled attack on Williams and designed to firmly establish the narrative set by Wilkins as the defining position of the convention. The link was made even more explicit after the governor's speech concluded, when the chair of the convention declared that deliberations on the Williams situation would be brought before the convention later in the week.[68]

In the meantime, however, Williams's Northern comrades took to the streets to protest his suspension and demonstrate support for his position of armed self-defense. As the convention got underway, Mae Mallory tuned into the coverage on local radio station WLIB, which proved a formative moment in her political evolution. In the struggle in Monroe she saw an opportunity to channel her analyses on self-determination and self-defense into a struggle for Black liberation that centered the experiences and needs of working-class Black women. "I heard it and I said 'My God, you know, this is only right,'"

Mallory remembered. "So instead of going to work that day I got up and went in the streets and organized some support for Robert Williams," a man she had never met.[69]

Mallory quickly called upon her connections with the Harlem Nine, including Pernella Wattley, and other Black women in her neighborhood to send telegrams to Roy Wilkins threatening to picket the convention if he did not "drop the charges against Rob."[70] Meanwhile, Williams's cousin Ora Mae Mobley had been busy writing letters to the editors of Black newspapers across the country, "publicizing Rob's position and giving him my support" in the weeks leading up to the convention. Now she mobilized members of the International Committee in Defense of Africa to stage a demonstration at the Coliseum.[71] To drum up support, the ICDA also hosted a rally in Harlem the night before the convention was set to kick off, where Williams addressed his comrades gathered at the Centra Barroom on 125th Street in preparation for the next day's fight.[72]

The idea of radical Black women picketing the NAACP's landmark convention in support of armed self-defense was met with predictably cool responses. When Mallory proposed the idea to Wattley and other members of the Harlem Nine, they gave her "some stupid excuse about how we could not let the whites downtown see us picket the NAACP."[73] Despite their fundamental disagreements with the NAACP's approach to the movement, many people were not willing to publicly criticize the legendary organization, for fear of playing into the hands of racist opposition and weakening the organization's reputation. These were strategic rather than principled decisions, which demonstrated both an embrace of respectability politics and a desire to work out organizational problems behind closed doors. The power imbalance within the organization between moderates in national leadership positions and more radical local leaders, however, made such a strategy untenable. Mallory later confessed to Rob and Mabel Williams that she was "so disgusted" with the response she received that she skipped the event altogether.[74]

Despite the disagreements and inherent risks around the demonstration, Ora Mobley and Eloise Moore carried on with the picket line to show their support for their comrades in Monroe. While the demonstration received no media coverage, it represented a rejection of respectability politics and an important expression of radical Black women taking a principled position of refusing to compromise on issues of armed self-defense, self-determination, and local leadership of working-class people. It also contributed to the emergence of the Crusader Family (aka Crusaders for Freedom), a local organization formed that summer in solidarity with Monroe, which would become an important node in Harlem's rapidly expanding network of Black radical organizers and a vehicle for political education and action.

THE NATION MEETS THE NATION

While convention delegates listened to Rockefeller's speech in the New York Coliseum and protestors walked the picket line outside, a startling documentary news program aired on Mike Wallace's television program *News Beat*. Viewers who tuned into channel 13 in New York that evening were greeted by the characteristically stern white reporter as he adjusted his footing and fidgeted with a stack of papers. "While city officials, state agencies, white liberals, and sober-minded Negroes stand idly by," Wallace began before finding his footing and fixing his gaze on the camera, "a group of Negro dissenters is taking to street corner stepladders, church pulpits, sports arenas, and ballroom platforms across the United States to preach a gospel of hate that would set off a federal investigation if it were preached by Southern whites."[75]

To illustrate Wallace's narration, the program cut to rare video footage of a gathering where Black men, dressed in suits and ties, and Black women, wearing flowing white robes and head scarves, sat on opposite sides of a hall watching a performance of a short play called *The Trial,* in which a symbolic white man was put on trial in a Black court for his crimes against humanity. When the spirited prosecutor exhorted the jury to bring back a verdict of guilty, the audience delivered their own verdict through a dignified yet thunderous applause. Returning to the *News Beat* studio, Wallace explained that this indictment echoed throughout major cities across the country and recited the predictable verdict of guilty. "The sentence," Wallace paused for dramatic effect, "is death." New Yorkers who were given their first look into the world of the Nation of Islam "were stunned," Wallace later recalled.[76]

Provocatively and problematically titled "The Hate That Hate Produced," the program was created as an exposé of the Nation of Islam, which Wallace referred to as "the most powerful of the Black supremacist groups" in the nation. Though Malcolm X and the NOI had gained heightened popularity and notoriety in New York City two years earlier following their intervention in the beating of Johnson X Hinton by the NYPD, white New Yorkers and many Americans in general knew next to nothing about the growing organization. "White journalism at that time didn't know who Malcolm was, who Elijah Muhammad was," Wallace explained, "so there was no attention being paid at that time." The news series changed that and provided white America—Wallace included—with a frightening glimpse into the organization's existence. "What I felt about Malcolm X when I first saw him on film," Wallace recalled in an interview, "was that he was a demagogue, racist."[77]

The broadcast was the idea of African American journalist Louis Lomax, a neophyte to Harlem who, like Wallace, had been shocked the previous summer when he first encountered the militant rhetoric that reverberated from nationalist street rallies in the neighborhood. Unfamiliar with the history and culture of street corner oration in Harlem, Lomax condemned such rhetoric as "inverse racism" and in an article he wrote for the *Baltimore Afro-American* even compared Black nationalists to the Ku Klux Klan, White Citizens Council, and Adolf Hitler.[78] Furthermore, Lomax's analysis, which reduced the complexities of the Nation of Islam's ideologies and programs to that of a Black counterpart to the KKK, took on a different meaning and had a different impact when reiterated by a white news anchor. Though they claimed that the report was made for interracial audiences in New York, it was clear that the two journalists sought to stoke fear among white New Yorkers and chasten moderate civil rights leaders for not reining in what they perceived as the growing threat of Black nationalism.

Despite its obvious attempt at fearmongering, "The Hate That Hate Produced" did not have the impact in Black communities that Lomax and Wallace had intended. While many white and some Black viewers were undoubtedly shocked by what they saw, the program also introduced Malcolm X to a younger generation of Black people, who were electrified by his rhetoric. "Malcolm X put words to the volcanic torrent of anger and frustration many of us felt with the Civil Rights Movement," Amiri Baraka (LeRoi Jones) recalled. Living downtown in Greenwich Village at the time, where he was ascending as a prolific poet, critic, and publisher in the Beat and jazz scene, Baraka experienced Malcolm's national emergence as a revelation. "When Malcolm stepped forward and began to teach Self Determination, Self Respect and Self Defense," Baraka later reflected, "it struck a chord deep within the soul of a wide spectrum of Black people, particularly Black youth."[79] While the broadcast exposed the NOI to the racist vitriol of white American society, the national visibility also proved a springboard for recruitment and expansion.

Though little known to Lomax, Wallace, and most white New Yorkers, the Nation of Islam was deeply rooted in Harlem's Black nationalist traditions, and the organization was only just beginning to blossom. In the two years since the beating of Hinton, the NOI had become the fastest growing organization in American cities, with its influence reaching across the nation and around the globe, owing in large part to the dogged efforts of its charismatic minister in New York. From 1955 to 1959, the number of temples grew from fifteen to fifty, with between five hundred and one thousand new converts joining the NOI every month.[80] Though operating within the doctrinaire constraints of the Honorable Elijah Muhammad's rather conservative theology, Malcolm invoked the inherently political implications of the Nation's ideologies and programs to locate the NOI within the context of local, national, and international struggles for Black liberation.

As working-class Black communities transformed local freedom struggles, Malcolm spoke to this base of people, who daily bore the brunt of white oppression. To Julian Mayfield, militant leaders like Malcolm X and Robert F. Williams represented a clear and direct challenge to the assumed leadership of middle-class organizations like the NAACP. Such a challenge, Mayfield explained in a 1961 article, was "inherent in the rapid growth of the militant, white-hating Muslim movement among working-class Negroes... who regard the efforts of the NAACP, the Urban League, and most religious and civic leaders with either disdain or despair, in the belief that they are doing too little, too timidly and too late."[81] The NOI's theology was particularly relevant for many Black people confined to ghettos in American cities, who saw the personification of the NOI's "white devil" theology in their daily experiences with police officers, teachers, employers, business owners, welfare caseworkers, city agencies, and everyday white New Yorkers. It was among this demographic that Malcolm and the NOI focused their organizing.

The Johnson X Hinton incident had put New York City on notice and earned Malcolm the respect of other Black leaders in Harlem. Between frequent trips to other temples across the country, including Boston, Detroit, Los Angeles, and Washington, DC, Malcolm tended to these relationships with a diverse array of local religious, political, Black nationalist, and civil rights leaders.[82] At the same time, he leveraged his newfound clout to call for Black organizations in Harlem to unite in a collective struggle against white supremacy. Speaking at a Marcus Garvey Day celebration hosted by the United African Nationalist Movement in August 1958, Malcolm X challenged Harlem residents to put aside their ideological differences and unite under a banner of Black Nationalism. "We can't look on ourselves as Republicans or Democrats, but as Black Nationalists. We can't look on ourselves as Baptists, but as Black Nationalists. We can't look on ourselves as Methodists, but as Black Nationalists. We can't look on ourselves as Masons or Elks, not as Americans, but as Black Nationalists," Malcolm repeated from the platform at the corner of 125th Street and 7th Avenue. "Is that right or wrong?" he called out to the thousands gathered at the bustling intersection. Malcolm drew the most energetic response of all the speakers that day when the crowd shouted back, "Right!"[83]

Malcolm's organizing efforts in these years also showed his development as an anticolonial and Pan-African thinker and organizer. In February 1959 he spoke at a meeting of the Ethiopian Coptic Forum alongside Dr. Tahseen Mohamed Besheer, the United Arab Republic representative to the United Nations, who condemned European colonialism and called for African and

FIG 5 Malcolm X speaks at a Marcus Garvey Day celebration at West 125th Street and 7th Avenue (now Adam Clayton Powell Jr. Blvd.) in Harlem on August 1, 1958. (Photo by Cecil Layne; Photographs and Prints Division, Schomburg Center for Research in Black Culture, The New York Public Library)

Arab solidarity. "We do stand for Arab and African Nationalism," Besheer proclaimed. "We have a full oneness with people of African descent."[84] In his address at an African Freedom Day rally in Harlem that May, part of which aired on "The Hate That Hate Produced," Malcolm built upon Besheer's remarks as he spoke about the connections between independence movements in Africa and Asia. "It has been since the Bandung Conference that all dark people of earth have been striding toward freedom," Malcolm declared. Instead of merely cheering on anticolonial struggles from a distance, however, he urged the enthusiastic crowd to "study the methods used by our darker brothers in Africa and Asia to get their freedom."[85] By the time the news series aired, in fact, Malcolm was on a three-week tour of the Middle East and Africa, traveling under the name of Malik El-Shabazz "so that my brothers in the East would recognize me as one of them."[86]

Police and policymakers in New York City did not miss the potential for more immediate and transformative social change that Malcolm's organizing held for liberating and mobilizing Black communities. For the NYPD, the Johnson X Hinton situation marked the NOI as a grave threat to law and order in the city. "From that point on," former Deputy Commissioner Robert Mangum explained, "the police department and the political people in New York City began to realize they had a significant force in the city to deal with."[87] The NYPD responded in the following years with an extensive operation to surveil, harass, and suppress the growing influence of Malcolm X and the NOI.

While Elijah Muhammad routinely cautioned against confrontations with the police, Malcolm refused to let unprovoked acts of police brutality against Muslims—especially Black women—go unchallenged. In April 1959 Muhammad raised concerns about the "all too frequent clashes with Law Enforcement Agents that we, the Believers of Islam, are being involved in."[88] To him, the legal and physical costs of clashes with police—in addition to the increased attention from law enforcement and exposure to repression—were not worth the price of the ticket in an arena where justice was seldom delivered. Whereas Malcolm preached a fire-and-brimstone message of an eye for an eye, Muhammad instructed his followers that "whenever an officer comes to serve a notice or to arrest you, you should not resist whether you are innocent or guilty."[89] The divergent positions that Malcolm and Muhammad took on the issue of resisting police violence and repression were reflective of more fundamental political fissures between the two men that were widening just below the surface.

Two specific cases illuminated the rising tensions between the NOI and NYPD, demonstrated Malcolm's evolving resistance to police repression, and fueled broader critiques of racist policing in New York City. In May 1958 two detectives stormed into the two-family home that Malcolm X and Betty Shabazz shared with other members of Temple No. 7 in East Elmhurst, Queens. Claiming they were looking for a woman who allegedly stayed in the ground floor unit, the detectives smashed a glass pane and forced their way into the home over the protests of John X and Yvonne X Molette. During the home invasion, the officers beat John X Molette, fired two shots into the house—barely missing Yvonne X Molette and the women and children inside—and threatened to shoot into Malcolm and Betty's apartment, where Betty was hiding with another woman. The detectives arrested six people, including a woman who was six months pregnant and a thirteen-year-old girl. The police later picked up the woman they were after in the Bronx (where she lived), suggesting that their search was a pretext for harassing and intimidating influential members of the Nation of Islam.[90] Malcolm and the NOI fought the spurious charges through the courts for over a year, demanding justice for Black women and children who had been terrorized by the NYPD as a form of political intimidation. During the trial in 1959, the Fruit of Islam secured the courtroom while "roving Muslim photographers patrolled the streets in the immediate area of the court, snapping pictures of any one who met their fancy," as one detective from the NYPD's Bureau of Special Services (BOSS) reported. The NOI's photo surveillance was part of a broader counterintelligence strategy to gather information, raise critical awareness by publishing police surveillance reports, and guard against infiltration by identifying and tracking police.[91]

While the trial was still unfolding in June 1959, NYPD officers in Brooklyn punched NOI member Roberta Sinclair in the face and arrested her when she tried to intervene in the wrongful arrest of her husband. At a meeting following the assault, an undercover FBI agent reported that Malcolm explained to congregants "that if anyone should strike their women," the person responsible "should be made so that he will not be able to strike another."[92] When NYPD commissioner Stephen Kennedy came to Harlem to speak a few days later, pledging that all new recruits would be trained to "develop an intelligent understanding of race relations," Malcolm confronted the police brass and demanded a meeting to discuss these recent incidents of police brutality against Black women. When Kennedy failed to show for the meeting two days later, Malcolm told Deputy Commissioner Walter Arm that the Nation of Islam did "not intend to let any man, regardless of race, police or otherwise, to molest our women." Infuriated at being kept waiting for over an hour just to be stood up, Malcolm delivered a stern warning to Kennedy's number two: "If we can't get justice from the law, then we'll have to seek justice elsewhere."[93]

A "NEAR RIOT" SHAKES NEW YORK CITY

The same evening "The Hate That Hate Produced" hit the airwaves, the frustrations and momentum swelling behind the "Negro revolt" in Harlem nearly reached a tipping point. The afternoon of July 13, while NAACP members convened in regional organization meetings at the Coliseum on Columbus Circle, Carmela Caviglione walked into the Regent Restaurant and Bar on 7th Avenue and 116th Street with a friend to have a drink.[94] The twenty-one-year-old Bronx resident of Puerto Rican and Italian descent was "apparently highly intoxicated," according to restaurant owner John Panuthos, when she walked in and excused herself to go to the restroom. After about forty-five minutes had passed, her companion asked the restaurant owner to help get her out of the bathroom. The two men pried open the door and asked two female employees to assist in removing Caviglione, who the men claimed was "very drunk" and "refused to leave." The two women managed to remove her from the restroom, but the struggle continued in the dining area, where Caviglione lodged herself in a booth and was reportedly "kicking, screaming, and swinging" at the employees as they tried to get her out of the restaurant.[95] "I was drinking a lot but I know what I'm doing when I'm drinking," Caviglione told a reporter later that evening, challenging Panuthos's account. "I didn't want to leave, that's all."[96]

As the struggle continued inside the bar, two white NYPD officers pulled up in their patrol car. Patrolman Norman Hammes entered the restaurant to get a cup of coffee, while Lieutenant John Angrist stayed in the car. Panuthos welcomed Hammes and asked the patrolman to help him remove the young woman from his restaurant. According to Panuthos, however, the struggle only intensified when Hammes intervened. "The way she was fighting," he told a reporter, "he had to use force to subdue her." Hammes, whom Panuthos described as "a little fellow," struggled as Caviglione was reportedly "doing everything in her power to try to maim him." Hammes slapped Caviglione and eventually yanked her up by her hair as he tried to remove her from the booth.[97] Having been called in for assistance, Angrist entered the restaurant, and the two officers dragged the young woman about forty feet from the restaurant to the patrol car while punching and kicking her along the way, according to a witness statement.[98] Unaware of the confrontation that had taken place inside, dozens of witnesses on 7th Avenue watched as two white officers manhandled a young woman with bronze skin and tight curls.

While bystanders on the crowded avenue looked on, the two officers struggled to force Caviglione into the car, eventually settling for confining her to the floor of the front seat underneath the dashboard. After finally securing her around 5:30 p.m., according to the same witness who lived across the street from the restaurant, the patrol car sped off up 7th Avenue. Within moments, however, the car swerved at 117th Street, smashing into the concrete median dividing the avenue. According to the officers, Caviglione had grabbed the wheel and stepped on the accelerator, causing the crash.[99]

Charles Samuel, a thirty-year-old Black postal worker who lived nearby, had been fixing a tire near the intersection when the patrol car crashed. As a crowd gathered around the spectacle of a wrecked NYPD vehicle, Samuel approached the car to see what had happened. Finding two white officers struggling with a young woman in the car, Samuel demanded to know why they were handling her so roughly. Angered by the questioning, Hammes got out of the car and grabbed Samuel, while simultaneously drawing his gun as the crowd drew closer. As Samuel struggled to free himself from the officer's grasp, Hammes fired his .38 caliber chrome-plated Colt, striking himself in the left hand before hitting Angrist in the lower back.[100]

Moments after the gunfire rang out, twenty patrol cars responding to a call for backup arrived on the scene. Caviglione and Samuel were whisked away to the infamous 28th Precinct on West 123rd Street, and the crowd followed in procession. Rumors of police brutality traveled quickly in Harlem, and in a scene reminiscent of the beating of Johnson X Hinton two years earlier, a crowd of nearly a thousand angry people soon surrounded the 28th Precinct to demand Samuel's release. That some in the crowd were unaware of what had actually provoked the demonstration reflected the prevalence of police brutality in the neighborhood. "I don't know what happened," one protestor told a reporter, "but I know these Harlem cops, and we oughta turn the station out."[101] With some among the crowd reportedly carrying bottles, bricks, and knives, it appeared to onlookers that Harlem residents were preparing to take justice into their own hands by storming the precinct to liberate Caviglione and Samuel.

As the crowd swelled in size and pulsed with anger, a "riot" seemed imminent for the second time in as many weeks. Just the weekend before, a crowd at 125th Street and 8th Avenue had pelted officers with objects to stop them from arresting two men before reinforcements arrived and dispersed the protest.[102] "I became scared when I saw the tension mounting outside the police station," State Senator James Watson told reporters after rushing to the scene with other officials to defuse the confrontation. Seeing people around him armed with "bricks, bottles, and knives," Watson took action.[103] Joined by Assemblyman Lloyd Dickens and middleweight boxing champion "Sugar" Ray Robinson—who owned a nightclub up the block—the unlikely trio managed to talk their way inside the precinct in hopes of negotiating a resolution with the police. Robinson, who Watson later commended for preventing "a serious situation from exploding into a race riot," coolly explained to high-ranking officers in the precinct that the crowd needed to see Samuel walk out of the precinct if they wanted to prevent open confrontation. The three men were then able to negotiate a compromise, by which the slew of charges facing Samuel, including felonious assault and inciting to riot, were reduced to a summons for disorderly conduct. In exchange, Robinson addressed the crowd to assure them that the police had not abused Samuel or Caviglione, even though he later admitted to reporters "the situation in the precinct didn't jibe with what I told the people . . . it was apparent the woman had been beaten."[104] Accompanied by his wife and the ad hoc negotiating team, Samuel walked out of the precinct, and the crowd slowly dissipated.

Although Charles Samuel walked free, Carmela Caviglione remained in a cell, beaten and afraid. Robinson's admission that he had deceived the crowd signaled a broader betrayal of Caviglione by the negotiators, protestors, and the Black press in the interest of preventing a more intense confrontation with police. "She had a split, bleeding upper lip and told me she was kicked and dragged by the hair by the police," Robinson told reporters after the fact. "She had obviously had a number of drinks but she was not incoherent as the cops reported. She was hysterical at times and seemed in great fear." Despite seeing and acknowledging the brutality Caviglione (pictured in fig. 6), suffered at the hands of the police, Robinson was clear in his position that "the most important thing right now is to stave off any crowd violence."[105] Though the young woman had been badly beaten, he was willing to sacrifice her right to safety and medical attention in favor of releasing Samuel and averting open confrontation with the NYPD.

FIG 6 Carmela Caviglione being questioned inside the 28th Precinct on July 13, 1959. (AP Wirephoto)

To add insult to injury, Caviglione's reputation was dragged through the mud by mainstream and Black newspapers alike. In addition to a report attributing the confrontation to "an angry, ill-informed crowd," the *Amsterdam News* also ran a front-page story the next week, detailing an interview with Caviglione inside the precinct. Featuring an unflattering photo of a detective pulling her up from a bench, the article revolved around her intoxication and portrayed her as "incoherent," "blubbering," kicking her feet "violently," and in a "near stupor."[106] Steeped in middle-class and moralistic views of respectability as a precondition for civil and human rights, such reports played into the hands of police accounts that used Caviglione's drinking and background to justify the beating they put on her.

From the initial confrontation inside the restaurant to the aftermath of the standoff at the 28th Precinct, the news coverage of the whole episode reeked of respectability politics and demonstrated a clear hostility toward

Caviglione based on her gender, perceived race, and substance use.[107] Drawing on racist stereotypes of nonwhite peoples, newspapers centered the accounts of Panuthos and his employees, who played up Caviglione's intoxication to justify the use of force against the young Puerto Rican woman.[108] News outlets spent far less time interviewing Samuel, Caviglione, and those who surrounded the precinct demanding their release (aside from Watson, Dickens, and Robinson), predictably skewing coverage to make the protest appear as an irrational and criminal response to a sensible and justifiable use of force.

Furthermore, while Samuel had his charges drastically reduced, the courts sought to make an example of Caviglione by holding her personally responsible for the actions of the police who beat her and the crowd that sought justice on her behalf. When her attorney sought to reduce her bail of $3,000 (approximately $32,425 in 2024) for charges of disorderly conduct and felonious assault, Felony Court Judge Louis Wallach denied the request. "It's just things like this—that's the way riots are created," Wallach lectured from the bench. "When an officer wants to make an arrest, these people want to create a revolution and I won't condone it."[109]

The confrontation outside the 28th Precinct made Harlem a political lightning rod as politicians, police, newspapers, and community leaders sought to explain the causes of the latest unrest and jostled to devise ways to curb any further trouble. In speaking to reporters about police abuse of the Nation of Islam two weeks before the "near riot," Malcolm X echoed the sentiments of many Black New Yorkers when he explained that the NOI had been waiting for the police to give them justice, but now, "I'm not responsible for anything that happens."[110] While the city narrowly avoided a violent confrontation that July, it had become clear to many that Harlem's Black communities were no longer willing to wait to receive justice—they were now fighting to seize it for themselves.

The "near riot" also represented an organic expression of Harlem residents' heightened demands for rights and power that had been growing in the previous days, weeks, and months. The collective anger that drew over one thousand people to spontaneously protest at the precinct that night was illustrative of a growing popular impatience with moderate approaches to civil rights advocacy, along with a swelling embrace of militant grassroots political action in the waning days of the 1950s. By the end of the decade, there was demonstrated—and growing—support in Harlem for local, national, and global Black freedom struggles that emphasized self-determination, self-defense, and local leadership of working-class people to achieve immediate rights and power. In turn, these local struggles were intersecting with and influencing national and global Black freedom struggles. Though these principles would become most closely associated with the Black Power movement in the latter half of the 1960s, radical grassroots struggles in Harlem led by Jesse Gray, Mae Mallory, Malcolm X, and others developed these tenets of Black Power from the late 1950s onward.

In the two weeks following the confrontation at the 28th Precinct, newspapers up and down the East Coast, and as far away as Sudan, carried stories of the altercation and rising racial tensions in Harlem, each seeking to explain the underlying causes that led residents to nearly storm the building.[111] Speaking to reporters the night of the incident, Borough President Hulan Jack attributed the conflict to rising racial tensions in the neighborhood, fueled by substandard housing, poor schools, and low-paying jobs. "The people of Harlem are in an angry mood," Jack said, "and the city's got to do something about it."[112]

As would be the case five years later when Harlem was rocked by a major uprising, media outlets and city officials, like Jack, employed the "powder keg thesis" to explain the causes of the confrontation. According to this common analysis of urban rebellions, forces of political, social, and economic oppression made powder kegs of Black communities, filling them with potentially explosive resentment that could be spontaneously sparked by an act of police violence. Though inherently flawed for denying people affected by systems of oppression any conscious political agency, the thesis nonetheless dominated mainstream explanations of what happened in Harlem that July. Subsequently, city officials launched a series of meetings, studies, and committees in attempts to drain some of the powder from the proverbial keg, while also taking measures to fasten down its lid.

These efforts represented mere concessions in an effort to appease moderate and middle-class Black leadership in Harlem, in hopes that they could cool the perceived hostility of the masses. However, it had become apparent over the previous two years that this class of leadership did not represent the interests of those most affected by systemic racism in Harlem. Notably absent from an emergency meeting called by Mayor Wagner on July 21 were representatives from grassroots organizations that embodied the growing spirit of militancy and self-determination among the Black working class in Harlem. Indeed, it was this growing militancy that city officials sought to suppress in the years following the "near riot" through increasingly militarized and oppressive policing.

By the start of the new decade, growing numbers of Harlem residents loudly demonstrated their disillusionment with moderate approaches to civil rights and began advocating for using more radical strategies and tactics to bring about Black liberation. Building on the neighborhood's Black radical traditions, grassroots organizers in the final years of the 1950s had begun to awaken and mobilize the masses to challenge and transform the political, social, and economic landscape of the nation's largest city. As James Hicks wrote a few months later, there was a "New Negro in Harlem" who was poised to mount a serious challenge to old ideas and institutions of power.[113]

3

THE LIMITS OF LIBERALISM IN HARLEM
1959-1960

> One day, to everyone's astonishment, someone drops a match
> in the powder keg and everything blows up. Before the dust has
> settled or the blood congealed, editorials, speeches, and civil-rights
> commissions are loud in the land, demanding to know what happened.
> What happened is that Negroes want to be treated like men.
> —JAMES BALDWIN, *"Fifth Avenue, Uptown," Esquire, 1960*

"**IT WAS NOT A RIOT,**" a ranking officer in the New York Police Department told a reporter as crowds dispersed from outside the 28th Precinct, "but it could easily have become one."[1] In the days that followed the arrest of Carmela Caviglione and Charles Samuel on July 13, 1959, it became evident the mass demonstration had signaled to city officials the potential that existed in Harlem for another rebellion. Just over a week earlier, the *Amsterdam News* had declared a "Negro revolt" was underway in Harlem, marked by the most "hostile and serious" collective mood since the 1930s, "when uptowners took measures into their own hands."[2] The provocative language invoked memories of 1935, when a rumor of police brutality triggered an uprising in Harlem. Though the protests outside the 28th Precinct did not escalate to the same level, most conscious observers in Harlem understood the "near riot" as a logical consequence of decades of oppressive resistance to struggles for civil rights, human rights, and political power. "If we were disposed to brag and boast," the *Amsterdam News* editorial staff declared a few days afterward, "we could scream in headlines: 'We knew it all the time!'"[3]

This brief yet powerful demonstration was a significant moment in the development of the modern civil rights movement in New York City. A large—and growing—population of Harlem residents, not necessarily affiliated with traditional civil rights organizations, showed that they could—*and believed they should*—do something about racial oppression and police violence. In so doing, they demonstrated the existence of a level of collective political consciousness in Harlem that could quickly translate into effective direct action, reflecting the influence of a more radical set of grassroots leaders in Harlem. Subsequent contestations over rights and power in Harlem in the wake of the unrest pointed to a growing popular disillusionment with liberal responses to issues of systemic racism. A growing number of local people engaged in Black freedom struggles in Harlem came to reject Northern liberalism, which had failed to resolve the underlying causes of political, social, and economic inequality for Black communities.

Sticking close to the script that Mayor Fiorello La Guardia had drawn up in response to the 1935 uprising in Harlem, Mayor Wagner announced the formation of a committee tasked with studying the conditions in Harlem that led to unrest, and to draw up recommendations of how city resources could be used more effectively to prevent future disturbances. As many Harlem residents quickly realized, these efforts were not designed to attack the structural foundations of racism in the city, but rather to offer a modicum of reform as a means of easing racial tensions. At the same time, city officials were also taking steps to prepare for the possibility of future disturbances through the militarization of the New York Police Department. The general futility of liberal commission politics to meaningfully address racial inequality in the city, coupled with an expanding police apparatus geared toward curbing resistance in the aftermath of the "near riot," contributed to a widening political gulf between grassroots activists, moderate civil rights leaders, and city officials and shaped the course of struggles for Black liberation in the years to come.

THE COMMITTEE ON HARLEM AFFAIRS

As news of a Harlem crowd nearly storming a police precinct traveled far and wide, city officials moved quickly to neutralize the threat of greater disorder. The following day, a group of Harlem politicians and officials gathered at city hall for a closed-session meeting with Deputy Mayor Paul O'Keefe. This July 14 meeting, described as "peace talks" by the *Amsterdam News,* was called by Manhattan Borough President Hulan Jack and attended by political leaders in Harlem, including State Senator James Watson and Assemblyman Lloyd Dickens, who had both been present outside the 28th Precinct. The purpose of the meeting, according to Dickens, was to "determine the general angle which brought about the situation" and to provide these political leaders with a forum to come up with recommendations to resolve the unrest.[4]

Although the meeting began with a thorough examination of the specific charges of police brutality that had triggered the demonstration, conversation shifted to "rising race tension" in Harlem. Jack charged that this tension was rooted in an increasing resentment of "inadequate housing, poor schools, unsanitary conditions, and low-paying jobs." He concluded that what was needed from the Wagner administration was a greater effort to establish channels of communication with Harlem residents to "make them feel as though they're part of the city."[5] To the borough president, the answer to relieving tensions was simple: make the government more accountable to the people, and make the people feel as though they had a voice in government.

Lloyd Dickens took Jack's recommendation a step further by demanding that Black citizens "be integrated from an executive standpoint" in all city departments, specifically citing the need for Black police captains to command Harlem precincts.[6] Though Dickens's demands for Black representation in city policy-making positions in Harlem vaguely resembled the calls of Black nationalists for community control and self-determination, the Black political class in Harlem seemed to be in general consensus that Harlem's potentially explosive problems could be solved through integrating the usual channels of representative government. At the conclusion of the meeting, Deputy Mayor O'Keefe smiled broadly as he posed for photos with the group of officials—along with Sugar Ray Robinson, who had helped negotiate the standoff at the precinct—and announced that he would personally investigate the situation and set up an appointment for the group to meet with Mayor Wagner.[7]

For his part, Mayor Wagner met with Police Commissioner Stephen Kennedy for a briefing on police responses to the protests. Kennedy had been active all week in mobilizing an increased police presence to curb any threat of further unrest. In an immediate response to the demonstration, Kennedy deployed an additional eighty-eight officers to the 28th Precinct. Warning against the continued threat of "race riots" two days later, Kennedy also sent police reinforcements to other predominantly Black neighborhoods in the city. These moves to expand the police presence in Black communities drew the ire of many Harlem leaders, who charged Kennedy with trying to create "a police state." NY NAACP officials Jawn A. Sandifer and L. Joseph Overton argued that the increased police deployment would only aggravate the situation, pointing out that oppressive policing was one of the leading factors in rising racial tensions in Harlem in the first place.[8]

Kennedy attacked these allegations as "outrageous" and complained to the press that the police were being made "scapegoats" for the various socioeconomic factors contributing to unrest in Harlem. The commissioner defended his actions by publicizing crime statistics for Central Harlem, which he described as "shocking," though he refused to provide statistics from other precincts for comparison.[9] Kennedy's manipulation of crime data to rationalize and justify the expansion of policing in Black communities did not go unchecked in Harlem, however. *Amsterdam News* editor James Hicks took Kennedy to task in an editorial column, pointing out that the commissioner had refused the request of *Amsterdam News* reporters for crime statistics for the 24th Precinct—a predominantly white neighborhood on the city's West Side with reportedly high crime rates. Hicks also argued that Kennedy's statistics did not match the monthly reports presented at meetings of the 28th Precinct Community Council.[10]

Furthermore, Kennedy couched his defense in fearmongering terms typical of Cold War–era repression of political dissent. "A race riot," Kennedy warned reporters, "could cause more destruction of community relations than an atom bomb." With such rhetoric of hyper-criminality and widespread destruction, Kennedy effectively convinced city officials, press outlets, and even some civil rights leaders that expanded police powers were necessary to prevent impending disaster.[11] In the following days, weeks, and months, Kennedy would build on this platform to further bolster the powers of the NYPD to enforce "law and order" in the city.

Mayor Wagner left his meeting with Kennedy feeling confident in the police commissioner's handling of the incident outside the 28th Precinct and declared the need to preserve "law and order" in the city. Like Kennedy, Wagner pointed to underlying problems rooted in economic inequality as the causes for "tensions" in Harlem. Speaking to reporters after the meeting, he argued that Harlem needed better housing, improved building conditions, more schools, more playgrounds, and "perhaps a closer relationship with the department heads involved." This last point proved to be the basis for his administrative responses to the problems he saw as contributing to the unrest in Harlem. Moments later, Wagner called for a meeting with community and political leaders in Harlem and city officials to "see whether we can work out better liaison—to have people give complaints more rapidly, and their hopes and aspirations."[12] It was clear that Harlem residents had drawn the attention of city hall to issues of inequality in the neighborhood. The next step for city hall was to figure out what answers they could come up with to make these issues less explosive.

The mayor invited a group of nearly ninety city officials and representatives from Harlem to city hall for an "initial exploration" of how city and community resources could be "more effectively utilized" to address the problems contributing to mounting protests.[13] Wagner had asked nearly every department head to attend, including the police commissioner, the commissioner of housing and buildings, the superintendent of schools, and many others whose departments were implicated in the oppressive living conditions in Harlem.[14] Notable among the Harlem political leaders in attendance at this July 21 meeting were Congressman Adam Clayton Powell Jr., Councilman Earl Brown, Assemblyman Dickens, Senator Watson, and Assemblywoman Bessie Buchanan. Also in attendance were several members of the clergy, civic leaders, and business owners. In his account of the meeting, Brown described the gathering as "the most imposing group of city officials ever in one room with Harlem citizens to discuss its problems."[15] Notably absent from the meetings convened by O'Keefe and Wagner, however, were many working-class representatives from local community organizations or grassroots civil rights leaders behind the "Negro revolt," who were better positioned to provide a meaningful diagnosis of the situation in Harlem. Furthermore, only twelve of the sixty-eight invited representatives from Harlem were women.[16]

Delegates to the meeting voiced a number of suggestions for the alleviation of oppressive conditions and the economic, political, and social empowerment of Harlem residents, but the topic of policing dominated the meeting and its press coverage. "Although bad housing conditions are considered to be Harlem's gravest problem," Brown argued in his regular column in the

Amsterdam News, "nobody uttered a single word about them."[17] Brown's claims were overstated: delegates repeatedly suggested improvements in education, housing, health, and sanitation policies and demanded representation in policy-making positions.[18] Though hyperbole, Brown's claims were nonetheless illustrative of a heightened popular focus on policing in Harlem. This attention was logical, since police actions had triggered the unrest and brought years of police brutality, abuse, and misconduct to the forefront of popular consciousness and conversation.

One of the most controversial discussions around policing arose when Powell and Buchanan requested that more Black officers be assigned to Harlem.[19] This request echoed the calls of Harlem residents who for years had demanded proportional representation in the police force, but the notion sparked hostile opposition. White and Black officials alike turned the suggestion that race be taken into account in public policy on its head and invoked the rhetoric of Southern segregation to discredit Powell and Buchanan. "Such an act of segregation is simply not right," Police Commissioner Kennedy told a press conference, adding that "rather than segregate the police department, we must continue to fight for a truly integrated city."[20] Meanwhile, Brown took the analogy a step further, arguing that Powell and Buchanan "took the same position that [Arkansas] Gov. Faubus and all other Southern white supremacists have taken about the race problem: Jim Crow the Negro and everything will be fine and dandy."[21]

The transcript of the meeting, however, showed that at no point in the proceedings did anyone suggest "Jim Crowing all Negro policemen" in Harlem, as Brown claimed.[22] Suggestions *were* made for greater integration of police in Harlem, interracial patrols, and new procedures for handling allegations of brutality.[23] Police Commissioner Kennedy deliberately mischaracterized requests for reform in an attempt to claim a moral high ground on race relations in the city. Furthermore, the commissioner found support for his defensive posturing among moderate Black leaders like Brown, who effectively appropriated the rhetoric of the civil rights movement to undermine demands for police accountability and Black representation in majority-Black precincts.[24] Misrepresenting criticism and masking intransigence with lofty rhetoric to gain popular support were tactics that the NYPD would employ frequently in the following years to gaslight Harlem residents, deceive the general public, and stymie demands for reform.

If the meeting produced little in the way of tangible benefits to improve social conditions, it did provide Harlem representatives with a rare opportunity to voice their concerns, complaints, and recommendations to such a collective of city officials. The most important achievement of the meeting, Hulan Jack wrote in a letter to Wagner, was the recognition that channels of communication must be established whereby "little people can come forward to intelligently speak for themselves to make complaints, offer suggestions and get results through their city government without fear or reprisals."[25] Judging by the influx of letters, telegrams, and phone calls to the borough president's office, these meetings did encourage Harlem residents to engage with their political representatives, and thereby with political action.[26] Perhaps sensing the precariousness of his own political standing as elections neared, Jack pled with the mayor to act on these grievances through concerted and systemic action. "The administration cannot afford to even think of letting these people down," he concluded, "they are with us and they expect and demand that we be with them." Although the borough president's professed faith in his constituents' loyalty to city government may have been political rhetoric, he nevertheless understood that the mayor needed to act in a meaningful way to address the deep-seated problems they faced or risk the alienation of his constituents from electoral politics.[27]

Just over a month later, Mayor Wagner did act when he announced the formation of the Committee on Harlem Affairs (CHA), an "action committee" that would assist his administration in "bringing more effective services" to Harlem. The committee was composed of five city officials and seventeen representatives from Harlem.[28] After an initial meeting on September 15, the CHA decided to form three subcommittees—on housing, education, and law enforcement—based on what they saw as the core issues in Harlem.[29] As Hulan Jack had suggested, these subcommittees were tasked with acting as liaison between Harlem residents and city officials and were set up to investigate conditions in Harlem in order to provide the mayor's office with recommendations for improvement.

From its inception, the CHA came under criticism from Harlem residents who had little faith that a city-sponsored committee would have any real impact on improving deeply rooted conditions in Harlem. In a sardonic critique of the mayor's "compulsion" for "government by committee," *New York Age* columnist Chuck Stone opined that the CHA had little chance for success. "Committees don't solve problems," Stone wrote, "votes, tough housing laws, court enforcement of these laws, and unbiased police protection solve problems."[30] *Amsterdam News* editor James Hicks also openly doubted that the committee would be able to implement any suggestions made to it.

As the CHA got to work, Hicks was invited to appear before both the Subcommittee on Law Enforcement and the Subcommittee on Housing. In his appearance before the former, Hicks claimed that his recommendations to integrate Black officers into policy-making levels of the NYPD were characteristically "twisted out of shape" by Kennedy to make him "appear as an advocate of racial segregation." After this experience, Hicks declined an offer to appear before the latter subcommittee, citing the malevolent rejection and misrepresentation of his earlier testimony.[31]

A lack of genuine community representation was also cited as a fundamental objection to the CHA from its inception. Shortly after its formation, Hicks described the committee as "a bunch of nice guys who don't know anything about the man in the street."[32] Although leaders from the NY NAACP, Urban League, and various civic associations were among the members of the CHA, Hicks's insight demonstrated the perceived disconnect between these types of moderate, middle-class-oriented organizations and the bulk of Harlem's working-class communities. Even though protesters had been in the streets all month, CHA member and president of the Peoples Civic and Welfare Association Glester Hinds bafflingly told reporters in late July that there was no tension in Harlem. Furthermore, Hinds charged, "All people, regardless of race, should let the law take its course."[33]

Published in the pages of the *Amsterdam News,* Hinds's remarks highlighted the psychological and political distance between the CHA and Harlem residents. Echoing the analyses of grassroots organizers like Ella Baker, Jesse Gray, Mae Mallory, and Malcolm X, Stone wrote, "The real persons who are going to reduce Harlem's problems to their lowest common denominator are not Mayor Wagner or his . . . committee, but the Negroes themselves."[34] If city officials were serious about resolving the problems facing Black communities, Stone reasoned, they needed to involve and listen to the people most directly affected by systemic racism.

Despite its inherent flaws and lack of popular support, the CHA went to work in Harlem at the dawn of the 1960s. For the next several months, the three subcommittees of the CHA met periodically to discuss their findings, write reports, and issue recommendations. These recommendations, analyzed below, are significant for understanding the ways that city and civic leaders proposed to solve what they viewed as the most pressing problems in Harlem at that time. Furthermore, the responses these recommendations received from the corresponding city commissioners offer insights into how city officials evaluated their own effectiveness in addressing issues of inequality in Harlem. They are also a metric by which to gauge the willingness of city officials to engage with citizens through the democratic process to reform government.

THE SUBCOMMITTEE ON EDUCATION

At the initial CHA meeting on July 21, representatives from Harlem repeatedly raised four main suggestions for improving education: improve the curriculum in Harlem schools, reduce split sessions, reduce overcrowding by transferring students to under-enrolled schools, and assign experienced teachers to Harlem.[35] To many Harlem parents and community members, none of these suggestions were new, since they had largely provided the basis of struggles waged for educational justice in Harlem over the previous five years in the wake of the *Brown v. Board* decision. Despite the efforts of local activists like Baker, Mallory, and Drs. Kenneth and Mamie Clark in these years, however, there had been little progress made by city hall toward fulfilling these demands.

From the outset, it became evident that the Subcommittee on Education was particularly troubled by the "de facto" segregation of Harlem schools, the issue for which the Harlem Nine had garnered national attention the previous year. Without mentioning these ongoing struggles for educational justice in their final report, the subcommittee criticized the Board of Education for failing to implement any of the recommendations of the Commission on Integration, which had been set up under the leadership of the Clarks and Ella Baker in response to the *Brown* decision. The implementation of these earlier recommendations, the subcommittee argued, was "essential to relieve tensions in Harlem." Furthermore, the subcommittee found that as a result of the board's sluggish and ineffectual posture toward these recommendations, there had actually been an *increase* in segregated schools over the previous five years.[36]

To resolve the problems associated with Harlem's separate and unequal schools, the subcommittee insisted that the Commission on Integration's recommendations be implemented, requested timely reports on the progress of school integration, and suggested that an additional committee be established to evaluate the conditions of each school in Harlem.[37] In his official response to these recommendations, however, Superintendent of Schools John Theobald offered little to those looking for action plans or guarantees to improve Harlem schools. Theobald balked at providing an answer as to why the commission's recommendations had not been implemented, rejected calls for an advisory committee to evaluate the conditions of schools, and promised that a progress report on desegregation would be forthcoming for the first time since 1957.[38] In essence, four months of work from the subcommittee produced only suggestions for further studies and reports of conditions in Harlem schools, but even these meager requests were rejected by the superintendent of schools.

THE SUBCOMMITTEE ON HOUSING

In a 1935 report, Mayor La Guardia's Commission on the Harlem Riot had laid out its suggestions for improving housing conditions in Harlem. The commission's primary points focused on the need for a planned housing program to address the shortage of sound units and better enforcement of housing codes. Additionally, the commission had encouraged Harlem tenants to organize and protest exorbitant rents and, if these failed, to engage in rent strikes. Deemed too "radical," the 1935 report was never publicly released, and the problems it addressed remained largely unchanged.[39] Nearly twenty-five years later, Harlem was still short on decent housing, building codes still weren't being enforced, and tenant organizers had begun to revive a dormant movement for housing justice.

Given the intractable nature of Harlem's housing problems over the previous two decades, the Subcommittee on Housing was treading on familiar ground as it began its work. Several suggestions were put forth to combat Harlem's "grave" housing problems at the July 21 meeting, centering on urban renewal and tenant displacement, enforcement of housing codes and laws, development of low and middle-income housing, and Black representation on Robert Moses's Committee on Slum Clearance.[40] Though overshadowed by the controversy over policing, these initial comments provided the foundation for the housing subcommittee's work in the following months.

The complexity of Harlem's housing problems was made clear in the subcommittee's report to Mayor Wagner that December. In an eight-page document that implicated eleven different city agencies, all three branches of city government, and several state and federal departments, the subcommittee recommended reforms pertaining to urban renewal and relocation, sanitation, building inspections and code enforcement, rodent control, housing development, and health care.[41] Of greatest concern to was the need for more housing units for low- and particularly middle-income residents, and the careful relocation of residents displaced by urban renewal projects.[42]

Of more immediate concern to many Harlem residents, however, were the dangerous conditions of apartments to which many low-income families were confined, as economic inequality, discriminatory housing practices, and low vacancy rates made it extremely difficult to find safe and affordable housing. These were the conditions that were bringing tenants out into the streets and filling the mailboxes of city officials with complaints. The subcommittee offered recommendations for strengthened building code enforcement and harsher penalties for negligent landlords, but the Department of Buildings deferred any response pending the passage of three bills in the city council to provide greater code enforcement powers to the city. In the interim, the Department of Buildings conducted a wave of inspections, turning up thousands of violations.

Though the subcommittee showed some signs of class bias favoring middle-class Harlem residents, Chairman Hope Stevens touched on a vital point in a post-report memo to Mayor Wagner. "We believe it to be the greatest importance," Stevens wrote, "that residents of the Harlem community be given proof that they are sharing in the development of the city through participation in its governmental functions at levels where their influence can be felt."[43] To Stevens, a degree of self-determination for Harlem's Black residents was imperative if hostilities toward city government were to be eased. More than any other area of racial discrimination, Stevens argued, housing inequality most directly contributed to a "psychological situation around which feelings of hostility with resulting tensions will continue to center." The nature of this "psychological situation," Stevens advised Wagner in conclusion, could be ameliorated if the mayor made efforts to empower Harlem residents by providing political representation at policy-making levels to promote a sense of collective agency. Stevens understood the political gravity of the housing question in Harlem, and his warning to the mayor proved prescient. Wagner's responses to the housing question had profound impacts on the direction of struggles for rights and power in the months and years that followed.

THE SUBCOMMITTEE ON LAW ENFORCEMENT

The heated public debate around the actions and policies of the NYPD in the immediate wake of the July 13 "near riot" swelled as the Subcommittee on Law Enforcement got to work. In early August five thousand people gathered at 125th Street and 7th Avenue for the annual Marcus Garvey Day celebration, with many hoisting photos of African nationalist leaders and carrying signs that read "Black Men of the World United to Down Police Brutality." Speaking alongside Bessie Phillips, Lewis Michaux, and other Harlem activists calling for united action and economic nationalism, United African Nationalist Movement President James Lawson blasted the NYPD for its rampant brutality against African Americans, called for Black police captains in Black neighborhoods, and demanded Stephen Kennedy's resignation as police commissioner.[44]

Though the nationalist leader had been painted as a dangerous militant in "The Hate That Hate Produced" documentary just weeks earlier, Lawson's comments at the rally were hardly radical, and certainly not unique. Indeed, his charges of police misconduct and demands for Black representation within the upper ranks of the NYPD had been brought up by others at the July 21 meeting and became major focal points of the Subcommittee on Law Enforcement's deliberations. For two months, this subcommittee held weekly

FIG 7 NYPD surveillance photo of demonstrators with the United African Nationalist Movement gathering on 7th Avenue (now Adam Clayton Powell Jr. Blvd.) during the Marcus Garvey Day celebration in August 1959. Signs read "Free Africa Now!"; "We Demand More and Better Jobs"; "We Demand Better Housing!!!" (Handschu Photograph Files, Municipal Archives, City of New York)

meetings and conferred with individuals and representatives of various organizations and city departments, including *Amsterdam News* editor James Hicks and the Black police union of the NYPD, the Guardians Association.

The political tug-of-war that ensued over the Subcommittee on Law Enforcement put a public spotlight on the NYPD's legacy of racist policing in Black communities and quickly overshadowed the work of the other subcommittees. In their November report, the subcommittee put forth nine recommendations for improving relations between the police and Harlem residents, including the appointment of a Black deputy commissioner, ending the common police practice of using Harlem as a training ground for rookie cops, improving race and human relations training for police, expanding public relations efforts, ending illegal searches and seizures, and increasing the number of Black officers on the force. In essence, the subcommittee's recommendations demonstrated a primary concern with improving the image of the police in Harlem through greater Black representation in the NYPD, improving interpersonal training, and curbing some of the most flagrant abuses commonly reported by Harlem residents. Notably absent from the report, however, was any mention or suggestion of disciplinary procedures for police officers who violated departmental policies or infringed upon the civil rights of Black citizens.[45]

Despite posing hardly any threat to the fundamental structures or powers of the NYPD, these recommendations were nonetheless met with a characteristically defensive response from Commissioner Kennedy. Doubling down on his previous refusal to hire more Black officers, Kennedy misrepresented the subcommittee's recommendation as an illegal quota system and declared that appointments in the NYPD would not be made "on the basis of politics, color, race or religion." Kennedy went on to describe his efforts to professionalize the police force and expand human relations training, and he professed his opposition to police misconduct while dismissing each concern laid out. As a way of deflecting responsibility for racial tensions in Harlem away from the NYPD, Kennedy audaciously explained that strained police-community relations in Harlem were a result not of police malfeasance but of citizens taking out their frustrations over racial oppression on officers who were merely trying to fulfill their duties to "protect the community as a whole."[46]

Kennedy's response received a predictably damning public rebuke from the members of the subcommittee and other public figures in Harlem. Subcommittee chairman Thomas Benjamin Dyett called Kennedy's comments a "vituperative outburst of fury" and suggested that the commissioner's hostility was based on his realization that tensions in Harlem had grown "steadily and even alarmingly" under his leadership.[47] A cofounder of New York City's first Black law firm in the 1920s (alongside George Hall and renowned Black communist William L. Patterson) and a member of the Mayor's Commission on Integration in the wake of the *Brown* decision, Dyett was no stranger to Wagner's committee approach to urban governance.[48] In his scathing critique, Dyett rebutted several of Kennedy's claims, drawing particular attention to illegal searches and seizures and the lack of Black officers. Expanding on the subcommittee's insistence on the "psychological importance" of having more Black officers in the NYPD, Dyett argued that Kennedy's failure to appoint a Black deputy commissioner could give the impression that the police commissioner "intends to maintain a lily-white staff." Furthermore, Dyett contended, the appointment of only white men as deputy commissioners "may in itself be telling evidence of discrimination."[49]

Black New Yorkers hardly needed Dyett to tell them what they already believed to be true. It certainly did not appear coincidental that in a police force of 23,000 there were only 1,200 Black officers (5.2%); that of 60 inspectors only one was Black (1.6%); that of 212 captains there was not a single Black officer; or that only 10 of 750 lieutenants were Black (1.3%).[50] The significance of Dyett's claim lay not in the observation of racial disparities but in the legal premise of his argument, which held that a disparate adverse impact of otherwise race-neutral policies on a particular racial group constituted evidence of racial discrimination. It would be another five years before this argument became codified in federal law through the passage of the 1964 Civil Rights Act. Like the Black mothers of the Harlem Nine a few months earlier, Dyett issued a challenge to the system of government-sponsored segregation in the city, which officials like Kennedy had tried to mask with rhetoric that professed allegiance to racial equality.

Dyett also took Kennedy to task for his apparent justification of illegal searches and seizures. Kennedy had justified these procedures by citing the alleged difficulties officers faced in making "split-second" decisions about the civil and human rights of those involved in an alleged crime.[51] "These split-second decisions," Dyett countered, "have at times included the shooting of teenagers running away from the scene of a crime, resulting in the handing out of a death sentence by an over-zealous or perhaps vicious policeman for an offense for which the Court of Appeals might hesitate to approve capital punishment."[52] While Kennedy tried to spin the lived experiences of Harlem residents into a narrative of police benevolence in the face of community hostility, Dyett provided a check on the commissioner's propagandistic interpretation. In the end, the advocacy from the Subcommittee on Law Enforcement far outpaced that of the other two subcommittees of the Committee on Harlem Affairs, yet it still proved largely ineffective in producing meaningful police reform.

Kennedy's continued intransigence also prompted Adam Clayton Powell Jr. to escalate his critiques of the embattled police commissioner in early 1960. As he had during the July 21 meeting at city hall, Powell again demanded greater Black representation among the ranks of the NYPD. During a February sermon before two thousand congregants at the storied Abyssinian Baptist Church on 138th Street, Powell berated Kennedy for his repeated refusals to comply with the recommendations of the CHA. Echoing Dyett's charge that the commissioner had created a "lily-white" department, Powell demanded Kennedy's resignation and called for Black representation at police headquarters "to prove there is democracy."[53]

About a month later, Powell doubled down on his sermon in a statement published in the *Pittsburgh Courier*. After explaining in detail his demands for Black representation in policy-making positions in the NYPD, Powell expressed concern over the patterns of police repression that frequently followed any public protests over police actions. "The immediate answer they get," Powell charged, "is an arrogant statement in the press from the Commissioner immediately followed by the dispatching of 'shock troops' to the area in an open attempt to intimidate the people." Powell's words certainly rang true for the "near riot" months earlier, and countless other protests of police misconduct and violence in previous years and decades. Repeating his demand for the commissioner to resign, Powell suggested that Mayor Wagner appoint "an interim board of responsible citizens to clean up the mess" in the NYPD. Powell insisted that as a basic tenet of a democratic society, police power must be subjected to civilian control "under the will of the people."[54] Kennedy's dogged refusal to submit to the will of the people in Harlem and throughout New York City reaffirmed for the congressman and his constituents the need to rein in a lawless department and fight for the realization of this democratic ideal. With Kennedy's hostility to sensible police reform supported by Wagner on one side, and surging demands for police accountability and community control on the other, the subcommittee's efforts served as tinder for the impending wildfire.

"MOB RULE" AND "CURBSTONE JUSTICE"

By the time Powell took to the pulpit to demand police accountability and Kennedy's resignation, two things had already become clear about the future of policing in Harlem. First, Kennedy demonstrated that the NYPD had absolutely no intention of implementing any reforms recommended by the Committee on Harlem Affairs. In what has become a common refrain among police commissioners in the years since, Kennedy cloaked the inherent racism of police violence with a narrative that blamed public hostility toward the NYPD for confrontations instigated by its officers. If the police "get no community support or are made scapegoats by a hostile community," Kennedy opined, "this has a tendency to breed resentment in the police." In Kennedy's estimation, confrontations between white police and Black communities resulted from misdirected anger over "racial prejudice" rather than racist policing, and therefore it was not the NYPD that needed reform but the communities they served.[55]

Second, the NYPD took the escalation of Black freedom struggles as a sign that racial unrest was likely to continue, and thus expanded its capacity to quell mass protests through both physical and covert suppression. Declaring his intention to "see that law and order are preserved" in Harlem, Wagner worked closely with Kennedy in the following months to increase police presence and power in majority-Black communities. Coupled with the arrival of Robert F. Williams in Harlem and the broadcast of "The Hate that Hate Produced," the protests during the summer of 1959 raised the specter of a looming insurrection in Harlem—and the NYPD was tasked with surveilling and suppressing the organizations and individuals deemed responsible.

In the weeks following the mass mobilization outside the 28th Precinct, police officers flooded into Harlem, Bedford-Stuyvesant, South Jamaica, and the East Bronx as part of Kennedy's plan to impose law and order amid growing protests against police violence. After previously using crime rates as justification for heightened policing, the commissioner next played up the existential threat of "mob rule." Speaking at an NYPD ceremony in early August, Kennedy alluded to the protests at the 28th Precinct when he warned against city streets being turned into courtrooms with police or mobs serving as judge and jury. "Curbstone justice is no justice at all," he proclaimed, "mob rule mocks justice and leads to anarchy. Eventually government in totalitarian form emerges."[56] Wagner followed suit, making explicit the city's position on the NYPD's responsibilities in suppressing protest in a commencement address at the Police Academy a week later. Wagner warned that any protests "will be put down according to the mandate given the police power by the constitution of the state and the charter of the city." Describing protests against police violence as "attempts to set up kangaroo justice on the streets," Wagner declared that "no group but constituted authority will rule anywhere."[57] This type of fearmongering rhetoric, typical of the Cold War era and continuously replicated in the decades since, largely served as a pretense to expand the powers of the NYPD to suppress protest in the months and years that followed.

Flooding majority-Black communities with white officers in the name of law and order that summer unsurprisingly led to hostile confrontations, often sparked by the actions of officers perceived as occupying forces. A few short weeks after the police beating of Carmela Caviglione, officers confronted another woman at the corner of 125th Street and 8th Avenue, just down the block from the New York NAACP office. An argument ensued, and the woman reportedly kicked one of the officers while passersby watched the situation unfold. *Amsterdam News* columnist Jimmy Booker reported that the confrontation drew about a hundred people to the busy intersection as the officers moved to arrest the unidentified woman. As the crowd closed in, however, the officers panicked and "turned, rushed to their patrol car, and drove off hurriedly."[58] Although the story received no apparent media attention outside Booker's column, the incident surely sent a message to the officers on the scene, those in their precinct, and the NYPD brass.

Two days later, a similar situation unfolded in the East Bronx, where police had been patrolling the neighborhood, "shoving people around," and generally harassing residents since the "near riot" in Harlem.[59] A confrontation began when detectives entered a luncheonette on Brook Avenue after staking out the shop for several days on suspicion that the proprietor was selling bootleg whisky. When the owner and an employee allegedly resisted arrest, they were roughed up and dragged out of the restaurant, along with a customer named Robert "Big Bob" Edwards. As Detectives Thomas Martino and Jeremiah O'Connor pushed Edwards to the ground, beat him over the head with a blackjack, and kicked him in the face, a crowd gathered to intervene. The detectives drew their guns on the owner, Tyson King, and others but holstered them for fear of shooting each other as the crowds drew nearer. The three hundred people who gathered to protect their neighbors from police violence allegedly worked over the officers and slashed their car tires before reinforcements arrived to disperse the crowd. The *New York*

Times carried the police account and stoked fears with the headline "300 in the Bronx Maul Detectives," yet investigations by the Bronx NAACP and *Amsterdam News* concluded that the incident was "provoked by the police themselves and their thoughtless actions which can only be termed as brutality." Nonetheless, when the dust settled, four Black people were charged with a litany of offenses, including inciting a riot, while the two detectives faced no consequences.[60]

With Robert F. Williams's presence in New York and the continued police repression of the Nation of Islam putting the public spotlight on debates around nonviolence and armed self-defense that summer, these conflicts demonstrated a growing popular militancy in New York City. Harlem residents read about Williams's armed self-defense against the Ku Klux Klan in the pages of *The Crusader* (circulated by Mae Mallory and the Crusader Family); listened to Williams, Malcolm X, and other street speakers call for protection against police and vigilante violence by any means necessary; and took direct action to protect themselves and their neighbors from rampant police brutality. For a brief moment, this popular practice of self-defense against police violence put the NYPD on the defensive, before police struck back in the late summer of 1959.

"GANG WARFARE," WHITE FEAR, AND POLICE BACKLASH

The rising tide of protest against police violence took place amid a rash of highly publicized violent crimes that summer. Attributed to youth gang activity, this widely reported crime wave sanctioned city and state officials to expand the powers and presence of the NYPD and expedite the city's carceral turn. In late August 1959 a fight on the Lower East Side resulted in the deaths of two teenagers, which the *New York Times* attributed to an "outburst of gang warfare."[61] The most high-profile and consequential conflict happened on August 30, when a group of Puerto Rican teens fatally stabbed two white teenagers in a playground fight on West 45th Street. Previous gang-related violence that year had largely involved teenagers in communities of color and received relatively scarce media attention, but the deaths of white teenagers now set the city into a frenzy. The story received front-page coverage in the *Times* for the next week, while radio stations stoked the flames through special broadcasts like "They Kill for Kicks."[62] Many of these reports stoked white fear in the city, referring to the teenage Puerto Rican suspects as "invaders" and demonizing one as "Dracula" because he had worn a cape during the fight.⁶³ Police Commissioner Kennedy joined the chorus as well, quoting FBI Director J. Edgar Hoover's warning that "the growing menace of youthful depredation is the core of the crime cancer in America." The next day, the commissioner quickly mobilized 1,400 officers to "fight against juvenile violence" in many of the same neighborhoods that had already received an influx of NYPD officers since mid-July.⁶⁴

To Kennedy, the killings were emblematic of a "rising tide of youth violence" since World War II, enabled by an unconcerned and complacent populace. The answer, to him, was obvious: the city needed more police. Local papers and city officials eagerly supported the commissioner's characteristic get-tough response. While Councilman J. Daniel Diggs called for a curfew on teenagers, Councilman Earl Brown urged police to preemptively "smash these gangs before their members commit crimes."⁶⁵ This selective sudden outrage over juvenile delinquency was not missed by many Black and Puerto Rican communities. "These civic leaders who have suddenly become hysterical, didn't lift a finger until they suddenly saw blood splashed across the doorways of their West Side apartment stoops," the *Amsterdam News* observed. "Then, typical of the Johnny-Come-Lately to anything, they want the Police Commissioner to line up and shoot everybody whom they suspect in their hysteria."⁶⁶

As Kennedy expanded police presence in majority-Black communities, Wagner convened with Governor Rockefeller, J. Edgar Hoover, and top city and state officials to coordinate responses. This coterie offered platitudes about the systemic factors behind juvenile delinquency, yet the primary local response was to empower the NYPD with more resources and the criminal justice system with greater punitive powers. Within a matter of days, Wagner acted swiftly in announcing a slate of punitive measures, including diverting $2.5 million from municipal programs to hire over a thousand additional police officers; expanding police patrols to "preserve law and order in the city and to rid the streets of the hoodlums"; ordering the review of past criminal court decisions thought to be too lenient; and calling on Rockefeller to expand state "work camps," residential treatment centers, and "correctional institutions" for youth offenders.⁶⁷ With additional officers dispatched primarily to working-class Black and Puerto Rican communities, this targeted expansion of policing was effectively designed to criminalize Black and Puerto Rican youth in retaliation for the death of two white teenagers. At the same time, these directives hastened the pace at which New York City was expanding its capacities to suppress Black dissent in response to the summer's protests against police violence.

The punitive responses of Rockefeller, Wagner, and Kennedy to rising protests and youth "delinquency" marked a decisive shift toward punishing crime rather than addressing its social determinants. "The social welfare agencies and their workers have done fine and effective work in the field of juvenile delinquency," Wagner said in early September. "But when organized gangs invade playgrounds and blindly and wantonly commit murder, the handling of the matter has passed from the social agency into the hands of the police."[68] Despite the progress that youth agencies and organizations had made during the first half of the twentieth century, by the dawn of the 1960s crime was being reframed as a racial issue that required the expansion of the state's punitive powers, rather than its social programs, to resolve. Through these tough-on-crime policies and rhetoric directed at Black and Puerto Rican communities, politicians empowered the NYPD to assert itself as the defender of the racist social order in Jim Crow New York.[69]

THE VIEW FROM OCCUPIED TERRITORY

This hyper-policing turned tragic in early September when a white NYPD officer killed a young Black woman in Harlem. Shortly after midnight on Labor Day, Patrolman James O'Connell apprehended a Black man on 116th Street for trying to start a truck with a screwdriver. When the man freed himself, O'Connell gave chase across 116th Street and down Manhattan Avenue, "crazily firing" from "several hundred yards away," the *Amsterdam News* reported. One of the eight shots that O'Connell sprayed the block with as he emptied and reloaded his gun struck twenty-year-old Delight Crawford in the temple as she sat on her Manhattan Avenue stoop. As Crawford's boyfriend and neighbors tended to her body on the sidewalk, O'Connell continued his pursuit, finally catching the man a few blocks away, breaking his jaw in the process.[70]

O'Connell was then questioned by an assistant district attorney, who recommended a verdict of "excusable homicide" to a grand jury the next day. Reporting on the incident that weekend, the *Amsterdam News* described the police actions of firing wildly on a crowded block as "downright insanity" and called for an investigation by Commissioner Kennedy.[71] "Nobody showed us any sympathy," Crawford's brother-in-law told reporters of their treatment by police, "in fact, the officer who did the shooting... never even came up to us and said he was sorry."⁷² Despite the obvious violence that hyper-policing was inflicting on Black and Puerto Rican communities, the matter received scant attention in mainstream media compared to the city's tough-on-crime responses to youth delinquency and the perceived lawlessness of protests against police violence.

To James Baldwin, the already overbearing—and now expanding—presence of police in Harlem that caused Delight Crawford's death was an unmistakable symbol of white supremacy. While city officials fell over themselves in their efforts to flood Black neighborhoods with more police while rendering the attendant human costs invisible, Baldwin interjected a searing critique of the functions of hyper-policing in Harlem. In a now-famous essay published in *Esquire* the following summer, Baldwin illuminated the material and psychological realities of life under police occupation. Like housing projects that signified the confinement of Black communities in Northern "ghettos," the police revealed "the real attitude" and "force of the white world," Baldwin contended, an attitude that could never be masked by liberal platitudes or civil rights commissions.⁷³ The primary function of the NYPD in Harlem and other Black communities, Baldwin argued, was to "keep the black man corralled up here, in his place," thereby facilitating and enforcing the continued racist exploitation and confinement of Black people with all the collateral damage swept under the rug. Harlem residents recognized the contradictions of policing in their communities, since cops could "swagger about in two's and three's controlling" the community but somehow vanished when people actually needed help.⁷⁴ As Baldwin's essay hit newsstands, Harlem residents were filling Borough President Hulan Jack's mailbox with complaints about the NYPD's lack of interest in protecting public safety uptown.⁷⁵

In addition to the NYPD's disregard for the lives of Delight Crawford and others caught in the crosshairs of the city's tough-on-crime clampdown, the constant police presence at mass meetings, street rallies, and protests further incensed Harlem residents. While officers had long been fixtures around the perimeters of street meetings, the escalation of police conflicts with the community in the summer of 1959 made their continued surveillance all the more unbearable. With police violence and suppression of dissent on the rise amid the swelling grassroots embrace of armed self-defense and anticolonial struggle, white patrolmen at street meetings personified the ubiquitous force of white opposition to Black liberation. Channeling

Harlem's anticolonial spirit, Baldwin described the NYPD's role in Harlem as analogous to "an occupying soldier in a bitterly hostile country."[76] To Baldwin, segregated communities were sites of confinement, exploitation, and extraction and therefore intrinsically connected with colonized African nations engaging in revolutionary struggle at the time of his writing. Baldwin here articulated what was becoming an increasingly popular sentiment in Harlem—the police were simply the hired guns for ensuring the economic and political interests of white landlords, business owners, and politicians.

The clear contempt that many Harlem residents had for the NYPD presented the department with two basic choices for addressing this tension: reform their practices or repress the people. As Kennedy's hostility to the CHA demonstrated, the former was summarily dismissed as the latter became departmental policy. Again, Baldwin perceptively explained the systemic rejection of reform and the attendant escalation of tensions and repression by articulating the psychological conflict he perceived to be consuming white officers. "The white policeman standing on a Harlem street corner finds himself at the very center of the revolution now occurring in the world," Baldwin explained, exposing him to "the anguish of the black people around him." The trepidation many white officers felt in these spaces was clearly reflected in their surveillance reports that summer and fall, selectively quoting speakers calling for self-defense against police and supporting armed revolutionary struggle in Africa.[77] Rather than attend to the discomfort of recognizing personal complicity in the oppression of Black people, Baldwin continued, these officers "become more callous, the population becomes more hostile, the situation grows more tense, and the police force is increased. One day, to everyone's astonishment, someone drops a match in the powder keg and everything blows up."[78] Kennedy and Wagner did not miss this logical progression and moved swiftly at the end of 1959 to empower the NYPD to fasten the lid on the powder keg Baldwin described.

THE FORMATION OF THE TACTICAL PATROL FORCE

While white cops walking the beat were an all-too-familiar sight in Harlem, the officers swaggering "about in two's and three's" Baldwin described as stalking Harlem's streets with swinging clubs were likely members of a new unit formed in the final days of the decade. In early December, Commissioner Kennedy made a decisive move to expand the NYPD's capacity to police working-class Black and Puerto Rican communities and clamp down on rising dissent. That month, he rolled out a new select unit that could be dispatched across the city to bolster the manpower of local precincts to deal with rising crime, gang violence, and uprisings. Known as the Tactical Patrol Force (TPF), the roving unit consisted of seventy-five physically imposing patrolmen—many ex-military—all over six feet tall, under the age of thirty, and armed with long nightsticks. Setting the tone for the years to come, Kennedy turned his commando squad loose on the city to come down hard on "the criminal" who "operates in the dark of night" and "preys upon the weak and the innocent."[79]

The thinly veiled us-versus-them subtext of Kennedy's remarks pitting righteous police against monstrous criminals spoke directly to the motivations of many officers who were selected to join the unit. In addition to the physical requirements, TPF commanders required that prospective officers score an average of 80 percent at the Police Academy and display a "distinct esprit de corps," or sense of mission, pride, and commitment to the unit's objectives.[80] For eager young patrolmen brimming with this "esprit de corps," assignment to the TPF represented a ticket into the real action of "knockaround" policing through an "elite, ass-kicking, crime-fighting, gut-busting squad."[81] In addition to their training in jujitsu for hand-to-hand combat, TPF recruits took a weeklong training course on such topics as civil rights, showing courtesy to the public, law of arrest, lawful use of force, and "the role of the policeman in a democratic society," all of which predictably proved futile in protecting the public from police abuse.[82] As the unit expanded in the following years, this training regimen would be supplemented with FBI and US Army recommended trainings on crowd psychology and riot control strategies.[83]

Following in the wake of the media frenzy over the fatal stabbing of the two white teenagers in Hell's Kitchen, the TPF effectively represented the personification of the law-and-order policies that city officials called for in response to popular paranoia over property crime, gang violence, and civil unrest in the city. "The unit can be called into any crime-plagued area quickly," the *New York Times* reported, "and can remain in the area until fears or tensions subside."[84] The formation of a tactical squad for this purpose followed the examples set by similar units in Chicago (1956), Cincinnati (1958), and San Francisco (1958), indicating a national trend toward what Chicago Police Superintendent Orlando W. Wilson called "aggressive preventive patrol." A leading figure in police professionalization in the postwar era, Wilson promoted aggressive crime prevention measures that were influential in the nationwide expansion of local police powers. These measures revolved around the saturation of specific neighborhoods with police patrols, including the use of stop-and-frisk procedures and vehicle checkpoints. Wilson described his strategy as "psychological warfare" because it "gives the impression of the police being everywhere."[85] In Harlem, that meant daily encounters with hostile patrolmen in every corner of the neighborhood.

As designed, the psychological and physical warfare waged by the TPF in Harlem exacerbated tensions between white police and the Black and Puerto Rican communities they prowled. The emergence of the TPF marked a decisive shift from its predecessor, the Emergency Services Unit. In addition to their function as a riot squad, ESU officers' day-to-day work had also included responding to the needs of the sick and injured. By contrast, TPF officers primarily dealt in intimidation and punishment. Whereas the ESU's reputation had been "more that of firefighters," the TPF quickly earned its image as "heavy-handed enforcers."[86] This type of aggressive policing was precisely what attracted many officers to the unit. "Most TPF cops had little patience with anyone who gave them a ration of shit," retired NYPD officer Robert Leuci explained in his memoir, "and it was also true that we didn't think of ourselves as social workers as some precinct cops did."[87] This mentality did not merely reflect police culture at the time—it reflected the tone deliberately set by Mayor Wagner in his response to the "near riot" and playground killings in Hell's Kitchen that summer.

Many TPF officers relished their image as the biggest, baddest unit in the NYPD. TPF officers patrolled seemingly every inch of Harlem, from basements to rooftops and alleys to hallways, with almost total license to define what justice meant on any given day. In his memoir, former TPF officer Jim O'Neil recalled his attraction to the kind of "instant justice" meted out by police in Harlem. "God, I loved the job back then," O'Neil wrote, reflecting on a time he watched a fellow white officer assault a Latino man with his nightstick on an East Harlem sidewalk, "when a cop could be a cop without fear of being accused of police brutality."[88] To O'Neil, Leuci, and many others in the TPF, a "cop being a cop" meant instilling fear into the communities they policed through occupation and wanton violence. "You looked at me crooked I'd come down like the hammers of hell," Leuci wrote of the TPF's habit of seeking revenge on civilians for the most minor transgressions.[89] With tacit endorsement from NYPD brass and no effective vehicle for police accountability, the TPF ran amok in Harlem, the East Bronx, Bedford-Stuyvesant, South Jamaica, and other majority-Black neighborhoods in the early 1960s.

Whereas Kennedy and Wagner hailed the TPF's emergence as a boon to the city's ability to effectively respond to rising crime rates and gang violence, the timing and tenor of the unit's formation sent a very clear message to Black New Yorkers about the city's intentions to suppress Black radicalism, particularly in Harlem. That summer's protests against police brutality and the ensuing hyper-policing of Black communities had further clarified for many Harlem residents the NYPD's function as the enforcement arm of white supremacy. As Baldwin articulated in his essay, "The badge, the gun in the holster, and the swinging club make vivid what will happen should his rebellion become overt."[90]

While newspapers heralded the deployment of the NYPD's new paramilitary unit, TPF shock troops flooded into Harlem and other majority-Black neighborhoods, bringing greater numbers of working-class Black and Puerto Rican residents into direct contact with white supremacy's enforcers. As Jack O'Dell would write in the pages of *Freedomways* several years later, following rebellions in Newark and Detroit, the formation of the TPF demonstrated that "state power at the local level is expanding its arsenal of weapons and troop reserves all in the name of 'riot control.'"[91] As the escalation of repressive policing provoked uprisings in greater frequency and scale in the following years, liberal rhetoric and minor reforms were increasingly overshadowed by sensational reports of rising crime rates in Black communities, calls for "law and order," and the suffocating expansion of the carceral state.

With police back on the offensive, the presence of officers at meetings and rallies in Harlem drew the ire of organizers, which in turn sharpened police hostility against the community. "Back then I didn't understand the rage I saw in their faces, the contempt," Leuci recalled of his days with TPF. "They felt we were intruding in their lives. And we were."[92] While TPF officers were able to perceive of the depth of resentment Harlem residents felt toward them, most were unwilling to consider their culpability and instead retreated into callousness. "Some of us were brutal and intolerant," Leuci admitted. "It absorbed us, inhabited us, and made us feel a kinship that is unknown to outsiders."[93] The formation of the TPF led to a predictable cycle of police hostility and violence. Adding further fuel to the smoldering fire, as the sit-in movement reenergized the Southern civil rights movement and inspired greater protest activity in New York City in the spring of 1960, the TPF expanded its operations in anticipation of escalating mobilization for Black liberation in the decade to come.

In an address to graduates of the city's police academy in April 1960, Mayor Wagner credited the TPF and the NYPD's new mobilization plan with increasing the department's "mobility and striking power in sudden emergencies." With this increased capacity, Wagner explained, the city was now capable of "bringing tranquility to disturbed situations that might have erupted in violence."[94] Amid media buzz and official praise of the elite crime-fighting squad, the ranks of the TPF grew exponentially. Just a month after the TPF's formation, Kennedy assigned an additional fifty men to the unit, nearly doubling its ranks to 125.[95] By 1963 the unit would boast a squad of 250 men,[96] and by the end of the decade, the TPF would grow to nearly a thousand officers.[97] In that span of time, the TPF also expanded their presence through an array of initiatives, including vehicle checkpoints, undercover patrols, and decoy units, further criminalizing and brutalizing Black and Puerto Rican communities throughout the city.

The emergence and rapid expansion of the TPF in late 1959 revealed that liberal handwringing and investigations by blue ribbon committees were little more than a façade for expanding the city's capacity to police Black communities and suppress future uprisings. Coupled with the NYPD's dogged resistance to the recommendations of the CHA for police reform in Harlem, the Wagner administration's targeted expansion of policing demonstrated a commitment to using the police to safeguard and entrench white supremacy in New York City.

Just days before his April 1960 graduation address to the police academy, Mayor Wagner attended a meeting of the Subcommittee on Law Enforcement to review their recommendations and discuss the general state of the Committee on Harlem Affairs. During the meeting, subcommittee member Jack Blumstein raised several points that were indicative of the general ineffectiveness of the CHA in resolving issues of inequality in Harlem. Despite the eight months of work put in by the three subcommittees of the CHA, Blumstein pointed out, racial tensions in Harlem were still high and "a spark could set off real trouble." "Positive action and quick help is needed," Blumstein argued, reiterating calls for a Black deputy commissioner and doubling the number of Black officers in the NYPD. Predicting further unrest in

Harlem amid demonstrations in support of the Southern sit-in movement as the summer neared once again, Blumstein insisted that Black communities needed to feel as though they had a voice in government and were "a part of the team to maintain law and order."[98] While the bulk of Blumstein's remarks and calls for even the most meager reforms were ignored, Wagner seized upon this latter point. With political will behind the CHA on the decline among city officials, the mayor largely turned his attention away from demands for police reform and toward the enforcement of "law and order."

The reason for the CHA's ineffectiveness was the very premise on which the committee had been founded. As conceived by Mayor Wagner, the purpose of the CHA was not to solve the problems of inequality caused by systemic racism in the city, but rather to ease racial tensions in Harlem through making the government appear more amenable to calls for Black equality and civil rights. "The best way to refuse to grapple with a problem," journalist Chuck Stone opined, "is to appoint a committee."[99] This government-by-committee approach to investigating racial tensions and refusing to act on recommendations to resolve them was exemplary of liberal approaches to issues of racial oppression in New York City. Rather than attempting to meaningfully address the root causes of inequality, this approach dealt with their symptoms to ensure order rather than to promote justice. Furthermore, while city officials were touting liberal reforms to disarm rising protests at the grassroots, they were also taking measures to militarize the city's police force to physically suppress surging demands for rights and power.

Because of its fundamentally flawed and limited premise, the CHA proved more effective in further straining relations between Black communities in Harlem and city hall than in cooling the volatile racial and political climate that had provoked unrest in the first place. Though there was little public faith from the start that the CHA would be able to enact any meaningful reforms in Harlem, the committee's inability to implement even the most conservative measures of reform affirmed residents' cynicism toward city government and its willingness to serve the interests of Black communities.

Furthermore, although one of the guiding principles of the committee was to promote greater dialogue between local people and city government, few efforts were actually made to include any representation from the ranks of those most adversely affected by the daily insults and assaults of systemic racism. As the Guardians Association suggested in a report to the Subcommittee on Law Enforcement, "The unfortunate, underprivileged, and unstable elements" must be represented in city government, for they were the "most likely group to cause a major community disorder."¹⁰⁰ With demands for Black rights and power surging locally and nationally, the rift between city hall and Harlem appeared to be only widening, despite the nominal efforts of the CHA to narrow the gap as the new decade began.

In July of 1960 Baldwin's gripping essay in *Esquire* magazine read like a direct critique of the cynical liberal responses to systemic racism and unrest in the wake of the 1959 "near riot" in Harlem. Using the housing situation faced by so many Black residents of Harlem as an entrée and central theme, Baldwin explained to readers, as few other writers could, why housing projects and policemen were hated in Harlem for the same reason: "Both reveal, unbearably, the real attitude of the white world, *no matter how many liberal speeches are made, no matter how many lofty editorials are written, no matter how many civil-rights commissions are set up* [emphasis added]." Having grown up in Harlem and born witness to the daily experiences of racial oppression there, Baldwin understood and expressed what few whites were able or willing to comprehend: liberal governance would not, and could not, improve or solve the conditions of a "ghetto." The only way a ghetto could be improved, Baldwin argued, was "out of existence."¹⁰¹

Despite the best efforts of city hall to undercut and contain Black demands for human rights and political empowerment in this period, however, grassroots organizers like Jesse Gray, Mae Mallory, and Malcolm X were succeeding in mobilizing and organizing Harlem residents in consciousness and in action. As more Harlem residents became increasingly aware of and impatient with the designed limitations of liberal governance for rectifying systemic racism in any meaningful way, support for more radical alternatives rose, and an already limited trust in city hall fell further.

The retrenchment of systemic racism in Jim Crow New York also came amid a wave of anticolonial revolutions sweeping across Africa and the Global South. As Harlem residents and activists increasingly realized that racial liberalism did more to protect white supremacy than dismantle it, many looked to liberation movements across the African diaspora for inspiration and instruction in winning their freedom. In doing so, they sparked a resurgence of Black radical internationalism in Harlem that would shape the course of the Black freedom movement at dawn of the 1960s.

4

THE SPIRIT OF BANDUNG
1959-1961

> They call us racial extremists. They call Jomo Kenyatta also a racial extremist and Tom Mboya a moderate. It is only the white man's fear of men like Kenyatta that makes him listen to men like Mboya. If it were not for the extremists, the white man would ignore the moderates. To be called a "moderate" in this awakening dark world today, that is crying for freedom, is to receive the "kiss of death" as spokesmen or leaders of the masses ... for the masses are ready to burst the shackles of slavery whether the "moderates" will stand up or not.
> —MALCOLM X, *1960*

THE SUMMER OF 1959 HAD proved to be a formative moment in the development of the Black freedom movement in Harlem. Influenced by the courageous armed resistance of Robert F. Williams in Monroe, North Carolina, the uncompromising rhetoric and resistance of the Nation of Islam, and local traditions of challenging police violence, the dramatic protests outside the 28th Precinct that July demonstrated a growing popular rejection of gradualism and an embrace of direct action and self-defense. The expansion of policing to repress dissent in the aftermath of the "near riot" was also instructive for Harlem residents, organizers, and intellectuals who were coming to see the NYPD as the enforcement arm of white supremacy in Jim Crow New

York. In coming to this conclusion at the dawn of the 1960s, Harlem activists were also finding common cause with and drawing inspiration from a wave of anticolonial liberation movements throughout the African diaspora, which sparked a revolutionary fervor among Harlem residents, organizers, and intellectuals in their local struggles for human rights and self-determination.

In the late 1950s, at a time when Black communities around the United States were organizing to take assertive action to demand their rights, anticolonial liberation struggles in Africa, the Diaspora, and throughout what was then called the Third World were reinvigorating international consciousness and Pan-Africanism in New York City. A historic gathering of Asian and African nations in Bandung, Indonesia, in 1955 had signaled the dawning of a new day after a long, dark night of European imperialism. Two years later, the people of Ghana celebrated their independence from British colonialism following a sustained anticolonial struggle led by Kwame Nkrumah, marking a watershed moment for escalating African liberation struggles on the continent and throughout the diaspora. Dozens of newly independent African nations emerged in the following years, many of which threw off the shackles of colonialism through armed struggle, activating the radical imaginations of Harlem residents who were beginning to see themselves as actors on the global stage of revolution.[1] Uniquely positioned as the nation's largest Black community in an international city that was home to the United Nations' world headquarters, by the late 1950s Harlem was reasserting itself as the capital of Black internationalism, anticolonialism, and anticapitalism in the United States.

Buoyed by the rising tide of global anticolonial struggle, a generation of Black Left, nationalist, and Pan-Africanist activists carried forward Harlem's storied radical traditions to chart the direction of the Black freedom movement in the city. This revolutionary consciousness had deep roots in Harlem, where organizations like the Universal Negro Improvement Association, the African Blood Brotherhood, and the Communist Party had mobilized and organized generations of African Americans in the early twentieth century. Building on this legacy, grassroots activists in the late 1950s channeled the "spirit of Bandung" into local organizing campaigns in Harlem, whereby working-class Black communities came to understand their lived experiences in Jim Crow New York within the context of global systems of racism, colonialism, and capitalism that were oppressing and exploiting African people throughout the diaspora. In doing so, local people refined their understanding of American racism, embraced more militant strategies and tactics to challenge it, and searched for new programs to achieve liberation in an era of global revolution.

HARLEM AND THE BANDUNG WORLD

The hardening of Cold War tensions between the United States and the USSR over competing political, economic, and imperial interests in the 1950s defined the terms of Black freedom struggles worldwide. As the United States audaciously declared itself the leader of the "free world" in the postwar era, Black liberal leaders sought to leverage these claims in their demands for full citizenship and "a share in American postwar prosperity."[2] Leaders like A. Philip Randolph and Adam Clayton Powell Jr. distanced themselves from their Left and popular front pasts and aligned with American foreign policy, embracing the position that "total diplomacy requires total democracy."[3] Such an embrace of American exceptionalism and foreign policy rested on a liberal understanding of racism as antithetical to American ideals, rather than as something inherent in American institutions. It also represented a strategy of moral suasion to pressure the United States to live up to these ideals for the benefit of its Black citizens. However, beyond its impotence in achieving Black equality, let alone liberation, this strategy primed the pump for marginalizing, red-baiting, and purging Black communists and fellow travelers. Furthermore, to be effective, these demands for federal protections and patronage required a near unquestioning embrace of American foreign interests, which, despite the material benefits of securing jobs for Black workers, effectively allowed the US government to use African Americans as pawns in advancing the interests of capital and empire in the 1950s.[4]

Although the political repression of the Cold War and McCarthyism curtailed the anticolonialist, anti-imperialist, and anticapitalist strands within the Black freedom struggle of the 1940s, a bridge generation of activists, artists, and intellectuals in Harlem kept the flame of radical Black internationalism burning through the 1950s and the emergence of the civil rights movement.[5] Energized by the 1955 Asian-African Conference in Bandung, Harlem activists cultivated grassroots Pan-Africanism, raised critical consciousness about the significance and meaning of African independence movements, and called residents into a global struggle for Black liberation.

Over the next five years, the "spirit of Bandung" was enlivened by the successes of anticolonial independence movements in Ghana (1957), Guinea

(1958), and Congo (1960) and the ongoing war for independence in Algeria. In 1960 alone, seventeen African nations gained their independence, charging Black freedom struggles in Harlem and throughout the United States with a revolutionary fervor. The Pan-African visions of Ghanaian President Kwame Nkrumah—who had spent time in Harlem in the 1940s—in particular inspired hope for a united international struggle to throw off the shackles of European colonialism.[6] In July 1958 Harlem residents caught the spirit of Bandung when Nkrumah paid them a special visit during a trip to the United States. An estimated 100,000 people lined the streets of Harlem to catch a glimpse of the revolutionary leader as he rode in an open car motorcade up 7th Avenue from 110th Street to a reception at the 369th Armory on 142nd and 5th Avenue, where he received a hero's welcome.[7] Nkrumah told the crowd that "back at home we think of the people of Harlem as our brothers" and referred to himself as "a son of Harlem," the place where he had "learned his politics" of Pan-Africanism and anticolonialism from Garveyites and street speakers during breaks from his studies at Lincoln University.[8] The energy and inspiration of Nkrumah's visit swept Harlem residents into the current of African liberation as Harlem became a destination for emergent African revolutionaries.

As anticolonial revolutions surged across the African continent, Black activists in Harlem worked to forge solidarity between continental and diasporic Africans based on shared experiences of oppression and resistance.[9] Through mass rallies, parades, cultural festivals, and literature, Black nationalist organizations nurtured racial pride, Pan-African identity, and grassroots anticolonial solidarity while inspiring new ideas and strategies for achieving Black liberation in the United States. For example, the African Nationalist Pioneer Movement's (ANPM) 1958 Marcus Garvey Day celebration featured a discussion, led by Carlos Cooks and Malcolm X, of the 1958 All-African People's Conference in Accra, where three hundred delegates from twenty-eight African nations, territories, and organizations met to debate strategies for achieving liberation (including debates around armed revolutionary struggle).[10] The International Committee in Defense of Africa (ICDA)—led by Black Left nationalists Ennis Francis and Eloise Moore—also organized a community forum on the Accra conference at the Hotel Theresa, featuring a report from Nigerian musician and activist Michael (Babatunde) Olatunji, who was a delegate to the conference.[11]

In recognition of the conference's proclamation of April 15 as African Freedom Day, the United African Nationalist Movement also began organizing annual celebrations in Harlem. In April 1959 an overflow crowd of six hundred people filled the Refuge Temple at 124th Street and 7th Avenue, where James Lawson, Bessie Philips, Malcolm X, and several African ambassadors spoke about African pride and liberation. Phillips, the longtime secretary of the UANM, told the audience they should be proud to call themselves African and reject the term "Negro," reflecting a growing embrace of self-naming among Black communities in Harlem. During his address, Malcolm X argued that Africans in the United States suffered under "the worst form of enslavement... mental bondage... unable to see that America is the citadel of white colonialism, the bulwark of white imperialism... the slavemaster of slavemasters." To free themselves, he urged Africans throughout the diaspora to unite against their common enemy and learn from the methods of African independence movements.[12] In subsequent years, African Freedom Day rallies created important opportunities for Harlem residents to connect with African independence leaders and diplomats to foster the collective sense of pride and unity that Philips and Malcolm X spoke of.

Inspired by the rising tide of Pan-Africanism and anticolonialism in the years since Bandung, Cooks and the ANPM issued a "Call to Convention" in August 1959, inviting a wide range of Black organizations to develop "a positive program of total unification of the African peoples of the world." On the eve of Marcus Garvey Day, delegates received messages of support from leaders across the diaspora as they unanimously endorsed resolutions to abolish the term "Negro," coordinate resources throughout the diaspora for the welfare and security of Black people, create African Community Leagues to advance economic self-determination in majority-Black communities, and create a Black united front with a goal of the "complete freedom of Africa."[13] In reflecting the spirit of Bandung, the convention's advocacy of racial pride, self-determination, and Pan-Africanism also anticipated key ideological and programmatic aspects of Black Power in the following years.[14]

The ANPM convention signified an emergent trend of Black Nationalists calling for united front formations in Harlem as part of broader Pan-African struggles for self-determination. At the 1959 African Freedom Day rally, for example, Malcolm X called for a "Bandung Conference in Harlem," arguing that Black Nationalist organizations "must come together before we can agree. We must agree before we can unite. We must unite before we can effectively face our enemy."[15] Through working cooperatively on rallies, forums, and celebrations in the years since Bandung, Black nationalist organizations that often sparred over their ideologies and programs laid the groundwork for cooperative action. Through these programs, the UANM, ANPM, NOI, and other Harlem nationalists carried Harlem traditions of Pan-Africanism, anticolonialism, and economic nationalism forward into a new era of struggle and laid foundations that Black united front formations would build upon in the years that followed.

The groundswell of Pan-African and anticolonial activity in Harlem also pushed the Nation of Islam to broaden its theological identification with Asia as the progenitor of the "Asiatic Black Man." In addition to Malcolm's evolving interest in African independence movements, grounded in his upbringing in a Garveyite household, this growing identification with Africa was also evident in the NOI's cultural programming through public bazaars. These events offered Black New Yorkers opportunities to both dispel racist myths about African inferiority and foster identification with the continent in casual community settings. The market festivals included educational exhibits, artisan booths selling African goods, cultural programming, and speeches. At the 1960 bazaar at the Rockland Palace, five thousand people visited exhibits, purchased African crafts, and watched a performance of *The Trial*, which had been featured the previous year in "The Hate That Hate Produced."[16]

By 1960, then, it had become clear that the wave of anticolonial revolutions washing across the African continent and throughout its diaspora had sparked the resurgence of Black radical internationalism in Harlem. As Black communities in Harlem came to see themselves as Africans, they were energized and empowered by their connections to a global majority rising up against white supremacy. For playwright Lorraine Hansberry, who had been active in Black Left anticolonialism through her work with the Harlem newspaper *Freedom* in the early 1950s, these years represented "one of the most affirmative periods in history." In a 1959 interview she described feeling "very pleased that those peoples in the world whom I feel closest to—the colonial peoples, the African peoples, the Asian peoples—are in an insurgent mood, and are in the process of transforming the world."[17]

A NATION WITHIN A NATION

The local, national, and global rise of Black nationalism in the late 1950s shaped and was shaped by Malcolm X's emergence as a formidable intellectual, teacher, and organizer in Harlem. Although two of his mentors, Audley

Moore and Vicki Garvin, had left Harlem by 1960, they laid the groundwork for a network of radical intellectuals, including Eloise Moore and John Henrik Clarke, who served as Malcolm's informal secular advisers in the early 1960s. "I became a part of a shadow cabinet that Malcolm had," Clarke later said. "I was the man in history and historical information, and historical personalities. There were other people on politics, another person occasionally on sociology, the diversity of people in this shadow cabinet, none of them Muslims, was equivalent to the faculty of a good university."[18] As he studied under grassroots intellectuals and activists in the early 1960s, Malcolm became a conduit for sharing Harlem's Black radical tradition through his public addresses and private teachings. The curriculum that he developed for his grueling weekly public speaking class in Mosque No. 7, according to NOI member Benjamin Karim (Benjamin 2X Goodman), was grounded in "geography, current events . . . American history, the history of colonialism."[19] Aspiring ministers were assigned readings from local, national, and global newspapers to promote an expansive worldview and foster the skills of critical inquiry and historical analysis that were central to Malcolm's own development and effectiveness as an intellectual and organizer.

Despite the increasing demands of leading Mosque No. 7, organizing new mosques across the nation, and managing his heightened public profile—all while continuing his education—Malcolm X took the lead in launching what would become one of the NOI's most effective initiatives, *Muhammad Speaks*. Following the media firestorm surrounding "The Hate That Hate Produced," the NOI sought to exercise greater agency over its image and recruit followers by producing and circulating its own literature. Though for years Elijah Muhammad had written columns in the *Pittsburgh Courier* and the *Los Angeles Herald-Dispatch*, the spotlight the NOI attracted by 1959 presented a prime opportunity for the Nation to launch its own publications to take control of the narrative and to reach its goal of adding one million converts by 1961.[20] After a short-lived attempt at publishing a magazine titled *The Messenger* in the fall of 1959, Malcolm X scored immediate, widespread success in launching *Muhammad Speaks* in May of 1960.[21] Printed out of a storefront office near Mosque No. 7, the tabloid-sized paper sold for fifteen cents and was billed as "a militant monthly dedicated to Justice for the Black Man." Bundles of the newspaper were swiftly delivered to mosques across the nation, and neatly dressed members of the Nation became regular fixtures on the streets of Harlem, where they hawked copies of the paper, setting up shop outside churches, NAACP meetings, street rallies, and any other place where Black people congregated.[22] Within two years, the newspaper had a circulation of over 50,000—the majority of whom were non-Muslim readers—and by 1963 *Muhammad Speaks* had the largest distribution of any African American newspaper.[23]

In addition to the tireless efforts of the NOI's ever-present sales force, the paper also drew non-Muslim readership by featuring columns from well-known writers who catered to the mood of Black communities in Harlem and the nation. The inaugural issue of *Muhammad Speaks* in May 1960 included articles on Marcus Garvey's legacy, police brutality against NOI members in New York, and a two-page spread on African independence movements since 1956 titled "Africa Moves Toward Freedom" and "Sun Sets on Colonialism."[24] As the paper grew over the next few years, the pages of *Muhammad Speaks* regularly included columns from notable Harlem writers Langston Hughes, John Henrik Clarke, and Sylvester Leaks, who helped shape the political takes of the widely circulated paper. Leaks was an activist who embraced self-defense and brought an international perspective—informed by Clarke's connections with African independence leaders—to his articles. Described by Julian Mayfield as a "militant writer, of great personal courage, sincerely dedicated to the cause of black freedom" who had an admirable quality of knowing when it was time to "lay down his pen, stop talking and wade in with his fists," Leaks had by 1961 become the head of Crusaders for Freedom and a fixture at street rallies and radical organizing campaigns.[25] Despite Elijah Muhammad's position on political abstinence, the paper's contributors and editors created a popular forum for Black nationalist, anticolonialist, and often anticapitalist discourse.[26]

In addition, Malcolm X was increasingly sought after for public debates and lectures on key issues in the Black freedom movement. He used these opportunities not only to correct misrepresentations of the NOI's theology as racist or hate mongering but also to explain his positions on Black nationalism, integration, anticolonialism, and self-defense. At a lecture at Boston University in May 1960, he devoted much of a two-hour question and answer session to explaining the NOI's position on the "nation question" and reparations. As "back salary" for generations of enslavement, Malcolm told the interracial crowd, Elijah Muhammad called for the United States to compensate Black Americans with "either a tract of land, or several states, wherein they could form their own government."[27] Although these aspects of the Nation of Islam's theology built upon generations of Black nationalist political organizing, in these appearances Malcolm exercised caution in explicitly commenting on the Black freedom movement, as mandated by Muhammad's position on political noninvolvement.

While most of Malcolm's public appearances at the turn of the decade were dedicated to explicating the theology and programs of the Nation of Islam, he also made efforts to forge unity among civil rights, religious, and nationalist organizations in Harlem. Having cut his teeth on the street corners of Harlem's grassroots nationalist scene, Malcolm knew that the sectarian nationalist groups competing for followers were stifling collective action. As John Henrik Clarke would describe the following year, the common cause of Black nationalism in Harlem was "being hampered by too many organizations and too many leaders with conflicting programs."[28] Harlem's political culture was diverse, and these conflicts largely stemmed from differing priorities and programs for achieving differing visions of Black freedom. With the likes of James Lawson, Carlos Cooks, Edward "Pork Chop" Davis, Bessie Philips, and many other veteran speakers and organizers staking claims to various corners and constituencies, Malcolm made a move in the spring of 1960 to bring together these nationalist factions, civil rights organizations, and community leaders under a common banner of Black liberation in Harlem.

In May 1960 an advertisement in the *New York Amsterdam News* announced a "huge 6-hour outdoor" rally to be held at the corner of 125th Street and 7th Avenue. Under a bold headline announcing this Harlem Freedom Rally, a photograph of a stone-faced Malcolm X heralded a call to religious, political, business, and civic leaders in Harlem. "Let us forget our religious and political differences. We must come together on the same platform in a great display of UNITY against our common enemy, and fight for one common cause ... complete and immediate FREEDOM for the Black Man in America." The list of speakers invited to the rally represented a veritable cross-section of Black political thought in Harlem, including several who had been involved in the mayor's Commission on Harlem Affairs the previous year. The expansive guest list included Roy Wilkins, Lester Granger, Martin Luther King Jr., A. Philip Randolph, Jackie Robinson, Hope Stevens, James Watson, Adam Clayton Powell Jr., James Lawson, and Sugar Ray Robinson.[29] Shortly after noon on May 28, an estimated four thousand people flocked to Harlem Square, where speakers blasted Louis X's "A White Man's Heaven Is a Black Man's Hell" from a stage set up in front of Lewis Michaux's bookstore.[30] On the grandstand, Bessie Philips, attorney Percy Sutton, Wallace Muhammad, jazz drummer Max Roach, Louis X, Hope Stevens, and Michaux looked out onto a bustling crowd on the streets and sidewalks where dozens raised signs with Elijah Muhammad's call "We Must Have Some Land."[31]

Rising to the podium, Malcolm began his address with calls for unity among Black leaders for the purpose of achieving the freedom, justice, and human rights so long denied by the American government. Far from offering a sentimental call for symbolic brotherhood, Malcolm explained that this unity in leadership must be built and directed from the grassroots. The purpose of the rally, he explained, was for the masses to become familiarized with "our leaders who have been acting as our spokesmen." Reflecting a growing local and national disillusionment with gradualist leadership in the wake of the July 1959 "near riot" in Harlem and the sit-ins throughout the South, Malcolm pointed to the need for local people to control their own movements. "We want to get behind leaders who will fight for us . . . leaders who are not afraid to demand freedom, justice, and equality," he declared. "We do not want leaders who are hand picked for us by the white man. We don't want any more Uncle Toms." Malcolm challenged the crowd to begin this process by building unity in their neighborhoods. From there, he argued, the people needed to "form a platform that will be good for all our own people, as well as for others," and give "intelligent active support to our political leaders" who would fight fearlessly and unselfishly for this platform of Black liberation.[32]

In this speech, Malcolm blended elements of the Nation of Islam's theology of moral conservatism, racial separatism, and economic nationalism with calls for self-determination, secular Black nationalism, and Pan-Africanism. Describing the twenty million Black Americans as constituting a "nation within a nation," Malcolm invoked the spirit of Bandung and cited his recent trip to Africa to call for "freedom from colonialism, foreign domination, oppression and exploitation." It was clear in his speech that Malcolm saw the Bandung conference and ongoing anticolonial liberation struggles as models for forging unity and building a grassroots revolutionary nationalist movement in the United States. Using Kenyan independence leaders Jomo Kenyatta and Tom Mboya as examples of "extremists" and "moderates," respectively, Malcolm explained the importance of "extremists" in advancing liberation struggles, despite the disparaging connotation of the term in mainstream media outlets. "To be called a 'moderate' in this awakening dark world today . . . is to receive the 'kiss of death' as . . . leader of the masses," Malcolm declared, "for the masses are ready to burst the shackles of slavery whether the 'moderates' will stand up or not."[33] With Harlem lawyer and businessman Hope Stevens as the only invited speaker to actually show up, though, it was evident that "moderate" leaders were generally unwilling to engage in talks with the "extremist" spokesman for the Nation of Islam at this point. The Harlem Freedom Rally nonetheless marked a significant entrée for Malcolm into coalition building in Harlem and was an early step toward his active engagement in united front organizing.[34]

Although his meteoric ascension was met with scorn from moderate civil rights leaders and white liberals, apprehension from Muhammad, and repression from law enforcement, Malcolm X was enthusiastically embraced by thousands of African Americans. From 1959 to 1961 the membership of Mosque No. 7 in Harlem rose from 1,125 members (569 of whom were considered "active") to 2,369 members (767 active).[35] By 1960 the Nation of Islam expanded to two hundred mosques nationwide with fifty thousand members, with tens of thousands more who never joined but sympathized with or actively supported the NOI's positions.[36] Much of this growth was due to Malcolm's organizational skills in building many of these mosques, as well as his liberatory rhetoric, which empowered thousands of Black people to break free from the chains of mental colonialism and embrace more radical action. Though he was still largely ostracized by mainstream civil rights leaders, it was evident that Malcolm's credibility among the masses in Harlem and other major cities was rapidly growing.

REVOLUTION COMES TO HARLEM

On New Year's Day in 1959, the era of anticolonial revolution appeared at the doorstep of the United States when a general strike in Cuba led US-backed dictator Fulgencio Batista to flee the island nation, signaling the victory of the guerilla army led by Fidel Castro. Unfolding just 250 miles off the coast of Miami and orchestrated by young, charismatic revolutionaries, the Cuban Revolution drew the attention of African American communities who were growing impatient with gradualism and stoked the radical imaginations of activists in Harlem who were seeking new directions to achieve Black liberation. While white politicians and corporations sought to exert influence on the new government to maintain colonial relations, Black communities were exhilarated by the prospects of what a successful anticolonial revolution in Cuba could mean for Black freedom struggles in the United States.

In the weeks following the revolution, the *Amsterdam News* and the *Baltimore Afro-American* circulated stories of shared experiences of discrimination and carried word that Castro vowed to "eliminate all forms of discrimination."[37] Reports of a triumphant people's army—led in large part by Afro-Cubans—over an oppressive dictatorship also captivated Black readers. In April of 1959 *Ebony* magazine reported on the history of Afro-Cuban freedom fighters and the heroism of Comandante Juan Almeida Bosque, who saw the revolution as a means of achieving racial justice.[38] "It seemed as if everyone knew his name and knew about his role and exploits in the revolution," Harlem organizer Bill Epton recalled of Almeida's influence in Harlem.[39] Reading this coverage through the lens of their own experiences with American racism, Black communities were drawing conclusions similar to those of Julian Mayfield, who wrote that "the important lesson in the Cuban experience is that social change need not wait on the patient education of white supremacists."[40] The revolution, rather, demonstrated the effectiveness—and to some, the imperative—of armed struggle to achieve Black liberation.

Despite the popular reception he received from Black communities, Castro and his revolutionary government quickly became a US target in the Cold War. The enactment of agrarian reform laws that spring and the nationalization of foreign corporations threatened the economic interests and imperial aspirations of US businesses and politicians who had profited handsomely under the Batista regime. American politicians and journalists made hay of Castro's imprisoning and executing Batista loyalists to protect against counterrevolution, but the handwringing over political executions rang hollow to many Black Americans who had watched Congress ignore the racist terrorism sweeping across the US South in the spring of 1959, most notably with the lynching of Mack Parker that April and continued Klan terrorism in Monroe.[41] While racist executions continued on the home front, US corporations, politicians, and media waged a decades-long anticommunist campaign of political repression, including an economic embargo and countless assassination attempts to overthrow the Cuban government. For Black organizers and intellectuals active in Left labor-led struggles in the post–World War II era, these repressive tactics were all too familiar, and many organized to actively support Castro's government.

In the spring of 1960 journalists Robert Taber and Richard Gibson organized an interracial group of thirty intellectuals, artists, and activists to challenge dominant narratives and to coordinate support for the revolutionary government. Dubbed the Fair Play for Cuba Committee (FPCC), the organization was launched that April with a full-page ad in the *New York Times,* which fact-checked mainstream news coverage of Cuba and offered a counternarrative of "the truth about revolutionary Cuba." The ad debunked American propaganda about the island while celebrating the promises of a young government that had, in its first year, built three thousand units of affordable housing and seven thousand classrooms, and created thousands of jobs in new industries.[42] In a city where Black communities had spent many years fighting for access to housing, schools, and jobs, the Cuban revolutionary government's haste in meeting the needs of the people won many admirers who looked to Cuba for inspiration.

Black nationalists and Leftists in Harlem played an important role in the growth of the FPCC and popular support for the Cuban Revolution. Of the thirty founding members of the committee, nearly one-third were Black New Yorkers, most of whom had been active supporters of Robert F. Williams, including James Baldwin, historian John Henrik Clarke, novelists John O. Killens and Julian Mayfield, and Williams himself.[43] Over the next few months, the FPCC's membership would grow to include scholar W. E. B. Du Bois, journalist William Worthy, and writer LeRoi Jones (later Amiri Baraka). Under the leadership of the Socialist Workers Party (which took over operations of FPCC in the fall of 1960) and with the surging support of Black nationalists, the committee quickly grew from three chapters with two thousand subscribers to its bulletin to twenty-seven chapters, forty student councils, and seven thousand members nationwide.[44]

Building on its narrative strategy, the FPCC fostered relationships between Black communities and the Cuban government by promoting tourism as an escape from Jim Crow and by sponsoring trips to the island for activists. In June of 1960 the FPCC provided Williams with the opportunity to visit the island as an official guest of Fidel Castro.[45] Writing for *The Crusader* as he packed his bags, Williams explained that the trip would offer him a chance to dispel the myth that "social justice must wait for a change of heart on the part of bigots" and to see how a "strong government that so desires can afford to grant all of its people equal protection under law."[46] As he toured the island, Williams shared his experiences in the pages of *The Crusader,* which Mae Mallory and the Crusaders for Freedom distributed throughout Harlem. He also lived without the indignities of Jim Crow or fear of violence for the first time in many years, explaining to readers that he was "enjoying the greatest freedom of my life in democratic revolutionary Cuba."[47] Williams's reports heightened the contradictions of American apartheid for readers of *The Crusader,* who marveled at Cuba's commitment to racial equality and the jobs, schools, land, and housing made possible by revolution.[48]

Weeks later, Williams was back in Cuba with a group of Black intellectuals, artists, and activists including Clarke, Mayfield, Jones (Baraka), critic Harold Cruse, and novelist Sarah E. Wright. The trip had been organized by the FPCC as a show of support for the revolutionary government and as an opportunity for Black artists and intellectuals to learn from the revolution. The group toured the island, learning about advancements in education, housing, and agrarian reform from government officials; making a pilgrimage to the Sierra Maestra mountains, where the revolution began; speaking with soldiers, artists, and local people; and generally basking in the afterglow of revolution.[49] These experiences were a revelation for many in the group, particularly Baraka, who previously understood revolution to be "one of those inconceivably 'romantic' and/or hopeless ideas."[50] Through the trip, revolution was made tangible—a living, breathing, evolving process organized by local people who had managed to overthrow a racist, US-backed colonial regime just off the coast of Florida.

The delegation returned carried by the global winds of anticolonial and anticapitalist revolution and eager to share what they learned with Black people in the United States who had grown impatient with the ever-delayed promises of equality. Writing in *Freedomways* the following year, Mayfield recounted a conversation with a militiawoman who had explained that the revolutionary government was less interested in changing the hearts and minds of bigots than in taking away their power to discriminate. Cuba's Right to Equality law, for example, imposed criminal penalties for business owners who practiced racial discrimination—including government seizure of the business until it proved it could be operated without discrimination. By comparing these measures with US responses to demands for Black equality, Mayfield reached the "inescapable conclusion" that neither US government officials nor the majority of white people felt "morally compelled to act against racism, and that they do, in fact, either actively or tacitly, condone it."[51] Mayfield had arrived at a fundamental question the Black freedom movement was beginning to reckon with. If racist oppression was intrinsic to the United States and could not be resolved through education, moral suasion, or litigation, what would it take for Black people to be free?

Harlem residents who were wrestling with this question got their own chance to witness the spirit of revolution in September 1960 when Fidel Castro arrived in New York for a visit to the United Nations. Sarah E. Wright was one of many Black New Yorkers who "felt that a piece of ourselves had been liberated" by the Cuban Revolution and were "glued to the radio, awaiting the announcement of Fidel's arrival."[52] When word came that Castro would be landing at Idlewild Airport (now John F. Kennedy) on September 18, Mae Mallory had just finished working a night shift. She quickly rounded up the Crusaders for Freedom to join a motorcade of five thousand people who weathered a rainy Sunday with flags, banners, and chants of "Venceremos" (We will win) to welcome the arrival of a revolutionary hero.[53] "Every Afro-American in his right mind supports Fidel Castro," Mallory wrote of the Cuban leader's popularity in Harlem, "even if he is afraid to do so publicly."[54]

While the motorcade's warm welcome demonstrated the anticolonial fervor in the city, the coarse treatment Castro received from US officials upon his arrival showed the strength of anticommunist and Cold War hostilities. The Cubans were treated as persona non grata by the State Department and mainstream media, jeered by Cuban exiles and anticommunist protestors, denied lodging, and eventually evicted from their hotel in midtown Manhattan. As the delegation prepared to camp out on the grounds of the United Nations in protest, Harlem leaders, who were quite familiar with this kind of treatment, mobilized to provide other accommodations for their comrades. Eager for an audience with the Cuban revolutionaries, Malcolm X sent word through Bob Taber of the FPCC that Harlem's Hotel Theresa would be a more suitable accommodation. A day after landing in New York, the Cuban delegation packed their bags and headed uptown to Harlem.[55]

When word got out that the Cuban premier was moving to the Hotel Theresa, two thousand New Yorkers of all political stripes flocked to 125th Street and 7th Avenue, braving the rain and rough police presence to celebrate Castro's arrival. The outpouring of support came, in part, from Castro's machismo and successes in achieving in a short period what many Harlem residents and organizers had been fighting for decades to realize. As the *New York Citizen-Call* explained, "To Harlem's oppressed ghetto-dwellers, Castro was that bearded revolutionary who had thrown the nation's rascals out and who had told white America to go to hell."[56] Even those who may not have given much attention to the Cuban Revolution could certainly identify with a man who was refused service and mistreated in Jim Crow New York.[57]

As Harlem residents flocked to the Theresa, members of the Harlem Writers Guild cut short a meeting and raced uptown to bear witness and join the ranks of "the poor, the abused, the disinherited . . . offering their protection and love to the leader of another poor, abused, and disinherited people."[58] Among the crowd they found filling the streets were Maya Angelou, Mae Mallory, and the Crusaders, who lined the police barricades along

125th Street, chanting "Viva Castro! Viva Fidel!" and carrying signs that read "Give em hell Fidel" and "Harlem loves Castro."[59] Mallory's embrace of Castro reflected her political evolution during this period, which included a rejection of moderate civil rights organizations and a budding embrace of self-determination, armed self-defense, Pan-African solidarity, and revolutionary nationalism—an evolution that signified a trending radicalization among working-class Black communities in Harlem between 1960 and 1964.

Castro's move uptown was a shrewd political maneuver in the chess game of Cold War propaganda. Harlem gave Castro a platform from which he could both denounce the hypocrisy of an imperial power that preached the virtues of democracy while practicing racial apartheid and also demonstrate solidarity with Black communities fighting for their liberation within the belly of the beast. While *Amsterdam News* editor James Hicks saw the move clearly as both a blow to the United States' Achilles heel in the Cold War and a "big lift" for the civil rights movement, Castro's critics and Black liberals—including Rep. Adam Clayton Powell Jr. (who had previously supported the revolution) and anticommunist NAACP leader Gloster Current—cynically claimed he was using Harlem residents as pawns in a geopolitical game.[60] The Baptist

FIG 8 A crowd of supporters gathers on 125th Street across from the Hotel Theresa during Fidel Castro's visit to Harlem in September 1960. (The Militant Photographic Collection, box 18, folder 10, Hoover Institution Library & Archives)

Ministers' Conference of Greater New York went so far as to send telegrams to President Eisenhower, Governor Rockefeller, and Mayor Wagner on behalf of their five hundred clergy members condemning Castro's attempts to make Harlem "a battleground for his ideologies and a cesspool for his doctrine of hate and greed."[61]

While moderate leaders were gnashing their teeth, many Harlem residents were clapping their hands for their guests of honor. Castro's move uptown was a sign of respect for the community and provided an opportunity for local people to become part of the revolutionary fervor sweeping the globe. At Harlem Square, Carlos Cooks, Edward "Porkchop" Davis, James Lawson, and other Black nationalists held daily rallies to harness the energy of the moment and call people into the global struggle for Black liberation.[62] Harlem residents were particularly excited to see Juan Almeida, a living example of a Black revolutionary fighter who had defeated American imperialism. Harlem residents showed their appreciation when Almeida strolled about the neighborhood, attracting thousands of followers eager to lay eyes on a man they saw as their "brother and our hero, too!" as Harlem organizer Bill Epton remembered.[63] Arriving amid a resurgent embrace of armed self-defense and anticolonialism in Harlem, the Cuban revolutionaries radicalized local people by demonstrating the possibilities of revolution, just as they had done for the intelligentsia who had visited Cuba that summer.[64]

Over the next week, Castro held court with foreign leaders, Black radicals, and local people in the heart of Harlem. "For a brief period," novelist Sarah E. Wright observed, "Harlem became a world capital." The Cuban delegation dined with hotel staff, met with heads of state—including Nikita Khrushchev, Gamal Abdel Nassar, Jawaharlal Nehru, and Kwame Nkrumah (all of whom were in town for the UN General Assembly)—and sought meetings with civil rights leaders, including L. Joseph Overton of the NY NAACP, Malcolm X, and Robert F. Williams.[65] The FPCC organized a reception in Castro's honor at the Hotel Theresa, where 250 activists, artists, and intellectuals, including Williams, Richard Gibson, LeRoi Jones, Julian Mayfield, and Ana Livia Cordero, gathered. Castro likened his experience of that reception to that of a man traveling through a desert who comes upon an oasis.[66] He, in turn, acknowledged Harlem for its hospitality and declared his solidarity with Black freedom struggles in his four-hour address to the UN General Assembly. In what the FPCC declared as "one of the most outstanding political documents of a generation," Castro recounted the history of US imperialism in Cuba and the triumphs of the revolutionary government, expressed solidarity with anticolonial revolutions in Africa and the Middle East, and pledged solidarity with all people seeking political and economic self-determination.[67]

Meanwhile, organizers used this opportunity to learn from the Cuban Revolution, build relationships with their Cuban comrades, and seize the momentum their presence offered. Malcolm X used his credentials as a member of the 28th Precinct Community Council to gain entrance to the Theresa through heavy police presence for a brief yet historic meeting in Castro's ninth-floor suite. As throngs of revelers milled about on the sidewalks outside, the two spoke cordially through interpreters about anticolonial movements in Africa and Latin America and their common struggles against American racism and imperialism.[68] After Malcolm voiced his support for the revolutionary government and assured Castro the masses in Harlem were not deluded by anti-Cuban "propaganda" in the US media, Castro expressed his solidarity with Pan-African liberation struggles. "We are all brothers. It is wonderful that 14 new African nations are in the United Nations," Castro said. "They are oppressed and exploited just as we are," he continued. "The new nations and we in Latin America are all African Americans."[69] Now enshrined in Harlem lore, the brief meeting demonstrated Malcolm's growing understanding of inherent connections between the Black freedom movement in the United States and anticolonial, anticapitalist, and armed revolutionary struggles unfolding in the Global South.[70]

For Mae Mallory, Castro's presence in Harlem made tangible the international context of the Black freedom movement and offered a unique vantage point to see the workings of US foreign policy. When the State Department offered to provide the Cuban delegation with free lodging after they were evicted from their hotel, which would have prevented their stay at the Black-owned Hotel Theresa in Harlem, Mallory pointedly questioned the motives of the federal government. "In this country of Free ENTERPRISE does it mean that people that the United States Gov't call UNFRIENDLY should live rent free rather than let a native born black man make one cent on his enterprise," Mallory charged, "or is there something that it would behove [sic] the black man in these United States to learn from Fidel Castro?"[71] In her analysis, these were calculated political moves that revealed a fundamental contradiction of American society. Recognizing that a capitalist society was willing to sacrifice the principles of free market trade, either to prevent Black businesses from earning money or to suppress international anticolonial and anticapitalist solidarity, clarified the centrality of racial oppression to US economic and foreign interests and marked an evolution in Mallory's critique of racial capitalism.

The rising tide of anticolonialism and anticapitalism in 1960 also stoked the radical imaginations of Black intellectuals and activists who built new organizations in New York City to forge this popular energy into collective action. Following his return from Cuba, LeRoi Jones (Baraka) began working his connections in the literary world to put together a group to raise political consciousness among downtown artists and intellectuals. The Organization of Young Men emerged from these efforts as an all-Black, "*highly militant* organization," including Harold Cruse, musicians Walter Bowe and Archie Shepp, journalist Calvin Hicks, and poet A. B. Spellman, who felt alienated from the mainstream civil rights movement and declared that "it was time to go on the offensive."[72] The group aligned themselves with "the majority of the peoples of the world" engaged in anticolonial struggles but asserted, "We must earn this brotherhood by acting."[73] Though by Jones's own admission the group lacked ideological cohesion and sense of direction, it nonetheless represented "a confirmation of rising consciousness" that resonated throughout the city and marked a "crucial step in Baraka's move toward Black Power."[74]

Meanwhile, Hicks organized another group, called the On Guard Committee for Freedom (OGFF), a Black nationalist and Pan-Africanist collective of writers and artists who launched a self-titled newspaper to advance anticolonial struggles at home and abroad. As part of an educational and action organization, committee members sought to "inspire our people to united mass action" and committed themselves to "an uncompromising, unswerving battle against all exploiters and forms of exploitation" through popular education and direct action. Operating from an understanding that Black Americans were living in the belly of the beast of racism and imperialism, the OGFF used its monthly newspaper to inform Black people "of the social conditions contributing to their oppression" as a pathway to engaging in "decisive action toward achieving their emancipation."[75] Though both organizations were mainly formed amid the Black literary scene on the Lower East Side, they increasingly looked to ground their political work uptown in Harlem. In the months that followed, many would put down their pens and horns and put up their fists in direct action.

While many activists and Harlem residents were being charged by the energy of revolution, many establishment civil rights leaders were trying to hold back the rising tide. Desperate to maintain control over the direction of the civil rights movement and stay in the good graces of politicians, media, and funders, moderate local and national Black leaders like the Baptist Ministers' Conference, Gloster Current, and even Rep. Adam Clayton Powell Jr. bowed to the anticommunist hysteria of the day and tried to distance their constituents from Castro's supposedly nefarious influence. After L. Joseph Overton unwittingly violated a directive not to accept any invitations from Castro without first consulting with the national office, Current and Roy Wilkins conspired to oust the NY NAACP president from his post later that year.[76] Fueled by Cold War anticommunism, gradualism, and respectability politics, the moderate leaders' hostility to the Cuban Revolution revealed the widening fissures between mainstream civil rights organizations and grassroots radicalism in Harlem at the start of a new decade.

"LUMUMBA BECAME EMMETT TILL"

Though the immediate exhilaration felt during Castro's ten-day visit faded, it nonetheless left a lasting mark on the collective consciousness of a generation of activists and local people. "What has always remained . . . of Fidel's visit," Sarah E. Wright recalled over thirty years later, "is a social vision immersed so deep in my heart it can never be dislodged."[77] Castro's arrival had a profound impact on the political development of other members of the Harlem Writers Guild (HWG) as well. Formed in 1950 as a writing salon for Black artists and intellectuals, including Wright, Killens, Clarke, Mayfield, and singer Abbey Lincoln, the guild included Left and nationalist intellectual-activists who remained unwavering in their politics in spite of the crushing weight of repression during the McCarthy era.[78] With the radical fervor of the postwar era showing renewed signs of life by 1960, members of the HWG brought the radical politics of that older era into more active organizational involvement in struggles for rights and power in Harlem.

The politics and activism of many HWG members were informed by close personal relationships with local, national, and global liberation struggles. While many guild members had roots in the South and felt a sense of immediacy from the firsthand reports of racist violence they received, Wright explained that "we were also at one with the seething ghettos of the North, our ears attuned to Malcolm's message."[79] And with 1960 dubbed the "Year of Africa" by the United Nations for the anticolonial revolutions sweeping the continent, HWG members immersed themselves in solidarity work for various armed liberation struggles and were instrumental in spreading anticolonial and Pan-Africanist consciousness in local Black communities.[80] Just months after Castro's visit to Harlem, local and global Black freedom struggles converged in New York City in an explosive way following the assassination of Congolese Prime Minister Patrice Lumumba.

The first leader of the newly liberated African nation, Lumumba rose to power in June of 1960 after being released from prison for his part in political uprisings against the Belgian colonial government the previous year.[81] Lumumba's charisma and bold defiance in the face of Belgian colonial oppression endeared him to African American radicals and aspiring revolutionaries. "Patrice Lumumba, Kwame Nkrumah, and Sékou Touré were the Holy African Triumvirate which radical black Americans held dear," HWG member Maya Angelou explained years later, "and we needed our leaders desperately."[82] As Western powers immediately conspired to undermine independence and maintain colonial influence, Lumumba's name rang out from Harlem rallies and protests in support of the revolutionary leader and in condemnation of US and European imperialism in Africa.

One of the most important figures in forging political relationships between Harlem activists and African independence leaders was Rosa Guy. A novelist, trade union activist, and cofounder of the HWG, Guy migrated to Harlem from Trinidad and was raised in a Garveyite household.[83] As African leaders arrived in New York in the spring of 1960, she went to the UN every day to bear witness to the rising tide of African independence washing ashore in the United States. Having drawn the attention of delegates whom she came to befriend, Guy was invited to receptions and given passes to attend UN Security Council debates, where she was often joined by fellow Garveyite Queen Mother Audley Moore.[84]

Guy's fluency in French was particularly useful in fostering close relationships between Congolese delegates and members of the HWG. As Calvin Hicks recalled, the delegates were largely isolated in New York because French was the only European language most of them spoke, so the HWG "became their family."[85] When Lumumba arrived in New York in late July 1960 to appeal to the UN for the withdrawal of counterrevolutionary Belgian troops, Guy joined his entourage, "going from place to place, standing as guards outside of doors, deciding who should or should not enter." After Lumumba's departure, Guy remained vigilant in the halls of the UN, listening to rumors of the swelling conspiracy to undermine his government and desperately lobbying delegates to support Lumumba and reject the separatist, neocolonial government.[86]

Through coverage from rallies, street speakers, and the Black press, Harlem radicals paid close attention as the situation in Congo escalated that fall. In late August, Lewis Michaux and James Lawson led a demonstration at the United Nations headquarters protesting UN involvement in Congo. Harkening back to Garvey's call of "Africa for Africans," the picketers carried signs reading "Congo for Congolese" and "UN Get Out of Congo."[87] Just days before Castro arrived in Harlem, Lumumba was again captured by neocolonial military factions backed by the United States, Belgium, and the UN, leading Harlem activists to use the global platform Castro's visit offered them to condemn US and UN intervention and to support their captured comrade. Wherever crowds gathered, activists carried signs supporting Lumumba and denouncing the unfolding coup, while Castro dedicated part of his UN address to condemning Western interference in Congo.[88]

While Lumumba's November escape offered a glimmer of hope that he could rally nationalist forces to regain control of Congo, that hope was quickly dashed when he and two allies were captured again on December 1.[89] In response, Harlem activists demonstrated at the United Nations to challenge US, European, and UN involvement in the coup d'état. The following week, a small group of Harlem women called the African American Women's Committee walked a picket line at the UN, declaring, "We are now ready to give our lives for the freedom of Africa and our children."[90]

The most significant protest at the UN that fall, though, was organized by the Cultural Association for Women of African Heritage (CAWAH), a new Black nationalist women's organization founded by HWG members Maya Angelou, Rosa Guy, Abbey Lincoln, and Sarah E. Wright.[91] On December 17 CAWAH and HWG picketed at the UN as part of a petition campaign to UN Secretary General Dag Hammarskjöld demanding that he secure Lumumba's release from prison and provide him with protection to govern; disarm and end the military rule of Colonel Mobutu (who had seized power through a CIA-backed coup d'état in September); expel all Belgian military forces; and place UN forces at the disposal of Lumumba and the central government to maintain unity and independence. CAWAH delivered these heady demands in the name of "an unbreakable bond to our Congolese brothers" and with full confidence that their outrage "represents that of the overwhelming majority of the Afro-American peoples."[92] Though CAWAH

FIG 9 Demonstrators gather outside the Hotel Theresa on September 24, 1960, during Cuban President Fidel Castro's stay, to protest the United Nations and support African independence movements. (Photographs and Prints Division, Schomburg Center for Research in Black Culture, The New York Public Library)

collected 1,500 signatures, the petition was largely ignored, and Lumumba was horrifically executed by separatist and Belgian soldiers on January 17, 1961, with the blessing of the UN and the US government.[93]

When the grisly assassination of Patrice Lumumba became public on February 13, 1961, Black radicals in the United States were incensed by what they (correctly) understood to be a calculated political assassination orchestrated by Western imperial powers and carried out by their neocolonial allies. The fallout from Lumumba's assassination was fast and furious in New York City, as radical activists and organizers of all stripes coalesced to protest the active roles played by the American government and United Nations in suppressing the interrelated struggles for African independence abroad and Black liberation at home. "Lumumba became Emmett Till and all the other black victims of lynch law and the mob," historian John Henrik Clarke explained in *Freedomways* the following year. "The plight of the Africans still fighting to throw off the yoke of colonialism and the plight of the Afro-Americans...

became one and the same."⁹⁴ Like the murder of Emmett Till nearly six years earlier, the assassination of Patrice Lumumba galvanized Black communities, who recognized the culprit of this vicious crime as the global system of white supremacy.

With the UN Security Council set to meet on February 15, 1961, members of CAWAH, the HWG, and the OGFF drew on their expansive connections with Black Left and nationalist groups to quickly mobilize a diverse coalition of radical organizations and local people for a demonstration at the UN. Though the Fair Play for Cuba Committee's Richard Gibson would later claim that "it was [Robert F.] Williams who inspired that much publicized and highly effective demonstration in the United Nations," it was Black women who turned that inspiration into organized action.⁹⁵ Indeed, it was CAWAH (with support from the HWG) that in about two days' time organized a mass demonstration at UN headquarters on 42nd Street.⁹⁶ One of the key architects of this ad hoc coalition was Rosa Guy, whose intimate connections with Congolese delegates had made Lumumba's assassination all the more personal for her and sharpened her resolve to protest this international lynching. It was through these relationships that Guy learned of the assassination before it was publicly announced, and she passed the news along to her comrades in CAWAH.⁹⁷

According to Angelou and Guy, the women initially planned to stage a symbolic protest at the UN, donning black veils and rising from their seats in a solemn protest when Adlai Stevenson began his announcement of Lumumba's death. Recognizing a need to connect their demonstrations with the masses, however, they decided instead to put the word out in Harlem—with the help of Lewis Michaux—to inform the people of Lumumba's death and drum up support for a much larger demonstration. Two days before the Security Council was scheduled to meet, Angelou, Guy, Lincoln, and other CAWAH members addressed an evening rally in front of Michaux's bookstore at the intersection of 125th Street and 7th Avenue. After Michaux warmed up the crowd, Abbey Lincoln stepped to the microphone and told the thousands gathered in Harlem Square that Lumumba was dead. "The whites killed a black man," she gravely informed the crowd, "another black man."⁹⁸ The following night, Robert F. Williams, who was staying with Rosa Guy while in New York, echoed CAWAH's call to action in a "fiery" speech at another Harlem street rally to generate support for the protest.⁹⁹ The crowds were livid and seized on the opportunity to join the women in their demonstration at the UN.

When the Security Council convened the morning of February 15, about seventy-five activists, many wearing black armbands or black veils, sat in small groups in the gallery, having made their way through the swirling crowd of protestors outside the building. Rosa Guy had used her connections with African delegates to secure passes, and each member handed theirs back to others in the line to gain entrance into the chambers.[100] On a dreary winter day, thousands of demonstrators were milling about on the sidewalks, seeking an outlet to channel their righteous anger. Just outside the chamber doors, scores of other activists representing CAWAH, HWG, OGFF, the Liberation Committee for Africa (LCA), and the Crusader Family waited in line to gain entrance.[101]

Despite the picket lines marching outside the building and the crowds trying to gain entry to the chamber, the Security Council session came to order and proceeded in normal fashion until Adlai Stevenson took to the podium and began his first formal speech as US representative to the United Nations. When Stevenson declared his support for UN Secretary General Dag Hammarskjöld, the man who had been responsible for Lumumba's protection, all hell broke loose.[102]

As Stevenson glibly announced US support for the man who many Africans and African Americans saw as complicit in the murder of Lumumba, Guy went to the chamber doors to give the signal for those waiting outside to enter. Meanwhile, her sister Mise "screamed and screamed, staring out at the podium as though indeed she were looking at Lumumba's coffin." The gallery erupted as security guards "rushed" at the women and dozens of protestors lashed out with cries of "Killers!" and "Murderers!" As the crowd chanted "Lumumba! Lumumba!" in unison, the chamber doors swung open and the throngs of activists who had been waiting outside rushed in, chanting "Uhuru! Ya Uhuru! [Freedom!]" while "bowling over" guards and shutting down the council session.[103] Chaos ensued as a wave of guards swept in to clear the room while protestors inside tussled with guards and white bystanders. Carlos Moore, an Afro-Cuban nationalist well known in the streets of Harlem, jumped on the back of a white man and brought him to the ground, while Maya Angelou watched as a "stout black woman" grabbed a white man by the jacket and "shook him like a dishrag."[104] A photographer snapped a picture of OGFF leader Calvin Hicks being dragged from the gallery by a group of guards that landed on the front page of the next day's edition of the *New York Times*.

Though Angelou did not identify the "stout black woman" in her autobiography, she likely saw Mae Mallory, who had been involved in coordinating the protests and had made her way inside the chambers that morning.[105] Mallory rushed to the defense of Carlos Moore, who was being beaten by four security guards. As she tried to push her way through a group of white spectators who had formed a human wall around the guards, they pushed her, broke her glasses, and hit her in the head. "Then I really got angry," she wrote in *The Crusader* weeks later. "All the pent up emotions that I'd suffered all my life from the hands of racist whites, overflowed." Surrounded by white men in the heart of the American empire, Mallory lashed out in defense of her comrade. After smashing her broken glasses into the face of one of the guards, she cracked him in the head with the heel of her shoe, then grabbed another guard by the necktie before she was dragged out of the chambers.[106]

As protestors and bystanders surged out of the room to escape the brawl and the influx of security guards, the conflict spilled out onto the sidewalk, where the thousands of protestors who had not been able to enter the building were energized by the news that a "riot" had taken place inside. While the crowd wanted "an extravagant disorder," as Maya Angelou remembered, the police on the scene "yearned for vindication."[107] From the steps of the building, a group of officers looked down on the crowd, "their eyes glittering," before charging at Mallory, Calvin Hicks, LeRoi Jones (Amiri Baraka), and Rolland Snellings (Askia Muhammad Touré), who were marching on the sidewalk. "They attacked us, clubs flying," Baraka later recalled in his autobiography.[108] Once again, Mallory demonstrated her willingness to defend herself and her comrades against state violence, fighting off two policemen whom she reportedly knocked unconscious.[109] "Mae put up a terrific battle," Baraka continued, "the police were sorry they ever put their hands on her."[110] Though Baraka and Mallory were forcibly stuffed into a paddy wagon, the protests continued throughout the day on the west side of 1st Avenue between 42nd and 43rd Streets. As the afternoon wore on, crowds shepherded by various Black Left and nationalist groups braved the cold and a zealous mounted police force to bring their protests to the Belgian Consulate and to Times Square, before regrouping in Harlem Square for a rally later that evening.[111]

As the city and nation reeled in the aftermath of the disruptive protest, demonstrations continued for the rest of the month. Three days later, members of the LCA and FPCC joined four hundred Cubans and Puerto Ricans in a picket at the UN, chanting "Viva Lumumba! Viva Fidel!" and carrying signs expressing solidarity with Congo and denouncing the Congolese separatists as "Colonial Uncle Toms."[112] The following week, the United African Nationalist Movement organized a funeral service in Harlem to collectively mourn Lumumba's death. Eloise Moore, who had been present at the UN protests, even acquired a casket for the funeral service held at Michaux's bookstore, where an effigy of Lumumba had lain in state since his death was announced.[113] Marching behind a banner proclaiming "They Have Lynched Our Savior," hundreds of mourners and drummers endured a cold rain as they processed down 7th Avenue to 125th Street, carrying the casket to Harlem Square, where the late revolutionary hero was eulogized by Harlem nationalists. The crowd intended to carry the casket to the United Nations but were prevented from doing so by a large police presence determined to prevent another "riot."[114]

The demonstration at the United Nations and the subsequent protests it inspired marked a watershed moment for Black freedom struggles in the city. Harlem activists raised popular consciousness about US complicity in the violent repression of anticolonial struggles in Africa, contributed to the popular resurgence of Pan-Africanism and anticolonialism, and demonstrated a willingness to engage in physical struggle against the enemies of Black liberation—both within the United States and throughout the diaspora.

Drawing energy and inspiration from the protests at the United Nations, Calvin Hicks, Rosa Guy, and Sarah Wright expanded their organizing efforts with the On Guard Committee for Freedom. In March OGFF sent out a mailer to formally announce its formation, share its positions on the global Black freedom struggle, and explain its program. Connecting the political repression of Black freedom fighters in the United States, the Congo, South Africa, and Ruanda-Urundi, OGFF nonetheless declared that there was reason to be hopeful, since "the Freedom March is on, and no amount of repression can or will stop the people in their drive for justice and liberty."[115] OGFF also acted on its calls for "united action on all things affecting civil rights" by merging with LeRoi Jones's Organization of Young Men to strengthen the coalitions formed through the UN demonstrations.[116] Like Jones, Hicks urged downtown Black artists and intellectuals to understand the vital links between art and politics and to engage in organized, collective struggle. Through OGFF, which operated out of Harlem, "downtown black bohemians" were brought together with uptown artists with roots in older Left and nationalist movements in Harlem, laying the foundations for the emergence of the Black Arts movement in the years to come.[117]

Meanwhile, former architect turned journalist Dan Watts used the furor over the protests to formally announce the formation of the Liberation Committee for Africa (LCA), which had been organized the previous year and was involved in the UN protest. The radical Pan-Africanist organization critiqued gradualism, demanded "immediate liberation," and embraced the activism of more militant leaders like Robert Williams, Malcolm X, and Mae Mallory.[118] In the wake of the UN demonstrations, the LCA carved out a major role in the production and dissemination of anticolonial, anticapitalist, and Pan-Africanist political thought through its literary organ, *Liberator*. The first edition, published in March 1961, was dedicated entirely to covering Belgian imperialism in Congo and the assassination of Patrice Lumumba. Through the monthly magazine, Watts, editor Lowell "Pete" Beveridge, and a cadre of radical intellectuals, artists, and writers offered action-oriented analyses of domestic and international struggles for Black self-determination. In the following years, the writings of this talented collective of writers, many of whom would influence the emergence of the Black Arts and Black Power movements, would play a formative part in promoting and shaping a popular radical political consciousness in New York City and beyond.[119]

LIBERALISM AND ITS DISCONTENTS

The fallout from the protests at the UN had intense local, national, and global reverberations. Not only did the protestors expose and oppose Western powers and white supremacy on an international stage, they also revealed the rapidly expanding gulf between mainstream, middle-class civil rights organizations, which were presumed to represent Black communities, and the radical activists and grassroots organizations, which were proving more capable of playing that role. "Harlem was in commotion," Angelou recalled, "and the rage was beyond the control of the NAACP, the SCLC or the Urban League."[120]

Newspaper coverage of the demonstrations in the following days and weeks revealed the liberal moderates' deep disconnect from popular sentiment in Harlem. Columns in the *New York Times* described the protests as "disgraceful," chided the "race consciousness" of Black nationalism as "an enemy of democracy," and warned of "extremist groups seeking to rouse American Negroes to a more militant attitude."[121] In Washington, the *New York Times* reported, US officials characteristically blamed "Communist agitators" for fomenting pro-Lumumba sentiments and orchestrating unrest, while newly elected President John F. Kennedy affirmed his support for the UN and alluded to Soviet involvement in Congo as justification for US intervention.¹²² In addition to blaming communists, media outlets frequently targeted the Nation of Islam as a scapegoat for this most recent racial unrest in New York City, despite its noninvolvement. In a national wave of fear mongering, Black newspapers like the *Norfolk Journal and Guide* described the NOI as "the most sinister of all Negro cults in the United States," while the *Washington Post* warned their readers that members of the NOI were "being conditioned and trained for the 'War of Armageddon' when the blacks—as they refer to themselves—will kill the whites."¹²³

The changing character of the Black freedom movement in Harlem also drew the attention of the NYPD. Police Commissioner Stephen Kennedy set his sights on Malcolm X, who he claimed was the chief instigator of the whole ordeal. Following a briefing with Kennedy and Deputy Commissioner Walter Arm, Adlai Stevenson singled out the "Black Muslims" as having been responsible for the disruption of his speech at the UN. Kennedy was reported to have described the NOI to Stevenson as "a fanatic Negro national cult, which is one of the most dangerous gangs in the city," adding that the NYPD had been actively investigating the group for the past few years.¹²⁴ These investigations had been carried out by the NYPD's counterintelligence unit, the Bureau of Special Services (BOSS), which escalated its surveillance of other Black nationalist organizations like the LCA and OGFF in the aftermath of the UN protests.

BOSS detectives were particularly troubled by the growth of Black nationalist organizations in the wake of the UN demonstrations, which gave them "reason to believe that persons interested in the 'Nationalist Movements' are also interested in the Communist Party."¹²⁵ Over the next few weeks, BOSS detectives infiltrated meetings of the LCA, OGFF, and UANM, taking note of attendees who had been involved in the UN protests, as well as "highly inflammatory remarks" against the United Nations that "paralleled the arguments of the communists."¹²⁶ As Black radical organizations continued to grow in the following years, BOSS expanded its counterintelligence efforts to surveil, infiltrate, and undermine the Black freedom movement in New York.

Meanwhile, moderate Black leaders joined the papers, politicians, and police in their condemnation of the UN protestors. *Amsterdam News* columnist Olga Pierce Lytle took aim at the "Harlem African Nationalists," chastising activists for not adhering to respectable forms of protest and suggesting that they "should have learned a little of the value and rewards of racial dignity from the 'sit-ins' intelligent protest of injustice."¹²⁷ City Councilman

Earl Brown decried the "disgraceful," communist-backed protestors, while National Urban League Executive Secretary Lester Granger described in his *Amsterdam News* column the "sick shame" he felt while "screaming men and women milled around the U.N. venting their ignorant frustrations or malicious anger."[128] United Nations Under-Secretary Dr. Ralph Bunche—who had overseen UN troops in Congo—went so far as to apologize for the behavior of his "duped" and "misled" fellow citizens. The conduct of the protestors, Dr. Bunche assured his colleagues, "was in no way representative of the American Negro's."[129] Such positions were characteristic of postwar Black liberals who toed the line of US Cold War foreign policy, embraced anticommunism, and threw activists under the bus to gain political favor for advancing integrationist, middle-class programs. Mainstream civil rights leaders like Roy Wilkins and Edward S. Lewis (Urban League of Greater New York) were sought out by reporters to provide the proverbial voice of reason, and they took advantage of the opportunity to offer their analyses of the problems facing Black communities and to promote their programs for solving them.[130]

In rejoinder, radical intellectuals and organizers, including James Baldwin, Lorraine Hansberry, and Malcolm X challenged the typical narratives spun by white commentators and moderate Black leaders. Over the next several weeks, Baldwin and Hansberry took turns making clear to readers of the *New York Times* that the conduct of the demonstrators at the UN was a far more authentic representation of the climate in Black America than Brown, Granger, and Bunche professed in their condemnations. In a lengthy article titled "A Negro Assays the Negro Mood," Baldwin swiftly rebuked the accounts of white pundits and "prominent Negroes" who blamed communist infiltration for the disruptive protests. "What I find appalling—and really dangerous," Baldwin opined, "is the American assumption that the Negro is so contented with his lot here that only the cynical agents of a foreign power can rouse him to protest." Baldwin characteristically challenged white readers to wake up to the realities of white supremacy in the Jim Crow North, while also calling attention to the complicity of Northern white liberals with their gradualist mentality toward Black equality. At bottom, Baldwin argued, the UN demonstrations sent a clear message to white America. "Any effort, from here on out, to keep the Negro in his 'place,'" he warned, "can only have the most extreme and unlucky repercussions."[131]

In her letter to the editor of the *New York Times* two weeks later, Hansberry piggybacked on Baldwin's assessment of African American identification with African liberation struggles, calling for Pan-African unity and placing the blame for Lumumba's assassination squarely on Euro-American imperialism. A gifted young playwright who had previously written for Paul Robeson's newspaper *Freedom* and recently received international acclaim following the Broadway debut of *A Raisin in the Sun,* Hansberry pulled no punches when it came to her rebuke of Dr. Bunche. Whereas Baldwin had merely alluded to the remarks of the UN under-secretary, Hansberry called him out by name and challenged his assumed right to speak on behalf of African Americans. "As so many of us were shocked and outraged at reports of Dr. Ralph Bunche's 'apologies' for the demonstrators," she wrote, "we were also curious as to his *mandate* from our people to do so." She concluded her letter with an apology to Mrs. Pauline Lumumba and the Congolese people for Bunche's remark.[132] Through this apology, Hansberry not only disavowed the leadership of moderate male "leaders" but also claimed such a role for herself and the masses of enraged African Americans.

For his part, Malcolm X refused to take the bait of the press, politicians, and police to denounce the protests to absolve the NOI of responsibility. Shortly after the UN demonstrations, Maya Angelou and Rosa Guy visited him at the Nation of Islam's restaurant on 116th Street in Harlem. Having witnessed the explosive anger over racial oppression swelling in Harlem, the two young writers feared that such fury would turn inward on the community if not channeled into organized action, and they decided to consult the NOI for guidance. While Malcolm conceded that the people of Harlem were rightfully enraged, he advised that "going to the United Nations, shouting and carrying placards will not win freedom for anyone, nor will it keep the white devils from killing another African leader. Or a black American leader."[133] Although he refused to endorse the demonstrations, to the frustration of Angelou and Guy, Malcolm nonetheless understood the importance of solidarity among Black radical and nationalist organizations and pledged to publicly affirm the validity of the protests. "I will say that yesterday's demonstration is symbolic of the anger in this country," Malcolm vowed. "That black people are saying they . . . will not always allow whites to spit on them at lunch counters in order to eat hot dogs and drink Coca-Cola."[134] To Malcolm, the resistance to racist oppression being waged in Congo, the American South, and Harlem were all connected in a global struggle for Black liberation, and he intended to use his platform to make those connections clear.

While insisting that the Nation abstained from any local, national, or international political involvement, and therefore, should not be implicated in the fallout from the protests, Malcolm made good on his promise in remarks to the *Amsterdam News*. "I am not Moise Tshombe and I will permit no one to use me against the nationalists," he explained in reference to the factionalist leader propped up by colonial powers to undermine the unity of liberation struggles in the Congo.[135] Though his active support for the demonstrations was constrained by Muhammad's conservative political doctrine, Malcolm supported them in spirit and offered the limited support that he was afforded as a minister of the Nation of Islam.

Though Malcolm actively disassociated the NOI from explicit political involvement amidst a whirlwind of abuse from the media and law enforcement (at the orders of Elijah Muhammad), he nonetheless used the platform the protests provided to expound his positions on Black Nationalism, the civil rights movement, anti-colonialism, and Pan-African liberation struggles. At a debate sponsored by the NAACP Youth Council at City College in early March, Malcolm X denounced integration as a solution to American racism and called for reparations in the form of land for a separate Black nation. "All over the world," Malcolm told the crowd of 300, "dark people are rejecting integration with their former oppressors." Reflecting the surging militancy in Harlem that the UN protests very clearly illustrated, Malcolm bluntly explained to the crowd "it'll take more than a cup of tea in a white restaurant to make us happy."[136] If Malcolm was unable to provide organizational support for Angelou and Guy in the wake of the UN demonstrations, he left little doubt that he stood in solidarity with them and shared this perspective with crowds by the hundreds and thousands that spring.

While the mainstream media and various levels of government explained away the political significance of the UN demonstrations, activists in Harlem mobilized the sentiments expressed by Baldwin, Hansberry, and Malcolm X and calculated their next steps for channeling this momentum into sustained, organized action. Most organizers recognized, as Baldwin had in his *New York Times* article, that the mass participation and explosive nature of the protests had as much to do with the assassination of Lumumba as they did with the socioeconomic conditions in Harlem created by systemic racism and maintained by many of the politicians, press, and police who had denounced the protests. Through the "spadework" of consciousness-raising by street corner speakers, grassroots organizers, and Black writers, Harlem residents came to better understand the international context of American racism, capitalism, and colonialism and began to see themselves as part of a global struggle for Black liberation. Now that local people in Harlem had been mentally and physically mobilized in defense of anticolonial liberation struggles, it was time to get organized.

For John Henrik Clarke, the confluence of radical organizing in the wake of the UN demonstrations marked the emergence of a new era in the Black freedom movement. The protests brought together a sense of collectivity among Black Left and nationalist groups in New York that "had not been seen for years, if ever."[137] This was a powerful manifestation, given the often-contentious sectarian disputes between Left and nationalist organizations in Harlem. In an article in *Freedomways* that fall, Clarke declared that this formative moment signaled the arrival of "the new Afro-American Nationalism," which he described as "a new manifestation of old grievances with deep roots." The flame of Harlem's Black radical tradition was now rekindled by the "international lynching of a black man on the altar of colonialism and white supremacy" at a time when the collective wounds from the domestic murders of Emmett Till and Mack Parker were still fresh.[138]

Cultivated by the grassroots efforts of organizations like the African Nationalist Pioneer Movement, the United African Nationalist Movement, and the Nation of Islam, and fueled by the emergence of new organizations grounded in old traditions, this New Afro-American Nationalism was characterized by a popular identification with Pan-African anticolonial liberation struggles, an appreciation of cultural heritage, demands for self-determination, and a rejection of middle-class leadership and integration as a panacea for American apartheid. Clarke understood this resurgent political consciousness to be a revolutionary proletarian movement against internal colonialism, which rejected bourgeois liberalism and fought to achieve personal and national liberation through the efforts of uncompromising independent local leadership. "In taking this historical step," Clarke observed, this new generation of grassroots activists, artists, and intellectuals had "turned away from a leadership that was begging and pleading to a more dynamic leadership that is insisting and demanding."[139] As a grassroots historian and participant observer, Clarke had his finger on the pulse of the movement in Harlem and saw the past, present, and future of Black freedom struggles converging in a moment of great possibility.

In the few years between the Cuban Revolution and the assassination of Patrice Lumumba, it became abundantly clear that the spirit of Bandung had come alive in Harlem as anticolonial revolutions in Africa and the Global

South were changing the landscape of domestic struggles for Black liberation. Inspired by African revolutionaries and nurtured by grassroots Black nationalist organizations, Black communities in Harlem and beyond were increasingly, according to Clarke, "looking back at their history and culture, and within themselves, for the spiritual and philosophical stimulus for their survival and direction."[140] In addition to the celebration of African heritage at Harlem parades, rallies, and bazaars, this growing identification with Africa as a source of pride became evident as many people rejected the term "Negro" and instead identified as "Black," "African," or "Afro-American." The rise of self-naming signified a rejection of the external and internal oppression that came with the term "Negro" and a collective demand for self-definition as a step toward self-determination.

Local people, activists, artists, and intellectuals also came to realize that solidarity with Pan-African, anticolonial, and anticapitalist struggles abroad required collective action at home. "No one is going to send a liberating army to rescue us," Mae Mallory wrote to Lorraine Hansberry in 1963. "Our liberation will come about through our own efforts."[141] The energy and examples of anticolonial struggles in Ghana, Cuba, and Congo stoked the radical imaginations of Harlem residents and activists like Mallory who envisioned new directions and possibilities for the Black freedom movement in the United States and took militant action to realize them. Through attending rallies and forums, studying revolutionary theory in the pages of *The Crusader, Liberator, On Guard,* and *Freedomways,* and joining local organizations, Harlem residents developed radical ideas about the ends and means of Black liberation and applied them to address colonial conditions in their communities.

The promise of African liberation followed by the peril of the first neocolonial coup against Patrice Lumumba enraged Black communities in Harlem and enlivened them to take bold, sustained action for Black liberation in the years that followed. "We held on to that rage," Rosa Guy recalled, "a rage that continued and became a part of us, a rage that went on to become part of the Black Revolution of the Sixties and the Seventies and the Black Power Movement."[142] In Harlem, this rage would propel the work of a broad array of emergent organizations in the early 1960s searching for concrete programs to channel the spirit of Bandung for Black liberation in the United States and beyond.

5

THE NEW AFRO-AMERICAN NATIONALISM

1961–1963

> Our freedom will depend on how much we are willing to fight and sacrifice for it. The harder we fight and the more we are willing to sacrifice will determine the extent and time of our freedom. No people have begged, pleaded or cried for their liberation. We shan't either. We must get up off our knees and fight back.
> —MAE MALLORY, *1963*

IN THE WAKE OF THE UN demonstrations, Harlem experienced a rebirth of Pan-African, Black nationalist, anticolonial, and anticapitalist grassroots activism as nationalist leaders and radical intellectuals brought revolutionary thought to street corners, salons, newspapers, and rallies. "A militant new generation has arisen," poet Rolland Snellings (Askia Touré) wrote in 1963. "Truly Garvey's 'cubs in the woods' have become majestic lions of the valleys and plains."[1] Inspired by anticolonial independence movements in Africa and the Caribbean, working-class Black communities made important contributions to this heightened radical consciousness in Harlem as they located their experiences in the Jim Crow North within global systems of oppression and exploitation. As local people, organizers, and intellectuals made these connections, many began to understand American racism as a form of internal colonialism and subsequently saw themselves as citizens of a "nation within a nation" who deserved and demanded self-determination.

Grassroots activists, tired of pleading with white liberals and Black moderates for civil rights, increasingly shaped the Black freedom movement in Harlem in the early 1960s. Dubbed the "New Afro-American Nationalism" by Dr. John Henrik Clarke in a 1961 *Freedomways* article, this new era of struggle was marked by a break with what singer and activist Abbey Lincoln called the "crumb-crunching, cocktail-sipping Uncle Tom leadership" class and an embrace of radical, working-class leaders who would fight for liberation and self-determination by any means necessary.[2] Accordingly, local people and activists talked less about civil rights and increasingly about freedom, while existing and emerging organizations shifted their focus to building grassroots power to fight for systemic change and Black liberation.

The New Afro-American Nationalism represented a dynamic and formative stage in the Black freedom movement in Harlem between 1961 and 1963. Forming a patchwork quilt of various Left, nationalist, and Pan-African traditions in Harlem, which represented different—often competing— ideas and programs for achieving Black liberation, artists, activists, intellectuals, and local people with a common goal of freedom debated liberal reforms, nonviolent resistance, armed self-defense, racial capitalism, self-determination, and revolutionary nationalism at venues ranging from street corners to theater stages. Harlem's radical popular culture came alive through mass rallies, street speakers, pickets, marches, performances, and meetings on a near daily basis, giving life to a collective sense of anger, power, and possibility. To harness the energy of such a heady political moment, organizers increasingly called for Black leaders of various stripes to set aside their ideological and programmatic differences to create a Black united front capable of upending white supremacy in the United States as part of an international struggle for Black liberation.

One of the most significant of these local activists was Mae Mallory, whose experiences exemplify how grassroots leaders theorized Harlem's place within national and global freedom struggles and applied these politics to local issues, promoting new strategies and tactics to achieve liberation. Mallory and her growing network of Black radical organizers in Harlem studied anticolonial revolutionary struggles in Africa and its diaspora, learned from their own organizing experiences, and worked to translate these lessons into concrete programs for Black liberation. In doing so, they forcefully challenged white supremacy in the Jim Crow North in ways that pushed the national civil rights movement in more radical directions in the early 1960s, while drawing the attention and ire of increasingly repressive local and federal law enforcement.

"UNLEASHING THIS BLACK POWER": SELF-DEFENSE AND SELF-DETERMINATION IN HARLEM

The rising tide of grassroots Black radicalism in Harlem in the wake of the UN demonstrations had a galvanizing influence on Mae Mallory's political development. Although from childhood she had claimed the right to self-defense and had actively organized in support of armed self-defense in Monroe, North Carolina, in the months and years following her clash with police at the United Nations, Mallory came to see armed struggle as a vital component of Black freedom struggles in Harlem and beyond.[3] Through organizing in solidarity with Monroe, Cuba, and Congo, Mallory hoped to inspire a more popular embrace of self-defense and armed resistance to achieve Black liberation. "Remember the school struggle started with just one then nine," Mallory wrote to a friend in 1963, so "perhaps the idea of self-defense will bear fruit the same as the idea of the school boycott."[4] As demonstrated by the recent UN demonstrations, Harlem was fertile ground for cultivating these sentiments.

The media fallout from the raucous protests was equally instructive. In the firestorm of scapegoating that sought to blame communists and Black nationalists—particularly the Nation of Islam—for the unrest, Mallory saw intentional efforts from the news media and government officials to drive wedges between Black organizations. She took this backlash as a sign that the budding unity between African American, African, and Caribbean people had finally struck a nerve in the Jim Crow North. Instead of causing divisions, the repression following the UN demonstration proved educational to Black radicals like Mallory and Malcolm X, who strengthened their resolve to forge a united front in its wake.

In an unpublished editorial written on behalf of Crusaders for Freedom, On Guard for Freedom, and the Black Liberation Movement in February 1961, Mallory warned that attempts to drive wedges between the Nation of Islam and Black communities were "doomed to failure" because there was "one thing that we have in common that supersedes other differences and that is a desire to rid ourselves of White Domination and exploitation."⁵ Echoing Malcolm X's earlier calls for a Black united front that reached across borders, oceans, and ideologies, Mallory explained that the assassination of Patrice Lumumba "taught us that the price of division is death and defeat for Black people and that only the forging of unity amongst us can ensure us of complete victory and liberation."⁶ While "Black Traitors" distanced themselves from the protests and condemned the actions of those involved, Mallory proudly declared that her organizations not only participated in calling for "death to the murderers of Patrice Lumumba" but were now rededicating themselves "to the task of unleashing this Black power" which had previously been "chained down" by Black moderates.⁷ In a little over a year's time, Mallory had gone from fighting city hall for educational justice in Harlem to calling for the destruction of white supremacy in the United States and throughout the African diaspora.

The organizing activities that Mallory dedicated herself to in the following weeks and months demonstrated this was no hollow threat. After President John F. Kennedy's failed attempt to overthrow Fidel Castro during the Bay of Pigs invasion two months later, Mallory joined a national group of militant Black leaders in issuing "A Declaration of Conscience," a manifesto warning the Kennedy administration that any attempt to overthrow the Cuban government would be met with an armed struggle in the United States. Although largely ignored by the media, writer and activist Julian Mayfield argued that the declaration "was a significant straw in the winds of change sweeping the earth, a warning that some Americans of African descent are prepared to lock arms with combatants against racism everywhere, even those who do not enjoy the approval of our State Department."⁸ As she became increasingly involved with anticolonial movements, Mallory clearly located her organizing work in Harlem within the vein of national and global revolutionary struggles.

Throughout the spring and summer of 1961, Mallory and the Crusaders organized rallies and events that illuminated a widespread embrace of militant struggle in Harlem and the widening gap between working-class Black communities and the moderate, middle-class leaders who were supposedly representing them. In May the Crusaders led local people in shutting down an NAACP rally in Harlem Square for refusing to allow Robert F. Williams to speak. In organizing to upstage the NAACP, the Crusaders both challenged their assumed leadership and created an opportunity for Harlem residents to learn about the successful use of arms to defend Black communities and secure civil rights. The majority of the three thousand in attendance, many carrying placards picturing Patrice Lumumba (as seen in fig. 10), shouted down speaker after speaker—even throwing eggs at Roy Wilkins—until the NAACP leaders gave in to their demands to hear Williams. The militant leader was met with a thunderous applause as he denounced the "Uncle Tom" leadership of the NAACP and urged Black communities to defend themselves against racist violence. After he finished speaking, Williams descended from the platform into a cheering crowd, who hoisted him on their shoulders and carried him through the streets.[9]

To mobilize popular support for self-defense, the Crusaders circulated fliers that spring citing the unpunished murders of Emmett Till and Mack Parker as evidence that "passive resistance is a fraud," while referring to Martin Luther King Jr. as a "phoney" and a "passive handkerchief head." In May they held another mass rally in Harlem Square to protest "southern injustice and brutality" and to critique the ineffective responses of "so-called leaders" in the face of unabated racial terror. The Crusaders circulated leaflets throughout Harlem ahead of the event, referring to the Second Amendment as the "first condition for our freedom" and inviting the community to join

FIG 10 Demonstrators carry signs showing Patrice Lumumba and heckle speakers during an NAACP rally at 125th Street and 7th Avenue in Harlem in May 1961. (Photo by Ed Bagwell; Library of Congress, Prints and Photographs Division, Visual Materials from the NAACP Records, [LC-USZ62-131068])

in the hanging in effigy of Alabama Governor John Patterson—a virulent racist whose opposition to integration had earned endorsements from the Ku Klux Klan.[10]

This growing power struggle in the local Black freedom movement drew national attention and contributed to a broader shift toward radical local leadership in campaigns for Black self-determination. Writing to congratulate Mallory on shutting down the NAACP rally in Harlem Square, Clark Atlanta University professor Dr. Lonnie Cross (Abdulalim A. Shabazz) declared, "The rout of the NAACP in Harlem ... proves beyond the shadow of a doubt that the NAACP and the whole of the black bourgeoisie do not speak for the black masses. They never did. They simply filled the void of the absence of the masses' own chosen leadership."[11] An active supporter of Williams and the Crusaders who would join the Nation of Islam's Atlanta Temple by the year's end, Cross understood that elevating leaders from working-class Black communities was a practice in self-determination that would facilitate broader social transformation. Furthermore, the successes of Mallory and the Crusaders in mobilizing thousands of local people demonstrated that self-defense was an issue Harlem residents could be effectively organized around.

The escalation of white terrorism in Monroe in the summer of 1961 demonstrated to Williams's Harlem supporters the impotence of nonviolent resistance and sounded the call for greater Northern involvement in the armed struggle in the South. These organizing efforts, in turn, led Harlem activists and intellectuals to embrace greater militancy to challenge white supremacy. By June members of the Crusaders, OGFF, Organization of Young Men (OYM), and Harlem Writers Guild (HWG) formed an ad hoc coalition called the Afro-American Alliance for Action (AAAA) to coordinate support for armed liberation struggles in Monroe and beyond. The minutes of their June meeting reveal a clear concern with economic inequality as a central pillar of the Black freedom movement, discussions about the creation of an independent Black state in the United States, and a near consensus on the position that "in forging their struggle Afro-Americans must separate themselves from whites."[12] Subsequent meetings focused on how to translate these positions into action, with an immediate interest in raising local, national, and global awareness of the struggle in Monroe and recruiting Harlem residents to get involved through rallies and picket lines.[13] To raise consciousness and support in early July, the AAAA distributed 25,000 leaflets in Harlem that briefly described the history of Klan violence in Monroe and highlighted the successes of armed self-defense in curbing white supremacist terrorism.

The right to armed self-defense was one issue that needed little debate, and raising funds for arms in Monroe became the coalition's primary campaign. Mayfield and Clarke had previously made trips to Monroe to deliver weapons, but the escalation of violence that spring and summer made the task more pressing. "Finally in 1961 when [Williams] was under heavy attack by the Klan, he called and asked for financial help," Mallory recalled, "so again, I went out and organized a rally to buy guns."[14] On July 10, while Conrad Lynn and Julian Mayfield addressed a rally at the United Mutual Auditorium in Harlem to spread the word about the situation in Monroe, Mallory and the AAAA held a meeting with the explicit purpose of raising money to purchase guns for Williams and his allies. An array of individuals and organizations contributed funds, including Vincent Copeland of the Workers World Party, Dan Watts of the Liberation Committee for Africa and *Liberator* magazine, *Negro Digest* editor Hoyt Fuller, several members of the OYM and Socialist Workers Party, and a handful of local people from Harlem and the Lower East Side. Through donations of $12.50 per gun ($132 in 2024), the AAAA was able to collect a total of $167.50 ($1,774 in 2024) that evening—enough to send thirteen firearms to Monroe.[15]

Because of its successes in drumming up local support for the militant Southern struggle, the AAAA drew the eye of the FBI. If Mallory was aware of the FBI's increasingly active surveillance programs at the time, she showed little regard for their actions when asked years later, declaring, "I didn't hide the fact that I was raising money to buy guns for black people in the South."[16] She refused to censor her right to self-defense in the face of governmental repression. Even if Mallory had been more discrete in her embrace of armed self-defense, it is doubtful she would have been able to evade the reach of local and federal surveillance agencies. The FBI had already begun keeping tabs on most of the activists in her network, including Williams, Julian Mayfield, LeRoi Jones, John Henrik Clarke, Hoyt Fuller, and John O. Killens and had an informant at the July fundraising meeting of the AAAA.[17] At the local level, the NYPD's counterintelligence unit, the Bureau of Special Services, was keeping a watchful eye on the Crusaders and various other organizations through undercover agents and confidential informants.[18] Mallory came to experience once more the repressive powers of the state the following month, when Robert and Mabel Williams called for reinforcements to come to Monroe.

THE MONROE DEFENSE COMMITTEE AND BLACK RADICALISM IN HARLEM

Throughout the summer of 1961, the correspondence Mae Mallory received from Mabel and Robert Williams grew increasingly alarming. "He called me up one day and he told me that they expected an attack by the Ku Klux Klan and that he would suggest that all of the people that wanted to come down there come," Mallory later recalled, "so Julian Mayfield and I went down."[19] They were joined in Monroe in August by a cadre of Freedom Riders from the Congress of Racial Equality (CORE) and Student Nonviolent Coordinating Committee (SNCC), who made the trip not only to lend support and draw attention but also to prove the effectiveness of nonviolent direct action in a crucible of racist violence. Mallory made it known, however, that she would not be walking on any nonviolent picket lines because of her steadfast position on self-defense.

This influx of support ratcheted up racist hostility in Monroe's white communities, who violently attacked the Freedom Riders, thereby proving the limitations and liabilities of nonviolent resistance. It also initiated a chain of events that culminated in the Williams family fleeing Monroe with Mae Mallory and Julian Mayfield.[20] Mayfield and the self-defense guard whisked the demonstrators away from mob violence to the safety of the Williams compound, where hundreds of angry Black residents prepared for a fight against Klan nightriders. As the sun began to set, a car approached carrying Charles and Mabel Stegall, known Klan members who had driven through the neighborhood the previous day with a banner reading "Open Season on Coons." As they once again rolled down the block, Mallory led an angry crowd to surround the black car and yank them out.[21] Realizing the consequences of the crowd harming a white couple on his front lawn, Robert Williams brought the Stegalls into the house for their protection, where Mallory kept watch over them.

As word of a hostage situation got out and circulated through the county, it appeared to Williams that a pogrom was coming, as state and federal law enforcement prepared for a raid on the house. Though the Stegalls had been allowed to leave safely under their own power, Williams was a marked man. To protect his comrades from slaughter and avoid the all-but-certain fate of being lynched by white police or mobs, the Williams family made the decision to flee Monroe. Armed for protection, they, along with Mallory and Mayfield, sped out of Union County in Mayfield's red Dodge Rambler and headed north to Harlem.[22]

News of the situation in Monroe traveled like wildfire. "Rob told me to get out in the event that, you know, nobody else can make it," Mallory later recalled. "Somebody had to get out, come back to New York and tell everybody what happened."[23] By the time they got to Harlem, the Williams family and Mallory had learned that they were wanted on charges of kidnapping the Stegalls, and they acted quickly to evade Southern "justice." While the Williams family covertly made their way to Cuba by way of Canada, Mallory fled to Cleveland, Ohio, to hide out with family and friends. For Mallory, going underground was not merely a means of staying out of jail but a means of staying alive. The horrors of the Southern justice system were well known—the lynching of Mack Parker was still fresh in popular memory—and Mabel Stegall may well have been speaking on behalf of the majority of Monroe's white population when she told reporters that "Mae Mallory ought to be strung up and if she ever come up to Union County she might get just that."[24]

Over the next month, the FBI conspired with local police departments to dig up information on Mallory and set up a national dragnet for her capture. Federal agents in New York interrogated Mallory's friends, family, and coworkers and made several visits to her mother's home, where they harassed and intimidated the elderly woman and Mallory's daughter, Patricia. Mallory's face circulated throughout the country on posters marked "Wanted by FBI," describing the thirty-four-year-old mother of two as someone with "a violent nature" who "reportedly carries a .22 caliber pistol concealed on her person." Through tapping phones lines and intercepting mail, the FBI finally got a lead in early October from their surveillance of Conrad Lynn, who had carelessly addressed a letter to Mallory in Cleveland.[25]

Federal agents acted quickly to put the screws to members of Mallory's extended family in Cleveland to ascertain her whereabouts, and on October 12 agents were at the door of her cousin's home where she was staying. "That Thursday about 25 members of the FBI came into the house with guns drawn and everything to arrest me," Mallory recalled. In that moment, her mind raced back to when she was a young girl in Macon and white police surrounded her aunt's house after Mallory punched a white girl in self-defense.[26] This time, however, the police didn't leave and Mallory was taken to the Cuyahoga County Jail. Though she was released on bond for five months, Mallory would spend the following year in jail fighting extradition to Monroe.

With Williams exiled in Cuba, Mallory jailed in Cleveland, and three others jailed in Monroe, a national network of activists in New York City,

Cleveland, and elsewhere rallied to defend their comrades. Within a matter of days, newspaper advertisements in several major Northern cities announced the formation of the Monroe Defense Committee (MDC). Described as a "broad, non-partisan defense committee" by executive secretary Calvin Hicks, the national organization, with headquarters on 125th Street, included an array of New York activists, artists, and intellectuals with ties to leading radical organizations, including the Crusaders, OGFF, CAWAH, AAAA, LCA, HWG, and CCH.[27] "The committee was organized and is sponsored by many individuals who may not agree with each other on the way in which full equality for Afro-Americans is to be achieved," Hicks explained in a letter seeking support for the group. "However, they do agree that the oppression, brutality and travesty of justice in Monroe, N.C. which forced Robert F. Williams to flee for his life must be rectified."[28] In addition to building a broad base of support for Williams and Mallory, the convergence of this array of activists and organizations in Harlem offered a promising sign for those who had been calling for a Black united front for many years.

Initially, the MDC positioned itself as an information organ responsible for countering the dominant narratives of white media outlets and politicians while raising national and global awareness about the true situation in Monroe. Through explaining the depths of racist violence in Monroe and exposing the culpability of government officials—including US Attorney General Robert F. Kennedy—the committee aspired to "achieve mass solidarity behind the fighting spirit of Monroe citizens and Robert F. Williams."[29] Articles from MDC members circulated throughout New York and the nation in the pages of *Liberator* and *Freedomways.* Posters with the headline "Save Mae Mallory!" appeared on utility poles throughout Harlem, reminding local people that their neighbor had fought and won against segregated schools in New York and was now "being persecuted because of her militant fight for Black Liberation."[30] Street rallies were organized in Harlem to educate the masses on the local, national, and global contexts and the importance of the struggle in Monroe. Fundraisers were also organized to contribute to legal expenses, and Ossie Davis dedicated a performance of his widely successful play *Purlie Victorious,* starring Ruby Dee, as a fundraiser for the MDC.[31] Through rallying broad popular support for Mallory, Williams, and the Monroe defendants, the committee was also advocating for the rights of Black people to defend themselves from racist violence and seek liberation by any means necessary.

Though the MDC's formation in New York offered a glimmer of hope for a united front of Black nationalist activists and organizations, the organization quickly became entangled in sectarian disputes with a rival organization called the Committee to Aid the Monroe Defendants (CAMD). The contestations over ideology, representation, and influence between the two organizations offer a lens into the long, messy histories of Left and nationalist factionalism that often got in the way of building united fronts in New York City. The CAMD effectively operated as an arm of the Trotskyist Socialist Workers Party under the leadership of white organizers Berta Green and George Weissman, which put the committee at odds with many of the MDC's Black nationalist members and those who had ties (former or existing) to the Communist Party. But the reality was more complicated than mere Left sectarianism.[32] In the estimation of Dr. Albert Perry, an associate of Williams in Monroe and the titular head of the CAMD, four main issues undergirded the division between the two committees: interracial organizing, support for the Freedom Riders, the banning of the word "Negro," and salaried officers.[33] For members of the MDC like Hicks and Jones (Baraka), however, the division hinged on their dedication to Black self-determination and the rejection of white leadership of Black political organizations, as well as their general disavowal of nonviolence as the only strategy for Black liberation.[34]

The Socialist Workers Party also had a reputation among young Black radicals in Harlem and the Lower East Side for taking over organizations like the Fair Play for Cuba Committee and imposing their ideological positions.[35] In an attempt to steer the direction of the fledgling MDC, the party offered financial support in exchange for making Berta Green an officer—a request that was swiftly rebuked by Hicks as a move "to dominate us rather than support us."[36] Conrad Lynn explained the matter quite frankly to Green in May 1963: "The basic reason is plain ... politically, the black people are no longer willing to accept white leadership of their cause."[37] While old-school Left sectarianism certainly informed the conflict, the issue that most concerned younger Black radicals was Black leadership of movements for Black self-determination. Despite the CAMD's contributions to supporting the Monroe defendants, their sectarian approach had "divisive and disorienting effects" on the Black freedom movement, driving wedges between former comrades and complicating efforts to build a Black united front.[38]

While acknowledging the important roles played by the CAMD in a letter she wrote to Mabel and Robert Williams in April 1963, after being released on $15,000 bond from the Cuyahoga County Jail, Mae Mallory argued that "it is obvious to all who care to see that in spite of all our disadvantages it was The Monroe Defense Committee that offered the leadership."[39] To Mallory, the rift between the MDC and CAMD also helped thrust a conversation about Black leadership of the Black freedom movement into national discourse. She credited the MDC in New York City with compelling Rep. Adam Clayton Powell Jr. to "denounce the NAACP, CORE, SCLC, etc. for the white domination in the leadership of Black organizations." Mallory was referring to a bold declaration Powell had made in Washington, DC, just weeks earlier. "The white man has given the Negro in America just about as much as he intends to," Powell stated. "We will achieve only that which we fight for and it can only be done by those organizations that are totally owned, controlled and maintained by the Negro people."[40] While Mallory qualified her commentary on the "opportunist" Powell's advocacy, she also credited the Harlem congressman with being "able to recognize the trend the liberation movement is taking."[41]

This "trend" of Black self-determination was a hallmark of the New Afro-American Nationalism Clarke had heralded in the pages of *Freedomways* two years earlier, following the UN demonstrations. "No people are really free," Clarke wrote, "until they become the instrument of their own liberation."[42] The positions on Black leadership and self-determination taken by Mallory and the MDC anticipated those that interracial organizations like the Northern Student Movement, CORE, and SNCC would embrace in the years that followed. It was clear to Mallory and many other Black activists that the physical and legal fights she and the Monroe defendants waged for nearly two years had helped to galvanize a radical liberation movement in Harlem and throughout the nation by 1963.

THE NEW AFRO-AMERICAN NATIONALISM

While the Monroe defendants and their supporters fought for freedom in the courts and in the streets, activists, artists, and intellectuals debated their ideological and organizational work in the pages of Left and nationalist publications. Characterized by a collective identification with Pan-Africanism and anticolonial liberation struggles, an appreciation of cultural heritage, and a rejection of bourgeois leadership and integration as pathways to Black liberation, the "New Afro-American Nationalism" was also based on the foundational analysis that African Americans constituted an internal colony of the United States—a nation within a nation.⁴³

In an era where revolutionary nationalist movements throughout the African diaspora were throwing off the chains of European colonialism and remapping the globe, activists and intellectuals increasingly began to understand the African American freedom struggle as one against internal colonialism. Segregated majority-Black urban communities like Harlem, where white people controlled most of the housing, businesses, employment, and politics, readily embraced this analysis. Amid the recent expansion of police powers and violence in response to community resistance, Harlem residents were also beginning to see the majority-white NYPD as an occupying force charged with protecting colonial interests, enforcing borders, and repressing challenges to the racist status quo.

Following an act of police brutality in December 1962, for example, members of the Nation of Islam walked a picket line carrying signs that read "20 Million American Negroes Are Suffering American Colonialism."⁴⁴ Accordingly, the big questions being debated in meetings, at street corner rallies, and in the pages of Black radical journals was what it would take to overthrow these colonial systems and achieve Black liberation. Charged by the energy of anticolonial revolutions, activists and intellectuals debated whether the growing embrace of armed self-defense was merely a militant tactic for achieving the moderate goal of integration or a pathway for bringing African Americans into anticolonial revolutionary struggle.

Among the most active figures in these debates was Harold Cruse, whose polemics in journals like *Liberator* and *Studies on the Left* provoked heated discussions and stimulated Black radical thought. Like many Black nationalists in Harlem, Cruse rejected the possibility, or even the value, of Black communities becoming fully integrated into the social, economic, political, and cultural institutions of the United States, and thus deemed the approach of mainstream civil rights organizations insufficient for achieving Black equality. Yet he also argued that in more radical organizations "programmatic ideas" were crucially absent, and in their absence "neither arms nor demonstrations nor protest marches mean very much." In a 1963 article in *Liberator,* Cruse characterized the struggle in Monroe as a local "rebellion" against "the American racial status quo," arguing that "a rebellion is not a revolutionary movement unless it changes the structural arrangements of the society or else is able to project programmatic ideas toward that end."⁴⁵ In other words,

African Americans could only achieve liberation and self-determination through revolution, which required seizing control of the levers of economic, political, and cultural power in society. The more radical factions of the Black freedom movement, in Cruse's thinking, had no concrete program for gaining control over these power structures and therefore were similarly incapable of achieving Black liberation. Although often patronizing coming from someone who wasn't much of an organizer and had few concrete programs of his own to offer, the critiques he offered in his essays would prove instructive for young Black radicals like Donald Freeman and Max Stanford (Muhammad Ahmad), who took them as a challenge.

These contemporary debates also provide a useful historical framework for analyzing the evolving radical thought of Harlem's "New Afro-American Nationalists" like Mae Mallory. On the one hand, Cruse was right that Mallory had not yet woven together her analyses of systemic racism, economic inequality, gender discrimination, nationalism, self-determination, and armed self-defense into a comprehensive program for Black liberation. In her writings, Mallory frequently pointed to the potential for armed self-defense to inspire the masses and provide the basis for organized struggle. However, the records of her correspondence and organizational activities during this period do not indicate that she had yet developed a plan as to how self-defense, as a tactic, fit within broader strategies for achieving economic, social, and political self-determination for Black communities.

A letter to Lorraine Hansberry in June 1963 is indicative of Mallory's general understanding of nonviolent direct action and self-defense at the time: "There is a very important principle involved here; one that must be resolved. The whole question of self-defense. Passive resistance may work for peripheral things such as the right to eat at a lunch counter, the right to use comfort stations and waiting rooms on a non-segregated basis. Passive resistance has helped to show the need for more militant action. No people under the sun ever won complete liberation by completely passive means."[46] While pointing to the need for "more militant action" and more expansive tactics to achieve economic, political, and social self-determination, however, Mallory did not explain in this or other letters how self-defense would help reach these ends beyond protecting communities who faced racist terrorism. At the same time, however, she was paying close attention to—and drawing inspiration from—the role of armed revolutionary struggles in Africa in the years since Lumumba's assassination. "I am personally impressed with the idea of a Pan African Army to liberate the whole of Africa the way the

Algerians liberated themselves," she wrote to Richard Gibson in August 1963. "It has been proven that a negotiated liberation isn't the most beneficial to the people."[47] Mallory's correspondence in these years reveals that she insisted on the right to self-defense as a means of protecting and expanding the arsenal of strategies and tactics available to those seeking Black liberation by any means necessary.

As Mallory continued to sharpen her evolving ideas on systemic racism and Black liberation, her actions in and subsequent flight from Monroe rendered her a central node in Black radical networks in Harlem and beyond. Emerging within the context of an increasingly radical political culture charged by the Cuban Revolution, the demonstrations at the UN, and escalating local and national struggles for human rights, the MDC and CAMD effectively parlayed Mallory's national persecution into a public referendum on state violence, armed struggle, Black nationalism, Pan-Africanism, and anticolonialism. According to Rosa Guy, the militant spirit embodied in the Monroe movement also inspired local people to push local and national freedom struggles in more assertive and radical directions. "Certainly," she wrote to Robert Williams in 1963, "the militant but limited stance the leaders are now taking is because of the millions of Robert Williamses behind them."[48]

In addition to fostering the development of grassroots militancy, the struggle to free Mae Mallory and vindicate Williams also created opportunities for a new generation of Black radicals to work with and learn from their movement elders.[49] Among those who found mentors in Black nationalism, Pan-Africanism, and armed struggle during this campaign were Donald Freeman, who forged relationships with CORE, the MDC, and the Nation of Islam through his organizing to support Mallory with the Afro-American Institute in Cleveland, and Max Stanford (Muhammad Ahmad), who met his future mentor, Queen Mother Audley Moore, at a "Free Mae Mallory Meeting" in Moore's home in Philadelphia.[50] Stanford was introduced to Moore through another mentor in Philadelphia, Ethel Azalea Johnson, a comrade of Robert and Mabel Williams and a confidante of Mae Mallory.[51] By the end of 1962, the duo helped form the Revolutionary Action Movement, a nascent revolutionary nationalist organization that would propel the radical trajectory of the Black freedom movement in the following years.

Mallory, however, was not merely an inspiration or coincidental connection for the budding revolutionaries. When Stanford and Stan Daniels were beaten and arrested at a protest against economic discrimination at a Philadelphia construction site in the summer of 1963, she wrote to Johnson offering

guidance, legal advice, and strategies for coordinating the pair's defense.⁵²
By the summer of 1963 it was clear that, just as Mallory's political development had been shaped by older generations of Black Left and nationalist thinkers and organizers in New York City, her own brand of grassroots militancy was now inspiring and influencing the evolution of freedom struggles across the country.

RONALD STOKES AND MALCOLM X'S POLITICAL THOUGHT IN TRANSITION, 1962–1963

Despite their lack of involvement in political action during the UN protests, Malcolm X and the Nation of Islam made undeniable contributions to the surging militancy of Black freedom struggles in New York City in the early 1960s. Though his affiliation with the Nation of Islam continued to constrict his involvement with the types of direct political action that Mae Mallory engaged in during these years, Malcolm X was very much in the thick of the same radical networks. Malcolm established close personal relationships with many of the most influential Black radical activists and intellectuals in Harlem, many of whom played active roles in the defense of Mallory and Williams. Whether on stages at Harlem Square, in television studios, or in private meetings, Malcolm made frequent contact with activists, intellectuals, and artists. Through these relationships, Malcolm inched toward an embrace of secular Black nationalism and revolutionary internationalism.

Though the theological nationalism and program of the NOI had empowered Malcolm to transform his life and reconnect with the Garveyite roots of his childhood, by 1962 they had become a drag on his political growth.⁵³ It was through the network of activists and intellectuals he cultivated in Harlem that Malcolm was able to continue his development in the early 1960s, in spite of the restrictions imposed by the NOI. In the summer of 1961, for instance, Malcolm joined a united front formation of Black civil rights, labor, Left, and nationalist leaders in response to another "near riot" in Harlem, likely caused by police violence.⁵⁴ As a member of this new Emergency Committee for Unity on Social and Economic Problems, Malcolm worked alongside Left-labor and civil rights leaders like A. Philip Randolph, Bayard Rustin, Percy Sutton, Anna Arnold Hedgeman, and L. Joseph Overton, as well as a who's who of Harlem's Black Left and nationalist leaders, including Bill Epton, Edward "Porkchop" Davis, James Haughton, Calvin Hicks, Lewis Michaux, Florence Rice, and Selma Sparks.⁵⁵

Malcolm's focus on policing in the Emergency Committee was informed by the escalation of police harassment of the NOI that year amid a broader crackdown on nationalist organizations and activities in the wake of the UN protests. After the second "near riot," the NYPD had once again flooded Harlem with members of its paramilitary Tactical Patrol Force and announced new regulations on nationalist street rallies, including a curfew and ban on speaking near crosswalks.⁵⁶ Though the NYPD had no evidence of its involvement in the conflicts, they predictably claimed the NOI had joined the fray and fueled the anger of the crowds.⁵⁷

Since the brutal police beating of Johnson X Hinton in 1957, surveillance of the NOI had become departmental policy for the NYPD. "They used every means they could to acquire as much information as they could about the Muslim movement," former Deputy Police Commissioner Robert Mangum later recalled.⁵⁸ That year, Harlem resident and police detective William DeFossett was assigned to serve as a "liaison" between the Nation of Islam and the NYPD.⁵⁹ While DeFossett coyly described himself as a "liaison," in reality he was running counterintelligence for the NYPD's Bureau of Special Services. Officially formed in 1946 as a descendant of the anticommunist "red squads," BOSS was tasked with investigating, infiltrating, and suppressing "subversive" organizations.⁶⁰ The most frequent targets for surveillance and suppression over the decades, unsurprisingly, were labor unions, the Communist Party, and Black nationalist organizations. So when activists with backgrounds in such organizations came together in 1961 to build a united front, the NYPD kept a watchful eye on the Emergency Committee through their man on the inside, Detective DeFossett, who used his affiliation with the 369th Infantry Regiment Veterans Association to gain a seat on the committee.⁶¹

Speaking at a rally to launch the Emergency Committee in September of 1961, Malcolm warned that until there was community control of police and real accountability for acts of violence, "there will always be police brutality, and the tensions between the people and the police will grow until uncontrolled violence explodes." As he had following the UN demonstrations, Malcolm refused to blame Harlem residents for resisting oppression and took "Uncle Tom Negro leaders" to task for being more critical of the people than the police.⁶² For Malcolm, the Emergency Committee offered a valuable learning experience in united front organizing, particularly around the issue of policing. Working alongside liberals and moderates who had previously been hostile to his positions, Malcolm developed strategies for police reform that would appeal to a broader base in Harlem without sacrificing his principles or politics. He would build upon this practical education the following year after another act of police brutality against the Nation of Islam in Los Angeles.

This type of political involvement drew reproach from Elijah Muhammad, who wrote to his top minister in early 1962 with instructions to abstain from political commentary in his public addresses, including any discussions of Black nationalism, which had been the crux of many of Malcolm's speeches throughout the previous year.[63] With the pace of local and national freedom struggles accelerating by the day, Malcolm felt he was being kept on the sidelines of history as Muhammad moved to reassert control and enforce the NOI's policy of political nonengagement. While adhering to Muhammad's restrictions, Malcolm X continued to engage in critical dialogue about Black liberation in his classes at Mosque No. 7, at street rallies, and in public addresses. Speaking to a full house at Adam Clayton Powell Jr.'s Abyssinian Baptist Church in the spring of 1962, Malcolm defended the Nation of Islam against charges of not backing up their militant rhetoric with concrete action. "Just because a man doesn't throw a punch doesn't mean he can't do so whenever he gets ready," he warned from the pulpit, "so don't play the Muslims and the nationalists cheap."[64] Though he publicly toed the line for the Nation, Malcolm privately sympathized with these critiques, which were swirling within Black communities. "Privately I was convinced that our Nation of Islam could be an even greater force in the American black man's overall struggle—if we engaged in more *action*," he later confessed. Malcolm privately predicted that if the Nation did not relax their nonengagement policy and actively participate in the Black freedom movement, it would find itself "one day suddenly separated from the Negroes' front-line struggle."[65]

Malcolm's concerns proved prophetic. Just weeks after he defended the Nation against charges of inaction in the face of injustice, the brutal murder of NOI member Ronald Stokes on April 27, 1962, by the Los Angeles Police Department posed a formative challenge for the Nation to back up its militant rhetoric of self-defense with concrete action.[66] The brutal killing of this unarmed Korean War veteran, whom an LAPD officer shot in the back, sent shockwaves through the Nation of Islam and through Black communities across the country, which waited with bated breath to see how the NOI, for all their fiery rhetoric, would respond.

For Malcolm, the police killing of Stokes was deeply personal. Malcolm had organized the Los Angeles mosque, and Stokes was an old friend who grew up only a few blocks from his sister Ella Collins in Boston.[67] Seeking justice through retribution, he rushed to Los Angeles to organize a response. "Malcolm was furious," recalled photographer Gordon Parks. "I expected that particular moment something really explosive to take over." Parks remembered an anxious Malcolm in Los Angeles, pacing, shaking his head, and repeating, "They're gonna pay for it, they're gonna pay for it."[68] Keenly aware of the rising murmurs within Black communities that the NOI was a paper tiger, Malcolm began preparing for a direct confrontation with the LAPD—to meet violence with violence. However, Muhammad ordered his minister to stand down, instead blaming Stokes's death on Malcolm's lack of faith.[69]

Malcolm X was fuming when he returned to New York City for a public forum to raise funds for the Monroe defendants hosted by the Socialist Workers Party on May 1.[70] As the last speaker to address the packed downtown meeting hall, Malcolm X pulled no punches in his verbal assault of the white supremacist society that had stolen the life of his friend. Making frequent comparisons between the LAPD and the Gestapo forces of Nazi Germany, Malcolm described what happened in Los Angeles as "one of the worst crimes, one of the most inhuman acts of atrocity that have ever been committed in a . . . so-called civilized society." To Malcolm, the murder of Stokes was the type of damning evidence of a morally bankrupt society that made the NOI's position against integration not only rational but imperative for Black survival. "I'd rather be dead," Malcolm declared, "than integrate into a society like this."[71]

The murder of Ronald Stokes solidified for Malcolm the necessity for Black Americans to defend themselves against the violence of white supremacy by any means necessary. Citing the armed anticolonial revolutionary struggles waged in Angola, Algeria, and Congo, Malcolm X argued that as a colonized people, Black Americans had the right to "defend ourselves from the atrocities that these white American colonialists have been inflicting against us." To Malcolm, Black Americans had been colonized by a people that had "perfected the art of hypocrisy to such high degree they'll stand up and make themselves look like angels in disguise when they've got blood of black people dripping from their mouths and dripping from their fingers." This rampant hypocrisy practiced by white supremacists and liberals alike was the fundamental basis for Malcolm's argument against integration. He concluded his fifteen-minute address: "We believe, that as you sow, so shall you reap. And if you're going to reap what you have sown, then we don't want to integrate with you."[72] Though he had not explicitly called for Black communities to take any action, thereby abiding by Muhammad's edict, it was clear that his patience had nearly worn out.

Black radicals in Harlem had also grown impatient with NOI rhetoric, which now appeared toothless. In an editorial in the May 1962 issue of *Liberator*, Dan Watts challenged Malcolm X to "reconcile his militant talk with the non-militant action of his followers." While he applauded the minister's truth telling about the "savagery and uncivilized nature of the white man," Watts argued that the NOI needed "more substantial weapons than the truth of Allah" to defend themselves against the police and other white supremacist forces.[73] Even some within the NOI grew dissatisfied with Muhammad's policy of noninvolvement in the movement. Benjamin Karim, one of Malcolm X's most trusted assistant ministers at Mosque No. 7, said that he and others felt they "should have been able to retaliate or train those people to retaliate."[74] Though Malcolm remained publicly silent, the NOI's inaction after Stokes's death proved a watershed in his relationship with Elijah Muhammad.

The contestation between Malcolm and Muhammad over the Nation's response to Stokes's murder marked the emergence of a new period in Malcolm's political development that would culminate in his departure from the Nation two years later. This period was characterized by Malcolm's efforts to define his political ideology of Black nationalism by moving beyond the Nation's theological focus and incorporating the Left, nationalist, and Pan-African teachings of his mentors in Harlem, like John Henrik Clarke and Eloise Moore.[75] In addition, Malcolm X took steps toward redefining his role in struggles for rights and power in Harlem: his renewed calls for a Black united front in the wake of the Stokes murder illustrated that he was attempting to steer the Nation of Islam into the currents of the national Black freedom movement.[76]

This change in course, in turn, was met by increased surveillance and repression from local, state, and federal law enforcement agencies. In New York, where the NYPD had been expanding its surveillance of Black radicals over the past five years, police began harassing members of the Nation with greater frequency in the summer of 1962. By the end of the year, this harassment and intimidation became so intense that Malcolm predicted "the time will come when the Muslims will not be able to leave their homes."[77]

Realizing that threats of divine retribution would do little to curb this suffocating repression, Malcolm made his first foray into civil disobedience in December, demonstrating his budding embrace of direct action in open defiance of Elijah Muhammad.

On Christmas Day 1962 two NOI members were arrested at gunpoint by two white NYPD officers at 42nd Street, near Times Square, for allegedly blocking a subway entrance while selling copies of *Muhammad Speaks*. When the men went to trial two weeks later on charges of assault, disorderly conduct, and inciting to riot, the NOI packed the courthouse while thirty members of the Nation picketed outside, carrying signs that read "America Is Against Human Rights" and "We Are Living In A Police State." After the two men were found guilty, the 250 Muslims who had been inside filed onto the sidewalk, where Malcolm X compared New York's criminal justice system to that of Mississippi and announced that "if the Muslims can't get justice in court then they will hold court in the street."[78] A month later, Malcolm made good on his promise when he led a demonstration in Times Square to protest the Christmas Day arrests and a recent police siege of the Rochester, New York, mosque which resulted in the brutal arrests of over a dozen Muslims.[79]

In the middle of the evening rush hour on February 13, 1963, Malcolm X and Joseph X (Yusef Shah) led two hundred members of the Fruit of Islam, carrying signs reading "America Violates the UN Charter on Human Rights" and "We Charge Genocide," in a solemn march along the sidewalks from Times Square to Rockefeller Center. As the pickets disrupted the flow of rush hour traffic, Malcolm and others distributed leaflets with the boldface heading "America has become a Police-State for 20 Million Negroes." The leaflet called out the hypocrisy of "political tricksters" like Governor Nelson Rockefeller, who denounced the racist violence of Southern segregationists while using "police-state methods to terrorize and suppress" Black New Yorkers.[80]

Malcolm also demonstrated his evolving internationalism in the leaflet, exposing the hollowness of US Cold War propaganda and exhorting Black communities in Harlem and throughout "the whole Dark World" to act in solidarity with their jailed brothers in Rochester. While the protest was an act of nonviolent direct action, the flyers made it clear that the demonstrators were prepared to return any violence inflicted upon them by police. "We must let the white man know that we will all go to jail today for what we believe. We will all fight for what we believe. We will all die for what we believe . . . but we must also let him know that we don't endorse the foolish philosophy of 'turning the other cheek' . . . We demand Justice or Death!!!!"[81] Though BOSS detectives hidden in plain sight kept a watchful eye on the demonstration, it appeared to observers that the NOI's willingness to stand their ground and fight back against political repression had, remarkably, kept the NYPD from interfering with their protest.[82]

The protest was uncharacteristic for both the Nation of Islam and the Times Square area. Demonstrations were technically illegal in New York's commercial hub, a fact that had been pointed out to Malcolm the day before by BOSS Detective William K. DeFossett. The detective's report illustrates Malcolm's intentions to engage in an act of civil disobedience—a tactic that betrayed the Nation's doctrines of nonengagement and obeying the law. Despite his clear intentions to coordinate a mass protest against police brutality and political repression, Malcolm X played coy to shield himself from accusations of such. Referring to the planned march as a "walk," Malcolm explained to DeFossett that he intended to merely "exercise his rights as an individual citizen to walk on the sidewalk in Times Square." If anyone were to walk in front or behind him, Malcolm explained, "that is his business." As the detective continued to badger him about what both men knew was a protest, however, Malcolm X eventually tipped his hand. "If we are going to get in trouble for nothing," he reportedly conceded to DeFossett, citing the arrest of the two Muslims in Times Square, "we might as well get in trouble for something."[83]

If Malcolm X felt constrained by Muhammad's order to stand down in Los Angeles following the Stokes murder, the Times Square protest represented an effort to break free. In his move toward secular nationalism, Malcolm was considering new tactics. And these tactics proved at least mildly successful in achieving immediate and longer-range results. As *Liberator* columnist Rose Finkenstaedt noted in her coverage of the protests, whereas "anonymous black men are murdered, beaten, and convicted with impunity day after day," Malcolm's actions resulted in dropped charges for one of the arrested Muslims and forced a parlay between him and Mayor Wagner regarding the NYPD's repression of the Nation of Islam. In Finkenstaedt's estimation, these minor victories offered important lessons to those involved in the Black freedom movement.[84]

Similarly, coverage in the Socialist Workers Party's newspaper *The Militant* concluded that by successfully challenging police repression and making clear to the NYPD that they were willing to fight and die that day, "the Muslims established a precedent in defense of free assembly, freedom of the press, freedom of speech, and freedom of religion."[85] While many in Harlem still criticized the Nation's noninvolvement, Malcolm's foray into organized political action demonstrated the influence of grassroots militancy on his political growth and marked the possibility of a new direction in 1963.

THE FREEDOM NOW PARTY AND THE POLITICS OF BLACK NATIONALISM

The rising tide of grassroots Black radicalism pushing Malcolm and other Harlem leaders in more radical directions was also forcing more mainstream presses to focus their attention uptown. In early June of 1963 *The New Yorker* sent staff reporters to Harlem to observe and describe the social, economic, and political conditions there for the magazine's predominantly white, middle-class subscribers. In their walking tour, the reporters happened upon a crowd of eight hundred people gathered at Harlem Square for a mass rally sponsored by the Harlem Anti-Colonial Committee.[86] The small group led by Bill Jones and Selma Sparks, a veteran of the Negro American Labor Council, counted among its few but distinguished members John Henrik Clarke, *Muhammad Speaks* editor Sylvester Leaks, journalist William Worthy, and Harlem Nine veteran Pernella Wattley, each of whom was also active in the campaign to free the Monroe defendants.[87] Billed as a protest against "black people's treatment in the white man's courts," the rally was organized to raise awareness of Mae Mallory's extradition fight, the ongoing legal struggle following the LAPD murder of Ronald Stokes, and the political persecution of Worthy.[88]

In their speeches to the enlivened crowd, Leaks and Conrad Lynn both encouraged the use of armed self-defense in struggles for Black self-determination. "We have guns, and we're going to make our presence felt," Lynn declared after deriding Dr. King's adherence to nonviolence in spite of the recent vicious attacks on protestors and bombings of his hotel room and his brother's home in Birmingham. "We have power," Lynn went on to say, as the crowd grew in size and vigor, "and we're going to use it!"[89] Leaks, who represented Malcolm X at the rally, expounded on Lynn's point in his address by declaring that African Americans in the South would have little trouble voting if they brought their rifles when they went to register.[90]

Whereas Leaks and Lynn spoke on the need for Black communities to seize political power by any means necessary, Worthy used his platform

FIG 11 Flyer for a June 1963 rally at Harlem Square organized by the Harlem Anti-Colonial Committee to protest the cases of Mae Mallory, William Worthy, and Ronald Stokes. (Handschu Files, Small Organizations, Harlem Anti-Colonial Committee, Municipal Archives, City of New York)

to denounce the repressive two-party system and called on Black voters to chart a new political course. With a presidential election looming large on the horizon amid growing frustrations with the Kennedy administration's inaction over civil rights and racist violence, engagement with electoral politics was becoming a key topic of debate within the Black freedom movement. To Worthy, the right to vote wasn't worth dying for if the candidates on the ballot were white men with no interest in Black liberation. Worthy argued that Black communities had to be in positions of power to control their own liberation, and thus proposed the formation of an independent Black political party. "Do you know what would happen if Fidel Castro were President of the United States instead of John F. Kennedy?" Worthy asked the audience to illustrate his point. "Ninety-five per cent of the police would have to flee to South Africa for political asylum. J. Edgar Hoover would be thrown into an integrated cell. If that didn't cure him, he'd be left there for life."[91] Worthy's point was well received by the sizable crowd, which laughed in appreciation and cheered in agreement.

By this point, few among the crowd at Harlem Square had any illusions of gaining civil rights—let alone Black liberation—through the national two-party system or the predominantly white liberal government of New York City. The rejection of white political power, repeated calls for armed self-defense, and the support of armed revolutionary struggles in Africa put the police stationed around the perimeter of the rally on edge as they bore witness to the crowd's collective anger. "There's going to be trouble," one observer stated plainly, citing the decades of systemic racism and police violence that the powers-that-be had refused to address in Harlem. "On a hot summer night," she predicted, "it wouldn't take much to set off a riot—not isolated violence but a kind of revolution."[92]

While there was no trouble that evening, the rally did mark the emergence of a new direction in Black politics and the Black freedom movement with the birth of the Freedom Now Party (FNP). Although in numerous interviews Lynn credited Worthy's speech as the impetus for creating the Freedom Now Party, the idea of forming an independent Black political party was deeply rooted in Harlem's Black radical tradition and had been discussed among Black Nationalist activists and intellectuals in New York City for some time before the June rally. During a meeting of the AAAA in Harlem two years earlier, Calvin Hicks had floated the idea of forming a political party, and several other members suggested that membership be limited to African Americans.[93] In the fall of 1962 Dan Watts and William Worthy appeared on a panel discussion televised by CBS where Watts queried whether the interests of Black people could only be served by "a political party of [their] own."[94] The proposition gained momentum the following spring when the televised racist brutality that Southern Democrats inflicted on the SCLC's Birmingham campaign added a greater sense of urgency and spurred some Black communities to seriously consider rejecting the national Democratic Party in favor of a progressive third party.[95]

In her reporting on the CBS discussion, which aired two days before President Kennedy's own televised announcement of an embargo of Cuba, *Liberator* columnist Rose Finkenstaedt argued "the interests of the black will never be considered until he becomes an independent political force." To Finkenstaedt, independent Black political power was not just a vehicle by which to achieve Black equality but also a means by which to fundamentally transform the political structures of the United States. "If the meaning of America is freedom, democracy, and anti-colonialism," she proposed, "the true interests of America will only be served through effective Black-led political power."[96]

Though Watts and Worthy may have had heady visions for such a party, they were also pragmatic. Worthy conceded that the party "cannot realistically anticipate meaningful 1964 victories at the polls." Explaining this first election cycle as a "training ground" for independent Black politics, Worthy declared, "1964 should therefore be regarded as the year for uniting and educating all militant forces in the black community."[97] The idea was already floating around Harlem, where Progressive Labor Party leader Bill Epton was formulating his campaign for councilman-at-large "as a means of introducing the concept of independent Negro political activity and action."[98]

With the New Afro-American Nationalism surging through its streets, Harlem was the logical choice for establishing the FNP's national headquarters after the party was officially launched at the March on Washington in August 1963. As the steady flow of demonstrators made their way toward the Lincoln Memorial, Lynn, Worthy, and several other FNP organizers distributed leaflets calling for a new political party with "an all-black slate and a platform for liberation." In their manifesto, titled "The Declaration of Washington," the organizers called for "all-black political action" that could "deliver knock-out punches to the enemies of equality" and promote economic justice, adequate housing, educational equality, and global self-determination.[99] As the crowds filtered out of the capital, the fledgling group met at the Park Sheraton Hotel to plan their next actions and establish the formal organization. After five hours of deliberations, a national committee was formed with Lynn as acting chairman and Wattley as corresponding secretary.

The formation of the FNP was met with polarizing receptions from white commentators and moderate civil rights leaders. It was immediately clear that demands for Black political leadership of Black communities made Northern white liberals very uncomfortable, and they responded with paternalistic arrogance and mischaracterizations of the FNP. In an editorial published two days before the March on Washington, the *New York Times* declared that the FNP would "extend racism into politics," increase divisiveness, and embolden white racists in the South. Further, the editorial cited the great progress African Americans had made in recent years and arrogantly claimed that the party's formation "implies a total misunderstanding of the nature of our political parties and the great flexibility of the American political system."[100] Similar sentiments were expressed in a letter to the editor of the *Amsterdam News*. "You are fighting . . . for freedom, equality, etc. and now fighting for segregation?" one writer pointedly queried, while offering a prediction that "confusion and violence will lose the gains made."[101] The responses of some conservative Black leaders echoed white liberal sentiments. Novelist and *Pittsburgh Courier* editor George Schuyler referred to Lynn and Worthy as "crackpots" in his dismissal of the FNP.[102] Such hostile responses to demands for Black self-determination reflected the general concerns and opposition of white communities to the FNP that would characterize popular responses to the emergence of "Black Power" in the coming years.

At the same time, some moderate civil rights leaders like Roy Wilkins offered tepid support for the FNP, demonstrating the successes of grassroots Black radicalism in shifting the scales of "acceptable" political thought and action. While stating that he "would hate to see purely racial political action in this country," Wilkins also conceded that "white people in the South have made the parties white parties, and the only logical answer for the Negro is to raise a black party."[103] Though Harlem residents, activists, artists, and intellectuals played a significant role in promoting Black nationalism at the grass roots, which prompted civil rights organizations to adopt similar political positions, Wilkins's response marked the entrance of Black nationalist political discourse into the mainstream of national civil rights leadership—even as he and others continued to publicly distance themselves from Black nationalist leaders.

Although the NOI's continued abstention from political involvement prevented Malcolm X from giving an explicit endorsement when asked for comment on the FNP, he did point toward the latent power the eight million unregistered Black voters across the nation possessed. If this massive base were activated and organized, Malcolm posited, "they would upset the entire political picture."[104] Malcolm made his position on the oppressive nature of the American political system characteristically plain at a June 1963 street rally in Harlem. "The Conservative is a wolf, he lets you know that he does not want you around. The Liberal is a fox, he pretends to be your friend," Malcolm explained to the crowd of 2,500 gathered at the corner of 115th and Lenox. "Both are dogs, and whatever the Negro chooses he is still in the doghouse."[105] Though Malcolm himself played no formal role in the organization of the FNP, his brand of nationalist thought contributed to this new direction in Black political action.

As the collective high from the March on Washington quickly receded that fall—particularly after the bombing of the 16th Street Baptist Church in Birmingham two weeks later—the FNP's national committee got to work in Harlem. In the minds of the more radical factions of the movement, and even in some of the mainstream leadership, the March on Washington had created a watershed from which organizations would need to emerge with new tactics and broader objectives, or risk losing precious momentum and leverage. From their office on 125th Street, Lynn, Wattley, and the FNP worked to move the focus of the national movement from protest to politics by coordinating a national grassroots political campaign ahead of the 1964 election cycle.

In contrast to the hierarchal status quo of the US two-party system, the national office of the FNP was designed to serve as a facilitating body, while the party's platform and policies were to be defined collaboratively at the grass roots. Worthy described his visions for the process in an article in *Liberator* in October 1963 in which he invited every reader to form "a study and action group of six to ten persons meeting regularly in homes, maintaining contact with other such groups in the same community, federating to form local committees for a Freedom Now Party, and working towards a founding congress of the new party."[106] Over the next several months, local and regional committees worked to develop a draft of the FNP's first platform.

Published by *Liberator* in early 1964, the FNP's inaugural program contained three platforms—economic, political, and cultural—to translate Black nationalist thought into political action. The economic platform contained provisions for collective ownership of multiple-dwelling housing in cities, nationalization of industries threatened by automation, a universal healthcare program, and federal aid for the "economic and cultural rehabilitation" of all Black communities. The political platform, for its part, cited the necessity of unified political action at local, regional, and national levels, flexibility and democratic participation in defining policies and programs, and the primacy of functional policies over emotional positions.[107]

The cultural platform was the most extensive and centered on a program of "cultural revolution." Likely influenced by FNP member Harold Cruse, the program uplifted African American artists and cultural institutions and sought alignment between the political, economic, and cultural aspects of revolutionary struggle—a stance that recognized the important contributions of Harlem artist-activists and anticipated the emergence of the Black Arts movement two years later. The FNP saw "cultural revolution" as the ideological basis for "healing the growing split" between nationalist and integrationist camps within the movement.[108] Through this platform, the FNP worked to build a united political front by forging a political organization capable of achieving structural changes in American society.[109]

FREEDOM NOW, MALCOLM X, AND REVOLUTIONARY NATIONALISM AT THE GRASS ROOTS

While Worthy, Lynn, and Wattley were busy building the framework for a national Freedom Now Party, Malcolm X had been actively promoting secular political action and the need for a Black united front at a series of street rallies in New York City in the summer of 1963. Speaking to a crowd of five hundred at a July rally in Brooklyn amid mass demonstrations against hiring discrimination at the construction site of the Downstate Medical Center, Malcolm renewed his calls for Black unity and announced that he would "no longer malign other black leaders."[110] Though members of the NOI did not participate in the demonstrations owing to their continued professed rejection of nonviolent direct action, a BOSS detective reported that Malcolm X "made it clear that if at any time the non-violent pickets are in need of Muslim aid they would be present to heed their call."[111] Now a year removed from Elijah Muhammad's order to stand down following the murder of Ronald Stokes, and on the heels of his bold stance in Times Square, Malcolm was once again forthright in his position on self-defense.

At the same time, he was also learning about armed resistance within Pan-African revolutionary struggles and its meaning for the Black freedom movement in the United States. At another Harlem rally in July 1963, Malcolm X was joined by Akbar Muhammad, Elijah Muhammad's youngest son, who had just returned from a semester at a university in Egypt. After Malcolm explained that Harlem's dire housing conditions were symptomatic of systemic racism, Muhammad issued a call "for unity for all black men in America and eventually for black men all over the world." Displaying a revolutionary Pan-African vision that would eventually lead to a split with his father, Akbar Muhammad informed the crowd of 2,500 that several African nations were prepared to break diplomatic relations with the United States. Muhammad reported that one of these nations was even "ready to support the black struggle in the US with money, arms, and know how."[112] Through his close rapport with leaders of newly independent African nations, Muhammad brought visions of Malcolm's earlier rhetoric about an armed African American anticolonial struggle in the wake of the Stokes murder out of the abstract and into the realm of possibility for those at the rally.

Like Mae Mallory, whose continued personal experiences with racist violence inspired her embrace of self-defense and then armed revolutionary struggle, Malcolm was pushed by the rampant state-sanctioned violence against members of the Nation of Islam and against protestors in Birmingham to support such a struggle in more explicit terms. Speaking at a street rally in early September, Malcolm chastised the co-optation of the recent March on Washington, berated the old guard leadership of the civil rights movement, and championed the emergence of younger Black leaders who were not afraid to pay the price of freedom. "You don't get freedom nonviolently, without bloodshed or by turning the other cheek," he explained to the thousand people gathered at 115th Street and Lenox Avenue. "You don't get freedom without being willing to fight for it."[113] Malcolm's call to action would take on an even greater sense of urgency a week later when a white supremacist's bomb ripped through the 16th Street Baptist Church in Birmingham, stealing the lives of four young Black girls. This revolutionary rhetoric, in turn, was attracting the attention of more militant activists who gravitated toward Malcolm X.

Coming amid a national wave of heightened militancy, direct-action confrontations, and white reactionary violence, Malcolm's Harlem street speeches that summer laid the groundwork for what would be his most significant public address to this point, at the Northern Negro Grass Roots Leadership Conference in Detroit that November.[114] The two-day conference provided generative space for a national cohort of radical grassroots organizers to collectively analyze the problems confronting urban Black communities, discuss organizing strategies, and build relationships and alliances. Though the specific conditions in their communities varied, the participants took steps toward developing a national strategy to combat systemic racism in the Jim Crow North. During a series of workshops the first day, Gloria Richardson, Selma Sparks, Dan Watts, Rev. Milton Galamison, Lawrence Landry, Stanley Branche, Jesse Gray, and others discussed and debated organizing strategies around self-defense and retaliatory violence, independent political action and interracial organizing, de facto segregation and educational justice, and economic empowerment and political boycotts.[115]

The next day, participants gathered again to lay the foundation for a national organization and to pass a series of resolutions: to build solidarity with global anticolonial struggles, support international labor organizing, organize a national boycott of schools, support the Freedom Now Party, advocate the use of self-defense, and support Mae Mallory's ongoing fight against extradition to North Carolina.[116] In addition to these resolutions, the constitution and by-laws emerging from the conference stated its continuing purpose as twofold: establishing closer ties and communication between

Northern Black grassroots organizations to reflect on lessons learned and develop strategies for the future, and advancing the principles of self-defense and uniting the "militant action forces" developing these principles into effective programs for Black liberation.[117]

The resolutions and constitution adopted at the conference illuminated how Northern grassroots organizers were pushing beyond the limits of racial liberalism and mainstream civil rights organizations in ways that offered a springboard for collective radical action and laid foundations for the emergence of the national Black Power movement.[118] They also reveal the influence of grassroots radicalism in Harlem on the national Black freedom movement, since many of the adopted resolutions were informed by ongoing struggles there and had already been informally adopted by local people over the past several years.[119] Thus, when it came time for Malcolm X to speak that evening, he was addressing an embodiment of the New Afro-American Nationalism that he and many of the other participants had cultivated in Harlem.[120]

Following addresses by William Worthy and Donald Freeman, Malcolm X ascended to the pulpit of the King Solomon Baptist Church on November 10 to the applause of the nearly two thousand people who had gathered there.[121] After reiterating his calls for a Black united front in opposition to a white "common enemy," Malcolm swiftly took up the complex topic of revolution and characteristically "made it plain" for those in the pews. Drawing from his studies of successful revolutions across the globe, including ongoing anticolonial struggles on the African continent, Malcolm distilled their lessons to offer a biting rebuke of the limited scope of moderate civil rights leaders and a charge to would-be Black revolutionaries.

According to his analysis, there was a decisive debate within the Black freedom movement between those who advocated a "Negro revolution"—a term popularized by news media to describe the escalation of the civil rights movement that year—and those who sought a "black revolution." The former represented the middle-class, liberal leadership, while the latter more closely resembled the New Afro-American Nationalism surging at the grassroots. For Malcolm, the distinctions between the two were clear in both their ends and means. "There's no such thing as a nonviolent revolution," Malcolm explained. "The only kind of revolution that is nonviolent is the Negro revolution." In real revolutions, he continued, oppressed and exploited communities did not seek integration with their oppressors. Rather, they sought self-determination by any means necessary and asserted their right to independence by claiming land through armed struggle. "A revolutionary wants land so he can set up his own nation, an independent nation," he argued. "These Negroes aren't asking for any nation—they're trying to crawl back on the plantation."[122] Malcolm's espousal of Black liberation and nation building through armed revolution marked a distinct evolution in his political thought and program. Whereas his previous speeches under the aegis of Elijah Muhammad had called for the United States, under threat of Allah's destructive wrath, to grant Black Americans monetary and territorial reparations to establish an independent Black nation, he was now suggesting that Black Americans act as their own liberators and take up the necessary tools to dismantle an oppressive society and build their own anew.

Malcolm X then invited the audience to consider what he saw as the historical roots of the division among the ranks in Black America that was stifling the emergence of a revolutionary Black united front. It was here that he most famously put forth his analogy of the "house Negro" and the "field Negro," which he had previously used on occasion. To Malcolm, the moderate leaders of the civil rights movement were the heirs of "house Negroes," who identified with their white masters and protected their interests as their own. "That house Negro loved his master, but that field Negro—remember, they were in the majority, and they hated the master," Malcolm explained. "When the master got sick, the field Negro prayed that he'd die." To Malcolm, this dichotomy between the "house Negro" and the "field Negro" was analogous to the differences between middle-class civil rights moderates and the working-class Black masses—a divergence that been playing out in Harlem over the previous decade and was now coming to characterize a broader rift within the national movement.

Driving his point home, Malcolm argued that as the enslavers of old had used the "house Negroes" to "keep the field Negroes in check," the "same old slavemaster today has Negroes who are nothing but modern Uncle Toms... to keep you and me in check, to keep us under control, to keep us passive and peaceful and nonviolent."[123] To support his claim, Malcolm pointed to the co-optation of the March on Washington by the Kennedy administration and white religious and labor groups who he argued had defanged the mass mobilization of its planned disruptive militancy. Through this analogy, Malcolm delivered his central message: the civil rights movement had run its course and it was time for a new generation—the descendants of the "field Negroes"—to forge a new path for achieving Black liberation.[124] To do so would require great sacrifice, Malcolm explained, instigating the crowd by accusing them that they were afraid to bleed. But from the pews, the voices of a new generation of Black revolutionaries rang out: "We'll bleed, Malcolm, we'll bleed!"[125]

The audio recording of Malcolm X's "Message to the Grass Roots" circulated around the country, marking the national emergence of the New Afro-American Nationalism. As they sat listening to his gripping speech that day, veteran organizers Gloria Richardson and Grace Lee Boggs noticed something different in Malcolm. "It seemed to me that he was coming just a little bit away from the sectarian kind of religion thing," Richardson later recalled. "It sounded like the preface that he always gave to those speeches was becoming more rote."[126] Richardson was now hearing firsthand what Harlem residents had noticed throughout that spring and summer. Boggs also took notice of the curt way in which Malcolm delivered his ordinarily effusive homage to Elijah Muhammad at the start of his speech. To Boggs, this seemingly trivial aspect of his powerful address was telling. "The tribute to Mr. Muhammad was so nominal and mechanical as contrasted with the passion and urgency in his 'off-the-cuff, down-to-earth chat' that I whispered into the ear of Rev. [Albert] Cleage who was sitting next to me on the platform, 'Malcolm's going to split with Mr. Muhammad.'"[127] Though Boggs had no way of knowing the impending firestorm that would embroil the Nation of Islam in the days following the assassination of John F. Kennedy and the revelations of Elijah Muhammad's infidelities, her intuition proved prescient. "After two decades of attending political meetings," Boggs later reflected, "my ear had become sensitized to the rhetorical changes that suggest that a radical political change is in the offing."[128]

Malcolm X's keynote address marked the apogee of a two-day conference that sought to reevaluate and redefine the Black freedom movement in the midst of what *Liberator* magazine dubbed "the year of violence."[129] The conference and historic speech represented a synthesis of the varying strands of Black nationalism, anticolonialism, Pan-Africanism, and revolutionary nationalism that local people and grassroots intellectuals cultivated as they sought to resist and transform the material conditions of life in the Jim Crow North.[130]

The grassroots organizing of Mae Mallory, Malcolm X, and their networks of Black radicals in the early 1960s largely marked a disavowal of working within the confines of the political system. Their contributions to the evolution of the Black freedom movement in Harlem and throughout the nation were based less on scoring piecemeal victories through policy reform than on forging, through struggle, a Black radical consciousness that would facilitate the emergence of a revolutionary force in the United States. This emphasis on militant tactics and radical imagination inspired Black communities to broaden their scope of political struggle and see themselves as part of an interconnected international revolutionary movement.[131] While both activists weathered state repression, along with the criticism of moderate, middle-class leaders of the civil rights movement and radical intellectuals alike for what they perceived as a lack of a practical program for change, these critiques failed to appreciate the formative contributions Mallory and Malcolm X made to the evolution of the national Black freedom movement in the early 1960s.

As part of a broad network of Black artists, activists, and intellectuals who fostered a radical popular culture in Harlem through street rallies, literature, music, media, and cultural fairs, Mallory and Malcolm X made profound contributions to the psychological, emotional, and intellectual liberation of Black people in the United States. While often overlooked in studies of social movements that focus on mobilizing material resources, in mobilizing the radical imaginations of Black communities, activists like Malcolm and Mallory provided the emotional and psychological catalysts for decolonizing the minds of oppressed people, thereby empowering them to engage in collective struggles for liberation.[132] Like Jesse Gray, who saw tenant organizing as a vehicle for drawing local people into broader struggles for Black liberation, Mae Mallory and Malcolm X sought to unleash the revolutionary potential of the Black masses through their radical analyses, grassroots organizing, and practical embodiment of the New Afro-American Nationalism in Harlem.

In doing so, this network of Black radical activists, artists, and intellectuals inspired the emergence of new organizations like the Revolutionary Action Movement and ACT (not an acronym) which organized young Black radicals to translate the New Afro-American Nationalism into concrete revolutionary programs capable of achieving Black liberation. At the same time, the resurgence of grassroots Black radicalism in Harlem unfolding alongside heightened political repression and racist violence also pushed national civil rights organizations like the CORE and the Northern Student Movement to change course. Thus by 1963 Harlem had become an epicenter of a seismic shift that was rapidly changing the terrain of the Black freedom movement.

6

INTERRACIAL ORGANIZING AND BLACK SELF-DETERMINATION

1960–1963

If we are successful ... in getting the support of the Black Nationalists including Malcolm X we will need to offset the impact of their participation by involving as much of the white community as possible. We are playing with dynamite. The nationalists have a stronghold in Harlem; and we may have to choose between the possibility of having them with us or against us.
—CARL ANTHONY, *1962*

If bigotry would slow down, then it might be possible to consider the argument of gradualism. The fact is that bigotry and indifference makes steady inroads into our communities and our fight must be hard, constant and effective. The Negro is like a man being strangled. We say stop the choking now, at once. You can't afford to be gradual about stopping a strangulation.
—GLADYS HARRINGTON, *1963*

AS THE CIVIL RIGHTS MOVEMENT surged across the nation in the summer of 1961, a group of Cornell University students left the scenic gorges of Ithaca, New York, to get a firsthand glimpse of what was happening on the front lines of the Northern movement in Harlem. Whereas other Northern students and activists joined the Freedom Rides into the Deep South that year to challenge segregation in interstate travel, the Cornell students were drawn to the resurgence of Black radicalism in New York City. The militant protests at the United Nations and subsequent emergence of the New Afro-American Nationalism created a gravitational pull that drew activists to Harlem as a key battleground in the national and global Black freedom movement.

As part of an initiative called "Project Understanding," the group of seven students visited Harlem to "learn from Lenox Avenue." "More than most streets in America," group member Danny Schechter wrote, Lenox Avenue had "a lesson to offer." Led by Bronx-native Schechter, the group experienced the realities of life and resistance in the Jim Crow North in Harlem. During their brief trip, the students saw churches and bars, Striver's Row and tenement blocks. They visited the Nation of Islam's Mosque No. 7 and ate bean pies while Malcolm X "spoke about soul." But the most effective teachers, Schechter reflected, were "the men who do nothing more than stroll down this broad promenade."[1]

Though a relatively minor undertaking, "Project Understanding" was part of a rising tide of concern about American racism and civil rights sweeping across college campuses. The previous year, Black students across the South had galvanized the civil rights movement with widely publicized sit-ins and ushered in a new phase of nonviolent civil disobedience and student activism. In a matter of months, these student activists were organized into the Student Nonviolent Coordinating Committee under the guidance of veteran organizer Ella Baker. SNCC's emergence from the sit-ins as an independent, youth-led grassroots organization marked a clear departure from the older bourgeois and clergy leadership of mainstream civil rights organizations. With the new decade still in its infancy, this generation of students—the age peers of Emmett Till—sparked what James Baldwin described as "a revolution in the consciousness of this country which will inexorably destroy nearly all that we now think of as concrete and indisputable."[2]

As a new wave of Southern student activism reinvigorated the civil rights movement, established organizations like CORE returned to national prominence through their active support of the sit-ins and their inception of the Freedom Rides in the spring of 1961. As part of this national campaign, the interracial organization mobilized Northern communities to engage in direct action campaigns in their own neighborhoods to support the Southern movement. As Black freedom struggles in the Jim Crow North escalated at the turn of the decade, however, Executive Director James Robinson recognized that "the Battle for Brotherhood is being lost in the great cities of the North while advances are painfully made in the South."[3] Fueled by the emergence of the New Afro-American Nationalism, this recognition revealed the need for the interracial organization to retool its programs to more effectively combat systemic racism in Northern cities.

CORE chapters quickly seized on the momentum generated by the Southern movement to wage local campaigns for fair housing, equal employment opportunities, and police reform. At the same time, local people in New York City and throughout the nation were pushing their local CORE chapters, and consequently the national organization, to adopt more radical strategies to achieve more immediate and expansive liberation in their own communities. In Harlem, specifically, Black communities saw CORE as only one possible vehicle for realizing their demands for human rights and self-determination. New York native and CORE member Jimmy McDonald expressed the way many Black residents of Harlem felt about interracial, nonviolent organizations like CORE during these years when he told an interviewer, "To hell with the way you go as long as you are on the road towards my freedom."[4]

In the wake of the Freedom Rides, another interracial organization joined CORE on the road toward Black liberation in Harlem. Growing out of a shared concern for supporting the student-led movement in the South, the Northern Student Movement drew waves of students from college campuses into Northern cities beginning in 1962. Largely organized by white college students on the pristine campuses of elite universities in the Northeast, the formation of NSM in the fall of 1961 marked the emergence of an interracial network of Northern students who saw their fate as intertwined with their Southern counterparts fighting for freedom hundreds of miles away. Drawn into the fledgling organization through its early fundraising campaigns for SNCC, most members subsequently came to see Northern cities as the next frontier of the civil rights movement. "New York is the most important city in America," Columbia University student Carl Anthony wrote in the summer of 1962. "A really dynamic student civil rights movement here would set the North on fire."[5] Like CORE, NSM quickly evolved as its members established "projects" in several Northern cities and became immersed in the Black radical traditions of communities in Philadelphia, Harlem, Boston, Detroit, and Hartford.

The evolution of both CORE and NSM in Harlem from 1960 to 1963 shows how local people shaped the emergence and direction of national organizations in ways that transformed broader struggles for Black liberation. Beginning as interracial organizations dedicated to supporting the Southern civil rights movement through fundraising and solidarity campaigns, by 1963 CORE and NSM had shifted their focus to grassroots organizing for Black liberation in the urban North. Through the active involvement and influence of local people and grassroots organizers, these organizations would transform their positions on integration, community organizing, self-determination, nationalism, and nonviolence and, in the process, emerge as leading forces in Northern Black freedom struggles.

SYMPATHY STRIKES AND CORE'S NATIONAL REVIVAL

News of the student sit-ins in Nashville, Tennessee, and Greensboro, North Carolina, swept across the nation in the early months of 1960, leaving few places or people untouched by the bold actions of young African American students willing to put their bodies on the line for desegregation and civil rights. Even in communities like Harlem, where struggles for rights and power were already in motion, the newspaper and television coverage of Southern students being attacked at lunch counters energized and inspired local people to take greater action. As the sit-ins spread across the South, civil rights organizations in New York mobilized protests of department stores like Woolworth and S. H. Kress to put economic pressure on the national chains to end their segregationist policies. Harlem became the locus for the emergence of solidarity protests in New York.

From February through October 1960, New York CORE was among a handful of organizations that led pickets, demonstrations, and sit-ins at department stores in Harlem and throughout the city. Two weeks after the February sit-ins in Greensboro captivated the nation, members of the New York and Columbia University chapters of CORE launched their first solidarity protests, often called "sympathy strikes," in New York City at the Woolworth store on the bustling corner of 125th Street and Lenox Avenue in Central Harlem. "Within a half hour the store was cleared of customers," Columbia University student and CORE picket captain Martin Smolin wrote. "Hardly anybody on this busy thoroughfare crossed our picket lines."[6] Over the next several weeks, CORE collaborated with a range of community leaders and organizations, including radical attorney and State Assemblyman Mark Lane, Mae Mallory and the Crusader Family, Congressman Adam Clayton Powell Jr., the NAACP, the International Ladies' Garment Workers Union, and Jesse Gray and the Lower Harlem Tenants Council (LHTC), as part of an ad hoc coalition to coordinate protests throughout the city.[7]

The high point of the protests came the first weekend of April, when CORE spearheaded the picketing of over eighty Woolworths across the city, culminating in a mass rally in front of the Hotel Theresa, where Bayard Rustin, Jackie Robinson, and A. Philip Randolph addressed a crowd of three thousand.[8] Though the pickets mobilized thousands and drastically reduced Woolworth's patronage in New York City that weekend, many CORE leaders saw these Northern protests as little more than a means of ending the practice of segregation in the South. "We don't want to put Woolworth stores and others out of business in the North by our picket lines," CORE field secretary Gordon Carey told reporters that weekend. "We just want to put justice in business in the South."[9]

Although its efforts in Harlem helped the national organization coerce Southern department stores and lunch counters to desegregate, NY CORE struggled to find its place within Harlem's political scene in 1960.[10] While predominantly Black organizations like the LHTC and the Crusader Family mobilized Harlem communities to join picket lines at local Woolworths as part of their broader programs for Black liberation, the mostly white demonstrators from NY and Columbia CORE were viewed as interlopers in a majority Black neighborhood. When the group of students first began walking the picket lines in Harlem that February, "many black pedestrians looked askance at the overwhelmingly white group."[11] In a neighborhood where Black nationalist rhetoric resonated from street corners and was increasingly characterizing grassroots political consciousness, white student protestors stuck out like a sore thumb.

However, through active outreach to local churches, civic groups, and politicians, NY CORE eventually managed to earn the endorsement of prominent leaders such as Adam Clayton Powell Jr., who agreed that the problem of segregation was a national issue and urged that all "American citizens interested in democracy stay out of these stores." Through their outreach and continued presence in front of multiple Woolworth stores, the NY CORE picket lines started to draw a larger proportion of Black demonstrators by the early spring.[12]

Despite the greater racial parity along the picket lines, the middle-class orientation of NY CORE's organizational policies and emphasis on respectability politics got in the way of building authentic coalitions with grassroots organizations and working-class communities in Harlem. When Jesse Gray, Horace Townsend, and the LHTC staged more raucous demonstrations at the picket line on 125th Street, CORE demonstrators confronted the LHTC leaders about the "extremely noisy" protest and their organization's "lack of discipline."[13] Although the organization scored a modicum of success in mobilizing Black communities in Harlem through their sympathy strikes, it was clear that CORE would need to reconsider its programs and policies at the local and national levels if the New York chapter was to get into step with grassroots political culture in Harlem.

In 1960 CORE grew exponentially from twenty-four to forty-nine chapters, but only a handful of chapters were outside the South, and most of these chapters were predominantly white.[14] To NY CORE member Marvin Rich, a white Army veteran who was also a member of CORE's National Action Council and its national community relations director, James Robinson's bureaucratic leadership style was inhibiting CORE's emergence as a front-line civil rights organization.[15] It also became increasingly untenable for a middle-class white man to head an organization fighting for Black equality. Rich and others in the national office understood that for CORE to build a mass movement they would need to appeal to greater numbers of Black people, specifically in working-class communities. NY CORE member Jimmy McDonald was just one of many who "resented the fact" that white men like Rich, Robinson, and field staffer Gordon Carey led the interracial organization.[16]

Things improved when James Farmer became national director in 1961. According to Rich, the decision to appoint Farmer represented the culmination of extensive internal efforts to shift CORE from "essentially a leader organization to a mass organization." More specifically, the National Action Council—CORE's governing body—realized Black leadership was vital for shifting CORE to a mass organization.[17] By hiring Farmer, a dynamic speaker with a magnetic personality, CORE sought to draw upon the successes of charismatic leaders like Martin Luther King Jr. and energetic college students who were effectively organizing Black communities in the South in the late 1950s. "Lots of things were done to make the organization more appealing to black masses," Rich recalled. Hiring Farmer to succeed Robinson "was done in part with that in mind" and represented a tacit acknowledgement of the need for Black leadership amid rising calls for Black self-determination.[18]

NEW YORK CORE MOVES UPTOWN

When Farmer became CORE's national director in February 1961, he made clear his intentions to bring the organization into alignment with the demands of Northern Black communities whose interests in Southern solidarity campaigns had waned. The twenty-year veteran of struggles for civil rights explained that the Northern chapters of the organization could not survive solely "on sympathy with the South," but needed to engage in local struggles that addressed the range of pressing needs in the North.[19] Farmer wasted little time in setting the organization's Northern agenda, telling *Amsterdam News* reporters just days after his appointment that CORE's top priorities would be "the complete wiping out of discrimination in housing" and "the end of segregation in employment" in New York City.[20] Despite the escalating struggles in the South, Farmer and others in the national office put a premium on organizing in the urban North, particularly in New York City, where CORE's national headquarters was located.

By the time Farmer dedicated the national office to open-housing campaigns in the city, NY CORE's housing secretary Gladys Harrington had already laid the groundwork. Born in Gainesville, Florida, in 1928, Harrington graduated from Florida A&M and participated in the 1956 Tallahassee bus boycotts before moving to the Black middle-class enclave of Corona, Queens, in the late 1950s.[21] A social worker by day, Harrington quickly established herself among the leadership of NY CORE. CORE member Doris Innis (née Funnyé) described Harrington as "a very strong woman" who "had a technique that was not abrasive or overly aggressive, but of making you feel she was asking you to do something important, that she had faith in you."[22] As chair of the housing committee, Harrington coordinated NY CORE's campaign to test the city's enforcement of its fair housing law by having white CORE members apply for rental units after Black applicants had been denied. In cases where Black applicants were denied but white applicants accepted, Harrington led demonstrations and sit-ins at rental offices, while also filing complaints with the city's Commission on Intergroup Relations.[23]

By the early 1960s there were two main approaches to organizing for improved housing conditions for Black communities in the urban North. The first was open-housing campaigns, an integrationist approach that sought to dismantle the personal, policy, and structural barriers that maintained and enforced segregated neighborhoods. Championed by Harrington and NY CORE, this approach was predicated on a belief that the key to ending housing inequality in New York was to allow Black families to live where they pleased. Black renters could not be as easily exploited by unscrupulous landlords and forced to live in crumbling apartment buildings because they would, in theory, have freedom of mobility that would break the slumlords' monopoly on housing.

The second approach was tenant organizing campaigns to build tenant power, improve housing conditions within working-class Black communities, and eventually gain public ownership of housing. Championed by Jesse Gray and the LHTC, the emphasis on building community power over open housing—which would displace and disperse it—was representative of the New Afro-American Nationalism surging through Harlem. This increasingly popular position rejected integration as the ultimate goal; instead, activists advocated militant grassroots organizing to develop economic, political, and social power within Black communities. Thus, whereas Harrington's mission was to break down the barriers that restricted Black residents to neighborhoods where substandard housing predominated, Gray and the LHTC organized tenants to fight for humane housing conditions as a transitional demand toward collective ownership and self-determination.[24]

Despite a handful of successes in securing housing for middle-class Black renters in Brooklyn, including housing for future NY CORE Chairman Clarence Funnyé in the summer of 1961, the impacts of CORE's open-housing drive were limited. By tailoring its organizing to suit the interests of the Black middle class, NY CORE effectively alienated working-class communities who stood to gain very little from integrated housing that they could not afford.[25] In addition, by leaning heavily on the city's Commission on Intergroup Relations to handle complaints of discrimination, CORE fell into the trap of advocating for civil and human rights through an apparatus of liberal governance that had already proven incapable of bringing forth any meaningful reforms. Yet despite these shortcomings, Harrington was influential in employing confrontational direct-action tactics, like sit-ins, to protest housing conditions—a tactic that would come to define CORE's approach to community organizing in Harlem after she was elected chair of NY CORE in late 1961.

Though the sit-in movement and open-housing campaigns of 1960 into 1961 buoyed CORE's national and local reputation, the membership of NY CORE remained dismally low. With a total base of less than fifty people, NY CORE paled in comparison to the number of members and supporters that other organizations in the city claimed.[26] In addition to the middle-class bias of their organizing efforts and protest ethos, NY CORE's bureaucratic membership policies largely discouraged active grassroots participation. Field staff were "instructed to zealously maintain CORE's tradition of 'closed membership'" by mandating that chapters restrict formal membership to "those who served a probationary period, participated in action projects, received approval from two-thirds of the chapter, and committed themselves to following the CORE Rules For Action."[27] In addition to its reputation as a white organization, this rigid membership process contributed to popular perceptions in Harlem that CORE only accepted people with a college education.[28]

Furthermore, operating out of a donated office space in mid-town Manhattan, NY CORE was a civil rights organization with no brick-and-mortar presence within the borough's largest Black community. Though many members of other groups, like the Harlem Writers Guild, Organization of Young Men, and On Guard Committee for Freedom, lived downtown or in Brooklyn, these groups recognized the importance of locating their organizational efforts in the streets of Harlem. Despite the momentum generated by the sit-ins and the minor victories scored in housing desegregation, these factors left NY CORE floundering in a city where Black communities were ready to move.

This began to change, however, when Farmer embarked on one of the most iconic campaigns of the civil rights movement. Farmer's appointment coincided with the organization's search for a new national campaign that would allow CORE to penetrate the Deep South with nonviolent direct action while launching the organization into the vanguard of the civil rights movement.[29] The same week that Harrington announced NY CORE's plans to apply the Gandhian tactics of nonviolent resistance to housing desegregation in New York City, a group of thirteen CORE members—including two from NY CORE—left the nation's capital on two buses headed South to launch the Freedom Rides. Aside from its larger national significance, this watershed campaign deeply influenced the development of NY CORE and local struggles in New York City. As with the sit-ins, the courage and brutality of the Freedom Rides energized and inspired working-class Black communities in Harlem to engage more actively in local struggles for rights and power. Whereas the sympathy strikes and other demonstrations had primarily drawn the support of white, middle-class protestors, by the summer of 1961 CORE saw an influx of working-class Black participation. A new wave of activists, who had grown disillusioned with liberal approaches to Black liberation and saw CORE as a potential vehicle for more assertive action in the wake of the Freedom Rides, steered the organization to adopt more radical objectives and use more militant tactics to achieve them in the months and years to follow.[30]

While NY CORE remained dedicated to its principles of nonviolence and integration during this period, some of its organizers sowed the seeds of Black nationalism that would flower in the coming years and cause a major rift among the New York chapters. As Farmer's appointment in early 1961 indicated, there were growing demands in New York and across the nation for Black leadership of CORE and other civil rights organizations. At the same time, NY CORE and other local chapters were fighting for the decentralization of national leadership, seeking greater representation in the decision-making process and greater autonomy for local chapters. Gladys Harrington herself expressed concern "that participation in the arm that is responsible for the day to day decisions (program and policy) of CORE by the areas and persons most affected is noticeably absent."[31] These struggles came to a head in the fall of 1961, when Harrington and former Executive Secretary James Robinson waged a successful struggle to democratize the national organization through restructuring the National Action Council.[32] These internal debates were significant, since they reflected broader demands for community control and self-determination within civil rights organizations as a means of achieving the same in American society writ large. "Perhaps, we are still in the throes of birth pains as a National Civil Rights organization and we have much to learn as well as do," Harrington acknowledged in advocating for local leadership in early 1962. "In the process, let us not lose faith with the people we are fighting with and for."[33]

Though Harrington and NY CORE struggled in 1961 and 1962 to come up with comprehensive direct-action programs that could effectively challenge systemic racism in the urban North, they did take important steps in that direction. Recognizing the need to develop new programs that would attract the active support and leadership of working-class Black communities, Harrington announced in September 1961 that NY CORE would be moving its office to Harlem. By November, NY CORE joined the NY NAACP in a building on bustling 125th Street. The branch was headed by newly elected President Percy Sutton, a respected attorney and emerging politician, who promised a "bold program" that would "give new life and meaning to the name of Harlem." In his first two months at the helm, Sutton made good on his promise by demanding more funding for Harlem Hospital, calling for the election of a Black mayor, and moving the branch office to 125th Street.[34]

To the editorial staff of the *Amsterdam News,* the close proximity of the two national civil rights organizations held the promise of a dynamic collaboration that could mobilize the masses in Harlem. "A hard-hitting youthful NAACP branch, working side by side from the same offices, with a free-swinging, two-fisted CORE unit should cause many who have been too long walking on their heels in this community to get back up on their toes again," an early November editorial predicted.[35] While Malcolm X's calls for a Black united front at this time had largely gone unanswered by integrationist leaders and organizations, the *Amsterdam News* saw the makings of a similar, if more moderate, coalition in CORE's move uptown. Though the editorial staff may have overestimated the influence of both the NAACP and CORE in Harlem at this time, they nonetheless recognized the impacts that a youthful organization that championed direct action could have on the realization of economic, political, and social justice in Harlem.

More than a symbolic gesture, the move to Harlem represented a formative moment in NY CORE's evolution as a community-based organization. "We are desperately trying to get more Negroes involved. That's why we moved to Harlem," one of the chapter's leaders said, acknowledging that most of the organization's efforts to that point had been geared toward "the bourgeois, the educated."[36] At its heart, CORE's move signaled a strategic decision to embed the organization within an emergent radical grassroots base in Harlem that had been driving Black freedom struggles in the city and beyond.

The grassroots base that CORE sought to attract with their move uptown was deeply influenced by Harlem's Black radical traditions, which in turn began to shape CORE organizers' actions. While participating in nonviolent direct-action protests, NY CORE members like Harlem native Peggy Trotter Dammond Preacely "heard Malcolm X speak at the local Muslim mosque, and we hung out late into the night at Micheaux's famous black bookstore on 125th Street."[37] In order to truly get their organization off the ground in New York City, the organization realized it would need to tap into Harlem's wellspring of Black radicalism that was informing political consciousness and action throughout New York City and the nation. In subsequent years, the very base that Harlem CORE sought to mobilize into a nonviolent movement for an open society would end up pushing the local and national organization to reconsider many of its fundamental positions on integration, self-determination, and nonviolence in the service of a more expansive program for Black liberation.

THE NORTHERN STUDENT MOVEMENT COMES TO HARLEM

By the time NY CORE made the move uptown, it had become clear that they weren't the only interracial organization being drawn to Harlem. As news of burning buses and bloodied Freedom Riders spread across the nation in the spring of 1961, stirrings among concerned college students in the North began to coalesce into coordinated action. In New Haven, Connecticut, a meeting with three Black students from Virginia Theological Seminary and College who had been involved with a sit-in campaign proved inspirational for Yale University sophomore Peter Countryman. The chance encounter with these Southern student activists "made the academic world seem pretty sterile" and moved the white philosophy major from Chicago to commit to the cause of racial equality.[38] At a conference sponsored by the New England Student Christian Movement that June, Countryman was chosen as chairman of a committee to "investigate the possibility of creating a Northern student civil rights movement."[39] The committee initially decided to coordinate a fundraising campaign to support the Freedom Riders in the South, but by October Countryman pressured the committee to pursue a more expansive program. "We felt at the time that something would have to be done about Northern problems," Countryman recalled. To truly reckon with these problems, he argued, would require forming an organization independent of the Student Christian Movement, "a Northern parallel to SNCC."[40]

That November, representatives from twenty college campuses gathered in New Haven to develop a program and structure for a national movement of Northern college students. "As students we can no longer disregard the challenge put to us by the indomitable spirit of the Southern student movement," the members of the fledgling organization declared in their founding document. "We are not free until they are free; their fight is now our fight; their burdens, ours also."[41] The first year of the fledgling Northern Student Movement's (NSM) involvement in civil rights activities was characterized by a two-pronged approach: providing support for the Southern student movement and developing programs to confront systemic racism in the Jim Crow North. By 1962 the NSM had raised $9,000 for SNCC's voter registration campaigns in the South and sent ten thousand books to Miles College in Birmingham, Alabama.[42] In addition to raising financial support for the Southern movement, NSM also understood the importance of raising individual awareness of the "urgency of the racial problem" in white communities largely untouched by the conflicts sweeping the nation.

As a Northern campus movement of predominantly white students, the NSM's initial target population was other white students who did not know racial oppression and had few ties to the Southern struggle.[43] Countryman and other NSM organizers initially understood the problem of American racism as "basically psychological" and "rooted in the individual," and therefore designed their early organizing efforts to confront racism and inspire political action on college campuses at a personal level.[44] To bring white college students off the sidelines, NSM organizers promoted a moral imperative based on their identities and privileges as college students to inspire empathy and compel students to become actively involved in the civil rights movement. Once this level of consciousness was established and mobilized, Countryman believed, students could then be organized "to concentrate on the less spectacular" problems of racial oppression in the North.[45] While hardly radical, these early efforts at raising awareness of racism among college students represented an effective entry point into local struggles in the Jim Crow North as a means of engaging in the national civil rights struggle.

Over the next several months, the emergent organization focused its energies on outreach and organizing on college campuses in the Northeast, primarily liberal arts colleges in New England, and took its first steps toward organized direct-action campaigns in the urban North. In April 1962 the NSM convened the Inter-collegiate Conference on Northern Civil Rights, drawing three hundred delegates from sixty colleges to the Bronxville campus of Sarah Lawrence College.[46] This founding convention educated students on the realities of racial discrimination in the urban North and called on the expertise of Northern civil rights leaders, such as Bayard Rustin, Kenneth Clark, Mark Lane, Paul Zuber, and Rev. Leon Sullivan, to explain how it could be effectively challenged.[47] Sullivan, a stalwart in civil rights struggles in Philadelphia and the uncle of Sarah Lawrence class president and NSM organizer Joan Cannady, spoke to students about a series of "selective patronage" campaigns he coordinated to successfully protest discriminatory hiring practices of several businesses.[48] Sullivan encouraged the students to undertake similar campaigns in their own cities, while also building more expansive programs for Black equality and liberation.

For Carl Anthony, a Black Philadelphia native and architecture student at Columbia University, the conference served as a springboard into the civil rights movement. Anthony was living on the Lower East Side with fellow Philadelphian and jazz musician John Churchville. Splitting time between the political hotbeds of the Lower East Side and Harlem, the two friends immersed themselves in the radical traditions of New York City, from communist study groups to Black nationalist street rallies. "I was in the University of the Streets and I was loving every single minute of it," recalled Churchville, who was especially inspired by Malcolm X.[49] Through these connections, Churchville learned of the Sarah Lawrence conference and invited Anthony to go with him. "It was wonderful introduction for me to the effectiveness of direct action and the power of social movements," Anthony recalled. "During the conference, I became a committed participant in the civil rights movement."[50] As did Churchville, who was recruited by SNCC staff at the conference to drive a donated bus to the organization's headquarters in Atlanta, where he stayed as a member of the field staff. While his roommate went South, Anthony immersed himself in Harlem and began laying the foundation for an NSM project there.

Emerging from the Sarah Lawrence conference with a sense of purpose, NSM members launched several nonviolent, direct-action campaigns that summer. Just north of the city in Rye, New York, one hundred students formed a day-long picket line outside an apartment complex to protest the landlord's refusal to rent to an African American family.[51] A few months later, the NSM sent busloads of students to join SNCC and CORE on the Eastern Shore of Maryland to participate in sit-ins at restaurants along Route 40 that refused to serve Black customers and to help with voter registration campaigns in Easton, Cambridge, and Chestertown—all with the broader goal of building a self-sustaining local movement through the promotion of "a community consciousness and an indigenous leadership among the Negroes."[52]

Through these experiences with direct-action campaigns, NSM organizers laid the groundwork for the young organization's growth. "We were really groping for awhile as to what we should do with Northern students in Northern areas," Countryman later reflected. Though inspired by SNCC, NSM organizers were unsure of how to apply their organizing methods in the North with a cadre of organizers whom Countryman described as "morally concerned about race" but "not political" and "without any experience at all." Eventually, they landed on an idea to bring college students into inner cities to tutor Black high school students.⁵³ The plan would create a pathway for college students to leverage their skills, privileges, and access to resources to confront the symptoms of systemic racism in public education in nearby cities. That summer, NSM field staff established tutorial programs in Philadelphia and Harlem.⁵⁴

Despite the efforts of community activists and organizers such as Ella Baker, Kenneth and Mamie Clark, Mae Mallory, and Paul Zuber over the previous decade, Black students in Harlem—and throughout New York City—largely remained in segregated, underfunded, and overcrowded schools. NSM organizers understood these persistent conditions of Harlem's schools to be symptomatic of a system that created and reinforced the institutional walls of urban "ghettos." "Our economics, our politics and our prejudiced social values are responsible for the underdeveloped ghetto," NSM organizer and Sarah Lawrence alum Kathie Rogers explained in an early position statement.⁵⁵ The fledgling NSM saw organizing to improve and expand educational opportunity as holding the potential to inspire "the awakening of the ghetto to the extent of its own power."⁵⁶

Following the lead of the Philadelphia Tutorial Project, the NSM formally launched a tutorial program in Central Harlem in July 1962.⁵⁷ A coordinating committee was formed that included Kathie Rogers, her fellow Crossroads Africa alumni and Bronx native Nan Bowe (née Murrell), and Carl Anthony, who had been working on a selective patronage campaign in Harlem that spring. Having recognized early on that any organizing efforts "must have the acceptance and active support of the community," the group began working with the Harlem Neighborhood Association, a community coalition of eighty church and civic groups, to build the organizational framework for what would become the Harlem Education Project (HEP).⁵⁸

HEP's tutorial program began that summer with a crew of twenty-five tutors recruited by NSM members from various colleges and universities and fifty Harlem students, known as "tutees." Twice a week, tutors would meet with small groups of students at the Harlem Neighborhood Association headquarters on West 133rd Street and the nearby YMCA for tutoring sessions in basic academic subjects.⁵⁹ By September 215 college students were tutoring Harlem students in biweekly sessions at five community centers. HEP also organized workshops in art, dance, and drama and launched a student newspaper called *The Harlem Voice,* which served as an important outlet for tutees like Sherron Jackson and the paper's editor Rufus K. Newlin to develop their emerging political consciousness by reporting on the national movement, local organizing work, and cultural events in Harlem.[60]

One often overlooked but vital aspect of HEP's educational programming was a series of public lectures and discussions on Black history and the civil rights movement. Prominent Black intellectuals and activists in Harlem led these weekly sessions, including scholar-activist and *Freedomways* associate editor Dr. John Henrik Clarke, sociologist Dr. Robert Johnson, and SNCC Chairman Chuck McDew. Discussions focused on "the historical and cultural heritage and contributions" of African American communities and on ongoing campaigns for rights and power led by civil rights organizations such as CORE, the NAACP, SNCC, and the NSM. These community sessions were designed "to draw the Harlem students into these activities in their own community through such action programs as voter registration projects and selective patronage campaigns."[61] Though the turnout for these sessions was generally smaller than for the tutorial sessions, the impact on the consciousness of students and tutors alike was no less significant. "They had almost the effect of a revolution on my mind," one student testified.[62] More than just a supplemental element of HEP's educational programming, these community sessions were indicative of a broader organizational focus on seeking Black liberation through educational empowerment.

INTERRACIAL ORGANIZING, BLACK NATIONALISM, AND "OPERATIONAL EDUCATION IN THE GHETTO"

The NSM's early involvement in Harlem, HEP tutor and eventual project director Andrea Cousins explained, was guided by the belief that "the power of community organization to sustain itself grows largely out of the sustained education of its constituents; and that a method of problem-solving must become part of local perspective, if that community is to become politically powerful."[63] Demonstrating the centrality of community power building and self-determination to HEP's mission, Cousins wrote that one of their primary objectives was "to bring the local population into greater control of their own lives, and consequently of the institutions which exerted power upon them."[64] Though this organizational focus on self-determination was complicated by the outsider status of many of NSM and HEP staff, the project sought the involvement of local Black leaders in organizing initiatives.

"Our idea was that the whole thing would eventually be taken over by local people," Cousins later recalled.[65]

Cousins had been introduced to the NSM as a student at Sarah Lawrence, when Countryman came to the campus "spreading the word about a northern Civil Rights Movement." Having grown up in an affluent, white liberal suburb in Connecticut, she experienced a "radical" political awakening at Sarah Lawrence that would shape her approach to organizing in Harlem.[66] During her junior year, after returning from a trip with Crossroads Africa to Guinea, where she saw Sékou Touré and learned about Marxism from peers, Cousins started volunteering at HEP's storefront office at 135th Street and 8th Avenue. There she met SNCC organizer Stokely Carmichael, who had grown up in New York City and was an occasional visitor to the office.[67]

Despite its connections with Harlem activists and its professed dedication to supporting community leadership, the interracial organization's presence in Harlem was met with a mixed reception. The NSM's arrival in Harlem coincided with a period of resurgent racial consciousness and Black nationalist organizing in the city. "Like black ghettoes throughout the country," Danny Schechter observed in 1962, Harlem "is reasserting its blackness."[68] Though Schechter was still a year away from joining the NSM, his appraisal of Harlem's rising racial consciousness and militancy closely resembled that of organizers on the ground, who expressed concern about the efficacy of an interracial organization entering this political space. Even before joining the NSM, Cousins was made explicitly aware of her place as a white woman in a political climate charged with revolutionary fervor. During her freshman year at Sarah Lawrence, she went with her African American "big sister" to a "huge African Nationalist program" in New York City where Miriam Makeba performed and Hubert Humphrey spoke. "As I was riding back on the train to Sarah Lawrence . . . she told me that when the revolution came, she would have to kill someone like me." The experience was "an eye opener" for Cousins and, though dramatic, foreshadowed real issues the interracial organization would have to navigate to organize effectively in Harlem.[69]

The realities of this racial dynamic led members of the interracial organization to engage in difficult, and often contentious, conversations about race and American society as they struggled to formulate a program for their involvement in the community. Local people often confronted NSM organizers in Harlem, including Peter Countryman, challenging their positions on integration and the assumed leadership roles of white students in predominantly Black communities. These critiques were also voiced within the NSM by organizers like Carl Anthony. At an October 1962 NSM meeting in New Haven, Anthony expressed his frustrations with having to interpret the lived experiences of racial oppression that informed Black political consciousness for his white comrades, and he criticized Countryman and others for failing to understand the situation in Harlem from the perspectives of local people. "The point that I'm trying to make," Anthony explained, "is that something is happening in Harlem which is causing black people to reject your kind of analysis. It's as simple as that."[70] Despite their frustrations with their white liberal peers, for the time being Black NSM organizers like Anthony saw their organization as Jimmy McDonald saw CORE—as a vehicle on the road to freedom. The issue at hand, however, was who was in the driver's seat.

As part of an organization with a stated goal of achieving an integrated society, NSM organizers needed to find a way to reconcile their integrationist ideals with rising demands for Black self-determination. From the outset of their involvement in Harlem, NSM organizers attempted to walk what they saw as a political tightrope. On one side, they recognized that to be successful in building programs in Harlem, they would need to tap into the ideological and programmatic base of Black nationalist groups. "For, the Malcolm X's of the generation have 'stirreth the eagles nest,'" HEP organizer Bob Knight noted, and "now it becomes our role to challenge that anger and channel that massive human resource into a sense of community."[71] On the other side, however, many organizers believed that to embrace the political zeitgeist of Black nationalism in Harlem risked alienating the moderate whites they sought to bring into the fold of the civil rights movement. "We are playing with dynamite," Anthony wrote to Countryman in 1962. "The nationalists have a stronghold in Harlem; and we may have to choose between the possibility of having them with us or against us."[72] To walk this tightrope meant that the NSM would need to develop an approach that "could encompass extreme points of view and communicate with either a nationalistic negroe [sic] or a cautious white," as one organizer put it.[73]

To work in this rocky political and organizational terrain, HEP operated under a broad ideological umbrella of building community power through education and action. During their time in Harlem, the interracial corps of tutors gained a more intimate understanding of systemic racism in the Jim Crow North and received training from veteran organizers like Carmichael, who led a training session on direct action during HEP tutor orientation in the summer of 1963.[74] Through these experiences, many tutors were inspired to take larger roles in local struggles for rights and power. "HEP has allowed me to act rather than just study," one tutor testified, "while at the same time it has made me more aware of the complexities of America's race problem and has encouraged me to look further and do more."[75] Another student who experienced a similar political awakening as a HEP tutor began working with the parents of his tutee to organize tenants to demand repairs of their building. Although the tutorial program did not present the "dramatic" mobilization of a student movement Carl Anthony initially hoped for, it brought hundreds of students into active engagement with struggles for educational justice and laid the groundwork for NSM's involvement in grassroots struggles for self-determination in Harlem.

THE SEALTEST BOYCOTT AND HARLEM CORE'S "GHETTO THRUST"

Like the NSM, Harlem CORE was also attempting to find its place in a political terrain shaped by the New Afro-American Nationalism. CORE leaders repeatedly pushed the organization to identify with the needs of working-class Black communities in Harlem. By 1962 nearly all of CORE's Northeastern branches had Black chairs, reflecting the earlier push for greater Black representation in leadership positions. Yet, the middle-class, integrationist focus of many of CORE's leaders and organizing campaigns, like the open-housing drives, had done little to win the allegiance of the working-class majority in Black communities in New York and elsewhere.[76] Recognizing this failure, local CORE leaders pushed for greater investment in mass movement building. Earlier that year the New York Metropolitan Area Coordinating Council, a confederation of CORE chapters in and around New York City, overwhelmingly endorsed a motion put forth by Long Island CORE Chairman Lincoln Lynch that the organization must make itself "more attractive to rank and file Negroes."[77] For Lynch, Gladys Harrington, and other CORE leaders in New York, the logical move to bring working-class Black communities into the fold of organized action was to address their immediate needs of fair employment opportunities and economic justice.

Though Harlem CORE had previously protested major corporations over discriminatory hiring practices, these early employment campaigns had the same shortcomings as those waged by the NAACP around this time, placing a handful of Black workers into middle-class jobs that remained out of reach to most of the community. In the end, "not one of New York CORE's employment projects brought worthwhile gains" between 1960 and 1962.[78] By early 1962, however, local struggles for economic justice and fair hiring practices were pushing CORE chapters and the national organization to reconsider their programs. In Harlem, where economic boycotts had a rich history and nationalist organizations routinely mobilized "Buy Black" campaigns, an ad hoc coalition organized a boycott of a white-owned steakhouse on 125th Street, and the nascent NSM was helping to orchestrate a boycott of a major dairy company. So when the national office announced that CORE would be taking a different line on issues of employment discrimination, its leaders were largely following the lead of Black communities that were already taking action.

CORE's first major action to end discriminatory hiring practices in blue-collar jobs came that fall, when the national office endorsed a boycott of Sealtest Dairy in New York City. Over the summer of 1962, Carl Anthony and a handful of other NSM members organized a coalition of religious, civil rights, and labor leaders to coordinate protests against the national dairy company, which employed only twelve Black and Puerto Rican workers among its workforce of 1,500 across four New York plants. When negotiations stalled in August after company representatives claimed they were "already doing everything in our power to employ qualified Negroes and Spanish-Americans," the NSM announced plans for a boycott.[79] CORE chapters in New York joined the boycott in the fall, and by December the national office threw its weight behind the campaign to win jobs for Black and Puerto Rican workers.

The Sealtest boycott provided the national office with an opportunity to test its new organizational emphasis on "compensatory hiring." "We used to talk simply of merit employment, i.e., hiring the best qualified person for the job regardless of race," field secretary Gordon Carey wrote that fall. "Now, National CORE is talking in terms of 'compensatory' hiring. We are approaching employers with the proposition that they have effectively excluded Negroes from their workforce for a long time and that they now have a responsibility and obligation to make up for their past sins."[80] CORE's demands for "compensatory hiring" during the Sealtest boycott signaled a new direction in struggles against employment discrimination in the urban North.[81]

This new direction was reflected in the demands that CORE and their allies presented to Sealtest in December. During negotiations, CORE leaders demanded that the company hire at least ten Black or Puerto Rican workers within thirty days and a minimum of fifty within a year; implement an affirmative action hiring plan to rectify the racial imbalance of their workforce; and meet with CORE representatives at ninety-day intervals to evaluate progress made toward these ends.[82] Although Sealtest representatives initially rejected these demands, the pressures CORE and the NSM put upon the company through the two-month boycott brought Sealtest back to the bargaining table in early 1963. While maintaining that its hiring practices "had not been discriminatory," Sealtest agreed to immediately hire ten Black or Puerto Rican workers and pledged to give "initial exclusive priority" in all job openings in 1963 to Black and Puerto Rican applicants.[83] Satisfied with this compromise as "evidence of the company's good faith," CORE called off the boycott in early February.[84]

The Sealtest boycott marked a turning point for CORE's national office in its embrace of more progressive programs to address systemic racism in employment opportunities. For Harlem CORE, the boycott marked the emergence of mass protests against employment discrimination that would take center stage in the city that summer. Implicit in this shift away from demands for token hiring and toward affirmative action programs was an organizational recognition of grassroots demands for systemic change, rather than piecemeal reforms. Harlem residents were increasingly unwilling to accept concessions in the form of a handful of white-collar Black workers being hired by a company while the unemployment rate in Harlem remained double that of white communities.

While the thrust for this change in CORE's approach came from grassroots efforts in Harlem, the shift was put into praxis in Harlem CORE largely through the efforts of Velma and Norman Hill. Upon arriving in New York from Chicago in the fall of 1962, the Hills sought to make CORE "more appealing to grass-roots people" through loosening membership restrictions, focusing on community organizing and local leadership, and undertaking campaigns that would benefit poor and working-class Black communities.[85] As chair of the branch's employment committee, Velma Hill pushed Harlem CORE to use the momentum generated by the Sealtest boycott to propel the chapter into greater involvement in employment campaigns as part of a broader "ghetto thrust."[86] To Norman Hill, a member of the national office's field staff, the Sealtest boycott represented a template that could be used not only to combat the "pattern of discrimination in all job categories" but also to "provide a direct alternative to the Muslims in terms of aims, programs, and results."[87]

Like Carl Anthony and the NSM, the Hills and Harlem CORE remained wary of cooperating with radical organizations like the Nation of Islam, even while they acknowledged their influence and tried to organize the same communities. As leaders of Harlem CORE continued to shift their focus to community organizing in the following months, the grassroots militancy of the working-class residents the chapter sought to recruit would push the organization to adopt more militant actions, setting the stage for dramatic confrontations with the city's power structure in the summer of 1963.

LOCAL LEADERSHIP AND THE NEIGHBORHOOD COMMONS PROJECT

While Velma Hill worked with Gladys Harrington and other Harlem CORE leaders to develop community leadership and action, the NSM began supporting hyperlocal organizing and "social action projects" to foster working-class leadership in Harlem neighborhoods through the Harlem Education Project. Like Jesse Gray, HEP organizers saw "quality of life" problems as issues that communities could be organized around, and in the fall of 1962 Peter Countryman advocated a national NSM focus on "SNCC drives, sel. pat. [selective patronage], and tutorial in one package . . . in Negro communities throughout the East."[88] Though HEP's involvement in selective patronage campaigns proved to be short-lived, the efforts provided organizers with an introduction to various leaders and organizers in the city, including Bayard Rustin, A. Philip Randolph, James Lawson, and Malcolm X, and laid a foundation for community-organizing campaigns.

While the tutorial programs remained the flagship initiative of the NSM from late 1962 to 1963, several organizers, including Carl Anthony, felt called in another direction. "There was a split," he later recalled, between those who saw the tutorials as "the main program" of HEP and those who were more interested in "direct action, political organizing."[89] While spearheading HEP's involvement in the selective patronage campaign, Anthony also began developing the organization's first social action project, the Neighborhood Commons. The project was inspired by the work of Karl Linn, a professor of landscape architecture at the University of Pennsylvania, who had been organizing communities in North Philadelphia to reclaim land razed by urban renewal projects for use as shared neighborhood spaces. From Linn, Anthony learned to notice the "hidden genius" of neighborhood residents, the wealth of underrecognized material and personal resources within communities, and the democratic practice of participatory planning.[90]

In May 1962 Anthony brought these lessons together in a proposal for the Neighborhood Commons project, which would organize neighborhood residents to transform vacant lots in Harlem into collective spaces for mutual aid, intergenerational support, and community organizing. In cooperation with Adam Clayton Powell's Associated Community Teams and the newly formed Harlem Youth Opportunities Unlimited, Anthony's proposal included plans for recruiting "indigenous leadership" through letter writing, canvassing, and working with local organizations, block clubs, churches, and community centers.[91] While soliciting community input and participation for the Commons, in the spring of 1963 Anthony, Linn, and HEP staff worked with the City Planning Commission on a survey of city-owned vacant lots to find a suitable location.[92] The location chosen for the project was a large debris-filled lot on 147th Street between Bradhurst and 8th Avenues. After gaining use of the land through the city's Department of Real Estate, HEP gained permission from landlords of buildings in the square block surrounding the lot to make use of their vacant basements and backyards for the Commons.[93]

Thinking beyond the conversion of vacant lots into pocket parks for badly needed recreational space, HEP organizers envisioned the project as a means of fostering community leadership and empowerment through active involvement in all aspects of its development. Using their connections with various community organizations, HEP staff recruited neighborhood teenagers and adults to work in cooperation with architectural students to design and build the Commons, while canvassing the neighborhood to crowdsource materials and tools to develop the lot.[94] HEP organizer Jean Doak recalled that one neighbor stole earth-moving equipment from his job to clear and level the lot, while other neighbors "had guns and they would shoot the rats that were bigger than cats." Meanwhile, Carl Anthony, his brother Lew Anthony, and other organizers worked with children in the neighborhood to build pigeon coops on the rooftops.[95] "All of their lives these people have been using their skills working for other people," Anthony told the *New York Times*, and "we want to show them what they can do if they use their skills for themselves."[96] The larger goal, then, for the Commons was not the piecemeal construction of recreational spaces but the demonstration of "how scattered resources can be brought together in a so-called 'slum community' to create a new reality."[97]

HEP organizers envisioned the Commons as a community hub where neighbors could build relationships, share visions and concerns, and develop plans for collective action. One of the fundamental goals of the project was to supplement the education of local students with practical experience in architecture, masonry, carpentry, horticulture, and commercial art to develop tools for practicing self-determination at a hyperlocal level.[98] In addition to the outdoor recreational space, HEP also renovated the unused basement-level spaces facing the lot for educational programming. By the fall of 1963, HEP was using these spaces for a science workshop where students studied and practiced game and computer theory, an office space for the Commons staff, and a photography studio, while plans were in place to establish a low-cost daycare center, music workshop, and gymnasium.[99]

Through the Neighborhood Commons project and the visibility gained from the tutorials, HEP provided a springboard for community leadership. "There was a lot of work on community organization," Andrea Cousins recalled, led in large part by Roscoe "Chick" Bradley.[100] A neighborhood

FIG 12 Members of the Northern Student Movement's Harlem Education Project gather during a block party on 147th Street between Bradhurst and 8th Avenues to launch the Neighborhood Commons project in July 1963. Clockwise from top left: Robert Knight, Carl Anthony, Lew Anthony, Bob Fletcher. (Photo, *Harlem Voice;* Walter P. Reuther Library, Archives of Labor and Urban Affairs, Wayne State University)

resident and community activist, Bradley began working with HEP in the spring of 1963 with another local resident, Earl Spence, to furnish and supervise a small gymnasium for teenage boys as part of the Commons.[101] In a few short months, Bradley established himself as the head of the 147th Street Neighborhood Council, HEP's community decision-making body, "which in democratic fashion was to determine the nature of block redevelopment."[102] Bradley's involvement with the Commons spurred a lifelong dedication to community organizing in Harlem and demonstrated that HEP's focus on local issue organizing was capable of supporting the development of local leaders. By the end of 1963, with the Commons underway, HEP moved from their storefront office on 8th Avenue and 135th Street up to a railroad apartment in a building on 147th Street that bordered the vacant Commons lot.[103] The relocation provided HEP organizers with a base within the community from which they could expand their tutoring, programming, and organizing initiatives.

This hyperlocal approach to community self-determination both reflected and contributed to the escalation of Black freedom struggles in Harlem and across the nation in the summer of 1963. As the movement evolved that summer, many HEP organizers began dedicating more of their time and resources to community organizing rather than to operating the tutorials, setting the stage for a major rift in the organization by the year's end. Though HEP and the NSM continued to organize around educational empowerment in various ways, including the establishment of Freedom Schools and support for school boycotts, the inherently limited scope of the tutorial program—critiqued by some as a "service program"—was no longer seen as a viable path toward Black liberation.[104] With the civil rights movement escalating, white violence raging in Birmingham and throughout the South, and the March on Washington looming large in public consciousness, NSM organizers felt a need to engage more assertively in the Northern struggle to achieve more immediate results. For both the NSM and CORE, this dynamic would lead organizers to launch new campaigns and form new organizations in the fight for Black liberation.

HARLEM CORE'S 1963 CONSTRUCTION PROTESTS

While NSM members and Harlem residents labored to build the Neighborhood Commons and foster community self-determination through education and organizing, Gladys Harrington and Harlem CORE sought to up the tempo of Black freedom struggles in New York City. Despite the nearly ten years of continued organizing efforts waged by local people and national organizations, few systemic changes had been won, while city officials, mainstream media, and white residents continued to preach patience and gradualism amid growing racist violence and Black protest nationwide. "If bigotry would slow down, then it might be possible to consider the argument of gradualism," Harrington told reporters in early 1963. "The fact is that bigotry and indifference makes steady inroads into our communities and our fight must be hard, constant and effective."[105]

Under Harrington's leadership, Harlem CORE grew substantially in the year leading up to the Sealtest boycott. Its active membership nearly quadrupled as the ranks began to swell with working-class Black members in the wake of the Freedom Rides.[106] Harrington earned a reputation as an effective organizer who was capable of mobilizing Harlem residents to engage in direct-action campaigns. While she remained dedicated to the principles of nonviolence and integration as the means to achieve Black equality and empowerment, her connections with Harlem's radical political culture spurred an increased militancy in her politics by 1963. Until 1962 Harrington's organizing campaigns had largely aimed at pressuring public officials to act in the interests of Black communities through moral suasion. By 1963, however, she and Harlem CORE signaled their intentions to gain economic, political, and social justice through more assertive means. "The Negro is like a man being strangled," Harrington declared in January 1963. "We say stop the choking now, at once. You can't afford to be gradual about stopping a strangulation."[107] Though she remained apprehensive about Black nationalists like Malcolm X, the influence of the popular Black radicalism he helped to shape was undeniable in her rhetoric.

The evolution of Harlem CORE's organizing became clear in the summer of 1963 in a direct-action campaign against employment discrimination at publicly funded construction projects. In the spring of 1962 Mayor Wagner announced long-awaited plans for a major construction project to renovate and expand Harlem Hospital. Promising "decent high-level medical and hospital care" for all, the city broke ground on the $48 million publicly funded project that fall as eight hundred residents gathered for the ceremonial event at 135th Street and Lenox Avenue.[108] The question of who would be employed in the projected three-year construction project was a pressing concern—particularly considering the massive public investment in the project. In a community where the unemployment rate was over twice that of predominantly white neighborhoods, few had reason to believe the economic windfall the construction project would bring to laborers in the construction trades would extend to Harlem residents.[109] The building and construction trade unions were notorious for discriminating against Black and Puerto Rican workers.[110] So when the plans were announced, many residents assumed the site would become, as the *Pittsburgh Courier* later predicted, a "beehive of skilled workers—lathers, brick-layers, electricians, plumbers, painters, etc., among whom Negroes would have been as scarce as hooded Klansmen on Seventh Ave. and 125th St."[111] In other words, Harlem residents and activists saw the Harlem Hospital project as a construction site in their neighborhood that they would pay for but not be allowed to work on.

Although racial discrimination in employment was technically illegal in New York City, the laws were laxly enforced, and it remained a particularly common practice in the construction industry. Restrictive apprenticeship training programs and union membership policies, along with "gentleman's agreements" and other forms of covert racism, skirted antidiscrimination laws and largely locked Black people out of union jobs.[112] Local 28 of the Sheet Metal Workers, for example, counted zero Black workers among its membership of 3,300.[113] When Black workers *were* hired in the construction trades, it was usually for what Dr. Kenneth Clark called "Negro jobs"—unskilled positions with "menial status, minimum wages, and little if any security."[114]

Adding to the economic anxieties and frustrations of Black workers, a study put out by the New York City Department of Labor that year predicted a decline of 70,000–80,000 unskilled and semiskilled jobs by the end of the decade.[115] In the local and national context of surging demands for Black rights and power, such economic insecurity in the face of a major publicly funded construction project that brought exclusively white workers into Harlem fueled resentment toward the hospital site. "Such a situation building up, this mass of unemployed and frustrated Negro youth, is social dynamite," the antipoverty program Harlem Youth Opportunities Unlimited warned of the dire state of the job market. "We are presented with a phenomenon that may be compared with the piling up of inflammable material in an empty building in a city block."[116] Though Harlem Youth Opportunities Unlimited was primarily concerned with what they saw as the pathological implications of unemployment in Central Harlem, the organization also noted that economic inequality had a way of drawing the community into collective struggles for equitable employment opportunities.

This was certainly the case in the summer of 1963, as a coalition of civil rights and labor organizations, including Harlem CORE, organized mass resistance to the Harlem Hospital construction in order to demand jobs for Black and Puerto Rican workers. Just weeks after police forces turned their dogs and hoses on children protesting in Birmingham, and days after journalist William Worthy called for a Freedom Now Party in Harlem, the Joint Committee for Equal Employment Opportunity announced plans to picket the Harlem Hospital construction site in early June after city officials and union leaders refused a meeting to discuss charges of employment discrimination on the project. "For years we have attempted through conferences, memoranda and interminable negotiations to make progress for Negro workers in the AFL building trades craft unions," NAACP Labor Secretary Herbert Hill declared. "This has been an exercise in futility."[117] Organizers seized on the refusal of city and labor leaders to even come to the negotiating table to mobilize collective outrage for direct action against the project.

As spokesperson for the coalition, which consisted of Harlem CORE, the NY NAACP, the Urban League, the Negro American Labor Council, the Workers Defense League, and the Association of Catholic Trade Unionists, Velma Hill (no relation to Herbert) announced that the Joint Committee for Equal Employment Opportunity demanded an immediate commitment from city officials, union leaders, and contractors "that discrimination against Negro and Puerto Rican construction workers will end." With work already underway on laying the foundation of the hospital buildings, Hill noted that of the sixty-four workers on the job, only nine (14%) were African American. Building on the affirmative action demands of the Sealtest boycott, Hill demanded that more Black and Puerto Rican workers be hired immediately to make up 35 percent of the workforce.[118]

To back up their demands with action, the joint committee canvassed the surrounding neighborhood to gauge the community's interest and investment in waging direct-action protests at the construction site. Organizers understood that their ability to put pressure on city officials and the unions relied on the active participation of local people to put their bodies on the line for jobs. Harlem CORE took the lead in distributing questionnaires door-to-door while the well-resourced Urban League contributed data processing equipment to analyze the results. "The survey indicated that we would receive strong community support for direct action at the project," CORE member Clarence Funnyé explained. While such a canvassing campaign may seem routine, it represented an important step for CORE in soliciting direction and taking leadership from the community and demonstrated how coalitions increased organizational capacities. By taking on the bulk of the ground game around the high-profile project, Harlem CORE seized on a prime opportunity to hit the streets and draw working-class people into the fold by fighting for decent jobs and membership in the building and construction trades unions in the heart of Harlem.[119]

On June 12 the Joint Committee for Equal Employment Opportunity led an interracial group of 150 protestors in an early morning picket line at the entrance of the construction site at 135th Street and Lenox Avenue. Coalition members had distributed leaflets throughout Harlem the night before, and a sound truck drove along the streets urging residents to join the picket line and shut down the construction site. Among the organizers that heeded the call that morning were Velma and Norman Hill, James Farmer, journalist Louis Lomax, and Harlem attorney Cora T. Walker. When workers arrived at the construction site around 7 a.m., they were greeted with chants of "If we don't work, nobody works" as groups of protestors sat down in front of the entrances on 135th and 136th Streets, barring workers and delivery trucks from entering the site. The predominantly white construction crew milled about outside the fenced-in site as the contractor pleaded with Herbert Hill

FIG 13 A group of protestors from Harlem CORE are surrounded by police officers as they sit down to block the entrance of the Harlem Hospital construction site in June 1963. (*The Militant/ Harlem Stirs*)

and other demonstrators to allow the workers to pass through their lines.[120] When the pickets refused to give way, police arrived and set up barricades to cordon off the protestors and keep the entrances to the site open.

With the demonstration foiled by police intervention, a phalanx of protestors broke through the barricade to block the entrance on West 136th Street with their bodies. "While the remainder of us were walking in the picket line singing that we would overcome one day," Lomax wrote, protestors "threw their bodies against the police and barricades to halt work at the hospital site."[121] As officers struggled to remove the group that had sat down to block the entrance, shoving and lifting people out of the way, reinforcements arrived, and three hundred officers flooded the intersection to keep the entrance clear by force.

Picketers shouted that the police were "working for Gov. Wallace" as officers manhandled the group of nonviolent demonstrators and shoved NAACP member Morris De Lisser up against a fence, leaving him hospitalized with head and neck injuries. The *Amsterdam News* coverage of the protest included a photo of a man lying on the ground in front of a police barricade after "being kicked and assaulted." Promising to file a formal complaint of police brutality against the NYPD, Herbert Hill said that the situation was "worse than Philadelphia," where police officers had beaten and arrested Revolutionary Action Movement (RAM) leaders Max Stanford (Muhammad Ahmad) and Stan Daniels two weeks earlier during a similar direct-action campaign against employment discrimination.[122]

Though the massive police presence broke the picket line and allowed workers to enter the site around 9 a.m., the dramatic confrontation compelled Deputy Mayor Paul Screvane, serving as acting mayor while Wagner was out of town, to warn that he would halt construction if the building trade unions "did not act immediately to end any discriminatory practices there."[123] Screvane's quick response was likely influenced by the uprisings that had rocked Birmingham a month earlier in response to police violence and racist terrorism during the SCLC's Birmingham Campaign. Following the bombings of the home of Rev. A. D. King and the A. G. Gaston Motel, which served as headquarters for the campaign, Black residents of Birmingham took to the streets to protect their community, destroy symbols of oppression, and physically challenge police complicity in the racist violence of Jim Crow.[124] Screvane's actions can be understood as measures to prevent a similar uprising in Harlem and to maintain the city's liberal image in comparison to the horrors of the Jim Crow South.

Screvane made good on his threat the following day when protests continued at the construction site. While demonstrators were back on the picket line at 6 a.m. that morning, again attempting to block the entrances to the site, leaders of the Building and Construction Trades Council met at Screvane's request to discuss the allegations of racial discrimination and develop a plan to address them. As the day dragged on, with the protestors awaiting word from Screvane on the outcomes of the meeting, the atmosphere grew increasingly tense. Several of Harlem's most notable Black nationalist leaders, including Malcolm X and James Lawson, looked on as groups of bystanders joined the demonstration, and protestors, including HEP tutee Sherron Jackson (Amina Rachman), lay down in front of cement trucks to block their deliveries.[125]

The protests were personal for Jackson, who was born at Harlem Hospital, lived a few blocks away, and walked the picket lines each day before catching the bus to school. Though only fourteen years old at the time, Jackson had already been involved with HEP, HARYOU, SNCC, and CORE, and held strong beliefs about integration and nonviolence as the pathways to Black equality. Noticing the fearlessness in the teenager's actions, Malcolm X called Jackson over and challenged her to think critically about her tactic of appealing to the moral conscience of the truck drivers by blocking the entrance with her body. Presuming that any white person had a moral conscience to appeal to, Malcolm explained, was "something that you ought to question given the history of what white people in this country have done to Black people." Malcolm's analysis of racism as an issue of power rather than morality was a revelation for Jackson. "When he left and I turned around to go back across the street to the demonstration," she recalled, "I went back and I got on the picket line but I never laid down in the street in front of a truck again."[126]

In the early afternoon, police assaulted protestors again when a group tried to barricade an open entrance to the site. Within minutes of the heavy police presence forcibly securing the entrance, however, word spread through the crowd that the construction workers had been ordered to stop, and the site was officially shut down. Screvane's order to halt construction pending an investigation over charges of discrimination was met with cheers from hundreds of protestors.[127] But despite the initial elation at the construction site, city hall's intervention was met with mixed reactions from organizers in Harlem. After conferring with Mayor Wagner, Screvane announced that the mayor would appoint a three-person committee to investigate the charges of racial discrimination in the construction industry. The move was characteristic of

Wagner's passive approach toward resolving injustice, which sought to soothe tensions in the city through commissions.[128] While Norman Hill welcomed Screvane's proposed committee investigation as "a step in the right direction," NAACP Labor Secretary Herbert Hill was less enthusiastic. To Hill, such a token response from city hall was "sheer fakery" and represented only "a further postponement for justice to the Negro worker in New York City."[129] Given the abject failure of the Committee on Harlem Affairs, formed in the wake of the 1959 "near riot," to produce any meaningful change, Wagner's government-by-committee routine was becoming increasingly threadbare.

Hill's assessment proved prescient. The mayor's "action committee," which characteristically had no representation from civil rights or community organizations, deliberated for nearly a month while the site remained closed, finally releasing a public report in mid-July. Without once using the word "discrimination," the committee's report detailed the exclusion of Black and Puerto Rican laborers in scores of construction unions in the city while lauding others for "actively trying to recruit more nonwhites." The committee offered a series of recommendations to open union membership to qualified Black and Puerto Rican workers through "voluntary compliance" from the building and construction trades unions.[130] In effect, the committee proposed that unions voluntarily desegregate with minor provisions for governmental oversight of the process—the type of resolution that seldom brought any meaningful change.

Community leaders criticized the shortcomings of the action committee's recommendations and demanded stronger action from city hall. The Joint Committee for Equal Employment Opportunity acknowledged that the mayor's committee "showed progress in thinking" but asserted that any program based on voluntary compliance remained weak and was "no substitute for meaningful action."[131] Spokesman Ramon E. Rivera announced that the joint committee would give the unions and building contractors ten days to study the recommendations of the mayor's committee and report back on how they would put the recommendations into action. If the unions failed to act, the joint committee would escalate their protests to force Mayor Wagner and Governor Rockefeller to shut down all city and state construction projects until the unions adopted a "meaningful program of integration." At the same time, the joint committee asked the mayor's committee to recommend legislative action to Wagner to force the unions to abide by such a program.[132]

While representatives of the joint committee convened with city officials and union leaders, the coalition's member organizations escalated their protests on the ground. In the second week of July, Gladys Harrington led a handful of CORE members in round-the-clock sit-ins at the offices of Mayor Wagner and Governor Rockefeller to demand legislative action for fair employment on publicly funded construction projects.[133] The sit-ins escalated to fast-ins by the end of the month, and during a forty-eight-hour fast in late July both Harrington and Bronx CORE member Tina Lawrence collapsed in the mayor's office.[134] Meanwhile, other CORE chapters used the momentum generated by the Harlem Hospital demonstrations to launch direct-action protests at publicly funded construction sites throughout the city, including the Rutgers Houses on the Lower East Side and Rochdale Village in Queens. In early July, Brooklyn CORE began picketing the construction site of the Downstate Medical Center, drawing thousands of protestors to the site and into the movement.[135]

Despite mass protests throughout the city that summer, the building and construction trades unions proved resilient in their efforts to maintain a lily-white membership while city and state officials provided little more than lip service to challenge their intransigence. Though over two thousand Black and Puerto Rican workers submitted applications for union membership to the City Labor Department by the end of the summer, only ten Black workers were accepted into construction unions by October.[136] This paltry number defied predictions made by the city's labor commissioner weeks earlier that at least six hundred Black and Puerto Rican workers would be admitted during this time.[137] Denouncing such dismal progress as "tokenism at its very worst," Gladys Harrington called for "a renewed attack on this shameful situation," and Harlem CORE began protests at the construction site of a new federal office building in Foley Square that fall.[138]

Taking place just blocks from city hall, the Foley Square demonstrations marked an escalation of protest tactics as well as police repression. Harrington and two other Harlem CORE members were arrested for climbing atop a crane to halt work on the construction site, just days after police brought out their mounted unit to forcibly suppress nonviolent protests there.[139] After more than a week of daily actions and police assaults on protestors at the site, Harrington led a two-hundred-person march from Harlem CORE's 125th Street headquarters to city hall to protest continued inaction from the mayor. Joined by another hundred marchers from Brooklyn, the eight-mile march culminated in a rally at city hall, where seven hundred people listened to speeches by Percy Sutton, James Peck, Mark Lane, Lincoln Lynch, and SNCC Chairman John Lewis, who called for the "mass nonviolent overthrow of segregation and racial discrimination."¹⁴⁰ The march and rally at city hall represented an impressive convergence of local and national civil rights leaders in New York City and marked an apex of sorts for the four months of dramatic protests against the construction industry in the city.

Such impressive mass action, however, failed to bring about the jobs, union memberships, and affirmative action policies Harrington and the joint committee demanded. When Mayor Wagner ordered work to resume on the Harlem Hospital project two weeks later, eleven of the sixteen workers onsite were African American, but neither city hall nor the Building and Construction Trades Council had agreed to any meaningful change in employment policies or practices, referring only a hundred out of 2,672 applicants for apprentice or journeymen positions in the unions. Again denouncing these limited gains as "tokenism," the joint committee objected to the resumption of work without a more systemic commitment to affirmative action policies from labor leaders and city and state officials.¹⁴¹ Mayor Wagner's characteristic insistence on gradualism, refusal to act on progressive demands to address employment discrimination, and deployment of the NYPD to suppress direct-action protests would lead organizers to embrace more radical strategies in their struggle for economic justice in the months that followed.

Though the dramatic protests that the Harlem Hospital demonstrations inspired fell short of winning equitable hiring in the building and construction trades, they nonetheless had profound impacts on the Black freedom movement in New York City. By the time work resumed on the Harlem Hospital site, the 151-day shutdown had cost the city over $75,000 ($774,000 in 2024 dollars), demonstrating to city and state officials the economic costs that continued racial inequality could incur.¹⁴² Furthermore, the confrontational tactics represented an escalation of protest activities throughout the city. Whereas national CORE leaders counseled local pickets during the "sympathy strikes" of 1960 to remain peaceful and orderly and to not obstruct businesses, by 1963 local people had pushed CORE leaders to adopt more assertive tactics, including civil disobedience and physical resistance to police intervention, to force physical confrontations and win concessions from businesses, unions, and city government. Organizers also came to realize the political power of shutting down public infrastructure and the potential of using this strategy to disrupt the functioning of the city to achieve more radical demands.¹⁴³

This escalation in tactics coincided with a fundamental shift in CORE's demands in the early 1960s. While CORE in 1960 wanted to create an "open society" by breaking the color barrier in employment or housing on a case-by-case basis, by 1963 Harlem CORE and other local chapters were forcing the national organization to adopt programs to organize community power within predominantly Black neighborhoods and demand more systemic changes in employment, housing, and policing. Inherent in this organizational evolution was a growing identification with the more radical demands of working-class Black communities in New York City. "What would have been big gains a year ago no longer are regarded by the rank and file," Velma Hill said in early 1964. "The result is a problem, restiveness among the members. They want to demonstrate if we do not get even bigger victories."[144]

At the same time, Harlem CORE's growing Black grassroots base brought the interracial organization into the fold of militant struggles for human rights, self-determination, and political power—the hallmarks of the New Afro-American Nationalism and later the Black Power movement. By the end of the summer, Gladys Harrington was calling for a Black united front at Harlem rallies with Malcolm X, Dan Watts, Bessie Phillips, and Cassius Clay (Muhammad Ali), and by the end of the year Left and nationalist members of Harlem CORE would split to form a more radical chapter.[145]

In the Northern Student Movement, the rising tide of Black radicalism in Harlem fostered the political development of Harlem Education Project organizers, who became acutely aware of housing conditions and started organizing tenants, while tutees like Sherron Jackson began working with Jesse Gray's Community Council on Housing (formerly known as the Lower Harlem Tenants Council) through her involvement with HARYOU's Leadership Training Workshop. The Harlem Hospital protests also proved transformative for Jackson, whose discussion with Malcolm X that summer inspired her to renounce her earlier positions on integration and nonviolence. While she maintained her relationships with HEP and HARYOU, by September Jackson was sharing a stage with Malcolm X at Harlem rallies, calling for Black people to unite "in the world wide revolution" and "stop turning the other cheek and fight force with force."[146] The budding relationships between HEP and radical grassroots organizers like Malcolm X and Jesse Gray also spurred the emergence of a new wing of the NSM, known as the Harlem Action Group, which would play a vital role in the emergence of a citywide rent strike that fall.

As the groundswell of Black radicalism was pushing the NSM to reconsider its mission and priorities, rising calls for Black self-determination made white leadership of the organization untenable—as CORE had concluded two years earlier. In September 1963 Peter Countryman stepped down from his post as national director to return to Yale and was succeeded by Bill Strickland, a Black Harvard graduate, Marine Corps veteran, and old friend of Malcolm X.[147] Coinciding with HEP's immersion in more radical grassroots organizing initiatives in Harlem, Strickland's arrival on the scene ushered in a new era for the NSM in New York and the nation. "It is becoming increasingly evident that 'civil rights' is no longer either an adequate term or an accurate description of the quest for full freedom which is now challenging our society," Strickland told a crowded conference at Columbia University that October. "It is also evident that an institutionalized system of disadvantage provokes just as dangerous a reaction in the overcrowded and under-resourced northern ghetto as in the more publicized and tragic south."[148] Strickland's stirring speech illustrated the systemic analysis of Northern racism that both NSM and CORE members alike had developed through their experiences in Harlem by 1963. Confronting this system through a grassroots movement for human rights and self-determination would require new ideas and bold programs, which would bring NSM and CORE to the front of Harlem's flowering radicalism as the city headed into what would be the most explosive year of an already turbulent decade.

7

RENT STRIKES AND REPRESSION

1963-1964

> People ask me why I spend all my time on heat and hot water and I say heat and hot water is the biggest organizing tool we have; it may even kick off the revolution in the ghetto.
> —JESSE GRAY, *1964*

IN EARLY DECEMBER 1963 New Yorkers tuned in to their local CBS station to watch an "examination of the Negro Revolution as it exists in Harlem." While the dramatic protests and violent backlash that surged throughout the South that summer commanded the attention of most national media outlets, the rising grassroots militancy in Harlem had drawn the gaze of the nation to its most famous Black community. "Instead of focusing on the Southern race problem," executive producer Fred W. Friendly stated in a press release, "The Harlem Temper" was intended to depict struggles for rights and power in Harlem "as a microcosm of the Negro in the North."[1]

The televised report opened with scenes of Black people walking about the sidewalks of a bustling 125th Street and gathering around stoops on residential blocks, while white reporter Harry Reasoner described the "invisible barriers of prejudice" that created "some of the worst of city slums." Most Americans were familiar with racist oppression in the South, having seen on the news "whites only" signs, police dogs set upon nonviolent protestors, and the destruction of Black churches, but far fewer understood the problems of Northern "ghettos" as part of a national system of institutional racism that knew no geographic bounds. If racial injustices existed in a Northern community where "full legal equality ... ostensibly already exists," Reasoner posited, then "how do we achieve real equality?"[2]

Through footage of Malcolm X, Lewis Michaux, and Adam Clayton Powell Jr. speaking forcefully at street rallies, and formal interviews with Jesse Gray, Gladys Harrington, Paul Zuber, and Thelma Johnson, among others, the hour-long program explored this question through the voices of those who had spent years in search of an answer. While "The Harlem Temper" aptly presented the breadth of political thought and action in Harlem, however, its producers and reviewers were critically mistaken in their conclusions that such a diverse political culture precluded collective action. "The kaleidoscope of opinions and impressions was so diverse as to create a canvas of total negation," a *Boston Globe* reporter noted.[3] Though seemingly irreconcilable, these debates around nonviolence, integration, nationalism, and self-defense were vital in forging a mass movement in Harlem as organizations searched for ways to achieve Black rights and power.

Although conflicting visions of the means and ends of Black liberation routinely hamstrung the development of united front formations in the early 1960s, by the time the CBS report aired in late 1963, interorganizational coalitions had emerged around various protest campaigns with much greater frequency. At the insistence of local people and activists, relatively moderate middle-class organizations like CORE and the NAACP embraced working-class community action and entered the fold of militant grassroots organizing. The Northern Student Movement similarly moved from service-oriented tutorial programs to community organizing for political power. And Malcolm X, as he escalated his calls for united action for Black liberation that summer, shared the stage with a diverse array of Black leaders, from staunch integrationist Gladys Harrington to radical anticolonial editor-activist Dan Watts.

These leaders' very different organizations now shared a common overarching goal: the immediate liberation of Black communities in the United States. To James Haughton, chair of the NY NAACP's Labor and Industry Committee, this nascent unity reflected a common recognition that the organizations that claimed to represent the people's interests must reflect their demands. "It's a matter of what the Negro people are demanding," Haughton said, dismissing questions about the supposed dichotomy between integration and separation in the Black freedom movement. "It's my understanding that they're neither demanding total separation, which is Malcolm's position, nor are they demanding total integration. They're demanding total equality."[4]

In the fall of 1963 these demands for total equality became manifest in a citywide rent strike that emerged from the grass roots in Harlem and galvanized local people, community groups, political leaders, and civil rights organizations throughout the city and across the nation. For Jesse Gray, whose radical organizing in Harlem bridged the Left-led movements of the post–World War II era with the radical insurgencies of the civil rights movement, the rent strikes served as a great unifying force. "Everybody in the community was around the basic struggle," Gray later said, "struggle unifies the community."[5] By centering the needs of some of the most economically exploited and politically oppressed communities in New York City, the rent strike movement of 1963–64 drew Black working-class communities into the forefront of a radical mass movement in Harlem.

Over the previous decade, working-class Harlem residents fueled the escalation of protest activity and demands for human rights and self-determination that pushed local and national civil rights organizations in more assertive radical directions. Inspired by Harlem's deeply rooted Black radical tradition, along with national and global liberation struggles, local people developed a revolutionary consciousness through the rent strikes, which stimulated the makings of a promising, if shaky, Black united front in Harlem. This chapter examines the emergence, evolution, and impact of the Harlem rent strikes of 1963–64 within the context of escalating demands of New York's Black and Puerto Rican communities for immediate rights and power. Through the rent strikes, thousands of working-class Black and Puerto Rican New Yorkers mobilized for racial justice in the city's economic, political, and social institutions. In response, the city government and its police force met this emerging movement, centered in Harlem, with increasingly repressive actions and policies. This dogged resistance to Black empowerment, in turn, spurred grassroots organizers to adopt more militant strategies and tactics as they fought to secure human rights and self-determination in Harlem and throughout the city.

THE REBIRTH OF THE RENT STRIKE MOVEMENT

If the March on Washington in late August 1963 had provided a sense of optimism and hope for many African Americans who looked forward to the promise of federal civil rights legislation, the bombing of the 16th Street Baptist Church in Birmingham just two weeks later tempered any sense of elation. Describing the racist attack as "one of the American answers to the march," James Baldwin and march organizer Bayard Rustin swiftly announced plans for nationwide mass demonstrations to protest the seemingly endless violence in the South. "It is not enough to mourn the dead children," Baldwin declared from Harlem. "What we must do is oppose and immobilize the power that put them to death."[6] Joined by Blyden Jackson of Harlem CORE, Baldwin and Rustin mobilized the collective anger throughout New York City into a protest of ten thousand New Yorkers at the federal courthouse in Foley Square one week after the deadly terrorist attack in Birmingham.[7]

In his widely published essays of the late 1950s and early 1960s, Baldwin had demonstrated a deep concern for explaining and analyzing the human impacts of racial discrimination in education, employment, policing, and housing in Harlem. Now, after the grisly murder of four young Black girls in Birmingham, Baldwin urged New Yorkers to confront these local manifestations of the same violent, national system through a "mass campaign of civil disobedience." "What would happen," Baldwin asked the crowd at the Foley Square protest that Sunday afternoon, "if Harlem refused to pay the rents for a month?"[8] Seemingly unbeknownst to Baldwin, a small group of tenants nine miles uptown had begun doing just that.

The notion was not a new one in Harlem, where rent strikes had been a staple of Left-led tenant movements during the Great Depression before reemerging with Jesse Gray's strikes in 1959. By the summer of 1963 rent strikes were once again creeping into the minds of Harlem tenants as city hall proved unwilling to enforce hard-won housing policies secured through tenant organizing over the past several years. Just weeks before the March on Washington, Gray threatened a strike at a 117th Street rally, urging the residents of the block's crumbling tenements to march on city hall and tell the mayor that "we are not going to pay any more rent on these blocks until the violations in our homes are corrected."[9] Called under the banner of "Civil Rights and Tenants Rights," the rally was one of three Gray and the Community Council on Housing (CCH) organized in lower Harlem that month, drawing the likes of Malcolm X, March on Washington organizer

Anna Arnold Hedgeman, former Borough President Hulan Jack, attorney Cora Walker, and Assemblyman José Ramos-Lopez. Sharing the stage with these formidable Harlem leaders, the CCH called for "stiff fines and long jail terms for landlords who refuse to obey the law."[10] With the March on Washington looming large in public consciousness, the rallies attempted to draw tenants out of their buildings and into the fold of organized political action by explicitly linking tenants' rights with civil rights.

While Gray organized tirelessly in his lower Harlem neighborhood, members of the Northern Student Movement (NSM) also moved into the field of tenant organizing that summer. Dissatisfied with the limited scope of their Harlem Education Project's (HEP) tutorial programs, several organizers wanted to develop local leadership and spur autonomous community action.[11] Inspired by the conditions they saw around them and the successes of SNCC in working with local people to build community-led movements, NSM members immersed themselves in tenant organizing in Harlem.[12] Like Jesse Gray and Jack O'Dell, NSM members saw Harlem tenements as the next frontier of the Black freedom movement.

By early July HEP workers had begun conducting housing surveys in the neighborhood near their office on 8th Avenue between 136th and 137th Streets. While canvassing the neighborhood, HEP organizers met Granville Cherry, an unemployed shipping clerk who lived in a railroad apartment at 2560 8th Avenue, just a few doors from the HEP office.[13] The apartment Cherry shared with his pregnant wife and six children was riddled with code violations, including broken windows, a broken toilet, crumbling walls, a leaking ceiling, and a horrible rat infestation.[14] To Cherry and the other tenants, these conditions were not isolated but rather symptomatic of racist oppression and exploitation in the Jim Crow North. "They believe," the *New York Times* wrote of the tenants, "that their troubles arise directly from the opportunities for exploitation that a racial ghetto affords white owners."[15]

Frustrated by the unchecked exploitation of their landlord, Daniel Fardella, an Italian American Bronx resident who collected rent but provided no services or repairs, Cherry formed a tenants council with the assistance and encouragement of HEP organizers. While Cherry organized his neighbors, Bob Fletcher and the HEP staff served as liaison between the tenants and landlord in an attempt to negotiate repairs of the building.[16] After two meetings with Fardella failed to bring any improvements, the newly formed tenants council decided to withhold their rents and make the repairs themselves.

When Fardella objected to the tenants repairing his building, the tenants council officially began a rent strike in September.[17] Garnering front-page coverage in the *New York Times,* the tenants of 2560 8th Avenue cranked up the heat on a simmering tenant movement and answered Baldwin's challenge in a resounding way.[18]

THE RENT STRIKE SPREADS

Within a matter of weeks, the rent strike scored immediate victories for the tenants and launched grassroots tenant organizing into the forefront of civil rights activity in the city. After Fardella failed to evict the tenants through court proceedings for nonpayment of rent, the city's Rent and Rehabilitation Administration (RRA) ordered a rent reduction in mid-October until the landlord resolved the violations in the building. Cherry and his neighbors had their rents reduced from $34 to $1 per month, thereby slashing the landlord's monthly revenue from the nine apartments in the building from $969.43 to $9.[19] While the tenants claimed victory against their landlord, believing the rent reductions would compel him to make the necessary repairs, the city patted itself on the back for resolving the issue and curbing the rent strike. Informing the *New York Times* that the rent strike was made "academic" by the rent reduction, the RRA pushed the narrative that tenants need only work through the prescribed channels of governmental agencies to solve their housing issues.[20]

If the RRA thought they dodged a bullet by ordering rent reductions, any sense of relief was dashed as word of Cherry's rent strike spread throughout the city. In a sermon at Abyssinian Baptist Church just days after the front-page article in the *Times,* Rep. Adam Clayton Powell Jr. celebrated the reemergence of the rent strikes and other economic protests in Harlem. "The way to make a man holler is to withhold his dollar," Powell declared from the pulpit, harkening back to the Left-led rent strikes and boycotts in Harlem during the Great Depression. Speaking at a press conference after the service, Powell announced that he would meet with James Baldwin that week to discuss plans for a national rent strike. Drawing on his own experience of leading a rent strike in Harlem in the early 1930s, Powell suggested that such a movement "is a good method of getting Northerners into the black revolution."[21]

While Powell used his pulpit to call for a national movement, "rent strike fever" was spreading rapidly throughout New York City. As word of Cherry's successful rent strike got out, other renters began organizing their own buildings to join the burgeoning tenants council. Just days after the RRA ordered the rent reductions, Mary King and Rita Jackson approached Cherry with a list of tenants in their buildings on the other side of 8th Avenue who were interested in joining the council. Like Cherry, the two Black women complained of gaping holes in the walls and ceilings, broken toilets, leaking pipes, fire hazards, and rats for roommates. "I wish I was the judge, I'd send the landlord to the electric chair," the superintendent of Jackson's building at 2577 8th Avenue told a reporter from the *Daily Worker*. "I'd do worse than that," Jackson followed, "I'd let him live here."[22] Inspired by Cherry's success, the two women worked diligently over the next several months to organize their buildings and expand the budding rent strike.

The *Daily Worker* heralded the organizing efforts of King and Jackson as evidence that "a fuse has been lit . . . by the rent strike victory," a flame that was spreading to other parts of the city. In early October Brooklyn CORE Chair Oliver Leeds threatened a rent strike in Bedford-Stuyvesant if tenants' demands for repairs were not met.[23] On the Lower East Side, NYU CORE and Mobilization for Youth, a social agency formed two years earlier to combat juvenile delinquency and organize working-class Black and Puerto Rican communities, both shifted their focus from service-based housing clinics to organizing tenants for collective action.[24] Uptown at Harlem CORE, which had established a housing clinic in December 1962, the housing committee moved away from conducting independent building investigations and toward organizing tenants associations "to confront landlords with 'direct action,' including pickets and rent strikes."[25]

This new emphasis on tenant organizing over open-housing campaigns was reflective of a broader trend in the city's Black freedom movement toward grassroots organizing and building community power for self-determination in Black and Puerto Rican communities. The embrace of housing as a primary vehicle through which community power could be mobilized was a direct recognition and outgrowth of Jesse Gray's decade of radical grassroots organizing in Harlem. Though Gray may not have organized the first rent strike of 1963, he had meticulously tilled the soil from which it grew.

In addition to sparking a mass mobilization around tenants' rights in the city, the birth of the rent strike on 8th Avenue proved an immediate boon for the NSM in Harlem. In Cherry, the NSM found the local leader they were looking for to jump-start a movement around housing. "He was articulate, he was committed, he was a hard worker, he was willing to take initiative, and distribute leaflets and talk to people," organizer Danny Schechter later recalled.[26] NSM organizers saw in Cherry's tenants council the potential for building a much broader social movement. "The real significance of this project," the *NSM News* reported that fall, "is that it indicates that the NSM philosophy of community action, community-led, is workable."[27] Cherry's emergence as a local leader lent the NSM "a kind of legitimacy," Schechter explained, through having "somebody in the neighborhood" emerge as a leader in a campaign swiftly spreading throughout the city.[28]

Cherry and NSM staff moved quickly to establish a new group dedicated to the grassroots organizing the rent strikes exemplified. Within a few short weeks, the ranks of Cherry's tenants council had grown to include a volunteer secretary and fieldworker, with plans to involve the neighborhood to a greater extent. The council also spurred the creation of the Harlem Action Group (HAG), an organization under the NSM umbrella dedicated to community organizing and political action. Operating out of the former HEP office at 2564 8th Avenue, the emergence of HAG through the rent strikes represented the culmination of simmering desires of organizers to move beyond the NSM's tutorial projects into more assertive direct-action campaigns. In mid-October, Cherry also announced the tenants council would be opening an office near the Neighborhood Commons at 307 West 147th Street "to continue and broaden the fight."[29]

In the following weeks, HAG staffers, including Bob Knight, Q. R. Hand, Jim Finch, and Julian Houston, used the momentum generated by Cherry's strike to expand their grassroots organizing efforts and bring more tenants into the fold of the rent strike. Going door-to-door in the neighborhood, HAG organizers distributed hundreds of leaflets to inform tenants of Cherry's recent victory against his landlord. Featuring newspaper coverage of Cherry's success alongside a photograph of a Black woman holding her young daughter in a crumbling apartment—a familiar scene for residents in many of the buildings they canvassed—the HAG flyers read, "2560 8th pays $1 a month rent so can you."[30] By the end of the month, HAG workers helped Mary King and Rita Jackson organize their buildings to formally join the collective rent strike.

THE CCH JOINS THE STRIKES

While HAG, CORE, and other civil rights organizations in New York began to focus their energies on tenant organizing, Gray and the Community Council on Housing (CCH) worked feverishly to capitalize on the sudden widespread attention on housing their ten years of groundwork had finally wrought. Though the CCH had not yet declared a rent strike, Gray and his small but committed group of organizers used the momentum from Cherry's strike to organize more buildings in their lower Harlem neighborhood.

At the same time, the CCH leveraged this increased attention to make more expansive and immediate demands on the city's power structure. Gray escalated his plans for a mass march on city hall in October 1963 to demand that the mayor "either order the courts to mete out stiffer penalties or invoke the receivership law" to rectify the rampant abuses of Harlem slumlords.[31] To drum up support for the march, the *Pittsburgh Courier* reported, CCH members conducted a month-long "house-to-house canvas of every building from 110th to 118th Streets from Park Avenue to Morningside Avenue to discuss with tenants the problems they face as a result of the neglect of landlords."[32] This diligent organizing work was necessary to help tenants overcome apprehensions about taking action against their landlords. In a city with a vacancy rate around 1 percent, many tenants had good reason to be wary of crossing their landlords and risking eviction. While some tenants were hesitant, others were eager to take action. At a CCH meeting in early October, tenants from 116th Street and 146th Street voted to withhold rents until all violations in their buildings were repaired.[33]

Despite CCH members' willingness to strike, Gray remained focused on coordinating that month's march. Gray's hesitation to launch a strike amid the tempting opening created by Cherry and HAG was indicative of his larger strategy. Rather than attempting to force slumlords to repair buildings in piecemeal fashion, Gray sought to coordinate a mass tenant movement to compel city authorities to undertake a mass rehabilitation of Black and Puerto Rican communities. Gray understood the inherently limited scope of targeting individual landlords for building repairs. Though these struggles were important in winning tangible victories for tenants, they required long, diligent organizing efforts to wrangle shiftless landlords and apathetic city agencies, efforts that seldom achieved the systemic change Gray envisioned. For a veteran organizer with radical visions for housing justice as a pathway to Black liberation, systemic problems required systemic solutions. Thus, by the fall of 1963 Gray increasingly focused his rhetoric and organizing on city hall, rather than individual slumlords. "The Harlem tenants," Gray told reporters in mid-October, "hold Mayor Wagner primarily responsible for the court's asserted coddling of slum owners."[34] By targeting the mayor, and thus personifying a complex system, Gray effectively challenged tenants in Harlem to develop a more systemic analysis of the broader power structure in New York City.

Gray's strategy brought some action from city hall. A week before the planned march, Mayor Wagner issued an alarming, if unsurprising, report on a recent wave of housing inspections conducted by the Department of Buildings. During what Commissioner Harold Birns described as the first "cellar-to-roof inspections in which every building on a block was visited," the department found forty thousand violations in 2,647 buildings in Harlem, Bedford-Stuyvesant, and the South Bronx. Of these buildings, 833 were referred for court action, 357 were recommended for rent reductions, and 50 were referred to the city's receivership process.[35] Whereas previous inspections in these same neighborhoods had only found four thousand violations, the dramatic tenfold increase revealed the severity of the housing crisis, along with the insufficiency of city resources dedicated to inspections and code enforcement.

With the housing crisis now a political fact, Gray and the CCH demanded the mayor "cut rents on buildings where there are violations, take over those buildings immediately and make repairs of the violations," all while inflicting stiffer punishments on recalcitrant landlords. Additionally, Gray told reporters the CCH would ask the mayor to establish a "non-biased, three-man arbitration board" to handle tenants' cases and to enforce the hard-won 1962 receivership law to order the city takeover of slum buildings "for rehabilitation at once."[36] For Gray, the expansion and swift enforcement of the receivership law was key to expediting repairs and improvements, because it empowered city authorities to circumvent intransigent landlords by completing repairs and billing landlords for the cost.[37] Significantly, Gray also saw the law as a transitional demand toward collective ownership of housing and self-determination for Black communities.[38] While working toward this longer-range program, Gray also told reporters after the mayor issued his inspection report that "what we want is action. Now."[39]

Wholly unimpressed by the inspection report, Gray led the planned march on city hall a week later. Though for two months he had predicted two thousand tenants would join in the protest, only two hundred showed up on a cold, rainy Monday afternoon. The protestors who did brave the weather spent three hours outside city hall, where they distributed leaflets listing the 110 buildings in lower Harlem that required immediate action and called on the city to take over every single building on 117th Street from 5th Avenue to Madison Avenue.[40] Despite the relatively low turnout, the protest served notice to city hall that tenants in Harlem made no distinction between tenants' rights and political power. While Gray met with the mayor's executive assistant inside city hall to present CCH demands, protestors outside chanted, "No action in '63, no votes in '64," sending a warning to Mayor Wagner that they were prepared to take their protests to the polls in the upcoming election year.[41] Returning to the crowd after his meeting, Gray made the point more explicit. "The Wagner Administration has proved that it is unable to handle the housing problem and we don't want him to come to Harlem next year to ask for votes."[42] Later that week, Gray announced plans for another demonstration at the City Housing and Redevelopment Board to continue pushing CCH's demands for the city takeover of all buildings on 117th Street, as well as the formation of an arbitration board. "We're tired of inspections. That's all they do in Harlem," Gray said at a meeting at the Dunlevy Milbank Community Center on West 118th Street. "We don't want inspectors. We want action!"[43]

As city hall floundered, tenants took action just days later when November rents were due. On the first of the month, HAG organizers announced that thirty-six tenants in the two buildings that Mary King and Rita Jackson had organized, across the street from Granville Cherry's apartment, had gone on strike.[44] Further downtown on the Lower East Side, NYU CORE announced that 110 tenants in six buildings had gone on strike after months of fighting for repairs through city agencies and the courts.[45] Three days later, the CCH followed suit when forty-five tenants in three buildings neighboring its storefront office on East 117th Street announced that they too had gone on strike. Though the CCH-organized rent strikes began with meager numbers, Gray predicted rapid growth. By the following weekend, Gray claimed, twelve more buildings would be on strike and by December the total number of buildings participating in the rent strike would eclipse a hundred.[46] Gray had his finger on the pulse of the community and felt that the people were ready to move. According to participant-observer Mark Naison, it was the "growing militancy" of the CCH's rank and file at meetings and protests over the previous weeks and months that prompted Gray to finally launch the strike in early November.[47]

THE EMERGENCE OF THE RENT STRIKE MOVEMENT

Bolstered by the participation and leadership of the CCH, the rent strikes quickly evolved from scattered actions to a coordinated movement by the beginning of December. Although more buildings had been on strike on the Lower East Side in early November, the CCH's organizational strength and charismatic leader quickly helped to establish Harlem as the epicenter of the rent strikes as tenants there joined in droves. Inspired by striking Harlem tenants, civil rights organizations, housing advocates, and civic groups throughout the city moved to organize their own communities to engage in rent strikes. Flyers distributed by the Metropolitan Council on Housing were illustrative of the rent strike fever that was spreading throughout the city: "IT'S TIME FOR US TO STRIKE BACK!" the flyer exhorted. "Harlem tenants organized rent strikes and are getting results. WE CAN DO THE SAME."[48]

Within a week of the CCH's involvement, the rent strikes drew the support of CORE's national office, which had previously kept Gray and the strikers at arm's length. "The rent strike has proven an effective weapon," James Farmer now told the *Amsterdam News* in early November, urging that "more of them should be employed by tenants having problems with indifferent slumlords."[49] Uptown, Harlem CORE's new chairman, Marshall England, threw his chapter's support behind the strikes as well. "We have talked with landlords, begged landlords and have met with a number of city agencies," England said in early December, but "so far the result has been nil." Calling for "massive rent strikes" in Harlem and Bedford-Stuyvesant, England argued that only "when the landlord is faced with no rents, then we get some action."[50]

Heralding the emergence of "a new and major weapon in the civil rights fight," the *New York Times* reported on December 1 that sixteen buildings were on strike in Harlem. At a community meeting called by the CCH at the Milbank Center later that day, tenants in thirty more buildings announced they would be joining the strike, bringing the total number of striking tenants in Harlem to 585 in over fifty buildings, according to Gray.[51] One of the tenants in these newly organized buildings was Elizabeth Evans, a mother of eight who spent her nights defending her three-month-old daughter's crib against attacks from rats in their West 118th Street apartment.[52] May Robinson, building leader of the rent strikers at 54 West 117th Street, also announced the participation of the tenants in her building. The tenants in

Robinson's building, including her next-door neighbor Elise McGee, complained of a terrible rat infestation, among myriad other health and safety violations. "There are more rats in this building than people," McGee said. "I'm here having tea and there they sit, looking me straight in the face." Other buildings on the street, like 15 East 117th Street, had no lock on the front door and had been without heat and hot water for months. Tenants of the building, like Muriel Jackson and building leader Doris Roper, resorted to gathering their children around gas stoves to keep warm at night, and heating up gallons of water on the stove each morning so that they could bathe before school.[53]

After Gray's right-hand man Major Williams announced at the community meeting that three thousand more tenants were willing to join the strike and encouraged younger activists to get involved, Gray laid out his strategy for the 130 tenant representatives in attendance. First, the CCH would urge the chief justice of the civil court to refuse to grant "slumlords the right to dispossess tenants when there are violations," given the meager vacancy rate in the city. Second, to dramatize the realities of their living conditions, tenants would show up to all future court cases with rubber rats tied around their necks. Lastly, Gray announced plans to picket the Department of Buildings to again demand cellar-to-roof inspections throughout lower Harlem.[54]

While laying out the legal side of the CCH's rent strike organizing plan, Gray, Williams, and the tenant organizers were also working out their strategies for dealing with landlords and city housing policies. Two days later, the CCH held a landlord-tenant meeting where thirty tenants directed their demands, as well as their frustrations, at the two landlords who had accepted the invitation to attend. Tenants seized the opportunity to air their grievances, but the only two landlords bold enough to attend passed the blame for decaying building conditions onto drug users in the neighborhood, a lack of capable superintendents, and the tenants themselves.[55]

It is highly doubtful that an organizer of Gray's experience had any illusions that such meetings would convince landlords to willingly repair their buildings. If anything, Gray helped to embolden striking tenants by providing a forum for them to directly confront their oppressors. The meeting served notice to previously evasive landlords that their tenants were learning their identities and would no longer allow them to remain in the shadows. Recognizing the futility of relying on slumlords to hold themselves accountable, Gray also doubled down on his calls for the city to invoke the receivership law to take over the striking buildings en masse as a first step toward "a mass rehabilitation of this ghetto." In essence, tenants would be waging their fight on two fronts. While pressuring the city to act swiftly and programmatically on the receivership law, Gray made it clear that in the meantime the CCH would take its fight directly to the landlords to demand immediate repairs.[56]

BUILDING COALITIONS FOR COLLECTIVE POWER

Coalition building was imperative to meeting the organizational demands of dealing with city and state officials, city agencies, and landlords, while also keeping up with the daily work of organizing and spreading the rent strikes. With tenants in buildings represented by HAG and the CCH engaged in rent strikes throughout November, the two organizations joined forces to form a working coalition in Harlem. The coalition was brokered by Danny Schechter, who was introduced to Gray through a mutual connection. "I went over there, and we said, 'Look, we're doing these rent strikes, we want to help organize and help you,'" Schechter later recalled. "He said, 'Great.' . . . and suddenly the thing started taking off in the winter."[57] The experience and expertise of Gray and the CCH was a boon for younger HAG organizers. NSM organizers like Schechter, Q. R. Hand, and Bob Knight, as well as national director Bill Strickland, who had been inspired by the organizing ethos of SNCC in the South, quickly developed strong ties and a close identification with the grassroots organizing tradition Gray and the CCH embodied. "I learned something very important from Jesse and the rent strikes," Strickland later recalled, "which was that the secret to real organizing is to get people to organize themselves."[58] By December HAG and the CCH had developed a working relationship, sharing resources, organizers, and a common vision for building grassroots political power in Harlem.

On December 15 the CCH called a mass rally at the Milbank Center to demonstrate surging popular support for the rent strikes and to encourage more Harlem tenants to join. While tenants were drawn in by leaflets exhorting them to take action against their landlords by joining the ranks of the now fifty-eight-building strike, the speakers at the rally laid the blame for New York's housing crisis squarely on city hall.[59] Gray criticized Wagner's vow to expedite rent reductions in buildings with code violations, arguing that rent reductions did not "put heat and hot water in a cold building."[60] Such weak responses from city hall, Gray argued—and the *New York Times* concurred—were little more than "a move to . . . stop the rent strike from spreading."[61] Gray maintained that city authorities had the legal power to rectify the housing crisis, yet lacked the political will to act in meaningful ways. "The rent strikers will not accept tokenism," Gray explained to reporters. "They are determined and prepared to continue the rent strike as long as it is necessary to rid the homes of rats, to achieve elementary services dictated by law and to eliminate all violations in existence on the buildings."[62]

In an effort to build a broad political coalition, the CCH invited politicians, clergy, civil rights, and labor leaders to speak at the Milbank Center.[63] With a bare cinder block wall as his backdrop, Adam Clayton Powell spoke fervently to the two hundred tenants who gathered. "If the City of New York doesn't take over the buildings, then I say we should have a march on City Hall," Powell declared. "Let's give Harlem the old spirit it used to have!"[64] After announcing that tenants in thirty-five more buildings had pledged to join the strike by New Year's Day, Gray doubled down on Powell's targeting of city hall by calling for a boycott of the Democratic Party writ-large if the city failed to immediately cut rents and take receivership of the buildings on 117th and 118th Streets. In an exciting bit of political theater, Powell seconded Gray's calls, declaring that he would "dump the Democratic Party" if no action was immediately taken to improve housing conditions in Harlem.[65] The mood was electric, and the various invited leaders in attendance quickly fell in line to back the surging rent strikes. Hulan Jack and Assemblymen Lloyd Dickens and José Ramos-Lopez all pledged their political support for the rent strike, while Rev. Richard Hildebrand pledged legal support from the NY NAACP. At the end of the meeting, Gray announced that a Rent Strike Coordinating Committee would soon be established to work on expanding the strike.[66]

The convergence of political, labor, religious, and civil rights leadership at the Milbank rally proved momentous for the rent strikes in particular and for broader grassroots Black freedom struggles in Harlem in general. The fervor stirred up by the rent strikes led the *Hartford Courant* to conclude two days later that there was "a storm gathering in Harlem."[67] The *Courant* proved perceptive, and by the end of the week the nascent Rent Strike Coordinating Committee had brought together a coalition comprising CCH, HAG, NAACP, CORE, HARYOU-ACT, a handful of block clubs and community groups, and several Harlem assemblymen and Democratic district leaders.[68]

Formed with the objective of coordinating a citywide rent strike to force "a mass rehabilitation of the ghettos," the coalition marked the emergence of the rent strikes at the vanguard of the Black freedom movement in the city.[69] "The great power blocs of the Harlem Community, the ministers and the politicians, were lining up behind the strike," Naison noted, "and CORE groups in Brooklyn and the Lower East Side were already beginning to organize their locales."[70] Additionally, the movement was beginning to spread across the nation, with groups of tenants in Providence, Chicago, and Cleveland all engaged in rent strikes by mid-December.[71] The decade of grassroots tenant organizing Gray and the CCH had undertaken in Harlem finally showed the makings of a mass movement in New York City and beyond.

"POWER IS SOMETHING THAT ONE MUST ORGANIZE"

The inaugural meeting of the Rent Strike Coordinating Committee was held on December 22 at the Mount Morris Presbyterian Church on 122nd Street. There, the group developed plans to recruit tenants in hundreds of other buildings in Harlem to expand the rent strike to a thousand buildings by early January. Representatives from seven organizations pledged field staff to distribute fifty thousand leaflets throughout Harlem in a door-to-door campaign to instruct tenants on how to organize their buildings and join the strike.[72] Despite the promise of the fledgling coalition, few of the participating organizations had much experience with tenant organizing. Thus, at its inception, as one student organizer noted, the committee was "little more than a list of supporters."[73] Though the NSM's national office brought in ten field secretaries to work as full-time organizers with HAG on the rent strikes, the bulk of the organizing work fell on Gray and the CCH.[74]

The nuts and bolts of the grassroots organizing campaign to build the rent strike movement drew from Gray's decade of organizing some of the most marginalized communities in New York City. Gray had earned the trust of working-class Black residents and built a reputation as the man people went to when they had problems with city agencies. Thanks to his consistently showing up for, and on behalf of, tenants, Naison noted, "there were buildings in Central Harlem where the name 'Jesse Gray' would open any door."[75] The impact of this groundwork was evident in how rapidly the rent strikes spread once the CCH got involved. In the six weeks after announcing their participation, the number of CCH-organized buildings on strike had grown from three to a reported fifty-eight.[76] "The only limit on the speed of organization," Naison explained, "seemed to be the time that was required to explain the mechanics of the strike."[77]

The "mechanics of the strike" included a process for organizing buildings that required extensive human and material resources. As Gray later explained, "I think power is something that . . . the Black community must organize, block-by-block, house-by-house, apartment-by-apartment."[78] For a rent strike to be successful, Gray believed the Black community would need to be organized into a united front capable of exerting power over slumlords and the various agencies, bureaucracies, and levels of city and state government. For a local, grassroots organization of working-class tenants, however, the resources necessary for such expansive organization were often in short supply. When the strikes began, the CCH "teetered on the edge of bankruptcy" and depended on membership dues and private donations from "wealthy radicals" to cover operating costs. The council's leadership consisted of four men, including Gray and Major Williams, who were the only two full-time organizers on staff and drew only meager subsistence salaries from the organization.[79] With such limited resources at their disposal, fostering local leadership was not only a guiding philosophy but also an organizational imperative.

The membership structure of the CCH reflected the organization's dedication to developing local leadership of social movements. "The organizers are all volunteers," Major Williams explained. "They live in the slums and know what the people are up against."[80] Unlike the tedious, bureaucratic membership policies of many CORE chapters which favored middle-class participation, the requirements for CCH membership were primarily action based. "This is one group where just signing up won't do a bit of good," one member explained. "You've got to pull your own weight if you want to get out of this mess."[81] Members were also required to pay monthly dues of one dollar, which guaranteed legal advice and representation during rent strikes. Though the dues were laxly enforced in a neighborhood where economic means were extremely limited, one of the intangible benefits of membership, as *Ebony* reported, was the "sense of security that springs from the knowledge that they are no longer alone in their fight against negligent landlords and rats."[82]

Pulling one's own weight in the CCH meant refusing to pay rent, organizing building meetings, and actively participating in weekly strategy meetings. To bring new members into the fold, the CCH placed a priority on leafleting neighborhood blocks, building by building, door by door. Organizers like

Peter Bailey spent countless hours meeting with tenants, "trying to get people to understand the rent strike, how the effective use of the rent strike could really... bring about changes."[83] When tenants expressed interest, they were instructed to organize a meeting in their building, where a building captain would be elected to serve as their representative in the CCH. The building captain was then responsible for attending weekly CCH meetings (as seen in fig. 14), to discuss problems and develop strategies.[84] "[Gray] would have weekly or nightly meetings—either emergency ones or ones planning what he was going to do the following week—where maybe one or 200 people could sit and talk and discuss it," Gloria Richardson recalled.[85] An occasional visitor to Harlem while engaged in her own militant struggles against racist violence in Cambridge, Maryland, Richardson became a close comrade of Gray and a regular around the CCH office and at meetings in 1964.[86] Through these meetings, tenant leaders not only received a political education from veteran organizers like Gray and Richardson but also took active part in shaping organizational policies and actions.

FIG 14 Harlem tenants gather in the basement of the Dunlevy Milbank Community Center at a weekly rent strike meeting of the Community Council on Housing in early 1964. Jesse Gray (*standing left*) asks people to raise their hands if they support a protest march on city hall. (Photo by Don Hogan Charles; *Ebony/Harlem Stirs*)

BLACK WOMEN LEADERSHIP IN THE RENT STRIKE MOVEMENT

Whereas the central leadership of the CCH consisted exclusively of men, Black women carried out the bulk of the organizing work. Indeed, "the strike in Harlem was run on a day-to-day basis by two women—Florence Rice and Anne Bradshaw—and women were numerically predominant on the city-wide strike coordinating committee."[87] Though little is known about Bradshaw, she was responsible for bringing her friend Rice into the organization. After working in defense manufacturing during World War II, Rice found work in a unionized garment shop and became active in labor and civil rights organizing as a member of the International Ladies' Garment Workers' Union. Reflecting on the influence of labor organizing on her political development, Rice explained, "That's when I began to understand how economics works, and once I began to understand economics, that's when I realized that I'd have to fight about it."[88]

It was through her background in labor organizing that Rice entered the fold of radical labor movements in Harlem. In the fall of 1961 she was part of the Emergency Committee for Unity on Social and Economic Problems, organized by A. Philip Randolph to demand a broad platform of initiatives to correct racist policies and practices in employment, housing, education, and policing in Harlem, working alongside the likes of Bayard Rustin, Malcolm X, James Haughton, Bill Epton, Selma Sparks, and Calvin Hicks.[89] While it is unclear whether Rice knew Gray personally prior to her involvement in the rent strikes, there was extensive overlap in the radical political circles the two veteran Left-labor organizers occupied, and both emphasized the importance of independent grassroots leadership for radical movement building.[90] "I find myself fighting many of the leaders who are supposedly representing us," Rice said in an interview for CBS's "The Harlem Temper" in the fall of 1963. "I would also like to see our leaders speak more accurate[ly] what the Black people in the community feel and not what the white power structure sets up—to speak for us."[91]

While Rice, Bradshaw, and Gray's close associate Maxine Green handled most of the day-to-day operations of the rent strikes for the CCH, it was Black and Puerto Rican women building leaders who were in the streets ensuring that "what the Black people in the community feel" was translating into organized action. Building leaders like Mary King, Rita Jackson, May Robinson, Doris Roper, Marjory Cruz, and Inocencia Flores were primarily responsible for mobilizing and organizing tenants. By Gray's standards, at least 75 percent of tenants in a building had to be on board before any collective action could be taken. With fifty-eight buildings on strike by mid-December, with an average of fifteen tenants per building, according to Gray's calculations, this meant that the cadre of building leaders, primarily Black and Puerto Rican women, were responsible for organizing over 650 families to engage in the rent strikes.[92] With Gray receiving most of the media spotlight during the strikes and the scholarly attention thereafter, these women organizers have gone underappreciated for their labor in building and expanding the rent strike movement.

As the cold of winter set in and the Christmas holiday approached, these women leaders found unlikely allies in the city's major newspapers. Aided by Gray's widely publicized, yet unsuccessful, calls for the Red Cross to declare lower Harlem a disaster area in late December 1963, reporters jumped at the chance to cover the heart-wrenching stories of families without heat and hot water on Christmas Day. The *New York Times* carried sobering stories of families in Harlem huddled around their gas stoves to stay warm.[93] "This is the worst Christmas we've had here," Mrs. Harrison Nelson told a reporter, with "no heat or hot water, but plenty of roaches and rats." She went on, "We got a Christmas tree set up in the front room but we can't enjoy it 'cause it's colder than the North Pole in here." Across the street, rent strike leader and mother of four Doris Roper said that her building had gone months without heat, hot water, or a superintendent. The building had broken windows on every floor and hallways cluttered with debris and fallen plaster. "I've had this oven on for the last two nights," she said, "and I guess it will stay on until someone decides to do something about this building."[94]

Though not often considered as such, these kinds of media exposés, for which Black and Puerto Rican women routinely opened their homes to reporters and inspectors, represented additional labor and contributions to the rent strike movement. Focused almost exclusively on Black and Puerto Rican mothers, these stories frequently occupied the front pages of several New York newspapers throughout December and elicited popular empathy and support for the burgeoning movement. Homer Bigart, a Pulitzer Prize–winning reporter for the *New York Times* who covered many of these stories, was said to have come out of one of the buildings on East 117th Street "quivering with anger" over the conditions he witnessed inside. "This is the worst thing I've seen in all my years of reporting," he told a publicity manager for the CCH that month. "I'll write anything you want."[95] Aided by this type of press coverage, fueled in large part by working-class Black and Puerto

Rican women, the rent strike movement became the premier political issue in New York City and "the cause célèbre of the civil rights movement in the North" by the end of 1963.[96]

THE CITY RESPONDS

As the Rent Strike Coordinating Committee and the news media continued to put pressure on city hall throughout December, token responses to the housing crisis became increasingly untenable. The rising tide of Black political power sent the city into "a state of complete and utter panic" by the year's end, as one prominent housing attorney explained.[97] Recognizing the potential political force of a citywide rent strike movement in an election year amid evolving national Black freedom struggles, city agencies scrambled to churn out proposals to address housing conditions and thereby curb the anger undergirding the strikes.

In early December three city agencies announced joint plans to develop 350 units of low-income housing through a massive redevelopment project on 117th and 118th Streets. "The ancient rat-ridden tenements to be cleared under this proposal make up one of the worst slum blocks in the city," Borough President Edward Dudley declared. However, while quality low-income housing was certainly needed in Harlem and throughout the city, the proposed development would have exacerbated the housing shortage by displacing five hundred families to build just 350 units.[98] Furthermore, such proposals ignored the demands of the CCH and striking tenants who favored rehabilitation over renewal. Rent strike leaders like Inocencia Flores balked at the idea of being relocated, asserting she would rather "stay here and change the system."[99]

While city officials floated housing reform initiatives, thirteen striking tenants from 16 and 18 East 117th Street were preparing for an appearance in civil court for nonpayment of rent. Though rarely analyzed as such, the rent strikes to this point were a mass display of civil disobedience. Withholding rent was an illegal and punishable offense, and the risk of eviction or financial penalties had prevented some tenants from joining the strikes. Scheduled for December 30, the court hearing represented the first legal test for the burgeoning movement, which Gray predicted would expand from fifty-eight to upwards of three hundred buildings by New Year's Day.[100]

Meanwhile, the Wagner administration worked feverishly to develop a comprehensive plan to head off the strikes. The day before the hearing, the rent administrator, Hortense Gabel, announced city hall would soon present a "bold plan to deal with the Harlem problem."[101] Though details were scarce, the *New York Times* declared Mayor Wagner was "forging new weapons to combat the slum conditions that have prompted Harlem's spreading rent strikes." These "new weapons," the *Times* reported, would likely include stiffer penalties for offending landlords, greater expediency of the city's receivership program, more frequent inspections, broader outreach efforts to inform tenants of their rights and duties, and a housing program to present to the state legislature.

Unmoved by Gabel's pledge, tenants brought their mounting protests into the courthouse downtown. Having previously found little justice through the courts, the CCH used the platform provided by the hearing to stage a dramatic demonstration. Gray and the CCH had urged the thirteen tenants to save every rat they killed in their apartments to bring into the courtroom as evidence against their landlords. Though court officers confiscated many of the dead rodents after learning of the plan in the newspapers, the tenants managed to smuggle in five rats under their coats.[102] The rats were never submitted as evidence, but the action received widespread media coverage, provided spectacular imagery for the proceedings, and marked the emergence of the rat as a potent protest symbol for the rent strikes.

The most significant moment of the court proceedings, however, came when Judge Guy Ribaudo delivered his ruling. Basing his decision on a 1930 law that permitted tenants in seriously neglected units to deposit their rents with the court, Ribaudo ruled that the tenants were within their rights in withholding rent for units where such "shocking" conditions existed. After deliberating with Gray, the tenants' legal team, and the landlord's attorney, Ribaudo declared that landlords could withdraw the rent money from the court to make repairs, but "only after the tenants' representative had approved."[103] Ribaudo's decision essentially established "a de facto receivership—court-controlled spending of rent money for repairs," which could achieve more immediate repairs than the sluggish process of the city's receivership law.[104]

Though Ribaudo announced in court that he did not condone the rent strikes, his decision nonetheless granted the movement legal sanction. Outside the courtroom, Gray declared the ruling a victory for the rent strikers and boldly announced that he expected the movement to grow to one thousand buildings within the next two weeks. "This gives us the push our campaign needs," Gray told reporters, since "the tenants now know they don't have to pay rent to landlords who do nothing for them. No services, no payment."[105] Seizing quickly upon the opportunity the legal victory offered, Gray led a march of a dozen tenants and organizers to the nearby offices of Hortense Gabel. Joined by Danny Schechter, Anne Bradshaw, and attorney Bruce Gould, Gray requested that Gabel reduce rents to one dollar in the buildings Ribaudo ruled on, arguing that tenants should not pay full rent while awaiting repairs—regardless of to whom the rent was paid. Though Gabel was hesitant to reduce rent on the two buildings in question, she did agree to immediately reduce rents on seven other CCH-organized buildings, demonstrating the heightened political leverage the CCH wielded following the Ribaudo ruling.[106]

Just days after the landmark decision, Mayor Wagner formally announced his action plan for addressing the city's housing problems. As part of a platform he described as a "pocketbook attack on the slumlord," Wagner urged the creation of special housing courts, increased building inspections, higher fines and jail sentences for landlords, a more streamlined process for verifying violations, and city support for a state bill to legalize rent strikes.[107] Later that week, he announced additional plans for a $1 million "anti-rat" program to be carried out by 148 new employees of the Health Department and reimbursed in part by billing landlords for the services.[108] The Wagner administration packaged these initiatives with a narrative that tenants ought to place their faith in city hall to address housing conditions rather than turn to independent grassroots action, which, to the mayor, had the undesirable potential to galvanize broader struggles for Black rights and power in the city.

Mayor Wagner's proposed broadside attack on slum conditions was met with decidedly mixed reactions from city officials, tenant organizers, and some members of the press. Though many city officials were motivated by fears of the potential power the rent strike movement wielded, many also embraced the impetus it provided for prioritizing housing reform. "Part of it was fear, part of it was relief," one member of the mayor's Housing Executive Committee said. "Finally it's out in the open—now we can do something."[109] Jesse Gray also cautiously welcomed the influx of political attention finally being paid to the city's housing crisis. "We are impressed with the Mayor's talk," the CCH leader announced in a press release, "however talk does not give heat and hot water."[110]

While Gray offered lukewarm support, other housing advocates were less reserved in their response to the proposed actions. R. Peter Straus, the head of radio station WMCA who had supported the women-led "Call to Action" call-in tenant advocacy service, called the mayor's proposal "a lot of hot air" and argued that the city already had "plenty of authority to make improvements under present laws."[111] As if to prove Straus's point, the following day *New York Telegram and Sun* reporter Woody Klein called attention to the mayor's dismal track record of promises made and routinely broken regarding housing reform. After listing fifteen proposals over the mayor's decade in office, Klein described the January 1964 program as "nothing more than a warmed-over version of past promises, with the possible exception of legalizing rent strikes." To further illustrate his point, Klein concluded with a quote from a conversation he had had with the mayor six years earlier: "There's nothing you can do about the slums, you know that," Wagner reportedly explained to Klein. "They're always going to be that way."[112] Despite the bombast that accompanied the mayor's most recent declaration of war on slumlords, his track record did little to instill confidence in Harlem tenants that city hall would take meaningful action to address the city's rampant housing crisis without sustained pressure from tenants and civil rights organizations.

Buoyed by the Ribaudo decision, the rent strike movement continued to gain momentum. Just days after the mayor unveiled his legislative program, Judge Fred Moritt ruled that five tenants in Red Hook represented by Brooklyn CORE "could live rent-free for as long as landlords failed to correct housing evils that menaced health and safety." Taking Ribaudo's earlier ruling a step further—and echoing the CCH's demands for sweeping rent reductions pending repairs—Moritt declared from the bench, "The landlord in extreme cases is not entitled to any rent until the conditions are remedied." Whereas Ribaudo had refused to condone the rent strikes, Moritt was less reserved in his rebuke of slumlords. "Some of the buildings are not fit for pigs to live in," Moritt told the court, adding, "If it takes the landlord two years to make the repairs, he gets no rent for two years. Period."[113] With the backing of the city's judiciary, the rent strike movement continued to spread rapidly throughout the city.

LOCAL STRUGGLE, NATIONAL MOVEMENT

Just days after the Moritt ruling, a broad coalition of tenants, civil rights, and labor organizations established the Lower East Side (LES) Rent Strike Committee.[114] "Harlem led the strikes," a newsletter that month declared. "Now a Lower East Side Rent Strike organization has alerted our area! The strike is growing."¹¹⁵ To help coordinate and energize the committee, its members invited Jesse Gray to participate in one of its initial meetings. "It was a very exciting coalition," Lower East Side activist Frances Goldin recalled. "He brought a kind of a gutsiness to the struggle [that] I don't think we would have had otherwise."¹¹⁶ With Gray's guidance and inspiration, the Lower East Side Rent Strike Committee quickly organized tenants in sixty Lower East Side buildings to join the citywide rent strike, which spread to ninety more buildings in the Bronx and Bedford-Stuyvesant by February.¹¹⁷ In the following weeks, Gray would collaborate with Lower East Side activists, including Jose Fuentes and Genoveva Clemente, to lead a torchlight parade of two hundred tenants downtown and to hold mass demonstrations at hotly contested rent-control hearings at city hall.¹¹⁸

Meanwhile, organizations uptown were actively discussing the potential the rent strike movement had for igniting the type of broader mass movement Gray envisioned all along. When the NSM Congress—a convening of organizers from the national office and chapter cities—met that month, attended by Peter and Joan Countryman, Q. R. Hand, Bayard Rustin, Danny Schechter, Bill Strickland, and others, the rent strikes were the predominant topic of conversation. After Rustin spoke about the broader meanings of the rent strikes for the national civil rights movement, Hand explained to the group that there was a "possibility that the [rent strikes] were the first movement in the North that is not all middle-class." To Strickland, the recent successes of the rent strike had the profound impact of awakening working-class Black communities to the power they held in their communities. This power, in turn, could be organized in a more expansive political and social movement for Black liberation. "The radical change in the mental attitude of the people," Strickland suggested, was contributing to the emergence of a powerful "multi-issue, cross-racial, and cross-class lines movement" and making Harlem the "Mississippi of the North."¹¹⁹ Over the next several weeks and months, organizers from the NSM, CCH, CORE, and several labor and Black nationalist organizations would work fervently to translate this grassroots power into a radical mass movement centered in Harlem.

As the rent strikes emerged at the vanguard of Black freedom struggles in New York City, a younger generation of organizers also joined the fray. One such organizer was Peter Bailey, an army veteran and Howard University student from Tuskegee, Alabama, who had taken a leave from college to join the movement in Harlem. Once there, Bailey became a regular at Malcolm X's street rallies at 116th Street and Lenox Avenue and participated in the Harlem Hospital and Downstate Medical Center protests in the summer of 1963 as a member of Harlem CORE. When the rent strike movement took off, Bailey quickly joined the ranks of the Rent Strike Coordinating Committee. "I went from CORE to Jesse Gray because I thought that he was doing something more immediate to the people," Bailey recalled.[120]

For Bailey and others of his generation who had grown increasingly disillusioned with the goal of integration, the rent strikes provided a training ground and entrée into the New Afro-American Nationalism that was coming to characterize the Black freedom movement in Harlem. Through tenant organizing, activists like Bailey gained experience in building a movement for community power and self-determination—central tenets of Black Left and nationalist organizing which would later define the Black Power movement. These experiences in the rent strike movement instilled in young activists "an extraordinary sense of exhilaration and even of historic destiny that drew people to the movement as the initiator of a new stage in the civil rights movement."[121]

The peak of this excitement came on January 12 at a rally called by the Rent Strike Coordinating Committee. The Lower East Side Rent Strike Committee had just announced its formation the previous day, and "rent strike fever" was in the air in the crowded gymnasium of the Milbank Center. As six hundred Harlem residents, civil rights activists, and representatives from tenant organizations throughout the city filed into the room, Jesse Gray sat alongside an array of local and national leaders, including John O. Killens, James Baldwin, Anna Arnold Hedgeman, Hulan Jack, Bill Strickland, SNCC Chairman John Lewis, Congressman William Fitts Ryan, Councilman Paul O'Dwyer, Assemblyman José Ramos-Lopez, and union leaders Leon Davis and Cleveland Robinson.

Addressing the crowd from behind a long table covered with posters mockingly depicting the Republican and Democratic Party mascots as rats, the speakers took turns declaring their support for the rent strike and denouncing the racism that undergirded housing inequality in Harlem.[122] After once again taking aim at city officials like Hortense Gabel, who, he declared, "acts just like any other slumlord and has got to go," Gray took the opportunity to announce another march on city hall at the end of the month to demand the extension of rent-control protections that were set to expire, as well as "to demand that the City jail all slumlords."[123] Gray also announced that plans were in place to form a citywide rent strike coalition to bring the full weight of Black and Puerto Rican renters on city hall.

While Gray laid out his program for the rent strikes, the most rousing speeches of the evening came from John Lewis and James Baldwin.[124] Baldwin spoke "as a witness" to the intrinsic relations between housing inequality in Harlem and systemic racism in the United States. "This is a revolution," he explained, and "it is going to be harder and harder and harder because the revolution has got to revise the entire system in order for us, as Negroes, to live and in order for the country to survive." In this assessment, Baldwin gave voice to the revolutionary ideology that informed Gray's housing activism. Challenging Harlem residents to locate their rent strikes within the context of global struggles for Black liberation, Baldwin declared this revolution "connects with the condition of black and dark people all over the world. One must be bold enough to see and say this." As his address came to a climax, Baldwin urged Harlem residents to bring this understanding to bear on their daily organizing work with the rent strikes to build a broader movement for confronting and overthrowing Jim Crow society in America. "Things *can* be corrected but only if we force them to act," Baldwin charged. "We know that the situation in the South was precipitated by the Negro people in the streets."[125] Echoing Baldwin's call to action, Strickland told the audience that "the rent strike is only the first stage in a social revolution where the people will gain control over their own lives."[126]

While Baldwin and Strickland issued an inspirational and forceful challenge to Harlem residents to engage in revolutionary struggle, John Lewis focused his remarks on the impacts of the rent strikes on national Black freedom struggles. Lewis began his address by telling the crowd he spent the previous night in a jail cell in Atlanta but made the rare decision to post bail in order to make it to Harlem that morning. To Lewis, the rent strikes represented "something very new and meaningful," not only to New York but also to the national movement. "Those of us who live and work in the Deep South have been following the struggle here in Harlem with great interest," Lewis explained, flipping the popular perceptions of Northern movements following in the wake of those in the South. "Some of us have been saying all along," he continued, "that when the masses get moving in Harlem, the masses in the whole nation will move."[127]

With the landmark March on Washington in the rearview mirror and the promise of the Civil Rights Act looming just over the horizon, Lewis acknowledged that new directions were needed to realize the fundamental goal of Black liberation. "If all over this nation, if during the next two weeks and February there is born a general rent strike you will see something very beautiful," Lewis predicted. "You will make 1963 look very petty and 1964 will be the year of the civil rights revolution."[128] The weight of Lewis's prophetic speech was not missed by the six hundred residents and activists in attendance, who cheered his remarks with a standing ovation and moving rendition of "We Shall Overcome."[129] After nearly a decade of active grassroots struggle in Harlem, Black and Puerto Rican residents and activists finally felt as though they were in the vanguard of the civil rights movement, rather than playing second fiddle to the highly visible struggles raging in the South. "At this meeting," one CORE leader expressed, "everyone caught the fever—Rent Strike . . . it seemed like the thing to do."[130]

Lewis was hardly filling the room with hot air when he told the crowd "the whole nation will move" once the Black masses in Harlem were in motion. By the time Lewis made these remarks, rent strikes were already underway in Providence, Chicago, and Cleveland, with others in the works in Los Angeles, New Orleans, Milwaukee, New Haven, Pittsburgh, Hartford, and Washington, DC, where SNCC launched its first rent strike later that month.[131]

Although the hyper-visibility provided by constant national news coverage helped introduce the concept of rent strikes to Black communities across the United States, Gray was also actively assisting various groups in coordinating and launching strikes in their own cities. "Jesse was frequently a resource person," Howard University student Phil Hutchings recalled. As a member of the SNCC-affiliated Nonviolent Action Group, Hutchings regularly made contact with Gray in both Harlem and Washington, DC. "We were playing with this idea of housing strikes, and thought who better to tell us and has experiences with housing strikes than Jesse Gray?" Hutchings said. "You just shot up the turnpike and you're in New York, or bring him down to interact and get [his] message."[132]

Furthermore, the grassroots militancy the rent strikes helped cultivate was now flowering in other struggles in New York City and beyond. In the years since the school boycott led by Mae Mallory and the Harlem Nine, the racial inequalities entrenched in the city's public school system remained. As civil rights organizations struggled to eke out any concessions from the Board of Education or city hall, frustrations mounted and plans for action escalated. By the winter of 1963 a massive citywide school boycott was in the works, spearheaded by Brooklyn organizer Rev. Milton Galamison, who had been at the front lines of major civil rights struggles in New York City for over a decade. Drawn from the same grassroots base as the rent strikes (Inocencia Flores was also an active supporter of the school boycott), the planned boycott reflected the same impatience with racial liberalism that fueled the rent strike movement.[133]

This grassroots militancy in New York City converged in the hours before the rally at the Milbank Center, when a group of radical organizers from across the country met in Harlem to discuss plans for coordinating similar direct-action campaigns on a national level. Having learned of the rent strikes and planned school boycott through the *Chicago Defender,* Chicago Friends of SNCC leader Lawrence Landry set up a meeting with Galamison to discuss the possibility of launching a nationwide school boycott. Joining the two civil rights leaders that day were Noel Day, an organizer with the NSM-affiliated Boston Action Group and husband of Harlem native and activist Peggy Trotter Dammond; Ruth Turner, leader of Cleveland CORE who had actively supported Mae Mallory during her extradition fight and had also coordinated rent strikes in Cleveland; Stanley Branche, chairman of the Committee for Freedom Now in Chester, Pennsylvania; James Bevel, a leader of the Nashville Student Movement, SNCC, and the SCLC; John Lewis; and Jesse Gray.[134]

During the daylong session, this impressive collective of radical grassroots organizers hammered out plans for the nationwide school boycott, which resulted in over one million students boycotting schools in thirty-two cities the following month. This summit also marked the first meeting of a new radical grassroots coalition known as ACT (not an acronym), which in the following months would grow to include Gloria Richardson, Harlem Parents Committee leader Isaiah Robinson, comedian and activist Dick Gregory, Washington, DC CORE leader Julius Hobson, Negro American Labor Council secretary Nahaz Rogers, and a newly independent Malcolm X.

By February it was becoming clear that the grassroots base of working-class Black and Puerto Rican Harlem residents mobilized through the rent strike movement was making far greater contributions to the evolution of the Black freedom struggle than many could have imagined when they took the first step of withholding their rent. Jesse Gray's vision for building a radical political movement through tenant organizing appeared on the verge of becoming a reality.

THE LANDLORDS AND CITY FIGHT BACK

As the winter stretched on in January and February 1964, the rent strike movement grew in size, scope, and militancy. On January 23 Gray and the CCH led tenants from Harlem and the Lower East Side in demonstrations at city hall to demand the extension of rent control legislation. While three hundred picketing women, men, and children circled the building, wearing rubber rats pinned to their lapels, chanting, and carrying signs reading "Wagner Stop Talking Start Acting," Gray led a contingency of tenants inside to disrupt the legislative hearings.[135] The scene inside the city council chamber was bedlam, with landlords and tenants alike removed from the room by police after waging disruptive protests. Gray was ejected for trying to seize the microphone, before later storming back into the chamber to declare the proceedings were "rigged" and leading the remaining tenants in a walkout. While Gray was outside, another woman tenant squared up with a landlord

FIG 15 NYPD surveillance photo of Jesse Gray (*center*) leading a picket line of rent strikers outside city hall in January 1964. (Handschu Photograph Files, Municipal Archives, City of New York)

who had assaulted an elderly tenant when he rose to address the council, forcing a recess to be called.[136] These physical confrontations at city hall, one observer noted, "convinced tenants that they must resist the landlords by all means."[137] At the same time, that the city council voted to extend rent control for another two years showed tenants that their protests were effective in winning tangible victories.

While the recent victories in civil court and city council galvanized striking tenants, they also drew a backlash from angry landlords who had grown accustomed to exploiting their tenants in peace. Frustrated by the loss of revenue and the barrage of demands for building repairs, landlords began to fight back against the movement by forcibly evicting striking tenants with the help of city marshals and police. This development was particularly concerning to Baldwin, who explained in a personal letter on behalf of the CCH that winter, "Landlords have been demanding—and getting—forcible evictions for non-payment of rent," and appealed for financial support for the rent strikers "engaged in the battle for better housing."[138]

The militancy displayed during the rent control hearings at city hall escalated days later when Harlem tenants clashed with a city marshal over the eviction of a striking tenant. Though the law required that a tenant be sent a preliminary eviction notice, Elizabeth Brown received only a twenty-four-hour notice that she was to be evicted from her third-floor apartment in a "burnt-out" building on 144th Street.[139] Despite Gray and the CCH securing a stay of eviction through the courts, the city marshal entered the apartment Brown shared with her sixteen-year-old son, Christopher, and moved all of their belongings onto the sidewalk. When Brown found her possessions on the sidewalk and her apartment padlocked, she called Gray, who quickly mobilized ten members of the CCH to break the lock and move the belongings back into the apartment.[140] The anti-eviction struggle resulted in a confrontation with the marshal, Reginald Thorpe, who Gray charged "roughed me up and one of his men punched me in the mouth" while a police officer on the scene "turned his head."[141] After the patrolman refused to arrest Thorpe for assault, Gray led a small protest at the nearby precinct, with demonstrators chanting, "The police must go" and "Brutality must go."[142]

Like the dramatic anti-eviction campaigns waged by the Communist Party and community organizers like Queen Mother Audley Moore during the Great Depression, Gray's confrontation with the city marshal aroused the ire of Harlem tenants against slumlords and the police alike. For the next two

FIG 16 NYPD surveillance photo of a demonstration outside the 30th Precinct on Amsterdam Avenue in late January 1964 protesting the brutality of City Marshal Reginald Thorpe during the eviction of Elizabeth Brown. (Handschu Photograph Files, Municipal Archives, City of New York)

weeks, the anti-eviction campaigns continued, with members of the CCH and HAG battling city marshals and the NYPD to prevent entry to apartments for carrying out evictions.

Just days after the first confrontation at Elizabeth Brown's apartment, members of the NYPD attempted to aid the city marshal in once again entering her apartment, despite a court order staying the eviction. After returning home from renewing the stay at civil court, Christopher Brown found police "trying to break through the back wall of the apartment" while members of the CCH barricaded the door. "There is no law for the people up here, the police work only for the landlords," Gray told reporters. Announcing a series of pickets at police headquarters to protest the NYPD's complicity with slumlords, Gray warned that "blood is going to flow if something isn't done."[143]

Another anti-eviction protest the following week tipped the scales. On February 7 a city marshal showed up at the apartment of rent striker Luther Brown (no relation to Elizabeth Brown), accompanied by police and a crew of laborers to carry out an eviction order. Over the past months, Brown had frequently complained to his landlord about violations in the apartment he shared with his sister and her five children on West 118th Street, to no avail. While CCH members scrambled to get a judge to issue a stay of the eviction ordered the previous night, Gray, Major Williams, Q. R. Hand, and others from the CCH and HAG joined Brown in physically barricading the apartment until the stay could be obtained.

While *Ebony* photographer Don Hogan Charles snapped pictures, the police "chopped down the door of the apartment and broke down the barricade," entering the apartment and arresting everyone inside. "You should've seen all the cops, man," Q. R. Hand said. "They came just out of nowhere, they had big paddy wagons out there, four or five patrol cars."[144] This time, rather than putting the family's possessions in the street, as they had with Elizabeth Brown, the marshal loaded the family's belongings into a moving van to prevent the CCH and HAG from moving them back inside. From a shared jail cell, Gray, Williams, Hand, and the other rent strikers worked out plans for protests that would "turn the tables on the police and expose them as the slumlords' tools."[145]

In their holding cell, the rent strikers drafted a leaflet for a demonstration at the 28th Precinct with a damning indictment of the NYPD. "When the slumlords are guilty of no heat, no hot water, and the rats biting our children, the police department does nothing," the leaflet read. "When tenants are being robbed, or when apartments are broken into, where are the police? Somewhere drunk? In some woman's apartment? In a garage asleep? Collecting graft and payoffs from prostitutes? Payoffs from number men or dope peddlers? But when it is time to illegally evict a tenant for a slumlord, the whole police department acts with great speed."[146] Each of these scenarios represented a common complaint against the NYPD and revealed a sharp contrast with the forceful police presence in Luther Brown's apartment just hours after an eviction notice was issued. The underlying critique of systemic racism and state repression in the leaflet was impossible to ignore, with the majority of landlords and police officers being white and the majority of Harlem tenants Black and Puerto Rican.

The following day, the CCH and HAG led picketers in demonstrations outside the 28th Precinct in Harlem and police headquarters downtown. Calling for the dismissal of the officers who arrested the rent strikers inside Luther Brown's apartment, protestors walked the picket lines with signs reading "Slumlord Cops Must Go" and "Arrest City Marshal Thorpe and his Slumlord-Supporting Goons." Later that evening, Gray and the building leaders of the CCH convened at the Mount Morris Presbyterian Church to discuss plans for increasing pressure on the NYPD, as well as strategies for continuing the rent strike.[147]

POLICE REPRESSION OF THE RENT STRIKE MOVEMENT

Though the protests outside the 28th Precinct and police headquarters achieved little in terms of concessions from the city or NYPD, the anti-eviction confrontations revealed more fully to many tenants the role of the police as the enforcement arm of white supremacy in the city. While much of Gray's organizing and rhetoric to this point had been dedicated to promoting a more systemic critique of housing inequality in the city, he had spent relatively little time confronting the role of the police. Certainly, few Harlem residents had any illusions about the NYPD, an overwhelmingly white department many saw as a corrupt, often abusive, occupying force in Harlem. "Rare, indeed, is the Harlem citizen . . . who does not have a long tale to tell of police incompetence, injustice, or brutality," James Baldwin wrote years earlier. "They represent the force of the white world, and that world's real intentions are, simply, for that world's criminal profit and ease, to keep the black man corralled up here, in his place."[148] Coming at a period of heightened political consciousness and collective action, the anti-eviction confrontations brought the true role of the NYPD into sharp relief for many Harlem residents.

For Q. R. Hand, coming face-to-face with the NYPD at Luther Brown's apartment after several months of witnessing police harassment and intimidation of rent strikers was a radicalizing experience. Speaking alongside Malcolm X at the Militant Labor Forum in May 1964, Hand recalled a visit tenant organizer Granville Cherry received the previous fall from the "King Cole Trio"—a notorious group of Black officers known for their corruption and heavy-handed administration of "law and order."[149] Most people on the block knew that the basement of Cherry's building was a hangout for top numbers runners and bankers, and that police were frequent visitors to the building to collect their cut for allowing the gambling ring to operate with their protection.[150] So when Cherry started a rent strike in a building that was a honey hole for the King Cole Trio, they paid him a visit. As Cherry was leaving his building, one of the plainclothes officers grabbed him while the other two kept lookout. "The guy worked Cherry over a little bit, [and] says, 'why don't you cut this stuff out, we don't want any trouble." The thinly veiled threat against Cherry, a "happy-go-lucky, good cat" who was merely trying to improve his family's housing situation, signaled to Hand that the problems they were dealing with extended far beyond housing policies.[151]

The increasingly repressive involvement of the NYPD in the rent strikes was part of the one-two punch that characterized liberal governance under the Wagner administration in New York City. With his left hand, the mayor promised to investigate and deliver legislative reforms to address demands for equality and justice in the city. By dressing up minor concessions as major policy advancements or appointing blue-ribbon commissions to investigate issues of inequality, the mayor sought to appease protestors and subvert demands for systemic change. With his right hand, the mayor dispatched the NYPD to curb protest and civil unrest through the surveillance, criminalization, and physical repression of activists and organizers.

The position of the NYPD in this regard became clear in early March of 1964, when Police Commissioner Michael Murphy declared at a meeting of six thousand officers that he would not allow civil rights leaders to "turn New York City into a battleground." Singling out Jesse Gray, Malcolm X, and Bronx CORE leader Herbert Callender, Murphy charged that these "extremist" leaders "see the struggle for [civil rights] only as a means to a personal end or as the weapon to create chaos in our community and weaken the structure of government."[152] Interestingly, it was these three Black leaders who had been among the most vocal about police corruption, brutality, and political repression in the preceding several weeks. Thus, not only did the police commissioner rally his rank and file against leaders of the Black freedom movement, he also attempted to delegitimize these leaders along with their legitimate claims against the NYPD and city hall. Murphy's rhetoric signaled the NYPD's intent to further criminalize Black dissent and set the stage for a looming showdown in the city.

THE DECLINE OF THE RENT STRIKE MOVEMENT

While school boycotts and struggles against police violence gained traction in Harlem in February 1964, the rent strike movement began to lose steam. Gray and the CCH continued the rent strikes throughout the spring, but as the weather warmed, the problems of heat and hot water became less acute, and the newspapers began to lose interest. The last major initiative of the rent strike movement came in early March, when Gray and the CCH joined a coalition of civil rights, labor, and tenant leaders, including James Farmer, Bayard Rustin, and Dorothy Height, for a march on the state capitol in Albany.

Joining forces with A. Philip Randolph's Committee for a $1.50 Minimum Wage and the National Association for Puerto Rican Civil Rights, the coalition chartered buses from New York City to go to Albany to demand a legislative program that reflected the joint economic and housing concerns of working-class Black and Puerto Rican residents. These demands included the establishment of a $1.50 minimum wage, a massive construction program for low-rent public housing, passage of emergency legislation to compel proper building code enforcement, legislation legalizing rent strikes, and substantial state aid for educational equality and school desegregation.[153] Although three thousand demonstrators from across the state braved snow and sleet to march on the state capitol, the governor was largely unmoved by the protest, and its leaders left disappointed. Speaking at a rally following the march, CORE leader Norman Hill told the thousands gathered that "only if we light fires all over the state, only if we disrupt and dislocate in a creative way, will we get what we want."[154]

The disappointment of the March on Albany served as an inglorious conclusion to the rent strike movement's prominence in New York City politics. By that point, as Mark Naison notes, "The aura of the cataclysmic power that had surrounded the rent strike in its early days had largely faded away."[155] While rent strikes would continue over the next year, several factors contributed to the movement's decline. First, despite the media spotlight and strong grassroots support garnered by Gray and the CCH, the movement was unable to win the full support of other civil rights and community organizations. Though the fifteen organizations that made up the Rent Strike Coordinating Committee provided some funding, publicity, and legal assistance for the movement, the bulk of the extensive organizing work needed to build a mass movement fell on the limited staff of the CCH and NSM.[156] This lack of support frustrated Gray, who blamed the rent strike movement's failure to reach his projected building totals on a lack of "adequate support from local civil rights organizations."[157]

Even when the local branches of national civil rights organizations, most notably CORE, were actively involved in organizing the rent strike movement, they received limited support from the national office. Although

James Farmer advocated for rent strikes when they emerged in November, the national CORE leader distanced himself from the strikes completely once the movement became identified with Jesse Gray. In a likely attempt to create separation between national CORE and Gray's background with the Communist Party, Farmer refused to make any public comment regarding the strikes and lent little institutional support.[158] Though the CCH had for a short while collaborated with larger tenant organizations in the city, including the Metropolitan Council on Housing, fundamental differences between the organizations' visions for tenant organizing also hampered any long-term coalition. While Gray and the CCH were attempting to "build a tenant movement that is trying to empower itself," as Gray's comrade Jack O'Dell later explained, the CCH viewed the council as more of "a social service thing."[159]

With such meager staffing, financial resources, and organizational support, the CCH lacked the institutional strength necessary to keep up with the rigors of tenant organizing while concurrently navigating and applying pressure on landlords and the vast network of city and state agencies involved in housing policy. Organizers were spread thin dealing with the courts, city agencies, and politicians, leaving little time for the "spadework" of street rallies, leafleting, and organizing buildings.[160] Even when the CCH scored a major victory with the Ribaudo decision in December 1963, the legal procedure established by the ruling was "difficult to employ, time consuming, and involved constant attention of volunteer or unpaid lawyers," thereby limiting its impacts for a cash- and resource-strapped grassroots organization.[161] Though some progress was made by March 1964, frustrations largely remained over slum conditions in Harlem as city hall made only minor concessions to demands for systemic change.

Though scholars have aptly pointed out how, by the spring of 1964, the rent strike movement became so bogged down in dealing with city agencies and the courts that the CCH more closely resembled a housing clinic than a radical social movement, the impacts of the rent strike stretched far beyond the realm of housing.[162] Given Gray's professed mission of forcing a mass rehabilitation of Black and Puerto Rican communities by transferring residential buildings from private to public ownership, the successes of the strikes in forcing housing repairs, rent deductions, and new legal and judicial policies can be considered marginal gains. However, while falling short of its lofty ambitions, the rent strike movement secured tangible victories for working-class tenants, built movement infrastructures, and supported the development of countless grassroots organizers, all of which made important contributions to the Black freedom movement in Harlem and beyond.

By the spring of 1964, the model of grassroots organizing Jesse Gray developed over more than a decade had pushed local and national civil rights organizations to embrace a militant grassroots approach to building Black community power in the Jim Crow North. The involvement of local CORE chapters in the rent strikes marked the culmination of a move away from a middle-class integrationist focus and toward self-determination for working-class Black communities. "We really have to step up our militancy," NY CORE rent strike coordinator William Reed acknowledged that spring. "We have to step it up . . . in organizing the Black people because our struggle is there for the Black people in the community."[163]

For the NSM, participation in the rent strikes prompted a major shift from the social service basis of the earlier tutorial projects to the transformative possibilities of community organizing. "The people who were administering the tutorials realized . . . there would be change only if the community organized itself to create change of its own," national NSM staffer Chuck Turner pointed out that spring.[164] This shift was reflected in mounting tensions over interracial organizing and a growing recognition of the need for local Black leadership of NSM projects. At an NSM Congress meeting in March 1964, organizers passed a motion introduced by Joan Countryman that "there should be no white girls in the ghetto." Arguing that the presence of white organizers gave the NSM a reformist "white image" and hamstrung the recruitment and development of local Black organizers, Bill Strickland explained that "the people we need want revolution" and that "liberation of society is our goal not integration."[165] For both CORE and the NSM, then, the radical grassroots ethos of the rent strikes served as a model for their own budding campaigns for Black Power and self-determination.

Most importantly, it was largely through participation in the rent strikes that thousands of working-class Black and Puerto Rican Harlem residents came into direct confrontations with the oppressive limitations of liberal governance in New York City and thereby developed an increasingly radical understanding of their position in Harlem as one of colonized peoples within a local, national, and global system of white supremacy. This radicalization was forged through door-to-door organizing, pickets in front of apartment buildings, mass rallies with local and national radical activists, protests inside courthouses, demonstrations at police precincts, all coupled with political education and exposure to Harlem's radical popular culture. As NSM rent strike organizer Danny Schechter's reflected, "For the first time, [the rent strikes] have involved deprived slum dwellers in a movement for substantive change. They have also expanded the political consciousness of the ghetto community and channeled frustrations into a socially effective response. By involving the 'welfare poor' in a movement for change, rent strikes have given thousands new dignity, self-respect, and a sense of empowerment. . . . As an organizing technique the rent strikes help nurture indigenous leadership and build organizations that can get involved in other activities (school boycotts, selective patronage, etc.)."[166]

And this, precisely, was a fundamental goal of Gray's tenant organizing—a revolutionary grassroots movement for Black liberation and Black Power in the nation's cities. "People ask me why I spend all my time on heat and hot water," Gray explained later that year, "and I say heat and hot water is the biggest organizing tool we have; it may even kick off the revolution in the ghetto."[167] And all that time needed to be spent on the ground in order to advance a revolutionary consciousness. "Real revolutionaries are out in the streets organizing people around their day-to-day problems," Gray explained. "Only if we do this can we organize the masses toward independent political struggle."[168] Gray's analysis of a revolutionary grassroots movement was forged in the same crucible of Black radical thought that shaped the development of some of the leading intellectuals and organizers of the Black freedom movement in New York City. And when Malcolm X split with the Nation of Islam in early March 1964 after a three-month suspension, the radical groundswell fostered by the rent strikes began to coalesce into the makings of a Black united front in Harlem.

8

THE TIME HAS COME
1964

Heretofore Harlem has been nonviolent. I think the leadership of Harlem would prefer that we remain nonviolent.... The problem isn't the leadership, the problem isn't even the masses of people, the problem is how long can you keep denying a people freedom and expect them to remain nonviolent. Turning your cheek once is fine, turning it twice is alright, but the third time you get a little bit sick of being slapped down. And you know if you don't hit back you're in trouble. I'm not advocating hitting back. I'm only saying that if we don't break through, somebody is going to get violent.
—THELMA JOHNSON, *December 1963*

This year, 1964 is going to be a violent one....
America is a house on fire—FREEDOM NOW—or let it burn,
let it burn. Praise the Lord and pass the ammunition!!!
—ROBERT F. WILLIAMS, *The Crusader, 1964*

IN APRIL 1964 CORE NATIONAL director James Farmer scheduled a series of meetings with New York City officials to negotiate demands raised by Harlem activists during spring campaigns around education, housing, employment, and policing. By that point, the rent strike movement was in its seventh month, the protests at Harlem Hospital had fueled demands for affirmative action hiring around the city, and the school boycotts marked the largest civil rights demonstration in the nation's history to date. Built on years of groundwork laid by Black radical organizers, these campaigns to address the material needs of working-class Black communities fostered the emergence of local leaders who developed more radical analyses of systemic racism and strategies for building and wielding Black Power in New York City. In the process, Harlem residents were met with increasingly hostile and repressive responses from the NYPD, prompting civil rights organizations to converge in opposition to police violence and repression. It was with this context in mind that Farmer told Police Commissioner Michael Murphy during an April meeting, "I am concerned about the summer, and that one of the key issues will be police brutality."[1]

The escalation of police brutality and repression behind Farmer's concern was a core component of the Wagner administration's response to recent developments in grassroots organizing in Harlem. Through the rent strike movement, the Community Council on Housing (CCH) had fostered the development of local leadership and forged solidarity with Puerto Rican communities in East Harlem to build tenant power. The Northern Student Movement's (NSM) participation in the rent strikes prompted a shift from interracial tutorial programs led by college students to Black-led grassroots community organizing for self-determination. Local chapters of CORE followed suit as working-class Black New Yorkers pushed the organization into the fold of militant struggle through direct-action protests at construction sites around the city and the formation of the radical East River CORE. Meanwhile, Black radicals who made up the New Afro-American Nationalism in Harlem gravitated around Malcolm X when he split with the Nation of Islam in March to form his own Black nationalist organizations. Individually, these developments were troubling to the Wagner administration. Collectively, they represented an emergent Black Power movement that posed a serious threat to the status quo of white supremacy in Jim Crow New York.

Instead of acceding to the demands of Black communities for human rights and self-determination, city officials deployed the NYPD to manage the symptoms of systemic racism and hold back the rising tide of Black radicalism. Throughout the spring of 1964, city and state policymakers expanded the powers and personnel of the NYPD under the guise of fighting rising crime rates and combating juvenile delinquency. With the active support of mainstream media, the NYPD stoked white fears of Black criminality as a narrative cover for expanding its capacity to suppress Black dissent and protect the status quo. Acts of everyday abuse and wanton brutality skyrocketed that spring as the NYPD increasingly dispatched its Tactical Patrol Force (TPF) and Bureau of Special Services (BOSS) to surveil and suppress working-class Black and Puerto Rican neighborhoods. The violence that predictably accompanied the heightened police presence in Harlem propelled residents to action and organizations to unite against what many saw as a police state.

As they came to see the police as an army of colonial occupation, Harlem residents organized to challenge police power through direct action, legal challenges, legislation, and eventually self-defense. With each successive challenge, Harlem residents became increasingly radicalized, while the Wagner administration doubled down on repression and prepared for war against Black communities. This escalation of repression, in turn, brought greater violence on Harlem residents, particularly Black youth, who were coming to embody the New Afro-American Nationalism in their resistance to oppression that spring. In its efforts to smash Black radicalism and prevent urban rebellions through a show of force, the Wagner administration actually provoked an open confrontation with Harlem residents who refused to submit to systemic racism and police terror. By July residents and activists had exhausted the prescribed channels of redress for their grievances against the city, and as Malcolm X predicted, many came to feel that the ballots hadn't worked and that it was time for the bullets.

POLICE TERROR IN EL BARRIO

Amidst the escalation of police repression that energized the rent strike movement, a wave of police killings of Puerto Ricans that fall and winter fueled emergent campaigns against police violence that forged solidarity between Black and Puerto Rican communities. In November 1963 police on the Upper West Side fatally shot Maximo Solero and Victor Rodriguez while they were in custody in the back of a patrol car. The two men had been arrested for loitering after a resident called in a noise complaint and were each shot in the chest and head while en route to the precinct on West 100th Street. While the privileging of police accounts in the *New York Times* justified the killings, Puerto Rican activists mobilized to demand justice for their slain compatriots.[2] The following day, labor organizer Gilberto Gerena-Valentin led six hundred protestors in a demonstration in front of the 24th Precinct that turned into an occupation of the building after the police captain refused to speak with them.[3] The bold protest, which was followed by a "near-riotous" march down Broadway that stopped traffic, brought Puerto Ricans into the fold of organized action against police brutality in the city.[4] It also compelled action from the city, as the NYPD pledged to launch a training program to reach "every cop on the beat" with "lectures on prejudice, patience, and respect for minority groups."[5]

These training programs were predictably insufficient at curbing police violence, and the simmering anger over the shootings boiled over three months later, on February 14, when an off-duty probationary patrolman fatally shot eighteen-year-old high school student Francisco "Frankie" Rodriguez. According to the police account, the patrolman walked out of a bar and attempted to break up a fight between several teenage boys at 92nd Street and 2nd Avenue. When the officer approached, Rodriguez allegedly swung at him with a knife and fled toward 2nd Avenue. The patrolman drew his service revolver and fired twice, the second shot hitting the teenager in the back of the head.[6] The grisly police shooting of a promising student and young father who had been recognized as "Boy of the Year" in 1962 for his commitment to community service left Puerto Rican communities throughout the city seething with anger.

In the weeks that followed, Black and Puerto Rican organizers launched a campaign against police brutality in East Harlem that coalesced with escalating struggles around housing and education. The day before the funeral services for Rodriguez, Gerena-Valentin took to the airwaves, charging the NYPD with acting as if they were "running a plantation" in East Harlem. As a representative of the newly formed National Association for Puerto Rican Civil Rights, he also urged participation in the citywide rent strike and affirmed the support of Puerto Rican communities for a second school boycott.[7] Meanwhile, Harlem ministers took to their pulpits to denounce police brutality and demand justice. "God help us when you and I, and more especially our children, are at the mercy of gunmen who are protected, paid and supported by our own government and by our own taxes," Rev. John H. Gill lamented to his East Harlem congregation.[8]

That afternoon, the East Harlem Tenants Council (EHTC) called on "the entire Negro and Puerto Rican community to unite" for a march on the 23rd Precinct on East 104th Street to demand an investigation of the police killings of Frankie Rodriguez, Maximo Solero, and Victor Rodriguez.[9] The EHTC had been formed in 1962 by Ted Velez, a young social worker and City College graduate who used his experiences working with Jesse Gray to begin organizing tenants in "El Barrio" of East Harlem.[10] With the support of the CCH, Harlem CORE, Downtown CORE, and Mobilization for Youth, the EHTC mobilized a protest that Sunday in which 250 Black and Puerto Rican activists marched from the EHTC headquarters on East 123rd Street to the 23rd Precinct, carrying signs and chanting "Assassins!" and "Down with Police Brutality." Outside the precinct, Velez called for a public inquiry into the shooting led by civilians, anticipating demands for an independent civilian review board that were beginning to emerge that winter.[11]

The next morning, five hundred mourners braved the cold for a funeral procession and protest march through the streets of East Harlem. The collective anger over the string of police killings simmered just beneath the surface during the nearly hour-long procession. While the march was mostly silent, there were "mutterings of hostility to the police," and rumors swirled that violence would break out, especially when marchers tried to halt the procession to stage a protest in front of the 23rd Precinct. The situation grew more tense when police ordered the mourners out of the street and onto the sidewalks, but the hearse kept driving and the procession continued.[12] While open confrontation with the NYPD was narrowly avoided, *The Worker* reported, the funeral march "conveyed an angry message to the police" and contributed to the emergence of a mass campaign against police brutality in Harlem that spring.[13]

The protests also provoked responses from city officials that only deepened hostilities. In announcing plans for a "Puerto Rican self-help project," Mayor Wagner and City Council President Paul Screvane characteristically avoided the issue of police violence by shifting responsibility onto Puerto Rican communities themselves. In response to the protests, NYPD Commissioner Michael Murphy came out swinging with a scathing call to "stop the flow of crocodile tears for 'the poor boys' who 'did not know what they were doing' with a knife in hand."[14] Other officers claimed that Puerto Ricans were taking out their frustrations over "bad housing, the rats and the slumlords" on the police, who should be forgiven when an officer "responds in kind—with hatred."[15] The following month, an organization of law enforcement and their supporters in the tristate area even named the officer who killed Rodriguez "patrolman of the month" for having "won the respect, confidence, and admiration" of his colleagues.[16]

Taken together, the inaction of city officials and the declaration of war by law enforcement sent a clear message to Black and Puerto Rican New Yorkers that battle lines had been drawn for a new stage of the struggle.[17] For many Puerto Ricans, these experiences with police brutality and state violence cast into sharper relief the daily realities of oppressive policing in their communities. "The Puerto Rican does not see the cop as a friend," one Puerto Rican leader explained to the *New York Times*. "He does not feel he can come to the station house for help. To him, the cop is someone who is there to oppress him."[18] Through their protests against state violence, however, it also became clear that "the Civil Rights Revolution has finally swept the Puerto Rican community into its orbit" as Black and Puerto Rican organizations forged alliances for collective action that spring.[19]

LIVING IN A POLICE STATE

The same day that Frankie Rodriguez was killed by the NYPD in East Harlem, state legislators in Albany passed two new bills to give police unprecedented power in New York State.[20] The stop-and-frisk and no-knock bills were introduced earlier that year by Republican Governor Nelson Rockefeller as part of a broad package of anticrime legislation to give law enforcement, in his words, "new tools and fresh efforts" in the "battle against organized and unorganized crime."[21] Motivated in part by a double-digit increase in crime rates since June 1963 reported by the NYPD, the two bills represented an effort to take the gloves off the city's police officers in what Rockefeller described as a "war on crime."[22] The stop-and-frisk bill—the first in the United States—gave police the authority to detain, question, and search any person they deemed "reasonably" suspicious. The law essentially legalized what was already a common police practice in Black communities. "A lot of us folks in Harlem thought that was the law already because they've been doing it that way for years," attorney Paul Zuber noted at a March rally.[23] The "no-knock" bill allowed police to execute search warrants on residences without knocking or announcing themselves as law enforcement.[24] While proponents of the new laws claimed they were imperative for clarifying and standardizing police policies to protect the rights of citizens, Black and

Puerto Rican New Yorkers had little doubt about the intentions and most likely targets of these new police powers.

Black media outlets warned of the dangers the new bills posed to Black communities. The *Amsterdam News* charged the laws would give "a green light" to "bigoted or sadistic police" and expressed its solidarity with civil rights organizations fighting their passage.[25] Even more concerning for *Liberator* columnist Robert Arnold was the green light the laws would give for suppressing radical political activity, predicting "a series of unprovoked raids, similar to the attack on the Muslim Temple in Los Angeles, which will further inflame the already tense racial situation."[26] With demands for police reform and oversight ignored for nearly a decade, it now appeared as though police abuse and repression of Black and Puerto Rican communities had won an official endorsement from the mayor and the state.

Harlem leaders mobilized to challenge the bills before they were signed into law. In late February representatives from twenty Harlem organizations, including the NAACP, CORE, and the Committee on Police-Community Relations—an East Harlem organization established in the wake of the recent killings—formed the Ad Hoc Committee for Fair Police Practice. The committee was formed to coordinate a direct-action campaign to pressure the governor to veto or repeal the two bills, to represent victims of police abuse, and to fight for the creation of an independent, civilian-led police review board.[27] Though previous campaigns around police brutality had forced the city to create a Civilian Complaint Review Board in 1953, it was operated internally by the NYPD and predictably did little to reduce police violence.[28] Coming on the heels of high-profile police killings that winter, the new laws revived demands for civilian oversight of the NYPD as a means of curbing police violence. While the committee moved quickly to organize protests outside the governor's apartment and office in Manhattan to demand he veto the bills, Rockefeller was undeterred.[29] With the active support of Mayor Wagner and Commissioner Murphy, the no-knock and stop-and-frisk bills were signed into law on March 3 over mounting opposition in Harlem.[30]

That weekend, the Ad Hoc Committee brought together a broad coalition of Black and Puerto Rican organizers, attorneys, clergy, and elected officials for a mass rally in front of the Hotel Theresa to publicly denounce the new legislation and demand its repeal. After Harlem attorney Basil Patterson explained the new laws and introduced the objectives of the committee to the crowd of three hundred, New York Congressman William Fitts

Ryan warned that the "clearly unconstitutional" laws would create "a police state" and likened their passage to the actions of a "demagogue or dictator."[31] Drawing connections to the killings of Solero, Victor Rodriguez, and Frankie Rodriguez, Puerto Rican leaders including Ted Velez, Hector Velez, and Assemblyman Jose Ramos Lopez called for Black and Puerto Rican unity and reiterated their prior demands for a civilian review board.[32] The most impassioned address came from Jesse Gray, whose recent encounters with police and city marshals informed his condemnation of the NYPD as the most "rotten, corrupt and degenerate" department in the nation. That these bills had breezed through the state legislature while code-enforcement bills to aid striking Harlem tenants were shot down fueled Gray's fury, which he directed at the twenty-five uniformed officers assigned to patrol the rally before joining the chorus of demands for a civilian review board.[33]

The swift organizational responses to what amounted to a direct attack on Black and Puerto Rican communities ensured that Rockefeller's anticrime measures would not be implemented in New York City without a fight. In the weeks and months before the new laws went into effect in July, police corruption, brutality, and repression would become the most pressing—and explosive—issues for the Black freedom movement in Harlem.

CAMPAIGNS AGAINST POLICE BRUTALITY

As the Ad Hoc Committee got to work, local chapters of CORE, NSM, and the Progressive Labor Movement (PLM) escalated their efforts to address the three "interrelated grievances" Black and Puerto Rican communities had with the NYPD: corruption and inefficiency, mistreatment and brutality, and repression of dissent.[34] Through campaigns to demand various reforms, organizers advanced new ideas about how to curb oppressive policing and developed more assertive strategies to achieve them. In doing so, these organizations predictably drew the attention and ire of the NYPD, which mobilized the resources of the state to undermine and suppress their rising demands.

The day before the Ad Hoc Committee rally, local CORE chapters staged a sit-in at Commissioner Murphy's office to protest police brutality, including the recent torture of thirty-five-year-old Bronx resident Jesse Roberts.[35] Members of Bronx, Brooklyn, and Harlem CORE arrived at police headquarters to present a series of demands, including the "abolition" of internal investigations, periodic meetings with civil rights organizations to improve police-community relations, and enhanced police training on civil rights. Most significantly, their demands for a civilian review board—comprising a board for each borough with members elected by legal and civil rights organizations and empowered to investigate complaints, terminate and deny benefits to officers, and submit findings to the district attorney for criminal prosecution—were reflective of an emergent struggle for community control of the police.[36] Finding Murphy absent from their scheduled meeting, Bronx CORE Chairman Rev. Herbert Callender, Howard Quander (Bronx CORE), and Brooklyn CORE Chairman Isaiah Brunson pulled out handcuffs and chained themselves to a metal grate near his door.[37] Joined by clergy and members of CORE and Progressive Youth for Puerto Rico, the group staged an hour-long "chain-in" until they were arrested and forcibly removed by police.[38] This bold direct-action protest jump-started a citywide campaign for an independent civilian review board spearheaded by CORE and the Ad Hoc Committee.

To the *New York Amsterdam News,* the chain-in—along with a sit-in on the Triborough Bridge led by East River CORE the same day—also marked opening day of the "1964 season of civil rights demonstrations." Having thrown out the opening pitch, Callender took the opportunity to announce, "We are just going to have to get more and more, larger and bigger demonstrations. We'll have to shock the officials and the public to get the city to face up to the realities of the day."[39] Commissioner Murphy took Callender's remarks as a threat and came out swinging the following week. In an address to six thousand police officers, Murphy announced he would not allow civil rights leaders—specifically Callender, Malcolm X, and Jesse Gray—to "turn New York City into a battleground" and declared the NYPD would "not be intimidated" from their duty to protect the city against "extremist violence." Murphy was particularly disturbed by a growing embrace of self-defense in Harlem, taking aim at Malcolm X as a "self-proclaimed 'leader'" who "openly advocates bloodshed and armed revolt." Published on the front page of the *New York Times,* Murphy's remarks were both an attempt to isolate and criminalize Black radical organizers and a call to arms for the NYPD to hold back the rising tide of Black radicalism.[40]

CORE was joined in its campaign by the NSM's Harlem Action Group (HAG), whose encounters with law enforcement during the rent strikes thrust organizers into struggles around policing. Working with HAG and CCH that winter, organizer Q. R. Hand developed a clear understanding of the relationships between police repression, abuse, corruption, and lack of protection in Harlem. Once the rent strikes got underway, Hand explained, "all of a sudden cops would be coming by much more often" to the street corners where they had previously permitted heroin dealers to set up shop and turned the other way when street fights broke out. Having witnessed the King Cole Trio's intimidation of Granville Cherry and having been arrested for blocking the illegal eviction of Luther Brown, Hand had a clear idea of the role of the police. "There's a particular reason uptown why the cops have to get their special tactical force up there," he explained. "It comes down to the fact that there are an awful lot of groups, not together as of yet, who are deciding, 'well we can't take this any longer. We can't take the bad housing, the rats, the roaches, the inferior schools.'"[41]

By the spring of 1964, such experiences led HAG organizers to begin shifting their focus to policing. In late March HAG Field Director Robert Knight sent a letter to Commissioner Murphy complaining that a patrolman had watched a Black teenager get jumped on 137th Street without intervening. Writing on behalf of "the unprotected citizens" of the community, Knight demanded an investigation and informed the commissioner that HAG had evidence to prove the officer's behavior was part of a pattern of police negligence in Central Harlem.[42] Knight's complaint was part of a common criticism of the NYPD for failing to protect Black communities from violent crime and property crime while offering protection to slumlords, drug dealers, and racketeers operating in Harlem. To raise awareness of the case as part of a developing campaign around policing, Knight made copies of the letter and distributed them in the neighborhood.[43]

As continued encounters with the NYPD led HAG to brainstorm programs for dealing with police violence, corruption, and negligence, organizers were also being influenced by emergent Black nationalist demands for community control of institutions. In a meeting of the NSM Congress the following week, Knight shared a proposal by East Harlem organizer Preston Wilcox for community control of urban renewal programs, which inspired discussions about community control of the police. During the discussion, HAG organizer Granville Cherry floated the idea of forming a "citizen's police force" to keep the community safe and to keep watch on police corruption with slumlords and hustlers.[44] Drawing on his earlier run-in with the King Cole Trio, Cherry conceived of the idea as a "group of community people assuming police powers in their area as protest of police brutality" and as a means of challenging what he described as the "police-hustler conspiracy."[45] While Cherry's idea never got off the ground, it laid the groundwork

FIG 17 Harlem Action Group Field Director Robert Knight (*left*) at a demonstration against police brutality in spring 1964. (Handschu Photograph Files, Municipal Archives, City of New York)

for NSM's involvement in campaigns for civilian oversight and anticipated demands for community control of the police and the formation of copwatch programs that would become key organizing initiatives during the Black Power era.

Through the rent strikes and its organizing around policing, HAG also began forging relationships with other Black radical organizations, such as the Harlem chapter of the Progressive Labor Movement. By the spring of 1964, the small but formidable organization had emerged at the forefront of struggles against police brutality in the city. Formed in 1962 by longtime communist and labor organizer Bill Epton following his expulsion from the CPUSA over his support of the Third World Marxism of Chairman Mao Tse-tung, the PLM advocated for working-class control of economic, social, and political institutions in Black communities as a path toward socialism, self-determination, and liberation.[46] Through his prior work with the Negro American Labor Council and the Emergency Committee for Unity on Social and Economic Problems, thirty-two-year-old Epton forged relationships with a wide array of Left and nationalist leaders in Harlem, including Malcolm X, Jesse Gray, James Haughton, Calvin Hicks, Florence Rice, and Selma Sparks. By late 1963 the New York chapters of PLM dedicated themselves to organizing in working-class Black and Puerto Rican communities around the issues of housing and policing, collaborating with Gray on the citywide rent strikes and challenging acts of police brutality and repression that fall and winter.[47]

Through direct-action protests and their weekly newspaper *Challenge,* the PLM organized around a series of demands informed by a systemic analysis of police repression. Following the police killings of Solero and Rodriguez, the West Side Progressive Labor Club attributed the shootings to a campaign of "police terror designed to keep Negro and Puerto Rican workers from fighting against the corrupt political and social forces that exploit them" and demanded murder charges and public investigations of police brutality led by a committee of Black and Puerto Rican workers.[48] Epton and the Harlem PLM built on these demands during the campaign against the Rockefeller anticrime laws. Denouncing the legalization of "police crime" against Black and Puerto Rican communities in a March flyer, the Harlem PLM declared police powers should be curbed by repealing the two "fascist laws," disarming the police, replacing Commissioner Murphy with someone elected by the people, and holding public trials of police accused of crimes. Furthermore, the Harlem PLM declared, "If the police cannot protect us, we must learn to protect ourselves!" anticipating an emerging embrace of self-defense against police brutality in Harlem that would gain in popularity as the summer approached.[49]

BALLOTS OR BULLETS

As the struggle against police brutality heated up in March, the *New York Times* broke the news that Malcolm X was leaving the Nation of Islam. In an interview with reporter M. S. Handler, Malcolm explained he could no longer be constrained by the Nation's restrictions on political action and engagement with the Black freedom movement. Despite these restrictions, Malcolm's immersion in Harlem's Black radical culture and forays into political action over the past several years had prepared him to assume a new role.[50] At a press conference three days later, on March 12, he announced the formation of a new Black nationalist organization, Muslim Mosque, Inc. (MMI). While the NOI's brand of Black nationalism had won broad support in Black communities over the years, its strict religious doctrines and practices kept many potential members from joining. Malcolm therefore adopted a more flexible structure for the MMI to encourage the participation of non-Muslim

Black members in building a broad-based organization. While speaking to the organization's long-range plans of building independent Black political power for self-determination, Malcolm also asserted the legal right to self-defense to protect Black communities in the meantime. "In areas where our people are the constant victims of brutality," he explained, "we should form rifle clubs that can be used to defend our lives and our property in times of emergency."[51] The statement reverberated throughout the nation, drawing the attention of Black radicals and law enforcement alike.

In the following weeks Malcolm X began working with Jesse Gray to organize resistance to police brutality and repression as part of their broader efforts to build a Black united front in Harlem. Two days after Malcolm's press conference, the two solidified their relationship in Chester, Pennsylvania, at the founding conference of ACT, a national federation of radical grassroots organizers to support local struggles and coordinate national campaigns for Black liberation.[52] The idea came from a January meeting in Harlem where organizers from several cities coordinated nationwide school boycotts that kept over one million students out of schools in 32 cities the following month, the most notable led by Rev. Milton Galamison in New York City.[53] When the NAACP, CORE, the Urban League, and the National Association for Puerto Rican Rights shunned Galamison's plans for another boycott in March, ACT took the lead in coordinating and mobilizing support. The day before the second boycott, Gray and Malcolm X called a mass rally in Harlem, where Malcolm explained he was "aligned with everyone who will take some action to end this criminal situation in the schools."[54] The following day, ACT members were on site at Galamison's Siloam Presbyterian Church in Brooklyn to coordinate protest actions. In spite of its abandonment by mainstream civil rights leadership, the boycott succeeded in keeping nearly 275,000 students out of school, including 50 percent of students in predominantly Black and Puerto Rican communities and 92 percent of students in Harlem.[55]

Building on the momentum of the boycott, Gray and Malcolm turned their attention to policing at a series of rallies following Commissioner Murphy's targeted attacks on them and Herbert Callender. The two repeated their demands for the commissioner's ouster, asserted the rights of Black communities to defend themselves, and demanded the creation of a civilian review board. Recognizing the inherent connections between policing, housing, education, and employment in Jim Crow New York, Gray and Malcolm X presented their resistance to police violence as part of a collective attack on

FIG 18 Malcolm X (*left*) addresses a rally at the Dunlevy Milbank Community Center in March 1964 in support of the second school boycott as Jesse Gray (*right*) listens. (Library of Congress, Prints and Photographs Division, NYWT&S Collection [LC-DIG-ppmsca-10454])

systemic racism. At a March 22 rent strike rally, Gray issued demands for Murphy's dismissal, alongside demands for a $1.50 minimum wage and a call for all Harlem residents to stop paying rent "until we get better education for our children." Malcolm seconded these demands and reasserted the rights of Black communities to practice self-defense when the government proved unable or unwilling to protect them from systemic racist violence. "I am indicting the government for not defending us," Malcolm proclaimed. "If the government can't do it then let us do it ourselves." Malcolm hardly needed to make any specific reference to the Rockefeller crime laws or the uptick in police brutality for the crowd of 250 to understand the premise of his comments.[56]

That same night, at the nearby Rockland Palace, the MMI held a rally to protest the Southern filibuster of the pending Civil Rights Act. Despite its promises of making citizenship a reality for African Americans, few Harlem leaders believed the legislation would solve the problems of systemic racism in the Jim Crow North. Nonetheless, Black radicals leveraged the filibuster in speeches to heighten contradictions and mobilize anger into action. At the outset, Malcolm X introduced Gray and Rev. Nelson C. Dukes as "strong Black Nationalists" and announced a series of forthcoming Sunday night rallies to expound on the MMI's positions.[57] In the course of this speech, which some described as among the best he ever gave, Malcolm laid the ideological groundwork for his nascent nationalist organization and introduced what would become one of his most iconic political analyses—the ballot or the bullet.[58] Predicting that 1964 would be the most explosive year in American history, Malcolm X explained that the Black freedom movement had reached a decisive moment in which Black Americans would win their freedom through either the ballot box or the barrel of a gun.

Though Malcolm coupled his call for "ballots or bullets" with plans for a massive voter registration drive, his message stretched beyond voting rights or electoral politics.[59] His emphasis on building political power was part of a broader strategy he was developing for achieving Black self-determination. Influenced by Gloria Richardson's position on Black independent politics—which she shared with him at ACT's founding conference and in the weeks since—Malcolm called for Black voters to register as independents and to strategically abstain from voting as a means of exercising greater leverage in electoral politics.[60] While the idea of Black independent politics wasn't new in Harlem, where Black radicals had launched the Freedom Now Party the previous summer, the Southern filibuster fueled a growing frustration with the Democratic Party's stranglehold on Black voters. Whereas Malcolm's position within the NOI had previously caused him to abstain from involvement with the FNP, his newfound independence allowed him to enter the political fray.

Beyond calling for Black communities to embrace new tactics to flex their political muscle, Malcolm urged his audiences to join any Black nationalist organization that taught people to "take over their own communities, politically and economically."[61] Specifically, he urged Black New Yorkers to unite in opposition to school segregation and the Rockefeller crime laws, which were designed to create a police state in Black communities to prevent their liberation. Malcolm explained that he saw school segregation as a form of internal colonialism, in which white outsiders controlled the educational institutions of Black communities.[62] Like Mae Mallory, he was not interested in Black students integrating white schools but rather in gaining Black community control over schools as a means of improving educational outcomes. As a consultant to ACT, Malcolm was part of planning meetings for the national school boycotts and pledged the MMI's support for these efforts so long as his allies didn't "compromise with the enemy."⁶³ Malcolm was clear that his solidarity with the school boycotts was not a sign that he was warming to integration but a demonstration of his commitment to building a broad-based Black united front.

While he did not articulate his plans for challenging the Rockefeller laws and rampant police brutality, Malcolm X was in the early stages of developing a strategy that included the use of organized self-defense to protect Black communities from racist violence and police repression. In laying out the MMI's future plans, Malcolm announced plans for a Black nationalist convention that spring, at which, he said, "we'll form whatever is necessary—whether it's a black nationalist party or a black nationalist army."⁶⁴ In presenting the looming threat of armed insurrection as a logical consequence of the continued resistance to civil and human rights for Black Americans, Malcolm characteristically articulated the feelings of many Harlem residents.

Over the next several weeks, Malcolm refined the analyses in "The Ballot or the Bullet" address before thousands of people at rallies in Harlem, Cleveland, and Detroit. On April 6 Mae Mallory joined him at an MMI forum at the Audubon Ballroom, just three weeks after being released on bond from a Monroe jail. After a nearly three-year legal battle against the kidnapping charges she faced in Monroe, Mallory was convicted in late February and sentenced to sixteen to twenty years in prison.⁶⁵ With bond posted by the Monroe Defense Committee pending an appeal, Mallory returned to Harlem in early April, where she resumed organizing while embarking on a national speaking tour entitled "Self-Defense in the Black Revolution."⁶⁶ Meanwhile, Malcolm grounded his continued calls for a Black united front within a broader international analysis of Black liberation struggles. Citing the type of rampant racist violence Mallory fought against in Monroe as evidence of the United States committing genocide against Black people, Malcolm insisted that the Black freedom movement now needed to shift its demands from "civil rights" to "human rights" as defined by international law.⁶⁷ To expedite this shift, Mallory privately pushed Malcolm to forge unity among advocates of radical self-defense by reconnecting with his old friend Robert F. Williams.⁶⁸

At the last of the MMI's series of rallies the following week, Malcolm announced his plans to embark on a three-week tour of Africa and the Middle East, hoping to build on Harlem's traditions of Black internationalism to forge alliances and study anticolonial revolutions. While many popular interpretations of his hajj to Mecca have focused on the reconsideration of his views on white people, Malcolm's trip was also a study abroad experience in the school of revolution. Like his comrades who had sought out revolutionary teachers and allies in the streets of Harlem and Havana over the past several years, Malcolm immersed himself in the revolutionary struggles that liberated African people from colonization. While learning from revolutionaries from Algeria, China, Cuba, and Ghana during his trip, Malcolm also sought their support for the coming Black revolution in the United States.[69] Whether it was through the ballot or the bullet, Malcolm understood that a minority revolution in the United States would require proactive solidarity from the Third World as part of an international struggle for human rights.

"A GUN AT THE HEART OF THE CITY"

As Malcolm prepared for his trip, the growing support for militant direct action at home was on full display when Brooklyn CORE announced plans to disrupt the opening of the 1964 World's Fair in Flushing Meadows, Queens. The fair had become a symbol of the contradictions of white opulence in the face of Black oppression that spring, particularly as the city extended a $40 million loan to the World's Fair Corporation, yet cried poverty when it came to resolving unsafe housing conditions.[70] These stark contradictions and an international platform made the World's Fair an ideal target for making demands on city officials.

On April 9 Brooklyn CORE announced plans to block all traffic to the fair on opening day unless Mayor Wagner implemented a plan to "end police brutality, abolish slum housing, integrate the construction and brewing industries, and provide integrated, quality education for all" by April 20. In a telegram to the mayor, CORE leaders blasted Wagner's brand of racial liberalism in Jim Crow New York. "For many years you have given lip service to the just demands of black people," the telegram read, "and for just as long, you and your agency heads have done everything in your power to thwart these demands." With the dramatic campaigns around employment, education, housing, and policing over the past year having failed to compel Wagner to act, Brooklyn CORE concluded that "more severe direct-action methods" needed to be taken if Black liberation was to be realized in New York.[71]

The plan for the "stall-in" was conceived by Brooklyn CORE Chair Isaiah Brunson on the heels of the chain-in at NYPD headquarters. Frustrated by the compromises of CORE's past campaigns, Brunson envisioned the stall-in as a disruptive tactic that would force city officials to act.[72] Brunson's plan also built on a sit-in on the Triborough Bridge (now the Robert F. Kennedy Bridge) that East River CORE staged the same day as the chain-in to protest overcrowded, underfunded, and dangerous schools in East Harlem. The strategy behind the action, which caused traffic jams throughout East Harlem, was to force white commuters to stop and take notice of conditions in Harlem and to take responsibility for resolving them.[73] Citing the power of just seven protestors to disrupt the city's infrastructure, East River CORE urged New Yorkers to imagine what could be accomplished "if all of us sat down on a bridge together, march on Mayor Wagner and Governor Rockefeller and the U.S. Congress together, and voted together."[74]

In response to East River CORE's challenge, Brunson called for thousands of drivers—with their gas tanks intentionally near empty—to get on the highways and bridges leading to Flushing Meadows on opening day, let their cars run out of gas, and create debilitating traffic jams. Those without vehicles would sit-in at subway stations and block trains to shut down public transit heading to Queens. In Brunson's analysis, the stall-in—which the city's traffic commissioner warned would "paralyze the whole city"—would force city officials to immediately meet their demands to avoid chaos.[75] "We have picketed, boycotted, sat-in, lied-in, etc. All our efforts have been in vain," he wrote just days before the planned action. "The time has come. The Power structure of this city, state, and country must be made to realize that we will accept palliation no longer."[76]

As opening day approached, the stall-in drew intense backlash from politicians, media, and white New Yorkers who were more affronted by the disruptive tactics than by the oppressive conditions that compelled Black New Yorkers to protest. Doubling down on its critique of the Triborough Bridge sit-in, the *New York Times* condemned the stall-in as a "hare-brained scheme" and criminal act that would "arouse the hostility of millions" and "do incalculable harm to their own cause."[77] Meanwhile, local and national politicians warned that the stall-in would fuel the opposition of Southern senators and compromise passage of the Civil Rights Act. Most of the efforts to suppress the proposed stall-in focused on criminalizing activists and marshaling the carceral powers of the state. While Mayor Wagner, who likened the action to holding "a gun to the heart of the city," mobilized thousands of police to patrol the routes to Queens and won an injunction from the New York State Supreme Court, city officials enacted a new traffic ordinance making it illegal to run out of gas on expressways, bridges, and tunnels under penalty of fine or imprisonment.[78] To supplement the expanded police presence, the World's Fair hired private security forces, which turned nearby warehouses into temporary "detention compounds" capable of holding six hundred people.[79] Created to suppress dissent, such actions also expanded a carceral dragnet in New York City that disproportionately targeted working-class Black and Latino residents.

Meanwhile, mainstream civil rights leaders denounced the protest and distanced themselves from its organizers. Claiming that the stall-in would "merely create confusion and thus damage the fight for freedom," James Farmer announced the suspension of Brooklyn CORE and warned other chapters they would share the same fate if they joined the protest.[80] Bayard Rustin and Martin Luther King Jr. played both sides, criticizing the stall-in as a "tactical error" while leveraging its media spotlight to urge "those in power to act vigorously to remove the conditions that give rise to what they consider extremist projects."[81] It was a standard play for the civil rights establishment which allowed them to maintain their standing with power brokers by throwing Black radicals under the bus.

Black radicals in Harlem and beyond showed up in solidarity, arguing that Black liberation would never be won through means deemed acceptable and respectable by people in power. Undeterred by threats from the national office, the Bronx, Harlem, and Queens CORE chapters threw their support behind the stall-in. The night before leaving for Africa, Malcolm X also expressed his support to the five hundred people who gathered for the MMI's final Sunday night forum. Joined by ACT comrades Gloria Richardson and Jesse Gray, Malcolm X couched his endorsement in terms of the need for greater militancy and for "lots of Mau Mau here," referring to the anticolonial fighters who liberated Kenya from British colonialism.[82] The stall-in also won the endorsement of ACT, which called the action "the next step in the black revolution" and planned solidarity protests across the nation at a meeting in Washington, DC, on April 18.[83] Gray rushed back to Harlem to organize a rally the next day with Brunson, Herbert Callender, and Marshall England. Under the headline "We Don't Need a World's Fair—We Need a Fair World," flyers urged New Yorkers to "tie up every highway and street... across the nation" until Brooklyn CORE's demands were met.[84] In Chicago, Lawrence Landry made plans for a solidarity stall-in, and Gloria Richardson and Stanley Branche pledged to send cars to New York from Cambridge and Chester.[85] New York City's sanitation workers union declared they "would not scab on anyone fighting for freedom or civil rights" and vowed its ten thousand workers would stay home if ordered to tow cars off the roadways.[86]

When opening day finally arrived, the national turmoil and cold rain led many fairgoers to stay home. With fewer commuters on the roads and a disappointing turnout from activists deterred by the massive police response, the disruptive potential of the stall-in never materialized. Out of the thousands of cars expected to participate, only a handful stalled out and were quickly removed with tow trucks, dump trucks, and bulldozers.[87] Instead, activists focused their energies on blocking subway traffic, which was met with police brutality and over a hundred arrests. Led by Bob Knight, HAG mobilized dozens of young activists to stall a subway train from Manhattan by pulling the emergency cord.[88] In Queens, protestors lay across subway tracks and blocked train doors with their bodies before police dragged them away, "gave merciless beatings" to five people who suffered severe head injuries, and arrested all twenty-three activists.[89] To Brunson, the violent arrests illuminated and validated the need for protests in the first place. "New York City is going to see a lot more of sitting-in and picketing on this police brutality case," he warned reporters at the scene. "Officials aren't going to be able to untie this city when we get through."[90] Days later, a group of twenty organizers, including Brunson, Callender, England, Galamison, and Gray, issued a statement challenging the criminalization of protestors, denouncing the "criminal brutality" of the NYPD, and calling for an injunction to forbid Mayor Wagner from ignoring the criminal negligence of slumlords, violations of fair employment laws, and neglect of children in segregated schools.[91]

Amid all the debate and controversy, the stall-in made one thing clear. The longer that city, state, and federal officials obstructed Black demands for rights and power, the more radical activists' strategies and tactics would become.[92] "Negroes are tired of waiting for promises to become realities," NSM director Bill Strickland explained in the organization's newsletter. "They are tired of listening to their 'friends'; and tired of being dependent upon someone else's timetable."[93] Though the stall-in was unsuccessful in meeting CORE's demands—largely because they gave the city too much time to mobilize opposition—it raised key ideological and tactical questions about the power of disruption for social change. As Strickland pointed out, the stall-in revealed that the struggle for civil rights was no longer about good intentions, morality, or the law but was "a battle of power."[94] And the threat of disabling a major city's infrastructure to win demands represented a new tool for wielding power in the Black freedom movement.

THE WAR ON BLACK YOUTH

Strickland's analysis was shared by Max Stanford (later Muhammad Ahmad), national field chairman of a recently formed revolutionary nationalist organization called the Revolutionary Action Movement (RAM). To Stanford, the stall-in demonstrated the ideological growth of Black radicals who now recognized they "were in a strategic position to disrupt the system."[95] Over the past year RAM had quietly emerged as a militant, youth-led Black radical organization with bases in Cleveland, Detroit, Philadelphia, and New York. Influenced by the theory of Harold Cruse and praxis of Robert F. Williams, RAM founders Donald Freeman, Wanda Marshall, and Stanford routinely looked to Harlem as they developed a program for fusing mass direct action with self-defense to "change the civil rights movement into a black revolution."[96]

With Robert F. Williams in exile, RAM saw Malcolm X as the driving ideological force behind Black revolutionary nationalism in the United States. Freeman was a frequent visitor to Mosque No. 7 as a college student in the early 1960s, and it was a formative meeting with Malcolm X in the fall of 1962 that prompted Marshall and Stanford to begin a pilot program for radical grassroots organizing in Stanford's hometown of Philadelphia. In November 1963 Freeman "cemented a personal and political convergence" with Malcolm when he opened for him at the Northern Negro Grass Roots Leadership Conference in Detroit. They kept in touch during Malcolm's suspension from the Nation of Islam that winter, and Freeman was at the press conference when Malcolm announced the MMI's formation in March 1964.[97] By the end of that month, Freeman was back in Harlem, strategizing with Malcolm about "how he could relate to RAM" and sharing the stage at an MMI forum, where he reportedly told the crowd that he and RAM were "prepared to 'get behind' Malcolm X in [the] struggle for freedom."[98] During these visits, Freeman built relationships with Black radical artists, intellectuals, and activists who made up the cultural arm of the New Afro-American Nationalism in Harlem, including Calvin Hicks, Rolland Snellings (later Askia Muhammad Touré), LeRoi Jones (later Amiri Baraka), Nan and Walter Bowe, Abbey Lincoln, and Dan Watts.[99] This network of Black radicals influenced RAM's development and offered Freeman fertile ground for cultivating a RAM cadre in the nation's largest city.[100]

Meanwhile, Marshall and Stanford learned some important lessons in Philadelphia that would shape RAM's work in New York. Through militant grassroots struggles around employment discrimination and racist policing, Stanford found that working-class Black people were ready to organize around self-defense and use more "aggressive" tactics for liberation. "We must control our own community, we must protect our own, we must obtain power to survive," Stanford declared in late 1963.[101] Like Mae Mallory and Malcolm X, RAM was trying to figure out how to translate popular support for self-defense into concrete strategies for self-determination.[102] Through their grassroots organizing and study of anticolonial revolutions, RAM came to see Black youth as the key. If organizers could channel their energy and anger into organized action, RAM believed, Black youth would act as a "catalyst" for making Black America "the vanguard of the world black revolution."[103]

RAM's focus on organizing Black working-class youth was part of a growing trend among community organizations in Harlem. Over the past decade, the city had invested a great deal of energy and resources to combat "juvenile delinquency" and youth gangs—primarily through expanded policing and detention—but did little to resolve their root causes. While few organizations shared RAM's interest in developing a youth liberation army, most shared a common belief that Harlem's future hinged on how Black youth responded to their oppression and exploitation. With the future of their communities under attack, organizations like Harlem Youth Opportunities Unlimited focused their work on developing youth leaders into a progressive force for social change. In doing so, HARYOU inevitably confronted the issue of racist policing and criminalization in Harlem.

As director of HARYOU, Dr. Kenneth Clark oversaw the development of initiatives to address "juvenile delinquency," amplify the voices of Black youth, and train a new generation of leaders in the Black freedom movement. Founded in 1962, HARYOU sought to move beyond a social service framework by empowering Harlem youth to shape the organization's direction while gaining experience in community organizing.[104] A key program was the Leadership Training Workshop, which brought together thirty-two youth leaders—including HEP activist Sherron Jackson and Pat Mallory (Mae Mallory's daughter)—in the summer of 1963 for a training and mentorship program on community organizing, Black history and culture, and building community institutions.[105] Participants spent the mornings working with veteran activists like Jesse Gray and John Henrik Clarke and the afternoons in group discussions facilitated by staff members, including Nan Bowe, where they reflected on their organizing experiences, analyses of social issues, and perspectives on the movement. Bowe taught the young activists about freedom fighters like Frederick Douglass and Mao Tse-tung, while encouraging them to develop their own ideas about social change through critical debates about organizing strategies.[106]

The most common and engaging debates during these sessions centered on nonviolence, self-defense, and revolutionary struggle. As the workshop progressed, many participants developed more critical analyses of integration and nonviolence as strategies for Black liberation. After declaring in an early session that she was "wholly for nonviolence" in a moral struggle for integration, Jackson found that her apprenticeship with Jesse Gray, participation in the Harlem Hospital protests (where she first met Malcolm X), and observations of the national movement that summer had sparked a change in her thinking.[107] By the fall, she came to see the movement as a struggle over power rather than morality which might require more radical tactics to win. "We're not going to go into the whole thing violently . . . we are asking the man for rights, we're asking him to give up certain values in terms of his system," she explained. "If he doesn't give them up, we have to take them. Now how you take them, is the question."[108] Like RAM, Jackson saw Black youth as the key to answering that question.[109]

As a step toward shouldering this massive responsibility, the young organizers were encouraged to broaden the base of their youth movement. "Go out to find the 'unaffiliated' kid, those who are hostile too. They are especially the ones you need," Harlem educational activist Thelma Johnson urged the group.[110] In the months following her directive, the reign of terror waged against Black and Puerto Rican teenagers by the NYPD became one of the leading causes of hostility among the Black youth HARYOU sought to organize. Through interviews with community members during the Leadership Training Workshop, the participants heard from dozens of teenagers and young adults about their experiences with police harassment, brutality, and corruption. As the police escalated their assault on Black communities in the spring of 1964, HARYOU was thrust into a case of police brutality that set the tone for the long, hot summers ahead.

On April 17 a group of Black and Puerto Rican teenagers on their way home from school knocked over a fruit stand on Lenox Avenue near 129th Street and started tossing apples and oranges at each other. What started as playful mischief changed when four NYPD officers stormed onto the block, snatching whoever they could and swinging their clubs at children and teenagers. While many scattered to escape the violence, others hurled fruit at the officers who were beating their peers and armed themselves with garbage can lids as shields against nightstick blows. The situation went from bad to worse when twenty-five officers who had been stationed nearby rushed in, clubs swinging and "smashing every kid that they see."[111] Neighbors who peered out their windows to bear witness looked down the barrels of service revolvers, as police aimed their weapons at open windows and rooftops, fearful of bricks and bottles raining down on them.[112] With the reinforcements violently taking control of the block, the police riot soon ended. Officers sped off to the 32nd Precinct, where they continued to savagely beat three teenagers and two adults they had arrested for daring to question their attacks. While their friends were being tortured, dozens of teenagers gathered outside the precinct chanting "Stop police brutality" and walking a picket line for three hours.[113]

In the days that followed, HARYOU staff member William "Willie" Jones set out to document witness accounts of what became known as the "Fruit Stand Riot" in order to bring charges of police brutality against the NYPD. In a community center on 130th Street, the thirty-five-year-old interviewed teenagers who recounted being targeted by police for protecting children from their nightsticks and later tortured while in custody. Daniel Hamm was walking up the block when he heard police sirens and children screaming and turned around to see what was happening. "I saw this policeman with his gun out, waving it in young children face with his billy [club] in his hand," the eighteen-year-old student explained. "He was shaking like a leaf and jumping all over the place and I thought he might shoot one of them, so I stepped in his way to keep from one of the kids getting hurt."[114] In return, the officer grabbed Hamm by the neck, threw him to the ground, and dug a knee into his chest before throwing him in the back of a police car. Hamm's friend Wallace Baker received similar treatment from two officers "who jumped on me and started beating me for nothing" after he stopped three police from beating another child with their nightsticks. Robert Rice was nearby and picked up a garbage can lid to shield Baker from the blows and others from officers who were pointing their guns all over the block. Robert Barnes Jr. told Jones that one Black officer pointed his weapon at Rice and told him "he was going to shoot him dead, right there on the street" if he didn't drop the lid. From the pained look he saw in their eyes, Jones could tell that these teenagers had "been through an experience no human being should have to go through."[115]

The most vicious beating was inflicted on Frank Stafford, a thirty-nine-year-old salesman who asked a group of police why they were beating a child. The officers wheeled about and beat him with their nightsticks as another pulled a gun on him. As Stafford tried to fend off the attacks coming from all sides, one of the officers "turned and jabbed the club in his eye" and continued beating him when he fell to the ground, writhing in pain. When Fecundo Acion, a forty-seven-year-old Puerto Rican seaman, approached and asked why they were beating Stafford, "they turned around and whipped that old man down to the ground" and took him to the 32nd Precinct with the others.[116] Inside the precinct, dozens of officers worked in shifts that evening to torture Acion and the others while they were handcuffed in a holding cell. "About thirty-five I'd say came into the room and started beating, punching us in the jaw, in the stomach, in the chest, beating us with a padded club . . . spit on us, call us niggers, dogs, animals . . . called us cop-fighters," Stafford recalled. The attack landed him in the hospital for two weeks and cost him his left eye.[117] The other four arrived in court the next day for their arraignments barely able to walk and covered with bandages and bruises.[118]

As he recorded their accounts, Jones was struck by the teenagers' determination to challenge the state violence they endured. Between interviews, he told the teenagers he had "never seen a more serious group of people in my life."[119] Just as their practice of self-defense marked them for retribution from the police, it also earned the support of many Harlem activists. The day after the Fruit Stand Riot, James 67X Shabazz organized an informal MMI meeting to "discuss police brutality" with Harlem residents, including Robert Rice.[120] For his part, Jones pledged to use his interviewing skills and resources to gather evidence for a lawsuit against the city for police brutality.[121] Like the teenagers who sparked the sit-in movement four years earlier, these young freedom fighters stirred Harlem to action.

The NYPD kept close tabs on the teenagers who dared to challenge police power in the days that followed, even staking out the community center while Jones conducted his interviews.[122] This surveillance detail went well beyond due diligence. In the month since Malcolm X launched the MMI and called for the formation of rifle clubs for self-defense, BOSS and the FBI had escalated their counterintelligence campaigns to suppress Black radicalism in Harlem by trying—in vain—to link Malcolm's calls for self-defense with organized acts of violence.[123] When Baker, Hamm, and Rice were arrested for practicing self-defense against police brutality, the NYPD and FBI saw a golden opportunity to clamp down on Black radicals by linking the teens to the MMI. Days after the Fruit Stand Riot, the NYPD began peddling a story to local journalists about a gang of Harlem youth influenced by Malcolm X and trained to attack white people. It was a common counterintelligence tactic: law enforcement would feed stories to media outlets to stoke racist fears and arouse popular sentiment in support of neutralizing threats to the status quo. While other outlets balked at the story, the NYPD and FBI finally found their man in *New York Times* reporter and Marine Corps veteran Junius Griffin when a white shopkeeper named Margit Sugar was killed in Harlem two weeks later.[124]

The fatal stabbing of a white woman in Harlem sparked a media firestorm fueled by fabricated accounts of antiwhite violence that facilitated a police occupation of Harlem. Working cooperatively with the FBI in their investigation, NYPD and BOSS detectives immediately identified those arrested during the Fruit Stand Riot as their prime suspects.[125] Within two days, the NYPD arrested six Black teenagers—including Baker, Hamm, and Rice—and fed fantastic stories to the *New York Times* about a militant Black gang roving the city attacking white people.[126] Lacking any physical evidence linking the teens to the killing, NYPD and FBI detectives relied almost exclusively on interrogating children and teenagers to prove their guilt.

The case rested on the confession of Robert Barnes Jr., a friend of the six who was at the Fruit Stand Riot and observed by police during Jones's interviews at the community center. The night of the killing, Barnes was sitting on his stoop when police approached, forced him into their car at gunpoint, and took him to the 28th Precinct, where he was peppered with leading questions and threatened with the electric chair if he didn't finger his friends for the crime. "They kept saying over and over again that they knew we were all black Muslims who wanted to kill white people and . . . we were members of a secret black group . . . until I finally said 'yes,'" Barnes later testified.[127] Detectives then used Barnes's confession to round up Baker, Hamm, Rice, Willie Craig, Ronald Felder, and Walter Thomas, who became known as the Harlem Six.[128] While Rice and Hamm confessed to the killing, they both claimed their confessions were coerced by police through the same violent tactics they used after the Fruit Stand Riot.[129]

On May 3 the *Times* published the first in a series of shocking stories by Griffin that linked the Fruit Stand Riot and the murder of Margit Sugar to a supposed gang called the "Blood Brothers." Working alongside joint investigations by the NYPD and FBI, Griffin wrote of a militant youth gang influenced by Malcolm X, skilled in martial arts, and "trained to maim and kill" white people.[130] Drawing from interviews with unnamed police officials and alleged gang members, Griffin claimed that the Blood Brothers had anywhere from sixty to four hundred members and "seized on the Fruit Riot as the means to expand their anti-white forces . . . and indoctrinate an increasing number of youths with militant anti-white sentiment."[131] Frequently implicating Malcolm X and James 67X Shabazz in his reporting, Griffin parroted reports from BOSS interrogations of teenagers like Barnes in which they were coerced to make outlandish statements about the supposed gang being influenced by Black nationalists who were "gathering arms ammunition and dynamite" for the "mass murder of whites."[132] Through his accounts of the supposed gang's clandestine judo training sessions, infiltration of community centers, rooftop perches, and plans to attack police officers, Griffin and the *Times* stoked a moral panic about Black radicalism, juvenile delinquency, and gang violence to manufacture consent for the repression of Black radicalism.[133]

The media frenzy cast a dark shadow over organizing campaigns in Harlem and put civil rights organizations on the defensive to both denounce antiwhite sentiments and disprove the existence of the Blood Brothers. With echoes of the antiwhite hysteria stirred up by *The Hate That Hate Produced* in 1959, the national NAACP took the bait and condemned the "incitement to hatred" preached by "Black racists," whom they likened to Southern segregationists like Ross Barnett and George Wallace.[134] While the press and civil rights establishment chided Black nationalists, Dr. Kenneth Clark disputed the "preposterous story," stating HARYOU had "not a single bit of evidence" that such a hate gang existed in Harlem.[135] Recognizing the media scare as a tool for political repression, the more progressive New York branch of the NAACP demanded that the state attorney general "put an end to the slanderous lies being propagated . . . by those who would impede the progress of the Negro freedom movement" and challenged law enforcement to produce evidence of the gang's existence.[136] Beyond Griffin's police sources and alleged interviews no such evidence was ever produced. By the fall, even BOSS quietly admitted there was no evidence that the gang existed, but nonetheless continued its investigations into "suspected anti-white groups, and other racist organizations."[137]

Meanwhile, Black radicals raised two incisive points in their assessments of the Blood Brothers firestorm. First, many read the lack of evidence as a clear indication that the story was fabricated by the state and fed to reporters to incite white panic and facilitate the repression of Black radicalism in Harlem.[138] Whenever resistance to oppression develops, RAM organizers explained, the state uses various means to create the "social conditions which will smash that development." Citing the rising tide of "anti police sentiments in Harlem" that spring, they argued that "the power structure wanted to frighten Harlems [sic] black community into submission to corrupt and brutal white racist cops" and "fabricated the case of the 'Blood brothers' to help create the social atmosphere they wanted."[139] RAM's analysis was shared by some moderates, including Harlem CORE Chairman Marshall England, who contended the "hysteria" was orchestrated by law enforcement, city officials, and the media to "create a climate of support" for the no-knock and stop-and-frisk laws in response to mounting opposition in Harlem.[140]

At the same time, other Black radicals suggested that if such an organization *did exist* in Harlem, it was a logical response to conditions caused by systemic racism and escalating repression. Speaking at the Militant Labor Forum on May 29, Malcolm X critiqued Black moderates who were "too quick to apologize for something that might exist that the power structure finds deplorable or finds difficult to digest." Having been on the receiving end of such denials following the broadcast of *The Hate That Hate Produced*, Malcolm understood that denouncements from moderates and liberals undermined the collective struggle for Black liberation. "I am one person who believes that anything the black man in this country needs to get his freedom right now, that thing should exist," he asserted.[141] Days later in the June edition of *Liberator* magazine, editor Dan Watts contended that whether or not the Blood Brothers existed, it should be no surprise if "the daily indignities heaped on the black community has produced an underground resistance movement, with all the weapons of guerilla warfare."[142]

By the time Watts penned his editorial, the existence or nonexistence of the Blood Brothers was largely immaterial. Borrowing heavily from the media playbook around the "near riot" in 1959 that facilitated the creation of the Tactical Patrol Force, the racist scare tactics inherent in Griffin's articles similarly enabled a heightened police presence in Harlem. By June the *Times* called for an immediate expansion of policing in the city, claiming "the overwhelming majority" of the population was "prepared to pay whatever bill is required to assure their physical safety."[143] At the same time, the moral and political panic also broadened popular discourse around self-defense and revolutionary violence as justifiable forms of resistance to white supremacy and police repression in Jim Crow New York. Nonetheless, by feeding sensational claims to a willing accomplice at the *Times,* the NYPD and FBI created a climate of fear in the city as a pretense for occupying Black communities to suppress rising Black dissent as the summer approached.

OCCUPIED TERRITORY

Police flooded into Harlem in the following weeks as part of a massive campaign to suppress Black radicalism in New York and beyond. "They are tightening the screws on Harlem," the Harlem PLM wrote in a May newsletter. "The police, the press, the politicians and all the other agents of the white power structure have launched a campaign of terror and slander . . . more vicious and more brutal than ever."[144] By expanding the operations of the NYPD's Tactical Patrol Force and Bureau of Special Services, the Wagner administration characteristically used police to manage the symptoms of oppression instead of resolving its root causes. In the process, the city turned Harlem into occupied territory that spring, provoking conflict and creating the conditions for mass resistance to state violence.

Every afternoon throughout May, a squad of fifty TPF officers—all over six feet tall, under the age of thirty, trained in judo, and carrying long nightsticks—arrived by bus at the 32nd Precinct to prowl the streets at night. The overwhelmingly white squads patrolled seemingly every inch of Harlem in pairs, from basements to rooftops and hallways to alleys, targeting areas where youth gangs and Black militants were reportedly operating.[145] With fears of a "long, hot summer" on the rise, Griffin's characterization of the Blood Brothers as a new type of gang "trained in karate" with "no geographical limitations" seemed to be a tailor-made narrative to justify the continued expansion of the TPF's operations as the summer approached.[146]

The TPF's expansion was carried out under an initiative Murphy introduced the previous year called "Operation Finecomb." In addition to busing squads of fifty officers into "high crime" areas for foot patrol, Operation Finecomb dispatched trios of officers to patrol the streets in marked and unmarked cars. While one officer drove, the other two would scan the block from the rear windows "ready to leap out as trouble appears."[147] As the Harlem PLM observed, each of these cars was like an "armed fortress, with riot guns, tear gas, helmets, and all of the other paraphanalia [sic] of a police state."[148] Operation Finecomb was one of three surveillance and suppression initiatives Murphy introduced that year, including Operation Taxicab, in which detectives surveilled communities from taxicabs, and Operation Decoy, in which officers dressed in drag to lure and entrap would-be muggers or purse snatchers.[149] Additional TPF tactics included vehicle checkpoints and illegal stop-and-frisk procedures, with Harlem residents "being rounded up on the streets, taken into hallways, and searched."[150] Yet another expansion of policing came in early June, when Mayor Wagner allocated $5 million to overtime pay for putting seven hundred extra patrolmen on the streets at night in response to continued outcries about Black youth crime. "I am determined to see that we are going to have law and order in this city of ours," Wagner declared after an emergency meeting with Murphy.[151] Taken together, Wagner's support for "law and order" and Murphy's "aggressive preventive patrol" tactics amounted to the hostile occupation and mass criminalization of Black and Puerto Rican communities as activists were mobilizing against the expansion of police powers.

As summer approached, many residents felt the TPF was preparing for war in Harlem. In May the Harlem PLM reported that riot gear was arriving at police precincts—which had become guarded "fortresses"—and plans were being made to contain and isolate Harlem in the event of an uprising.[152] As part of their preparations for riot control, the TPF conducted training drills in which squads of a hundred officers marched in formation down Lenox Avenue and 125th Street, fanning out to tactical positions—including rooftops and subway entrances—when they reached an appointed destination.[153] While Murphy continued to publicly downplay the threat of unrest that summer, the actions of his troops in Harlem suggested the city was preparing for open confrontation with its residents.

While the TPF was supposed to "lower the temperature" in Harlem and "keep it from reaching the boiling point," their presence did more to escalate tensions than resolve them.[154] As the Youth Committee of Harlem CORE explained in a mid-May telegram to Wagner and Murphy, "The continued presence of the Tactical Patrol Force in Harlem tends to provoke rather than prevent racial explosions."[155] Even some police acknowledged this; one Black officer told Griffin that TPF officers were "apt to explode community tensions by their very direct application of the letter of the law."[156] The negative impacts were felt almost immediately in Black and Puerto Rican communities as "young, white, 'trigger-happy' cops" responded to minor street crimes and protests with extraordinary violence. Over the next three months, residents reported over three hundred cases of police brutality to the Harlem Defense Council, an organization formed by the Harlem PLM in May to protect the community from police violence.[157]

Less than a week after the Fruit Stand Riot and just a day after brutalizing protestors during the World's Fair stall-in, the NYPD shot yet another Puerto Rican teenager in the back. Patrolman Maurice Mulligan shot fourteen-year-old Abraham Ortega in the Upper West Side after he allegedly snatched a woman's pocketbook and took off running. Ortega survived and was placed under arrest while he recovered in the hospital, and Mulligan faced no disciplinary action. While the *New York Times* buried the story deep in the next day's paper, the newly formed Action Committee Against Police Brutality mobilized Harlem residents to protest the escalating assaults against Black and Puerto Rican teenagers.[158] Drawing comparisons to the fatal police shootings of Solero, Rodriguez, and Frankie Rodriguez, the Action Committee organized a protest at the 24th Precinct, where sixty adults and thirty children walked the picket line carrying signs that read "Disarm the Thugs in Blue" and "Killer Cops Must Pay For Their Crimes."[159]

Three weeks later, in mid-May, police assaulted men, women, and children during a demonstration to demand a traffic light near an elementary school in Central Harlem. After years of parents asking and being ignored, HARYOU, East River and Harlem CORE, the Harlem Parents Committee, and the Community Council on Housing organized a hundred protestors to block the intersection to compel the city to act. The city responded by sending fifty police officers, who punched, kicked, and shoved women and children, while an officer in plainclothes picked a fight with a man before beating and arresting him. After police forcibly cleared the street and arrested four people—including HARYOU youth leaders—protestors marched on the nearby 25th Precinct, shouting "Police brutality!" and attempting to free another woman who police arrested on the way. Activists then occupied the intersection outside the precinct to protest the beatings and arrests before police once again forcibly cleared the street and arrested seven more, including CCH leader Major Williams.[160] The shooting of Abraham Ortega and the violent repression of nonviolent protests by the NYPD illuminated the clear and present dangers of life in a police state and fueled organizing campaigns to challenge police power.

Less obvious were the NYPD's expanding counterintelligence operations through its clandestine BOSS unit. Within days of the Blood Brothers story breaking, forty Black undercover detectives were sent into Harlem to investigate antiwhite gang violence as part of the city's broader counterintelligence strategy against Black radical organizations. Agents posted up in locations where gang members reportedly hung out, including restaurants, bars, and community centers, where they gathered intelligence by questioning social workers and staff about teenagers suspected of being Blood Brothers.[161] By feeding Griffin information from the coerced statements of juveniles about supposed MMI members who "moved into and out of youth gangs in

Harlem," the NYPD created a narrative cover for expanding their counterintelligence operations as the summer neared.[162]

Under the Wagner administration, the NYPD broadened the scale and scope of BOSS operations to keep pace with the resurgence of Black radicalism in New York City.[163] BOSS agents hid in plain sight at protests, rallies, and meetings of civil rights and Black nationalist organizations in Harlem, taking note of militant rhetoric, future plans, and known radicals in the crowd. Surveillance reports were filed alongside newspaper coverage and organizational literature and compiled into dossiers on individuals and organizations which totaled over one million by 1968.[164] In addition to informing counterintelligence strategies, BOSS used these dossiers for retribution against activists by sharing information with courts, employers, and government agencies. After a CORE demonstration against police brutality in November 1963, BOSS ordered an investigation of communists and "trouble makers" in the organization, which they later used to discredit activists who brought allegations of brutality before the Civilian Complaint Review Board in January 1964.[165]

BOSS also worked closely with the FBI's counterintelligence program (COINTELPRO) to suppress Black radicalism in New York.[166] In February 1964 BOSS and the FBI launched a joint investigation into Black radical organizations in the city, with a particular focus on Bill Epton, Jesse Gray, and Malcolm X.[167] In the months that followed, FBI Director J. Edgar Hoover tried obsessively to link Malcolm and the MMI to arms and acts of violence.[168] Having tried in vain to implicate the MMI in the Fruit Stand Riot and murder of Margit Sugar, by June Hoover had installed illegal wiretaps in Malcolm's home and the MMI office and expanded efforts to infiltrate the organization with informants and undercover agents.[169]

While the NYPD remained hostile to desegregating its overwhelmingly white force, they made exceptions for recruiting Black detectives—particularly military veterans—to infiltrate organizations, gather intelligence, and exert influence.[170] In an August 1961 memo, BOSS Commander Sanford Garelick laid bare the unit's confidential counterintelligence methods: "Infiltration of the organization's ranks; Direct contact with the organization leaders by Negro police officers; Close cooperation and exchange of data with Federal and State investigative agencies; Intensive investigation and constant surveillance of the members and activities of the members."[171] Using militant rhetoric and bold actions to establish radical credentials, earn the respect of organizers, and ascend to leadership positions, Black agents used their influence to gather higher-level intelligence and advocate illegal actions to facilitate the arrest of organizers, evoke public condemnation, and ultimately dismantle organizations.[172]

By the spring of 1964 BOSS had dozens of agents in Harlem and exploited the crime scare to recruit more. Over the past several years, BOSS had routinely assigned agents in response to emerging threats to the status quo—especially when organizations dared to challenge police power. Following the police beating of Johnson X Hinton in 1957, BOSS tapped Detective William K. DeFossett to serve as a "liaison" to the Nation of Islam and use his proximity to Malcolm X to gather intelligence on the NOI, CORE, the Monroe Defense Committee, the Emergency Committee, and others in the years that followed.[173] Shortly after Malcolm's Times Square protest against police brutality in early 1963, BOSS recruited Korean War veteran Adolph "Abe" Hart to infiltrate the NOI.[174] After several months, Hart was reassigned to the Harlem PLM when they began to expand their campaigns against police brutality that fall. When Malcolm X established the MMI and called for organized self-defense, BOSS tapped navy veteran Gene Roberts to investigate the organization's members, plans, and acquisition of weapons.[175] And the day after the Fruit Stand Riot, BOSS recruited air force veteran Raymond A. Wood to infiltrate Bronx CORE amid their escalating campaigns against police brutality.

Posing as twenty-seven-year-old law student named Raymond Woodall, Wood hit the ground running, joining sit-ins on the opening day of the World's Fair; attending meetings of Brooklyn, East River, and Harlem CORE chapters; and establishing himself as a committed and increasingly radical activist.[176] Described by one Harlem CORE member as "the prototype of the new Negro militant," within two months Wood was named Bronx CORE's housing chairman and elected as a delegate to CORE's national convention.[177] Once embedded, his BOSS handler pressured him to deliver evidence the NYPD could use to discredit and dismantle the organization. In May Wood proposed a plan to members of Harlem and East River CORE to blow up national monuments, including the Statue of Liberty.[178] Finding no takers, in late June he convinced Herbert Callender to place Mayor Wagner under citizen's arrest for permitting employment discrimination on publicly funded construction projects. After announcing their plans as part of CORE's ongoing campaign against racism in the construction industry two weeks earlier, Callender, Wood, and John Valentine were arrested at city hall on July 15 when they tried to place Wagner under arrest. While Wood and Valentine were given a court date and released that afternoon, the judge had Callender committed to the psychiatric ward of Bellevue Hospital, where he spent five days.[179]

This setup accomplished two objectives for the NYPD. First, it created an opportunity to tarnish the reputation of a key figure in the struggle against police violence by arresting Callender on the steps of city hall and publicly questioning his sanity. Since Callender had previously been singled out by Commissioner Murphy as an "extremist" trying to "create chaos" in the city, the judge's extraordinary decision to commit him to Bellevue amounted to a public humiliation to undermine his credibility and influence. Second, Wood's high-profile arrest—which was covered along with his photograph in the *New York Times*—earned him recognition he could use to infiltrate more radical organizations.[180] In the months and years that followed, Wood used these credentials to infiltrate RAM, HARYOU, the Freedom Now Party, the Black Liberation Front, the Organization of Afro-American Unity, the Black Panther Party, and other radical groups, with disastrous consequences at nearly every turn.

FIG 19 Undercover BOSS detective Ray Wood (aka Raymond Woodall) in police custody following his arrest for the attempted citizen's arrest of Mayor Wagner at city hall on July 15, 1964. (Photo by Walter Albertin; Library of Congress, Prints and Photographs Division, NYWT&S Collection [LC-DIG-ds-17340])

Taken together, the expansion of the TPF and BOSS in response to rising Black militancy turned Harlem into a veritable police state in the spring of 1964. While the media rationalized the aggressive expansion of policing with sensational reports of Black criminality that stoked white panic, residents felt the suffocating weight of the state bearing down. With Harlem already saturated with law enforcement, Commissioner Murphy declared in mid-May that "even more manpower" would be deployed to enforce "the climate of law and order in New York." Despite Murphy's pledge to turn "the threat of a long, hot summer into a cool, calm and constructive period of progress," it became increasingly clear the city was preparing for conflict as it rolled out its riot control strategy that spring.[181] Murphy's hollow rhetoric about "progress" belied the Wagner administration's continued refusal to accede to demands for Black rights and power in the city. Instead of taking action to address systemic racism, Wagner characteristically leaned on political repression as he in effect declared war on Black communities as the summer neared.

RESISTING POLICE POWER

With the NYPD engaged in what the Harlem PLM described as "an unprecedented reign of terror," residents and activists challenged the police occupation of Harlem through direct action, legislation, and self-defense. Drawing parallels with the "police state tactics" of Nazi Germany, apartheid South Africa, and the Jim Crow South, that May Harlem residents took to the streets in large numbers to challenge police violence and pressure city officials to enact reforms, including a new bill to create an independent civilian review board.[182] At the same time, Black radicals drew from traditions of self-defense in organizing Harlem communities to physically resist the police occupation and protect themselves against police brutality. These complementary strategies coalesced by late June, when the united front long called for by Black radicals finally emerged with the formation of the Organization of Afro-American Unity (OAAU).

Throughout May and June, HAG, the Harlem PLM, and the Mothers Defense Committee rallied around the Harlem Six to demand reforms and justice for victims of police violence through direct-action protests. On June 5 HAG organized a protest at the 32nd Precinct—the site of police torture during the Fruit Stand Riot—to demand an end to police brutality and raise bail money for Frank Stafford. Additionally, HAG demanded the repeal of the Rockefeller laws and called on city officials to dismiss Commissioner Murphy, fire the three officers who assaulted Stafford, and enact a recently proposed bill to create a citizens review board.[183] The following week, the Harlem PLM held a demonstration at the site of the Fruit Stand Riot, where Bill Epton denounced the "Gestapo" tactics of the NYPD and predicted "an all-out police war against Harlem this summer."[184] Speaking after Epton, Harlem Six parents Mildred Thomas and Mary Hamm announced the formation of the Mothers Defense Committee to fight for their sons' freedom and protect Harlem youth from police violence. "We mothers stopped feeling sorry for ourselves when we saw that our children were being railroaded," Thomas later wrote in *Liberator*. "We decided to join together and fight back."[185] Having been abandoned by mainstream civil rights organizations amid the Blood Brothers hysteria, the Mothers Defense Committee—like the Monroe Defense Committee before them—found support among Harlem radicals, including Epton and Mae Mallory. While Epton mobilized demonstrations and recruited attorneys Conrad Lynn and William Kunstler, Mallory worked behind the scenes, likely helping craft their language for fliers, petitions, and public statements.[186]

Meanwhile, the Ad Hoc Committee on Fair Police Practice mobilized support for civilian oversight of the NYPD. Since their formation in early March, the committee continued to pressure lawmakers to repeal the no-knock and stop-and-frisk laws and to create an independent civilian review board. While making little progress on the former, they gained steam on the latter when city council member Theodore Weiss introduced a bill in early April to establish a board composed entirely of civilians to investigate allegations of police brutality, recommend disciplinary action, and advise the mayor on policies to curb police brutality.[187] The Weiss bill became a political lightning rod in the city, as the struggle for a civilian review board offered a tangible objective to build political unity around.

To coordinate a broad-based campaign to pass the bill, CORE and the NAACP expanded the Ad Hoc Committee into the City Wide Committee for Fair Police Protection. Coalition members included CORE and NAACP chapters from across the city, HAG, the Puerto Rican Committee for Civil Rights, and the Workers' Defense League.[188] Beyond merely rallying support for a piece of legislation they saw as "inadequate," the City Wide Committee organized around more expansive demands for civilian oversight. In addition to the provisions of the bill, they demanded the appointment of board members in consultation with civil rights organizations and expanded powers for the civilian review board to subpoena witnesses, discipline officers found guilty (rather than just recommending disciplinary action), and access all police facilities twenty-four hours a day to investigate the kinds of brutality and torture that followed the Fruit Stand Riot.[189] Meanwhile, member organizations like Bronx CORE called for a decentralized civilian review board with local boards elected by legal and civil rights organizations in each borough, while HAG pushed for an amendment to the bill that would create precinct-level review boards as a step toward establishing community control over police in Black and Puerto Rican communities.[190]

In mid-May the City Wide Committee officially launched their campaign to expand the Weiss bill and pressure city council to move it out of committee for a vote. To build momentum, they organized two weeks of protest actions at precincts where police brutality had taken place, while gathering signatures on petitions and encouraging residents to put pressure on their council representatives. On June 4, for its first public event, the committee organized a mock civilian review board to hear complaints of police brutality submitted to CORE. Made up of ten representatives of community, religious, labor, and civil rights organizations, including James Farmer, ACLU founder Roger Baldwin, former judge and educational activist Hubert Delany, and Northern Student Movement Director Bill Strickland, the board hoped to "mark a turning point in the ghastly story of police brutality in New York City."[191] Commissioner Murphy predictably declined their invitation to attend, denouncing the hearings as "kangaroo courts" and "public lynchings."[192] After hearing several cases—including those of Jesse Roberts, Maximo Solero and Victor Rodriguez, and Frankie Rodriguez—the board ruled "the time has come for the police department of New York to cease being its own prosecutor, judge and jury."[193] While the mock review board did little to advance the stalled legislation, it did help draw media attention to the ongoing campaign for a civilian review board.[194] Followed by continued pickets at "hot precincts," Murphy's office, and city hall, the proceedings illuminated the shortcomings of the current review board and demonstrated what a more just system of police oversight could look like.[195]

Instead of joining the City Wide Committee, the Harlem PLM announced the formation of a "united people's committee against police brutality" in mid-May. "We in Harlem have just about reached the peak of our endurance. We have nothing to lose," they declared. "We have only one alternative: to organize ourselves into a militant force to protect ourselves against this pro-fascist police state. We must organize apartment-by-apartment, house-by-house, block-by-block—the entire community—to resist the attacks upon us."[196] By the end of the month, the committee was formalized as the Harlem Defense Council (HDC) under the leadership of Bill Epton. At biweekly June rallies at the site of the Fruit Stand Riot, Epton announced the council's plans to organize both a cop-watch program and a network of residents trained to defend against acts of police brutality.[197] By July the HDC reportedly organized Black youth near their office on Lenox Avenue and 127th Street to watch out for police violence and give a signal for people nearby to physically intervene when necessary.[198] While many Harlem residents had long supported self-defense in the South and at times intervened in acts of police brutality, the formation of organized units to defend Black communities against police violence was a new development in response to unrelenting state violence.

The HDC's position on self-defense was bolstered in late June by the formation of the Organization of Afro-American Unity (OAAU). After several months of secretive meetings with longtime Left nationalists in Harlem like John Henrik Clarke and John O. Killens, and with younger transplants like Lynn Shifflett, Peter Bailey, and Muriel Gray, the organization began to take shape upon Malcolm's return from Africa in late May. Malcolm's return also drew Max Stanford back to Harlem to help build the new organization in tandem with RAM.[199] At a June 22 rally, Malcolm X described the Rockefeller laws as among "the most oppressive laws in history," called for Harlem residents to unite in opposition to police violence, and hinted that a major announcement was forthcoming.[200] The following weekend, he announced the OAAU's formation as a grassroots revolutionary nationalist organization that would unite Black communities throughout the diaspora in "an all out militant fight for human rights."[201] With the goal of building a national Black united front, the group saw Harlem as a strategic location to develop a mass-based organization that would serve as a model for other cities.[202] Planning meetings throughout May and June revolved around finding "the one issue, housing, jobs, police brutality—whatever it may be, that the community is concerned with most and wage a resolute struggle around it in order to galvanize the masses."[203] With the Rockefeller laws set to take effect on July 1 amid escalating police brutality and repression, the founding members decided that police brutality and the new laws were "prime issues" for the OAAU to immediately organize around.[204]

The OAAU's program around policing blended consciousness-raising, direct action, victim support, and self-defense into a comprehensive plan to build community power through challenging the police occupation in Harlem. To raise awareness and bring people into the struggle, organizers would develop educational literature and "systematically canvass Harlem" to prepare the community to "defend those who are arrested resisting the anti-Negro" laws. To organize mass resistance, a communications system would be developed "to get masses of people together on short notice," while plans were laid for a silent funeral march to "symbolize our intention to bury" the laws. To support survivors and victims of police violence, a twenty-four-hour hotline would be established for residents to report abuse and request assistance. To defend against the looming escalation of police violence, organizers would offer "formal training in the art of self-defense" as well as "psychological defense" against the daily assaults of life in occupied territory.[205] OAAU members would be expected to join and work from within various organizations to mobilize people and resources into a mass campaign against police violence and build a united front for Black Power in Harlem.

In working out their program, the OAAU members wrestled with two strategic questions. Considering the expansion of counterintelligence operations and repression over the past few years, should their defense strategy be made public or kept confidential? The debate was prompted in part by comments Malcolm X made in a mid-June interview in which he stressed the rights of Black people to fight for their freedom by any means necessary, including the use of self-defense and guerilla warfare. Having witnessed the firestorm surrounding his earlier calls for rifle clubs, others in the group—including Stanford—believed Malcolm's public stance was premature and feared it would invite government repression to destroy the fledgling organization. They resolved that the OAAU would maintain its position on self-defense as a constitutional right, while RAM would operate underground to organize a guerilla formation known as the Black Liberation Front.[206]

At the same time, organizers confronted the question of how to address issues of public safety in Harlem without subjecting residents to racist police violence. The OAAU's founding members knew people had real concerns about crime, drugs, and violence in their communities which needed to be addressed if they were to build a mass movement around policing. Realizing that their calls to "reduce the excessive number of cops in Harlem" risked alienating some community members, OAAU founders called for public safety committees that would "take a stand on crime in Harlem and continue to make our community a better place to live."[207] In also calling for guardianship and mentorship programs to address "juvenile delinquency" and for community clinics to treat people with drug addictions, the OAAU urged Black communities to take responsibility for "regaining our people who have lost their place in society" without relying on the state for rehabilitation or incarceration as solutions to social conditions caused by state violence.[208] These were not bourgeois approaches to crime and vice, but transitional steps to address immediate problems caused by systemic racism while working to resolve their root causes.

By the time of its launch on June 28, the OAAU had already recruited an impressive collective of radical organizers. Attorney and former NY NAACP chair Percy Sutton served as the organization's legal adviser, John Henrik Clarke as its research director. Heading up its cultural and educational programs were jazz artist and Cultural Association for Women of African Heritage organizer Abbey Lincoln, Monroe Defense Committee and HARYOU organizer Nan Bowe, and ACT and RAM organizer Herman Ferguson. The OAAU's positions on electoral politics were informed by the Freedom Now Party and Gloria Richardson's strategies around independent politics and bloc voting to wield Black political power; their economic platform was influenced in part by Jesse Gray's analysis of housing exploitation as a form of internal colonialism.[209] Walter Bowe and Max Stanford advised on self-defense and assigned RAM cadre Khaleel Sayyed to form an internal security apparatus.[210] The budding united front also drew support from Ossie Davis, Ruby Dee, Bill Epton, Jesse Gray, Conrad Lynn, Ora Mobley, Jack O'Dell, Gloria Richardson, Bill Strickland, and William Worthy, all of whom had played formative roles in shaping the Black freedom movement in Harlem over the past decade or more.

As the city deployed the NYPD to suppress Black radicalism, the OAAU drew from Harlem's traditions of anticolonialism and Pan-Africanism in calling for "an unrelenting struggle against police brutality" as a means of uniting Black communities to rid themselves of exploitation and oppression by any means necessary.[211] In early July Malcolm X repeated his calls to internationalize the Black freedom movement and announced plans to bring the United States before the UN on charges of human rights violations against African Americans. Malcolm's address at a July 5 OAAU meeting at the Audubon Ballroom followed remarks by one of his protégés, former HEP and HARYOU activist Sherron Jackson, who channeled the spirit of Bandung as she explained to the four hundred gathered that a "wind of change" was blowing across the United States, "similar to the one which led to freedom for Ghana, the establishment of the underground in South Africa and the organizing of the Mau Mau in Kenya." While a decade of grassroots struggles for civil rights, human rights, and self-determination had won some tangible changes and forged a radical popular culture in Harlem, by the summer of 1964 the repressive limits of racial liberalism and the concurrent expansion of police violence left residents and activists exasperated and radicalized. Jackson concluded her remarks with a clarion call to Harlem. "Freedom is never given, it must be taken," she exhorted, "and the time for the black man to take his freedom is now."[212]

THE TIME HAS COME

After several months of resistance and anticipation, the stop-and-frisk and no-knock laws finally went into effect July 1. Having failed to pressure lawmakers to repeal them, organizers turned their focus to protecting residents from police abuse and developing a legal strategy to overturn the laws. In late June the NY NAACP announced an emergency six-day work week to support the community during the anticipated fallout from the expansion of police powers in Harlem, while the Harlem Lawyers Association announced they would seek a test case to build a legal challenge around.[213] Meanwhile, the HDC and the OAAU organized working-class Black communities to defend themselves against police violence and build power to fight for self-determination. Threatened by the emergence of united front groups to challenge police power, the NYPD and Wagner administration worked frantically to hold back the rising tide of Black radicalism in the city. By the middle of July, the city's determination to violently repress Black dissent instead of resolving its root causes led many Harlem residents to seek more radical means of achieving human rights and provoked the first urban uprising of the "long, hot summers."

While the campaign around the Weiss bill galvanized Black and Puerto Rican communities, it also energized opposition from police, politicians, and white New Yorkers who condemned calls for police accountability as an attack on the thin blue line protecting the city from crime, violence, and political anarchy. On June 16 Murphy appeared before the city council's Committee on City Affairs for a public hearing at which he denied any "pattern of brutality" existed, lauded the current internal review board, and denounced civilian oversight as an "attack against law enforcement" that would "create situations where police officers would hesitate to act." Throughout his address, Murphy incited fear that police were under siege from Black radicals and criminals who would engulf the city "in a sea of confusion, contradiction and chaos" if police powers were curbed by a civilian review board.²¹⁴

After concluding his remarks, Murphy strode out of city hall to applause from hundreds of his officers. Upon learning of the hearing, the Patrolmen's Benevolent Association quickly mobilized 1,200 uniformed, pistol-carrying off-duty officers to fill the council chambers and gather on the steps of city hall in protest. In a memo to 26,000 NYPD officers the week before the hearing, the PBA's president, John Cassese, called the Weiss bill "a threat to every policeman" and urged members "to do your share in preventing a breakdown of law and order."²¹⁵ As the hearing got underway that morning, hundreds of patrolmen gathered outside in a show of force and prevented civilians, journalists, and activists from entering.²¹⁶ When it was his turn to address the committee, Cassese railed against the Weiss bill as a communist plot to undermine the NYPD and likened civilian oversight to "holding a gun to the policeman's head."²¹⁷ By characterizing demands for reform as calculated attacks on police, Murphy and Cassese sought to delegitimize and criminalize the Black freedom movement while stoking a racist backlash in the city to heighten police power.

The narrative strategy the NYPD and city hall used to combat the Weiss bill reflected their broader efforts to expand police authority and criminalize dissent. Two days before the public hearing, the MMI held a meeting on police brutality where Malcolm X described Harlem as a police state being run by Commissioner Murphy. After months of trying to link the MMI with gun clubs, the FBI was eager to learn from an informant that Malcolm had appeared with eight bodyguards armed with rifles.²¹⁸ While openly carrying long guns was legal in New York City at the time, Murphy and Wagner pounced on the opportunity to criminalize firearms and clamp down on organized self-defense. At Murphy's insistence, Wagner asked the city council ten days later to enact a local law to prohibit carrying rifles and shotguns in public. Pushed by Murphy and Wagner and endorsed by the *Times* as a deterrent to violent crime and protection for police, the city council passed the law within two weeks, while the Weiss bill withered in committee.²¹⁹ By restricting civilian access to arms while expanding police powers, the Wagner administration affirmed and strengthened the state's monopoly on violence in response to mounting challenges to its authority.

By that point, it was clear to many Harlem residents that the expansion of police power was a core part of the city's commitment to maintaining the racist status quo. With the city engaged in what the Harlem PLM described as "a campaign of terror and intimidation," Black radicals prepared Harlem residents to defend themselves and, in Malcolm's words, to "declare war on oppression."[220] As the new gun law breezed through the city council in late June, Mae and Pat Mallory distributed thousands of copies of an explosive new edition of *The Crusader* throughout Harlem. Under an illustration of a giant Black warrior setting fire to a city, Robert F. Williams challenged readers to question the efficacy of nonviolence for achieving Black self-determination and to seriously consider the possibility of armed revolutionary struggle in the United States.[221] "It is becoming next to impossible for Negroes to conduct a 'peaceful' demonstration in America," he observed. "Our only logical and successful answer is to meet organized and massive violence with massive and organized violence. Our people must prepare to wage an urban guerrilla war of self-defense," through which Black people would develop and wield the power necessary to wage a revolutionary struggle for Black liberation.[222]

With echoes of his declaration in Monroe five years earlier, Williams denounced the state's monopoly on violence as he called on Black communities to prepare for revolutionary struggle. "This year, 1964 is going to be a violent one," he predicted. "America is a house on fire—FREEDOM NOW!—or let it burn, let it burn."[223] To prepare for delivering this ultimatum, Williams included lessons about organized self-defense from Monroe and basic instructions for making homemade weapons and developing urban defense strategies. Molotov cocktails and acid bombs could be easily made and thrown from rooftops at night to "make the streets impossible for racist cops to patrol," he wrote. Government vehicles could be incapacitated by pouring sugar into gas tanks, and roads could be blocked by using homemade spike strips to blow out car tires.[224] Much like the stall-in, these tactics were meant to enable members of a minority population to leverage their familiarity with the built environment and infrastructure of their neighborhoods to exert greater power over the larger city.[225]

Recognizing collective outrage was mounting "in direct proportion to the amazing increase in police terror," the OAAU, HDC, and RAM worked to harness the righteous anger of militant, yet unaffiliated Black youth and women, disaffected Black workers, and local people into a struggle for survival and liberation.[226] In the July edition of *Liberator*, RAM cadre Rolland Snellings (Askia Muhammad Touré) called for civil rights organizations to recruit and take leadership from the "caste of warriors" who preferred bars, cafés, and pool halls to meetings, rallies, and demonstrations. Using "Mose" as a metonym for "the fighting man of black America," Snellings argued there could be no Black liberation "without 'Mose' and our militant, young soul-sisters who make up the angry, exploited masses" who would "NEVER rally to a basically suicidal, masochistic movement such as non-violence in a police state."[227] By consistently rejecting Black youth who did not adhere to white, middle-class standards of respectability, mainstream civil rights organizations deprived the Black freedom movement of a powerful force in the battle for liberation.[228] Snellings concluded his article with a clear directive to Black America: "Unchain your hero, unchain the mighty lion, and gird yourself to meet the gathering storm!"[229]

The winds of change Sherron Jackson forecast finally brought the gathering storm to Harlem on July 16 when another Black teenager was fatally shot by a white police officer. That morning a group of teenagers were sitting on a stoop on East 76th Street waiting for summer school to begin when the white superintendent of the building sprayed them with a hose, telling them he would "wash all the black off you."[230] James Powell, a fifteen-year-old Bronx resident who had worked as a youth organizer for the March on Washington the previous summer, likely pictured the firehoses turned on children in Birmingham as he went across the street to confront the man while other students began hurling bottles and trash can lids. After chasing the superintendent into the building, Powell walked back out the front door as thirty-six-year-old off-duty lieutenant Thomas Gilligan approached with his revolver drawn. A six-foot, two-hundred-pound military veteran with a history of disarming armed suspects, Gilligan was in a shop next door when he heard the commotion and came out to investigate. Claiming the five-foot-six-inch, 122-pound Powell charged at him with a knife, Gilligan fired three shots, two of which fatally struck Powell in the chest and abdomen. Dozens of witnesses disputed Gilligan's account, claiming Powell did not have a knife and the officer opened fire as Powell came out the doorway.[231] For many Harlem residents, it was like the Frankie Rodriguez case all over again—a nonwhite high school student gunned down by a white off-duty cop—and few had cause to expect any justice for the victim or punishment for the killer.

A crowd of students quickly gathered, growing in size and anger as police flooded onto the block while James Powell lay motionless on the sidewalk. When officers tried to physically disperse the crowd that swelled to three hundred, the students stood their ground, yelling, "This is worse than Mississippi!" and pelting officers with bottles, cans, and chunks of cement. In the two hours it took a hundred TPF officers to finally disperse the crowd, representatives of the NY NAACP, East River CORE, and national CORE arrived at the nearby 19th Precinct to issue a series of demands, including an independent investigation of the police killing. East River CORE Chairman Blyden Jackson announced plans for a noon protest at the precinct the next day, while students planned their own demonstration at the site of the shooting.[232] With Mayor Wagner out of town, Murphy announced that the NYPD and district attorney would conduct a "thorough investigation" and offered no further comment.[233] With no faith in the police, district attorney, courts, or mayor to deliver justice for Powell, activists organized to put pressure on the legal system to demand it.

The next morning, under the watchful eye of fifty members of the TPF, seventy-five people—mostly Black teenagers—walked a picket line, chanting "Killer cops must go!" and carrying signs that read "Stop Killer Cops." When school let out at noon, another 150 students joined in before marching nine blocks to the 19th Precinct to link up with the East River CORE demonstration. As police cordoned off the block, a fifteen-year-old from Monroe, North Carolina, distributed PLM leaflets and reportedly told the protestors that in his hometown "if the cops shoot a Negro, we arm ourselves and get that cop worse than he got us." Meanwhile, members of the OAAU arrived to interview witnesses and urged the students not to let the police "push you around."[234] Though Malcolm X was in Cairo to meet with members of the Organization of African Unity, he was closely following the situation in Harlem. While the students were protesting, Malcolm was delivering a statement before the Organization of African Unity, in which he urged African leaders to charge the United States with human rights violations in the United Nations and asserted the right of Black people to defend themselves. "Our young people have reached the point of no return," he declared. "From here on in, if we must die anyway, we will die fighting back, and we will not die alone."[235] Though the demonstration at the precinct fizzled out as the afternoon wore on, Malcolm's warning proved prescient as Harlem prepared for Powell's wake the following day.

On Saturday afternoon over three hundred people filtered through a Central Harlem funeral home where James Powell's body lay in an open casket.[236] After paying their respects, some likely made their way down to 115th Street and Lenox Avenue, where the Harlem PLM, HDC, and the Mothers Defense Committee were hosting a joint rally. Speaking alongside mothers of the Harlem Six and other victims of police violence, Bill Epton called for the dismissal and prosecution of Gilligan, the resignations of Murphy and Wagner,

FIG 20 Police observe demonstrators gathered on East 76th Street to protest the police killing of James Powell. (Photo by Marion S. Trikosko; Library of Congress, Prints and Photographs Division, U.S. News & World Report Magazine Collection [LC-U9-12259 frame 1])

and a mass demonstration the following weekend.[237] Throughout the day, OAAU members circulated the organization's first newsletter, which laid out the facts of the case, condemned police officials and the white press for "creating the atmosphere for the killing" of Black youth, called for punishment of the "killer" cop, and urged Black adults to organize a self-defense apparatus to protect Black children from racist police violence.[238] As that rally ended, another began at 7th Avenue and 125th Street, where hundreds gathered for a rally organized by local CORE chapters. Notably absent was Bronx CORE Chair Herbert Callender, who remained in Bellevue's psychiatric ward following his attempted citizen's arrest of Mayor Wagner three days earlier. Once the CORE speakers concluded, they opened the floor to UANM leader James Lawson and Rev. Nelson Dukes. In an electrifying twenty-minute speech, Dukes told the crowd it was time to stop talking and start acting by marching on the nearby precinct to deliver their demands.[239]

As the sun began to set, hundreds of Harlem residents silently marched two blocks down 7th Avenue and one block west to the notorious 28th Precinct. As they approached, *Amsterdam News* columnist James Booker reported, they were joined by another hundred people from the neighborhood who had grown "tired of seeing brutality victims stream in and out of the 123rd St. slaughterhouse."[240] In a scene reminiscent of the "near riot" of July 1959, several hundred Harlem residents surrounded the precinct, threatening to storm the building. Several protestors who tried to force their way inside to demand Gilligan's arrest were met by a squad of police who pushed them back across the street as bottles and garbage can lids began flying. Meanwhile, Rev. Dukes and Ernest Russell from East River CORE told the precinct commander they would not leave until Commissioner Murphy personally came to Harlem to announce Gilligan's suspension. When police responded by setting up barricades between the people and the precinct, some protestors fought back while others sat down on the sidewalk, refusing to move. The precinct commander then ordered his men to arrest anyone showing signs of resistance, and police quickly and roughly dragged dozens of protestors inside the precinct. More bottles and debris rained down from rooftops in response as reinforcements stormed out of the precinct with clubs swinging to force back the swelling crowd.[241]

Within moments, a TPF bus arrived, and fifty officers stormed onto the block using their long nightsticks to clear the street of men, women, and children "until 123rd Street was covered with blood."[242] While Harlem residents fought back in self-defense, two more buses carrying a hundred TPF officers arrived and established barricades at both ends of the block. On 7th Avenue, a crowd of over five hundred surrounded the police blockade as reinforcements from around the city continued to flood into Central Harlem. Amid the standoff, an officer grabbed a bullhorn and shouted to the crowd, "Why don't you go home?" Channeling the spirit of Bandung in the face of occupying forces, a voice from the crowd yelled back, "We are home—this is our home, baby!" Police responded with a yell of "Charge!" as a phalanx of TPF officers vaulted the barricades and plowed into the crowd with clubs swinging.[243]

The crowd broke into smaller clusters as the police gave chase, brutalizing anyone they caught. "It was like a war by the cops against anything that appeared black," Booker reported.[244] With police running roughshod before their self-defense units were fully established, Harlem residents fought back in any way they knew how. "These resistance fighters were mainly the youth who had overwhelming support of the community," the HDC reported. "Unarmed, unorganized, improvising and offering resistance through sheer 'guts' they instilled fear in the hearts of the ruling class."[245] About half an hour after police stormed through the barricades, a Molotov cocktail hurled by a young freedom fighter exploded next to a police car and flames danced across the street. Police nearby whirled about, drawing their revolvers and firing wildly at the rooftops above their heads as the first sounds of gunfire rang out through the night sky. Harlem unchained its mighty lion, and the long, hot summers began.

CONCLUSION

AS THE SMOKE BEGAN TO clear in Harlem and nearby Bedford-Stuyvesant, newspapers across the country carried article after article covering the "riots" spreading throughout the Northeast. Alongside dramatic photographs of broken windows and people running from the police ran columns in which reporters, politicians, police, and civil rights leaders offered their explanations of the recent unrest in the nation's cities. With explanations ranging from condemnations of "looters" and "rioters" with no regard for law and order, to descriptions of the hopelessness and despair that created a powder keg in the "ghetto," to accusations that "irresponsible civil rights leaders" and communists incited the "riots" with their campaigns against police brutality, it was hard to find a person who did not have an opinion on the cause or meaning of the uprisings.[1] Despite the range of reactions, there was general agreement that action was needed in Harlem and elsewhere to address the explosive symptoms of systemic racism. The disagreement lay in what (or who) was responsible for the uprising and what should be done about the situation.

The responses from city hall were characteristic of the Wagner administration's general position toward the Black freedom movement over the previous decade. In a televised address as the uprising began to ebb, Wagner stuck close to the well-worn script of his one-two punch of liberal governance. With his left hand, he explained to Harlem residents that he empathized with their "needs and problems in regard to housing and jobs and discrimination and the education of your children" and made familiar promises to "go all out to remedy injustice" and "reduce inequality." With his right hand, Wagner blamed the uprising on "tough young ones" who were "ready for violence . . . and full of resentment and hate" and declared "the mandate to maintain law and order is absolute, unconditional and unqualified." Furthermore, the mayor warned that "illegal acts, including defiance of or attacks upon the police" would not be tolerated and that the city would not be "browbeaten by prophets of despair, or by peddlers of hate."[2] To Harlem residents, the message was abundantly clear. "There was nothing new in Wagner's statement," NY NAACP President Rev. Richard Hildebrand observed, while reiterating demands for a civilian review board over the mayor's continued objections.[3]

While the Wagner administration characterized the "riot" as both a consequence of racist oppression *and* an expression of Black criminality, many Harlem activists characterized "the battle of Harlem" as a rational response to unyielding systemic racism and unrelenting police violence.[4] To activist and *Muhammad Speaks* columnist Sylvester Leaks, the cause of and solution to the collective anger behind the uprising was simple. "If the premise is accepted that black anger has its roots in fundamental social, political and economic oppression—then its corollary must be that only a fundamental change will cool it." Yet, as Leaks explained, "most of the present white leaders will not and cannot accept this premise."[5] Instead of acceding to the fundamental changes demanded by Black radicals for a decade, the state attempted both to assuage Black anger through lofty promises and minor concessions and to contain it with an expansion of the carceral state.

To John O. Killens, the uprising was the outcome of a dialectical struggle between the demands of Black communities for rights, power, and self-determination and the determination of the state to maintain white supremacy. "The instinctive reaction of the white power structure is to keep the lid on by brute force—the police. Little is done about the steam; little about the fire . . . and the pressure builds up against the lid. The answer is more force," Killens explained. "This is the final contradiction: the white man's fear of the oppressed leads to an intensification of police brutality which inexorably sharpens the anger, hatred and, finally, the militancy of the Negro people."[6] Through the mayor's consistently meeting legitimate Black demands for rights and power with his velvet glove–iron fist routine for over a decade, the Wagner administration revealed the repressive nature of liberalism and the illegitimacy of white state power in the Jim Crow North. In the process, the state catalyzed the radicalization of local people and an emergent Black Power movement.

While police militarization is usually perceived as a political response to urban rebellions, the expansion of policing—intended to suppress Black radicalism, enforce white supremacy, and prevent unrest—actually precipitated the uprisings in Harlem and elsewhere. As the Harlem Defense Council reported, "The period between April and mid-July was so filled with acts of cruelty committed by policemen and sanctioned by the political bosses that one supreme act of cruelty was enough to spark a rebellion against police terror."[7] Acts of police brutality are commonly cited as the catalysts of the urban rebellions of the 1960s and beyond, yet their singularity is created by the context in which they occur, that of escalating police violence and resistance. As W. E. B. Du Bois explained in 1917, "The cause of war is preparation for war."[8] As the Black freedom movement evolved in Harlem, the state increasingly mobilized the police to enforce the status quo of white supremacy and ultimately declared war on Black communities in the spring of 1964. As the repression escalated, grassroots organizers developed more radical ideas, strategies, and tactics to achieve the fundamental changes that would bring Black liberation. Fueled by surging demands for human rights, political power, and self-determination, Harlem residents refused to submit to white state power and fought back against police violence after years of demands for systemic change being routinely met with political obstruction and state violence. "The wonder is that it took so long for our patience to wear thin," Killens reflected.[9]

The fatal shooting of James Powell on July 16, then, served as a singular example of the force of the white world pressing down on a rising Black nation. By rebelling against the white power structure in the days that followed, Harlem residents demonstrated their allegiance to a challenge Mae Mallory had thrown down three years earlier: "the task of unleashing this Black power until the world is rid of White domination and exploitation."[10] As city after city exploded in the weeks, months, and years that followed, it was clear that Harlem residents were not alone in their task. When Harlem erupted, local people shouted down Bayard Rustin's pleas for calm and called for Malcolm X to come home from Africa to give direction to the uprising. When Rochester followed suit a week later, the masses in the streets of western New York declared, "Don't give us [Martin Luther] King, give us Jesse Gray."[11]

For their part, Gray and Malcolm X sought to organize the power of the rebellion into a revolutionary movement for Black liberation. In December 1964 Gray delivered the keynote address at the founding conference of the Federation for Independent Political Action, one of several attempts at building united front formations in the wake of the rebellion, which brought together grassroots organizers to "initiate and coordinate struggle for independent political power."[12] Building on the foundations laid by the Northern Negro Grass Roots Leadership Conference and the subsequent work of ACT, the conference featured speeches by Malcolm X and Isaiah Brunson and workshops led by Gray, Rev. Milton Galamison, James Haughton, Bill Strickland, and John Henrik Clarke. Citing many of the issues Harlem organizers had challenged over the past decade, the conference called for "mass organized political action" to advance "the black revolution."[13]

In his keynote address, Gray wove together the major threads of Harlem's emergent grassroots Black Power movement in a clarion call for revolutionaries to organize "the mass reservoir of black power" in cities around the country. The inability of the movement—even in the wake of a rebellion—to achieve fundamental change in the city was a clear sign that new directions had to be sought. "Unless we begin to move beyond all the major struggles we have gone through for the last years, school boycotts, rent strikes, sit-ins and all the rest of them," Gray explained, "the present political power will let us continue to do this year in and year out." While he recognized the power demonstrated through the rebellion, Gray argued that Harlem's revolutionary potential was being hamstrung by a lack of "unified, organized black political power" and a lack of real revolutionary leadership. The answer, he explained, was not to break down the walls of the "ghetto" but for "real revolutionaries" to "go down to the streets and organize the people" around their day-to-day problems and "make it a healthy place to live." Through this "spadework" of grassroots organizing, working-class Black communities would build the power to seize control of the political, economic, educational, and cultural institutions in their communities. The work of building unity and power, Gray explained to the all-Black gathering, required independent Black leadership and "must develop . . . our pride in being black." Highlighting the national context of local issues and struggles, Gray declared the only way to change "the jim crow policy" of the federal government was "to bring a true revolutionary movement into being."[14]

Beyond articulating the ideologies and strategies of Harlem's Black Power movement cultivated over decades by radical grassroots organizers, the

Federation for Independent Political Action conference was also formative in the emergence of Black Power in other northern cities. Following the conference, Detroit organizer James Boggs wrote, "Militant black leaders from all over the country . . . went back into their communities to link the idea of black power with concrete struggles."[15] In May 1965, just months after the conference and weeks after the assassination of Malcolm X, the Organization for Black Power was formed in Detroit to coordinate local struggles into a national movement.[16] Identifying the police as the enforcement arm of white supremacy and "an occupying force of absentee landlords, merchants, politicians, and managers," the organization developed plans for organizing Black communities to defend against repression and seize political, economic, and cultural power in American cities as part of a national struggle for Black state power.[17] Founded by members of ACT, the OAAU, and RAM, the Organization for Black Power emphasized radical grassroots organizing around material conditions and visions of creating liberated territories as part of a national and global freedom struggle, clearly reflecting the political thought and organizing of Jesse Gray, Mae Mallory, Malcolm X, and other radical grassroots organizers in Harlem.[18] Though short-lived, the organization was an important benchmark in the emergence of the national Black Power movement and demonstrated the national influence of grassroots organizing in Harlem.

The history of the Black freedom movement in Harlem from 1954 to 1964, then, is vital to understanding the emergence of the Black Power movement and the arrival of the long, hot summers. To honestly reckon with the outbreak of rebellions in Harlem and elsewhere in the mid-1960s requires a thorough analysis of the preceding periods of organized resistance to systemic racism and state violence. Through this decade of struggle, radical grassroots organizers in Harlem nurtured a popular political consciousness that emphasized Black self-determination, community control of political, social, and economic institutions, a broader focus on human rights over civil rights, Black indigenous leadership of organizations, cultural nationalism, an identification with Pan-African freedom struggles, a fundamental critique of racial capitalism, and a disavowal of nonviolence as an ideology. The evolution of the Black freedom movement in Harlem during these formative years clearly demonstrates that the Black Power movement emerged alongside the civil rights movement and illuminates how attempts to hold back the rising tide of Black Power provoked the 1964 Harlem uprising.

When urban rebellions are delegitimized and criminalized as senseless violence or subversive plots, these narratives give cover to even greater repression with incalculable collateral damage in Black and Latino/a communities, as evidenced by the devastating national legacies of the War on Crime and the bloody wake left by the FBI's COINTELPRO. As Bill Strickland reflected years later, "If rebellion is legitimate, then America is illegitimate—and so, therefore, you must always define the behavior as illegitimate."[19] By denying conscious political agency to those who rise up against systemic racism and state violence, such narratives stoke popular backlash against legitimate demands for rights and power, enable the retrenchment of the more repressive elements of racial liberalism, and ultimately reify the state's monopoly on violence. To challenge these perceptions of popular uprisings against state violence and systemic racism in the 1960s is to provide vital space for developing a more critical framework for understanding their recurrence in the twenty-first century.

ACKNOWLEDGMENTS

This book is a testament to the support, labor, and love of a vast network of people who have inspired, encouraged, and sustained my growth as a scholar, educator, and person. I carried this project with me through many life changes over fifteen years as I moved from New York, to Massachusetts, back to New York, to Newark, and finally to Detroit. In each place, I found communities who have supported and guided my work, ultimately helping bring this book to life. This has been a long, challenging project, and the depth of my gratitude to those who have been there along the way cannot possibly be measured within these pages. I've done the best I could with the time and resources available to me and humbly offer this book as a contribution to our collective understanding of the Black freedom movement and to the field of Black studies. I hope any gaps or errors will serve as openings for other scholars to improve on and expand our knowledge of the movement in Harlem and New York City.

I began working on this project as an undergraduate history major at Wagner College. I will always be grateful to the faculty there, especially Rita Reynolds, who saw something in me as a student and invested in my development as a scholar. As I pursued my master's degree in education, Rita continuously pushed me to pursue a PhD in Black studies, despite my insistence that I was done with school. Eventually she won out and shepherded my application to her alma mater, the W. E. B. Du Bois Department of Afro-American Studies at UMass Amherst. It was also Rita who encouraged me as an undergraduate to apply for an internship at the Schomburg Center for Research in Black Culture, where the research for this book began many years ago. My time immersing myself in Harlem's history at the Schomburg was transformative. Thank you, Dierdre Hollman, for your mentorship and for allowing me to spend my down time in the archives.

Rita, thank you for starting me on my way and for your continued mentorship and friendship in the years since.

The intellectual community the Du Bois Department cultivated at UMass has guided my political development and shaped the evolution of this book. I am profoundly grateful to the faculty of the department, past and present, for laying and expanding the intellectual, political, and institutional groundwork for so many of us to pursue degrees in Afro-American studies. Thank you, Professors Ernest Allen Jr., John Bracey Jr., A. Yemisi Jimoh, Toussaint Losier, Karen "Kym" Morrison, Britt Rusert, Amilcar Shabazz, Manisha Sinha, Jim Smethurst, Bill Strickland, Ekwueme Michael Thelwell, and Steven Tracy. I am also grateful to Tricia Loveland for her support, friendship, and steadfast dedication to the department. A special thanks goes to Jim Smethurst, Bill Strickland, Toussaint Losier, and Chris Tinson for serving on my dissertation committee and for their continuous guidance, labor, and encouragement throughout the years. Thank you as well to David Glassberg and Marla Miller for showing me the ropes of public history and for hosting Robin D. G. Kelley as a writer-in-residence, whose visit to one of our classes was a lightbulb moment in the development of this book.

Bill Strickland was the first person I met in the Du Bois Department, and he quickly took me under his wing. I owe much of my intellectual, political, and professional growth to his mentorship over the years in the classroom, at the Monkey Bar or Johnny's Tavern, over dinner in New York, and more recently on the phone. Strick taught me to be thorough in my research, clear in my writing, fearless in presenting my analysis, and generous with time, resources, and connections. He also connected me with countless movement veterans, including Junius Williams, who brought me to Newark and has been another cherished mentor over the past decade. Finishing this book is bittersweet, since I can't give you a copy to mark up and critique, but I hope it makes you proud.

A close community of scholars, friends, and mentors have provided endless support and sustenance over the years. Thank you to my family from the Du Bois Department, including Nadia Alahmed, Shawn Alexander, Biko Caruthers, Julia Charles-Linen, Rosa Clemente (also Justice and Alicia), Markeysha Davis, Nneka Dennie, Crystal Donkor, Stephanie Evans, Don Geesling, David Goldberg, Trent Masiki, Zebulon Miletsky, Kelli Morgan, Johanna Ortner, Ousmane Power-Greene, Rita Reynolds, Jacinta Saffold, David Swiderski, Chris Tinson, Crystal Webster, Bob Williams, and Karla Zelaya. Special thanks to Julia Bernier, Carlyn Ferrari, and Kelly Giles for their continued love and friendship as we "get through this thing called life" in academia. Thanks to the late Richard Gassan for giving me an affordable place to live in Amherst and to his brother Larry for his friendship in the years since. Thanks as well to Laura Heisig, Ian Tapscott, and Caitlin Kelley for giving me a soft place to land in Northampton and for the community we built together. I am also grateful for the support of scholars I met through the Columbia University Institute for Research in African-American Studies Summer Teachers and Scholars Institute who have become dear friends, particularly Lauren Broussard and Aja Lans. Thanks to Samuel K. Roberts, Zoraida Lopez-Diago, and Elizabeth Sarah Ross for their work in fostering this kind of community.

Newark and Detroit have been home for the past eight years I've worked on this book. I am grateful to Junius Williams and Antoinette Ellis-Williams for welcoming me home in Newark and for their steadfast support, guidance, and fellowship in the years since. Mr. Williams, I'm grateful Strick vouched for me, and I cherish the work we've done together and your friendship and mentorship along the way. Thanks as well to Jae, James, Gabrielle, Addil, Kai, Kaleena, Jillian, Daniel, and Linda McDonald Carter for their friendship, conversations, and making Newark home. Thanks also to Komozi Woodard, a generous scholar and welcoming mentor who has helped shape my thinking and connected me with people and resources to support this work. In Detroit, I've been privileged to work alongside, learn from, and be in community with people who have helped me grow as a scholar, writer, teacher, activist, and friend. Thanks to Shakeb Ahmed, Dan and Dorothy Aldridge, Carolyn Baker, Val Baker, Rae Baker, Marcia Black, Mama Lila Cabbil, Rhiannon Chester-Bey, Charles Ezra Ferrell, David Goldberg and Beth Cole, Derrielle Goodwin, Martina Guzmán, Peter Hammer, Aysha Jamali, Jamon Jordan, Frank Joyce and Mary Anne Barnett, Marian Kramer-Baker, Helen Moore, Martha Prescod Norman Noonan, Ann Rall, Baba Charles Simmons, Lloyd Simpson, Herbert and Dayja Taylor, Rod Toneye, and Zach Weedon.

I'm also grateful to friends, colleagues, mentors, and editors who have helped shepherd this project from a dissertation into a book. David Goldberg and Shawn Alexander have been champions of this project and helped connect me with presses and editors. Thanks to Brandon Proia for seeing value in this project and working with me through the proposal process. A big thank you to Julia Bernier, Say Burgin, and David Goldberg for reading chapters and proposals, offering invaluable feedback, and helping me work through challenges. I've been fortunate to work with attentive, supportive, and talented editors at UVA Press who generously helped transform my rough dissertation into a more polished book. Nadine Zimmerli has been a joy to work with and went above and beyond to review lengthy chapters, help me develop arguments and structure, and generally teach me how to write a book, all during a time of pandemic and uprisings while carrying a heavy workload. Beth Colón Pizzini has been a gift in spotting gaps in the manuscript and helping get the book across the finish line. Thanks as well to Mark Naison, Jeanne Theoharis, and the other reviewers for their gracious critiques and feedback to help improve the book. Lastly, thanks to Ruth Melville for carefully copyediting the manuscript and Jenny Lillich for creating the index.

None of this work could have been possible without the labor of librarians and archivists. The Schomburg Center for Research in Black Culture is where this project began over fifteen years ago and has provided the archival bedrock the project is built on. Thank you to all of the archivists who have worked in the Manuscripts, Archives and Rare Books Division (particularly Alexsandra Mitchell), the Moving Image and Recorded Sound Division, and Photographs and Prints Division (particularly La Tanya Autry). Archivists at the New York City Municipal Archives, particularly Ken Cobb, Dwight Johnson, Zach Kautzman, Rossy Mendez, and Carlos Ramos, have been immensely helpful in accessing city records and photographs, including the NYPD's vast surveillance files. Thank you for all your work in processing and making this invaluable, sinister collection accessible. Special thanks to Brian Woodman at Washington University Libraries for sharing the transcripts of the interviews from *Malcolm X: Make It Plain* from the Henry Hampton Collection. Thank you as well to all the archivists at the Tamiment Library and Robert F. Wagner Labor Archives at New York University Libraries, Columbia University Libraries, the Division of Rare and Manuscript Collections at Cornell University Library, the Walter P. Reuther Library, Archives of Labor and Urban Affairs at Wayne State University, and the Hoover Institution Library and Archives at Stanford University. Professors Ernest Allen Jr. and the late John H. Bracey Jr. merit special recognition for their commitment to archiving records of Black nationalist organizations and the Black Power movement through the Black Power Movement Microform Collection and Professor Allen's legendary CD-ROM collections. Lastly, thanks to Carolyn Baker and the General Baker Institute, John H. Bracey Jr., Say Burgin, Joseph R. Fitzgerald, David Goldberg, Marilyn Lowen, Pat Murphy,

Bill Strickland, and Junius Williams for generously sharing materials from your research and collections with me.

This book is also the product of countless hours of oral history interviews and conversations with movement veterans. I owe a profound debt of gratitude to Dan and Dorothy Aldridge, Carl Anthony, Leroy Baylor, L. Pete Beveridge, John H. Bracey Jr., Elsie Chandler, John Churchville, Joan Countryman, Andrea Cousins, Gloria Richardson Dandridge, Jean Doak, Bob Fletcher, Q. R. Hand, David Henderson, Phil Hutchings, Frank Joyce, Marilyn Lowen, Kathie Rogers McQuarrie, Pat Murphy, Tom Roderick, Dorothy Stoneman, Bill Strickland, C. E. Wilson and Carol Fineberg, and Rod Toneye, each of whom graciously shared memories and stories with me. I am deeply humbled and grateful that you have entrusted me with writing parts of your histories.

Portions of my work on this book have been supported by internal awards from Eastern Michigan University, which provided necessary financial support for research travel and a brief reprieve from a 4/4 teaching load. The Department of Africology and African American Studies, the College of Arts and Sciences "Game Above" Professional Development Award, and the Provost's Research Support Award all provided funding to cover production costs and indexing. Thanks to all the students I've had the privilege of teaching over the past five years in various capacities. Your curiosity, drive, and fire have sustained me through the grueling workloads. Lastly, I want to express my deep respect for my fellow academic workers laboring under heavy teaching and service loads while still putting out serious scholarship.

I could not have written this book without the love and support of my family. My parents, Maureen and Brian Blackmer, have been a constant source of encouragement and support. One the daughter of a professor and the other a first-generation college graduate, you both have instilled in me a deep appreciation and love of learning, for which I am grateful. Thanks for pushing me to get the PhD, supporting me through the process, and being proud of where it's brought me. My grandmother, Virginia "Giggle" Brennan, was a lover of history and constant cheerleader over the years. Thank you for loving and supporting me, Gig. My siblings, Kyle and Megan, along with their families have been a consistent source of love, encouragement, and joy. I hope Tommy, Cora, Joseph, Louie, Bear, Ben, and Jake will read this one day and be proud of their Uncle Pete. To my friends Michael and Paul, and cousins Jack, John, and Paul, thanks for always putting me up and making time to hang out during research trips back to New York. Finally, to my partner Fitz (Nicole Fitzmaurice), thank you for loving and supporting me throughout this journey—even when I made it hard, with the long nights and weekends hunched over the computer and away from you. You're my rock and I couldn't have done this without you.

NOTES

ABBREVIATIONS

AMP	August Meier Papers, Schomburg Center for Research in Black Culture, New York Public Library
BOEC	Board of Education Collection, New York City Municipal Archives
CORE	The Papers of the Congress of Racial Equality, 1941–1967 [microfilm], Schomburg Center for Research in Black Culture, New York Public Library
HHC	Henry Hampton Collection, Washington University Libraries
HHP	Harry Haywood Papers, Schomburg Center for Research in Black Culture, New York Public Library
HJP	Hulan Jack Papers, New York City Municipal Archives
JCGF	John Carro General Files, New York City Municipal Archives
JHP	James Haughton Papers, Schomburg Center for Research in Black Culture, New York Public Library
JOP	Jack O'Dell Papers, Schomburg Center for Research in Black Culture, New York Public Library
KMP	Kenneth Marshall Papers, Schomburg Center for Research in Black Culture, New York Public Library
MCHR	Metropolitan Council on Housing Records, Tamiment Library and Robert F. Wagner Labor Archives, New York University Libraries
MMIFBI	Muslim Mosque Incorporated FBI Files
MMP	Mae Mallory Papers, Walter R. Reuther Library, Archives of Labor and Urban Affairs, Wayne State University
MRFWP	Robert F. Wagner Papers, New York City Municipal Archives

MXC	Malcolm X Collection, Schomburg Center for Research in Black Culture, New York Public Library
MXFBI	Malcolm X FBI File
NSM	Northern Student Movement Records, Schomburg Center for Research in Black Culture, New York Public Library
NYAN	*New York Amsterdam News*
NYPDIR	New York Police Department Intelligence Records, 1930–1990, New York City Municipal Archives
NYT	*New York Times*
OHALC	Oral History of the American Left Collection, The Tamiment Library and Robert F. Wagner Labor Archives, New York University Libraries.
RAM	The Black Power Movement Microform Collection: Papers of the Revolutionary Action Movement, 1962–1996
RBOHC	Ralph Bunche Oral History Collection, Moorland-Spingarn Research Center, Howard University
RFWP	The Black Power Movement Microform Collection: The Papers of Robert F. Williams

INTRODUCTION

1. Halstead et al., *Harlem Stirs*, 62.
2. Purnell and Theoharis, *The Strange Careers of the Jim Crow North.*
3. Halstead et al., *Harlem Stirs*, 62.
4. Biondi, *To Stand and Fight.*
5. Halstead et al., *Harlem Stirs*, 62.
6. Halstead et al., *Harlem Stirs*, 62.
7. Halstead et al., *Harlem Stirs*, 64.
8. Halstead et al., *Harlem Stirs*, 64.
9. Osofsky, *Harlem;* King, *Whose Harlem Is This, Anyway?;* Makalani, *In the Cause of Freedom;* James, *Holding Aloft the Banner of Ethiopia;* Cronon, *Black Moses;* McDuffie, *Sojourning for Freedom;* Blain, *Set the World on Fire;* Naison, *Communists in Harlem;* Greenberg, *Or Does It Explode;* Horne, *Black Liberation/Red Scare;* Griffin, *Harlem Nocturne;* Harris, *Sex Workers, Psychics, and Numbers Runners;* Biondi, *To Stand and Fight;* Essien-Udom, *Black Nationalism;* Fearnley and Matlin, *Race Capital?;* Smith and Sinclair, *The Harlem Cultural/Politics Movements;* Sugrue,

Sweet Land of Liberty; Erickson and Morrell, *Educating Harlem;* Smethurst, *The Black Arts Movement;* Tinson, *Radical Intellect;* Purnell and Theoharis, *The Strange Careers of the Jim Crow North;* Felber, *Those Who Know Don't Say;* Taylor, *Fight the Power;* Flamm, *In the Heat of the Summer;* Christopher Hayes, *The Harlem Uprising.*

10. OAAU Working Paper, June 6, 1964, MXC.
11. Robinson, *Black Marxism.*
12. William Strickland, speech at College Conference at Columbia, October 25, 1963, unmarked clipping, box 76, folder 24, AMP.
13. Throughout the book, I explore the common experiences of oppression and exploitation faced by Black and Puerto Rican communities as racialized "minorities" in New York City. Many Puerto Ricans are descendants of the African diaspora with shared histories of colonization, slavery, and resistance, which fostered solidarity with Black communities in urban spaces. As Sonia Song-Ha Lee explains, "Not only were Puerto Ricans and African Americans racialized as 'non-white' in parallel ways, but they also utilized their racial and ethnic identities as sites of political mobilization through mutual collaborations and contestations of power." While differences in language, national identity, religion, neighborhoods, etc., often led Black and Puerto Rican communities to form separate grassroots organizations, there was a common investment in Black liberation and Third World independence that nurtured solidarity movements and illuminates the anticolonial internationalism of the Black freedom movement in Harlem. Lee, *Building a Latino Civil Rights Movement,* 4–6; Beth Colón Pizzini, email correspondence with author, October 4, 2024.
14. Payne, *I've Got the Light of Freedom,* 264, 404.
15. Dittmer, *Local People;* Payne, *I've Got the Light of Freedom;* Crosby, *Civil Rights History.*
16. My analysis of "identity politics" here is informed by The Combahee River Collective Statement. See Keeanga-Yamahtta Taylor, *How We Get Free,* 15–28.
17. King, *Whose Harlem Is This, Anyway?;* McAdam, *Political Process and the Development of Black Insurgency;* Morris, *The Origins of the Civil Rights Movement;* Louis, *And We Are Not Saved;* Payne, *I've Got the Light of Freedom.*
18. King, *Whose Harlem Is This, Anyway?,* 5–6.
19. Joseph, "Waiting *till the* Midnight Hour," 6–17; Rhonda Y. Williams, *Concrete Demands;* Joseph, *Waiting 'Til the Midnight Hour;* Joseph, *The Black Power Movement.*
20. Baldwin, *The Fire Next Time,* 94.
21. For works on self-defense in the Southern civil rights movement, see Cobb, *This Nonviolent Stuff'll Get You Killed;* Tyson, *Radio Free Dixie;* Umoja, *We Will Shoot Back.* For works that explore self-defense in the Northern civil rights movement, see Ahmad, *We Will Return in the Whirlwind;* Cruse, *The Crisis of the Negro Intellectual;* Joseph, *Waiting 'Til the Midnight Hour;* Sugrue, *Sweet Land of Liberty;* Clarence

Taylor, *Fight the Power*; Tinson, *Radical Intellect*; Rhonda Y. Williams, *Concrete Demands*.

22. Purnell and Theoharis, *The Strange Careers of the Jim Crow North*, 6–9, 20; Miller, *Managing Inequality*, 4–5.
23. Abu-Lughod, *Race, Space, and Riots*; Felker-Kantor, *Policing Los Angeles*; Flamm, *In the Heat of the Summer*; Christopher Hayes, *The Harlem Uprising*; Hill, *Strike the Hammer*; Hinton, *America on Fire*; Hinton, *From the War on Poverty*; Horne, *Fire This Time*; Levy, *The Great Uprising*; Taylor, *Fight the Power*; Felber, *Those Who Know Don't Say*; Suddler, *Presumed Criminal*; Theoharis, *A More Beautiful and Terrible History*.

1. A "RISING TIDE" COMING IN

1. Rampersad, "Introduction," x–xi.
2. Locke, "Harlem," 630.
3. James Weldon Johnson, "The Making of Harlem," 639.
4. Haley and Malcolm X, *The Autobiography of Malcolm X*, 79–125; Marable, *Malcolm X*, 39–100.
5. Rhonda Y. Williams, *Concrete Demands*, 20–22.
6. Cronon, *Black Moses*.
7. Rosenwaike, *Population History of New York City*, 190.
8. Sales, *From Civil Rights to Black Liberation*, 59.
9. Munro, *The Anticolonial Front*, 161.
10. Bobo, "Carlos Cooks," 22–23.
11. Cooks, "Gamal Abdel Nassar; Marcus Garvey Day," 76–79.
12. Clarke, "The New Afro-American Nationalism," 287.
13. "Join the United African Nationalist Movement Now!," 1958, box 44, folder 14, Small Organization Files, NYPDIR.
14. "What We Know!," "Buy Black Shopper's Directory," and "Code Afric," *The Black Challenge*, 1959. Thanks to Professor Ernest Allen Jr. for preserving and digitizing the records of Black nationalist organizations like the ANPM in his legendary CD-ROM archives.
15. For a more extensive analysis of the Bandung conference, see Munro, *The Anticolonial Front*, 203–46.
16. "The Issue at Bandung," *NYAN*, April 2, 1955; "African Nationalists Call Conference Aug. 1," *NYAN*, May 14, 1955.
17. Von Eschen, *Race Against Empire*, 150–52.
18. NY FBI Report, "Malcolm K. Little," November 17, 1959, MXFBI.
19. Von Eschen, *Race Against Empire*, 172; Munro, *The Anticolonial Front*, 214.
20. Goldman, *The Death and Life of Malcolm X*, 53.

21. Rivera, "Carlos Cooks and Garveyism," 157; Sinclair, "Harlem Street Speakers," 39–42.
22. Mathes, "Scratching the Threshold," 363–96.
23. Goldman, *The Death and Life of Malcolm X,* 53.
24. Sinclair, "Louis H. Michaux," 43–48.
25. John Henrik Clarke, interview with Blackside.
26. Gore, "From Communist Politics to Black Power," 71–81; McDuffie and Woodard, "If You're in a Country," 514–19.
27. McDuffie and Woodard, "If You're in a Country," 507–16.
28. McDuffie and Woodard, "If You're in a Country," 521; Queen Mother Audley Moore, interview with Mark Naison.
29. Joseph, *Waiting 'Til the Midnight Hour,* 13.
30. Haley and Malcolm X, *The Autobiography of Malcolm X,* 218.
31. Haley and Malcolm X, *The Autobiography of Malcolm X,* 221.
32. Sonia Sanchez, interview with Blackside.
33. Haley and Malcolm X, *The Autobiography of Malcolm X,* 221.
34. Griffin, "Ironies of the Saint," 214-29.
35. Goldman, *The Death and Life of Malcolm X,* 55.
36. "The Second Emancipation," *NYAN,* May 22, 1954.
37. C. G. Fraser, "Harlem Students Learn Inferiority," *NYAN,* May 1, 1954.
38. Back, "Exposing the 'Whole Segregation Myth,'" 69; Biondi, *To Stand and Fight,* 246.
39. HARYOU, *Youth in the* Ghetto, 163–65; Glass, "From Sword to Shield."
40. Harlem Parents Committee, "The Education of Minority Group Children in the New York City Public Schools, 1965," 1–2, ERIC Institute of Education Sciences, https://eric.ed.gov/?id=ED010784.
41. Burrell, "Black Women as Activist Intellectuals," 91–92.
42. Biondi, *To Stand and Fight,* 241; Burrell, "Black Women as Activist Intellectuals," 91–92.
43. Louis E. Burnham, "Negro Children Branded!," *Freedom,* April 1954.
44. "Permanent Committee to Carry Out Resolutions of Conference," *Freedom,* April 1954.
45. Back, "Exposing the 'Whole Segregation Myth,'" 69; Biondi, *To Stand and Fight,* 246.
46. Ransby, "Cops, Schools, and Communism," 36.
47. Burnham, "Negro Children Branded!" As historian Martha Biondi points out, New York City was one of the first places in which the *Brown* decision inspired organizing campaigns for desegregation, owing in large part to the work of organizers like Baker, Delany, the Clarks, and Rev. Milton Galamison. Biondi, *To Stand and Fight,* 246.
48. Ransby, "Cops, Schools, and Communism," 37.
49. Ransby, "Cops, Schools, and Communism," 34–35.

50. Biondi, *To Stand and Fight*, 168–69.
51. Ella Baker, "Developing Community Leadership," 345–51.
52. Ransby, "Cops, Schools, and Communism," 32–33.
53. Ransby, "Cops, Schools, and Communism," 37.
54. Ransby, "Cops, Schools, and Communism," 38.
55. Back, "Exposing the 'Whole Segregation Myth,'" 72.
56. "Statement Presented to Mayor Robert F. Wagner by Delegation of Parents, Thursday, September 19, 1957, Read by Ella J. Baker," box 60, folder 691, HJP.
57. Back, "Up South in New York," 315–17; Back, "Exposing the 'Whole Segregation Myth,'" 70.
58. Mallory, interview with Malaika Lumumba, 16–17.
59. Tyson, *Radio Free Dixie*, 189; Rhonda Y. Williams, *Concrete Demands*, 66.
60. Rhonda Y. Williams, *Concrete Demands*, 67; Back, "Exposing the 'Whole Segregation Myth,'" 72.
61. Mallory's critiques of the Communist Party's language and messaging is also instructive for analyzing the party's limitations in connecting with working-class communities in New York City. "I went to all these meetings and there these people sat, black and white, you know, saying words like international proletariat, democratic centralism, and it was a different kind of language. I didn't know what in the world these people were talking about." Mallory, interview with Lumumba, 9–11.
62. Mallory, interview with Lumumba, 11.
63. Mae Mallory, "Maladjusted Follower," *NYAN*, November 24, 1956.
64. Mallory, *Letters from Prison*, 29; Mae Mallory Statement to the Board of Education Public Hearing, January 17, 1957, box 261.2, folder 14, BOEC; Burrell, "Black Women as Activist Intellectuals," 98–99.
65. See Sara Slack, "New Site Selected for PS 10," *NYAN*, June 1, 1957; Earl Brown, "New School for Harlem," *NYAN*, March 23, 1957.
66. For more on Mallory and Ella Baker as "activist intellectuals," see Burrell, "Black Women as Activist Intellectuals," 89–112. For a more extensive analysis of gender roles and representations within struggles around educational justice in late 1950s New York, see Back, "Exposing the 'Whole Segregation Myth,'" 78–81.
67. Mallory, *Letters from Prison*, 30.
68. "Jim Crow School Case to High Court," *NYAN*, July 6, 1957.
69. Paul Zuber Statement to the Board of Education Public Hearing, January 17, 1957, box 261.2, folder 13, BOEC.
70. Mae Mallory Statement to the Board of Education Public Hearing, January 17, 1957, BOEC.
71. Draft of Mayor Robert F. Wagner's Statement to the Federal Civil Rights Commission, February 2, 1959, box 60, folder 696, MRFWP.
72. Letter from Algernon Black to Robert F. Wagner, May 27, 1957, box 60, folder 689, RFWP.

73. For more on the Commission on Integration, including the roles of parents, civil rights activists, teachers unions, and the opposition to integration from white New Yorkers, see Back, "Up South in New York," 154-244; Clarence Taylor, "Harlem Schools and the New York City Teachers Union," 148-56.
74. Hubert T. Delany Statement to the Board of Education Public Hearing, January 17, 1957, box 261.2, folder 13, BOEC.
75. Baker, "Developing Community Leadership." For more on resistance to school desegregation and popular white backlash, see Back, "Exposing the 'Whole Segregation Myth,'" 68-71; Back, "Up South in New York," 242-43.
76. Jesse H. Walker, "Theatricals," *NYAN,* January 17, 1959.
77. "Protests School, Arrested on Welfare Charge," *NYAN,* June 29, 1957.
78. Mallory, interview with Lumumba, 15.
79. Mallory, interview with Lumumba, 15-16.
80. Gray, interview with Katherine M. Shannon, 1-2; Gold, *When Tenants Claimed the City,* 116-17.
81. The progressive CIO, which had split from the more conservative American Federation of Labor (AFL) in 1935, became popular among members of the Black working class in the 1930s-40s for resisting Jim Crow and organizing black workers. O'Dell, *Climbin' Jacob's Ladder,* 12.
82. O'Dell, *Climbin' Jacob's Ladder,* 13.
83. Gray, interview with Shannon, 3.
84. During World War II, Smith worked alongside Eleanor Roosevelt and Paul Robeson to win the appointment of former Garveyite Hugh Mulzac as the first Black captain of the Merchant Marine. Biondi, *To Stand and Fight,* 8. For more on Smith and the NMU, see Horne, *Red Seas.*
85. Jack O'Dell, interview with James Early.
86. Gray, interview with Shannon, 3; Gray, interview with Harry Haywood. The "Black Belt" thesis contended that African Americans constituted an oppressed nation and therefore had a right to self-determination and to form their own nation-state in the Black Belt South.
87. Though there has been scholarly debate surrounding Jesse Gray's affiliation with the Communist Party, an interview between him and Harry Haywood makes Gray's affiliation with the party a matter of historical fact. See Gray, interview with Haywood.
88. Naison, *Communists in Harlem,* xvii-xviii.
89. Queen Mother Audley Moore, interview with Mark Naison. See also Moore, interview with Ruth Prago. Moore eventually left the party in 1950 when it became apparent to her that they lacked the radical racial consciousness necessary to build a movement for Black liberation and empowerment.
90. Navasky, *The O'Dell File,* loc. 458; Gold, *When Tenants Claimed the City,* 117.
91. Although Roberta Gold notes that Gray was purged from the NMU "around 1952," the details surrounding his ouster remain unclear. The last available record

of his affiliation with the NMU was as a representative of the Maritime Peace Committee at a "mass memorial meeting" held for the Martinsville 7 and John Derrick on February 12, 1951. Gray appeared alongside Paul Robeson and Sidney Poitier at the meeting. See "Mass Memorial Meeting," *NYAN,* February 10, 1951.

92. O'Dell initially went south to organize with the CIO's Operation Dixie and the Southern Negro Youth Conference before returning to New York.
93. Gray, interview with Haywood.
94. Gold, *When Tenants Claimed the City,* 117.
95. Engels, *The Housing Question,* 58.
96. Engels, *The Housing Question,* 58.
97. Gold, *When Tenants Claimed the City,* 117.
98. Johnstone, "The Tenants' Movement," 252–54.
99. Gold, *When Tenants Claimed the City,* 117.
100. Untitled news clipping, *New York Herald Tribune,* November 29, 1964.
101. Navasky, *The O'Dell File,* loc 458; Gold, *When Tenants Claimed the City,* 117; Sugrue, *Sweet Land of Liberty,* 403; Biondi, *To Stand and Fight,* 209. Gray joined the ALP around 1952 following his ouster from the NMU and immediately became involved in political organizing. That year he led a committee to run former communist City Councilman Ben Davis—then imprisoned under the Smith Act—for state assembly in New York City's 11th Assembly District on the Freedom Party ballot. Offering a glimpse of the showmanship and radical rhetoric that he would come to be known for in the years to follow, Gray compared the Davis campaign to "electing Kwame Nkrumah from a Ghana jail." Horne, *Black Liberation/Red Scare,* 260.
102. Schwartz, "Tenant Power in the Liberal City"; Sugrue, *Sweet Land of Liberty,* 403; Carroll, *Mobilizing New York,* 61.
103. HARYOU, *Youth in the Ghetto,* 105–6.
104. Lipsky, *Protest in City Politics,* 43.
105. "Excerpts from Panuch Report to Wagner on Need For New Housing Board," *NYT,* March 10, 1960; J. Anthony Panuch, *Building a Better New York,* Final Report, Mayor's Independent Survey on Housing and Urban Renewal, 1960, https://archive.org/details/buildingbetterne00newy/mode/1up; Gold, *When Tenants Claimed the City,* 122–23.
106. HARYOU, *Youth in the Ghetto,* 107–8.
107. "Harlem Tenants Live in Dread of . . . Death by Fire," *Freedom,* January 1955.
108. "Harlem Tenants Live in Dread of . . . Death by Fire," *Freedom,* January 1955. NYU Libraries has created a digital archive of its collection of editions of *Freedom:* https://dlib.nyu.edu/freedom/.
109. Schwartz, "Tenant Power in the Liberal City," 141–53.
110. Jesse Gray, "Harlem Tenants Fight Evictions and Proposal to Decontrol Rents," *Freedom,* March 1953.
111. Lipsky, *Protest in City Politics,* 56.

112. "Harlem Homeowners Fight Jimcrow Mortgage Policies," *Freedom,* February 1955.
113. Harlem Tenants Council, "Tenants! Know Your Rights!," undated, box 25, folder 39, MCHR.
114. Gray, interview with Shannon, 12.
115. "Rent Office to Help Two Evicted Families," *NYAN,* December 19, 1953; Jesse Gray, "Defends Work of the Tenants Council," *NYAN,* February 6, 1954.
116. "Tenant Group Lists 100 Slum Landlords," *NYAN,* May 15, 1954; Lipsky, *Protest in City Politics,* 56; "Say Inspector Never Visited Condemned House," *NYAN,* June 19, 1954.
117. For more on how tenants organized to resist Title I in New York City, see Schwartz, "Tenant Power in the Liberal City" 153-72. For a national analysis of slum clearance and urban renewal programs, see Anderson, *The Federal Bulldozer.*
118. Richard Lincoln, "Review Plan to Increase Jim Crow, Cut Negro Vote," *NYAN,* April 11, 1953.
119. George B. Murphy Jr., "Harlem Tenants Organize as Housing Crisis Deepens," *Freedom,* February 1953.
120. Schwartz, "Tenant Power in the Liberal City," 162; "Urge Civic Groups to Aid in Work," *NYAN,* February 19, 1955; "Asks Probe of Harlem Project Site," *NYAN,* February 12, 1955.
121. "Sponsors Boycott Housing Meeting," *NYAN,* January 31, 1953; "500 Tenants Attend UL Housing Meet," *NYAN;* Murphy, "Harlem Tenants Organize as Housing Crisis Deepens."
122. Jesse Gray, "Harlem Tenants Fight Evictions and Proposal to Decontrol Rents," *Freedom,* March 1953.
123. Murphy, "Harlem Tenants Organize as Housing Crisis Deepens."
124. Gold, *When Tenants Claimed the City,* 72-73.
125. Gray, interview with Shannon, 14-15.
126. "The Housing Headache," *NYAN,* May 26, 1954.
127. James Booker, "1,000 Protest Housing Projects," *NYAN,* April 21, 1956.
128. FBI Investigation Report, April 19, 1956, box E8, Gray, Jesse Williard, Federal Records National Advisory Commission on Civil Disorders (Kerner Commission), Lyndon Baines Johnson Library. Thanks to David Goldberg for sharing this file with me.
129. Biondi, *To Stand and Fight,* 72-73. For extended analyses of postwar police abuses and struggles for reform in New York City, see Biondi, *To Stand and Fight;* M. S. Johnson, *Street Justice.*
130. Powell, *Marching Blacks,* 158-59.
131. Biondi, *To Stand and Fight,* 72-73.
132. Biondi, *To Stand and Fight,* 193; "Justice Delany Raps Brutality," *NYAN,* June 2, 1951.

133. Biondi, *To Stand and Fight,* 60.
134. "Justice Delany Raps Brutality," *NYAN,* June 2, 1951.
135. M. S. Johnson, *Street Justice,* 22–25.
136. Ransby, *Ella Baker and the Black Freedom Movement,* 156–57.
137. Ransby, *Ella Baker and the Black Freedom Movement,* 156–57; M. S. Johnson, *Street Justice,* 224; Cannato, *The Ungovernable City,* 156.
138. Hudson, "Police Review Boards and Police Accountability," 523.
139. M. S. Johnson, *Street Justice,* 227.
140. "Police make It Easier for Public to File Complaints of Brutality," *NYT,* May 16, 1955.
141. "Boy, 9, Says Cops Brutally Beat Him," *NYAN,* May 21, 1955.
142. Huie, interview with Blackside.
143. Ogbar, *Black Power,* 39.
144. Biondi, *To Stand and Fight,* 206–7.
145. Earl Brown, "Aroused Race," *NYAN,* October 8, 1955.
146. T. J. Sellers, "Wave of Terror Sweeps Miss.!," *NYAN,* October 8, 1955. According to Sellers, Mamie Till Bradley was scheduled to make an appearance at the rally but suffered a "nervous collapse" days before and was hospitalized.
147. Sellers, "Wave of Terror Sweeps Miss.!"
148. Ogbar, *Black Power,* 39.
149. Joseph, *Waiting 'Til the Midnight Hour,* 9–11; Rhonda Y. Williams, *Concrete Demands,* 68–69; "Moslem Victim's Own Story of Cops' Brutality," *NYAN,* May 18, 1957; James L. Hicks, "Riot Threat as Cops Beat Moslem," *NYAN,* May 4, 1957.
150. Joseph, *Waiting 'Til the Midnight Hour,* 9–11; Rhonda Y. Williams, *Concrete Demands,* 68–69; Hicks, "Riot Threat as Cops Beat Moslem."
151. Hicks, "Riot Threat as Cops Beat Moslem."
152. Hicks, "Riot Threat as Cops Beat Moslem."
153. Haley and Malcolm X, *The Autobiography of Malcolm X,* 236.
154. Joseph, *Waiting 'Til the Midnight Hour,* 11.
155. Goldman, *The Death and Life of Malcolm X,* 55.
156. Goldman, *The Death and Life of Malcolm X,* 60.
157. Goldman, *The Death and Life of Malcolm X,* 60.
158. Goldman, *The Death and Life of Malcolm X,* 59.
159. Joseph, *Waiting 'Til the Midnight Hour,* 19.
160. Sales, *From Civil Rights to Black Liberation,* 43.

2. "THE NEGRO REVOLT"

1. "President's July 4 Message," *NYT,* July 4, 1959.
2. "Harlem Is Seething with Grim Unrest," *NYAN,* July 4, 1959.

3. Back, "Up South in New York," 307–8.
4. Back, "Exposing the 'Whole Segregation Myth,'" 72.
5. Loren B. Pope, "21 Negro Pupils Are Kept Home on Charge of Segregation Here," *NYT*, September 9, 1958.
6. Back, "Exposing the 'Whole Segregation Myth,'" 73.
7. Back, "Exposing the 'Whole Segregation Myth,'" 73–74.
8. Sara Slack, "We'd Rather Go to Jail': Defy Court's Order in School Boycott," *NYAN*, December 13, 1958.
9. Back, "Exposing the 'Whole Segregation Myth,'" 75.
10. Back, "Exposing the 'Whole Segregation Myth,'" 73–76.
11. Back, "Exposing the 'Whole Segregation Myth,'" 77–78.
12. Back, "Up South in New York," 338; Sara Slack, "Community Halts Woman's Eviction," *NYAN*, October 4, 1958.
13. "Protests School, Arrested on Welfare Charge," *NYAN*, June 29, 1957.
14. Sara Slack, "Receives Threats in School Suits," *NYAN*, August 3, 1957.
15. Harry Haywood, "Black Political Power: The Next Stage in the Afro-American Liberation Struggle," box 5, folder 1, HHP.
16. Back, "Exposing the 'Whole Segregation Myth,'" 81.
17. Gold, *When Tenants Claimed the City*, 117.
18. O'Dell, interview with James Early; Navasky, *The O'Dell File*, loc. 497–502.
19. Gold, *When Tenants Claimed the City*, 130.
20. Gold, *When Tenants Claimed the City*, 130.
21. Though some communist-influenced American Labor Party clubs had toyed with the idea of organizing "block groups" in the late 1940s and early 1950s to promote grassroots political mobilization, the idea was never acted upon. Schwartz, "Tenant Power in the Liberal City," 144.
22. O'Dell, interview with Early; Gold, *When Tenants Claimed the City*, 118; "Tenants Rally Set Sept. 19," *NYAN*, September 10, 1960.
23. O'Dell, interview with Early; Gold, *When Tenants Claimed the City*, 149.
24. Gray, interview with Shannon.
25. O'Dell, interview with Early; Gold, *When Tenants Claimed the City*, 149.
26. Schwartz, "The New York City Rent Strikes," 547.
27. At the time, the New York City Housing Authority did not have any agency dedicated to coordinating relocation for residents displaced by developments. The lack of relocation agencies in communities impacted by urban development became a locus of organizing against urban renewal and for community control of development in Northern cities in the 1960s.
28. Jesse H. Walker, "Powell Calls Jack 'Stooge' Of Enemy," *NYAN*, April 5, 1958.
29. Gray, interview with Shannon, 14–15.
30. "Ask Hearing on Rent Control," *NYAN*, January 17, 1958; "See Rent Controls Getting Extension," *NYAN*, February 28, 1959.
31. "1,000 Tenants Got Mad, Got Petitions, Got Action," *NYAN*, April 4, 1959.

32. "1,000 Tenants Got Mad, Got Petitions, Got Action."
33. Office of the Mayor Press Release, "Slum-Combat Inspection Team Program," November 25, 1958, box 148, folder 2083, MRFWP.
34. The 1960 Census showed a rate of 2.3 "deaths from home accidents" per 10,000 population count in Harlem, as compared to 1.2 for the rest of New York City. HARYOU, *Youth in the Ghetto,* 107–8.
35. Edith Evans Asbury, "Agent for 2 Harlem Tenements Is Fined $75 for 99 Violations," *NYT,* July 2, 1959.
36. George Barner, "Angry Tenants on Rent Strike," *NYAN,* July 4, 1959.
37. Barner, "Angry Tenants on Rent Strike."
38. Sugrue, *Sweet Land of Liberty,* 404.
39. "Negro Revolt: Harlem Is Seething with Grim Unrest," *NYAN,* July 4, 1959.
40. Barner, "Angry Tenants on Rent Strike."
41. George Barner and Sara Slack, "Revolt Spreads," *NYAN,* July 11, 1959.
42. Barner and Slack, "Revolt Spreads."
43. "Williams Returns to Speak Again," *NYAN,* July 11, 1959.
44. Tyson, *Radio Free Dixie,* 143.
45. Tyson, *Radio Free Dixie,* 143.
46. Tyson, *Radio Free Dixie,* 143.
47. Earl Brown, "They Lynched Us All," *NYAN,* May 16, 1959.
48. "We Printed It," *NYAN,* May 23, 1959.
49. Tyson, *Radio Free Dixie,* 149.
50. Dickson and Roberts, "Negroes with Guns."
51. Dickson and Roberts, "Negroes with Guns."
52. McDuffie, "We Owe a Debt to Her," 135–58; Sweeting, *Nobody Gave Me Permission,* 40.
53. Tyson, *Radio Free Dixie,* 205.
54. Tyson, *Radio Free Dixie,* 205.
55. Tyson, *Radio Free Dixie,* 145–47.
56. Tyson, *Radio Free Dixie,* 70.
57. Sweeting, *Nobody Gave Me Permission,* 29–31; "Mothers Press for a New PS 157, M.," *NYAN,* March 15, 1958.
58. "Williams Hearing to Hear Recording," *NYAN,* June 6, 1959; "Williams Returns to Speak Again," *NYAN,* July 11, 1959.
59. Tyson, *Radio Free Dixie,* 205.
60. Memo from Director to Charlotte SAC [Special Agent in Charge], June 18, 1959, RFWP.
61. Memo from J. J. Middleton to A. H. Belmont, May 6, 1959, RFWP.
62. Memo from Director to Charlotte SAC, June 18, 1959, RFWP.
63. Tyson, *Radio Free Dixie,* 149–65.
64. Cobb, *This Nonviolent Stuff;* Umoja, *We Will Shoot Back.*
65. Lomax, *The Negro Revolt,* 101–2.

66. Tyson, *Radio Free Dixie,* 162–63.
67. Farnsworth Fowle, "Governor Wants Housing Bias Law Similar to City's," *NYT,* July 14, 1959.
68. Tyson, *Radio Free Dixie,* 162–63.
69. Mallory, interview with Lumumba, 17.
70. Letter from Mae Mallory to Mabel and Robert F. Williams, June 3, 1963, box 1, folder 2, MMP.
71. Mobley was joined in her letter writing by Williams's Aunt Estelle (Williams) Johnson, who wrote to the *Amsterdam News* in late June to critique Wilkins and publicly support her nephew's position. Estelle Johnson, "An Aunt Speaks," *NYAN,* June 20, 1959.
72. "Williams Returns to Speak Again," *NYAN,* July 11, 1959.
73. Letter from Mae Mallory to Mabel and Robert F. Williams, June 3, 1963, box 1, folder 2, MMP.
74. Letter from Mallory to Mabel and Robert F. Williams, June 3, 1963.
75. Lomax et al., "The Hate That Hate Produced."
76. Lomax et al., "The Hate That Hate Produced"; Mike Wallace, interview with Blackside.
77. Wallace, interview with Blackside.
78. Louis E. Lomax, "Harlem, Saturday Night," *Baltimore Afro-American,* July 19, 1958; Lomax, *The Negro Revolt,* 164.
79. Baraka, "The Black Arts Movement," 12.
80. Ula Yvette Taylor, *The Promise of Patriarchy,* 74; Marable, *Malcolm X,* 135.
81. Julian Mayfield, "Challenge to Negro Leadership," *Commentary,* April 1961.
82. Marable, *Malcolm X,* 130–39.
83. "Jack, Powell, Brown All Agree on Garvey," *NYAN,* August 9, 1958; "Celebrate Marcus Garvey Day," *NYAN,* July 19, 1958.
84. Sara Slack, "Arab-African Ties Tight, Says Egyptian," *NYAN,* February 14, 1959.
85. NY FBI Report, "Malcolm K. Little," November 17, 1959, MXFBI.
86. Sales, *From Civil Rights to Black Liberation,* 67.
87. Robert Mangum, interview with Blackside.
88. Marable, *Malcolm X,* 159–60.
89. Marable, *Malcolm X,* 159–60.
90. "3 Moslems Seized as Police Fighters," *NYAN,* May 24, 1958. For more on the NYPD raid of the East Elmhurst home, see Marable, *Malcolm X,* 150–54, and Felber, *Those Who Know Don't Say,* 96–102.
91. Felber, *Those Who Know Don't Say,* 97–100.
92. NY FBI Report, "Malcolm K. Little," November 17, 1959, MXFBI.
93. "Kennedy Pledges Racial Fairness," *NYT,* June 21, 1959; "Moslems Didn't Get to See Commissioner," *NYAN,* June 27, 1959.
94. Carmela Caviglione (maiden name) also appears in newspaper coverage as Carmela Perez (married name). According to the *Amsterdam News,* all the records

from the case used her maiden name, so most newspaper coverage followed suit. She was married to Raymond Perez, also of the Bronx. "Crowd Melted Away After Clerk's Release," *NYAN,* July 18, 1959.
95. For details of the incident at the Regent Restaurant and Bar, see "Crowd Melted Away"; "Harlem Tensions Cited in Flare-Up," *NYT,* July 15, 1959.
96. George Barner, "Victim's Own Story," *NYAN,* July 18, 1959.
97. "Crowd Melted Away."
98. Al Nall, "Notarized Riot Statement: 'The Cop Dragged Her Out by Her Hair . . . ,'" *NYAN,* July 18, 1959.
99. Nall, "Notarized Riot Statement"; "Crowd Melted Away."
100. Nall, "Notarized Riot Statement"; "Crowd Melted Away."
101. "Sidelights of the 'Riot,'" *NYAN,* July 18, 1959.
102. "Near Riot at 125th St.," *NYAN,* July 11, 1959.
103. Nall, "Notarized Riot Statement."
104. "Harlem Tensions Cited in Flare-Up," *NYT,* July 15, 1959; Herman Chauka, "1,000 Harlem Demonstrators Protest N.Y. Police Violence," *The Militant,* July 20, 1959.
105. Chauka, "1,000 Harlem Demonstrators."
106. "Crowd Melted Away"; Barner, "Victim's Own Story."
107. Although her resistance to police brutality sparked a major protest against police violence and triggered critical public conversations about systemic racism in Harlem, Carmela Caviglione was treated as disposable and undeserving of the very civil and human rights her protest was used to advance. As an intoxicated woman who did not adhere to gendered notions of respectability, Caviglione was cast aside and left to fend for herself, while the men who had defused the situation were looked on as heroes and symbols of Black masculinity.
108. "Crowd Melted Away."
109. "Crowd Melted Away." Caviglione later pled guilty to the disorderly conduct charge and received a suspended sentence, while the felony assault charge was reduced to assault in the third degree. "Woman Who Set Off Near Riot Pleads Guilty," *NYAN,* August 8, 1959.
110. "Moslems Didn't Get to See Commissioner," *NYAN,* June 27, 1959.
111. On August 22, 1959, the *Amsterdam News* carried an editorial written by Malcolm X from Khartoum, stating that "racial trouble in New York occupied prominent space on the front pages here and in other parts of Africa yesterday." Malcolm X, "Africa Eyes Us," *NYAN,* August 22, 1959.
112. "Harlem Tensions Cited in Flare-Up," *NYT,* July 15, 1959.
113. James Hicks, "Another Angle: Powell's Power," *NYAN,* June 11, 1960.

3. THE LIMITS OF LIBERALISM IN HARLEM

1. "Sidelights of the 'Riot,'" *NYAN*, July 18, 1959.
2. "Harlem Is Seething with Grim Unrest," *NYAN*, July 4, 1959.
3. "Time To Act," *NYAN*, July 18, 1959.
4. Nall, "Notarized Riot Statement," *NYAN*, July 18, 1959.
5. "Harlem Tensions Cited in Flare-Up," *NYT*, July 15, 1959.
6. Nall, "Notarized Riot Statement."
7. "Discuss Alleged Police Brutality in Harlem," *Norfolk Journal and Guide*, July 25, 1959.
8. Peter Kihss, "4 Negro Areas Get Extra Police Units," *NYT*, July 16, 1959.
9. Kihss, "4 Negro Areas Get Extra Police Units."
10. James L. Hicks, "Another Angle: Somebody's Lying," *NYAN*, July 25, 1959.
11. Kihss, "4 Negro Areas Get Extra Police Units."
12. Peter Kihss, "Mayor Calls Parley on Harlem; Seeks Liaison to Ease Tension," *NYT*, July 17, 1959.
13. Executive Memorandum from Mayor Robert Wagner to City Commissioners, box 64, folder 743, Subject Files, MRFWP.
14. "City Officials at the Meeting of the Mayor with Harlem Community Representatives at City Hall on Tuesday, 2:30 p.m., July 21, 1959," box 78, folder 966, MRFWP.
15. Ibid. Other notable figures invited were Eugene Callender, Kenneth Clark, Hubert Delany, Dorothy Height, Glester Hinds, L. Joseph Overton, Jackie Robinson, Sugar Ray Robinson, Robert Weaver, and Paul Zuber. Earl Brown, "The City Hall Meeting," *NYAN*, August 1, 1959.
16. "City Officials at the Meeting of the Mayor."
17. Brown, "The City Hall Meeting."
18. Memorandum from Joyce Phillips Austin to Deputy Mayor Paul T. O'Keefe, August 7, 1959, box 109072B, folder 249, JCGF.
19. "Commissioner Balks at More Colored Harlem Police," *Norfolk Journal and Guide*, August 1, 1959.
20. "Commissioner Balks at More Colored Harlem Police."
21. Brown, "The City Hall Meeting."
22. Brown, "The City Hall Meeting."
23. Memorandum from Joyce Phillips Austin to Deputy Mayor Paul T. O'Keefe, August 7, 1959, box 109072B, folder 249, JCGF.
24. Brown even went so far as to describe Kennedy as "the knight fighting for racial integration in his department." Brown, "The City Hall Meeting."
25. Letter from Hulan Jack to Mayor Robert Wagner, August 3, 1959, box 3, folder 72, MRFWP.
26. Correspondence from constituents during this period can be found in the Hulan Jack Papers in the New York City Municipal Archives.
27. Letter from Hulan Jack to Mayor Robert Wagner.

28. Office of the Mayor Press Release, September 10, 1959, box 5, folder "Housing, 1958-9," HJP.
29. Robert F. Wagner Press Release, August 1959, box 109072B, folder 249, JCGF. The structure and functions of the CHA closely resembled a similar committee formed by Mayor La Guardia following the 1935 Harlem rebellion. Abu-Lughod, *Race, Space, and Riots,* 142–43.
30. Chuck Stone, "Okay, Harlem, You're a Malted Milkshake," *New York Age,* undated news clipping, box 109072B, folder 249, JCGF.
31. Letter from James Hicks to Robert Lowe, February 23, 1960, box 109072C, folder 251, JCGF.
32. "'Tensions' in Harlem," *Baltimore Afro-American,* September 26, 1959.
33. "You Said It," *NYAN,* July 25, 1959.
34. Stone, "Okay, Harlem, You're a Malted Milkshake."
35. Memorandum from Joyce Phillips Austin to Deputy Mayor Paul T. O'Keefe, August 7, 1959, box 109072B, folder 249, JCGF.
36. Initial Recommendations Submitted by the Subcommittee on Education, December 23, 1959, box 109072B, folder 250, JCGF.
37. Initial Recommendations Submitted by the Subcommittee on Education.
38. Letter from John Theobald to Robert F. Wagner, December 16, 1959, box 109072B, folder 250, JCGF.
39. Abu-Lughod, *Race, Space, and Riots,* 144.
40. Memorandum from Joyce Phillips Austin to Deputy Mayor Paul T. O'Keefe.
41. "Initial Verbatim Recommendations Submitted by the Subcommittee on Housing," December 11, 1959, box 109072C, folder 251, JCGF. At no point does any mention of expanding Black homeownership seem to have been made, despite only 17 percent of nonwhite households in New York City being owner occupied as compared to 40 percent of white households. Gold, *When Tenants Claimed the City,* 112.
42. Memorandum from Hope R. Stevens to Mayor Robert Wagner, February 9, 1960, box 109072C, folder 251, JCGF.
43. Memorandum from Hope R. Stevens to Mayor Robert Wagner.
44. "Nationalists Demand Kennedy's Dismissal," *NYAN,* August 8, 1959.
45. Recommendations of the Subcommittee on Law Enforcement, November 12, 1959, box 109072C, folder 251, JCGF.
46. Letter from Stephen P. Kennedy to Mayor Robert F. Wagner, January 14, 1960, box 109072B, folder 249, JCGF.
47. "Comments on Recommendations of Sub-Committee on Law Enforcement," February 19, 1960, box 109072C, folder 252, JCGF.
48. The following sources offer a useful starting point for learning more about Dyett's underacknowledged life and career: Back, "Up South in New York," 340n76; Hughes, *Letters from Langston,* 13, 352–53; Dagbovie, *African American History Reconsidered,* 175; Dinkins, *A Mayor's Life,* 38–45; J. Clay Smith,

Emancipation, 400; Dr. Kenneth B. Clark, interview with Ed Edwin, August 3, 1976, *Notable New Yorkers,* Columbia University Libraries Oral History Research Office, http://www.columbia.edu/cu/lweb/digital/collections/nny/clarkk/transcripts/clarkk_1_8_310.html.

49. "Comments on Recommendations of Sub-Committee on Law Enforcement," February 19, 1960, box 109072C, folder 252, JCGF.
50. "'Commissioner Ought to Resign': Powell Blasts N.Y. Police Dep't," *New Pittsburgh Courier,* March 5, 1960.
51. Letter from Stephen P. Kennedy to Mayor Robert F. Wagner, January 14, 1960, box 109072B, folder 249, JCGF.
52. "Comments on Recommendations of Sub-Committee on Law Enforcement."
53. Emanuel Perlmutter, "Powell Demands Kennedy Resign," *NYT,* February 8, 1960.
54. "Commissioner Ought to Resign."
55. Peter Kihss, "4 Negro Areas Get Extra Police Units," *NYT,* July 16, 1959; letter from Stephen P. Kennedy to Mayor Robert F. Wagner, January 14, 1960, box 109072B, folder 249, JCGF.
56. "Police Head Bids Public Aid Force," *NYT,* August 4, 1959.
57. "Mayor Proclaims Faith in Kennedy," *NYT,* August 18, 1959.
58. Jimmy Booker, "Uptown Lowdown," *NYAN,* August 8, 1959.
59. Al Nall, "Give Lie to Bronx 'Riot,'" *NYAN,* August 15, 1959.
60. "300 in the Bronx Maul Detectives," *NYT,* August 10, 1959; Nall, "Give Lie to Bronx 'Riot'"; Harry Ring, "The Two Cops Pulled Their Guns But Were Afraid to Use Them," *The Militant,* August 17, 1959; "Four Arraigned in Bronx Melee," *NYT,* August 11, 1959; "Police Called 'Brutal,'" *NYT,* August 13, 1959; "Flareup in Bronx," *NYAN,* August 15, 1959; "Bronx NAACP Leader Explains His Stand," *NYAN,* August 22, 1959; "Riot Indictments Found Against 4," *NYT,* August 14, 1959.
61. "2 Youths Are Slain in Midtown Attack," *NYT,* August 30, 1959; Emanuel Perlmutter, "10 Deaths Laid to Youth-Gang Action This Year," *NYT,* September 1, 1959.
62. Richard F. Shephard, "3 Programs Set on Delinquency," *NYT,* September 3, 1959.
63. "New York: Death in the Streets," *NYT,* September 6, 1959; Peter Kihss, "Wagner Will Add 1,080 Policemen to Fill Out Force," *NYT,* September 3, 1959.
64. Peter Kihss, "1,400 City Police Shifted to Fight on Youth Crimes," *NYT,* September 1, 1959.
65. Kihss, "1,400 City Police Shifted."
66. "The Hysterical Ones," *NYAN,* September 12, 1959.
67. Peter Kihss, "Attack on Gangs Is Ordered Here by City and State," *NYT,* September 4, 1959.
68. "Prime Suspect in Teen Slayings Seized in Bronx," *NYT,* September 2, 1959.
69. Suddler, *Presumed Criminal,* 125.
70. "Bystander Slain in Police Chase," *NYT,* September 8, 1959; "—She Never Knew What Hit Her," *NYAN,* September 12, 1959; "Insanity (An Editorial)," *NYAN,* September 12, 1959.

71. "—She Never Knew What Hit Her"; "Insanity (An Editorial)."
72. "Cop's Stray Bullet Kills Girl in Harlem," *Baltimore Afro-American,* September 19, 1959.
73. Baldwin, "Fifth Avenue, Uptown: A Letter from Harlem," in *Nobody Knows My Name,* 63–65.
74. Baldwin, "Fifth Avenue, Uptown," 65.
75. Letter from Hulan Jack to Stephen Kennedy, August 11, 1960, box 6, folder "Police Dept.," HJP.
76. Baldwin, "Fifth Avenue, Uptown," 66.
77. Memo from Detectives Richard D. Lazarus and Ernest B. Latty to Commanding Officer, BOSS, August 16, 1959, box 02-045343, folder 5, NOI Files, NYPDIR; memo from Ernest B. Latty to Commanding Officer, BOSS, November 10, 1959, NOI Files, NYPDIR.
78. Baldwin, "Fifth Avenue, Uptown," 67.
79. "New Tactical Patrol Force Takes to the Streets," *NYT,* December 2, 1959.
80. John P. Callahan, "On the Bronx Beat, 225 Elite Policemen," *NYT,* April 8, 1967.
81. Leuci, *All the Centurions,* 44; O'Neil, *A Cop's Tale,* 18.
82. Guy Passant, "6-Footers to Man New Police Squad," *NYT,* December 1, 1959.
83. M. S. Johnson, *Street Justice,* 256.
84. Passant, "6-Footers to Man New Police Squad."
85. Elkins, "Battle of the Corner," 79–83.
86. Lardner and Repetto, *NYPD,* 254–55.
87. Leuci, *All the Centurions,* 103.
88. O'Neil, *A Cop's Tale,* 32.
89. Leuci, *All the Centurions,* 56.
90. Baldwin, "Fifth Avenue, Uptown," 65–66.
91. J. H. O'Dell, "July Rebellions and the 'Military State,'" 295–96.
92. Leuci, *All the Centurions,* 46–47.
93. Leuci, *All the Centurions,* 58–59.
94. Remarks by Mayor Robert F. Wagner at Police Graduation Ceremony, April 11, 1960, box 101, folder 1199, MRFWP.
95. "Police Head Inducts 97 Rookies," *NYT,* January 5, 1960.
96. Alfred E. Lewis, "Tough Tactical Force Cuts Street Crime in New York," *Washington Post,* April 28, 1963.
97. M. S. Johnson, *Street Justice,* 256.
98. Remarks of Mr. Jack Blumstein, Meeting of Mayor with Subcommittee on Law Enforcement, April 7, 1960, box 109072B, folder 249, JCGF.
99. Stone, "Okay, Harlem, You're a Malted Milkshake."
100. Memo from the Guardians Association to the Harlem Affairs Committee, September 30, 1959, box 109072B, folder 249, JCGF.
101. Baldwin, "Fifth Avenue, Uptown," 63–65.

4. THE SPIRIT OF BANDUNG

1. Rhonda Y. Williams, *Concrete Demands*, 72.
2. Von Eschen, *Race Against Empire*, 146.
3. Von Eschen, *Race Against Empire*, 149.
4. Von Eschen, *Race Against Empire*, 149–87.
5. On repression, see again Von Eschen, *Race Against Empire*, 186–87.
6. Robin J. Hayes, *Love for Liberation*, 39–40.
7. "New York Highlight Will Be Harlem Visit," *NYAN*, July 19, 1958; "100,000 Harlemites Welcome Nkrumah," *Baltimore Afro-American*, August 2, 1958.
8. Dr. Sinclair Drake, "5,000 Cheer Nkrumah In Harlem Welcome," *Atlanta Daily World*, July 30, 1958; "We're Brothers—Nkrumah," *NYAN*, August 2, 1958; R. J. Hayes, *Love for Liberation*, 39–40.
9. Von Eschen, *Race Against Empire*, 150–52.
10. "Celebrate Marcus Garvey Day," *NYAN*, July 19, 1958. On the AAPC Accra conference, see R. J. Hayes, *Love for Liberation*, 74–75; Munro, *The Anticolonial Front*, 257; Plummer, *In Search of Power*, 50, 70–72.
11. "A True Report on the 'All African Peoples Conference,'" January 25, 1959, Broadsides Collection, Schomburg Center for Research in Black Culture.
12. Investigation Report of Detective Ernest B. Latty, April 15, 1959, United African Nationalist Movement, box 44, folder 14, Small Organizations, NYPDIR; Essien-Udom, *Black Nationalism*, 243–44.
13. Robert Harris, preface to *Carlos Cooks and Black Nationalism*, xviii–xix; Essien-Udom, *Black Nationalism*, 53–54; "African Pioneer Movement Plans for 'Real Marcus Garvey Day,'" *NYAN*, August 15, 1959.
14. Later that year Harlem orator Richard B. Moore published *The Name "Negro,"* urging Black Americans to identify as "Afro-Americans." Harris, introduction to Cooks, *Carlos Cooks and Black Nationalism*, xviii; McDuffie, "We Owe a Debt to Her," 147–49.
15. Felber, *Those Who Know Don't Say*, 29–30.
16. Memo from Francis M. Sullivan to Chief Inspector, April 12, 1960, Large Organization Files, box 29, folder 11, NYPDIR; Felber, *Those Who Know Don't Say*, 30–31, 203n95.
17. Quoted in Munro, *The Anticolonial Front*, 203.
18. Clarke, interview with Blackside.
19. Karim, interview with Blackside. Elijah Muhammad ordered the renaming of NOI temples as mosques in February 1960 following his return from a pilgrimage to Mecca. Marable, *Malcolm X*, 169.
20. Lincoln, *The Black Muslims in America*, 132.

21. Lincoln, *The Black Muslims in America*, 132-33; Marable, *Malcolm X*, 163; Strickland, *Malcolm X*, 84.
22. Strickland, *Malcolm X*, 107; Lincoln, *The Black Muslims in America*, 133.
23. Marable, *Malcolm X*, 163; Lomax, *When the Word Is Given*, 73, 147.
24. *Muhammad Speaks* 1, no. 1 (May 1960); Hussain, "Dreaming Differently About Freedom," 327.
25. Mayfield, "And Then Came Baldwin," 168.
26. Smethurst, *The Black Arts Movement*, 181-82.
27. "Malcolm X Defends Muhammad at Boston U.," *NYAN*, March 5, 1960; "Defends Muslim Leader at Meet," *Chicago Daily Defender*, March 15, 1960.
28. Clarke, "The New Afro-American Nationalism," 286.
29. "Harlem Freedom Rally," *NYAN*, May 21, 1960.
30. Marable, *Malcolm X*, 170.
31. Memo from Ernest B. Latty to Commanding Officer, May 30, 1960, box 02-045030, folder 6, NOI Files, NYPDIR; memo from Bernard F. Mulligan to Chief Inspector, June 1, 1960, NYPDIR. The slogan was also the headline of the first edition of *Muhammad Speaks* that came out the same month.
32. Lomax, *When the Word Is Given*, 128-29.
33. Lomax, *When the Word Is Given*, 132.
34. Marable, *Malcolm X*, 170.
35. Marable, *Malcolm X*, 196.
36. Sales, *From Civil Rights to Black Liberation*, 66.
37. C. W. Mackay, "Fantastic! Inside Cuba," *Baltimore Afro-American*, January 31, 1959; M. A. Lockhart, "Adam Powell in Castro Spotlight," *NYAN*, January 24, 1959; Cliff Mackay, "So This Is Havana," *Baltimore Afro-American*, February 3, 1959.
38. Plummer, "Castro in Harlem," 137.
39. Mealy, *Fidel and Malcolm X*, 18-19.
40. Mayfield, "The Cuban Challenge"; Tyson, *Radio Free Dixie*, 222; Hall, *Ten Days in Harlem*, 82.
41. "NAACP Wires Tell Congress to Act Now," *NYAN*, May 2, 1959.
42. "What Is Really Happening in Cuba?," *NYT*, April 6, 1960.
43. "What Is Really Happening in Cuba?"; Tyson, *Radio Free Dixie*, 224.
44. Tyson, *Radio Free Dixie*, 235-37.
45. Tyson, *Radio Free Dixie*, 235-37; Joseph, *Waiting 'Til the Midnight Hour*, 29.
46. Robert F. Williams, "Why I Am Going to Cuba," *The Crusader*, June 18, 1960.
47. *The Crusader* 1, no. 52 (June 25, 1960): 2.
48. "Greetings from Cuba," *The Crusader*, June 18, 1960; "Negro Leader Calls Cuba's Schools an Example to the U.S.A.," *The Crusader*, June 25, 1960.
49. For personal accounts of the trip to Cuba, see Jones, "Cuba Libre"; Clarke, "Journey to the Sierra Maestra"; Mayfield, "The Cuban Challenge"; Baraka, *The Autobiography of LeRoi Jones*; Cruse, *The Crisis of the Negro Intellectual*.

50. Jones, "Cuba Libre," 61.
51. Mayfield, "The Cuban Challenge."
52. Mealy, *Fidel and Malcolm X*, 21.
53. Mae Mallory, "Fidel Castro in New York," September 1960, box 2, folder 10, MMP.
54. Mallory, "Fidel Castro in New York."
55. Mealy, *Fidel and Malcolm X*; "The True Story: How Castro Came to the Theresa," *NYAN*, October 1, 1960. For more detailed accounts of Castro's time in New York and its broader significance, see Hall, *Ten Days in Harlem*; Plummer, "Castro in Harlem."
56. Mealy, *Fidel and Malcolm X*, 49.
57. Mayfield, "The Cuban Challenge," 185.
58. Mealy, *Fidel and Malcolm X*, 22.
59. Mallory, "Fidel Castro in New York"; Killens, *Black Man's Burden*, 114–15. Mallory can be seen holding a sign reading "Stand-Up in the Struggle for Negro Liberation in America" with other members of the Crusaders in the photos section of Mealy, *Fidel and Malcolm X*.
60. James L. Hicks, "Our Achilles Heel," *NYAN*, September 24, 1960.
61. James Booker, "Castro Leaves an Unruffled Harlem," *NYAN*, October 1, 1960.
62. Booker Johnson, quoted in Mealy, *Fidel and Malcolm X*, 29.
63. Mealy, *Fidel and Malcolm X*, 19.
64. Mealy, *Fidel and Malcolm X*, 53.
65. Mealy, *Fidel and Malcolm X*, 21; Tyson, *Radio Free Dixie*, 234; Smethurst, *The Black Arts Movement*, 113; Hall, *Ten Days in Harlem*, 94.
66. Mealy, *Fidel and Malcolm X*, 22; Hall, *Ten Days in Harlem*, 108–11; Plummer, "Castro in Harlem," 14–41; Tyson, *Radio Free Dixie*, 234–35.
67. Hall, *Ten Days in Harlem*, 170.
68. It was also rumored among radicals that the two revolutionaries had discussed the prospects of armed revolutionary struggle in the United States. See Ture and Thelwell, *Ready for Revolution*, 536.
69. James Booker, "Castro Talks," *NYAN*, September 24, 1960; Aida Alami, "The Man Who Drove Malcolm X Around and Introduced Him to Fidel Castro," *Africa Is a Country*, November 2, 2017, http://africasacountry.com/2017/11/the-man-who-drove-malcolm-x-around-and-introduced-him-to-fidel-castro/.
70. For more on the meeting between Malcolm X and Fidel Castro, see Mealy, *Fidel and Malcolm X*; Hall, *Ten Days in Harlem*.
71. Mallory, "Fidel Castro in New York," September 1960, box 2, folder 10, MMP.
72. Baraka, *The Autobiography of LeRoi Jones*, 248; LeRoi Jones, "An Organization of Young Men," April 18, 1961, box 2, folder 21, MMP.
73. Jones, "An Organization of Young Men."
74. Baraka, *The Autobiography of LeRoi Jones*, 248; Smethurst, *The Black Arts Movement*, 345.

75. The slogan of OGFF's newspaper was "The Truth Shall Make You Free." On Guard Committee for Freedom, "If You Want to Read a Newspaper That 'Tells It like It Is'...," box 34, folder 70, Small Organizations Files, NYPDIR.
76. He was succeeded by Percy Sutton, who won the election later that year. Hall, *Ten Days in Harlem*, 94.
77. Wright, "The Lower East Side," 596.
78. Smethurst, *The Black Arts Movement*, 118.
79. Wright, "The Lower East Side," 594.
80. Wright, "The Lower East Side," 594.
81. Lowell "Pete" Beveridge, "The Death of Lumumba," *Liberator* 1, no. 1 (March 1961).
82. Angelou, *The Heart of a Woman*, 170.
83. Rhonda Y. Williams, *Concrete Demands*, 70; Guy, "Castro in New York."
84. Guy, "Castro in New York."
85. Smethurst, *The Black Arts Movement*, 118; Calvin Hicks, interview with The HistoryMakers.
86. Guy, "Castro in New York"; Dworkin, *Congolese Love Song*, 228–29; Rivera, "Carlos Cooks and Garveyism," 130n48.
87. Memo from Detective Patrick R. Vecchio to Commanding Officer, BOSS, August 21, 1960, BSS 201-m, Correspondence Files, NYPDIR.
88. Hall, *Ten Days in Harlem*, 164.
89. R. J. Hayes, *Love for Liberation*, 84–85.
90. The African American Women's Committee was led by Anna Levy and based in Lower Harlem. Memo from Detective Robert O. Bystricky to Commanding Officer, BOSS, December 8, 1960, BSS 301-m, Correspondence Files, NYPDIR.
91. Smethurst, *The Black Arts Movement*, 118.
92. Sarah E. Wright was named on the petition as the chairwoman of CAWAH's Petition Committee. "Help Lumumba Free the Congo," December 7, 1960, Correspondence Files, NYPDIR; memo from Detective Thomas E. Fitzgerald to Commanding Officer, BOSS, December 17, 1960, BSS 318-m, Correspondence Files, NYPDIR.
93. For more on the assassination of Patrice Lumumba and its impact on Black radicalism in the United States, see Tinson, *Radical Intellect*, 17–22; R. J. Hayes, *Love for Liberation*, 69–89; Dworkin, *Congolese Love Song*.
94. Clarke, "The New Afro-American Nationalism," 285.
95. Tinson, *Radical Intellect*, 18. Like Gibson, Timothy Tyson also credits Williams with "inspiring" the demonstration at the UN, but credit for breaking the news of Lumumba's assassination and initiating the demonstration at the UN must be given to the Black women of CAWAH who orchestrated the event. Tyson, *Radio Free Dixie*, 237.
96. Smethurst and Williams both credit CAWAH for organizing the protests at the UN. Joseph, *Waiting 'Til the Midnight Hour*, 39–40.

97. Angelou, *The Heart of a Woman,* 170.
98. Angelou, *The Heart of a Woman,* 169–80.
99. "No Apology," *The Crusader,* March 4, 1961; Tyson, *Radio Free Dixie,* 237; Guy, "Castro in New York."
100. Guy, "Castro in New York."
101. "Riot in Gallery Halts U.N. Debate," *NYT,* February 16, 1961; Joseph, *Waiting 'Til the Midnight Hour,* 38–42; Tinson, *Radical Intellect,* 17–18; Rhonda Y. Williams, *Concrete Demands,* 70. According to Mallory, only twenty-eight tickets had been given out for the Security Council meeting, all of which went to white people. Thinking quickly, the group accepted tickets to a meeting of the Narcotics Committee—which met on the same floor as the Security Council—and pushed their way into the chambers. New York Correspondent, "I Was There," *The Crusader,* March 4, 1961.
102. Tinson, *Radical Intellect,* 17–18.
103. "Riot in Gallery Halts U.N. Debate," *NYT,* February 16, 1961; Joseph, *Waiting 'Til the Midnight Hour,* 38–42; Angelou, *The Heart of a Woman,* 182–87; Guy, "Castro in New York."
104. Angelou, *The Heart of a Woman,* 187.
105. Tinson, *Radical Intellect,* 18.
106. Mallory shared her account of the protest anonymously in *The Crusader.* New York Correspondent, "I Was There," *The Crusader,* March 4, 1961. See also Tyson, *Radio Free Dixie,* 237.
107. Angelou, *The Heart of a Woman,* 187–88.
108. Angelou, *The Heart of a Woman,* 188; Baraka, *The Autobiography of LeRoi Jones,* 267–68.
109. Lynn, *There Is a Fountain,* 163.
110. Baraka, *The Autobiography of LeRoi Jones,* 268.
111. "Riot in Gallery Halts U.N. Debate," *NYT,* February 16, 1961.
112. Philip Benjamin, "400 Picket U.N. in Salute to Castro and Lumumba," *NYT,* February 19, 1961.
113. Queen Mother Audley Moore, interview with Mark Naison; memo from Detective William K. DeFossett to Commanding Officer, BOSS, March 7, 1961, BSS 87-m, Correspondence Files, NYPDIR.
114. "Hold 'Funeral' For Lumumba," *Chicago Daily Defender,* February 28, 1961; "Harlem Funeral in Absentia Is Set for Lumumba," *Hartford Courant,* February 23, 1961; "Harlem Drums Beat Knell for Lumumba," *Washington Afro-American,* March 7, 1961.
115. Letter from Virginia Hughes to friend, March 20, 1961, BSS 143-m, Correspondence Files, NYPDIR.
116. According to Hicks's interview with The HistoryMakers, the merger was suggested by musician and OYM member Walter Bowe.
117. Smethurst, *The Black Arts Movement,* 119.

118. Tinson, "The Voice of the Black Protest Movement," 3–4.
119. Tinson, *Radical Intellect*, 20.
120. Angelou, *The Heart of a Woman*, 196.
121. "The Hoodlums," *NYT*, February 16, 1961; "Harlem 'Nationalism,'" *NYT*, March 5, 1961; Peter Kihss, "Negro Extremist Groups Step Up Nationalist Drive," *NYT*, March 1, 1961.
122. "Riot in Gallery Halts U.N. Debate," *NYT*, February 16, 1961.
123. Jack Fox, "What Was Behind Riot at UN?," *Norfolk Journal and Guide*, March 4, 1961; George E. Sokolsky, "These Days: The Nation of Islam," *Washington Post*, February 25, 1961.
124. "Muslims to Sue Adlai Stevenson," *NYAN*, February 25, 1961.
125. Memo from Edward W. Byrnes to Chief of Detectives, January 15, 1962, box 19, folder 52, Small Organization Files, NYPDIR.
126. Memo from Sanford D. Garelick to Commanding Officer, BOSS, March 2, 1961, BSS 52, Correspondence Files, NYPDIR.
127. Olga Pierce Lytle, "Queens Private Line," *NYAN*, February 25, 1961.
128. "Negroes Picket U.N. Without Riots," *Washington Post*, February 17, 1961; Lester Granger, "Manhattan and Beyond," *NYAN*, February 25, 1961. In a subsequent column in September 1960, Granger went so far as to call Lumumba a "scoundrel," "rascal," and "communist stooge" in a continued diatribe against the "immaturity" of Black radicals organizing against colonialism. Granger, "Manhattan and Beyond," *NYAN*, September 17, 1960.
129. "Bunche Deplores Riot by Negroes in Council," *NYT*, February 18, 1961.
130. Peter Kihss, "Negro Extremist Groups Step Up Nationalist Drive," *NYT*, March 1, 1961.
131. James Baldwin, "A Negro Assays the Negro Mood," *NYT*, March 12, 1961. The article was later republished in *Nobody Knows My Name* under the title "East River, Downtown: Postscript to a Letter from Harlem."
132. Lorraine Hansberry, "Congolese Patriot," *NYT*, March 26, 1961.
133. Angelou, *The Heart of a Woman*, 196–98.
134. Angelou, *The Heart of a Woman*, 198–200.
135. "Muslims to Sue Adlai Stevenson," *NYAN*, February 25, 1961.
136. "In City College Debate: Muslims' Malcolm X and NAACP's Wright Clash," *New Pittsburgh Courier*, March 11, 1961.
137. Smethurst, *The Black Arts Movement*, 118.
138. Clarke, "The New Afro-American Nationalism," 285.
139. Clarke, "The New Afro-American Nationalism," 285.
140. Clarke, "The New Afro-American Nationalism," 294.
141. Letter from Mae Mallory to Lorraine Hansberry, June 1, 1963, box 1, folder 2, MMP.
142. Guy, "Castro in Harlem," 7.

5. THE NEW AFRO-AMERICAN NATIONALISM

1. Rolland Snellings, "The New Afro-American Writer," *Liberator* 3, no. 10 (October 1963): 10.
2. Clarke, "The New Afro-American Nationalism," 287.
3. Attorney Conrad Lynn stated in his autobiography that Mallory was arrested and charged with assault. "I represented her against the assault charge and we won," Lynn claimed. "The police were too embarrassed to admit what a woman had done to them, and their case fell apart." Lynn, *There Is a Fountain,* 163.
4. Letter from Mae Mallory to Jeanne, June 23, 1963, box 1, folder 2, MMP.
5. In his autobiography, Baraka states that Mallory was a member of On Guard. Though her records do not indicate any formal association with OGFF, it is evident that she worked in close cooperation with the group. Baraka, *The Autobiography of LeRoi Jones,* 267; letter from Mae Mallory to Sir, February 1961, box 2, folder 10, MMP.
6. Letter from Mallory to Sir.
7. Letter from Mallory to Sir.
8. Other members included Conrad Lynn, James Boggs, John Henrik Clarke, Julian Mayfield, William Worthy, Ossie Davis, Ora Mae Mobley, and Calvin Hicks. Lynn, *There Is a Fountain,* 171; Mayfield, "The Cuban Challenge," 189.
9. Crusaders For Freedom, "Militant Mass Protest Causes NAACP to Abandon Rally And Turn It Over to Robert Williams!," May 17, 1961, box 2, folder 10, MMP.
10. "How Long Will We Turn the Other Cheek?," box 2, folder 10, MMP.
11. Letter from Lonnie Cross to Mae Mallory, May 22, 1961, box 1, folder 1, MMP.
12. The meeting was attended by Mae Mallory, Robert F. Williams, John Henrik Clarke, Ossie Davis, Calvin Hicks, Conrad Lynn, Julian Mayfield, and Ora Mae Mobley. "Meeting of Afro-Americans, June 14, 1961," box 2, folder 4, MMP.
13. "Preparations for Activity for Action for Gaining Support for Rob Williams, June 29, 1961," box 2, folder 4, MMP.
14. Mallory, interview with Lumumba, 18.
15. Pledges for donations from July 10, 1961, Meeting of AAAA, box 2, folder 3, MMP; "LCA Finances Arms for Defense of Afro Americans in Monroe, N.C.," *Liberator* 1 (July 1961): 2.
16. Mallory, interview with Lumumba, 18.
17. FBI record of Julian Mayfield, "F.B. Eyes Digital Archive," Washington University Libraries, http://omeka.wustl.edu/omeka/exhibits/show/fbeyes/mayfield.
18. Minutes of a meeting of the Crusaders for Freedom on June 10, 1961, suggest that the group may have suspected they had been infiltrated. "Meeting Minutes of the Crusaders for Freedom," June 10, 1961, box 2, folder 10, MMP.
19. Mallory, interview with Lumumba, 18.

20. For more expansive narratives of the conflicts in Monroe, see Robert F. Williams, *Negroes with Guns,* 75–110; Tyson, *Radio Free Dixie,* 262–86; Forman, *The Making of Black Revolutionaries,* 193–211.
21. Tyson, *Radio Free Dixie,* 278.
22. Tyson, *Radio Free Dixie,* 282–83.
23. Mallory, interview with Lumumba, 22.
24. Tyson, *Radio Free Dixie,* 280.
25. Foong, "Frame Up in Monroe," 45–46, 69.
26. Mallory, interview with Lumumba, 18.
27. Among the MDC's many notable sponsors were James Baldwin, John Henrik Clarke, Richard Gibson, LeRoi Jones (Amiri Baraka), Shirley Graham, Julian and Ana Mayfield, Gerald Quinn, Bayard Rustin, Dan Watts, Max Roach, Abbey Lincoln, Ruby Dee, Ossie Davis, Sylvester Leaks, Ramona Garrett, and Jesse Gray.
28. Tinson, *Radical Intellect,* 34.
29. "Monroe, North Carolina Victims of Racial Injustice Need Your Help," *Baltimore Afro-American,* October 21, 1961.
30. Sinclair, "Mae Mallory Harlem Activist," 61.
31. Flyer for benefit performance of *Purlie Victorious* for Monroe Defense Committee, RFWP.
32. Here I disagree with Harold Cruse, who characterized the conflict as basically an ideological one between Trotskyists and communists. Cruse, *The Crisis of the Negro Intellectual,* 369–70.
33. Letter from Albert E. Perry to Calvin Hicks, September 30, 1961, RFWP. Though many supporters of the MDC applauded the Freedom Riders for escalating the tempo of the movement through exposing the naked brutality of Southern racism, Dan Watts and others also criticized the Freedom Riders for announcing their plans and adherence to nonviolence in advance, so as to welcome violence against defenseless demonstrators.
34. Baraka, *The Autobiography of LeRoi Jones,* 249–50; Cruse, *The Crisis of the Negro Intellectual,* 368–70.
35. Smethurst, *The Black Arts Movement,* 144–45.
36. Cruse, *The Crisis of the Negro Intellectual,* 368–70; Baraka, *The Autobiography of LeRoi Jones,* 249–50.
37. Letter from Conrad J. Lynn to Berta Green, May 7, 1963, RFWP.
38. Cruse, *The Crisis of the Negro Intellectual,* 369.
39. Mae Mallory, "Memo from a Monroe Jail," 211; letter from Mae Mallory to Mabel and Rob Williams, April 10, 1963, RFWP.
40. "Welcome Home, Adam," *Liberator* 3, no. 5 (May 1963): 2.
41. Mallory, "Memo from a Monroe Jail," 211; letter from Mallory to Mabel and Rob Williams.
42. Clarke, "The New Afro-American Nationalism," 295.
43. Cruse, "Revolutionary Nationalism and the Afro-American."

44. "Victims, Not 'Merchants,' of Hate," *The Militant,* February 18, 1963.
45. Harold Cruse, "Rebellion or Revolution? (1 of 3)," *Liberator* 3, no. 10 (October 1963): 20. The three-part article was later republished in a volume of Cruse's essays under the same title.
46. Letter from Mae Mallory to Lorraine Hansberry, June 1, 1963, box 1, folder 2, MMP.
47. Letter from Mae Mallory to Richard Gibson, August 24, 1963, box 1, folder 2, MMP.
48. Letter from Rosa Guy to Robert F. Williams, July 4, 1963, RFWP.
49. Farmer, *Remaking Black Power,* 48; Donald Freeman, "The Cleveland Story," *Liberator* 3, no. 6 (June 1963): 7–8.
50. Farmer, *Remaking Black Power,* 48; Freeman, "The Cleveland Story," 7–8.
51. Rhonda Y. Williams, *Concrete Demands,* 80–81.
52. Letter from Mae Mallory to Ethel Azalea Johnson, June 9, 1963, box 1, folder 2, MMP.
53. Sales, *From Civil Rights to Black Liberation,* 60–61.
54. McCandlish Phillips, "200 More Policemen Assigned to Harlem," *NYT,* July 30, 1961; George Barner, "The Riot Story," *NYAN,* August 5, 1961; Harold L. Keith, "Leaders Bury Differences, Merge: New York Group Formed to Uplift Negro Masses," *New Pittsburgh Courier,* October 7, 1961.
55. For more on the Emergency Committee and Malcolm X's political development, see Felber, *Those Who Know Don't Say,* 85–119.
56. "Good Rules," *NYAN,* September 16, 1962.
57. Phillips, "200 More Policemen Assigned to Harlem."
58. Mangum, interview with Blackside.
59. DeFossett, interview with Blackside.
60. Lardner and Reppetto, *NYPD,* 189; Donner, *Protectors of Privilege,* 49, 156; *Handschu v. Special Services Division, et al.,* May 18, 1971; Caulfield, *Caulfield, Shield #911-NYPD,* 23.
61. Although DeFossett's identity as a police officer was known to the Nation of Islam and the public in Harlem (he was identified as NYPD in a photo in the *New York Amsterdam News* following the 1959 "near riot"), it is highly unlikely he disclosed his affiliation with BOSS. In this way, he was able to use community policing as a cloak for his surveillance of the NOI. Felber, *Those Who Know Don't Say,* 87, 114.
62. Felber, *Those Who Know Don't Say,* 104–5.
63. Marable, *Malcolm X,* 202.
64. Marable, *Malcolm X,* 204.
65. Haley and Malcolm X, *The Autobiography of Malcolm X,* 289.
66. In addition to killing Stokes, over seventy LAPD officers indiscriminately beat and opened fire on NOI members, leaving seven shot, one paralyzed, and dozens injured. Marable, *Malcolm X,* 205–8; Felker-Kantor, *Policing Los Angeles,* 25.
67. Strickland, *Malcolm X,* 81–82.

68. Gordon Parks, interview with Blackside.
69. Parks, interview with Blackside; Marable, *Malcolm X,* 208–9. Although constrained by Muhammad, Malcolm built on his experience with the Emergency Committee to spearhead the formation of a coalition of community organizations to challenge the racist violence of the LAPD. For more on Malcolm's role in organizing a Black united front following the murder of Ronald Stokes, see Felber, *Those Who Know Don't Say,* 120–50.
70. The other speakers were William Worthy, James Farmer, and Bayard Rustin. Malcolm X, "The Challenge of Racism," May 1, 1962, RFWP. There is a handwritten note on the flyer saying that Malcolm had requested that the CAMD not be named as a sponsor, "to keep his religious skirts clear of any political charge."
71. Malcolm X, "The Challenge of Racism," May 1, 1962, https://www.youtube.com/watch?v=WA_YixhCP2g/.
72. Malcolm X, "The Challenge of Racism."
73. Dan Watts, "Unarmed Afro-Americans Beaten by Armed Police," *Liberator* 2, no. 5 (May 1962): 3.
74. Benjamin Karim, interview with Blackside, 42.
75. Sales, *From Civil Rights to Black Liberation,* 73.
76. Upon returning to New York, Malcolm continued working toward united front formations around police brutality in Harlem. Edward Silberfarb, "War Chants from a Muslim Rally," *New York Herald Tribune,* July 22, 1962.
77. Marable, *Malcolm X,* 215.
78. Memo from John L. Kinsella to Chief Inspector, January 12, 1963, box 02-045343, folder Nation of Islam, 1964, NYPDIR; "More Persecution of the Muslims," *Workers World,* January 11, 1963.
79. For more on the Rochester Mosque, see Hill, *Strike the Hammer,* 33–50.
80. "America has become a Police-state for 20 Million Negroes," box 02-045343, folder Nation of Islam, 1964, NYPDIR.
81. Memo from John L. Kinsella to Chief Inspector, February 14, 1963, NYPDIR.
82. Robert Franklin, "Black Muslim Demonstration Protests Police Persecution," *The Militant,* February 25, 1963.
83. Memo from John L. Kinsella to Chief Inspector, February 14, 1963, box 02-045343, folder Nation of Islam, 1964, NYPDIR.
84. Rose L. H. Finkenstaedt, "A Black Muslim Story: Never on Christmas," *Liberator* 3, no. 3 (March 1963): 16–18.
85. Robert Franklin, "Black Muslim Demonstration Protests Police Persecution," *The Militant,* February 25, 1963.
86. "The Talk of the Town," *The New Yorker,* June 15, 1963.
87. Tinson, *Radical Intellect,* 61. Wattley had also been an active member of the FPCC.
88. Worthy was arrested following a trip to Cuba for the Cold War crime of "failing to travel with a valid passport." Flyer for Harlem Anti-Colonial Committee Rally,

NOTES TO PAGES 167-172   341

box 2, folder 18, MMP. For more on Worthy's arrest under the McCarran Act, see Joseph, *Waiting 'Til the Midnight Hour,* 47–51.
89. "The Talk of the Town."
90. "Harlem," *Liberator* 3, no. 7 (July 1963): 19.
91. "The Talk of the Town."
92. "The Talk of the Town."
93. "Meeting of Afro-Americans, June 14, 1961," box 2, folder 4, MMP.
94. Rose H. L. Finkenstaedt, "Needed: An Afro-American Political Party," *Liberator* 2, no. 11 (November–December 1962): 5.
95. William Worthy, "An All Black Party," *Liberator* 3, no. 10 (October 1963): 18. At the same time, there were also Black radicals who were considering the possibilities of taking over local levels of the Democratic Party. In February 1963 Jesse Gray announced his candidacy for Democratic district leader of the 16th Assembly District, declaring that "regardless to how good a white man is, he cannot speak for us." Following his announcement, the *New Pittsburgh Courier* reported that "Mr. Gray is of the opinion that in any area predominantly populated by Negroes or Puerto Ricans, a Negro or Puerto Rican should be at the helm of that district." "New York Political Roundup," *New Pittsburgh Courier,* February 23, 1963.
96. Finkenstaedt, "Needed," 5.
97. William Worthy, "Our Power Can Change the World," Michigan Committee for a Freedom Now Party, September 1963, box 2, folder 12, MMP.
98. William Epton, "An Alternative Policy: Political Power," *Liberator* 3, no. 9 (September 1963): 15–16.
99. "The Declaration of Washington," August 28, 1963, Michigan Committee for a Freedom Now Party, September 1963, box 2, folder 12, MMP; Joseph, *Waiting 'Til the Midnight Hour,* 84–87.
100. "Racism in Politics," *NYT,* August 26, 1963.
101. Justus Seebode, "Why 3rd Party?," *NYAN,* September 14, 1963.
102. George S. Schuyler, "The World Today," *New Pittsburgh Courier,* September 7, 1963.
103. "Wilkins Warns of Racial Trouble If Congress Fails on Civil Rights," *New Pittsburgh Courier,* September 14, 1963.
104. Marable, *Malcolm X,* 267.
105. Memo from Det. Ernest B. Latty to Commanding Officer, June 30, 1963, box 02-045343, folder Nation of Islam, 1964, NYPDIR.
106. Worthy, "An All Black Party," 18–19.
107. "Freedom Now Party: Draft National Platform," *Liberator* 4, no. 2 (February 1964): 4–5.
108. "Freedom Now Party: Draft National Platform," 4–5.
109. While the FNP was launched and had its national headquarters in New York, the Michigan FNP would become its most impactful branch. For more on the

Michigan FNP, see Dillard, *Faith in the City;* Ward, *In Love and Struggle;* Rhonda Williams, *Concrete Demands.*

110. Memo from John L. Kinsella to Chief Inspector, July 29, 1963, box 29, folder 7, Large Organization Files, NYPDIR.
111. Memo from John L. Kinsella to Chief Inspector.
112. Memo from Frederick Jenoure to Commanding Officer, July 17, 1963, box 7, folder 29, Large Organization Files, NYPDIR.
113. Memo from Ernest B. Latty to Commanding Officer, September 9, 1963, box 7, folder 29, Large Organization Files, NYPDIR.
114. *Liberator* 3, no. 12 (December 1963); Joseph, *Waiting 'Til the Midnight Hour,* 56–58.
115. Harley, "Chronicle of a Death Foretold," 190; Ward, *In Love and Struggle,* 311.
116. First Draft, Constitution and By-Laws of the Northern Negro Grass Roots Leadership Conference, 1963, MMP; Ward, *In Love and Struggle,* 312, 394n69.
117. First Draft, Constitution and By-Laws of the Leadership Conference.
118. Ward, *In Love and Struggle,* 312.
119. The specific influence of Mae Mallory was evident, as the resolution supporting her fight against extradition was the longest of the thirteen and immediately preceded the declaration of support for self-defense.
120. Indeed, many of the comments, analogies, and turns of phrase Malcolm X used in his address that night were drawn from speeches he had given in Harlem over the past several months.
121. Lowell "Pete" Beveridge, "King's Dilemma," *Liberator* 3, no. 12 (December 1963): 3; Sterling Gray, "Architect of a Revolution," *Liberator* 3, no. 12 (December 1963): 8–9.
122. X, *Malcolm X Speaks,* 4–10.
123. X, *Malcolm X Speaks,* 10–12.
124. Ward, *In Love and Struggle,* 313.
125. Among those shouting "We'll bleed!" were General Baker, Charles Simmons, Luke Tripp, and John Watson, who were members of Uhuru, a radical youth-led organization in Detroit that organized militant campaigns against housing discrimination and police violence and laid foundations for the emergence of the League of Revolutionary Black Workers. Norman Richmond, "Malcolm X in the 21st Century," *Counterpunch,* May 17, 2017.
126. Gloria Richardson, interview with Blackside, 16.
127. Grace Lee Boggs, *Living for Change,* 129.
128. G. L. Boggs, *Living for Change,* 129.
129. Lowell Pete Beveridge Jr., "1963: Year of Violence," *Liberator* 4, no. 1 (January 1964): 7–9.
130. Cedric Johnson, *Revolutionaries to Race Leaders,* 50.
131. Farmer, *Remaking Black Power,* 48.
132. Sales, *From Civil Rights to Black Liberation,* 43; Ngũgĩ wa Thiong'o, *Decolonising the Mind.*

6. INTERRACIAL ORGANIZING AND BLACK SELF-DETERMINATION

1. Schechter, "Discovering Harlem," 32.
2. Baldwin, "The Dangerous Road," 262.
3. Letter from James Robinson to New Yorkers, November 30, 1959, CORE.
4. Jimmy McDonald, interview with James Mosby, 24.
5. Letter from Carl Anthony to Peter Countryman June 19, 1962, box 8, folder 10, NSM.
6. Martin Smolin, "The North: 'We Walk So They May Sit,'" in CORE, "Sit Ins: The Student Report," May 1960, box 02-045329, CORE Files, NYPDIR.
7. Gray and LHTC Director Horace Townsend led one of the more colorful protests when demonstrators carried a casket on a picket line in front of the Woolworth's on 116th Street to signify the death of Jim Crow. Memo from Ernest B. Latty to Commanding Officer, February 25, 1960, Large Organization Files, NYPDIR.
8. T. R. Bassett, "3,000 Picket in Harlem to Aid South Sitdowners," *New York Herald Tribune,* April 3, 1960; "First Sit-In Staged at Store Here," *New York Herald Tribune,* April 3, 1960.
9. "Plan Stepped Up Picketing," *NYAN,* April 9, 1960.
10. By July 1960, when the stores in Greensboro began serving Black customers, Woolworth had begun to desegregate its stores in twenty-seven Southern cities. Within the next few weeks, ninety towns in eleven Southern states reported changes in their local store's racist policies. Meier and Rudwick, *CORE,* 111–12.
11. Purnell, *Fighting Jim Crow,* 38.
12. Purnell, *Fighting Jim Crow,* 38.
13. Meier and Rudwick, *CORE,* 111.
14. Meier and Rudwick, *CORE,* 126.
15. Meier and Rudwick, *CORE,* 126–31.
16. McDonald, interview with Mosby, 11.
17. Marvin Rich, interview with James Mosby, 11–12.
18. Rich, interview with Mosby, 12.
19. Meier and Rudwick, *CORE,* 131, 182.
20. "CORE Gets New National Director," *NYAN,* February 4, 1961.
21. Letter from Marvin Rich to Paul Berger, April 20, 1961, accessed at www.harlemcore.com. The CORE Project, a digital archive organized by scholar L. E. J. Rachell, is an invaluable resource for scholarship on the histories and legacies of the Congress of Racial Equality in New York City. See www.corenyc.org.
22. Doris Innis, interview with August Meier, October 12, 1971.
23. "CORE Starts Direct Action Drive Here," *NYAN,* May 14, 1960; "Housing Bias Victims Stage Realty Sit-In," *NYAN,* August 20, 1960.
24. For a more thorough exploration of the open housing versus tenant organizing debate, see Sugrue, *Sweet Land of Liberty,* 400–448.

25. Meier and Rudwick, *CORE*, 183-84. The two-bedroom apartment CORE helped Clarence Funnyé secure was rented for $141 per month in 1961, totaling $1,692 for the year, which was nearly half of the median income ($3,480) of Central Harlem residents in 1960. HARYOU, *Youth in the Ghetto*, 133.
26. Meier and Rudwick, *CORE*, 151.
27. Meier and Rudwick, *CORE*, 151.
28. Innis, interview with Meier.
29. McDonald, interview with Mosby, 19.
30. Meier and Rudwick, *CORE*, 144-46.
31. Letter from Gladys Harrington to Alan Gartner, January 6, 1962, CORE.
32. Meier and Rudwick, *CORE*, 144-46.
33. Letter from Gladys Harrington to Alan Gartner.
34. For news coverage of Sutton's election and the branch's move to Harlem, see "Sutton Is NAACP President," *NYAN*, December 24, 1960; "Sutton Airs NAACP Program," *NYAN*, December 31, 1960; "Sutton to Discuss NAACP Fight in NYC," *NYAN*, January 14, 1961; "NAACP Seeks Salvage, Plans 125th St. Move," *NYAN*, February 4, 1961.
35. "Welcome," *NYAN*, November 4, 1961.
36. Meier and Rudwick, *CORE*, 198.
37. Preacely, "It Was Simply in My Blood," 166.
38. R. W. Apple Jr., "The Ivy League Integrationists," *The Reporter*, February 14, 1963.
39. Apple, "The Ivy League Integrationists"; "Northern Student Movement," box 5, folder 4, NSM; Tobierre, "Black Power Does Not Come," 23-24.
40. Peter Countryman, interview with Katherine Shannon, 2.
41. "Definitive Statement of the Northern Student Movement Coordinating Committee of New England (in New Haven)," box 8, folder 5, NSM.
42. "Northern Student Movement," box 5, folder 4, NSM; Bill Strickland, "NSM Goals & History, and Other Reflections," box 4, folder 13, NSM.
43. Peter Countryman, "With Our Minds Stayed on Freedom," *Fellowship*, November 1, 1963.
44. Letter from Peter Countryman to Anne Marting, February 16, 1962, box 11, folder 8, NSM.
45. Apple, "The Ivy League Integrationists."
46. Tobierre, "Black Power Does Not Come," 26-28.
47. Tobierre, "Black Power Does Not Come," 26-28; United States National Student Association Press Release, April 11, 1962, BSS 196-m, NYPDIR.
48. Apple, "The Ivy League Integrationists"; Tobierre, "Black Power Does Not Come," 38-40; Countryman, *Up South*, 181.
49. Churchville, *Driven!*, 5-8.
50. Anthony, *The Earth, the City*, 54-55.
51. Tobierre, "Black Power Does Not Come," 31; "Northern Student Movement," box 5, folder 4, NSM.

52. Tobierre, "Black Power Does Not Come," 32; "Northern Student Movement." While in Maryland, young organizers were also introduced to veteran CORE organizers like James Farmer, Gladys Harrington, Julius Hobson, and Blyden Jackson, and to Gloria Richardson in Cambridge. Author interview with Gloria Richardson Dandridge, April 19, 2018.
53. The idea was inspired by Joan Cannady Countryman's father, Bill Cannady, who was a counselor at Gratz High School in Philadelphia. Countryman, interview with Shannon, 7–8.
54. "Northern Student Movement," box 5, folder 4, NSM; Bill Strickland, "NSM Goals & History, and Other Reflections," box 4, folder 13, NSM.
55. Kathie Rogers, "Some Facts About the N.Y.C. Public School System," box 8, folder 12, NSM.
56. "A Statement of the Aims and Philosophy of the Harlem Education Project and a Prospectus for the Summer of 1963," box 8, folder 11, NSM; Bill Strickland, "NSM Goals & History, and Other Reflections," box 4, folder 13, NSM.
57. Harlem Educational Project, "Get Hip with HEP," box 8, folder 10, NSM.
58. Kathie Rogers McQuarrie, interview with author, February 13, 2021; Northern Student Movement, "Summer Tutorials—1962," box 76, folder 24, AMP.
59. Northern Student Movement, "Summer Tutorials—1962."
60. Andrea Cousins and Quentin R. Hand, "Harlem Education Program, Inc. Prospectus: September 1963–September 1964," box 8, folder 11, NSM.
61. Harlem Educational Project, "Get Hip with HEP."
62. Northern Student Movement, "Summer Tutorials—1962."
63. Andrea Cousins, "Harlem: The Neighborhood and Social Change," April 2, 1964, Junius Williams Collection, in author's possession.
64. Cousins, "Harlem."
65. Andrea Cousins, interview with author, October 19, 2017.
66. Cousins, interview with author, October 19, 2017.
67. Cousins, interview with author, October 19, 2017. Carmichael came by the HEP offices from time to time, even participating in a HEP tutor orientation program in June 1963, where he spoke about direct action on a panel with NSM staffers Carl Anthony, Bob Knight, Roger Siegel, and Kathie Rogers. The Harlem Education Project, "Tutor Orientation," June 28–29, 1963, box 8, folder 10, NSM.
68. Schechter, "Black Nationalism," 37.
69. Cousins, interview with author, October 19, 2017. Cousins was likely describing the Africa Freedom Day Rally at Hunter College in April 1961. See "Kenneth Kaunda African Freedom Day Speaker," *NYAN*, April 8, 1961.
70. Carl Anthony, "Harlem," in Northern Student Movement, "Negro Militancy in the North," October 21, 1962, box 76, folder 24, AMP.
71. Robert F. Knight, "An Analysis of the Community," undated, box 8, folder 12, NSM.
72. Letter from Carl Anthony to Peter Countryman, June 19, 1962, box 8, folder 10, NSM.

73. Letter from Barbara to Tom, October 15, 1962, box 8, folder 10, NSM.
74. The Harlem Education Project, "Tutor Orientation," June 28–29, 1963, box 8, folder 10, NSM.
75. Cousins and Hand, "Harlem Education Program, Inc. Prospectus," box 8, folder 11, NSM.
76. Meier and Rudwick, *CORE*, 196.
77. Meier and Rudwick, *CORE*, 196.
78. Meier and Rudwick, *CORE*, 188.
79. "Sealtest Fact Sheet," January 1963, CORE.
80. Meier and Rudwick, *CORE*, 191–92.
81. For more on CORE's influence on the emergence of struggles for affirmative action, see Purnell, *Fighting Jim Crow*, and Goldberg and Griffey, *Black Power at Work*.
82. "Sealtest Fact Sheet," January 1963, CORE.
83. Meier and Rudwick, *CORE*, 192.
84. Unmarked clipping of CORE press release, 1963, CORE.
85. Norman Hill, interviews with August Meier, May 24, 1969, December 15, 1970, and August 2, 1971, box 56, folder 8, AMP; Velma Hill, interview with August Meier, July 1971, box 56, folder 8, AMP.
86. Velma Hill, interview with August Meier.
87. Meier and Rudwick, *CORE*, 208.
88. Letter from Peter Countryman to Carl Anthony, October 3, 1962, box 8, folder 10, NSM Records.
89. Carl Anthony and Jean Doak, interview with author, November 10, 2019.
90. Anthony, *The Earth, the City*, 47.
91. "HEP Prospectus for Neighborhood Commons Project," box 8, folder 12, NSM. For more on Associated Community Teams (not to be confused with the radical grassroots federation ACT), see Cazenave, *Impossible Democracy*, 99–104.
92. "The Neighborhood Commons Project," August 1963, Patricia Murphy Collection, in author's possession.
93. "Prospectus: Harlem Education Program, Inc.," box 8, folder 11, NSM.
94. "Prospectus: Harlem Education Program, Inc."
95. Author interview with Carl Anthony, Andrea Cousins, Jean Doak, David Henderson, Marilyn Lowen, and Kathie Rogers McQuarrie, February 20, 2021.
96. "Harlem Back Lot to Become a Park," *NYT*, undated clipping, box 76, folder 24, AMP.
97. "HEP Prospectus for Neighborhood Commons Project," May 1962, box 8, folder 12, NSM.
98. "A Statement of the Aims and Philosophy of the Harlem Education Project and a Prospectus for the Summer of 1963," box 8, folder 11, NSM.
99. Letter from A. W. Finch and James D. Cook to Hortense Gabel, in Andrea Cousins and Quentin R. Hand, "Harlem Education Program, Inc. Prospectus: September 1963–September 1964," box 8, folder 11, NSM.

100. Cousins, interview with author, October 19, 2017.
101. Letter from A. W. Finch and James D. Cook to Hortense Gabel.
102. Cousins, "Harlem," 3.
103. Cousins, "Harlem," 2–3.
104. The Commons also influenced an evolution of the tutorial program toward a sustainable, community-controlled model. Letter from Gordon Davis to Robert Hess, June 23, 1964, box 5, folder 6, NSM.
105. Thomas A. Johnson, "Freedom Now or Gradualism Fight on in L.I.," *Pittsburgh Courier,* January 12, 1963.
106. Innis, interview with Meier.
107. Johnson, "Freedom Now or Gradualism Fight."
108. "Mayor Sets October to Begin Expansion of Harlem Hospital," *NYT,* June 6, 1962; "New Building Begun at Harlem Hospital," *NYT,* November 1, 1962.
109. HARYOU, *Youth in the Ghetto,* 246.
110. For more on employment discrimination in the construction industry, see Goldberg and Griffey, *Black Power at Work.*
111. Thomas A. Johnson, "Job Protest at Hospital Site Jolts Gotham," *New Pittsburgh Courier,* June 29, 1963.
112. Clark, *Dark Ghetto,* 38.
113. "Promise Mass Action on Building Trade Unions," *NYAN,* June 8, 1963.
114. Clark, *Dark Ghetto,* 38.
115. HARYOU, *Youth in the Ghetto,* 252–53.
116. HARYOU, *Youth in the Ghetto,* 247.
117. "Promise Mass Action on Building Trade Unions."
118. Samuel Kaplan, "Race Group Plans Hospital Pickets," *NYT,* June 12, 1963.
119. "1962–63 Annual National Convention Report on New York CORE Activities," CORE; Clarence Funnyé, "New York CORE: Report to the National Convention at Durham, North Carolina July 1–5, 1965 for the period from July, 1964 to July, 1965," CORE.
120. Samuel Kaplan, "Unions Here Get Warning on Bias," *NYT,* June 13, 1963; "3 in Harlem Biracial Demonstration Injured During Clash with Police," *Washington Post,* June 13, 1963; "Pickets, Police Brawl at N.Y. Hospital Site," *Chicago Daily Defender,* June 13, 1963; "300 Cops Present: Pickets Clash at Hospital Site," *NYAN,* June 15, 1963.
121. The group included Herbert Hill, Norman Hill, Velma Hill, Gladys Harrington, Urban League Industrial Relations Director Ramon Rivera, CORE member William Mahoney, and NAACP members Morris De Lisser and Isaiah Brunson (who would later become head of Brooklyn CORE). Louis Lomax, "Tomorrow's Leaders," *Ebony,* September 1963, 42; Ahmad, *We Will Return in the Whirlwind,* 114.
122. Kaplan, "Unions Here Get Warning on Bias"; "3 in Harlem Biracial Demonstration Injured"; "Pickets, Police Brawl at N.Y. Hospital Site"; "300 Cops Present: Pickets Clash"; Ahmad, *We Will Return in the Whirlwind,* 105–8.

123. Kaplan, "Unions Here Get Warning on Bias"; "3 in Harlem Biracial Demonstration Injured"; "Pickets, Police Brawl at N.Y. Hospital Site"; "300 Cops Present: Pickets Clash."
124. Claude Sitton, "50 Hurt in Negro Rioting after Birmingham Blasts," *NYT,* May 13, 1963.
125. Samuel Kaplan, "City Halts Work at Site in Harlem," *NYT,* June 14, 1963.
126. Amina Rahman, interview with Blackside, 9–11.
127. Kaplan, "City Halts Work at Site in Harlem."
128. "Rights Picketing at Fair Construction Is Planned," *NYT,* June 15, 1963.
129. Kaplan, "City Halts Work at Site in Harlem."
130. Clayton Knowles, "City Panel Gives Job Racial Plan," *NYT,* July 12, 1963.
131. The Joint Committee for Equal Employment Opportunity also released their own demands, including admission of all qualified Black and Puerto Rican journeymen into the unions, the opening of apprenticeship programs for Black and Puerto Rican workers at twice their proportion of the city's population, and a requirement that such skilled workers need only pass a test to gain admission to a building trades union. Samuel Kaplan, "Job-Equality Group Demands Unions Here Admit Minorities," *NYT,* July 8, 1963; Samuel Kaplan, "Job Plan Scored by Racial Group," *NYT,* July 13, 1963.
132. Kaplan, "Job Plan Scored by Racial Group."
133. "Sit-Ins Maintain Two Vigils Here," *NYT,* July 14, 1963.
134. "General Roundup Of 'Revolution,'" *NYAN,* July 27, 1963.
135. For more on the Downstate Medical Center campaign, see Purnell, *Fighting Jim Crow.*
136. "Only 100 Names Go to Labor Unions," *NYAN,* September 21, 1963; Malcolm Nash, "Big Six Pickets Building Unions," *NYAN,* November 9, 1963.
137. "City Aide Confident Unions Will Accept 600 Negroes Soon," *NYT,* September 2, 1963.
138. Malcolm Nash, "Harlem Hospital Site Costing City $500 a Day," *NYAN,* October 19, 1963.
139. "NYC Losing $1400 a Day in Harlem," *NYAN,* October 26, 1963; "CORE Assails Mayor on Mounted Police," *NYT,* October 17, 1963. The heavy police presence at Foley Square was supplemented by the NYPD's counterintelligence unit, the Bureau of Special Services (BOSS), which conducted surveillance operations and deployed agents provocateurs to incite conflicts with police as a pretext for breaking up the protests. See CORE, Large Organization Files, NYPDIR.
140. "500 March Here for Job Equality," *NYT,* October 21, 1963; Jo Holly, "Long Island, Inside Out," *Pittsburgh Courier,* October 26, 1963.
141. Theodore Jones, "Negroes Denounce Resumption of Hospital Job," *NYT,* November 14, 1963; "Only 100 Names Go to Building Unions," *NYAN,* September 21, 1963.
142. "Work Starts Again at Harlem Hospital Site," *NYAN,* November 16, 1963.

143. Ahmad, *We Will Return in the Whirlwind,* 114–15.
144. Norman and Velma Hill, interview with August Meier, February 1964.
145. Memo from John Kinsella to Chief Inspector, August 13, 1963, NYPDIR.
146. Memo from Frederick Jenoure to Commanding Officer, September 17, 1963, box 9, folder 27, Large Organization Files, NYPDIR. For more on Jackson's earlier positions on nonviolence, see the folder "HARYOU Leadership Training Workshop," KMP.
147. Countryman, *Up South,* 189.
148. William Strickland, speech at College Conference at Columbia, October 25, 1963, unmarked clipping, box 76, folder 24, AMP.

7. RENT STRIKES AND REPRESSION

1. "CBS Will Report on 'The Harlem Temper,'" *Cleveland Call and Post,* November 30, 1963.
2. Friendly, "The Harlem Temper," December 11, 1963, accessed at https://www.youtube.com/watch?v=gf9RDF6T4AY&t=350s/.
3. Percy Shain, "Portrait of Disunity in Northern Negroes," *Boston Globe,* December 12, 1963.
4. Friendly, "The Harlem Temper."
5. Gray, interview with Shannon, 24.
6. Albin Krebs, "Day of Mourning for Bomb Victims," *Boston Globe,* September 19, 1963.
7. Terry Smith, "Nationwide Throngs Mourn Child Bomb Victims," *Boston Globe,* September 23, 1963; Peter Kihss, "Rallies in Nation Protest Killing of 6 In Alabama," *NYT,* September 23, 1963.
8. Kihss, "Rallies in Nation Protest Killing."
9. "Harlem Housing Ills Laid to Landlords and Mayor," *NYT,* August 4, 1963.
10. Community Council on Housing, "The Tenants News," August 1963, box 5, folder 9, JHP.
11. "Northern Student Movement Prospectus, September 1963–June 1964," box 4, folder 2, NSM.
12. Gold, *When Tenants Claimed the City,* 120.
13. "Successful Rent Strike Rocks Harlem," *NSM News,* December 1, 1963, box 76, folder 26, AMP; "HEP Program Report," August 7, 1963, box 8, folder 12, NSM.
14. McClandish Phillips, "Harlem Tenants Open Rent Strike," *NYT,* September 28, 1963.
15. Phillips, "Harlem Tenants Open Rent Strike."
16. "HEP Program Report," August 7, 1963, box 8, folder 12, NSM; Marilyn Lowen Correspondence Collection, in author's possession; Bob Fletcher, interview with author, September 11, 2019.

17. "Rent Strikes Rocks Harlem: The People Take the Lead," January 28, 1964, box 76, folder 26, AMP.
18. Phillips, "Harlem Tenants Open Rent Strike."
19. "Harlem Rents Cut to $1 After Strike," *NYT,* October 12, 1963.
20. "Harlem Rents Cut to $1 After Strike"; Lipsky, *Protest in City Politics,* 58–59.
21. "Rep. Powell Preaches Anti-Santa Claus Sermon," *Hartford Courant,* September 30, 1963; Martin Arnold, "City Aide Chides Building Unions," *NYT,* September 30, 1963; "Adam Powell Joins List of Boycott Supporters," *Pittsburgh Courier,* October 5, 1963.
22. Fred Gilman, "Harlem Strike Makes City Act on a Slumlord," *Daily Worker,* October 15, 1963; Fred Gilman, "Victory in Harlem Spreads Struggle Against Slumlords," *Daily Worker,* October 22, 1963.
23. Halstead et al., *Harlem Stirs,* 50.
24. Schwartz, "Tenant Power in the Liberal City," 173–76; For more on Mobilization for Youth, see Carroll, *Mobilizing New York.*
25. Schwartz, "The New York Rent Strikes of 1963–1964," 548–49.
26. Gold, *When Tenants Claimed the City,* 120.
27. "Successful Rent Strike Rocks Harlem," *NSM News,* December 1, 1963, box 76, folder 26, AMP.
28. Gold, *When Tenants Claimed the City,* 120.
29. Fred Gilman, "Harlem Strike Makes City Act on a Slumlord," *Daily Worker,* October 15, 1963.
30. Harlem Action Group Flyer, 1963, box 31, folder 17, MCHR.
31. "Tenants Picket Landlord," *NYAN,* October 19, 1963.
32. "March Protesting Slum Conditions Will Be Staged by Tenants," *Pittsburgh Courier,* October 12, 1963.
33. "March Protesting Slum Conditions."
34. "Tenants Picket Landlord."
35. "Tenants Unimpressed by Mayor's Housing Report; Still Plan March," *NYAN,* October 26, 1963.
36. "Tenants Unimpressed by Mayor's Housing Report."
37. The receivership law took years to pass in the New York State Legislature. In early 1960 the New York City Council called upon the Republican-controlled state legislature to pass a receivership bill introduced by State Senator James Watson. Gray brought a "mass delegation" of tenants from the LHTC to Albany that February to demand the bill's passage, along with other legislative acts to improve housing conditions in Harlem, and continued to advocate for its passage. The law was finally passed in 1962, though the city proved resistant to taking on the costs and responsibilities of wielding its new powers to improve housing conditions in Harlem. "Council Asks State Back Watson Bill," *NYAN,* February 20, 1960; Gold, *When Tenants Claimed the City,* 119.
38. Gray, interview with Shannon, 13.

39. "Tenants Unimpressed by Mayor's Housing Report."
40. "150 Harlem Tenants Picket City Hall in Slum Protest," *NYT,* October 29, 1963.
41. Lipsky, *Protest in City Politics,* 58–59; "Only 200 at City Hall Rally," *NYAN,* November 2, 1963.
42. "Only 200 at City Hall Rally."
43. "Only 200 at City Hall Rally."
44. "110 Tenants Begin Rent Strike Here," *NYT,* November 2, 1963.
45. "Harlem Boycott on Rents Spreads," *NYT,* November 5, 1963; "110 Tenants Begin Rent Strike Here."
46. "Harlem Boycott on Rents Spreads."
47. Naison, "The Rent Strikes in New York," 18–19.
48. "Fed Up Tenants Say to Slumlords: 'No Repairs?' No Rent!," box 31, folder 17, MCHR.
49. Naison, "The Rent Strikes in New York," 18.
50. Martin Arnold, "Rents Withheld by Slum Tenants," *NYT,* December 1, 1963.
51. Arnold, "Rents Withheld by Slum Tenants."
52. Homer Bigart, "Rent Strike Gains Momentum Here," *NYT,* December 18, 1963.
53. Bigart, "Rent Strike Gains Momentum Here."
54. Martin Gansberg, "Tenants in 34 Tenements Join Growing Rent Strike in Harlem," *NYT,* December 2, 1963.
55. Fred Gilman, "Rent Strike Spreading in Harlem," *The Worker,* December 8, 1963.
56. Gilman, "Rent Strike Spreading in Harlem."
57. Gold, *When Tenants Claimed the City,* 121.
58. Bill Strickland, interview with author, October 20, 2017.
59. "Mass Rent Strike Rally," December 15, 1963, box 31, folder 17, MCHR.
60. "Harlem Rent Strike Tenants Push Early City Hall Action," *Pittsburgh Courier,* December 14, 1963.
61. "Powell Urges City Hall March to Support Harlem Rent Strike," *NYT,* December 16, 1963.
62. "Harlem Rent Strike Tenants Push Early City Hall Action."
63. "Mass Rent Strike Rally."
64. "Powell Urges City Hall March."
65. George Todd, "Blame City Hall," *NYAN,* December 21, 1963.
66. "Powell Urges City Hall March."
67. "There Is a Storm Gathering in Harlem," *Hartford Courant,* December 17, 1963.
68. Lipsky, *Protest in City Politics,* 62; Homer Bigart, "Rent Strike Gains Momentum Here," *NYT,* December 18, 1963; "Rent Strike Plan Pushed in Harlem," *NYT,* December 23, 1963. HARYOU and Associated Community Teams (ACT) joined forces around 1962 to collaborate on a grant proposal for a community action program to address mental health and juvenile delinquency issues in Harlem. It was a contentious coalition and eventual merger, with Kenneth Clark (HARYOU) and Adam Clayton Powell Jr. (ACT) competing for influence and resources. For more on HARYOU-ACT, see Cazenave, *Impossible Democracy,* 85–135.

69. Bigart, "Rent Strike Gains Momentum Here."
70. Naison, "The Rent Strikes in New York," 21.
71. "R.I. Slum Dwellers Plan Rent Strike," *Chicago Daily Defender,* October 17, 1963; "Westsiders Wage Rent Strike, Picket Bldg.," *Chicago Daily Defender,* December 7, 1963; Allen Howard, "Hough Citizens Blast City's Housing Policy," *Cleveland Call and Post,* December 21, 1963.
72. "Rent Strike Plan Pushed in Harlem," *NYT,* December 23, 1963.
73. Joel Edelstein, "Rent Strike: What, When, How," January 1964, box 76, folder 26, AMP.
74. "Rent Strikes Rocks Harlem: The People Take the Lead," January 28, 1964, box 76, folder 26, AMP.
75. Naison, "The Rent Strikes in New York," 19.
76. Lipsky, *Protest in City Politics,* 62.
77. Naison, "The Rent Strikes in New York," 19.
78. Gray, interview with Shannon, 5.
79. Naison, "The Rent Strikes in New York," 19.
80. Halstead et al., *Harlem Stirs,* 52.
81. "Rent Strike in Harlem," *Ebony,* April 1964.
82. "Rent Strike in Harlem."
83. Peter Bailey, interview with Robert Martin, 23.
84. Joel Edelstein, "Rent Strike: What, When, How," January 1964, box 76, folder 26, AMP; Halstead et al., *Harlem Stirs,* 52.
85. Richardson Dandridge, interview with author, April 19, 2018.
86. Richardson Dandridge, interview with author.
87. Lawson, Barton, and Joselit, "From Kitchen to Storefront," 263.
88. Gold, *When Tenants Claimed the City,* 132–33. For more on Florence Rice, see Rice, "It Takes a While to Realize," 275–87.
89. Rice was also a member of A. Philip Randolph's Negro American Labor Council and joined Haughton, Epton, and National Maritime Union veteran Josh Lawrence in a little-known struggle to build a more militant, "fighting NALC," resulting in a series of purges by Randolph. For more on the Emergency Committee and Rice's involvement in the "Fighting NALC" struggle, see box 2, folder 5; and box 3, folder 10, JHP.
90. By the time the rent strikes got underway, many of Rice's comrades were also throwing their support behind the nascent movement. In mid-December, Haughton pushed the NY NAACP's militant Labor and Industry Committee to organize regular fundraising events for the CCH. In early 1964 Malcolm X also lent his support to the rent strikes and forged relationships with Gray and Gloria Richardson en route to forming the radical organization ACT that spring.
91. Friendly, "The Harlem Temper," December 11, 1963.
92. Community Council on Housing, "Rent Strike!!," December 1963, box 5, folder 9, JHP.
93. Homer Bigart, "Rent Striker Bids for Red Cross Aid," *NYT,* December 25, 1963.

94. Theodore Jones, "Bleak Day Spent by Rent Strikers," *NYT,* December 26, 1963.
95. Naison, "The Rent Strikes in New York," 22.
96. Naison, "The Rent Strikes in New York," 22.
97. Naison, "The Rent Strikes in New York," 23n30.
98. Lawrence O'Kane, "Housing Proposed Above 2 Schools," *NYT,* December 17, 1963.
99. Jackson, "Harlem's Rent Strike and Rat War," 61.
100. George Todd, "Tenants Planning Rat Exhibition," *NYAN,* December 28, 1963; Samuel Kaplan, "Slum Rent Strike Upheld by Judge," *NYT,* December 31, 1963.
101. Lipsky, *Protest in City Politics,* 63.
102. George Todd, "Tenants Planning Rat Exhibition," *NYAN,* December 28, 1963; Kaplan, "Slum Rent Strike Upheld by Judge."
103. Kaplan, "Slum Rent Strike Upheld by Judge"; Gold, *When Tenants Claimed the City,* 124-25; Lipsky, *Protest in City Politics,* 63-64. According to Gold and Lipsky, Ribaudo was alerted to the seldom-used law by Columbia University law professors allied with Mobilization for Youth.
104. Gold, *When Tenants Claimed the City,* 124-25.
105. Kaplan, "Slum Rent Strike Upheld by Judge."
106. Kaplan, "Slum Rent Strike Upheld by Judge."
107. Martin Arnold, "Reaction Is Mixed to City Slum Plan," *NYT,* January 7, 1964; Gold, *When Tenants Claimed the City,* 125; Lipsky, *Protest in City Politics,* 65-66.
108. Lipsky, *Protest in City Politics,* 66.
109. Lipsky, *Protest in City Politics,* 90.
110. Lipsky, *Protest in City Politics,* 66.
111. Naison, "The Rent Strikes in New York," 24; Lipsky, *Protest in City Politics,* 66.
112. Woody Klein, "Through the Years: How Not to Fight Slumlords," *New York Telegram and Sun,* January 8, 1964.
113. Charles Grutzner, "Court Halts Rent for 'Unfit' Slums," *NYT,* January 9, 1964. For more on the Moritt decision, see Gold, *When Tenants Claimed the City,* 126-27; Lipsky, *Protest in City Politics,* 66-68.
114. The coalition was brought together by Mobilization for Youth and included Downtown and NYU CORE, Puertorriqueños Unidos, the Metropolitan Council on Housing, and several other organizations. Gold, *When Tenants Claimed the City,* 126-27; Lipsky, *Protest in City Politics,* 67; Carroll, *Mobilizing New York,* 53-54.
115. Carroll, *Mobilizing New York,* 53.
116. Gold, *When Tenants Claimed the City,* 127.
117. Carroll, *Mobilizing New York,* 54.
118. Gold, *When Tenants Claimed the City,* 127; Halstead et al., *Harlem Stirs,* 80-88.
119. Tobierre, "Black Power Does Not Come," 65; Minutes: Meeting of NSM Congress, January 17-18, 1964, New York, box 1, folder 14, NSM.
120. Bailey, interview with Martin, 22.
121. Naison, "The Rent Strikes in New York," 28.

122. Halstead et al., *Harlem Stirs*, 60–64; Lipsky, *Protest in City Politics*, 67; Harlem Action Group, "Attention All Tenants," January 1964, box 76, folder 26, AMP.
123. "Jim Baldwin Sparks Harlem Rent Strike," *NYAN*, January 18, 1964; Emanuel Perlmutter, "March Is Planned by Rent Strikers," *NYT*, January 13, 1964.
124. Baldwin's participation in the rent strike rally was secured by Bill Strickland, who visited Baldwin's home at the request of Jesse Gray to ask the internationally renowned writer to attend and speak. Strickland, interview with author, May 31, 2018.
125. The transcript of Baldwin's address can be found in Halstead et al., *Harlem Stirs*, 62.
126. "500 at Rent Strike Rally Hear Lewis, Baldwin, Strickland Call for Rent Revolt," *NSM News*, February 10, 1964, Pat Murphy Collection, in author's possession.
127. The transcript of Lewis's address can be found in Halstead et al., *Harlem Stirs*, 64.
128. Halstead et al., *Harlem Stirs*, 64.
129. "Jim Baldwin Sparks Harlem Rent Strike," *NYAN*, January 18, 1964.
130. Naison, "The Rent Strikes in New York," 28.
131. "Harlem Rent Strike Seeks 'Push' from Rights Groups," *Pittsburgh Courier*, January 18, 1964; "NECAP Is Considering Harlem Type Rent Strike," *Hartford Courant*, January 6, 1964; Dan Day, "Capitol Spotlight: Rent Strike Is New Civil Rights Weapon," *Atlanta Daily World*, January 7, 1964; Rasa Gustaitis, "Tenants Start First 'Rent Strike' in District," *Washington Post, Times Herald*, January 25, 1964.
132. Hutchings, interview with author, January 26, 2017.
133. Gold, *When Tenants Claimed the City*, 135–36. For more on the 1964 school boycotts in New York City, see Taylor, *Knocking at Our Own Door*.
134. Landry, interview with Britton, 24; Allen Howard, "Ruth Turner Quits Comfy School Post to Battle Bias," *Call and Post*, January 25, 1964; "James Bevel," SNCC Digital Gateway, accessed April 27, 2018, https://snccdigital.org/people/james-bevel/.
135. Halstead et al., *Harlem Stirs*, 80–87.
136. Lipsky, *Rent Strikes in City Politics*, 68; Lawrence O'Kane, "City Hall Crowds Disrupt Hearing on Rent Control," *NYT*, January 24, 1964.
137. Halstead et al., *Harlem Stirs*, 87.
138. Letter from James Baldwin, undated, box 31, folder 17, MCHR.
139. "Rent Strike Movement Grows in New York: HAG Joins Tenants to Fight Illegal Evictions," *NSM News*, February 10, 1964, Pat Murphy Collection, in author's possession.
140. "Eviction Causes Harlem Scuffle," *NYT*, January 30, 1964.
141. "Jesse Gray Charges He Was Roughed Up," *NYAN*, February 1, 1964.
142. "Eviction Causes Harlem Scuffle."
143. "Rent Strike Due to Double in Size," *NYT*, February 1, 1964.
144. Militant Labor Forum, "The Harlem Hate-Gang Scare," May 29, 1964, Moving Image and Recorded Sound Division, Schomburg Center for Research in Black Culture.

145. Halstead et al., *Harlem Stirs,* 88–100.
146. Halstead et al., *Harlem Stirs,* 99.
147. Halstead et al., *Harlem Stirs,* 88–100; Bernard Stengren, "Police Are Picketed over Slum Eviction," *NYT,* February 9, 1964.
148. Baldwin, *Nobody Knows My Name,* 65–66.
149. For more on the King Cole Trio, see Flamm, *In the Heat of the Summer,* 61–62.
150. Militant Labor Forum, "The Harlem Hate-Gang Scare."
151. Militant Labor Forum, "The Harlem Hate-Gang Scare."
152. Emanuel Perlmutter, "Murphy Says City Will Not Permit Rights Violence," *NYT,* March 16, 1964; Lipsky, *Protest in City Politics,* 71–72.
153. "March on Albany—March 10th, 1964," box 25, folder 27, MCHR; Fred Powledge, "Civil Rights and Labor Groups Join for March on Albany Today," *NYT,* March 10, 1964.
154. Fred Powledge, "3,000 in Rights Protest March on Albany in Snow," *NYT,* March 11, 1964.
155. Naison, "The Rent Strikes in New York," 32.
156. Naison, "The Rent Strikes in New York," 26.
157. "Harlem Rent Strike Seeks 'Push' from Rights Groups," *Pittsburgh Courier,* January 18, 1964.
158. Naison, "The Rent Strikes in New York," 26–27. Like Farmer, NAACP executive secretary Roy Wilkins essentially shunned the rent strike movement.
159. Gold, *When Tenants Claimed the City,* 130. In addition to these political divisions between Gray and mainstream civil rights or housing organizations, there were also personal differences among organizers that often complicated coalition-building efforts. The minutes of NSM meetings from this period suggest that many organizers were critical of Gray's leadership style within coalitions and some others were skeptical of his political motives. Q. R. Hand told me that he was sometimes wary of Gray in these years but later came to appreciate his methods and effectiveness as an organizer. Q. R. Hand, interview with author, November 10, 2019.
160. Naison, "The Rent Strikes in Harlem," 40–41.
161. Lipsky, *Protest in City Politics,* 64.
162. See Naison, "The Rent Strikes in New York"; Schwartz, "Tenant Power in the Liberal City"; Lipsky, *Protest in City Politics;* Gold, *When Tenants Claimed the City.*
163. Militant Labor Forum, "The Harlem Hate-Gang Scare."
164. Fred Powledge, "Rights Activists Expanding Goals," *NYT,* March 28, 1964.
165. In a letter to Bayard Rustin in April 1964, Strickland further explained that "the building of indigenous leadership is severely hampered by white leadership" and sought his participation in a conference to clarify strategies for NSM's summer projects. The NSM Congress reversed the decision two months later, but it was reinstated by Strickland in August 1964. NSM Congress, March 27–28, 1964, box 1, folder 14, NSM; letter from Bill Strickland to Bayard Rustin, April 22, 1964, box 8, folder 13, NSM. For more on NSM's move away from interracial

organizing, see Burgin, *Organizing Your Own,* 29–69; Tobierre, "Black Power Does Not Come," 68–70.
166. Schechter, *News Dissector,* 40.
167. "Jesse Gray Tells Plans In New York: The Rent-Strike Season Is On," *National Guardian,* November 11, 1964.
168. Jesse Gray, "The Black Revolution—A Struggle for Political Power," December 19, 1964, Federation for Independent Political Action Conference, box 15, folder 6, JHP.

8. THE TIME HAS COME

1. Fred Powledge, "Farmer and Murphy Discuss Complaints Board," *NYT,* April 28, 1964.
2. Fernández, *The Young Lords,* 70–72; "Policeman Kills 2 in Patrol Car," *NYT,* November 16, 1963; "Inquiry Upholds Killing by Police," *NYT,* November 17, 1963; "2 Slain by Police Linked to Holdup," *NYT,* November 23, 1963.
3. Fernández, *The Young Lords,* 71.
4. Jack Roth, "Police Cleared in Slaying of 2," *NYT,* April 9, 1964; Gertrude Samuels, "I Don't Think the Cop Is My Friend," *NYT,* March 29, 1964.
5. Peter Kihss, "Police Assailed by Puerto Ricans," *NYT,* February 24, 1964.
6. "Father, 18, Accused of Pulling a Knife, Slain by Policeman," *NYT,* February 19, 1964.
7. Kihss, "Police Assailed by Puerto Ricans."
8. "2 Clerics Accuse Police in Killing," *NYT,* February 24, 1964.
9. East Harlem Tenants Council Press Release, February 23, 1964, Small Organizations, Police Brutality Clippings, NYPDIR.
10. Velez began organizing with Gray and the LHTC around 1960, and two years later used his experience and connections to establish the EHTC. Under the leadership of Velez and Tony Williams, the EHTC followed the organizational and tactical models of the CCH and developed a "network of building captains" to promote indigenous leadership and a self-sustaining movement among Puerto Rican renters. For more on Velez's background, see Schwartz, "Tenant Power in the Liberal City," 177; Gold, *When Tenants Claimed the City,* 134–35; Lee, *Building a Latino Civil Rights Movement,* 151–52, George Todd, "E. Harlem Leader Fights Slumlords," *NYAN,* May 2, 1964.
11. Memo from Jack Barnathan to Commanding Officer, BOSS, February 22, 1964, BSS 78-m (1964), Correspondence Files, NYPDIR; Kihss, "Police Assailed by Puerto Ricans."
12. Albin Krebs, "A Funeral March with Lurking Hostility," *New York Herald Tribune,* February 25, 1964; Robert Trumbull, "Rodriguez Youth Is Mourned by 300," *NYT,* February 25, 1964.

13. Fred Gilman, "Demand Mayor Probe Cop Slaying of Youth," *The Worker,* March 1, 1964.
14. Murphy's remarks also came in response to legislation introduced by Harlem State Senator Jerome L. Wilson that would have barred police from carrying their service revolvers when off duty. "East Side Seething over Youth's Death," *NYAN,* February 29, 1964; Trumbull, "Rodriguez Youth Is Mourned by 300."
15. Samuels, "I Don't Think the Cop Is My Friend."
16. Thomas Johnson and Joseph Gelmis, "CORE Pickets Murphy," *Newsday,* March 21, 1964.
17. Although the officers who killed Solero and Rodriguez were later transferred out of the area, two separate grand juries declined to indict any of the officers involved in the three killings. Jack Roth, "Police Cleared in Slaying of 2," *NYT,* April 9, 1964; "Grand Jury Finds No Case in Shooting by a Patrolman," *NYT,* May 7, 1964.
18. Samuels, "I Don't Think the Cop Is My Friend."
19. Mike Davidow, "City Hall March Sunday Will Protest March Slaying," *The Worker,* March 1, 1964.
20. Layhmond Robinson, "Legislators Pass Anticrime Bills," *NYT,* February 19, 1964.
21. "Text of Governor Rockefeller's Message to the Members of the Legislature," *NYT,* January 9, 1964.
22. Flamm, *In the Heat of the Summer,* 56–57; "Text of Governor Rockefeller's Message."
23. "New Police Laws Scored at Rally," *NYT,* March 8, 1964.
24. Robinson, "Legislators Pass Anticrime Bills"; Felber, *Those Who Know Don't Say,* 157. The package also included legislation to create a new state agency to coordinate information and data sharing between local and state law enforcement agencies. "State Data Pool for Crime Urged," *NYT,* January 6, 1964.
25. "A Bad Law," *NYAN,* March 7, 1964.
26. Robert Arnold, "Rockefeller's Police State," *Liberator* 4, no. 6 (June 1964): 4–5.
27. Letter from Basil Patterson, March 3, 1964, BSS 100-M 1964, Correspondence Files, NYPDIR.
28. Hudson, "Police Review Boards," 523; M. S. Johnson, *Street Justice,* 222–34; Chronopoulos, "Police Misconduct, Community Opposition," 648.
29. Martin Arnold, "NAACP and CORE to Fight Bills Increasing Police Powers," *NYT,* February 29, 1964; "Governor Picketed by Foes of Search and Seizure Bills," *NYT,* March 2, 1964; Douglas Dales, "Rockefeller Signs Bills Increasing Powers of Police," *NYT,* March 4, 1964; "NAACP Pickets Rocky," *NYAN,* March 7, 1964.
30. Douglas Dales, "2 Bills Prepared on Police Search," *NYT,* January 21, 1964; Dales, "Rockefeller Signs Bills."
31. "New Police Laws Scored at Rally," *NYT,* March 8, 1964.
32. "Stop-and-Frisk' Law Blasted by Speakers at Harlem Rally," *The Militant,* March 16, 1964; Memo from John J. O'Connor to The Chief Inspector, March 11, 1964, BSS 100-M 1964, Correspondence Files, NYPDIR.

33. Gold, *When Tenants Claimed the City,* 128; "New Police Laws Scored at Rally."
34. Chronopoulos, "Police Misconduct, Community Opposition" 16.
35. "CORE Sounds Commissioner," *NYAN,* March 7, 1964; Bronx CORE Newsletter, March 6, 1964, box 02-045329, CORE Files, NYPDIR.
36. Bronx CORE Newsletter, March 6, 1964.
37. Brunson had been among the protestors who shut down the Harlem Hospital construction site the previous summer and had established himself in Black radical circles through his work on the rent strikes in the months since.
38. "Chain-in at Police Headquarters, Sitdown on Bridge," March 12, 1964, CORE.
39. Malcolm Nash, "Spring Bringing 'Open Season' On," *NYAN,* March 14, 1964.
40. Emanuel Perlmutter, "Murphy Says City Will Not Permit Rights Violence," *NYT,* March 16, 1964.
41. Militant Labor Forum, "The Harlem Hate-Gang Scare."
42. Letter from Robert Knight to Police Commissioner Murphy, March 22, 1964, Harlem Action Group, Small Organization Files, NYPDIR.
43. Memo from Thomas V. Pendergast to The Chief Inspector, May 19, 1964, Harlem Action Group, Small Organization Files, NYPDIR. As it reacted to many activists who challenged police power, BOSS responded to Knight's complaints by placing him under surveillance. BOSS records show sensational, likely fabricated claims from an informant that Knight was "planning to actually provoke policemen into using force against them, even by attacking police with knives" and even had a "plan to kill the Police Commissioner." Detectives were also concerned about white women coming to the HAG office, women who "actually teach kids to demonstrate"; the presence of outside agitators who "speak and spark their meetings"; and connections with "Puerto Rican Nationalist Groups" that "produce and store arms" in the neighborhood. See files in Harlem Action Group, Small Organization Files, NYPDIR.
44. NSM Congress, March 27–28, box 1, folder 14, NSM.
45. Cherry's description is documented in handwritten notes on a copy of the proposal that Knight circulated at the NSM Congress. Local Advisory Committee Proposal, March 1964, Pat Murphy Collection, in author's possession.
46. Progressive Labor Party, "Vote Epton First!," 1965, box 34, folder 5, Large Organization Files, NYPDIR; William Epton, "An Alternative Policy: Political Power," *Liberator* 3, no. 9 (September 1963): 15–16. For more on the influence of Mao Tse-tung on the evolution of Black radicalism in the United States, see Kelley, *Freedom Dreams,* chapter 3.
47. Gold, *When Tenants Claimed the City,* 127; Halstead et al., *Harlem Stirs,* 80–88.
48. West Side Progressive Labor Club, "Two New Police Killings," November 1963, in "Subversive Influences in Riots, Looting, and Burning Part 1": Hearings Before the House Committee on Un-American Activities, 90th Congress, 2nd session, 1968, 982.

49. Harlem Progressive Labor Club, "Rockefeller Legalizes Police Crime," March 1964, box 8, folder 13, NSM.
50. M. S. Handler, "Malcolm X Splits with Muhammad," *NYT*, March 9, 1964.
51. X, *Malcolm X Speaks*, 18–22.
52. Among the sixty representatives from various Northern organizations were Jesse Gray and Herman Ferguson from New York, Stanley Branche from Chester, comedian and activist Dick Gregory, Lawrence Landry and Nahaz Rogers from Chicago, Gloria Richardson from Cambridge, MD, and Julius Hobson from Washington, DC. The gathering built on relationships forged at the Northern Negro Grass Roots Leadership Conference in Detroit. Harley, "Chronicle of a Death Foretold," 190; Ward, *In Love and Struggle*, 311; "Minutes: National Temporary Freedom Day Committee Meeting," Chester, PA, March 14, 1964. Thanks to Joseph R. Fitzgerald for sharing this document with me, along with several emails between him and Gloria Richardson Dandridge about the formation of ACT.
53. Landry, interview with Britton; email from Gloria Richardson Dandridge to Joseph R. Fitzgerald, June 24, 2014. For more on the NYC school boycotts, see Clarence Taylor, *Knocking at Our Own Door*.
54. Martin Arnold, "Galamison Sees Boycott Success," *NYT*, March 16, 1964.
55. Leonard Buder, "School Boycott Is Half as Large as the First One," *NYT*, March 17, 1964; "Boycott: Split Down Middle—In Leadership and Support," *Pittsburgh Courier*, March 21, 1964.
56. George Todd, "Malcolm X Explains His Rifle Statement," *NYAN*, March 28, 1964.
57. Edward Murrain, "Angry at Filibuster in Senate: Malcolm X Launches Drive 'Boycott Democratic Party,'" *Pittsburgh Courier*, March 28, 1964.
58. X, *Malcolm X Speaks*, 23. As editor George Breitman notes, the central tenets of the speech Malcolm gave at this rally, along with three others held that month, provided the basis for an early April talk in Cleveland titled "The Ballot or the Bullet," which is remembered as one of his most iconic public addresses.
59. Murrain, "Angry at Filibuster in Senate"; Marable claimed that, "at its core," the address was about the "importance of voting rights." Marable, *Malcolm X*, 302–7.
60. Fitzgerald, *The Struggle Is Eternal*, 182–84; David Herman, "Malcolm X to Organize Mass Voter Registration," *The Militant*, April 6, 1964.
61. Murrain, "Angry at Filibuster in Senate."
62. David Herman, "3,000 Cheer Malcolm X at Opening Rally in Harlem," *The Militant*, March 30, 1964; X, *Malcolm X Speaks*, 42–43.
63. "Minutes: National Temporary Freedom Day Committee Meeting," Chester, PA, March 14, 1964.
64. Herman, "3,000 Cheer Malcolm X At Opening Rally."
65. "Mae Mallory, Monroe N.C., Four to Appeal Lengthy Jail Sentences," *Philadelphia Tribune*, March 3, 1964.
66. "Release N.C. Kidnap Prisoners on Bail," *Chicago Daily Defender*, March 23, 1964; Mae Mallory FBI File, Part 01 of 03, FBI Records: The Vault.

67. Marable, *Malcolm X,* 305; David Herman, untitled article, *The Militant,* April 13, 1964.
68. Although Malcolm supported Williams during his trips to New York in 1959, Mallory found it troubling—and damaging to Black radical unity—that he had been relatively quiet in the years since. "I think it would be beneficial to Rob the case and the over all struggle if Malcolm would let it be known that he is furthering the program that was started by Robert F. Williams. . . . This is what I want him to do and I am going to get him to admit this if I can," she wrote in a letter to Mabel Williams just days before returning to Harlem. Letter from Mae Mallory to Mabel Williams, March 30, 1964, folder 009051-014-0808, RFWP.
69. Malcolm X, "We Are All Blood Brothers," *Liberator* 4, no. 7 (July 1964): 4–6.
70. As National CORE Director James Farmer pointed out in a stern rebuke of the city's real estate commissioner, who had earlier argued that the receivership law was fiscally irresponsible, the cost of removing violations from 1,000 buildings at $20,000 per building would have been $20 million—half of the amount provided to the World's Fair and a fraction of a percent of the city's budget. Lipsky, *Protest in City Politics,* 70.
71. William Bundy, "Call for World's Fair Stall-in Gives Boost to Rights Battle," *The Militant,* April 20, 1964; Halstead et al., *Harlem Stirs,* 112. For more thorough coverage of the stall-in, see Purnell, *Fighting Jim Crow,* 237–65.
72. Purnell, *Fighting Jim Crow,* 248.
73. East River CORE Press Release, March 6, 1964, box 02-045329, folder "CORE (1 of 3)," CORE Files, NYPDIR.
74. "CORE Sitters, Sprawlers Disrupt Cop HQ & Triboro," series 5, folder 252251-022-0958, CORE.
75. Bundy, "Call for World's Fair Stall-in Gives Boost."
76. Purnell, *Fighting Jim Crow,* 259.
77. "The Stall-In," *NYT,* April 21, 1964.
78. "It's Illegal to Run Out of Gas in N.Y.C. Now," *Chicago Daily Defender,* April 15, 1964; "Union May Aid 'Stall-in' by Halting Tow Service," *Baltimore Afro-American,* April 25, 1964.
79. "N.Y. 'Snarl-In' May Paralyze Biggest City," *Chicago Daily Defender,* April 22, 1964.
80. Purnell, *Fighting Jim Crow,* 258; Simon Anekwe, "B'klyn CORE Defies Farmer, Pushes Fair Stall-In Plan," *NYAN,* April 18, 1964. Farmer was joined by other civil rights leaders, including Whitney Young, John Lewis, Roy Wilkins, A. Philip Randolph, and Dorothy Height in publicly denouncing the stall-in. "'Stall-Ins' Hit by Organization Heads," *Atlanta Daily World,* April 18, 1964; "Big 6 Frowns on Stall-In," *Baltimore Afro-American,* April 25, 1964.
81. "Dr. King Urges Initiative Defeat," *Los Angeles Sentinel,* April 30, 1964; "FBI Aids South, Rev. King Claims," *Chicago Daily Defender,* April 29, 1964; Lillian S. Calhoun, "Confetti," *Chicago Daily Defender,* April 23, 1964.

82. Memo from SAC [Special Agent in Charge], New York, to Director, FBI, April 13, 1964, reel 1, section 1, MMIFBI; David Herman, "Malcolm X Details Black Nationalist Views," *The Militant,* April 20, 1964.
83. Untitled news clipping, box 8, folder 12, Large Organization Files, NYPDIR. ACT also welcomed Brunson into the organization during the meeting. "New Coalition of Rights Leaders Meets," *The Militant,* April 27, 1964; "Daley Threatens Stall-Ins Arrests," *Chicago Daily Defender,* April 21, 1964.
84. Memo from Ernest B. Latty to Commanding Officer, BOSS, April 20, 1964, box 8, folder 12, Large Organization Files, NYPDIR.
85. "Daley Threatens Stall-Ins Arrests"; Bundy, "Call for World's Fair Stall-in Gives Boost."
86. "Union May Aid 'Stall-in' by Halting Tow Service," *Baltimore Afro-American,* April 25, 1964.
87. "Bloody Battle Marks Start of World's Fair," *Chicago Daily Defender,* April 23, 1964.
88. George Todd, "First Stall-In on Northern Blvd.," *NYAN,* April 25, 1964.
89. George Levan, "Rights Movement Wins Top Billing at Fair's Open," *The Militant,* April 27, 1964; "Bloody Battle Marks Start of World's Fair"; Purnell, *Fighting Jim Crow,* 260.
90. Sara Slack, "They Could Have Arrested Him Then," *NYAN,* April 25, 1964.
91. Simon Anekwe, "Tough-Minded B'klyn CORE Group Never Considered Stopping Stall," *NYAN,* April 25, 1964; Levan, "Rights Movement Wins Top Billing."
92. Purnell, *Fighting Jim Crow,* 263.
93. Bill Strickland, "On Stall-ins," *NSM News-Observer,* May 5, 1964.
94. Strickland, "On Stall-ins."
95. Ahmad, *We Will Return in the Whirlwind,* 114–15.
96. Ahmad, *We Will Return in the Whirlwind,* 101.
97. Freeman, *Reflections of a Resolute Radical,* 71–72.
98. Memo from FBI NY to FBI Director, April 3, 1964, reel 1, section 1, MMIFBI.
99. Freeman, *Reflections of a Resolute Radical,* 49–62.
100. According to Ahmad, Isaiah Brunson was one of dozens of RAM cadre working to build a revolutionary nationalist movement by infiltrating larger organizations and steering them in more radical directions. Ahmad, *We Will Return in the Whirlwind,* 114–15.
101. "Black Americans: Prepare for a Living Hell: Unite Now or Perish," *Black America* 1, no. 7–8 (November–December 1963).
102. RAM's political analysis was being shaped by Williams's comrade Ethel Azalea Johnson, who shared her knowledge of organizing around armed self-defense, and Queen Mother Audley Moore, who tutored RAM cadre on Pan-Africanism and Marxism-Leninism. Ahmad, *We Will Return in the Whirlwind,* 101.
103. Max Stanford, "Orientation to a Black Mass Movement: Part 2," folder 010629-001-0256, RAM.

104. HARYOU, *Youth in the Ghetto,* 22–31; Erickson, "HARYOU," 171n9.
105. Erickson, "HARYOU," 171; Appendix IV, Leadership Training Workshop for the HARYOU Associates, box 2, KMP.
106. Memo from LJ Pires to James Jones, Ken Marshall, August 29, 1963, box 2, KMP.
107. Harlem Youth Opportunities Unlimited, Forum Discussion on Civil Rights by HARYOU Associates, undated, box 2, KMP.
108. Friendly, "The Harlem Temper."
109. Harlem Youth Opportunities Unlimited, Inc., Leadership Training Workshop "End of Program" Banquet, September 5, 1963, box 2, KMP.
110. Memo from Laura Pires to Jim Jones, Ken Marshall, July 26, 1963, box 2, KMP.
111. These reinforcements were likely able to respond so quickly because of a new targeted enforcement program that Police Commissioner Michael Murphy introduced months earlier to combat youth crime. In early February Murphy announced that two hundred plainclothes detectives and patrolmen would be deployed as "crime combat teams" in twenty-five "high hazard" areas. The initiative was particularly directed at policing youth, as Murphy announced that felony arrests of sixteen- to twenty-year-olds had increased by 13.6 percent over the past year. Martin Arnold, "New Patrol to Fight Rising Crime Rate," *NYT,* February 5, 1964; Nelson, *The Torture of Mothers,* 18–19.
112. Nelson, *The Torture of Mothers,* 3–4.
113. "75 In Harlem Throw Fruit at Policemen," *NYT,* April 18, 1964.
114. HARYOU Interviews, April 20, 1964, box 18, folder 4, Large Organization Files, NYPDIR.
115. HARYOU Interviews, April 20, 1964.
116. HARYOU Interviews, April 20, 1964.
117. For Stafford's account of the assault in the street and torture in the 32nd Precinct, see Nelson, *The Torture of Mothers,* 4–9.
118. HARYOU Interviews, April 20, 1964; "Lawyer for 5 Tells Court Police Roughed Up Clients," *NYT,* April 19, 1964.
119. HARYOU Interviews, April 20, 1964.
120. Memo from New York FBI to Director, May 8, 1964, reel 1, section 2, MMIFBI.
121. HARYOU Interviews, April 20, 1964. During the arraignment two days earlier, defense attorney George Sena also used the opportunity to level charges of brutality against the NYPD. The charge was quickly dismissed by Judge Maurice W. Grey, who told Sena to take his complaints to Commissioner Murphy. "Lawyer for 5 Tells Court."
122. According to Jones, two officers continually walked by and peered in the window throughout the interviews. When he left the community center, "there was three or four of them on the corner, looking at us." Nelson, *The Torture of Mothers,* 56.
123. See reel 1, section 1, "Mar.–Apr. 1964," and section 2, "May–Jun. 1964," MMIFBI.
124. Ted Poston, "Violence in Harlem," *Midstream* 10, no. 3 (September 1964): 27. As Flamm points out, while Griffin maintained the veracity of his reporting,

other veteran reporters in New York similarly believed the story was fabricated. Flamm, *In the Heat of the Summer,* 71–73.

125. As James Baldwin explained in his report on the Harlem Six two years later, the Fruit Stand Riot wasn't the first run-in that the six teens had had with the NYPD. The boys kept pigeons, and police previously tried to arrest them at gunpoint as part of rooftop sweeps targeting Black youth. "They refused to go to the precinct... and their exhibition of the spirit of '76 marked them as dangerous," Baldwin reported. Mildred Thomas similarly told reporters, "They had pigeon coops on the roof and they were forced to move them... the police hound them constantly and several of the boys grew up disliking the police." James Baldwin, "A Report from Occupied Territory," *The Nation,* July 11, 1966; Les Matthews and George Barner, "They Still Can't Prove That 'Blood Gang' Lie!," *NYAN,* May 23, 1964.

126. "3 Youths Seized in Harlem Killing," *NYT,* May 1, 1964.

127. "Good News for the Harlem Four: State's Witness Swears Affidavit Negating Testimony," *Liberation News Service,* July 8, 1972; "Singing a Different Tune," *NYT,* July 9, 1972. According to attorney William Kunstler, the assistant district attorney met with Barnes over forty times before delivering his initial testimony, suggesting that his account was likely coerced, as other members of the Harlem Six also claimed. Barnes recanted his testimony in 1973, leading to the eventual release of Baker, Craig, Felder, and Thomas. Lacey Kosburgh, "Harlem Six Jury to Get Case Soon," *NYT,* January 23, 1972.

128. "3 Youths Seized in Harlem Killing"; Martin Arnold, "2 Held in Killing Admit Another; Will Be Questioned on 2 More," *NYT,* May 2, 1964. Like Baker, Hamm, and Rice, Craig had also been at the Fruit Stand Riot and witnessed the police beatings of his friends that day. Suddler, *Presumed Criminal,* 150.

129. Suddler, *Presumed Criminal,* 143; Nelson, *The Torture of Mothers,* 25.

130. Junius Griffin, "Whites Are Target of Harlem Gang," *NYT,* May 3, 1964.

131. Junius Griffin, "Harlem: The Tension Underneath," *NYT,* May 29, 1964.

132. Memo from FBI New York to Director, May 4, 1964, reel 1, section 2, MMIFBI; Memo from SAC New York to Director, FBI, May 6, 1964, reel 1, section 2, MMIFBI; Junius Griffin, "Police in Harlem Hunt Gang Chiefs," *NYT,* May 8, 1964.

133. Griffin supplemented his police sources and alleged interviews with fabricated accounts of Willie Jones's interviews, which he shared with the reporter. Nowhere in the recordings was there any mention of gang activity, Malcolm X, or Black nationalism. Griffin then shared transcripts of the tapes and a draft of his next article with BOSS detectives, which suggests Griffin not only received information from law enforcement but also supplied it. Nelson, *The Torture of Mothers,* 54–60; HARYOU Interviews, April 20, 1964, box 18, folder 4, Large Organization Files, NYPDIR; Junius Griffin, "Anti-White Harlem Gang Reported to Number 400," *NYT,* May 6, 1964; Griffin, "Harlem: The Tension Underneath."

134. Junius Griffin, "40 Negro Detectives Investigate Anti-White Gang," *NYT,* May 7, 1964; Felber, *Those Who Know Don't Say,* 159–60.
135. New York FBI Memo, May 7, 1964, reel 1, section 2, MMIFBI.
136. Junius Griffin, "N.A.A.C.P. Assails Reports of Gang," *NYT,* May 11, 1964.
137. Commanding Officer, BOSS, to Chief of Detectives, September 5, 1964, BSS 164 1964, Correspondence Files, NYPDIR.
138. Felber, *Those Who Know Don't Say,* 160.
139. "The Man Who Shot Malcolm X," *Black Vanguard* 1, no. 3 (March 20, 1965).
140. Matthews and Barner, "They Still Can't Prove That 'Blood Gang' Lie!"
141. X, *Malcolm X Speaks,* 65.
142. Daniel H. Watts, "Harlem... 'Blood Brothers,'" *Liberator* 4, no. 6 (June 1964): 3.
143. "Violence in the City," *NYT,* June 1, 1964.
144. Harlem Progressive Labor Movement, "Harlem Unite: Let Us Defend Ourselves!," May 1964, box 34, NYPDIR.
145. Griffin, "Harlem: The Tension Underneath," *NYT,* May 29, 1964.
146. Griffin, "Whites Are Target of Harlem Gang," *NYT,* May 3, 1964.
147. Alfred E. Lewis, "Tough Tactical Force Cuts Street Crime in New York," *Washington Post,* April 28, 1963.
148. Harlem Progressive Labor Movement, "Harlem Unite."
149. Lewis, "Tough Tactical Force Cuts Street Crime."
150. Lewis, "Tough Tactical Force Cuts Street Crime"; Harlem Progressive Labor Movement, "Harlem Unite."
151. Homer Bigart, "Wagner Bolsters Police on Subway to Deter Attacks," *NYT,* June 3, 1964.
152. Harlem Progressive Labor Movement, "Harlem Unite."
153. Black Liberation Commission of the Progressive Labor Party, "The Plot Against Black America," 1966, in author's possession.
154. Griffin, "Harlem: The Tension Underneath."
155. "Says Cops Provoke It," *NYAN,* May 16, 1964.
156. Griffin, "Harlem: The Tension Underneath."
157. Black Liberation Commission of the Progressive Labor Party, "The Plot Against Black America."
158. "Boy, 14, Shot by Policeman When He Fails to Halt," *NYT,* April 24, 1964; memo from John Caulfield to Commanding Officer, BOSS, April 14, 1964, BSS 178 M 1964, Correspondence Files, NYPDIR.
159. "Pickets at Police Station Protest Shooting of Youth," *NYT,* April 28, 1964; memo from Jack Barnathan and Francis Koopman to Commanding Officer, BOSS, April 27, 1964, BSS 201 M 1964, Correspondence Files, NYPDIR.
160. Junius Griffin, "11 Are Arrested in Harlem Clash," *NYT,* May 20, 1964; "Arrest 4 Parents in Fight for Light; Brutality Charged."
161. Griffin, "40 Negro Detectives Investigate Anti-White Gang"; Griffin, "Harlem: The Tension Underneath." According to Griffin, by the end of May community

centers were "working closely with the police, turning over information on any youth suspected of being a Blood Brother." As Carl Suddler explains, the deputization of community centers and youth services as arms of the surveillance state has been an important but underrecognized form of institutional surveillance. Suddler, *Presumed Criminal.*

162. Junius Griffin, "Police in Harlem Hunt Gang Chiefs," *NYT,* May 8, 1964.
163. Wagner described the counterintelligence work of BOSS as a "very key part of the department," which allowed him to "keep check on all sorts of different groups and infiltrate" developing threats to the status quo. Reminiscences of Robert Ferdinand Wagner from oral history, 1979, Columbia Center for Oral History, Columbia University Libraries, 651.
164. *Handschu v. Special Services Division, et al.,* May 18, 1971, 15; Donner, *Protectors of Privilege,* 157–58; Emanuel Perlmutter, "Police Intelligence Unit Watches Racial Activity," *NYT,* July 27, 1964. BOSS even set up a PO box under the inconspicuously named "Political Science Society," which they added to mailing lists of organizations to obtain a direct feed of newsletters, pamphlets, and other literature.
165. Memo from Henry Taylor to Civilian Complaint Review Board, January 16, 1964, CORE Files, NYPDIR.
166. Felber, *Those Who Know Don't Say,* 45; Bouza, *Police Intelligence,* 34, 140.
167. Jack Mallon, William Federici, and Henry Lee, "Blame Hate Groups, Red & White, for Harlem Terror," *New York Daily News,* July 22, 1964.
168. Memo from SAC, NY, to FBI Director, March 26, 1964, reel 1, section 1, MMIFBI; memo from J. Edgar Hoover to Chicago and NY, March 23, 1964,
169. Memo from Director to SACs, May 22, 1964, reel 1, section 2, MMIFBI; Malcolm X FBI File, 100-399321, section 11, serials 109–26; memo from SAC, NY, to Director, June 1, 1964, reel 1, section 2, MMIFBI; memo from Director to SAC, NY, June 4, 1964, reel 1, section 2, MMIFBI.
170. Caulfield, *Caulfield, Shield #911-NYPD,* 83; Donner, *Protectors of Privilege,* 162–63; *Handschu v. Special Services Division, et al.,* May 18, 1971, 31; Felber, *Those Who Know Don't Say,* 114.
171. Memo from Sanford D. Garelick to Commanding Officer, August 7, 1961, box 02-045343, Large Organization Files, NYPDIR. This memo was sent to the chief of police in Portland, OR, in response to a request for information on how the NYPD dealt with Black radical organizations, specifically the Nation of Islam. As the counterintelligence agency of the nation's largest city, BOSS played a major role in shaping a national surveillance network through exchanging information and strategies with other municipalities and federal agencies.
172. Donner, *Protectors of Privilege,* 170–73.
173. William DeFossett, interview with Blackside.
174. Kaplan, "We Accuse"; Hart, *Memoirs of a Spy,* vi.
175. Gene Roberts, interview with Blackside; Marable, *Malcolm X,* 422.

176. Wood and Salado, *The Ray Wood Story;* Felber, "Malcolm X Assassination"; Rachell, "Incognegro" and "Incognegro, Part II."
177. Susan Brownmiller, "View from the Inside: I Remember Ray Wood," *The Village Voice,* June 3, 1965.
178. Wood also proposed robbing liquor stores to raise money for East River CORE. That fall, he infiltrated the RAM-affiliated Black Liberation Front and used the Statue of Liberty plan to frame Robert Collier, Khaleel Sayyed, and Walter Bowe, who were also members of the OAAU's security detail, days before Malcolm X was assassinated. Rachell, "Incognegro" and "Incognegro, Part II."
179. Donner, *Protectors of Privilege,* 175; Rachell, "Incognegro, Part II"; Wood and Salado, *The Ray Wood Story,* 40–41; Theodore Jones, "CORE Aide Is Sent to Bellevue for Attempt to Arrest Wagner," *NYT,* July 16, 1964.
180. Ulasewicz, *The President's Private Eye,* 156–57.
181. Michael J. Murphy, "Civil Rights and the Police: A Compilation of Speeches by Police Commissioner Michael J. Murphy," New York City Police Department, 1964, 22–24; Francis X. Clines, "Policemen Exhaust Their Ammunition in All-Night Battle," *NYT,* July 20, 1964.
182. Harlem Progressive Labor Movement, "Harlem Unite: Let Us Defend Ourselves!"
183. Harlem Action Group flier, May 1964, box 8, folder 13, NSM; handwritten notes from June 1964, box 8, folder 13, NSM.
184. Memo from Commanding Officer, BOSS, to Chief Inspector, June 15, 1964, box 34, folder 3, Large Organization Files, NYPDIR.
185. Mildred Thomas, "Harlem Mothers Organize to Save Their Sons," *Liberator* 4, no. 8 (August 1964): 10.
186. Though little documentation exists regarding Mallory's involvement, her archives include literature on the Harlem Six, and she references the case in fliers for her Organization of Militant Black Women. In addition to the unmistakable likeness of their name to the Monroe Defense Committee, the rhetoric and analyses in the Mothers Defense Committee fliers, as well as Mildred Thomas's article in *Liberator,* are suggestive of Mallory's involvement. Mallory continued her fight for the Harlem Six with her Organization of Militant Black Women as part of a broad, multi-issue platform "to be free by any means necessary." Organization of Militant Black Women leaflet, September 1964, box 2, folder 20, MMP.
187. Civilian Complaint Review Board, No. 498, New York City Council (1964), box 25, folder 37, MCHR.
188. City-Wide Committee for Fair Police Protection letter, May 13, 1964, box 25, folder 37, MCHR.
189. City-Wide Committee for Fair Police Protection letter.
190. Bronx CORE Newsletter, March 6, 1964, box 02-045343, CORE Files, NYPDIR; Harlem Action Group flier, May 1964, box 8, folder 13, NSM; handwritten notes from June 1964, box 8, folder 13, NSM.

191. "Police Brutality Hearing," box 24, folder 9, NSM; Thomas Buckley, "Unofficial Citizen Panel to Study Accusations of Police Brutality," *NYT,* May 23, 1964; Martin Gansberg, "CORE Sets Up Panel to Hear Police Charged with Brutality," *NYT,* June 5, 1964.
192. Buckley, "Unofficial Citizen Panel to Study Accusations of Police Brutality"; "Police Brutality Hearing."
193. Gansberg, "CORE Sets Up Panel to Hear Police Charged."
194. Executive Director's Report, 1964, box 1, folder 2, NSM.
195. City Wide Committee on Fair Police Protection, May 29, 1964, CORE; "CORE Pickets Seek Civil Police Panel," *NYT,* June 10, 1964.
196. Harlem Progressive Labor Movement, "Harlem Unite: Let Us Defend Ourselves!"
197. Memo from Commanding Officer, BOSS, to Chief Inspector, June 15, 1964, box 34, folder 3, Large Organization Files, NYPDIR; memo from Anton Weidinger to Commanding Officer, BOSS, June 27, 1964, box 34, folder 3, Large Organization Files, NYPDIR.
198. Report of William C. Kash, September 16, 1964, box E8, Epton, William Leo, Jr., Federal Records NACCD (Kerner Commission), Lyndon Baines Johnson Library. Thanks to David Goldberg for sharing this file with me.
199. Ahmad, *We Will Return in the Whirlwind,* 122–23; Ahmad, "Working with Malcolm X," Muhammad Ahmad (Max Stanford), Writings, Undated, folder 010629-017-0242, RAM.
200. "Dignity Plus Manhood Plus Freedom Equal Human Rights: A United Front Is a Victorious Front," June 22, 1964, box 14, folder 4, MXC; David Herman, "Malcolm X Announces Rally to Launch New Organization," *The Militant,* June 29, 1964.
201. OAAU Working Paper, June 6, 1964, box 14, folder 3, MXC.
202. OAAU Working Paper, June 6, 1964.
203. "Notes on an Organization and Possible Issues Around Which to Struggle and Raise the Level of Consciousness of the People," box 14, folder 3, MXC; Felber, "Harlem Is the Black World," 203.
204. OAAU Working Paper, June 6, 1964.
205. OAAU Working Paper, June 6, 1964; OAAU Working Paper, June 14, 1964, box 14, folder 3, MXC; "Notes on an Organization and Possible Issues Around Which to Struggle."
206. Sales, *From Civil Rights to Black Liberation,* 106; Ahmad, *We Will Return in the Whirlwind,* 172.
207. OAAU Working Paper, June 6, 1964.
208. Statement of Basic Aims and Objectives of the Organization of Afro-American Unity, June 28, 1964, in Clarke, *Malcolm X: The Man and His Times,* 335–42.
209. Felber, "Harlem Is the Black World"; Sales, *From Civil Rights to Black Liberation,* 106–10.

210. Ahmad, "Working with Malcolm X."
211. Statement of Basic Aims and Objectives of the Organization of Afro-American Unity, June 28, 1964.
212. Memo from Ernest B. Latty to Commanding Officer, BOSS, July 6, 1964, BSS 334 M 1964, Correspondence Files, NYPDIR.
213. Executive Secretary's Report, June 1964, box 4, folder 1, JHP; "Harlem Warns City on Stop Frisk Law," *NYAN,* July 4, 1964.
214. Murphy, "Civil Rights and the Police," 31-32.
215. "Midnight-to-8 Shift Does Second Tour at City Hall," *NYT,* June 17, 1964; M. S. Johnson, *Street Justice,* 233.
216. Fred Gilman, "Anti-Brutality Bill Bottled Up; Police Pressure Hearing," *The Worker,* June 23, 1964; letter from Jane Benedict to Robert F. Wagner, June 23, 1964, box 25, folder 37, MCHR; Charles G. Bennett, "Police Decry Bill for Review Panel," *NYT,* June 17, 1964.
217. Bennett, "Police Decry Bill for Review Panel"; Gilman, "Anti-Brutality Bill Bottled Up."
218. Memo from SAC, New York, to Director, FBI, June 15, 1964, reel 1, section 3, MMIFBI.
219. Charles G. Bennett, "Rise in Cab Fares Meets Roadblock," *NYT,* July 8, 1964; "Guns in the City," *NYT,* June 26, 1964.
220. Harlem Progressive Labor Movement, "The Plot Against Black America"; "Dignity Plus Manhood Plus Freedom Equal Human Rights: A United Front Is a Victorious Front," June 22, 1964, box 14, folder 4, MXC.
221. "The Racist U.S.A.—The Torch of Retribution," *The Crusader,* May–June 1964, 1; letter from Anne Olsen to Rob and Mabel Williams, September 1, 1964, RFWP.
222. "USA: The Potential of a Minority Revolution," *The Crusader,* May–June 1964, 5-7.
223. "USA: The Potential of a Minority Revolution," 5-7.
224. "USA: The Potential of a Minority Revolution," 5-7.
225. While police, politicians, and the press often seize on the kinds of rhetoric and information Williams shared as evidence that uprisings or rebellions are planned and coordinated by subversive organizations (in order to criminalize and suppress dissent), I make no such claim here. The ideas and tactics of Williams, Malcolm X, and others were rational conclusions for the survival and liberation of Black communities in a city and nation that met legitimate demands for rights and power with violence and terrorism.
226. Harlem Progressive Labor Movement, "The Plot Against Black America."
227. Touré explained in the article that "Mose" was "a complimentary name derived from the pharaohs: Thutmost, Ahmose, Ramose, etc." Rolland Snellings, "Unchain the Lion," *Liberator* 4, no. 7 (July 1964): 20-21.
228. In response to sensational racist stories in June about random acts of violence in the subways committed by Black teenagers, Roy Wilkins denounced "Negro hoodlums," "punks," and "Harlem and Brooklyn morons"

for "undercutting and wrecking the gains" made by the civil rights movement. "Wilkins Denounces Negro 'Hoodlums,'" *NYT*, June 24, 1964.
229. Snellings, "Unchain the Lion."
230. Theodore Jones, "Negro Boy Killed; 300 Harass Police," *NYT*, July 17, 1964. For more detailed coverage of the series of events surrounding Powell's murder and the subsequent rebellion in Harlem, see Flamm, *In the Heat of the Summer,* and C. Hayes, *The Harlem Uprising.*
231. "Text of Report by District Attorney on Investigation into Gilligan Case," *NYT*, September 2, 1964; Jones, "Negro Boy Killed"; C. Hayes, *The Harlem Uprising*, 110–12; Flamm, *In the Heat of the Summer,* 10–15.
232. Jones, "Negro Boy Killed"; C. Hayes, *The Harlem Uprising,* 113–15.
233. Theodore Jones, "Teen-Age Parade Protests Killing," *NYT,* July 18, 1964.
234. Shapiro and Sullivan, *Race Riots,* 12–15.
235. Malcolm X Address to the Organization of African Unity, July 17, 1964, box 1, folder 6, OAAU Papers, Schomburg Center for Research in Black Culture.
236. "Mother Hysterical at Boy's Bier," *NYT,* July 19, 1964.
237. Progressive Labor Party, "The Case of Bill Epton," January 1968, 1, in author's possession; Harlem Defense Council, "Police Terror in Harlem," 5, box 18, folder 19, James and Grace Lee Boggs Papers, Walter P. Reuther Library, Archives of Labor and Urban Affairs. For BOSS detective Abe Hart's account of the rally, see Hart, *Memoirs of a Spy,* 76–81.
238. Peter Bailey, OAAU Newsletter, July 18, 1964. Thanks to the late Prof. John H. Bracey Jr. for sharing this document with me.
239. Paul L. Montgomery, "Night of Riots Began with Calm Rally," *NYT,* July 20, 1964; Flamm, *In the Heat of the Summer,* 80–81; C. Hayes, *The Harlem Uprising,* 116–17.
240. James Booker, "As Jimmy Booker Saw the Rioting," *NYAN,* July 25, 1964.
241. Montgomery, "Night of Riots Began with Calm Rally"; C. Hayes, *The Harlem Uprising,* 117–18; Harlem Defense Council, "Police Terror in Harlem," 5–6.
242. Harlem Defense Council, "Police Terror in Harlem," 5–6.
243. Montgomery, "Night of Riots Began with Calm Rally"; Flamm, *In the Heat of the Summer,* 84–85; C. Hayes, *The Harlem Uprising,* 117–18.
244. Booker, "As Jimmy Booker Saw the Rioting."
245. Harlem Defense Council, "Police Terror in Harlem," 5–6.

CONCLUSION

1. For a sampling of news coverage, see Junius Griffin, "Harlem Businessmen Put Riot Losses at $50,000," *NYT,* July 21, 1964; "Harlem and the Police," *NYT,* July 21, 1964; Peter Kihss, "Screvane Links Reds to Rioting," *NYT,* July 22, 1964.

2. "Text of Wagner's Radio-TV Appeal for Restoration of Law and Order in City," *NYT,* July 23, 1964, 12. Commissioner Murphy was even more direct, explaining that "in our estimation, this is a crime problem and not a social problem." "Texts of Screvane and Murphy Appeals," *NYT,* July 20, 1964.
3. Flamm, *In the Heat of the Summer,* 180.
4. Ossie Sykes, "Harlem Report," *Liberator* 4, no. 9 (September 1964): 4-5.
5. Sylvester Leaks, "Writer Underscores Basic Facts Behind Riot That Shocked the World," *Muhammad Speaks,* August 14, 1964.
6. Halstead et al., *Harlem Stirs,* 40.
7. Harlem Defense Council, "Police Terror in Harlem," 1965.
8. Du Bois, "Of the Culture of White Folk," 442.
9. Killens, *Black Man's Burden,* 93.
10. Letter from Mae Mallory to Sir, February 1961, box 2, folder 10, MMP.
11. Flamm, *In the Heat of the Summer,* 101-2, 220.
12. These included the United Council of Harlem Organizations (Harlem Unity Council) and OAAU, each of which sought to build united front formations to translate the power of the rebellion into concrete programs for Black liberation. Notable members of the Unity Council included HARYOU, HAG, OAAU, UANM, NAACP, HWG, Freedom Now Party, East River CORE, and the Eloise Moore Memorial Committee. Memo from Commanding Officer, BOSS, to Chief Inspector, August 24, 1964, BSS 419-M, Correspondence Files, NYP-DIR. For more on the Harlem Unity Council and the OAAU after the rebellion, see Felber, *Those Who Know Don't Say,* 161-64; Felber, "Harlem Is the Black World," 207-8.
13. The conference also featured an address by Victoria Gray of the Mississippi Freedom Democratic Party, who was in Harlem along with Fannie Lou Hamer at the invitation of Malcolm X and Bill Strickland to generate support for the MFDP. The workshop topics were education (Galamison), housing (Gray), unemployment (Haughton), political action for institutional change (Strickland), and culture (Clarke). Program for a Political Action Conference: The Black Revolution—A Struggle for Political Power, box 14, folder 3, MXC.
14. Jesse Gray, "The Black Revolution—A Struggle for Political Power," Keynote Address at the Federation for Independent Political Action Conference, December 19, 1964, box 15, folder 6, JHP.
15. J. Boggs, "The City Is the Black Man's Land," 44-47.
16. According to Rhonda Y. Williams, Malcolm X declined an invitation from Max Stanford (Muhammad Ahmad) to help build the OBP. Williams, *Concrete Demands,* 109.
17. J. Boggs, "The City Is the Black Man's Land," 44-47; Ahmad, *We Will Return in the Whirlwind,* 143. According to Ahmad, "The purpose was to raise the position that the struggle for black power was a struggle for black state power and not just for black independent political power" and the purpose of OBP was to

"organize the African-American people to politically take over large metropolitan areas in the 1970s."
18. Among those in attendance at the OBP's founding conference were James and Grace Lee Boggs, Don Freeman, Jesse Gray, Julius Hobson, Nahazz Rogers, and Bill Strickland. Ahmad, *We Will Return in the Whirlwind,* 143.
19. Strickland, interview with Mosnier.

BIBLIOGRAPHY

MANUSCRIPTS AND ARCHIVES

BLACK POWER MOVEMENT MICROFORM COLLECTION

The Papers of Robert F. Williams
Papers of the Revolutionary Action Movement, 1962–1996

ERNEST ALLEN JR. COLLECTION

The Black Power Movement CD-ROM

LYNDON BAINES JOHNSON LIBRARY

National Advisory Commission on Civil Disorders

NEW YORK CITY MUNICIPAL ARCHIVE

Board of Education Collection
John Carro Files
Hulan Jack Papers
New York Police Department Intelligence Records, 1930–1990
Robert F. Wagner Papers

SCHOMBURG CENTER FOR RESEARCH IN BLACK CULTURE, NEW YORK PUBLIC LIBRARY

John Henrik Clarke Papers
James Haughton Papers
Harry Haywood Papers
Kenneth Marshall Papers

August Meier Papers
Northern Student Movement Records
Jack O'Dell Papers
The Papers of the Congress of Racial Equality, 1941-1967 [microfilm]
Malcolm X Collection [microfilm]

TAMIMENT LIBRARY AND ROBERT F. WAGNER LABOR ARCHIVES, NEW YORK UNIVERSITY LIBRARIES

Metropolitan Council on Housing Records
Oral History of the American Left Collection
Printed Ephemera Collection on the National Maritime Union

WALTER P. REUTHER LIBRARY, ARCHIVES OF LABOR AND URBAN AFFAIRS, WAYNE STATE UNIVERSITY

James and Grace Lee Boggs Papers
Mae Mallory Papers

WASHINGTON UNIVERSITY LIBRARIES

Henry Hampton Collection

INTERVIEWS

Anthony, Carl, Andrea Cousins, Jean Doak, David Henderson, Marilyn Lowen, and Kathie Rogers McQuarrie. Interview with author. February 20, 2021. Zoom.
Anthony, Carl, and Jean Doak. Interview with author. November 10, 2019. Berkeley, CA.
Bailey, Peter. Interview with Robert Martin. September 4, 1968. RBOHC.
Clarke, John Henrik. Interview with Blackside, Inc. June 30, 1992. HHC.
Countryman, Peter. Interview with Katherine Shannon. January 11, 1968. RBOHC.
Cousins, Andrea. Interview with author. March 20, 2021. Zoom.
———. Interview with author. October 19, 2017. Northampton, MA.
DeFossett, William. Interview with Blackside, Inc. June 23, 1992. HHC.
Fletcher, Bob. Interview with author. September 11, 2019. Telephone.
Gray, Jesse. Interview with Harry Haywood. April 6, 1975. HHP.
———. Interview with Katherine M. Shannon. July 26, 1967. RBOHC.
Hand, Q. R. Interview with author. November 10, 2019. Vallejo, CA.

Hicks, Calvin. Interview with The HistoryMakers. October 15, 2004.
Hill, Norman. Interview with August Meier. August 2, 1971. AMP.
———. Interview with August Meier. December 15, 1970. AMP.
———. Interview with August Meier. May 24, 1969. AMP.
Hill, Norman, and Velma Hill. Interview with August Meier. February 1964. Box 56, folder 8, AMP.
Hill, Velma. Interview with August Meier. July 1971. AMP.
Huie, William Bradford. Interview with Blackside, Inc. August 30, 1979. HHC.
Hutchings, Phil. Interview with author. January 26, 2017. Telephone.
Innis, Doris. Interview with August Meier. October 12, 1971. Box 56, folder 9, AMP.
Karim, Benjamin. Interview with Blackside, Inc. June 27, 1992. HHC.
Landry, Lawrence. Interview with John H. Britton. September 7, 1967. RBOHC.
Mallory, Mae. Interview with Malaika Lumumba. 1970. RBOHC.
Mangum, Robert. Interview with Blackside, Inc. June 23, 1992. HHC.
McDonald, Jimmy. Interview with James Mosby. November 5, 1969. RBOHC.
McQuarrie, Kathie Rogers. Interview with author. February 13, 2021. Zoom.
———. Interview with author. January 15, 2021. Telephone.
Moore, Queen Mother Audley. Interview with Mark Naison. 1972. OHALC.
———. Interview with Ruth Prago. December 23, 1981. OHALC.
O'Dell, Jack. Interview with James Early. May 13, 1997. JOP.
Parks, Gordon. Interview with Blackside, Inc. 1992. HHC.
Rahman, Amina. Interview with Blackside, Inc. 1992. HHC.
Rich, Marvin. Interview with James Mosby. November 6, 1969. RBOHC.
Richardson Dandridge, Gloria. Interview with author. April 19, 2018. Telephone.
———. Interview with Blackside, Inc. July 1, 1992. HHC.
Roberts, Gene. Interview with Blackside, Inc. June 30, 1992. HHC.
Sanchez, Sonia. Interview with Blackside, Inc. March 7, 1989. HHC.
Strickland, William Lamar. Interview with author. May 31, 2018. New York, NY.
———. Interview with author. October 20, 2017. Amherst, MA.
———. Interview with Joseph Mosnier. September 23, 2011. US Civil Rights History Project, Library of Congress.
Wagner, Robert Ferdinand. Reminiscences of Robert Ferdinand Wagner: oral history. 1979. Columbia Center for Oral History, Columbia University Libraries.
Wallace, Mike. Interview with Blackside, Inc. October 12, 1988. HHC.
Wilson, C. E., and Leroy Baylor. Interview with author. March 2, 2018. New York, NY.

SECONDARY SOURCES

Abu-Lughod, Janet. *Race, Space, and Riots in Chicago, New York, and Los Angeles*. Oxford University Press, 2007.

Ahmad, Muhammad. *We Will Return in the Whirlwind: Black Radical Organizations, 1960–1975.* Charles H. Kerr, 2007.

Alami, Aida. "The Man Who Drove Malcolm X Around and Introduced Him to Fidel Castro." *Africa Is a Country,* November 2, 2017.

Anderson, Martin. *The Federal Bulldozer: A Critical Analysis of Urban Renewal, 1949–1962.* MIT Press, 1964.

Angelou, Maya. *The Heart of a Woman.* Bantam, 1997.

Anthony, Carl. *The Earth, the City, and the Hidden Narrative of Race.* New Village Press, 2017.

Back, Adina. "Exposing the 'Whole Segregation Myth': The Harlem Nine and New York City's School Desegregation Battles." In *Freedom North: Black Freedom Struggles Outside the South, 1940–1980,* edited by Jeanne F. Theoharis and Komozi Woodard. Palgrave Macmillan, 2003.

———. "Up South in New York: The 1950s School Desegregation Struggles." PhD diss., New York University, 1997.

Baker, Ella. "Developing Community Leadership." In *Black Women in White America,* edited by Gerda Lerner. Vintage, 1992.

Baldwin, James. "The Dangerous Road Before Martin Luther King." In *The Price of the Ticket: Collected Nonfiction 1948–1985,* by James Baldwin. St. Martin's-Marek, 1985.

———. *The Fire Next Time.* Vintage International, 1991.

———. *Nobody Knows My Name.* Dell, 1962.

Baraka, Amiri. *The Autobiography of LeRoi Jones.* Lawrence Hill Books, 1997.

———. "The Black Arts Movement." In *SOS—Calling All Black People: A Black Arts Movement Reader,* edited by John H. Bracey Jr., Sonia Sanchez, and James Smethurst. University of Massachusetts Press, 2014.

Biondi, Martha. *To Stand and Fight: The Struggle for Civil Rights in Postwar New York City.* Harvard University Press, 2003.

Blain, Keisha N. *Set the World on Fire: Black Nationalist Women and the Global Struggle for Freedom.* University of Pennsylvania Press, 2018.

Bobo, Nab Eddie. "Carlos Cooks: African Nationalism's Missing Link." In Smith and Sinclair, *The Harlem Cultural/Politics Movements.*

Boggs, Grace Lee. *Living for Change: An Autobiography.* University of Minnesota Press, 2016.

Boggs, James. "The City Is the Black Man's Land." In *Racism and the Class Struggle: Further Pages from a Black Worker's Notebook,* by James Boggs. Monthly Review Press, 1970.

Bouza, Anthony J. *Police Intelligence: The Operations of an Investigative Unit.* AMS Press, 1976.

Burgin, Say. *Organizing Your Own: The White Fight for Black Power in Detroit.* New York University Press, 2024.

Burrell, Kristopher Bryan. "Black Women as Activist Intellectuals: Ella Baker and Mae Mallory Combat Northern Jim Crow in New York City's Public Schools During the 1950s." In *The Strange Careers of the Jim Crow North: Segregation and Struggle*

Outside of the South, edited by Brian Purnell and Jeanne Theoharis, with Komozi Woodard. New York University Press, 2019.

Cannato, Vincent J. *The Ungovernable City: John Lindsay and His Struggle to Save New York.* Basic Books, 2001.

Carroll, Tamar W. *Mobilizing New York: AIDS, Antipoverty, and Feminist Activism.* University of North Carolina Press, 2015.

Caulfield, John. *Caulfield, Shield #911-NYPD.* iUniverse, 2012.

Cazenave, Noel A. *Impossible Democracy: The Unlikely Success of the War on Poverty Community Action Programs.* SUNY Press, 2007.

Chronopoulos, Themis. "Police Misconduct, Community Opposition, and Urban Governance in New York City, 1945-65." *Journal of Urban History* 44, no. 4 (2015): 643-68.

Churchville, John Elliott. *Driven! Remembrance, Reflection, and Revelation.* Infinity, 2013.

Clark, Kenneth B. *Dark Ghetto: Dilemmas of Social Power.* Harper Torchbooks, 1965.

Clarke, John Henrik. "Journey to the Sierra Maestra." *Freedomways* 1 (Spring 1961): 32-35.

———, ed. *Harlem USA.* A&B Books Publishers, 1971.

———, ed. *Malcolm X: The Man and His Times.* With A. Peter Bailey and Earl Grant. Africa World Press, 1990.

———. "The New Afro-American Nationalism." *Freedomways* 1, no. 3 (Fall 1961): 285-95.

Cobb, Charles. *This Nonviolent Stuff'll Get You Killed: How Guns Made the Civil Rights Movement Possible.* Duke University Press, 2015.

Cooks, Carlos. "Gamal Abdel Nassar; Marcus Garvey Day (May-December 1955)." In *Carlos Cooks and Black Nationalism from Garvey to Malcolm,* edited by Robert Harris, Nyota Harris, and Grandassa Harris. Majority Press, 1992.

Countryman, Matthew. *Up South: Civil Rights and Black Power in Philadelphia.* University of Pennsylvania Press, 2006.

Cronon, E. David. *Black Moses: The Story of Marcus Garvey and the Universal Negro Improvement Association.* University of Wisconsin Press, 1969.

Crosby, Emilye, ed. *Civil Rights History from the Ground Up: Local Struggles, a National Movement.* University of Georgia Press, 2011.

Cruse, Harold. *The Crisis of the Negro Intellectual: A Historical Analysis of the Failure of Black Leadership.* Quill, 1984.

———. "Revolutionary Nationalism and the Afro-American." In *Rebellion or Revolution?,* by Harold Cruse. William Morrow, 1968.

Curvin, Robert. *Inside Newark: Decline, Rebellion, and the Search for Transformation.* Rutgers University Press, 2014.

Dagbovie, Pero Gaglo. *African American History Reconsidered.* University of Illinois Press, 2010.

Dickson, Sandra, and Churchill Roberts, dirs. *Negroes with Guns: Rob Williams and Black Power* 2005. San Francisco: California Newsreel, 2005.

Dillard, Angela D. *Faith in the City: Preaching Radical Social Change in Detroit.* University of Michigan Press, 2007.

Dinkins, David N. *A Mayor's Life: Governing New York's Gorgeous Mosaic.* PublicAffairs, 2013.

Dittmer, John. *Local People: The Struggle for Civil Rights in Mississippi.* University of Illinois Press, 1995.

Donner, Frank. *Protectors of Privilege: Red Squads and Police Repression in Urban America.* University of California Press, 1992.

Du Bois, W. E. Burghardt. "Of the Culture of White Folk." *Journal of Race Development* 7, no. 4 (1917): 434–47.

Dworkin, Ira. *Congolese Love Song: African American Culture and the Crisis of the Colonial State.* University of North Carolina Press, 2017.

Elkins, Alexander B. "Battle of the Corner: Urban Policing and Rioting in the United States, 1943–1971." PhD diss., Temple University, 2017.

Engels, Friedrich. *The Housing Question.* Leopard Books, 2016.

Erickson, Ansley T. "HARYOU: An Apprenticeship for Young Leaders." In Erickson and Morrell, *Educating Harlem.*

Erickson, Ansley T., and Ernest Morrell, eds. *Educating Harlem: A Century of Schooling and Resistance in a Black Community.* Columbia University Press, 2019.

Essien-Udom, E. U. *Black Nationalism: A Search for an Identity in America.* Dell, 1968.

Farmer, Ashley D. *Remaking Black Power: How Black Women Transformed an Era.* University of North Carolina Press, 2017.

Fearnley, Andrew M., and Daniel Matlin, eds. *Race Capital? Harlem as Setting and Symbol.* Columbia University Press, 2019.

Felber, Garrett. "'Harlem Is the Black World': The Organization of Afro-American Unity at the Grassroots." *Journal of African American History* 100, no. 2 (Spring 2015): 199–225.

———. "Malcolm X Assassination: 50 Years on, Mystery Still Clouds Details of the Case." *The Guardian,* February 21, 2015.

———. *Those Who Know Don't Say: The Nation of Islam, the Black Freedom Movement, and the Carceral State.* University of North Carolina Press, 2020.

Felker-Kantor, Max. *Policing Los Angeles: Race, Resistance, and the Rise of the LAPD.* University of North Carolina Press, 2018.

Fernández, Johanna. *The Young Lords: A Radical History.* University of North Carolina Press, 2020.

Fitzgerald, Joseph R. *The Struggle Is Eternal: Gloria Richardson and Black Liberation.* University Press of Kentucky, 2018.

Flamm, Michael. *In the Heat of the Summer: The New York Riots of 1964 and the War on Crime.* University of Pennsylvania Press, 2017.

Foong, Yie. "Frame Up in Monroe: The Mae Mallory Story." MA thesis, Sarah Lawrence College, 2010.

Forman, James. *The Making of Black Revolutionaries.* University of Washington Press, 2000.
Freeman, Don. *Reflections of a Resolute Radical.* Self-published, 2017.
Friendly, Fred W. "The Harlem Temper." CBS. New York, NY, December 11, 1963.
Glass, Michael R. "From Sword to Shield to Myth: Facing the Facts of *De Facto* School Segregation." *Journal of Urban History* 44, no. 6 (2018): 1197–226.
Gold, Roberta. *When Tenants Claimed the City: The Struggle for Citizenship in New York City Housing.* University of Illinois Press, 2014.
Goldberg, David, and Trevor Griffey, eds. *Black Power at Work: Community Control, Affirmative Action, and the Construction Industry.* Cornell University Press, 2010.
Goldman, Peter. *The Death and Life of Malcolm X.* University of Illinois Press, 1979.
Gore, Dayo F. "From Communist Politics to Black Power: The Visionary Politics and Transnational Solidarities of Victoria 'Vicki' Ama Garvin." In *Want to Start a Revolution? Radical Women in the Black Freedom Struggle,* edited by Dayo F. Gore, Jeanne Theoharis, and Komozi Woodard. NYU Press, 2009.
Greenberg, Cheryl Lynn. *Or Does It Explode? Black Harlem in the Great Depression.* Oxford University Press, 1991.
Griffin, Farah Jasmine. *Harlem Nocturne: Women Artists and Progressive Politics During World War II.* Basic Civitas, 2013.
———. "'Ironies of the Saint': Malcolm X, Black Women, and the Price of Protection." In *Sisters in the Struggle: African American Women in the Civil Rights–Black Power Movement,* edited by Bettye Collier-Thomas and V. P. Franklin. NYU Press, 2001.
Guy, Rosa. "Castro in New York." *Black Renaissance* 1, no. 1 (October 1996): 10–20.
Haley, Alex, and Malcolm X. *The Autobiography of Malcolm X as Told to Alex Haley.* Ballantine, 1992.
Hall, Simon. *Ten Days in Harlem: Fidel Castro and the Making of the 1960s.* Faber and Faber, 2020.
Halstead, Fred, et al. *Harlem Stirs.* Marzani & Munsell, 1966.
Hampton, Henry, and Steve Fayer. *Voices of Freedom.* Bantam, 1990.
Harlem Youth Opportunities Unlimited [HARYOU]. *Youth in the Ghetto: A Study of the Consequences of Powerlessness and a Blueprint for Change.* HARYOU, 1964.
Harley, Sharon. "'Chronicle of a Death Foretold': Gloria Richardson, the Cambridge Movement, and the Radical Black Activist Tradition." In *Sisters in the Struggle: African American Women in the Civil Rights–Black Power Movement,* edited by Bettye Collier-Thomas and V. P. Franklin. NYU Press, 2001.
Harris, LaShawn. *Sex Workers, Psychics, and Numbers Runners: Black Women in New York City's Underground Economy.* University of Illinois Press, 2016.
Hart, Adolph "Abe." *Memoirs of a Spy.* 1st Books, 2004.
Hayes, Christopher. *The Harlem Uprising: Segregation and Inequality in Postwar New York City.* Columbia University Press, 2021.
Hayes, Robin J. *Love for Liberation: African Independence, Black Power, and a Diaspora Underground.* University of Washington Press, 2021.

Hill, Laura Warren. *Strike the Hammer: The Black Freedom Struggle in Rochester, New York, 1940-1970.* Cornell University Press, 2021.

Hinton, Elizabeth. *America on Fire: The Untold History of Police Violence and Black Rebellion Since the 1960s.* Liveright, 2021.

———. *From the War on Poverty to the War on Crime: The Making of Mass Incarceration in America.* Harvard University Press, 2016.

Horne, Gerald. *Black Liberation/Red Scare: Ben Davis and the Communist Party.* International Publishers, 2020.

———. *Fire This Time: The Watts Uprising and the 1960s.* Da Capo, 1997.

———. *Red Seas: Ferdinand Smith and Radical Black Sailors in the United States and Jamaica.* New York University Press, 2005.

Hudson, James R. "Police Review Boards and Police Accountability." *Law and Contemporary Problems* 36, no. 4 (1971): 515-38.

Hughes, Langston. *Letters from Langston: From the Harlem Renaissance to the Red Scare and Beyond,* edited by Evelyn Louise Crawford and MaryLouise Patterson. University of California Press, 2016.

Hussain, Khuram. "Dreaming Differently About Freedom: Malcolm X and *Muhammad Speaks.*" *Journal of African American Studies* 24, no. 3 (September 2020): 319-36.

Jackson, Mandi Isaacs. "Harlem's Rent Strike and Rat War: Representation, Housing Access and Tenant Resistance in New York, 1958-1964." *American Studies* 47, no. 1 (Spring 2006): 53-79.

James, Winston. *Holding Aloft the Banner of Ethiopia: Caribbean Radicalism in Early Twentieth-Century America.* Verso, 2020.

Johnson, Cedric. *Revolutionaries to Race Leaders: Black Power and the Making of African American Politics.* University of Minnesota Press, 2007.

Johnson, James Weldon. "The Making of Harlem." *Survey Graphic* 53 no. 11 (1925): 635-39.

Johnson, Marilynn S. *Street Justice: A History of Police Violence in New York City.* Beacon, 2003.

Johnstone, Charles. "The Tenants' Movement and Housing Struggles in Glasgow, 1945-1990." PhD diss., University of Glasgow, 1992.

Jones, LeRoi. "Cuba Libre." In *Home: Social Essays,* by LeRoi Jones. William Morrow, 1966.

Joseph, Peniel E., ed. *The Black Power Movement: Rethinking the Civil Rights–Black Power Era.* Routledge, 2006.

———. *Waiting 'Til the Midnight Hour: A Narrative History of Black Power in America.* Holt, 2006.

———. "Waiting *till the* Midnight Hour: Reconceptualizing the Heroic Period of the Civil Rights Movement, 1954-1965." *Souls* 2, no. 2 (2000): 6-17.

Kaplan, Joseph. "'We Accuse': The Harlem Rebellion, Bill Epton's Anti-Carceral Activism, and the Rise of the Surveillance State." *Gotham Center for New York City History,* August 24, 2021.

Kelley, Robin D. G. *Freedom Dreams: The Black Radical Imagination.* Beacon, 2022.
Killens, John Oliver. *Black Man's Burden.* Pocket Books, 1969.
King, Shannon. *Whose Harlem Is This, Anyway? Community Politics and Grassroots Activism During the New Negro Era.* New York University Press, 2015.
Lardner, James, and Thomas Repetto. *NYPD: A City and Its Police.* Henry Holt, 2000.
Lawson, Ronald, Stephen Barton, and Jenna Weissman Joselit. "From Kitchen to Storefront: Women in the Tenant Movement." In *New Space for Women,* edited by Gerda R. Wekerle et al. Westview Press, 1980.
Lee, Sonia Song-Ha. *Building a Latino Civil Rights Movement: Puerto Ricans, African Americans, and the Pursuit of Racial Justice in New York City.* University of North Carolina Press, 2014.
Leuci, Robert. *All the Centurions: A New York City Cop Remembers His Years on the Street, 1961–1981.* William Morrow, 2004.
Levy, Peter B. *The Great Uprising: Race Riots in Urban America During the 1960s.* Cambridge University Press, 2018.
Lincoln, C. Eric. *The Black Muslims in America.* Beacon, 1961.
Lipsky, Michael. *Protest in City Politics: Rent Strikes, Housing and the Power of the Poor.* Rand McNally, 1970.
Locke, Alain. "Harlem." *Survey Graphic* 53, no. 11 (1925): 629–30.
Lomax, Louis E. *The Negro Revolt.* Harper & Row 1962.
———. *When the Word Is Given.* Signet, 1963.
Lomax, Louis E., Mike Wallace, and Ted Yates Jr. "The Hate That Hate Produced." *News Beat,* WNTA-TV. New York City, NY, July 23, 1959.
Louis, Debbie. *And We Are Not Saved: A History of the Movement as People.* Doubleday, 1970.
Lynn, Conrad. *There Is a Fountain: The Autobiography of Conrad Lynn.* Lawrence Hill Books, 1993.
Makalani, Minkah. *In the Cause of Freedom: Radical Black Internationalism from Harlem to London, 1917–1939.* University of North Carolina Press, 2011.
Mallory, Mae. *Letters from Prison by Mae Mallory: The Story of a Frame Up.* Monroe Defense Committee, 1963.
———. "Memo from a Monroe Jail." *Freedomways* 4, no. 1 (1964): 203–14.
Marable, Manning. *Malcolm X: A Life of Reinvention.* Penguin, 2011.
Mathes, Carter A. "Scratching the Threshold: Textual Sound and Political Form in Toni Cade Bambara's 'The Salt Eaters.'" *Contemporary Literature* 50, no. 2 (2009): 363–96.
Mayfield, Julian. "And Then Came Baldwin." In *Harlem USA,* edited by John Henrik Clarke. A&B, 1971.
———. "Challenge to Negro Leadership." *Commentary,* April 1961.
———. "The Cuban Challenge." *Freedomways* 1, no. 2 (Summer 1961): 185–89.
McAdam, Doug. *Political Process and the Development of Black Insurgency, 1930–1970.* University of Chicago Press, 1982.

McDuffie, Erik S. *Sojourning for Freedom: Black Women, American Communism, and the Making of Black Left Feminism.* Duke University Press, 2011.

———. "'We Owe a Debt to Her, She Taught Us How to Think': Eloise Moore and Her Impact on Queen Mother Moore and Twentieth-Century Grassroots Black Nationalism." *Palimpsest: A Journal on Women, Gender, and the Black International* 7, no. 2 (2018): 135-58.

McDuffie, Erik S., and Komozi Woodard. "If You're in a Country That's Progressive, the Woman Is Progressive." *Biography* 36, no. 3 (Summer 2013): 507-39.

Mealy, Rosmari. *Fidel and Malcolm X: Memories of a Meeting.* Ocean Press, 1993.

Meier, August, and Elliott Rudwick. *CORE: A Study in the Civil Rights Movement, 1942-1968.* Oxford University Press, 1973.

Miller, Karen R. *Managing Inequality: Northern Racial Liberalism in Interwar Detroit.* New York University Press, 2015.

Morris, Aldon. *The Origins of the Civil Rights Movement: Black Communities Organizing for Change.* Free Press, 1984.

Munro, John. *The Anticolonial Front: The African American Freedom Struggle and Global Decolonization, 1945-1960.* Cambridge University Press, 2017.

Naison, Mark. *Communists in Harlem during the Depression.* University of Illinois Press, 1983.

———. "The Rent Strikes in New York." *Radical America* 1, no. 3 (November-December 1967): 7-49.

Navasky, Victor S. *The O'Dell File: A Kindle Single.* Victor S. Navasky, 2014. Kindle.

Nelson, Truman. *The Torture of Mothers.* Beacon, 1965.

Ngũgĩ wa Thiong'o. *Decolonising the Mind: The Politics of Language in African Liberation.* James Currey, 2006.

O'Dell, J. H. "The July Rebellions and the 'Military State.'" *Freedomways* 7, no. 4 (Fall 1967): 288-301.

O'Dell, Jack. *Climbin' Jacob's Ladder: The Black Freedom Movement Writings of Jack O'Dell,* edited by Nikhil Pal Singh. University of California Press, 2010.

Ogbar, Jeffrey O. G. *Black Power: Radical Politics and African American Identity.* Johns Hopkins University Press, 2004.

O'Neil, Jim. *A Cop's Tale—NYPD The Violent Years.* With Mel Fazzino. Barricade Books, 2009.

Osofsky, Gilbert. *Harlem: The Making of a Ghetto.* Elephant Paperbacks, 1996.

Payne, Charles M. *I've Got the Light of Freedom: The Organizing Tradition and the Mississippi Freedom Struggle.* University of California Press, 2007.

Plummer, Brenda Gayle. "Castro in Harlem: A Cold War Watershed." In *Rethinking the Cold War,* edited by Allen Hunter. Temple University Press, 1998.

———. *In Search of Power: African Americans in the Era of Decolonization, 1956-1974.* Cambridge University Press, 2013.

Powell, Adam Clayton, Jr. *Marching Blacks.* Dial Press, 1973.

Preacely, Peggy Trotter Dammond. "It Was Simply in My Blood." In *Hands on the Freedom Plow: Personal Accounts by Women in SNCC,* edited by Faith S. Holsaert et al. University of Illinois Press, 2010.

Purnell, Brian. *Fighting Jim Crow in the County of Kings: The Congress of Racial Equality in Brooklyn.* University of Kentucky Press, 2013.

Purnell, Brian, and Jeanne Theoharis, eds. *The Strange Careers of the Jim Crow North: Segregation and Struggle Outside of the South.* With Komozi Woodard. NYU Press, 2019.

Rachell, L. E. J. "Incognegro: How Law Enforcement Spies on Black Radical Groups." *History News Network,* October 6, 2019.

———. "Incognegro, Part II: How New York Law Enforcement Worked to Destroy CORE." *History News Network,* March 21, 2021.

Rampersad, Arnold. Introduction to *The New Negro: Voices of the Harlem Renaissance,* edited by Alain Locke. Touchstone, 1997.

Ransby, Barbara. "Cops, Schools, and Communism: Local Politics and Global Ideologies—New York City in the 1950s." In *Civil Rights in New York City: From World War II to the Giuliani Era,* edited by Clarence Taylor. Fordham University Press, 2011.

———. *Ella Baker and the Black Freedom Movement: A Radical Democratic Vision.* University of North Carolina Press, 2003.

Rice, Florence. "It Takes a While to Realize That It Is Discrimination." In *Black Women in White America,* edited by Gerda Lerner. Vintage, 1992.

Rivera, Pedro R. "Carlos Cooks and Garveyism: Bridging Two Eras of Black Nationalism." PhD diss., Howard University, 2012.

Robinson, Cedric. *Black Marxism: The Making of the Black Radical Tradition.* University of North Carolina Press, 1983.

Rosenwaike, Ira. *Population History of New York City.* Syracuse University Press, 1972.

Sales, William W., Jr. *From Civil Rights to Black Liberation: Malcolm X and the Organization of Afro-American Unity.* South End Press, 1994.

Schechter, Danny. "Black Nationalism: The Ghetto Seeks Identity." In *News Dissector: Passions, Pieces, and Polemics, 1960–2000,* by Danny Schechter. Akashic Books, 2001.

———. "Discovering Harlem." In *News Dissector: Passions, Pieces, and Polemics, 1960–2000,* by Danny Schechter. Akashic Books, 2001.

Schwartz, Joel. "The New York City Rent Strikes of 1963–1964." *Social Science Review* 57, no. 4 (1983): 545–64.

———. "Tenant Power in the Liberal City, 1943–1971." In *The Tenant Movement in New York City, 1904–1984,* edited by Ronald Lawson and Mark Naison. Rutgers University Press, 1986.

Shapiro, Fred C., and James W. Sullivan. *Race Riots: New York 1964.* Thomas Crowell, 1964.

Sinclair, Abiola. "Harlem Street Speakers of the 1960s." In Smith and Sinclair, *The Harlem Cultural/Politics Movements*.
———. "Louis H. Michaux: The Bookman." In Smith and Sinclair, *The Harlem Cultural/Politics Movements*.
———. "Mae Mallory Harlem Activist." In Smith and Sinclair, *The Harlem Cultural/Politics Movements*.
Smethurst, James. *The Black Arts Movement: Literary Nationalism in the 1960s and 1970s*. University of North Carolina Press, 2005.
Smith, J. Clay, Jr. *Emancipation: The Making of the Black Lawyer, 1844-1944*. University of Pennsylvania Press, 1993.
Smith, Klytus, and Abiola Sinclair, eds. *The Harlem Cultural/Politics Movements 1960-1970: From Malcolm X to "Black Is Beautiful."* Gumbs and Thomas, 2005.
Stanford, Maxwell C. "Revolutionary Action Movement (RAM): A Case Study of an Urban Revolutionary Movement in Western Capitalist Society." MA thesis, Atlanta University, 1986.
Strickland, William. *Malcolm X: Make It Plain*. With Cheryl Greene. Viking, 1994.
Suddler, Carl. *Presumed Criminal: Black Youth and the Justice System in Postwar New York*. New York University Press, 2019.
Sugrue, Thomas. *Sweet Land of Liberty: The Forgotten Struggle for Civil Rights in the North*. Random House, 2008.
Sweeting, Ora Mobley. *Nobody Gave Me Permission: Memoirs of a Harlem Activist*. With Ezekiel C. Mobley Jr. Xlibris, 2000.
Taylor, Clarence. *Fight the Power: African Americans and the Long History of Police Brutality in New York City*. New York University Press, 2019.
———. "Harlem Schools and the New York City Teachers Union." In Erickson and Morrell, *Educating Harlem*.
———. *Knocking at Our Own Door: Milton A. Galamison and the Struggle to Integrate New York City Schools*. Columbia University Press, 1997.
Taylor, Keeanga-Yamahtta. *How We Get Free: Black Feminism and the Combahee River Collective*. Haymarket, 2017.
Taylor, Ula Yvette. *The Promise of Patriarchy: Women and the Nation of Islam*. University of North Carolina Press, 2017.
Theoharis, Jeanne. *A More Beautiful and Terrible History: The Uses and Misuses of Civil Rights History*. Beacon, 2018.
Tinson, Christopher M. *Radical Intellect: "Liberator" Magazine and Black Activism in the 1960s*. Chapel Hill: University of North Carolina Press, 2017.
———. "'The Voice of the Black Protest Movement': Notes on the *Liberator* Magazine and Black Radicalism in the Early 1960s." *Black Scholar* 37, no. 4 (Winter 2008): 3-15.
Tobierre, Elizabeth. "'Black Power Does Not Come Out of the Sky': The Emergence of Black Power Politics in the Northern Student Movement, 1961-1968." BA thesis, Duke University, 2014.

Ture, Kwame, and Eukweme Michael Thelwell. *Ready for Revolution: The Life and Struggles of Stokely Carmichael (Kwame Ture).* Scribner, 2005.

Tyson, Timothy. *Radio Free Dixie: Robert F. Williams and the Roots of Black Power.* University of North Carolina Press, 1999.

Ulasewicz, Tony. *The President's Private Eye: The Journey of Detective Tony U. From N.Y.P.D. to the Nixon White House.* With Stuart A. McKeever. MACSAM Publishing, 1990.

Umoja, Akinyele Omowale. *We Will Shoot Back: Armed Resistance in the Mississippi Freedom Movement.* New York University Press, 2014.

Von Eschen, Penny. *Race Against Empire: Black Americans and Anticolonialism, 1937-1957.* Cornell University Press, 1997.

Ward, Stephen. *In Love and Struggle: The Revolutionary Lives of James and Grace Lee Boggs.* University of North Carolina Press, 2016.

Williams, Rhonda Y. *Concrete Demands: The Search for Black Power in the 20th Century.* Routledge, 2015.

Williams, Robert F. *Negroes with Guns.* Marzani & Munsell, 1962.

Wood, Reggie, and Lizzette Salado. *The Ray Wood Story: Confessions of a Black NYPD Cop in the Assassination of Malcolm X.* Madera Enterprises, 2021.

Wright, Sarah E. "The Lower East Side: A Rebirth of World Vision." *African American Review* 27, no. 4 (Winter 1993): 596.

X, Malcolm. *The Autobiography of Malcolm X.* With Alex Haley. Ballentine Books, 1992.

———. "The Challenge of Racism." New York, NY, May 1, 1962. Audio recording. https://www.youtube.com/watch?v=WA_YixhCP2g/.

———. *Malcolm X Speaks: Selected Speeches and Statements.* Edited by George Breitman. Grove Press, 1990.

INDEX

Italicized page numbers refer to illustrations.

Africa: and Accra, 114; and African and Arab solidarity, 73-74; and African Freedom Day, 74, 114, 115; and African nationalist leaders, 94, 115; Algeria in, 114, 163, 270; and All-African People's Conference (1958), 114; Angola in, 163; and anticolonialism, 128, 131, 137, 143-44, 145, 147, 157, 163, 269-70, 272; and Black Americans, 22, 144; and colonized African nations, 104, 112, 113-14, 131, 270; and Congo, 13, 114, 131, 132, 136, 137, 138, 140, 141, 142, 144, 147, 163; diasporic movements from, 157, 315n13; Egypt in, 173; and European imperialism, 131, 138; and Ghanaians, 49, 112, 113, 270; Ghana in, 144, 293; Guinea in, 113, 195; and independence struggles, 20, 49, 73-74, 104, 110, 112, 113-14, 120, 130-31, 133-34, 137, 138, 144, 145, 158-59, 163, 169, 175, 270, 272, 293, 303; and independent African nations, 173, 293; and International Committee in Defense of Africa, 21; Kenya in, 272, 294; and media in, 326n111; Kwame Nkrumah, 49, 112, 114; and Michael (Babatunde) Olatunji, 114; Ruanda-Urundi in, 137; South Africa in, 137, 168, 288, 293; Sudan in, 81; unification of peoples of, 115; and United Nations, 128, 130-31; and United States, 131, 138-39; Western interference in, 136; and "Year of Africa," 130-31

African Americans: and African American Women's Committee, 132; and African Blood Brotherhood, 112; and African development, 19; and African independence, 66; and African liberation struggles, 140-41; and American political system, 170, 172, 319n86; and anticolonialism, 18, 20; and artist-activists, 172; and Black anger, 302; and Black churches, 35; and Black communities, 121, 268; and Black consciousness, 35; and Black liberation, 268; and Black men, 24, 29, 94, 128, 129; and Black migrants, 3, 15-16, 22; and Black mothers, 53-57, 96; and Black nationalism, 157, 268-69; and Black politics, 29-30, 35-36, 37, 56-57, 87, 113, 268-69; and Black radicalism, 4, 5, 8, 20, 34, 35-36, 56, 131, 294; and Black women, 7, 15, 22, 24, 27, 28-29, 30, 35, 56-57, 61, 64, 75, 87; and Black workers, 206, 212; and Black youth, 14, 16, 45, 71, 256, 275; and Fidel Castro, 125; and celebration of heritage, 144; and children, 25, 30, 56, 61, 75, 174; and citizenship, 43, 113, 265; and civil rights, 182; and colonialism, 163; and communism, 112, 113; and community rights, 8; and Congo, 132, 163;

African Americans (*continued*)
and criminalization of youth, 101; and Cuban Revolution, 124; and cultural centers, 15-16; and desegregation, 182; and education, 25, 30-33, 34, 123; and employment, 123; and equality, 28, 29, 34, 35, 83, 154, 218; and freedom, 268, 294, 296; fury of, 141; Great Migrations of, 15, 16; and Guardians Association, 95, 109-10; and guerilla warfare, 296; and Harlem, 4-5, 7, 15-17, 18, 104, 269; and "The Hate That Hate Produced," 70, 71; and housing, 36-37, 123, 192; and human rights, 110, 120, 159, 255, 269, 291, 293, 294, 305; and inequality, 84; and integration, 9-10, 26, 32, 96, 240; and justice, 297; and liberation, 157-58; and liberation of Africa, 20, 112, 115; and lynch mobs, 24; and militancy, 138, 302; and National Memorial African Bookstore, 18; and National Negro Labor Council, 18; and nation within a nation, 120; and New Negro movement, 15-16; in New York City, 123, 288, 291; in the 1970s, 370-71n17; in the North, 215; and Organization of Afro-American Unity, 5, 287, 288, 291-93, 294, 298; and Pan-Africanism, 140; and police charges, 100; and police militarization, 303; and political power, 169; and population, 18, 38; and racial identity, 19; and racial pride, 18, 19, 115; and racist terrorism, 122; and rebellions of the 1960s, 9; and religion, 72; repression of, 165, 166, 296; and revolution, 241; and self-defense, 28, 163, 266, 298, 299; and self-determination, 7, 9, 19, 115, 144, 146, 157-58, 264, 294, 319n86; and slavery, 111, 115, 118, 176; and solidarity with Africans, 133-34, 143-44, 147, 157; in the South, 2-4, 28, 49, 167, 291; and spirit of Bandung, 115; and strangulation, 179, 204; and Student Nonviolent Coordinating Committee (SNCC), 194; and students, 182, 194; and term "Negro," 115, 144, 331n14; and Emmett Till murder, 134, 143, 149, 180; and UN protestors, 140; and violence, 296; and white supremacy, 72, 134; and working-class Black communities, 7, 8-9, 28, 113, 150, 176; and Xavier University, 34. *See also* African diaspora; Harlem, New York City; newspapers

African Community Leagues, 115

African diaspora, 5, 6, 9, 13, 19, 20. *See also* Black freedom movement; Harlem, New York City

African Nationalist Pioneer Movement (ANPM), 19-20, 21, 114, 115, 116, 143

Afro-American Alliance for Action (AAAA), 150-51, 154, 169

Afro-American Institute, 159

Ali, Noble Drew, 17

American Civil Liberties Union (ACLU), 44, 290

American Labor Party, 37, 65, 323n21

Angelou, Maya, 125, 131, 132, 134, 135, 136. *See also* Malcolm X

Anthony, Carl, 179, 181, 192, 193, 196, 197. *See also* Northern Student Movement (NSM)

Asia, 20, 74, 112, 113, 116

Bailey, Peter, 239-40, 291

Baker, Ella, 6, 16, 25, 27-30, 32, 56-57. *See also* grassroots organizing; National Association for the Advancement of Colored People (NAACP); New York City; organizers

Baker, Wallace, 277, 278

Baldwin, James: and equality for Black people, 83, 140, 142, 241; and *Esquire* essay, 103, 110; essays of, 218; and Harlem, 1, 2, 3, *3*, 10, 103, 104, 218; and Harlem Six, 363n125; and housing conditions, 1, 220, 241, 245; and landlords' responsibilities, 2, 220; and mass demonstrations, 218; and "A Negro Assays the Negro Mood," 140; and racial discrimination, 218; and rent strikes, 220,

240, 354n124; and rent strike speech, 1-2, 3, 6, 241; and revolution in consciousness, 180; and role of NYPD, 248; and self-determination, 9; and transforming institutions, 2; and UN protests, 142; and white police officers, 104, 107; and white supremacy, 103, 107; and Robert F. Williams, 123
Bandung, Indonesia, 20, 112, 113, 115
Baptist Ministers' Conference of Greater New York, 126-27, 130
Baraka, Amiri (LeRoi Jones), 71, 123, 124, 127, 129, 136. *See also* Black freedom movement
Barnes, Robert, Jr., 279, 280
Bates, Daisy, 30
Batista, Fulgencio: and dictatorship, 121, 122; regime of, 122
Belgium, 132, 133, 138
Bellevue Hospital, 286, 299
Besheer, Dr. Tahseen Mohamed, 73-74
Beveridge, Lowell "Pete," 138
Birmingham Baptist Church bombing, 171, 174, 218
Black, Algernon, 31
Black Arts movement, 137, 138, 172
Black freedom movement: and ACT, 178, 266, 268; and activists, 4, 6-8, 10, 52, 54, 56-57, 113, 115-16, 119-21, 128, 137, 144, 173, 183, 184, 253, 266, 293; and African diaspora, 110, 112, 113-15, 137, 147; and African Freedom Day, 114-15; and anticapitalism, 128; and anticolonialism, 113-16, 118, 128, 144, 177, 315n13; and armed resistance, 173; and armed self-defense, 150-51, 167, 169; and armed struggle, 10, 111, 114, 128, 131, 150, 173-74, 296; and Amiri Baraka, 151, 155; and Birmingham protesters, 174, 208; and Black anger, 302; and Black communities, 172, 174, 302; and Black equality, 209, 217; and Black history and culture, 275-76; and Black leadership, 155-56; and Black liberation, 155, 158, 168, 183, 241, 266, 276; and Black Liberation Front, 287; and

Black nationalism, 138, 139, 143-44, 172, 177, 216; and Black politics, 167-72, 216, 268; and Black Power movement, 305; and Black radicalism, 5, 8, 11-12, 13, 14, 52, 66, 110, 111-13, 116, 143, 144, 155, 157-58, 171, 274; and Black working class, 145; and Black youth, 275-76; and capitalist societies, 305; and collective action, 216, 221; and colonialism, 157; and Communist Party (CPUSA), 139; and community organizers, 8, 12, 13, 52, 57, 203, 293; and community organizing, 6-8, 13, 200-203, 275-76; and courts' treatment of Black people, 167; and Crusaders for Freedom, 118, 183, 337n18; and cultural nationalism, 305; and "cultural revolution," 172; diversity of, 7, 175; and economic issues, 56, 150; and education, 8, 52, 53-57; and electoral politics, 293; and employment, 8, 56, 181; and freedom, 166-67; and Freedom Rides, 181, 190, 204; and Garveyism, 18, 116; and global movement, 3, 4, 7, 8-9, 63, 66, 81, 113-14, 116, 130, 137; and Harlem, 2-5, 6, 7, 13, 14, 39, 63, 65-66, 80-81, 113-15, 130, 139, 146, 180; and Harlem Youth Opportunities Unlimited (HARYOU), 280; and Calvin Hicks, 161, 169, 233, 264; and housing, 8, 39, 52, 57-63, 172, 240; and human rights, 305; and improvement of living conditions, 7, 60-63; and integrationists, 13, 63, 217, 276; and internationalism, 315n13; and Sherron Jackson, 297; and justice, 137; and John O. Killens, 302, 303; and Bob Knight, 273; and leadership, 150, 296-97; and Leadership Training Workshop, 275-76; and *Liberator*, 169, 172, 177, 260, 281, 289, 296-97; and liberty, 137, 281; and local people, 81, 159; and Conrad Lynn, 171, 172, 173, 289, 293, 337n3; and Malcolm X, 118-19, 160, 178, 265, 292, 293; and Julian Mayfield, 151, 152; and militancy, 144, 150, 151, 159, 160, 178, 242, 274, 281, 296-97; and minimum wage, 267; and Monroe, North

Black freedom movement (*continued*)
Carolina, 111, 151, 152, 154; and Audley Moore, 159; and National Association for the Advancement of Colored People (NAACP), 56, 63, 281; and national movement, 3, 4, 6–7, 8, 9, 13, 164, 178, 235, 241, 242, 266; and New Afro-American Nationalism, 146; in New York City, 56, 63, 80–81, 110–12, 137, 138, 212, 229–30, 253; in New York State, 139; and nonviolence, 152, 155, 167, 209, 216, 276, 297; in the North, 8, 13, 52, 212, 241; and On Guard Committee for Freedom (OGFF), 150, 154, 187, 334n75; and Pan-Africanism, 113–16, 138, 144, 177, 305; and parents' boycott of schools, 53–57; and police reform, 260; and policing, 8, 10, 11–14, 52, 98, 265, 273, 302–3; and political consciousness, 138, 143–44; and power, 81, 150, 158, 167, 221, 273, 276, 302; and racial equality, 190, 302; and racial pride, 114; and racial unrest, 98, 302; and racist oppression, 124, 302; and radical organizing, 81, 113; and rejection of nonviolence, 10, 150, 155, 296, 305; and religious groups, 173; and rent strikes, 239, 241; and resistance histories, 11, 13–14, 114; and Revolutionary Action Movement, 159, 178, 208, 274–75; and riots of 1964, 302–4; and self-defense, 63–65, 81, 118, 147, 150, 216, 267, 276, 281, 292, 293; and self-determination, 56–57, 81, 138, 150, 155, 156, 167, 171, 184, 190, 214, 221, 255, 296, 302, 305; and separation from whites, 150, 217; and sit-in movement, 190; and solidarity with Asians, 116; in the South, 151, 184; and spirit of Bandung, 293; and Max Stanford, 292, 293; and Ronald Stokes, 173; and struggle for rights, 305; student involvement in, 190; and systems of oppression, 2, 6, 7, 10–12, 30–31, 56, 166, 302; and United African Nationalist Movement (UANM), 139; and Dan Watts, 174, 213, 216, 338n33; and white supremacy, 116, 302, 303; and Robert F. Williams, 151, 154, 155, 159, 254, 274, 296; and working-class leadership, 81; and William Worthy, 173, 175, 206, 293, 340n88; and Paul Zuber, 216, 259. *See also* Africa; grassroots organizing; Monroe Defense Committee (MDC); New Afro-American Nationalism

Black Liberation Front, 292, 366n178
Black Liberation Movement, 147
Black nationalists, 13, 17–22, 23, 29, 35, 49. *See also* Haywood, Harry; Malcolm X; Nation of Islam (NOI); New Afro-American Nationalism; newspapers; organizers; United African Nationalist Movement (UANM)
Black Panther Party, 287
Black Power: and ACT, 305; and Amiri Baraka, 129; and Black communities, 10, 49, 50, 109–10, 144, 237, 239, 303; and Black liberation, 239, 253, 296; and Black political power, 235, 370–71n17; and Black radicalism, 9–10, 138, 303; and community power, 240, 292; and cop-watch programs, 264; and cultural power, 305; and Detroit, 305; in Harlem, 292, 304–5; and Harlem uprising, 305; and human rights, 213; and mass movements, 216, 235; and national movement, 175, 305; in New York City, 255; in the North, 9, 10, 14, 304–5; and Organization for Black Power, 305, 370–71n17, 371n18; and organizations, 216; and Pan-Africanism, 115; and the police, 305; and police violence, 292; and political consciousness, 138, 304; and political power, 213, 304; and racial consciousness, 23; and racial pride, 115; and rage, 144; rise of, 4, 9, 14; and self-defense, 10, 81, 292; and self-determination, 6, 9, 81, 115, 213, 240, 252, 266; and state repression, 9, 292; tenets of, 81; and transformative power, 9; and white communities, 171; and white supremacy, 305; and working-class leadership, 10, 81

INDEX   391

Blood Brothers, 279-80, 281, 282, 284, 289, 364-65n161
Blumstein, Jack, 108, 109
Booker, Jimmy, 99
bookstores, 18, 21, 66, 119, 134, 137. *See also* Harlem, New York City
Bosque, Juan Almeida, 122, 127
Bowe, Nan, 193, 274-75, 293
Bowe, Walter, 129, 274, 293, 335n116, 366n178
Bradley, Roscoe "Chick," 202-3
Bradshaw, Anne, 233, 237
Branche, Stanley, 243, 272
Briggs, Cyril, 22
Brown, Earl, 30, 45, 46, 64, 87-88, 101. *See also* New York City
Brown, Elizabeth, 245, 246, 247
Brown v. Board of Education, 25, 26, 27-28, 31, 33, 40. *See also* civil rights; New York City; racism; United States
Buchanan, Bessie, 87, 88
Bunche, Dr. Ralph, 140, 141
Burnham, Louis, 26, 38
Buy Black campaigns, 19-20, 198

Callender, Herbert, 249, 262, 266, 272, 273, 286-87. *See also* Congress of Racial Equality (CORE)
Callender, Reverend Eugene, 30, 54
Canada, 153
capitalism, 3, 9, 19, 26, 63, 112. *See also* Black freedom movement; Harlem, New York City; Mallory, Mae; newspapers; United States
carceral system: and Angola Prison, 34; and the incarcerated, 23; and Massachusetts state prisons, 17; ministers in, 23; of New York, 302; in the South, 34; in the urban North, 4, 271, 272
Carey, Gordon, 183, 184
Caribbean, 9, 145, 147
Carmichael, Stokely (Kwame Ture), 195, 196, 345n67
Cassese, John, 295

Castro, Fidel: army of, 121, 122; and Bay of Pigs, 148; and Black consciousness, 130; and Black freedom struggles, 127, 168; and Congo, 132; and Cubans and Puerto Ricans, 136; and discrimination, 122; execution of opposition to, 122; government of, 122; and Harlem, 126, 127, 131, 132, 333n55; influence of, 130; New York visit of, 124-28, 130, 133; and self-determination, 128; and solidarity with anticolonial revolutions, 127-28; and US imperialism, 126, 127; and Robert F. Williams, 123
Caviglione, Carmela, 76-77, 78, 79, 79, 80, 83. *See also* Harlem, New York City
Cherry, Granville, 219, 220, 221, 222, 223, 225, 248-49. *See also* organizers
Chicago, Illinois, 15, 22, 105, 230, 242, 272
China, 270
Churchville, John, 192
City Wide Committee for Fair Police Protection, 289-90
civil disobedience, 53, 59, 165, 166, 180, 212. *See also* New York City
civil rights: and affirmative action, 212; and A. G. Gaston Motel, 208; and Ella Baker, 27, 49, 53; and Roger Baldwin, 290; and Black civil rights leaders, 160, 185; and Black communities, 47, 50, 52, 71, 80-81, 88, 95, 103, 138, 140, 148-49, 185, 187, 194, 255; and Black equality, 35-36, 45, 47, 49, 84, 109, 109-10, 214; and Black freedom movement, 269; and Black history, 194; and Black liberation, 146, 169, 176; and Black moderates, 146; and Black nationalism, 196; and Black Power, 305; and Black radicalism, 262, 274, 296-97; and Black revolution, 274; and Black students, 180; and Black women organizers, 30, 50, 53-57; and *Brown v. Board of Education,* 47, 49; and civilian review board, 290; and Civil Rights Congress, 18, 44; and coalitions, 137, 250; and collective action, 259; commissions on, 83, 110; and Cuban Revolution, 130;

civil right (*continued*)
and demonstrations of 1964, 262; and direct-action campaigns, 192, 194; and educational justice, 27–28, 30, 34, 194; and federal intervention, 47; framework of, 6; and Freedom Rides, 180; and freedom schools, 54; and Gloster Current, 130; and grassroots activists, 146, 294; and Harlem orators, 21; and housing as an issue, 38–39; and integrationism, 24, 47, 52, 319n73; and Kennedy administration, 168; and leadership, 29, 30, 66, 67, 71, 72, 84, 87, 127, 129–30, 140, 146, 171, 174, 180, 229, 243, 249, 250, 255, 262, 266, 272, 296–97, 301; luminaries of, 6; and March on Washington, 218, 219, 241, 297; moderate approaches to, 69, 80, 81, 82, 84, 126, 130, 297; and moderate leaders, 121, 130, 140, 170, 171, 175, 176, 178; modern era of, 5, 9, 17, 23, 34, 35–36, 40, 45, 50, 52, 84; and Montgomery bus boycott, 47; and National Association for Puerto Rican Civil Rights, 250, 257; and national movement, 4, 6, 8, 9, 12, 13, 19, 21, 43, 47, 50, 52, 71, 72, 147, 176, 178, 179, 180–82, 191, 192, 194, 203, 217, 241–42; and New England Student Christian Movement, 190; and New York City, 12, 17, 24, 30, 31, 40, 44, 45, 46, 49–50, 51–57, 79, 80, 84, 242, 249; and nonviolence, 180, 192, 211–12, 338n33; in the North, 50, 52, 185, 190, 235, 241–42, 272; Northern movement for, 180, 211–14, 315n13; and NYPD, 95, 105; organizations for, 5, 6, 9, 13, 24, 25, 30, 31, 45, 46, 50, 52, 53, 54, 84, 119, 126, 130, 138, 140, 157, 171, 180–82, 184, 185, 187, 188–89, 194, 206, 217, 226, 238, 250–52, 261–62, 280, 289; and organizing, 233; and police reform, 27, 44–45; and policing, 260, 261–62; and power, 273; and Puerto Rican Committee for Civil Rights, 289; and Puerto Rican community, 259; and racial liberalism, 52; and racial oppression, 84; and rebellions of the 1960s, 9; rejection of, 9–10; and rent strike movement, 235, 239–42, 250; resistance to, 269; and revolution, 241–42; and sanitation workers union, 272–73; and school boycotts, 255; and school desegregation, 31–32; and segregation, 180, 211–12; and selective patronage, 193, 194; and self-defense, 10, 67, 315n13; and sit-in movement, 180, 182; and Southern civil rights movement, 3–4, 9, 10, 24, 50, 52, 57, 108, 180–81, 190–91, 242, 315n13; and Southern Negro Youth Conference, 57; and tenant organizing, 61, 218–19; and tenants' rights, 43, 218–19; and trade unions, 212; and urban renewal projects, 42; and voter registration, 190–91, 192, 194; and white supremacists, 67; and Roy Wilkins, 140, 149, 171, 368–69n228; and working-class Black communities, 8–9, 35, 61; and young activists, 50, 129, 190–94. *See also* civil disobedience; Civil Rights Act (1964); grassroots organizing; National Association for the Advancement of Colored People (NAACP)

Civil Rights Act (1964), 96, 241, 265, 267–68, 271

Clark, Dr. Kenneth, 25, 91, 191, 193, 205, 275. *See also* Harlem, New York City

Clark, Dr. Mamie, 25, 91, 193

Clarke, Dr. John Henrik: as adviser of Malcolm X, 117, 164; and Black communities, 144; and Black freedom movement, 143, 151, 156, 304; and Black nationalism, 119, 143; and colonialism, 133–34, 143; and culture, 370n13; FBI surveillance of, 151; and *Freedomways*, 156, 194; and Harlem Anti-Colonial Committee, 167; as a Harlem writer, 65, 118; and Harlem Writers Guild, 130; as an historian, 123, 133, 143; and Leadership Training Workshop, 275; and New Afro-American Nationalism, 13, 146; and Organization of Afro-American Unity, 291, 293

Clay, Cassius (Muhammad Ali), 213

Clemente, Genoveva, 239

Clydebank tenants, 37, 38-39
Cobb, Charles, 10
Cold War, 20, 86, 99, 113, 122, 125. *See also* United States
Columbia University, 182, 183, 214
Committee to Aid the Monroe Defendants (CAMD), 155, 156, 159
communism, 5, 20, 22, 27, 29, 33. *See also* African Americans; Gray, Jesse; Harlem, New York City; Marxism; United States
Community Council on Housing (CCH), 154, 213, 218-19, 223, 224, 225. *See also* grassroots organizing; Gray, Jesse; Harlem, New York City
Congress of Industrial Organizations (CIO), 34
Congress of Racial Equality (CORE): and Ad Hoc Committee for Fair Police Practice, 260, 261, 262; and affirmative action, 346n81; assertive tactics of, 212-13, 261, 262, 273; and autonomy for local chapters, 188; and Black communities, 181, 184, 185, 189, 197, 198, 199, 204, 206-8, 252; and Black leadership, 156, 184, 185, 188, 197, 204; and Black nationalism, 159, 188, 189, 213; and Black political empowerment, 204; and boycott of Sealtest Dairy, 198, 199, 204; and Bronx CORE, 211, 249, 261-62, 272, 286, 290; and Brooklyn CORE, 211, 221, 230, 238, 261-62, 270, 272; and Isaiah Brunson, 262, 270-71; and Herbert Callender, 299; and civil rights movement, 8, 13, 178, 180-84, 194, 223, 272; and class, 186, 187, 197, 231; as Committee for Racial Equality, 59; and community power, 213; and demonstrations, 299; and direct action, 204, 211, 212, 255, 262, 270, 271; and East River CORE, 255, 271, 286, 298, 366n178, 370n12; and economic justice, 197-98; and education, 254-55, 270; and employment, 181, 185, 197-98, 199, 204-8, 211, 213, 254-55, 270; and James Farmer, 251, 254, 255, 272, 290; and Freedom Rides, 152, 180, 187-88, 204; and Clarence Funnyé, 186, 206; and Harlem CORE, 197, 199-200, 203-7, 211, 213, 218, 221, 226, 240, 258, 261-62, 272, 281, 283; and hiring discrimination, 197-99, 204-5, 206; and housing fairness, 181, 185-86, 187, 197, 213, 221, 223, 226, 254-55, 270; and human rights, 181, 213, 214; and increase in membership, 204; and integration, 189-90, 197, 252, 270; as an interracial organization, 181, 182, 184, 213, 214; and Blyden Jackson, 218, 298; and leadership of Black organizations, 156, 214; and local people, 182, 199; and Long Island CORE, 197; and mass movements, 197, 199, 239; and Jimmy McDonald, 196; and militant tactics, 188; National Action Council of, 184, 188; and nonviolence, 187, 188, 189, 190; in the North, 185-90; and NY CORE, 182, 183-90, 225, 252; and NYU CORE, 221; open housing drive of, 186; and picketing, 212, 221; and police reform, 181, 289-90; and policing, 213, 254-55, 286; and political power, 213; and protests, 198, 199, 209, 211, 212; and William Reed, 252; and rent strikes, 221, 229, 239, 250-52; and Marvin Rich, 184; rules for action of, 187; and Ernest Russell, 300; and school boycotts, 266; and self-determination, 181, 188, 189-90, 213; and sit-ins, 192, 211, 262; and social justice, 204; and the South, 184, 185, 187; and strikes, 212, 230; and students, 209; surveillance of, 286; and tenant organizing, 186, 223, 238; and Ruth Turner, 243; Washington, DC, CORE, 243; white members of, 184; and working-class communities, 184, 213, 216. *See also* Farmer, James
Cooks, Carlos, 18, 19, 21, 114, 115, 119, 127
Cornell University, 179
Countryman, Peter, 190, 191, 192, 195, 200, 214. *See also* organizers
Cousins, Andrea, 194, 195, 202
Craig, Willie, 279

Crawford, Delight, 102, 103
Crawford, Samuel, 44
Cross, Dr. Lonnie (Abdulalim A. Shabazz), 150
Crusader, The, 100, 110, 123, 136, 144, 296
Crusaders for Freedom, 123, 125–26, 147, 148, 149–50, 151. *See also* Black freedom movement; New York City
Cruse, Harold, 124, 129, 157, 158, 172, 274
Cuba: and affordable housing, 123; and Afro-Cubans, 122; and agrarian reform, 124; and Amiri Baraka, 129; and Bay of Pigs, 148; and Black communities, 123; Black intellectuals in, 123–24; and Cuban Revolution, 13, 122–23, 124, 125, 127, 144, 159; and discrimination, 124; and education, 123, 124; and Fair Play for Cuba Committee (FPCC), 155; flight of Fulgencio Batista from, 121; government of, 127; Havana in, 270; and housing, 123, 124; jobs in, 123; and Kennedy administration, 148; and land, 123; and Malcolm X, 270; and Mae Mallory, 147, 148; and nationalization of foreign corporations, 122; news coverage of, 122–23; and racial equality, 123; and Right to Equality law, 124; Sierra Maestra mountains in, 124; and tourism, 123; US embargo of, 169; US imperialism in, 127; and Robert F. Williams, 123–24; and Williams family, 153. *See also* Fair Play for Cuba Committee (FPCC)
Cultural Association for Women of African Heritage (CAWAH), 132–34, 135, 154, 293, 334n92, 334n95

Daniels, Stan, 159, 208
Davis, Benjamin, Jr., 43, 320n101
Davis, Edward "Pork Chop," 21, 119, 127, 161
Davis, Leon, 240
Dee, Ruby, 154, 293
Delany, Judge Hubert, 25, 32–33, 43, 290
Delany, William, 44
Democratic Party, 229, 240, 268, 341n95, 370n13

Dewey, Governor Thomas, 39
Dickens, Lloyd, 78, 80, 85, 87, 229
Diggs, J. Daniel, 101
Dittmer, John, 6
Douglass, Frederick, 18, 276
Du Bois, W. E. B., 35, 123, 303
Dukes, Elbert, 45
Dukes, Rev. Nelson C., 268, 299, 300
Dunlevy Milbank Community Center, 1, 3, 6, 225, 226, 228. *See also* Harlem, New York City
Dyett, Thomas Benjamin, 95–96, 97

Ebony, 122, 231, 247
Eisenhower, President Dwight, 46, 51, 127
Engels, Friedrich, 36
England, Marshall, 226, 272, 273, 281
Epton, Bill, 122, 127, 161, 170, 233, 264, 298. *See also* organizers
Evers, Medgar, 64
eviction protection law, 42

Fair Play for Cuba Committee (FPCC), 122–23, 124, 125, 127, 134, 136. *See also* Cuba
Farmer, James, 184, 185, 187, 188, 207, 226, 250. *See also* Congress of Racial Equality (CORE)
Faubus, Governor Orval, 28, 88
Federal Housing Act, 40
Federation for Independent Political Action, 304–5
Felder, Ronald, 279
Finch, Jim, 222
Finkenstaedt, Rose, 169
Foley Square demonstrations, 211–12, 218
Francis, Ennis, 65, 66, 114
Freedom Now Party (FNP), 168–74, 206, 268, 287, 293, 341n109
Freedomways, 107, 124, 133, 143, 144, 146. *See also* Clarke, Dr. John Henrik; Monroe Defense Committee (MDC)
Freeman, Donald, 158, 159, 175, 274

Fruit Stand Riot, 277-78, 279, 280, 283, 286, 288. *See also* Harlem, New York City
Fuentes, Jose, 239
Fuller, Hoyt, 151

Gabel, Hortense, 236, 237, 240
Garrett, Ramona, 34
Garvey, Marcus: and Africa, 132; and anticolonialism, 19; and Black generations, 145; and Black nationalism, 17; and economic nationalism, 18, 19; and Garveyism, 65, 114; and Jamaica, 18; legacy of, 118; and Marcus Garvey Day Parade, 19; as an orator, 21; and Pan-Africanism, 5, 19, 21; as a race leader, 16; and racial pride, 18; and Universal Negro Improvement Association (UNIA), 17, 18, 19
Garvin, Vicki, 22, 35, 117
Germany, 163, 288
Gibson, Richard, 122, 127, 159
Gilligan, Thomas, 297, 298, 300
Global South, 3, 110, 128, 143-44
Godfrey Nurse Houses, 41, 42, 58
Goodman, Benjamin (Benjamin Karim), 49, 117, 164
Granger, Lester, 119, 140, 336n128
grassroots organizing: and ACT coalition, 243, 272, 304, 359n52; and Action Committee Against Police Brutality, 284; and activists, 148-50; activities of, 6, 8, 14, 18, 28, 35, 38-39, 51-52, 56-57, 60, 61-62, 63, 69, 71, 114, 137, 150, 230-32; and Ad Hoc Committee for Fair Police Practice, 289; and affirmative action, 198-99; and armed self-defense, 68-69, 292; and Ella Baker, 53, 56, 58, 180; and Black and Puerto Rican parents, 28, 33; and Black communities, 27, 33, 35, 36-37, 38, 52, 57, 60, 84, 112, 120, 184, 239, 265, 304; and Black liberation, 57, 113, 120, 203, 274-75, 296-97, 304; and Black nationalism, 118, 195; and Black political power, 293, 304; and Black politics, 5, 6, 7-8, 18, 25, 35, 36-37, 69, 177-78; and Black radicalism, 177-78, 240, 274-75, 296-97; and Black women, 61, 68-70, 134, 233-35, 296; and Black working-class, 35, 36-37, 57, 61, 206, 296; and Black youth, 296-97; and boycott of junior high schools, 53-57; and boycott of Sealtest Dairy, 206; and Isaiah Brunson, 304; and building demolitions, 41; and campaign about police, 263, 266-68; and canvassing, 201, 206-7, 219, 223; and civilian review board, 266; and civil rights movement, 49-50, 52, 53, 57, 223, 294; and coalition building, 228-30; and coalition on employment, 206-7, 210-11; and collective action, 28, 39, 59, 60, 119, 201, 202, 221; and Communist Party (CPUSA), 245; and community control of police, 263-64; and Community Council on Housing (CCH), 231-33, 244, 245, 258; and community organizing, 9, 16, 38-39, 41-42, 57, 182-83, 186, 194-95, 199-200, 225, 226-35, 239, 240, 275-76; and community power, 194, 231, 239, 240; and community resources, 8, 231; and cop-watch programs, 264; and demonstrations, 56, 69, 208, 285, 289, 299; and direct action, 196, 200, 204, 206-7, 208, 222, 243, 256, 291; and economic boycotts, 35; and economics, 233; and education, 2, 6, 8, 12, 25, 26, 27, 28, 30-34, 53-57, 70, 193-94, 196-97, 202, 257; and emotions, 50; and employment, 2, 6, 8, 27, 33-34, 52, 56, 208, 266-67; and flyers, 168, 226, 265, 272, 289; and freedom, 47, 196, 289; and Rev. Milton Galamison, 304; and grassroots organizations, 8, 27, 28, 57-58, 195-97; in Harlem, 3, 4-16, 27, 36, 38-43, 52-59, 110, 168, 195, 214, 221, 223-30, 241-42, 255, 265, 289; and Harlem Action Group, 223, 229, 273; and Harlem Defense Council, 290-91, 296; and Harlem Nine, 53-57; and Harlem rebellions, 11; and HARYOU-ACT, 229, 351n68; and heat and hot water, 215, 227,

grassroots organizing (*continued*)
228, 234; and housing, 2, 8, 12, 13, 27, 36, 38-43, 52, 57-63, 186, 197, 220-35, 257, 265; and integration, 195; and intellectual resources, 50; and interracial organizing, 252; and Joint Committee for Equal Employment Opportunity, 206, 207, 212; and labor organizations, 18, 22, 206, 207, 209, 229, 233; and leadership, 195, 216, 229, 231, 304; and legalizing rent strikes, 250; and letter writing, 201; and local people, 8, 27, 29, 50, 87, 112-13, 120, 134, 195-96, 216, 225, 230-32; and Lower East Side (LES) Rent Strike Committee, 238-39, 240; and Malcolm X, 178; and Mae Mallory, 178; and mass demonstration at United Nations, 134-35, 137; and mass marches, 35, 223-25; and material conditions, 305; and members' dues, 231; and militancy, 13, 59-60, 62-63, 65, 80, 81, 112-13, 148, 175, 176, 200, 216, 225, 290-91, 296; and minimum wage, 250; and monthly donations, 231; and Mothers Defense Committee, 288, 289; and Muslim Mosque, Inc. (MMI), 278, 295; and nationwide school boycott, 243; and network with Monroe, North Carolina, 65, 69, 70; in New York City, 6, 8, 11, 12, 27-28, 51-57, 190-200, 216, 220-35, 229-33; and the 1920s-40s, 18; in the 1950s, 27-28, 29, 52-57, 68-70, 80; in the 1960s, 148-50, 226-30, 272, 284; in the North, 182, 228; and Northern Black organizations, 175, 272; and NYC stall-in, 271, 272, 273, 274, 283; and NY NAACP, 27, 59; and oppressive power structures, 271-72, 296; and Organization of Afro-American Unity, 296; and organized defense, 296; and parents as activists, 28, 30-31, 34, 53-57; in Philadelphia, 274; and picketing, 182, 183-84, 206, 207, 208-9, 211, 227, 244, 246, 247-48, 252, 271, 273, 284; and policing, 2, 8, 13-14, 52, 208, 209, 256-59, 265, 273, 284, 288-92, 300; and political action, 19, 28, 30-31, 33-34, 36-37, 56-57, 216, 289-92; and political consciousness, 177-78, 227; and politicians, 229, 230; and power, 4, 12, 28, 35, 52, 56-57, 58, 186, 231, 275; and protests, 35, 40, 44, 56, 265; and Puerto Rican residents, 6, 28, 265; and Puerto Rican workers, 206; and radical leaders, 84; and radical organizing, 3, 8, 40, 68-70, 118; and radio programs, 28, 68; and A. Philip Randolph, 233, 250; and rent strikes, 35, 60-63, *62*, 240, 241, 250, 252-53, 255, 257; and Revolutionary Action Movement (RAM), 274-75, 296; and school boycotts, 253, 257, 268-69; and school desegregation, 25, 53-56; and selective patronage, 253; and self-defense, 274-75, 291-92; and self-determination, 4, 6, 57, 69, 81, 186, 194, 202, 203, 240, 275; and sit-in movement, 120, 186, 207-8, 261, 271, 273, 286; in the South, 57, 58, 120, 228; and "spirit of Bandung," 112; and Bill Strickland, 252, 273, 274, 290, 293, 304, 306, 370n13; and Student Nonviolent Coordinating Committee (SNCC), 209, 228; and systems of oppression, 30-31, 81, 82; and tenant organizing, 6, 13, 18, 22, 34, 35, 36, 37, 38-43, 57-63, 92, 186, 218-39, 243, 251-53, 321n117; and Title I, 321n117; and unjust evictions, 40; and Robert F. Williams, 134, 138; and working class, 8, 28, 30, 35, 36-37, 39, 40, 41, 42, 52, 57, 112, 183. *See also* Northern Negro Grass Roots Leadership Conference; organizers

Gray, Jesse, *244*, *267*; and ACT, 272; assault of, 245; base building strategy of, 40; and Black communists, 35-36, 56; and Black freedom, 81; and Black leadership, 341n95; and Black liberation, 178, 241, 303-4; and Black nationalism, 268; and black power, 304; and black pride, 304; and Black radicalism, 253, 304; and Chester, Pennsylvania, 266; and civilian review board, 261; and civil rights struggle, 249; and collective action, 233–34; and collective ownership of housing, 224, 251; and Communist Party (CPUSA), 58, 251, 319n87, 320n101; and Community Council on Housing (CCH), 249–50, 251; and coordination of marches, 223–25, 236–37, 240; and Federal Bureau of Investigation (FBI) investigations, 42; and Glasgow, Scotland, 37; as a grassroots organizer, 1, 11, 12, 34, 35, 36, 37–43, 49, 50, 52, 59, 61, 90, 110, 174, 200, 215, 217, 218–19, 221, 223–25, 226, 227, 229, 230, 231, 236–38, 240, 242, 251–52, 264, 272, 273, 276, 305, 320n101, 355n159; and Harlem Action Group, 213; and Harlem Tenants Council, 37, 38, 39–43; and heat and hot water, 247, 249–50, 253; and housing inequality, 248, 293; and Leadership Training Workshop, 275; and Left-labor organizers, 233; and Lower Harlem Tenants Council (LHTC), 43, 57, 58, 59, 60–61, 183, 184, 186, 213, 343n7; and Commissioner Murphy, 262; and National Maritime Union (NMU), 35, 319–20n91, 320n101; and nationwide school boycott, 243; and nation within a nation, 319n86; and New Orleans, Louisiana, 34; and North Carolina, 42; and oppressive power structures, 35, 36, 42, 43; police investigation of, 285; and policing, 246–48, 266–67; and rent control, 60; and rent strikes, 217, 218, 230, 231, 239, 240, 241, 242, 243, 244, 248, 250, 251, 265, 267, 304; and school boycotts, 304; and segregated street car seating, 34; and sit-in movement, 304; and SS *Washington,* 35; and tenant movement, 58, 60–61, 62, 178, 223–25, 230–32, 235, 236–37, 243, 244–45, 247, 251, 253, 258; and Tunica, Louisiana, 34. *See also* Community Council on Housing (CCH); Lower Harlem Tenants Council (LHTC)

Gray, Muriel, 291

Great Britain, 37, 49
Green, Berta, 155
Green, Maxine, 233
Gregory, Dick, 243
Griffin, Farah Jasmine, 24
Griffin, Junius, 279, 280, 281, 282, 283, 284. *See also* New York Police Department (NYPD)
Guy, Rosa: and French language, 131; and Marcus Garvey, 131; as a grassroots organizer, 134, 137; and Harlem Writers Guild, 132; and Malcolm X, 141, 142; and militancy, 159; and rage, 144; and support for Lumumba, 131–32; as a union activist, 131; and United Nations, 131, 134, 135, 142

Hall, George, 96
Hamer, Fannie Lou, 370n13
Hamm, Daniel, 278, 279
Hammarskjöld, Dag, 132, 135
Hammes, Norman, 76–77
Hand, Q. R., 222, 228, 239, 247–48, 262–63, 355n159
Hansberry, Lorraine, 116, 140–41, 142, 144, 158
Harlem, New York City: and activists, 13, 17, 18, 20, 22, 27, 30–31, 34, 35, 37, 50, 57–58, 66, 94, 112, 113, 114, 115–16, 119, 121, 127, 131, 132, 134, 137, 139, 141–46, 154, 156, 157, 174, 186, 187–88, 194, 202–3, 205, 228, 233–35, 240, 284, 288, 302; affordable housing in, 59, 60, 92, 93, 235; and African diaspora, 5, 112, 113–14, 116; and African heritage, 144; and "African Nationalists," 139; and Alexander Hamilton Houses, 58–59, 60; angry crowds in, 77–78, 80, 85, 161, 169, 297; anticapitalism in, 145; and anticolonialism, 20, 103–4, 112, 114, 115, 116, 127, 131, 145, 270, 293; and armed self-defense, 103, 127, 146, 293, 297; and Black and Puerto Rican workers, 205; and Black business ownership, 19–20, 87; and Black communities, 13–14, 16, 19–20,

398 INDEX

Harlem, New York City (continued)
24-25, 49, 60-63, 80-82, 87, 106, 107, 112, 115, 116, 118, 126, 131, 144, 157, 165, 242, 247, 252, 256, 293, 294; and Black governmental representation, 19, 85, 87, 88; and Black internationalism, 269; and Black Leftist organizations, 143, 160-61; and Black liberation struggles, 113-16, 119, 121, 127, 142-43, 144, 147, 157, 181, 182, 203, 229-30, 253-55, 315n13; and Black migrants, 22; and Black nationalism, 35, 71, 74, 85, 112, 114, 115-16, 119, 127, 145, 157, 164, 171, 179, 183, 192, 196, 209, 291; and Black nationalists and Leftists, 123, 127, 137, 146, 157, 196, 217, 291; and Black politics, 21, 22, 35, 85, 88-89, 93, 114, 119, 127, 157, 170, 171-72, 189, 268; and Black radicalism, 5, 8, 9, 10, 12, 13, 14, 18, 21, 35, 52, 63, 65, 66, 74, 82, 107, 110, 113, 117, 127, 137-38, 143, 144, 147, 155, 156, 157, 159, 169, 175, 178, 181, 189, 204, 213, 214, 217, 256, 272, 278, 280-81, 288, 294; and Black students, 25-26, 30, 193; and Black women activists, 53-57, 68-70, 156; as the Black world, 1, 4, 5; and Black youth, 291; and boycott of public schools, 34, 53-55, 203; and building fires, 38, 41, 61; businesses in, 19-20, 87, 157; and capitalism, 142, 146; and Fidel Castro, 126, *126*, 127; and Carmela Caviglione, 99, 325-26n94, 326n107, 326n109; and challenges to police, 256, 288; and "Children Apart" conference, 25, 26-27; and Christian churches, 23, 24, 46, 59, 97, 162; and civil rights struggle, 4, 9, 10, 21, 27, 44-47, 84, 96, 239; and Dr. Kenneth Clark, 280; and collective action, 144; and colonialism, 142-43; and Committee on Harlem Affairs (CHA), 84, 89-97, 98, 108-10, 119, 210; and Committee on Police-Community Relations, 260; and Communist Party (CPUSA), 29, 35, 37, 65; and Community Council on Housing (CCH), 226, 228, 229, 230, 230-31, 233, 234, 235, 236, 237, 246, 247-48, 255; and community organizing, 16, 18-19, 30, 39, 59, 200-203, 219-20, 223-35, 236; community politics in, 8, 16, 39, 49, 93; and Ana Livia Cordero, 127; and Cornell students, 180; and crime data, 86; and crime laws, 281, 291; and Cuban Revolution, 125, 143; and cultural production, 5, 15, 16, 18, 114, 178; and daycare centers, 202; deaths in, 61; and "de facto" segregation, 91; and demands for justice, 257-58; and democratic process, 91; demonstrators in, *133*, 299; as destination for migrants, 3, 15-16; diasporic movements in, 8; and direct action, 260, 274, 288; and displacement of Black residents, 41, 42, 59-60; and displacement of tenants, 40-41, 93, 235; and drugs, 292, 293; and Dunlevy Milbank Community Center, 229, 232, 240, 243, 267; and East Harlem schools, 271; and East Harlem Tenants Council (EHTC), 257-58; and economic boycotts, 19, 198; and economic inequality, 87, 93, 205; and economic nationalism, 19, 20, 94; and education, 25-26, 30-31, 34, 52, 53, 54-56, 66, 87, 88, 89, 91-92, 148, 193-97, 202, 203, 218, 219, 233, 263, 301-2, 370n13; employment in, 81, 85, 157, 197-200, 204-6, 218, 233, 291, 301-2, 370n13; and evictions, 59, 263; and freedom, 4, 19, 20, 49, 146; and Fruit Stand Riot, 289, 290, 291, 363n125; and grassroots organizations, 289-94; and grassroots radicalism, 130, 200; gymnasium in, 202; and Harlem Action Group, 225, 228, 246, 247, 263, 264, 288-90, 370n12; and Harlem Defense Council, 283, 294, 298, 300, 303; and Harlem Democratic Party, 52; and Harlem Hospital, 48, 189, 204-5, 206, 209, 211, 212, 213, 240, 255, 276; and Harlem Nine trials, 54, 56; and Harlem Parents Committee, 243; and Harlem Square, 6, 21, 127, 134, 136, 137, 148, 149,

160, 167, 168, 169; and Harlem Tenants Council, 18, 38-43; and Harlem Trade Union Council, 22; and Harlem Writers Guild, 18, 125, 130-31, 132, 134, 135, 150, 187; and Harlem Youth Opportunities Unlimited (HARYOU), 284, 287; and Gladys Harrington, 200, 203, 204, 211, 213, 216; and "The Hate That Hate Produced," 98, 280; health and sanitation in, 38, 88, 92-93, 227; Hotel Theresa in, 125, 126, 127, 128, 133, 183, 260; and housing as an issue, 110, 157, 173, 186, 213, 218, 219-20, 223-38, 240-41, 263, 291, 301-2, 370n13; housing crisis in, 1, 38, 39, 40-41, 58-59, 61, 81, 85, 87-88, 92-93, 224, 236-38; and human rights, 112, 217, 303, 326n107; and integration, 88, 186, 216; as an international hub, 5-6, 13, 127; and juvenile delinquency, 103, 275, 293, 351n68; labor movements in, 233; landlords' control in, 18, 38, 39, 40, 41, 42, 61, 62, 93, 219, 223, 245; and law enforcement, 89-90, 94-97, 98, 257, 288; and James Lawson, 127, 209; and Lenox Terrace Apartments, 42; Lincoln Project in, 55; living conditions in, 9, 13, 37-38, 40, 41, 60, 61, 84, 85, 87, 89, 92-93, 142, 167, 215, 219, 226, 227, 229, 231, 234, 236, 251, 263; and local and federal government, 24-25, 38-45, 84, 85-97, 109-10, 120, 205-20, 217, 231, 236; and local leaders, 203, 219, 230-32, 255, 264; and local people, 206-7, 217, 219, 231-32; location of, 5, 129; and marches, 146, 211, 292; and Marcus Garvey Day, 72, 94, 114; mass rallies in, 45-48, 46, 83, 114, 146; and Julian Mayfield, 127, 130, 148; media in, 100-101; and Lewis Michaux, 134, 137, 216; and militancy, 142, 195, 215, 280, 291; and money for guns, 151; and Mothers Defense Committee, 298; and "Negro Revolt," 52, 76, 83, 87; and nonviolence, 10, 254; and NY CORE, 188, 189; and Organization of Afro-American Unity, 299, 370n12; and organized defense, 10, 291-92; and Pan-Africanism, 113, 114-16, 131, 145, 146, 293; police brutality in, 6, 10, 11-12, 24, 44-46, 76-77, 83, 85, 88, 94, 99-100, 106-7, 208, 255-58, 260, 263, 264, 277-79, 283-84, 288, 289-91, 300, 301, 326n107; and police repression, 255, 260, 280-81, 288, 292, 293, 294; and policing, 233, 246-49, 255-63, 275, 279, 281-86, 289, 290-92, 302, 303; and political action, 370n13; and political consciousness, 49, 81-82, 84, 110, 113-14, 130, 146, 150, 183, 189, 194, 196, 217, 248, 252-53, 290-91; and political power, 157, 169, 225, 228, 229-30, 303; and potential riots, 12, 78, 80, 81, 82, 83-84, 86, 99, 110, 120, 160, 169, 210, 281, 299-300; and power, 50, 80, 81-82, 84, 93, 130, 146, 164, 182, 187, 215, 217, 294; and Peggy Trotter Dammond Preacely, 243; protests in, 12, 45-46, 59, 78, 86, 90, 98, 100, 103, 111, 131, 149, 187, 199, 206-13, 220, 240, 252, 276, 277, 284, 288, 299-300; and public health problems, 38; and public safety, 292; and Puerto Rican residents, 76-77, 106, 107, 198-99, 233, 234-35, 242, 243, 247, 252, 255-57, 294; and Puerto Rican students, 25-26; and Puerto Rican workers, 206; and Puerto Rican youth, 14, 283-84; race relations in, 75, 80-81, 85, 88, 283; and racial consciousness, 195; racial inequality in, 1-3, 4, 6, 10-12, 53, 83-84, 91-92, 93; and racial oppression, 110, 141, 196; and racial pride, 18, 21; racial tensions in, 86, 87, 90, 93, 95-96, 103-4, 106, 108, 109; rage in, 138; rallies in, 154, 157, 167, 168-69, 173, 183, 192, 213, 218-19, 228, 229, 252, 266-68, 272, 288, 298; and rebellion in 1964, 10, 11, 12, 13-14, 299-301, 302-4, 369n230; rebellions in, 83, 84, 92, 215, 256, 294, 299-301, 303-4, 305; and recreational space, 201, 202; religious leaders in, 119;

Harlem, New York City (*continued*)
and rent reductions, 39; rent strikes in, 1–2, 3, 6, 11, 35, 61–63, 92, 225, 239, 240–41; and rent strikes of 1963–64, 13, 217, 218–42, 249–50, 255, 263, 267; and school boycotts, 53, 249, 266, 267; and school conditions, 25–26, 30, 81, 85; and school segregation, 53, 91; science workshops in, 202; and segregated communities, 157; and self-defense, 12, 14, 104, 111, 256, 262, 265, 274, 276–78, 288, 291, 294, 295–96, 300; and self-determination, 12, 19, 20, 52, 85, 93, 112, 146, 196, 197, 203, 217, 294, 303; significance of, 4, 12, 35; and sit-in movement, 109, 182, *207*, 278; and social justice, 189; Speakers' Corner in, 6, 21; and Earl Spence, 203; and spirit of Bandung, 20, 113–14, 143–44, 300; and state violence, 278, 293; and Stephen Foster Houses, 60; and struggle for rights, 2–6, 10, 11–13, 80–82, 113; and Subcommittee on Housing (CHA), 92–93; and Subcommittee on Law Enforcement (CHA), 94–97; and summers of the 1960s, 174, 177, 294, 300–301; and systems of oppression, 81–82, 294, 303; teachers in, 30, 91; tenant movement in, 1, 18, 37–43, 59–63, 92, 218, 220–40, *232*, 255; and traditions of resistance, 112, 114, 293–94; and treatment of rent strikers, 248–49; and United African Nationalist Movement (UANM), 136, 143; and UN protests, 142, 145, 147, 159; and urban renewal projects, 41–42, 92, 93; and victim support, 291, 292; and violence, 256, 259, 263, 278, 279, 298, 300, 301, 302; and Mayor Wagner, 104; and white people, 157, 279; and white students, 25–26; white supremacy in, 2–3, 252; and Robert F. Williams, 98, 111, 123, 127, 148, 149, 150; and will of people, 97; and Woolworth store, 182; and working-class Black communities, 7, 10, 30, 37, 41, 60, 81, 87, 90, 148, 187–88, 197, 217, 243, 275, 294. *See also* African diaspora; Dunlevy Milbank Community Center; Godfrey Nurse Houses; Neighborhood Commons Project; Powell, Adam Clayton, Jr.

Harlem Anti-Colonial Committee, 167, 168
Harlem Education Program (HEP), 193–97, 200–203, 209, 214, 219, 222
Harlem Freedom Rally, 119–21, *120*
Harlem Lawyers Association, 294
Harlem Neighborhood Association, 193
Harlem Nine, 53–57, 69, 91, 96, 167, 242
Harlem Renaissance, 5
Harlem Six, 279, 288, 289, 298, 363n125, 363n127
"Harlem Temper, The," 215–16, 233
Harlem Tenants Council (HTC), 18, 37, 38–43. *See also* Lower Harlem Tenants Council (LHTC)
Harlem Trade Union Council, 22
Harlem Unity Council, 370n12
Harlem Youth Opportunities Unlimited (HARYOU), 201, 205, 209, 213, 275–76, 277. *See also* Black freedom movement; Harlem, New York City
Harrington, Gladys, 179, 185, 186, 187, 188, 197. *See also* Harlem, New York City; New York City
Harrison, Hubert, 21
Harvard University, 214
Haughton, James, 161, 216–17, 233, 264, 304
Hayes, Roland, 15
Haynes, Carrie, 53, 54, 55
Haywood, Harry, 22, 35, 56
Hedgeman, Anna Arnold, 160, 219, 240
Hicks, Calvin, 129, 131, 135, 137, 154, 155. *See also* Black freedom movement; New Afro-American Nationalism
Hicks, James, 82, 86, 89–90, 95, 126, 136
Hill, Herbert, 206, 207–8, 210
Hill, Norman, 199, 200, 207, 210, 250
Hill, Velma, 199, 200, 206, 207, 213
Hinds, Glester, 90
Hinton, Johnson X, 12, 47, 48, 49, 70, 72. *See also* New York Police Department (NYPD)

INDEX 401

Hobson, Julius, 243
Hoover, J. Edgar, 66, 67, 101, 168, 285
Housing Question, The (Engels), 36
Howard University, 239, 242
Hughes, Langston, 118
human rights, 4, 10, 12, 13, 52, 79, 84, 269. *See also* African Americans; Black Power; Congress of Racial Equality (CORE); Harlem, New York City; liberalism; Malcolm X; Nation of Islam (NOI); New Afro-American Nationalism; United States
Humphrey, Hubert, 195
Hunton, Alphaeus, 20

Intergroup Committee on New York's Public Schools, 25, 27, 33, 43
International Committee in Defense of Africa (ICDA), 65, 66, 69, 114
International Ladies' Garment Workers Union, 183, 233

Jack, Hulan, 81, 89, 103, 219, 229, 240
Jackson, Jacob, 44
Jackson, Rita, 221, 222, 225, 233
Jackson, Sherron (Amina Rahman), 209, 213, 275, 276, 293, 294. *See also* Black freedom movement
Jewish communities, 37
Jim Crow society: and activists, 123, 180, 343n7; and Black working class, 319n81; and education, 30, 31; indignities of, 123; and "Negro Revolt," 51–52; in New York City, 7, 8, 9, 10, 16, 21, 25, 26, 30, 31, 38, 43–44, 52, 59–60, 102, 110–12, 125, 266–67, 270, 281; in the North, 2, 3, 4, 5, 9, 10, 16, 21, 25, 26, 30, 31, 38, 51, 52, 63, 140, 145, 147, 174, 177, 180, 181, 191, 196, 219, 252, 266–67, 302; and racial oppression, 38, 42, 88, 111–12, 270; and racial segregation, 31; and rent strikes, 51; and resistance from Labor, 319n81; and the South, 2, 3–4, 31, 34, 43, 88, 208, 241, 288; and systems of oppression, 145; and urban renewal projects, 40–42; and US policy, 304; and white state power, 302–3; and white supremacy, 140, 255, 281
Johnson, Dr. Robert, 194
Johnson, Thelma, 216, 254, 276
Jones, Bill, 167
Jones, LeRoi. *See* Baraka, Amiri
Jones, William "Willie," 277, 278, 279, 363n133

Kennedy, President John F., 138, 148, 168, 169, 176, 177
Kennedy, Robert F., 154
Kennedy, Stephen, 75, 85, 86–87, 88, 90, 94. *See also* New York Police Department (NYPD)
Kenyatta, Jomo, 111, 120
Khrushchev, Nikita, 127
Killens, John O., 1, 123, 130, 151, 240, 291. *See also* Black freedom movement
King, Dr. Martin Luther, Jr., 53, 119, 149, 167, 184, 272, 303
King, Mary, 221, 222, 225, 233
King, Rev. A. D., 208
King, Shannon, 8
King, Tyson, 99
Knight, Bob, 196, *202,* 222, 228, 263, *264.* *See also* Black freedom movement
Ku Klux Klan, 64, 71, 100, 122, 150, 151. *See also* United States

Landry, Lawrence, 243, 272
Lane, Mark, 183, 191, 211
Latin America, 128
Lawrence, Tina (Zungara Tina Lawrence), 211
Lawson, James, 18, 19, 21, 94, 115, 119, 299. *See also* Harlem, New York City; New York City
Leaks, Sylvester, 118, 167, 302
Lewis, Edward S., 140
Lewis, John: and civil rights, 1, 6, 243; and nonviolence, 211–12; and racial

Lewis, John (*continued*)
discrimination, 211-12; and rent strikes, 241-42; and segregation, 211-12; as a Southerner, 3-4; and Student Nonviolent Coordinating Committee (SNCC), 211, 240

liberalism: and Black equality, 113, 140; and Black liberals, 140; and civil rights, 186; and human rights, 186; and justice, 109; and liberal reforms, 146; limits of, 8, 10, 84, 109; in New York City, 11, 84, 109, 110, 186, 242, 252; and Puerto Rican residents, 252; and race, 175; and racial liberalism, 242, 270, 294, 306; and racism, 110, 113; rejection of, 12, 84, 110, 143; and repression, 302; and state power, 11; and Wagner administration, 249, 302; and white liberals, 10-11, 121, 140, 169, 170; and working-class Black communities, 252

Liberation Committee for Africa (LCA), 135, 136, 137-39, 151, 154

Liberator, 6, 138, 144, 151, 154, 157, 169. *See also* Black freedom movement

lien laws, 39

Lincoln, Abbey, 130, 132, 134, 146, 274, 293

Lincoln, Richard, 41

Lincoln University, 114

Lindsay, Mayor John, 45

Linn, Karl, 200, 201

Little Rock, Arkansas, 49, 55, 56

Little Rock High School, 28, 49

Locke, Alain, 15

Lomax, Louis, 67-68, 71, 72, 207, 208

Los Angeles Police Department (LAPD), 162, 163, 167, 339n66, 340n69

Lower Harlem Tenants Council (LHTC), 43, 57-59, 60, 61-62, 63. *See also* Community Council on Housing (CCH); Gray, Jesse

Lumumba, Patrice: assassination of, 13, 131, 133, 134, 135, 138, 141, 142, 143, 148, 158, 334n93, 334n95; and Belgian oppression, 131, 138; capture of, 132; and communism, 336n128; and Cubans and Puerto Ricans, 136; funeral for, 136-37; neocolonial coup against, 144; and New York City, 131, 136-37; on placards, 149, *149;* and rule of Colonel Mobutu, 132; and United Nations, 132, 133

Lumumba, Pauline, 141

Lynch, Lincoln, 197, 211

Lynching Northern Style: Police Brutality, 43, 45

Lynn, Conrad, 151, 153, 155, 167, 169, 170. *See also* Black freedom movement

Lytle, Olga Pierce, 139

Makeba, Miriam, 195

Malcolm X, *267,* 280, 291; and ACT, 268-69, 272; advisers of, 117; and African pride and liberation, 115, 116, 142; and Maya Angelou, 141, 142; and anticolonialism, 73-74, 116, 118, 120, 269; and armed resistance, 173; and armed struggle, 175, 176, 269; assassination of, 305, 366n178; and "Ballot or the Bullet" speech, 268, 269, 359n58; and Bandung Conference, 20, 115, 120; and Black freedom movement, 118-20, 128, 217, 269; and Black independent politics, 268; and Black liberation, 13, 18, 25, 50, 72, 81, 111, 114, 116, 118-20, 141, 142, 162, 176, 269, 281, 304, 368n225; and Black nationalism, 21-23, 72-73, 116-19, 120, 142, 160, 162, 164, 179, 196, 204, 265, 268, 269, 274, 291; and Black people, 71, 72, 111, 130, 214; and Black political empowerment, 25, 30, 49, 50, 114, 116, 119, 120, 121, 178, 266, 269; and Black radicalism, 140, 160, 291; in Boston, Massachusetts, 17, 18; and call for unity, 119, 120, 148, 173, 175, 189, 213, 216; and Fidel Castro, 128, 333n68; and challenges to police, 340n69; and Chester, Pennsylvania, 266; and civil rights movement, 142, 192, 243, 249; and coalition building, 121; contribution of, 178; and criminal justice system, 165; and Cuban revolutionaries, 125, 127; and demonstration in Times Square, 165; and desire for land, 175–76; and direct action, 165; and dispersal of crowd, 48; and education, 268–69; as Malik El-Shabazz, 74; and Emergency Committee for Unity on Social and Economic Problems, 160–62, 340n69; family of, 17, 22; and Marcus Garvey, 17, 18, 116; and grassroots bases, 49, 72, 177, 213; as a grassroots organizer, 11, 12, 49, 50, 52, 72, 74, 90, 110, 116–17, 121, 162, 165, 166, 177, 200, 213, 233, 268, 305; and Harlem, 264, 276, 370n13; and Harlem youth, 278–79; and "The Hate That Hate Produced," 74, 281; and history of colonialism, 117; and human rights, 269, 270; and integration, 118, 142, 163–64, 213, 269; and internationalism, 165, 293; and Joseph X, 165; and justice, 76, 80, 163, 166; and Benjamin Karim, 164; and King Solomon Baptist Church, 175; and Sylvester Leaks, 167; as Malcolm Little, 17, 22; and Los Angeles mosque, 163; and Marcus Garvey Day, 71–72, 72; and Mecca, 270; and militancy, 138, 167, 268, 270, 272, 285; and Militant Labor Forum, 248, 281; and Audley Moore as mentor, 116–17; and Eloise Moore, 164; and *Muhammad Speaks*, 117; and Commissioner Murphy, 262; and Muslim Mosque, Inc. (MMI), 265–66, 268, 269, 272, 274, 278, 285; and nation building, 176; and Nation of Islam, 48, 49, 70–72, 117–21, 141–42, 162, 163, 164, 173, 174, 189, 265, 268; and nonviolence, 175, 213; and Northern Negro Grass Roots Leadership Conference, 274; as an orator, 21, 23, 142, 162, 163–64, 171, 174, 175–77, 216, 268, 293, 304, 342n125; and Organization of African Unity, 298; as a Pan-Africanist, 22–23, 72, 164, 173; and the police, 43, 48, 49, 74–76, 100, 139, 161–62, 165–67, 269, 285, 295; and police brutality, 295; and police reform, 162; and political consciousness, 24, 165, 174; and politics, 171, 173, 174, 176, 265–66, 268; popularity of, 47, 70, 71; and power, 48, 49, 171, 268; and protection of women, 75; and protests, 49, 141–42, 209, 218, 286; and racial pride, 24; and racial problems in New York, 326n111; and rejection of nonviolence, 174, 256; and resistance to police violence, 266–67; and return to Harlem, 17, 18, 22, 25; and revolutions, 175–76, 269–70, 274; and rifle clubs, 266, 278, 292; and secular nationalism, 166; and self-defense, 65, 71, 118, 173, 266, 269, 275, 278, 292, 295; and self-determination, 71, 268; and self-respect, 71; spiritual awakening of, 17; and split with Elijah Muhammad, 177; and split with Nation of Islam, 253, 255, 265, 268; and Ronald Stokes's death, 162–63, 164, 340n69; surveillance of, 74; and Temple No. 7, 17, 18, 23, 65, 75, 117, 162, 164, 274; and tours of Africa and Middle East, 74, 120, 269–70, 272, 291; and trial in 1959, 75; and 28th Precinct Community Council, 128; and UN protests, 160; and uprising in 1964, 303; and violence, 163; and voter registration, 268; and Mayor Wagner, 166; and white imperialism, 115; and white supremacy, 17; and Robert F. Williams, 65, 66, 269, 360n68; wiretaps of, 285; youth of, 17, 22. *See also* Nation of Islam (NOI)

Mallory, Mae, *32;* and African diaspora, 148; and Algeria, 158–59; and anticolonialism, 148; and armed self-defense, 126, 147, 148–49, 151, 152, 158; and armed struggle, 173; and Black liberation, 13, 29–30, 50, 68, 81, 144, 145, 146–48, 154, 158, 159, 178, 333n59; and Black moderates, 148; and Black power, 148, 303; and boycott of public schools, 34, 53, 54, 55, 56–57, 147; and capitalist societies, 128–29; and Fidel Castro, 125, 128; in Cleveland, Ohio, 153; and Communist Party (CPUSA), 29, 318n61; and coordination of protests, 183; and *The Crusader*, 100, 123, 136, 296; and Cuban revolutionaries, 125;

Mallory, Mae (*continued*)
and Cuyahoga County Jail, 153, 155; and daughter Patricia, 31, *32*, 153, 275, 296; and "A Declaration of Conscience," 148; defense of, 160, 337n3; and economic inequality, 158; and educational justice, 148, 318n66; and educational outcomes, 268; eviction of, 34, 55; extradition fight of, 167, 174, 243; FBI search for, 153; felony charges of, 33–34; and forging of unity, 148; and fundraising for arms, 151; and gender discrimination, 158; as a grassroots organizer, 11, 12, 29–31, 34, 49, 50, 52, 55, 56–57, 90, 110, 125, 147, 148, 150, 151, 158, 177, 193, 305; and Harlem, 29, 30, 52, 53, 54, 55, 56–57, 66, 110, 153; and Harlem Nine, 242; and Harlem Six, 366n186; and Harlem Square rally, 150, 168; and housing project, 66; importance of, 178; and Ethel Azalea Johnson, 159; and Junior High School Coordinating Committee, 53; and justice in education, 91; lawsuit of, 31, 32; and legal advice, 160; and Macon, Georgia, 28, 31; and "maladjusted Negroes," 51; and Keefer Mallory, 29; and militancy, 138, 144, 148, 154, 158, 160, 366n186; and Monroe, North Carolina, 159, 269; and Muslim Mosque, Inc. (MMI), 269; and nationalism, 158; and nonviolent direct action, 158; and On Guard Committee for Freedom (OGFF), 337n5; and Organization of Militant Black Women, 366n186; and Pan-Africanism, 158–59; as a parent, 28, 29, 31, 33, 55; and the police, 43, 147; political evolution of, 126, 147, 160; and prison time, 269; and public schools, 30–33, 53, 54, 56, 154; and revolution, 269; and self-defense, 269, 275, 342n119; and self-determination, 56, 68, 126, 158; and son Keefer Jr., 34; and surveillance agencies, 151; and systemic racism, 158, 159; threats to, 56; and UN protests, 135–36, 147; and violence, 136; and Mabel and Robert Williams, 152, 155; and working-class Black women, 68–69

Mangum, Robert, 74
March on Washington, 170, 171, 172, 174, 176, 203. *See also* civil rights
Marshall, Wanda, 274
Marxism, 35, 195, 264
Mayfield, Julian, 65, 72, 118, 122, 123, 124. *See also* Black freedom movement; Harlem, New York City
Mboya, Tom, 111, 120
McDew, Chuck, 194
McDonald, Jimmy, 181, 184, 196
McKay, Claude, 16
Metropolitan Council on Housing, 57, 226, 251
Michaux, Lewis, 18, 21, 66, 94, 119, 132. *See also* Harlem, New York City
Mobley, Ora Mae, 65, 66, 69, 293
Monroe Defense Committee (MDC): and anticolonialism, 159; and armed struggle, 159; and Black leadership, 155–56, 293; and Black nationalism, 155, 159; and Black self-determination, 156; formation of, 154–55; and Freedom Riders, 155, 338n33; and *Freedomways*, 154; and fundraisers, 154; and interracial organizing, 155; and Mae Mallory, 154, 156, 159, 289; mission of, 154; and Pan-Africanism, 159; and salaried officers, 155; and state violence, 159; surveillance of, 286; and white leadership, 155
Moore, Audley, 16, 18, 21, 22, 29, 35, 65, 319n87. *See also* Black freedom movement; Malcolm X; New York City
Moore, Carlos, 135, 136
Moore, Eloise, 18, 22, 65, 69, 114, 117, 139. *See also* Malcolm X
Moore, Richard B., 18, 21, 331n14
Moritt, Judge Fred, 238
Moses, Robert, 40–41, 93
Muhammad, Akbar, 173
Muhammad, Elijah: and Black nationalism, 18, 162; and call for black unity, 173; and call for land, 118, 120; and Malcolm X, 121, 162, 163, 164, 165, 166, 176, 177; and Mecca, 331n19; and NOI recruitment,

47, 72; and NOI temples as mosques, 331n19; and noninvolvement in politics, 164, 173; and origins of Black Americans, 22; political positions of, 118, 142; popularity of, 71; and resisting police repression, 74; theology of, 72, 74; writings of, 117

Mulzac, Hugh, 18

Muslim Mosque, Inc. (MMI), 265, 267, 268, 269, 272, 274. *See also* Malcolm X; New York Police Department (NYPD)

Nassar, Gamal Abdel, 127

National Association for Puerto Rican Rights, 266

National Association for the Advancement of Colored People (NAACP): and armed self-defense, 66, 67, 68, 69; Ella Baker as president of, 27–28, 36; and Black freedom movement, 280; and Bronx NAACP, 100; and civilian review board, 302; and civil rights, 24, 27, 51, 68, 183, 194; and Committee for Fair Police Practice, 260; and Gloster Current as leader, 126; and debate, 142; and Morris De Lisser, 208; and direct-action campaigns, 28–29; and employment discrimination, 53, 197, 206; gun clubs of, 64, 65; and Harlem, 138, 210; and Harlem Square rally, 148–49, 150; and Rev. Hildebrand, 229, 302; and Labor Secretary Hill, 210; and leadership, 149, 156; and local people, 8, 27, 68, 69–70; meetings of, 117; and Monroe, North Carolina, 64, 68; New York branch of, 25, 27, 36, 66, 76, 86, 90, 127, 130, 188, 189, 206, 216, 229, 280, 294, 298, 302, 352n90; and 1959 convention, 62, 67–70; and nonviolence, 67, 68; and people's demands, 216–17, 298, 302; and police brutality, 44, 208, 289; and purging of communists, 27, 36; and racism, 280; and rent strikes, 229; and school boycotts, 266; white and moderate supporters of, 67; and Roy Wilkins, 66, 67, 68; and Robert F. Williams as leader, 62–69, 72; and working-class action, 216. *See also* civil rights; New York State; organizers; United States

National Association for the Advancement of Colored People Legal Defense Fund, 43

National Maritime Union (NMU), 34–35, 36, 58

National Negro Congress, 22

National Negro Labor Council, 22

National Urban League, 44, 72, 138, 140, 266. *See also* Urban League of Greater New York

Nation of Islam (NOI): and "Asiatic Black Man," 116; Atlanta Temple of, 150; and Black communities, 147–48, 162, 163, 164, 200, 265; and Black nationalism, 17–18, 22, 47, 72, 118, 147, 255, 265; and Black people, 18, 23, 47, 70–72, 116, 117–18; brutality against, 118; charges for members of, 165; and coalition against development, 59; and colonialism, 157; and controversy, 177; and demonstrations, 141, 157, 160; and economic nationalism, 120; and education, 21, 117; and empowerment, 49, 71; and Donald Freeman, 159; and Fruit of Islam, 48, 75, 165; growth of, 71–72; and Harlem restaurant, 141; and "The Hate That Hate Produced," 70–71, 116, 117; and human rights, 165; ideologies of, 71, 72; and integration, 163; and justice, 74, 117; in Los Angeles, 162, 163; and Malcolm X, 268, 274; militancy of, 47; moral code of, 23; and Muslims, 48, 49, 72, 74, 139, 162, 164, 165, 166, 173; national temples of, 72, 117, 121, 150, 165; and nation within a nation, 118–19; and New Afro-American Nationalism, 143; and New York Police Department, 49, 74–76, 100, 161, 164, 165; and noninvolvement in politics, 167, 171, 265; and number of members, 49, 72, 121; and Pan-Africanism, 21, 116; police abuse of, 80; police harassment of,

Nation of Islam (NOI) (*continued*) 161, 164; and police surveillance, 75, 161; political nonengagement of, 162, 166; programs of, 17–18, 72, 119, 160; and protection of women, 76; and protests, 165; public bazaars of, 116; and racial pride, 23; and racial separatism, 120; and racial unrest, 139; and recruitment in Harlem, 23–24, 47, 48–49, 71, 117, 121; and rejection of direct action, 173; repression of, 166; resistance of, 110–11; and self-defense, 67, 162; and self-determination, 67, 120; and Ronald Stokes's death, 339n66; surveillance of, 74; and Temple No. 7, 17, 21, 24, 47, 58, 117, 121, 180; theology of, 25, 72, 116, 118, 119, 120, 160, 164; and "War of Armageddon," 139; and white people, 70–71, 72; and Robert F. Williams, 65, 66–67; and working-class communities, 23

Negro American Labor Council, 167, 264, 352n89

Nehru, Jawaharlal, 127

Neighborhood Commons Project, 200–203

New Afro-American Nationalism: and activists, 146, 180, 274; and African Americans, 156–57, 255; and anticolonial revolutions, 5, 143, 157; and armed self-defense, 157; and Black equality, 157, 170; and Black liberation, 156, 157, 170; and Black nation within a nation, 156–57; and Black revolution, 175; and Black youth, 256; and education, 170; and Harlem, 170, 178, 256, 274; and Calvin Hicks, 274; and housing, 170; and human rights, 213; and integration, 143, 157; and Malcolm X's "Message to the Grass Roots," 177; and Pan-Africanism, 143, 146, 156; and political landscape, 197; and political power, 213; and racial capitalism, 146; and rejection of bourgeois leadership, 156; and rejection of integration, 186; and rent strikes, 240; and revolution, 178; and self-determination, 143, 146, 156, 170, 213; and spirit of Bandung, 13; and traditions of resistance, 143, 146, 175, 181; and Dan Watts, 274

New Negro Movement, 14–15, 82

newspapers: and African independence movements, 118; anticapitalist discourse in, 118; *Baltimore Afro-American*, 71, 121–22; and Homer Bigart, 234; and Black liberation, 129; and Black nationalism, 138; and Black newspapers, 69, 71, 79, 118, 121–22, 129, 139, 260; *Boston Globe*, 216; *Challenge*, 265; *Chicago Daily Defender*, 243; and communists, 139; *The Crusader*, 100, 110, 123, 136, 144, 296; *Daily Worker*, 221; and democracy, 138; *Freedom*, 20, 22, 26, 38, 116, 141; *Guide*, 139; *The Harlem Voice*, 193–94; *Hartford Courant*, 229; and James Hicks, 48, 49; and international papers, 81; and Woody Klein, 238; and "Little Rock Nine of Harlem," 53–54; and local papers, 101; *Los Angeles Herald-Dispatch*, 117; and Malcolm X's class, 117; *The Militant*, 166; *Muhammad Speaks*, 6, 117–18, 165, 167, 302, 332n31; *New York Age*, 89; *New York Amsterdam News*, 6, 20, 25, 29, 40, 41, 42, 44, 45, 48, 49, 51–52, 53, 61, 63, 64, 79, 83, 84, 85, 86, 87–88, 89, 90, 95, 99, 100, 101, 102, 110, 119, 121–22, 126, 139, 140, 142, 170, 185, 189, 208, 226, 260, 262, 299, 325n71; *New York Citizen-Call*, 125; *New York Telegram and Sun*, 44, 238; *New York Times*, 51, 61, 68, 99–100, 105, 110, 122–23, 135, 138, 140, 142, 170, 201, 219, 226, 228–29, 234, 236, 256, 259, 262, 265, 279, 280, 281, 284, 287, 295; *Norfolk Journal*, 139; *Pittsburgh Courier*, 97, 117, 170, 205, 223; and policing, 281, 287; and radical intellectuals, 145; and rent strikes, 250; and "riot" coverage, 301; and segregation, 170; and Emmett Till murder, 45; *Washington Post*, 139

New York City: and activists, 153–54, 156, 160, 187, 195, 203–4, 210, 237–39, 250, 273, 274; and affirmative action, 255; and affordable housing, 235, 250;

African leaders in, 131; and African Nationalists, 195; and anticapitalism, 129; and anticolonialism, 125, 129, 131; and "anti-rat" program, 237; and armed self-defense, 100; and Ella Baker, 33, 36, 44, 49, 91; and Bedford-Stuyvesant, 98, 107, 224, 226, 239, 301; and Belgian Consulate, 136; and Black communities, 26, 28, 32, 37-38, 40-42, 44-45, 51-52, 59-63, 84-97, 101, 103, 108, 109, 186, 213, 221, 223, 240, 250, 251, 259, 266, 288, 290, 315n13; and Black consciousness, 129; Black law firm in, 96; and Black liberation struggles, 26-27, 270-71; and Black nationalism, 129, 160, 169; and Black Power, 5-6, 10-11; and Black radical thought, 4, 5, 7, 13-14, 52, 129, 180, 274; and Black students, 32, 33, 53, 55, 91; Black workers in, 210, 211; and Black youth, 205, 283, 299; and Board of Education (BOE), 26, 28, 31-32, 33, 53, 54, 55, 91, 242; and boycott of public schools, 53-54, 55, 242-43, 266; and the Bronx, 5, 75, 98, 99-100, 107, 180, 219, 224, 239, 261, 297; Brooklyn in, 5, 29, 64, 75, 173, 186, 187, 211, 266; and Councilman Earl Brown, 139-40; and *Brown v. Board of Education,* 53, 54, 91, 96, 317n47; and building code enforcement, 250, 261; and building inspections, 236, 237; and City College, 142, 258; and City Planning Commission, 201; and civil disobedience, 235; and climate of fear, 288; Commission on Integration of, 26, 32, 91, 96, 319n73; and Commission on Intergroup Relations, 185, 186; and Committee on Harlem Affairs (CHA), 108-10; and communism, 41, 68, 139, 140, 155, 161, 192, 295, 301, 318n61; construction industry in, 205, 209, 210, 212, 270; and cost of racial inequality, 212; and crime laws, 294-95; and crime rates, 98, 107; and Crusaders for Freedom, 154; and de facto segregation, 55, 56, 91, 96; and de jure segregation, 33; and democracy, 26, 97; demonstrators in, *299;* and Department of Buildings, 93, 224, 227; and Department of Housing and Building, 39, 62; and Department of Labor, 205, 211; and desegregation, 187, 210; and displacement of Black and Puerto Rican residents, 41, 58-60; Domestic Relations Court of, 54, 55; and Edward Dudley, 235; and education, 5, 25-28, 30-33, 34, 53-55, 56, 89, 91-92, 242, 266-67; and employment discrimination, 51, 205, 206, 208, 209-12, 274-75, 286; and employment laws, 273; and equal opportunity, 55; and evictions, 40, 42, 245-47, 248; and exploitation of Black renters, 38, 39, 41, 186; and fair housing law, 185; and fast-ins, 211; and Rev. Milton Galamison, 266; and gang-related violence, 100-101, 102, 107, 278-79; Greenwich Village in, 71; gun laws in, 295, 357n14; and Gladys Harrington, 211, 212; and "The Hate That Hate Produced," 76; and hazardous buildings, 221, 227, 270; and health and safety, 238; Health Department of, 237; and housing, 5, 26, 31, 33, 34, 36, 37-38, 39, 40-43, 55, 57-63, 87, 89-90, 92-93, 185-86, 187, 218-38, 258, 266-67, 270, 273, 321n117, 328n41; and Housing and Rent Committee, 38; Housing Authority of, 55, 323n27; and housing codes, 92-93, 219, 224, 228; and housing courts, 237; housing crisis in, 224, 228-29, 235, 236, 237-38; importance of, 181; and inequality, 10-11, 25-26, 28, 31-32, 53, 55, 108-9, 185-86, 302; and integration of schools, 32-33, 319n73; and Superintendent William Jansen, 33; and Joint Committee for Equal Employment Opportunity, 210, 212, 348n131; judiciary of, 238, 278; and juvenile delinquency, 255, 275, 280; and killings of Puerto Ricans, 256-58; and killings of teenagers, 297-99; lack of relocation agencies in, 323n27; and Mayor Fiorello La Guardia, 84, 92; and

408 INDEX

New York City (*continued*)
landlords' repairs, 219–20, 236–38, 245; and Latino residents, 272; and law and order, 109, 283, 288, 301, 302; and law enforcement, 89–90, 98, 104–10, 259–61, 271–72, 278–81, 283, 288; and James Lawson, 127, 132, 200; and Left and nationalist factionalism, 155; and Left political organizing, 36, 57, 107–8, 125, 160–62; and legalizing rent strikes, 237, 238; and Mae Mallory, FBI search for, 153; and Manhattan, 5, 85, 125, 187, 260, 273; and marches, 298; mass demonstration in, 17, 28, 44–45, 48, 211–12, 218, 239; media in, 12–13, 45, 48, 87–88, 89, 90, 102–3, 105, 107, 108, 117–18, 119, 130, 132, 138, 147, 154, 164, 166, 167, 182, 204, 215–16, 222, 234–38, 250, 255–56, 258, 265–66, 271, 278–79, 284–85, 288, 290, 295, 299; and Lewis Michaux, 161; and money for building repairs, 236–37; and Monroe defendants, 163; and Audley Moore, 131, 245; and no-knock law, 294; and nonwhite people, 210, 297, 328n41; and NY NAACP office, 99; and Deputy Mayor O'Keefe, 85, 87; and Pan-Africanism, 112, 129; and penalties for landlords, 236; and police brutality lawsuit, 278; and police brutality settlement, 48; and police reform, 288, 294–95; and policing, 5, 10, 11, 12–13, 24, 43, 47–48, 74–76, 84, 85–89, 92, 94–108, 109, 111, 218, 266–67, 278; and political power, 169, 225; and population growth, 38; and potential riots, 257; power structure of, 2, 10–13, 34, 43, 223–24; private development of, 40–42; protests in, 12, 99, 100, 102, 133, 134–36, 137, 139, 140, 141, 143, 156, 161, 165, 166, 180, 182–83, 198, 210–12, 225, 236, 244–45, 247–48, 255, 257, 258, 262, 270–71, 273, 290, 295, 298; Public Schools of, 30–33; and Puerto Rican communities, 26, 32, 37, 38, 59, 101, 108, 217, 221, 223, 240, 250, 251, 256, 257, 258–59, 290, 315n13; and Puerto Rican students, 32, 53, 55, 266; Puerto Rican workers in, 210, 211; Queens in, 5, 51, 75, 185, 211, 270, 271, 273; and racial oppression, 2–3, 5, 7, 10–11, 12, 40–41, 80–81, 109, 110; racial tensions in, 80–81, 84, 85, 108–9, 110, 288, 295–96; and racist status quo, 295–96; rallies in, 153–54, 173, 288, 291, 299; Rent and Rehabilitation Administration of, 220, 221; rent control in, 39, 42, 239, 240, 244–45; and rent reductions, 220, 221, 224, 228, 229, 237, 238; rent strikes in, 217, 220, 236, 237, 238, 239, 240–43, 250; and repression, 256, 294; and residential segregation, 31, 33, 38; and riot control, 288; and school desegregation, 32, 33, 51, 55, 56, 250, 317n47; and school segregation, 25–26, 28, 31, 33, 53, 154, 268, 273; school teachers in, 26, 28, 32, 33; and sit-in movement, 107–8, 109, 139, 185, 187; solidarity protests in, 182; and South Jamaica, 98, 107; and Staten Island, 5; and stop-and-frisk law, 294; and summers of the 1960s, 7, 109, 173, 186, 206, 282–83, 288; and surveillance of Black leaders, 67, 74; and takeover of slum buildings, 224–25, 227–29; and tenants' rights, 221, 236; Times Square in, 136, 165, 166, 173, 286; and traffic jams from stall-in, 271, 272; and United Nations, 131, 132, 133, 134–35, 136, 137, 138, 139, 140, 141, 143, 147, 156, 180; and urban renewal programs, 263, 321n117, 323n27; and use of vacant lots, 201; and violence, 262, 280, 281, 285, 295, 297, 302, 368–69n228; and voting, 271; and Mayor Wagner, 81, 84, 85–86, 87, 89, 93, 96, 97, 98–99, 102, 106, 107, 108, 109, 127, 204, 208, 209–12, 223, 228, 236, 237, 238, 244, 249, 258, 260, 270, 271, 273, 283, 286, 295, 298, 299, 301–2, 365n163; Wagner administration in, 12, 14, 28, 31, 85, 108, 225, 235, 238, 255, 256, 282, 285, 288, 294, 301, 302; and white landlords, 38; white residents of,

33, 51, 55, 72, 100, 204, 271, 278–79, 294, 319n73; white supremacy in, 7, 10–11, 12, 14, 43, 108; and Robert F. Williams, 65, 134, 160; and Woolworth stores, 183, 343n7; and working-class Black communities, 53, 186, 221, 230–31, 239, 272, 274–75; and zoning policies, 31, 32, 33, 53. *See also* Harlem, New York City; New York Police Department (NYPD)

New York Police Department (NYPD): and accountability, 97, 107, 161, 290, 294; and Lieutenant Angrist, 76, 77; and Walter Arm, 75, 76, 139; and assaults on teenagers, 284; and attack on protesters, 136; and benefits for officers, 262; and Black and Puerto Rican youth, 276–78; and Black communities, 86, 88, 95, 96–99, 100–102, 104–5, 245–46, 259–60, 262, 276, 278, 282–87; and Black nationalists, 139, 161, 280; and Black officers, 85, 88, 90, 94, 95, 96, 97, 108, 248, 277, 283, 285–86; and Black radicalism, 255, 280, 284–86, 287, 293, 295; and Black rights, 43, 95; brutality of, 43, 44, 45, 47–48, 70, 75, 76–79, 88, 94, 99, 100, 157, 161, 162, 166, 248, 249, 255, 256, 257, 258, 261, 264, 265, 267, 269, 270, 273, 276–78, 278, 281, 283–86, 288, 289, 290, 293, 294, 300, 362n121; and Bureau of Special Services (BOSS), 139, 151, 161, 166, 173, 256, 278, 279, 280, 284–86, 288, 339n61, 348n139, 363n133, 365n163, 365n164; and Civilian Complaint Review Board (CCRB), 44–45, 260, 285; and civilian review board demands, 261, 262, 266, 288, 289–90, 294–95; and climate of fear, 281, 295; and coerced confessions, 279; and Committee on Harlem Affairs (CHA), 104; and Communist Party (CPUSA), 161; complaints against, 247, 249, 256, 257, 258, 260–61, 262, 263, 283, 298; corruption of, 43, 249, 261, 262–63, 276; and counterintelligence methods, 284–86, 292, 365n163; and crime, 105, 106, 255, 259, 263, 265, 282, 283–84, 286, 294, 362n111; and William DeFossett, 161, 166, 286, 339n61; and democratic society, 105; and discipline for police officers, 95, 284, 290; and Robert Edwards, 99; and efforts to dismantle CORE, 286; and Emergency Services Unit, 106; and Federal Bureau of Investigation (FBI), 44, 105, 279, 285; and gangs, 105, 279, 280, 282, 284–85, 363n133; and Junius Griffin, 363n133, 364–65n161; and gun laws, 295–96; and Harlem occupation, 279, 282–85, 292; and Harlem Six, 363n127; and Johnson X Hinton, 74, 77, 161, 286; and illegal searches and seizures, 95, 96; and interracial patrols, 88; and justice, 106, 290; and Commissioner Kennedy, 95–96, 97, 98, 101, 102, 104, 105, 107, 139; killings of, 44, 96, 102, 256–58, 259, 260, 261, 265, 284, 290, 297–99, 303, 357n17; and law and order, 86, 99, 105, 248, 260–61, 283, 294–95; and Robert Mangum, 74, 161; and Thomas Martino, 99; militarization of, 84; and mob rule, 98–99; and Maurice Mulligan, 283, 284; and Commissioner Murphy, 249, 255, 258, 260, 261, 262, 263, 265, 266, 267, 282, 283, 288, 289, 290, 294–95, 298, 362n111, 362n121; and Muslim Mosque, Inc. (MMI), 284–85; and Nation of Islam, 74–75, 139, 166, 365n171; and "no knock" bill, 259, 260–61; and NYC stall-in, 273; and James O'Connell, 102; and Jeremiah O'Connor, 99; and Operation Decoy, 282; and Operations Finecomb and Taxicab, 282; and oppressive policing, 82, 86, 104, 106–8, 261, 282; and Abraham Ortega shooting, 283–84; and Patrolmen's Benevolent Association, 295; and picketing protesters, 208; and police abuse, 45, 105; Police Academy of, 99, 105; and police cars, 282, 300; and police commissioners, 44, 75, 86–87, 88, 94, 96–97, 98, 101, 104; and police

410 INDEX

New York Police Department (NYPD) (*continued*)
  reform, 97, 104, 108; and policing youth, 362n111, 363n125, 364-65n161; and political intimidation, 75; and potential riots, 44, 84, 86, 94, 97, 98-99, 100, 106, 111, 137, 161, 281, 283; powers of, 99, 102, 106, 108, 157, 255, 259-60, 263, 265, 283, 284, 294-96; presence of, 125, 166, 261, 271, 272, 281, 283, 348n139; and pressure from activists, 247-48, 260-61, 265, 284, 290, 295, 298; and public safety, 103; and Puerto Rican communities, 104-5, 259-60, 283; and punishment for police, 299; and race relations, 75, 86, 88, 95, 98, 110, 283; and racist policing, 49, 75, 95, 98, 103, 104-5, 108; and racist status quo, 157, 303; and repression of protest, 11, 13-14, 98-99, 108, 111, 212, 281, 283, 284, 300, 303; resistance to, 300, 303; resources for, 101; and Francisco Rodriguez shooting, 257, 258, 259, 261, 284, 290, 297; and speaking ban, 161; and stop-and-frisk procedures, 106, 259, 260, 261, 282, 289; and surveillance of Black communities, 103, 104, 106, 248-49, 256, 278, 282; and surveillance of Black radicals, 164, 244, 285-86, 358n43, 365n171; and surveillance of Nation of Islam, 161, 286, 339n61; and Tactical Patrol Force (TPF), 104-8, 161, 256, 281, 282, 283, 288, 297, 300; and terror, 256, 265, 276, 282, 288, 296, 303; and torture, 261, 277, 278, 288; training of, 44, 95, 105, 257, 262, 283; and undercover agents, 284, 285, 286; and UN protests, 142; and use of force, 80, 105, 136, 208, 211, 358n43; victims of abuse of, 260, 288, 289, 297, 298; and violence, 75, 81, 84, 97, 98, 99, 100, 102, 103, 106, 107, 108, 111, 136, 157, 160, 161, 169, 208, 249, 256, 257, 258-60, 263, 266-67, 273, 276-79, 283-84, 288, 289, 291, 292, 294, 297, 298, 300, 302; and Arthur Wallander, 43; and white police officers, 98, 99, 102, 103, 104, 106, 247, 283, 297; and white supremacy, 14, 103, 107, 111, 248. *See also* Thorpe, Reginald
New York Public Library, 58
New York Society for Ethical Culture, 31
New York State, 280-81; Albany in, 30, 41, 60, 250, 259; and Black communities, 102-3, 106-8, 197, 267, 282; compulsory education law of, 54; and construction projects of, 211; and crime laws, 259, 267, 268, 269, 289, 291, 294; and crime rates, 259; criminal justice system in, 101; and education equality, 250; and employment, 55, 210-11; expansion of policing in, 101-2, 106-8, 259-61, 282-83, 288, 294, 303; and housing, 55, 59, 236; and integration, 210; Ithaca in, 179; and juvenile delinquency, 101-2; and law enforcement, 164, 258-59, 357n24; and NAACP branch, 25, 27, 36, 44, 45, 46, 59, 63, 86; and police power, 99; and political dissent, 55; Public Schools of, 25-26, 30-33, 43, 54, 55; and Puerto Rican communities, 102-3; rent control in, 60; and rent strikes, 237, 250; Rochester in, 165, 303; and Governor Rockefeller, 165, 210, 211, 259, 260, 261, 265, 267, 268, 271; Rye in, 192; and school desegregation, 250; and segregation, 25, 54-55, 68; and state violence, 259, 282, 291; Supreme Court of, 31, 271; and Urban League of Greater New York, 140; and white state power, 4, 282, 302-3; and white supremacy, 46, 303; and Robert F. Williams, 100; work camps of, 101; and youth agencies, 102
Nkrumah, Kwame, 127, 131
nonviolence, 10, 64, 67, 68, 100, 146. *See also* Black freedom movement; civil rights; Malcolm X; Student Nonviolent Coordinating Committee (SNCC)
North Carolina, 63, 64, 65, 66, 67, 68. *See also* United States
Northern Negro Grass Roots Leadership Conference, 174-77, 304

Northern Student Movement (NSM), *202;* and Carl Anthony, 198, 200–201, *202;* and Black equality, 191–93, 194, 214; and Black leadership, 252; and Black radicalism, 214, 273; and boycott of Sealtest Dairy, 199; and campaigns against police, 261; and Joan Cannady, 191; and civil rights organizations, 13, 178, 190–91, 194, 195; and community organizing, 216, 222, 228; Congress of, 239, 263; director of, 6; and education, 200, 203, 216; and Freedom Schools, 203; and Harlem, 193, 194, 195, 196, 197, 200; and Harlem Action Group, 213, 222–23, 230, 262; and housing, 222–23; and "indigenous leadership," 192, 355n165; and integration, 196, 252; and Inter-collegiate Conference on Northern Civil Rights, 191–92; as an interracial organization, 182, 195, 196, 214; and local people, 182, 195–96, 222; and nonviolent direct action, 192; in Philadelphia, 193; and picketing, 192; and policing, 262; and political power, 216; and rent strikes, 213, 230, 239, 250, 252, 252–53, 255, 262; and Danny Schechter, 252–53; and selective patronage, 200; and self-determination, 156, 214, 255; and social action projects, 200; student involvement in, 181, 190–91, 255; and Student Nonviolent Coordinating Committee (SNCC), 190, 192, 194, 195, 200, 219, 228; and Rev. Leon Sullivan, 191; and tenant organizing, 213, 219, 222–23; and tutoring of Black students, 193, 219, 255; and white communities, 191; and working-class leadership, 200. *See also* Harlem Education Program (HEP); Strickland, Bill

O'Dell, Jack, 34, 35–36, 37, 57; and Black freedom movement, 293; and Communist Party (CPUSA), 58; and *Freedomways*, 107; in the South, 320n92; and tenant movement, 58, 219, 251
O'Dwyer, Paul, 240

O'Neil, Jim, 106
On Guard Committee for Freedom (OGFF), 129, 134, 135, 137, 139, 147. *See also* Black freedom movement
Organization of Afro-American Unity (OAAU), 288, 291–94, 296, 298–99, 305, 366n178, 370n12
Organization of Young Men (OYM), 129, 137, 150, 151, 187
organizers: and ACT, 266, 293; and Lew Anthony, 201, *202;* and anticolonialism, 52, 112; arrests of, 286; and Peter Bailey, 232; and Ella Baker, 47, 53, 90, 193, 318n66; and Amiri Baraka (LeRoi Jones), 137; and Black and Puerto Rican organizers, 260, 261–62; and Black consciousness, 142; and Black equality, 204; and Black liberation struggles, 5–7, 11, 12, 13, 19, 34–35, 52, 57, 66, 110, 111–12, 119, 127, 142–43, 146–47, 182, 275, 303; and Black nationalism, 19, 35, 52, 65, 66, 116–17, 263; and Black radicalism, 35, 66, 255; and Black revolution, 275; and Black women activists, 53–57, 66; and Black youth, 276; and Grace Lee Boggs, 177; and James Boggs, 305; and Isaiah Brunson, 273; and Joan Cannady, 191; and Granville Cherry, 263; and coalitions, 260; and Communist Party (CPUSA), 35–36, 264; and communities' resources, 7; and Community Council on Housing (CCH), 239, 262; and community organizers, 1, 6–7, 12, 13, 18–19, 22, 53–54, 57, 219, 228, 239; and Joan Countryman, 239, 252; and Peter Countryman, 239; and crime laws, 294; and Harold Cruse, 158; and Marjory Cruz, 233; and Cuban Revolution, 128; and Noel Day, 243; and dealing with courts, 251; and de facto segregation, 174; and demonstrations at United Nations, 137–38; and desegregation, 317n47; and direct action, 206, 212, 345n67; and Jean Doak, 201; and economic justice, 212; and education, 52, 53–54, 66, 174,

organizers (*continued*)
192–93; and empowerment, 253; and Bill Epton, 265, 285, 289, 291, 293; and Herman Ferguson, 293; and Bob Fletcher, 219; and Inocencia Flores, 233, 235, 242; and Freedom Now Party, 170; and Donald Freeman, 159; and Rev. Milton Galamison, 242, 273, 317n47; and Ramona Garrett, 34; and Gilberto Gerena-Valentin, 257; in Harlem, 122, 209, 231–35, 253, 305; and Harlem Youth Opportunities Unlimited (HARYOU), 293; and Dorothy Height, 250; and housing, 52, 57–63, 233–35; importance of, 12; and integration, 204; and leadership, 53, 204, 231, 233; and Left-labor organizers, 233, 264; and local people, 52, 53, 56–57, 195–96, 217; and militancy, 204, 217; and Nashville Student Movement, 243; and national movements, 239; and "nation within a nation," 145–46; and New York City, 49–50, 52, 56–57, 110, 160, 195–96, 203–4, 231–32, 238–39; and nonviolence, 204; and NY NAACP, 46; and Pan-Africanism, 52, 65, 137; and police repression, 262–63; and policing, 52, 107; and political action, 174, 304; and political consciousness, 50, 52, 305; and power, 52, 57, 212, 304; and Puerto Ricans, 6, 257–58; and race, 192; and radical organizers, 174, 217, 243, 266, 293; and revolution, 125; and Eloise Richardson, 59; and Gloria Richardson, 293; and Bayard Rustin, 239, 250, 272, 303; salaries of, 231; and school boycotts, 266; and self-defense, 174, 175; and self-determination, 52; and sending supplies, 65; and Student Nonviolent Coordinating Committee (SNCC), 243; and support for Castro's government, 122; and tenant organizers, 1, 6, 34, 35, 37–39, 41, 61, 66, 92, 230–33, 236–37, 238, 251–52; and traditions of resistance, 17, 82; and volunteering, 231; and Cora T. Walker, 207, 219; and white supremacy, 52; and Preston Wilcox, 263; and working-class Black communities, 50, 52, 68–69; and workshops, 174. *See also* Baker, Ella; Countryman, Peter; Gray, Jesse; Harlem Education Program (HEP); Harrington, Gladys; Malcolm X; Mallory, Mae; O'Dell, Jack; Rustin, Bayard

Overton, L. Joseph, 86, 127, 130, 160

Pan-Africanism, 9, 18, 19, 21, 22, 34. *See also* Black freedom movement; Harlem, New York City; Malcolm X; New York City; organizers
Panuthos, John, 76
Parents Committee for Better Education, 30, 31, 54
Parents in Action Against Educational Discrimination, 28, 31, 53, 54
Parker, Mack Charles, 63, 64, 122, 143, 149, 153
Parks, Rosa, 30
Patterson, Governor John, 150
Patterson, William L., 96
Payne, Charles, 6
Peck, James, 211
Perry, Dr. Albert, 155
Philips, Bessie, 21, 94, 115, 119, 213
Polier, Justice Justine, 54–55, 56
Powell, Adam Clayton, Jr., 229; and Abyssinian Baptist Church, 162, 220; and Associated Community Teams, 201; and Black people as police, 97; and Fidel Castro, 126; and civil rights movement, 21, 130, 183; and democracy, 97, 113, 183; and direct-action tactics, 60; and "Don't Buy Where You Can't Work" Campaign, 22; and Harlem, 16, 59, 87, 88; and Harlem Freedom Rally, 119; and housing conditions, 229; and investigation of Title I projects, 41; and leadership of Black organizations, 156; and mass civil disobedience, 59; and national rent strikes, 220–21; and police accountability, 98; and protest of police brutality, 44; and "rising tide" of activism, 43; and street rally, 216

Powell, James, 297, 298, 299, 303, 369n230
Progressive Labor Movement, 261, 264–65, 288, 289, 290–91, 296. *See also* Harlem, New York City
Progressive Labor Party, 170
Puerto Rican communities, 6, 28, 33, 38, 41, 44. *See also* Harlem, New York City; New York Police Department (NYPD); New York State
Purlie Victorious (Davis), 154

quota systems, 95

racial justice, 48, 217
racism: and agency, 306; and American racism, 128, 129, 142, 145–46, 169, 180, 191, 204, 218, 306; and antiwhite sentiment, 280; and Black communities, 11, 36–37, 38, 41, 43, 88, 93, 102, 103, 112, 122, 280; and "Black supremacist groups," 70; and Black workers, 205–7; and *Brown v. Board of Education,* 45; and colonialism, 124; and construction industry, 286; and "crime waves," 43; de facto, 2; and desegregation, 343n10; and discrimination in NYC, 301–2; and discriminatory housing practices, 93, 192, 213; and education, 53–57, 233; and employment discrimination, 37, 96–97, 197–99, 205, 213, 233; and gender, 7, 29; and global racism, 148; and Harlem, 81, 96–97, 112, 205, 281; and hate, 118; and hiring practices, 34, 96, 97, 173, 191; and housing, 233, 240; and inequality, 1, 10–11, 25–26, 28, 31–32, 215–16, 240; and integration, 150; and justice for victims, 48; and landlords, 37, 38; and lending practices, 37; and lynching, 43, 63–64, 122; and Malcolm X, 71; and militant rhetoric, 71; and minority groups, 257; and myths about Africa, 20; and Nation of Islam, 118; in New York City, 34, 37–38, 47–48, 54, 56; and New York Police Department, 49, 96; and nonwhite people, 80, 315n13; in the North, 1–5, 6, 10, 11–12, 17, 31–32, 52, 165, 188, 191, 214, 215, 216; and oppression, 302; and policing, 43–44, 48, 52, 75, 80, 96, 98, 103–4, 216, 233, 274, 275, 278, 280–81, 292, 295, 299; and politics, 170, 171; and popular culture, 24, 215–16; and popular sentiment, 279; and power, 209; and "Project Understanding," 180; and Puerto Rican residents, 80; and racial apartheid, 126; and racial discrimination, 96, 124, 185, 191, 205, 209, 211–12, 218; and racial oppression, 2–3, 10–11, 12, 23, 24, 29, 38, 49, 191, 215–16, 219; and racial segregation, 54, 185; and racist terrorism, 158; raising awareness of, 191; and religion, 7; resistance to, 5, 6, 17, 111–12; and segregated schools, 1, 6, 12, 31; and sexuality, 7; and slumlords, 40; and slums, 215, 216; and the social order, 102; and solidarity of communities, 315n13; in the South, 1, 3, 10, 28, 31, 35, 63, 64, 122, 130, 149, 152, 153, 165, 169, 170, 214, 215–16, 218, 338n33, 343n10; and Southern segregationists, 280; and state violence, 305; and subway violence, 368–69n228; and systemic racism, 2–3, 4, 5, 6, 7, 9, 10–11, 12, 16, 23, 26, 28, 43, 54, 56, 81, 84, 90, 109, 110, 113, 142, 158, 159, 169, 173, 174, 181, 188, 190, 193, 196, 199, 214, 218, 241, 247, 255, 256, 267, 281, 288, 293, 301, 302, 305, 306, 326n107; and trade unions, 211; and violence, 18, 43, 44, 45, 48, 63, 64, 122, 130, 149, 152, 154, 165, 168, 173, 178, 204, 208, 216, 266–67, 269, 278, 292, 299; and Mayor Wagner, 288; and white Americans, 71, 124, 136, 153; and white hostility, 17, 56, 152; and white racists, 170; and white supremacy, 45, 46, 122, 138, 248, 303; and zoning policies, 31. *See also* Jim Crow society
Raisin in the Sun, A (Hansberry), 141
Ramos-Lopez, José, 219, 229, 240, 261
Randolph, A. Philip, 21, 113, 119, 160, 183, 200. *See also* grassroots organizing
Reasoner, Harry, 215, 216

receivership law (1962), 224, 227-28, 236, 350n37, 360n70
Reid, William, 60
Rent Strike Coordinating Committee, 229, 230, 233, 235, 240, 250
reparations, 118, 142, 176, 178
Republican Party, 240
Revolutionary Action Movement (RAM), 276, 280, 281, 287, 291, 292. *See also* grassroots organizing
Ribaudo, Judge Guy, 236, 237, 238, 251
Rice, Florence, 161, 233, 264
Rice, Robert, 278, 279
Richardson, Eloise, 59
Richardson, Gloria, 174, 177, 232, 243, 268, 272. *See also* organizers
Rivera, Ramon E., 210
Roach, Max, 119
Roberts, Jesse, 261, 290
Robeson, Paul, 38, 141
Robinson, Cleveland, 240
Robinson, Jackie, 119, 183
Robinson, James, 181, 184, 188
Robinson, May, 226-27, 233
Robinson, "Sugar" Ray, 78, 80, 85, 119
Rockefeller, Governor Nelson, 60, 68, 70, 101, 102, 127. *See also* New York State
Rodriguez, Francisco "Frankie," 257-59, 261, 284, 290, 297
Rodriguez, Victor, 256, 258, 261, 265, 284, 290
Rogers, Kathie, 193
Rogers, Nahaz, 243
Roper, Doris, 233
Rustin, Bayard, 160, 183, 191, 200, 218, 233, 303. *See also* organizers
Rutgers Houses, 211
Ryan, William Fitts, 240, 260-61

Samuel, Charles, 77, 78, 80, 83
Sanchez, Sonia, 24
Sandifer, Jawn A., 86
Sarah Lawrence College, 191, 195
Schechter, Danny, 180, 195, 222, 228, 237, 239

Scottsboro Boys, 29, 35
Screvane, Paul, 208, 209, 210, 258
Sealtest Dairy, 198, 199, 204, 206
Shabazz, Betty, 75
Shabazz, James 67X, 278, 280
Sharkey-Brown-Isaacs Bill, 31
Shepp, Archie, 129
Sinclair, Roberta, 75
slavery, 15, 111, 115, 118, 176
Snellings, Rolland (Askia Muhammad Touré), 136, 145, 274, 296-97
socialism, 264
Socialist Workers Party, 123, 151, 155, 163, 166
Solero, Maximo, 256, 258, 261, 265, 284, 290
Southern Christian Leadership Conference, 53, 138, 156, 169, 208, 243
Southern civil rights movement, 3-4, 10, 24, 52, 57, 63-64. *See also* civil rights
Soviet Union, 113, 138
Sparks, Selma, 161, 167, 174, 233, 264
Spellman, A. B., 129
Stafford, Frank, 277, 278, 288, 289
Stanford, Max (Muhammad Ahmad), 158, 159, 208, 274, 275, 291. *See also* Black freedom movement
Stegall, Charles, 152, 153
Stegall, Mabel, 152, 153
Stevens, Hope, 93, 119, 120-21
Stevenson, Adlai, 134, 135, 139
Stokes, Ronald, 162, 163, 164, 166, 167, 168. *See also* Black freedom movement
Straus, R. Peter, 237-38
Strickland, Bill, 6, 214, 228, 239, 240, 241. *See also* grassroots organizing
Student Nonviolent Coordinating Committee (SNCC), 3, 152, 156, 180, 181, 190-92. *See also* grassroots organizing; Northern Student Movement (NSM)
Sugar, Margit, 279, 285
Survey Graphic, 14, 16
Sutton, Percy, 160, 188-89, 211, 293

Taber, Robert, 122, 125
Tallahassee bus boycotts, 185

INDEX   415

Taylor, Dr. Gardner, 55
Theobald, John, 54, 91-92
Thomas, Walter, 279
Thorpe, Reginald, 245, 246, 247
Till, Emmett, 45, 46, 47, 50, 63, 133. *See also* African Americans
Touré, Sékou, 131, 195
Townsend, Horace, 184
Trial, The (play), 70, 116
Tse-tung, Mao, 264, 276
Tshombe, Moise, 142

Umoja, Akinyele, 10
United African Nationalist Movement (UANM), 21, 59, 72, 94, *94*, 114-15, 116. *See also* Harlem, New York City
United Committee Against Alexander Hamilton Houses (UCAAH), 59-60
United Nations, 12, 73, 112, 124, 127, 128. *See also* Africa; New York City; United States
United States: and African independence, 19-20, 114; and African nations, 173; and aggressive policing, 105-6; Alabama in, 56, 167, 239; and American exceptionalism, 113; and anticolonialism, 121, 169; and anticommunism, 122; Arkansas in, 28, 88; Army of, 105; Atlanta, Georgia, in, 53; bigotry in, 179; Birmingham, Alabama, in, 191, 203, 206, 208, 218, 297; and "Black Belt," 35, 319n86; and Black communities, 36-37, 88, 112, 118, 179, 215, 242, 305-6, 368n225; and Black equality, 169, 216-17, 218; and Black freedom movement, 128, 204; Black liberation in, 114, 119, 120, 121, 133, 137, 144, 216; and Black nationalism, 120, 123, 176, 274; and Black political parties, 169-72; and Black revolution, 270, 274; and Boston, Massachusetts, 17, 72, 163, 181; and *Brown v. Board of Education*, 55; Cambridge, Maryland, in, 232; and capitalist societies, 129; and Cincinnati, 105; and civil rights movement, 3-4, 112, 241-42, 243; Cleveland, Ohio, in, 159, 230, 241-42, 243, 269, 274; and the Cold War, 126, 130, 140, 165, 340n88; and communism, 27, 36, 37, 57, 68, 125, 138, 140; and compensation for Black Americans, 118; Congress of, 19, 46, 122, 271; Connecticut in, 195; and de facto racial subordination, 2; and de facto segregation, 26, 55; and de jure racial subordination, 2; and de jure segregation, 2, 55; and democracy, 52, 126, 169, 172; Detroit in, 72, 107, 174, 181, 269, 274, 342n125; and educational justice, 54; and Eisenhower's Fourth of July address, 51; and embargo of Cuba, 169; and employment discrimination, 51, 197-99; and equal opportunity, 51; and Federal Bureau of Investigation (FBI), 42, 44, 66-67, 75, 101, 151, 278, 279, 306; and Florida, 124, 185; foreign interests of, 113; foreign policy of, 140; and freedom, 51, 52, 169, 254; and genocide, 269; Great Depression in, 5, 22, 29, 35, 59, 218, 220, 245; and Hartford, Connecticut, 181, 242; hate in, 70-71, 72; and human rights, 293, 298; and imperialism, 128, 129, 131, 141; and an independent Black state, 150, 157; and integration, 140, 157; and justice, 51, 120, 183; and Ku Klux Klan, 152, 205; and labor-led struggles, 35-36; and Lansing, Michigan, 17; and Latino/a communities, 305-6; Los Angeles in, 72, 162, 166, 242, 260; and lynching, 133, 152, 153; Maryland in, 192; McCarthyism in, 18, 27, 113, 130; and Merchant Marine, 34, 319n84; Miami in, 121; Mississippi in, 45, 46-47, 63, 64, 165, 297; Mississippi River in, 34; and Monroe, North Carolina, 122, 147, 150, 151, 152-53, 157, 296, 298; and Nashville, Tennessee, 182; and nationwide protests, 204; and nationwide school boycott, 243; and nation within a nation, 145-46, 156-57, 178; Newark in, 107; and New Haven, Connecticut, 190, 242; and North Carolina, 174, 182; Philadelphia in, 18, 159, 181, 200, 208, 274; police-state methods in, 165, 303; political parties

United States (*continued*)
in, 172; and presidential elections, 168; and racial equality, 34, 36, 124, 197; and racial oppression, 36-37, 45-46, 124, 141; and racial segregation, 25-26, 34, 182, 183; and racial violence fears, 67; and rebellions of the 1960s, 10, 11, 12, 215, 305-6; and rent strikes, 230, 241-42, 243; and San Francisco, 105; and school boycotts, 266; school segregation in, 25-26, 28, 49; and Second Amendment, 149; and the South, 141, 183, 203, 215, 218; State Department of, 125, 128, 148; and stop-and-frisk bill, 259; and summer of 1963, 159-60, 203; Supreme Court of, 25, 45, 55; and tenant organizing, 230; and truth, 51; and United Nations, 132, 293, 298, 334n95, 335n101; and violence, 150-51, 163, 173-74, 190, 203, 206, 208, 215, 218, 303, 306; Washington, DC, in, 25, 72, 138, 156, 170, 242, 272; and white people, 125, 164, 179, 335n101; and white Southern justice system, 63, 64; and white supremacists, 46, 50, 88, 143, 163, 164; and white supremacy, 146, 147, 148, 150, 150-51, 163, 174; and Woolworth stores, 343n10; and World War II, 233; and youth violence, 100-102. *See also* carceral system; Chicago, Illinois; civil rights; Harlem, New York City; Jim Crow society; New York State; North Carolina
universal healthcare, 172
Universal Negro Improvement Association (UNIA), 17, 18, 19, 112
University of Pennsylvania, 200
Unleashing Black Power (Blackmer), 4, 5, 6, 7, 9, 11-12
Urban League of Greater New York, 41, 59, 72, 90, 140, 206, 266

Valentine, John, 286
Velez, Hector, 261
Velez, Ted, 258, 261, 356n10
voting rights, 47, 268

Waddy, Viola, 53, 54
Wagner, Mayor Robert F., 28, 31, 33, 54, 55, 60-61. *See also* New York City
Wallace, George, 280
Wallace, Mike, 70, 71, 72, 208
Wallach, Judge Louis, 80
War on Crime, 306
Watson, James, 78, 80, 85, 87, 119
Wattley, Pernella, 69, 167, 170, 172, 173
Watts, Dan, 137, 138, 151, 164, 169, 170, 281. *See also* Black freedom movement; New Afro-American Nationalism
Weiss, Theodore, 289, 290, 294, 295
Weissman, George, 155
White, Governor Hugh, 46
White Citizens Council, 71
Wilkins, Roy, 66, 67, 68, 69, 119, 130. *See also* civil rights
Williams, Mabel, 151, 159
Williams, Major, 227, 231, 247, 284
Williams, Robert F., 64, 65, 66, 67, 68, 69. *See also* Black freedom movement; grassroots organizing; Harlem, New York City; Malcolm X; National Association for the Advancement of Colored People (NAACP); New York State
Wilson, Orlando W., 105-6
Wood, Raymond A., 286, 287, *287,* 366n178
World's Fair (1964), 270, 273, 283, 286, 360n70
World War I, 16
World War II, 17, 22, 34, 43, 101, 122. *See also* United States
Worthy, William, 123, 167-68, 169, 170, 171, 172. *See also* Black freedom movement
Wright, Sarah E., 124, 127, 130, 132, 137

Yale University, 190, 214

Zuber, Paul, 31, *32,* 54, 60, 191, 193. *See also* Black freedom movement

RECENT BOOKS IN

THE CARTER G. WOODSON INSTITUTE SERIES
Black Studies at Work in the World

The Evolution of a Rural Free Black Community: Goochland County, Virginia, 1728–1832
REGINALD D. BUTLER, EDITED BY PETER S. ONUF

Roses in December: Black Life in Hanover County from Civil War to Civil Rights
JODY LYNN ALLEN

The Struggle for Change: Race and the Politics of Reconciliation in Modern Richmond
MARVIN T. CHILES

A Little Child Shall Lead Them: A Documentary Account of the Struggle for School Desegregation in Prince Edward County, Virginia
BRIAN J. DAUGHERITY AND BRIAN GROGAN, EDITORS

We Face the Dawn: Oliver Hill, Spottswood Robinson, and the Legal Team That Dismantled Jim Crow
MARGARET EDDS

Keep On Keeping On: The NAACP and the Implementation of Brown v. Board of Education *in Virginia*
BRIAN J. DAUGHERITY

Schooling Jim Crow: The Fight for Atlanta's Booker T. Washington High School and the Roots of Black Protest Politics
JAY WINSTON DRISKELL JR.

The Punitive Turn: New Approaches to Race and Incarceration
DEBORAH E. MCDOWELL, CLAUDRENA N. HAROLD, AND JUAN BATTLE, EDITORS

www.ingramcontent.com/pod-product-compliance
Lightning Source LLC
Chambersburg PA
CBHW061817010226
39060CB00036B/881